HISTORY OF GWINNETT COUNTY GEORGIA

By

JAMES C. FLANIGAN

1818 - 1943

Volume I

Southern Historical Press, Inc.
Greenville, South Carolina

This volume was reproduced from
An 1943 edition located in the
Publisher's private Library
Greenville, South Carolina

All rights reserved. No part of this publication may be reproduced,
stored in a retrieval system, transmitted in any form, posted
on to the web in any form or by any means without
the prior written permission of the publisher.

Please direct all correspondence and orders to:

www.southernhistoricalpress.com
or
SOUTHERN HISTORICAL PRESS, Inc.
PO Box 1267
375 West Broad Street
Greenville, SC   29601
southernhistoricalpress@gmail.com

Originally published: Hapeville, GA, 1943
Copyright 1943 by James C. Flanigan
ISBN #0-89308-977-X
All rights Reserved.
Printed in the United States of America

The Author

JAMES C. FLANIGAN

This Volume

Is dedicated to every one who has contributed to the development of Gwinnett County and who believes with MACAULAY that "A people which takes no pride in the noble achievements of remote ancestors will never achieve anything worthy to be remembered by remote descendants;" and it is also especially dedicated

To

My daughter, NELL, and to all children whose lives have been shadowed by affliction, but whose minds are bright and cheerful, with the hope that its pages may contribute to their entertainment and pleasure and at the same time warm their hearts with a deeper love for their native county.

From presentments of the Grand Jury at the September term of the Superior Court of Gwinnett County, 1939:

Therefore be it resolved by this Grand Jury that J. C. Flanigan be authorized to compile and assemble the history of Gwinnett County as early as can conveniently be done.

T. D. McDANIEL, Foreman.
J. E. SHAFER, Clerk.
G. W. Shell, T. C. Rutledge, W. A. Griswell, W. D. Smith, J. E. Jacobs, E. G. Singleton, N. W. Buice, B. F. Summerour, J. T. White, Sr., M. H. Mason, W. W. White, E. B. Peeples, J. S. Bennefield, C. W. Johnson, W. R. Pruett, C. S. Gunter, O. Z. Cox, O. R. Juhan, G. W. Pharr, Jr., J. F. Wages, M. L. Adams.

CLIFFORD PRATT, Judge,
Piedmont Circuit.

FRANK SIMPSON,
Solicitor General.

From presentments of the Grand Jury at the March term of the Gwinnett Superior Court, 1942:

We are informed that Mr. J. C. Flanigan, who was requested by a former Grand Jury to write a history of Gwinnett County, has responded to the Grand Jury's request and the history of the county, covering a period of 125 years, has been practically completed. We recommend that the history be published.

O. E. BUCHANAN, Foreman.
O. E. UPSHAW, Clerk.
W. E. Green, J. O. Moore, Sr., C. A. Spain, G. S. Crow, I. D. Buice, Holman Puckett, Carl Pirkle, J. W. Guthrie, R. M. Higgins, C. T. Jacobs, J. T. Simonton, Eugine Gilbert, W. H. Hutchins, E. L. Smith, Gaines Ivy, A. M. Garner, J. F. Atkinson, W. T. Griswell, Jim Crow, W. A. Griswell, W. T. Corley.

CLIFFORD PRATT, Judge.

HOPE STARK,
Solicitor General.

PREFACE

Judge R. B. Whitworth was appointed county historian in 1930 and two years later Mr. G. W. Jacobs, of Washington, was appointed his assistant. They collected material from various sources, but never, so far as I know, did they compile the history itself. Judge Whitworth unfortunately suffered a stroke of paralysis in 1937 and died about two years later. In his passing the county lost one of its best and most outstanding citizens.

In September, 1939, the Grand Jury requested that I undertake the work of compiling the county's history. Such material as seemed to be important that was turned over to me by Judge Whitworth and Mr. Jacobs has been used. I have interviewed many prominent men and women, scanned books and newspapers, examined records in the libraries and archives in Atlanta, and sought information from interesting people from New York to Mexico. What is related here, however, is but a part of the story.

I wish to express my gratitude to everyone whose assistance made this history possible.

JAMES C. FLANIGAN.

TABLE OF CONTENTS

Chapter		Page
I.	THE INDIANS	1

Treaties, Civilization, Suwanee Old Town, House of Worship, Trails, Upper Creeks, Cherokees, Government Organized, Indian Names, Family Life, Sequoia, Graves.

II.	FORT DANIEL	8

Fort at Hog Mountain, Muster Rolls, Brandy for Soldiers, Gilmer at Standing Peachtree, Marker Dedicated.

III.	GEOGRAPHY AND GEOLOGY	19

Location, Drainage, Topography, Climate, Rocks and Minerals, Flora and Fauna.

IV.	CREATION OF GWINNETT COUNTY	24

Name, Gwinnett Part of Colony, Boundaries, Elections and Courts at Elisha Winn's, First County Officers, Temporary Courthouse, County Site Purchased, List of First Taxpayers, Census of 1820.

V.	LAND DISTRIBUTED BY LOTTERY	48

County Surveyed, Four Land Districts, The Lottery, Gwinnett Drawers, Fourth District Drawers, Fifth District Drawers, Sixth District Drawers, Seventh District Drawers, Gwinnett Citizens Who Drew Lots in Monroe and Houston Counties.

VI.	EARLY COUNTY EVENTS	68

First Settlers, Smashing a Saloon, Early Court Records, Early Schools.

VII.	PROSPEROUS YEARS, 1830-1860	98

Plantation Supplants the Farm, Trial of the Missionaries, Battle of Shepherd's Plantation, Removal of Indians, Cherokee Lottery, Gwinnett Pensions, A Strange Transaction, Most Unusual Case, Slave Owners 1820-1860, Plantation Owners 1860.

Chapter		Page
VIII.	CONFEDERATE STATES OF AMERICA	188

Company A 42nd Infantry, Company B 42nd Infantry, Company C 3rd Btn., Sharpshooters, Troop C 10th Cavalry, Company C Gwinnett Guards, Battery D 9th Artillery, Company E 8th Infantry, Company F 35th Georgia Regiment, Company F 24th Georgia Infantry, Company H 16th Infantry, Company H 10th Cavalry, Company H 35th Infantry, Company I 55th Infantry, Company I 16th Infantry, Troop I 16th Cavalry, Company K 36th Infantry, Troop K 16th Cavalry, Company D 16th Cavalry, Yankees Overrun the County, Yankees Lynch Negro, Confederate Pensioners, Letters from Soldiers, Diary of Major Simmons.

IX.	THE NEW ERA	246

Freedman's Bureau, Ku Klux Klan, Courthouse Burned, Railroads, Farmers Alliance, Cotton Bagging Wedding, Spanish-American War.

X.	THE MULTIPLYING YEARS, 1900-1942	260

Advent of Automobile, Paved Roads, The World War, The New Deal, Salute to Gwinnett County, Industries, Vital Statistics, Gwinnett Lawyers, Physicians and Dentists.

XI.	PUBLIC SCHOOLS OF GWINNETT COUNTY	293

XII.	WRITINGS OF MAJOR WINN	320

Rev. John S. Wilson, D.D.	Richard Saye
James Bracewell	Asahel R. Smith
Isham Williams	Captain John Beasley
Elisha W. Chester	Daniel Liddell
Daniel R. Arnold	Levi Loveless
William Maltbie	David Spence
James Russell	Robert Steel Brown
Rev. Anslem Anthony	David Richardson
Rev. Hosea Camp	Laurence Family
Nathan L. Hutchins	Abraham Martin
Elder James Hale	The Berry Family
Henry P. Thomas	James Hawthorne
Dr. Philo Hall	James Jackson
Jesse Rambo	Evan Howell
Hamilton Garmany	William King
John and Henry Cupp	John Sammon
John Rogers	Richard Whitworth
Thomas P. Hudson	Robert S. Adair
Moses Liddell	John Lietch
William Nesbit	David Pruett
John C. Whitworth	John Stuart and Wife
William Baugh	Isaac Adair
Dr. James M. Gordon	Solomon Hopkins

Gwinnett County Court House
Lawrenceville, Ga.

CHAPTER I

THE INDIANS

THE TERRITORY within the limits of Gwinnett County was claimed and occupied at different times by the Creek and the Cherokee Indians. It is probable that the Creeks appeared in the territory first. However, the Cherokees were here for a long period before the creation of the county. The territory was ceded to the United States by both Indian nations in formal treaties executed by representatives of the federal government and the two Indian tribes.

In a treaty signed at Hopewell, South Carolina, November 28, 1789, the Cherokees ceded to the United States all territory lying north and east of a line running through Kentucky, Tennessee, North and South Carolina, including that section of Georgia from the Tugaloo river to Currahee mountain, thence a straight line to the head of the south fork of the Oconee river, called the Appalachee. That part of Gwinnett county east of the Appalachee river passed into the possession of the United States by a treaty with the Creek Indians executed in New York City, August 7, 1790, the Creeks ceding all territory north and east of a line from the Tugalo river to the top of Currahee mountain, thence to the source of the main south branch of the Oconee river, called the Appalachee, thence down the middle of the Appalachee to the Ocmulgee river. By the same treaty it was provided that the head or source of the Appalachee should be determined by a United States surveyor, assisted by three old citizens of the state appointed by the governor, and three Indian chiefs, who were to assemble for that purpose on the first day of October, 1791, at Rock Landing, near Milledgeville. The line from the top of Currahee mountain to the head of the Appalachee and down that river for twenty miles or more, if necessary, was to be marked by cutting the trees over a strip twenty feet wide and chopping standing trees on each side of the line.

On July 3, 1817, at the Cherokee agency in Tennessee, the chiefs, headmen and warriors of the Cherokee nation ceded all lands north and east of a line from the High Shoals of the Appalachee river, thence westwardly to the Chattahoochee river along the boundary line between the Creek and Cherokee nations; thence up the Chattahoochee river to the mouth of Souque creek. This included all the land in the county not ceded in the treaties mentioned above. However, the Creeks at one time occupied this section and to obviate future trouble a treaty was made with that nation on June 22, 1818, at the Creek agency on the Flint river by which agreement the Creeks ceded all lands beginning at the High Shoals of the Appalachee river, thence to the Ulcofauhatchie (Alcova) river, thence up the Ulcofauhatchie to where the Hightower trail crosses same, thence along the said Hightower trail to the Shallow Ford on the Chattahoochee river, thence up the said Chattahoochee river to Suwanee Old Town, thence by a straight line to the head or source of the Appalachee river, thence down said river to the High Shoals.

Currahee mountain, mentioned in the above treaties, is a few miles north of Toccoa, near the Habersham-Stephens county line.

The head of the south fork of the Oconee river, called the Appalachee, is located near Hog Mountain. The Appalachee river in the treaty signed at Hopewell is called the south fork of the Oconee river and in the treaty negotiated in New York it is referred to as the main south branch of the Oconee river. In those early days the Appalachee was called the south branch and the Mulberry the middle branch of the Oconee river. Both the south and middle branches, of course, flow into the Oconee.

The Indians left very little permanent physical evidence of their long stay in Gwinnett County. They opened no highways, built no bridges, erected no dwellings, established no schools. They pitched their wigwams here and there, cultivated patches of corn and beans and sustained their families on the game of the forest and the fish of the creeks and rivers. They played many games, attended ceremonial festivals, went to war, worshipped the Great Spirit and then died as have all men since the world began.

Suwanee Old Town

Suwanee Old Town was an Indian settlement or village on the Chattahoochee just above the mouth of Suwanee creek. This village was of such importance that it was mentioned in treaties executed between the Indian nation and the United States. Maps of that early date show the location of Suwanee Old Town. Trails or paths from all directions centered there. And it is believed that Suwanee Old Town had been the site of a village for perhaps hundreds of years. There the Indians lived from generation to generation. There they fished and hunted; there the chiefs, headmen and warriors gathered to discuss questions of war and peace; and there young braves and comely princesses romanced as they canoed along the shaded banks of that famous old river.

Across the river in Forsyth county at Shakerag is an Indian mound. There is a mound on the Neely farm, half a mile from Buck Creek and a quarter of a mile from the Chattahoochee. The Inferior Court records show that in an application to open a certain road in that community mention is made of a mound near which the road was to run.

Sites of Indian villages or camping places have been located in many sections of the county. Broken pottery, pipes, arrowheads, axes, beads and tomahawks have been found at Freeman's mill, on the Dr. Moore farm in Harbins district, at the junction of Pamatree creek and Alcova river, in Bay Creek district, at various places near Snellville, on Yellow river and other places in the county. Pottery from these sites are types known in Georgia archaeology by the names of Lamar Stamped, Check Stamped, Simple Stamped and Dunlap Fabric Impressed. Lamar pottery precedes the best known historic period and may have been in use in Georgia about the time of De Soto's arrival. The other types of pottery mentioned are, in general, earlier.

In Goodwin's district there is a site of an Indian village or camp. It was located near a spring on the Maddox farm. It was claimed by Columbus Atkinson, who lived in that community and was well acquainted with the early history and traditions of that section, that this village was occupied by the Indians from prehistoric times and up to their removal from this territory. It is a tradition that the Indians erected a house of worship at this village, using a material known as soapstone. The quantity of large stones on this site would seem to indicate that a house or temple of large proportions stood there. The stones lay in heaps near the spring, many of which have been carried away by farmers in the community. There is no quarry of soapstone in the community and the stones must have been secured some distance away in another locality. There is a hill of soapstone near Oakland and it is probable the stones were quarried there. Whether these stones once housed generation after generation of men and women who lived there or gathered there to worship the Great Spirit, or whether they were used for a fort or council hall, the fact remains that they were there when the first white man passed that way.

A rock house, erected by the Indians, stood on a rocky ridge on the Thomas W. Brownlee farm two or three miles north of Snellville. Small flint-like rocks were used. The structure was round in shape, twelve or fifteen feet in diameter and had seats of stone all around the wall inside.

Trails

Indian paths or trails threaded the country from ocean to ocean. In this county the trails were narrow, usually two to three feet wide. Indians in this section traveled single file, one after the other. The Okoloco trail was the original boundary line between Gwinnett and Jackson counties and ran through Snodon, later Jug Tavern, now Winder, on by Cedar Hill, County Line academy, Bethabra Baptist Church, Thompson's Mill and intersected another trail towards Gainesville. Another trail ran along the ridge south of the Chattahoochee and is now known as Peachtree road. Trails extended from Suwanee Old Town north and south. The Hightower

Trail crossed the Chattahoochee at Shallow Ford and ran south and was made the boundary line between Gwinnett and DeKalb counties. Other paths extended from these more important trails to various camps and villages in the interior of the county.

The most important path was the Hightower Trail. It came from the Cherokee territory in northwest Georgia and was a popular route from that section on to High Shoals and Augusta. For centuries, perhaps, the Indians traveled this path, sometimes on pleasure, sometimes to market, sometimes on hunting expeditions, and sometimes to war. "Along this trail in later years they traveled to market with their peltries and articles of their own manufacture such as moccasins beautifully ornamented with beads, bead pockets, baskets and other notions, which they exchanged for things as their wants might require or their crude fancy might crave. They generally spent a week in the city effecting their sales and purchases; and then, packing their goods on their ponies, they would take up their line of march for their homes. It was a long journey from the Coosa or Hightower river to Augusta then. Our imagination pictures a hundred or more of these tawny people of the forest consisting of warriors, squaws and pickaninnies, the men clothed in hunting shirts, buckskin leggins, moccasins on their feet and turbans or handkerchiefs tied around their heads; the women with their short frocks reaching to their knees, with red shawls or scarfs around their shoulders, carrying their papooses on their backs, often in a nude state, and wending their way moodily in single file to the big town of the white man far away.

"Many a grotesque scene was enacted by these rude people in these journeyings which are lost to the white man, but is probably preserved by tradition to the remnant of the tribe now living beyond the Mississippi. There is something peculiarly interesting in the Indian character. When sober they were taciturn, quiet and good humored; when imbibing fire water, they were garrulous and noisy. His oratory was of no mean order and is remarkable for pithiness and dry sarcasm. The most pleasing traits in the character of these strange people are their reverence for age, their affection for their children, their high notions of honor and their keen sense of justice. Before the introduction of the Bible and the Christian religion among them, they had a general idea that the good would be rewarded and the bad punished. Far away to the west a pleasant land was prepared in which the hunter, after death, would pursue his favorite employment in the midst of an abundance of game, a stranger forever to want and fear."

UPPER CREEKS

The Creek Indians occupied middle and south Georgia and bore the names of Upper Creeks and Lower Creeks. The former occupied this county at one time. There is a legend that they came from the far West. Their language, customs, dress, games and religious belief and mode of worship differed little from that of other tribes. In 1802 Georgia surrendered its territory extending from its present western boundary to the Mississippi river and the United States agreed to extinguish the title of all the territory in the state then owned by and in the possession of the Indians. The United States made no effort to carry out this agreement until 1825 when a treaty was executed at Indian Springs by General William McIntosh on behalf of the Creek nation and the commissioners of the United States. This treaty extinguished the title of the Creek Indians to all the territory occupied by them in this state. The treaty was ratified by the Senate of the United States and signed by President James Monroe. Many of the chiefs, headmen and warriors opposed the treaty and on Saturday morning, May 1, 1825, a large body of them surrounded the house of General McIntosh, set it on fire, shot him, and threw his body into the flames.

The Creek Indians were required to leave the state; the ceded lands were surveyed and the entire territory covered by this treaty was distributed among the people of the state by lottery.

The Cherokees

The Cherokee Indians were in the territory now known as Georgia when De Soto made his voyage through this country. They belonged to that branch of American Indians known as the Iroquois, their ancestral home being farther north. For reasons unknown the tribe migrated south and settled in the lower part of the Allegheny mountains and the Piedmont regions south of the mountains. They aided the British in the Revolutionary War and the War of 1812 which greatly embittered loyal Americans against them, and thereafter constant were the disputes between them, often resulting in war and bloodshed.

Ministers of several denominations were sent into the Cherokee nation and schools and missions were established in several communities. Some white men married Indian women and white girls married Indian braves. The intermarriages appeared beneficial, for many of the leading men of the Cherokee nation were halfbreeds. The missions and schools were eminently successful. Many Indians united with the churches and the schools were crowded with Indian youths eager to learn.

The territory claimed by the Cherokees embraced some 40,000 square miles in Tennessee, North Carolina, Alabama and Georgia, reaching as far south as Gwinnett county. The nation moved its capital from Tennessee to New Echota in 1819, a site two or three miles from the city of Calhoun, in Gordon county. Here buildings were erected, a government established, courts set up and the Indians gave themselves to the pursuits of agriculture and stock-raising. Instead of war and the chase they turned to the pursuits of civilized men; instead of guns and the tomahawk, they learned to know the hoe and plow, the spinning wheel and loom, the music of the saw and hammer and the benefits of religion and morality.

The nation was divided into several districts or states. Delegates were chosen to meet at the capital and a constitution was adopted, patterned after the Constitution of the United States. Judges were elected to preside over the courts and enforce the laws of the nation, and churches and schools flourished. The Cherokee Nation in 1827 adopted its constitution, and that document declared the Nation to be a free and independent country with complete and sole jurisdiction over all its territory to the exclusion of the authority of any other state or nation.

Indian Names

The larger streams in this county and section were given names by the Indians. Chattahoochee, Appalachee, Alcova and Oconee are Indian names. Chattahoochee means marked or pictured rock or stone; the Indian name for Alcova is Ulcofauhatchie, hatchie meaning creek, and the first part of the name Anglicized to Alcova. Yellow river was called Coc-lau-pou-chee; Mulberry, Tish-ma-gu; Cedar creek, Ip-se-quil-ta; Oconee, E-to-ho or Ekwoni; Cedar Hill, Po-ga-nap; Sno-don was a village at Jug Tavern, now Winder.

When the white man moved into the county, he designated the smaller streams with such prosaic names as Beaver Ruin, Buck, Ivy, Rocky, Sweetwater, Haynes and No Business.

Family Life

Prior to the settlement of this continent by the white race, the family life of the aborigines differed little from that of all primitive people in other parts of the world. Some tribes were polygamous, others, for the most part, monogamous. "Marriage is of a simple nature," says one writer, "and of no other form than mutual consent of the parties. The future husband makes presents of skins and provisions at the cabin of the father of his intended; after the meal there is a dance, they sing of the war exploits of the ancestors of the husband. Next day the oldest man presents the wife to the parents of the husband. That is the entire ceremony."

Bartram says: "Amongst some of the Creeks I was informed the mystery is performed after the following manner: When a young man has fixed his affections and is determined to marry, he takes a cane or reed, such as they stick down at the hills of their bean vines for their support. With this, after having obtained her parents' consent, he repairs to the habitation of his beloved, attended by his friends and associates, and in the presence of the wedding guests, he sticks his reed down, upright in the ground; when soon after his sweetheart comes forth with another reed, which she sticks down by the side of his, and they are married. Then they exchange reeds, which are laid by as evidence or certificates of the marriage, which is celebrated with feasting, music and dancing."

There was a diversity of marriage rites. For instance Swan describes it thus: "The man, to signify his wishes, kills a bear with his own hands and sends a panful of the oil to his mistress. If she receives the oil, he next attends and helps her hoe the corn in her field; afterwards plants her beans; and when they come up, he sets poles for them to run upon. In the meantime he attends her corn until the beans have run up and entwined their vines about the pole. They then take each other for better or worse and are bound to all intents and purposes."

When the white people began to covet the beautiful lands lying in the Sautee and Nacoochee valleys the Indians, or part of them, moved to what is now Chattooga county and settled on a lovely landscape that has since been called Alpine. Among them was George Guess, or Gist. He was born in 1770 in the Sautee valley in White county. His father was a wandering German peddler named Guess and his mother was an Indian girl whom the peddler married and soon afterward abandoned. The boy evinced great mechanical skill and at an early age he became an expert blacksmith and silversmith. He invented an alphabet of eighty-five characters, and the Cherokees were the first of all American Indians to have a written language.

The hundred and twenty years since the Indians were removed from this county have effaced all markers and mounds that at one time pointed out the last resting places of these primitive people. The Lanier mountain at Snellville was used by them as a graveyard for their dead. Broken pottery, arrow heads, tomahawks, pipes and other fragments of their handiwork were found in great abundance near the Snellville cemetery.

Chapter II

FORT DANIEL

DURING the War of 1812 forts were erected at points along the frontier. The Indians aided the enemy and the safety of the people who lived along the dividing line between the white settlers and the Indians at once became an important question. The woods swarmed with painted warriors eager to use their scalping knives and tomahawks. The settlers along the frontier were in imminent danger.

At that time Jackson County extended to the Appalachee River, and from its source near Hog Mountain northeast to the Franklin County line. The source of the Appalachee near Hog Mountain was the most western point on the frontier. Many families lived in the section from the source of the Appalachee near Hog Mountain to Jug Tavern and between the Mulberry and Appalachee rivers. Even at that early time Hog Mountain was an important place. Prominent families had settled near by. Stores were opened and a lively trade was carried on with the Indians and the white settlers. Maltbie's store did a flourishing business for years. Bogan's store was a noted center of activity and trade for a long time.

Hog Mountain was selected as a site to locate a fort. The exact location of the fort is well known. It was erected on the highest point in the community where one could see in all directions. It stood on a hill about a quarter of a mile from the crossroads at Hog Mountain on the land now (1942) owned by R. H. Burel. The forest on all sides, for quite a distance, was cut away. In the center of the clearing a "blockade and stockding" was constructed by soldiers and the fort was garrisoned by officers, spies and volunteers during the war.

The fort bore the name of Fort Daniel, presumably for General Allen Daniel, and Captain Nehemiah Garrison was in command of the soldiers when the fort was erected. It appears from the record that Isham Williams lived in the community and furnished a quantity of beef to the soldiers stationed there. Williams lies in his grave near the residence of Rolla Williams, three miles west of Lawrenceville, and his descendants live in the county now and are among its most highly respected citizens.

The following documents give information about Fort Daniel. These documents were copied from original records on file in the State Department of Archives in Atlanta.

Fort Daniel Records

In obedience to orders from Brigadier General Beall, your Captain Nehemiah Garrison will take the requisite measures to cause all the men who labor on the fort near Hog Mountain as well as the Soldiers who are or may be detached for the defence of the fort aforesaid to be regularly and duly returned and to grant proper vouchers therefor.
28th November, 1813.

TANDY KEY, Major,
Commanding the 25th R. G. M.

Muster Roll of Company Stationed at Hog Mountain

Muster Roll of a company of militia under the command of Captain Nehemiah Garrison detached by order of Brig. Gen. Frederick Beall of the 21st of November, 1813, from the 25th Regiment of Georgia Militia (in the absence of Captain Walton Harris). Commanded by Major Tandy Key for the purpose of building a blockade and stockding near the Hog Mountain in Jackson County.

No.	Rank	Names	Commencement of Service	Termination of Service
	Captain	Nehemiah Garrison	Nov. 31, 1813	Dec. 14, 1813
1.	Sergeant	Isaac Busson	Nov. 22, 1813	Dec. 2, 1813
2.	Private	Wm. Lyle	Nov. 22, 1813	Dec. 2, 1813
3.	Private	Elisha Burson	Nov. 22, 1813	Dec. 2, 1813
4.	Private	Johnathan Betts	Nov. 22, 1813	Dec. 2, 1813
5.	Private	Dolphin Lindsey	Nov. 22, 1813	Dec. 2, 1813
6.	Private	Thomas Koker	Nov. 22, 1813	Dec. 2, 1813
7.	Private	John Bostwick	Nov. 22, 1813	Dec. 2, 1813
8.	Private	Elisha Oliver	Nov. 22, 1813	Dec. 2, 1813
9.	Private	James Tate	Nov. 22, 1813	Dec. 2, 1813
10.	Private	John Lyle	Nov. 22, 1813	Dec. 2, 1813
11.	Private	Thomas Nicks	Nov. 22, 1813	Dec. 2, 1813
12.	Private	John Stanley	Nov. 22, 1813	Dec. 2, 1813

Men reporting themselves under the second draft:

1.	Private	Mathew McKnight	Dec. 3, 1813	Dec. 10, 1813
2.	Private	Henry King	Dec. 3, 1813	Dec. 10, 1813

Men reporting themselves under the third draft from Colonel R. Jones' Regiment:

No.	Rank	Name	Commencement of Service	Termination of Service
1.	Sergeant	Alexander Beard	Dec. 2, 1813	Dec. 14, 1813
2.	Private	Bradley Thomas	Dec. 2, 1813	Dec. 14, 1813

No.	Rank	Name	Commencement of Service	Termination of Service
3.	Private	James Seay	Dec. 2, 1813	Dec. 14, 1813
4.	Private	James McMurry	Dec. 2, 1813	Dec. 14, 1813
5.	Private	Charles Strickland	Dec. 2, 1813	Dec. 14, 1813
6.	Private	Moses Betts	Dec. 2, 1813	Dec. 14, 1813
7.	Private	Richard Strickland	Dec. 2, 1813	Dec. 14, 1813
8.	Private	Samuel Hughs	Dec. 2, 1813	Dec. 14, 1813
9.	Private	Wm. Post	Dec. 2, 1813	Dec. 14, 1813
10.	Private	Jerimiah Twidwell	Dec. 2, 1813	Dec. 14, 1813
11.	Private	Thomas Wortham	Dec. 2, 1813	Dec. 14, 1813
12.	Private	James Pyron	Dec. 2, 1813	Dec. 14, 1813
13.	Private	John Phipps	Dec. 2, 1813	Dec. 14, 1813

I do certify, on honor, that muster rolls exhibit a true statement of the commencement and termination of a service of a detachment of militia stationed on the frontier of Jackson County as mentioned in the above caption and that the remarks set opposite the names are accurate and just.
June 17th, 1814.

NEHEMIAH GARRISON,
Captain, Commanding.

Muster Roll of Militia under command of Captain Joseph Whorton in the service of the State of Georgia stationed on the frontier of Jackson County in pursuant to General orders issued November 12, 1813.

No.	Rank	Name	Beginning of Service	Termination of Service
1.	Private	Wm. Armer	Jan. 5, 1814	Mar. 5, 1814
2.	Horseman	Charles Austin	Jan. 5, 1814	Mar. 5, 1814
3.	Horseman	David Anglin	Jan. 25, 1814	Mar. 5, 1814
4.	Horseman	Mitchel Bennett	Jan. 5, 1814	Mar. 5, 1814
5.	Horseman	Thomas Beard	Jan. 5, 1814	Mar. 5, 1814
6.	Private	Alexander Beard	Jan. 5, 1814	Mar. 5, 1814
7.	Sergeant	Danl. Busson	Jan. 5, 1814	Mar. 5, 1814
8.	Private	Wm. Bell	Jan. 5, 1814	Mar. 5, 1814
9.	Private	Wm. Bowles	Jan. 5, 1814	Mar. 5, 1814
10.	Private	Richard Cruce	Jan. 5, 1814	Mar. 5, 1814
11.	Private	Robbin Chandler	Jan. 5, 1814	Mar. 5, 1814
12.	Private	John Crayton	Jan. 5, 1814	Mar. 5, 1814
13.	Private	Wm. Combs	Jan. 5, 1814	Mar. 5, 1814
14.	Private	Andrew Cunningham	Jan. 5, 1814	Mar. 5, 1814
15.	2nd Sergt.	James Cash	Jan. 5, 1814	Mar. 5, 1814
16.	Private	Wm. Giddins	Jan. 5, 1814	Mar. 5, 1814
17.	Private	Ezekial Green	Jan. 5, 1814	Mar. 5, 1814
18.	Private	Hardy Howard	Jan. 5, 1814	Mar. 5, 1814

No.	Rank	Name	Beginning of Service	Termination of Service
19.	Private	Petter Haney	Jan. 5, 1814	Mar. 5, 1814
20.	Private	Harry Kolb	Jan. 5, 1814	Mar. 5, 1814
21.	Private	John Kanady	Jan. 5, 1814	Mar. 5, 1814
22.	Private	Jacob Millsaps	Jan. 5, 1814	Mar. 5, 1814
23.	Private	John McMullin	Jan. 5, 1814	Mar. 5, 1814
24.	Private	Shelton McGuier	Jan. 5, 1814	Mar. 5, 1814
25.	Horseman	Wm. McGinnis	Jan. 5, 1814	Mar. 5, 1814
26.	Horseman	Thomas Niblack	Jan. 5, 1814	Mar. 5, 1814
27.	Private	Wiley Pierce	Jan. 5, 1814	Mar. 5, 1814
28.	Horseman	John Pierce	Jan. 5, 1814	Mar. 5, 1814
29.	Private	Jno. Robertson	Jan. 5, 1814	Mar. 5, 1814
30.	Private	Howard Smith	Jan. 5, 1814	Mar. 5, 1814
31.	Private	James Spurgin	Jan. 5, 1814	Mar. 5, 1814
32.	Private	Fleming Staten	Jan. 5, 1814	Mar. 5, 1814
33.	Private	Seabourn Scroggins	Jan. 5, 1814	Mar. 5, 1814
34.	Private	Nathaniel Venable	Jan. 5, 1814	Mar. 5, 1814
35.	Private	Wm. Venable	Jan. 5, 1814	Mar. 5, 1814
36.	Private	Wm. Watts	Jan. 5, 1814	Mar. 5, 1814
37.	Private	Adam Williamson	Jan. 5, 1814	Mar. 5, 1814
38.	Private	William Wilson	Jan. 5, 1814	Mar. 5, 1814
39.	Private	Sherwood Horton	Jan. 5, 1814	Mar. 5, 1814
40.	Private	Wm. Ward	Jan. 5, 1814	Mar. 5, 1814
41.	Private	Henry Wilson	Jan. 5, 1814	Mar. 5, 1814
42.	Private	Hesikiah Williams	Jan. 5, 1814	Mar. 5, 1814
43.	Private	John Williamson	Jan. 5, 1814	Mar. 5, 1814
44.	Private	Samuel Winstead	Jan. 5, 1814	Mar. 5, 1814
45.	Private	James Willson	Jan. 5, 1814	Mar. 5, 1814
46.	Horseman	Abraham Whorton	Jan. 5, 1814	Mar. 5, 1814
47.	1st Sergeant	Wm. Clements	Jan. 5, 1814	Mar. 5, 1814
48.	Ensign	Josiah Hickman	Jan. 5, 1814	Mar. 5, 1814
		Benjamin Pounds		

Georgia, Jackson County:

I, Joseph Whorton, Captain and Commander of a detachment of Soldiers stationed at Fort Daniel in the county and state aforesaid, do certify that seventeen soldiers were stationed at the above Camp or Fort for the space of sixty days, viz., from the fifth day of January, 1814, to the fifth day of March, 1814, both days inclusive, and rations were issued to said soldiers under the contract of Dudley Jones amounting to One Thousand and Twenty. And I also certify that two horses was stationed at the aforesaid Camp or Fort sixty days, and that forage rations was issued for said horses amounting to One Hundred and Twenty forage rations under the contract of said Dudley Jones.

Given under my hand this 29th day of April, 1814.

JOSEPH WHORTON, Captain,
Commandant.

Georgia, Jackson County:

Pursuant to the above orders I caused to be issued to the Troops regularly detached and the Volunteers under my command in the execution of Fort Daniel, near the Hog Mountain in Jackson County, ten gallons and one fourth of good Brandy which I certify to have been consumed by the aforesaid Troops and Volunteers in said service; also certify that the above brandy to have been received of Tandy Key, of said county.

Given under my hand this 13th of November, 1813.

NEHEMIAH GARRISON, Captain,
Commanding Fort Daniel.

N.B.: The charge for the brandy was $1 per gallon.

I Certify that myself and Major J. T. Terrell furnished the Troops and Volunteers, under my command, Six Gallons and a Half of brandy from the above orders for part of their rations due them for whilst in erecting of Fort Daniel in Jackson County.

Given under my hand this 13th of December, 1813.

NEHEMIAH GARRISON, Captain,
Commanding Fort Daniel.

Georgia, Jackson County:

Pursuant to the above orders I have caused to be issued to the Troops regularly detached and Volunteers under my command in the execution of Fort Daniel, near the Hog Mountain in Jackson County, ten bushels and a half of corn meal which I certify to have been consumed by the aforesaid Troops and Volunteers in said service, and also certify that quantity of meal to have been furnished by James Clements of said county.

Given under my hand this 13th of December, 1813.

NEHEMIAH GARRISON, Captain,
Commanding Fort Daniel.

N. B.: The price of the meal, fifty cents per bushel. Carriage to the mill, from thence to the fort, $1.50.

Georgia, Jackson County:

Pursuant to the above orders I have caused to be issued to the Troops regularly detached and Volunteers under my command in the execution of Fort Daniel, near the Hog Mountain in Jackson County, nine hundred and forty-four pounds of beef which I certify to have been consumed by the aforesaid Troops and Volunteers in said service, and also certify that quantity of beef to have been furnished by Isam Williams, of said County, who, on that occasion, supplied the Troops and Volunteers as a patriot should have done.

Given under my hand this 13th of December, 1813.

       NEHEMIAH GARRISON, Captain,
        Commanding at Fort Daniel.

N.B.: The charge for the beef was $3 per hundred.

The State of Georgia
To Dudley Jones, Dr.
 29th day of April, 1814.
  To 104 rations issued to spies stationed at
  Fort Daniel, @ 18 cents, 3 mills $19.03
  To 104 forage rations issued to spies' horses,
  @ 40 cents $41.60

Georgia, Jackson County:

I, Joseph Whorton, Captain and Commander at Fort Daniel, do certify that two spies were stationed at the above fort during the term of fifty-two days, commencing on the thirteenth day of January, 1814, and ending on the fifth day of March, 1814, both days inclusive, and that rations were issued to said spies and their horses under the contract of Dudley Jones, amounting to 104 rations and 104 forage rations.

 Given under my hand this 29th day of April, 1814.

       JOSEPH WHORTON, Captain,
        Commandant.

The State of Georgia,
To Dudley Jones, Dr.
  To issuing rations of provisions to seventeen
  Soldiers, sixty days, at 18 cents 3 mills per
  ration amounting to 1,020 rations $186.66
  To 120 forage rations @ 40 cents per ration .... $ 48.00

State of Georgia,
To Chas. Price, Dr.
  To 3¾ gallons whiskey @ 62½ cents per gallon ...... $ 2.34½
  To one Runlett .... .75
  One bushel salt 4.00
  One Waggonerary Arms to Hog Mountain 3.00

                  $10.09½

I certify that the above was furnished and performed by Mr. Charley Price on my requisition certified by me this 26th day of May, 1814.

       NEHEMIAH GARRISON, Captain,
        Formerly Commanding Fort. Daniel.

The State of Georgia,
To Isham Williams, Dr.
    For 944 pounds of beef furnished by him to the Militia stationed at Fort Daniel in Jackson County under the command of Captain Garrison at $3 per hundred $28.32

To James Clements,
    For 10½ bushels corn meal furnished as above at 50 cents per bushel $5.25
    Hauling the corn to the mill, thence to the Fort 1.50

                                                              6.75

To Tandy Key,
    For 10½ gallons of brandy at $1 per gallon, furnished as above 10.25

To Tandy Key and Nehemiah Garrison,
    For 6½ gallons of brandy furnished as above at $1 per gallon, the price in the certificate not stated . 6.50

To Charles Price,
    As per account herewith rendered for sundries 10.09¼

                                                             $61.91¼

GEORGIA JACKSON COUNTY FEDERAL ROAD

                                              14th January 1827

His Excellency G M Troup—

    Sir: In The Year 1813, I Was Classed in The first Class According to The Classification of The Militia of This State and Agreeable to Executive Orders.

    I Vollunteered for Sixty days Service, and Was Stationed at The hogmountain Fort, Which Agreeable To Orders Was to be in Lieu of a Six Months Tour, And Was at That Time Received as Such by The Authority of The State.

    And Your petitioner Whishes Your Honour to Say Whether he has legally Served his Six Months Tour or Not, And Whether you Think he With others in like Circumstances is Entitled to an Extry draw in the land lottery Agreeable to The late Act of The legislature giving an Extra draw to The Soldiers, That Served in The late War—

    And in So doing You Will Oblige a True friend And Well Wisher,
                        Yours With high Esteem—

    Sir if You Think This Worty of an Answer You Will be So Good as to Address Kellogs Office

REVERSE	Jacob Braselton paid 12½ His Excellency G M Troup Milledgeville Georgia paid 12½
Jefferson J. C. Ga 20th Jany 1827	Jacob Braselton 1827

(Original on file, Department of Archives, Atlanta)

GILMER AT STANDING PEACHTREE

It became necessary, in the opinion of army officials, to establish another fort farther out in the Indian territory. The war-like attitude of the Indians required, if it did not demand, that the frontier be so strongly garrisoned that there would be little, if any, danger of the Indians' invading the white settlements. Accordingly, George R. Gilmer, a young lieutenant of the 43rd Regiment, and who was later governor, was ordered to advance into the territory west of Hog Mountain and erect another fort. In his book, "Georgians," Gilmer refers to this expedition in the following words: "In October, 1813, I received a commission as first lieutenant in the 43rd Regiment. I marched with recruits, without arms except refuse drill muskets, and a small quantity of loose powder and unmoulded lead. My appointed station was on the banks of the Chattahoochee, about 30 or 40 miles beyond the frontiers of the state, near an Indian town, not far from where the Georgia Railroad now crosses the Chattahoochee River. I was ordered to build a fort. A few days after I arrived at the standing peachtree," etc.

Lieutenant Gilmer, with his recruits, probably men stationed at Fort Daniel at Hog Mountain, marched thirty miles into the Indian territory and erected a fort at Standing Peachtree. This necessitated the opening of a road from Fort Daniel, at Hog Mountain, to Gilmer's new fort at Standing Peachtree, thirty miles from Hog Mountain. This road immediately became the most important road in this section of the state. It connected Fort Daniel at Hog Mountain with the fort at the Standing Peachtree on the Chattahoochee, thirty miles from Hog Mountain. The road was called Peachtree Road from the time it was opened for travel and it still is called Peachtree Road. The original Peachtree Road, therefore, extended from Hog Mountain to the Standing Peachtree.

A history of this road and some incidents connected with its construction will not appear out of place in this narrative. The opening of the road connecting the two forts was an important event of that day. And two young men, who were employed both in marking out the road and in opening it up for travel, became two outstanding citizens of Gwinnett County. They were William Nesbit and Isham Williams.

PEACHTREE ROAD OPENED

The officer whose duty it was to have this road constructed was probably Captain Nehemiah Garrison, who was in command of the detachment of soldiers when Fort Daniel was erected; and the next officer in rank was Lieutenant George R. Gilmer, afterwards prominent in Georgia as a member of congress and governor of this state. Writing in 1873 Judge R. D. Winn refers to this event as follows:

"There is probably but one man now living who assisted to garrison that post; and that man is our venerable and respected fellow citizen, James Stanley, now nearly ninety years of age. It became necessary to establish another post in communication with this one farther out in the Indian country; and the commandant at Fort Daniel procured the services of Robert Young, Isham Williams and William Nesbit, who were stock raisers and well acquainted with the country, to mark out the route. These three men, accompanied by Lieutenant Gilmer and a detachment from the fort, proceeded to the task by following the trail leading from the white settlement to Hog Mountain and from there to Suwanee Old Town or to the settlement of John Rogers, near the mouth of Suwanee Creek." They followed this trail to where it crossed the ridge, known since as Peachtree ridge, and then followed this ridge to an old Indian settlement near the Chattahoochee River where Montgomery's ferry was afterwards established in what later became Fulton County. The road thus surveyed terminated at the old Indian settlement; and it was generally understood that at this settlement there was a solitary peachtree of large size, and the place ever afterwards was called The Standing Peachtree, and the road thus marked out connecting the two forts was called Peachtree Road, and is so called at the present time. Hence Peachtree Road, Peachtree Creek and Peachtree Street.

"Nesbit, one of the party employed to mark out the road, was then a young man of wonderful activity and swift of foot as the following incident will show. On traveling the route for the proposed road, a wild turkey, disabled in one of its wings, ran across their way and Nesbit took after it and soon captured it. He was more successful than was Joe Hill in a similar race afterwards. Joe was a large backwoodsman in the early settlement of the county, large in body, but moderate in intellect, and still less in education and the use of language. He spent his time in the woods with his rifle, all the property he had, and got his living by killing deer, turkeys, bears and other wild game. On one of his hunts he shot a large gobbler and broke its wing. Throwing down his gun, he pursued it at the top of his speed for four miles and it was nip and tuck. On going down hill, Joe would 'crease' on it, but going up hill it would 'juce' away. Joe Hill was a brother of Josh Hill, a worthy fellow citizen who lived near the Appalachee, the scene of Joe's race with the turkey, and who, when a big boy, walked from Augusta to his home on the Appalachee, 140 miles, eating during the trip but one meal, a few bites with a wagoner who had stopped by the roadside to feed his team and eat dinner.

"After this road was marked out, or surveyed, it was important that it be constructed or opened up. Isham Williams, William Nesbit and Bob Young were employed to grade or construct the road, each one agreeing to furnish some hands, and William Nesbit was to superintend the work.

"I am able," continued Judge Winn, "to give a list of the persons engaged in opening of the road, as one of them, Hiram Williams, is still living, a valued citizen of the county and held in high esteem by his fellow citizens. William Nesbit was 'boss.' John Young, Lewis Lawly, John Lawly, and a negro man did the work; and Hiram Williams and Gustin Young, who were boys, drove the cart. Isham Williams and Bob Young, who accompanied the party, were generally on picket duty, looking out for Indians who were then on the war path. On the evening before reaching the end of the road, as they were getting far down the Chattahoochee and in proximity to the Indian settlements, Young thought it advisable that he and Williams should go off on a reconnoissance, lest the Red Skins give them a surprise, and accordingly, they mounted their horses and rode off. When night came, Nesbit and his men struck camp, built a fire, fed their stock and prepared supper for themselves. While eating they heard, to their dismay, a clear and shrill 'whoop, whoop, whoope-e-e!' All dropped their cups and, alarmed, rose to their feet, for it was evidently an Indian war-whoop, and all eyes were turned to Mr. Nesbit, and the two boys placed themselves near him. Soon again, and nearer, 'whoop, whoop, whoope-e-e' rang out and the whole party took to the woods and secreted themselves. Mr. Nesbit kept the boys near him. Soon galloping horses were heard approaching the campfire and the voice of Williams calling for Nesbit was recognized, greatly to the relief of Mr. Nesbit and his party. The fearful war whoop had emanated from him as a bit of mischief, 'to try the metal of the boys.'

"The road was opened and for doing the work the contractors were paid $150.00. Bob Young, referred to above, was a character. His like has seldom been seen and will seldom be seen hereafter. He was original in his looks, in his language, in his habits, and in the character of his mind. Wholly illiterate, with no knowledge of books except the great book of nature from which he drew liberally, he was a man of superior sense, superior judgment, and had stored up, from observation, a large fund of information that was valuable to him and his friends. While a confirmed infidel, perhaps an atheist, he was true to his word, faithful to his honor, truthful to the fullest extent. His word, his promises and his integrity were never questioned by those who knew him. He always wore his hair tied in a 'queue' which he prized most highly and of which he was proud to the day of his death."

Fort Daniel Marker

A memorial to the officers and soldiers who erected the fort and who were stationed there was dedicated Sunday afternoon, October 5, 1941. The marker stands on the roadside near the site where the fort was erected. The inscription on the marker reads as follows:

"Just south, in sight of this spot, stood Fort Daniel, provided by legislative act of 1812, completed December 14, 1813, under orders of Brigadier General Frederick Beall and Major Tandy Key, commanding the 25th Regiment Georgia Militia. Captain Nehemiah Garrison and Captain Joseph Whorton were among the officers in direct charge. This post defended by troops and volunteers and its intelligence service proved a bulwark against hostile British and Indian incursions."

The county historian asked and received the aid of the Division of State Parks in securing the marker. The Hugh L. Holt Post, American Legion, sponsored the program. The Sunbury Chapter, Daughters of the American Revolution, of Winder, participated in the exercises, and addresses were made by John C. Houston, Robert Lee Avary, and Judge Clifford Pratt.

Chapter III

GEOGRAPHY AND GEOLOGY

Location

IN AGE, Gwinnett is the 39th county, and is situated on the ridge between Atlanta and Athens. It is bounded on the north by the Chattahoochee River, on the east by Hall and Barrow Counties, on the south by Walton and Rockdale, and on the west by DeKalb and Fulton. Atlanta is only thirty miles west of Lawrenceville; Stone Mountain rears its head just across the county line; Athens, with its University of Georgia, lies sprawled over a hill at the junction of two paved highways that traverse this county, and Gainesville is scarcely more than a dozen miles beyond the county line on another highway that sweeps across the northern part of the county from Atlanta to Washington.

Gwinnett is one of the large counties, having an area of 440 square miles, or approximately 281,600 acres, divided into 3,800 farms. It is well watered and well drained. The ridge running east to west, a short distance south of the Chattahoochee, forms a watershed that separates the drainage basin of the Chattahoochee from the basin of the Altamaha. The Appalachee rises near Hog Mountain. The Little Mulberry rises a short distance east of Hog Mountain. The Alcova rises in part within the corporate limits of Lawrenceville, but the main branch of that stream rises near Sunny Hill school. The Yellow river has two or three springs in Lawrenceville, but its most northern source is near Rock Springs Methodist Church in Hog Mountain district. Of the four rivers that rise in this county, the Little Mulberry and the Appalachee flow into the Oconee, while the Alcova and the Yellow rivers unite and form the Ocmulgee.

There are many creeks that wind their way through the county. Among them are Richland, Suwanee, Bush, Crooked, Ivy, Level, Wild Cat, Redland, Jackson, Sweetwater, Beaver Ruin, Downing, Pamatree, Bay, Haynes, No Business. All the rivers and larger streams had high banks and carried several feet of water and were alive with fish of various kinds at the time the county was created and the pioneers came into its borders.

Topography

There are no mountains in the county, though some of the hills east of Hog Mountain are referred to as mountains by the natives. Along the rivers are some hills and there is also much fertile land, called bottoms, on these rivers. The low lands on the Chattahoochee produce enormous yields of corn and other crops. The larger part of the county is comparatively level. In the southern part of the county there are outcroppings of granite much like that found at and near Stone Mountain.

The altitude at Lawrenceville is between 1,000 and 1,200 feet. Other portions of the county are a few feet less.

CLIMATE

The climate is mild and healthful. A killing frost is seldom seen before the tenth of November and March usually ushers in peach blossoms and the cheerful notes of the bluebird. White's "Historical Collections of Georgia," under date of 1854, gives the names of several citizens who lived to a ripe old age: Daniel Clower, 87; John Lawrence, 85; Stephen Harris, 90; Jonathan Johnson, 80; Lewis Deshons, 80; Owen Andrews, 90; Edward Johnson, 87; Sarah Hunt, 81; Mrs. Shaddock, 100; Mr. Hunt, 100; George Wilson, 100; John Davis, 110; George Thrasher, 93.

The average temperature is about 55 F., and the average rainfall annually is about 50 inches. Growing season, six and a half months.

ROCKS AND MINERALS

The Hall County gold belt attains much greater commercial importance in Gwinnett county than in the counties to the southwest. Mining developments have so far been quite limited in extent, but enough has been done to prove the presence of some well defined quartz veins, yielding ore of a very good grade. The more important mining operations have been carried on in the vicinity to Buford, a town in the northwestern part of the county on the main division of the Southern Railroad.

The gold belt traverses the northeast corner of the county and closely parallels the Southern Railway from which it is distant only about a mile on the northwest. The close proximity of this portion of the Hall County gold belt to stations on the main division of an extensive railway system, together with easy accessibility to Atlanta, the most commercially important city of the State, gives the Gwinnett County deposits unusual advantage of location.

The majority of the auriferous quartz veins examined were found to cut the trend of the enclosing formations at a distant angle. In some of the veins, that have been worked, galena is a conspicuous sulphide.

At the Piedmont mine it occurs in considerable quantities, and is reported at this locality as being argentiferous.

Harris Property—This property, on Lot 275, 7th district, is about a mile northeast of Suwanee. Two quartz veins occur here within something like a hundred yards of each other. It is reported that one of these veins was mined before the Civil War. A sample taken from the southern vein and assayed by the Survey gave only a trace of gold.

Suwanee, or Level Creek Mine—This mine is about four miles west of Buford on Lot 289, 7th district. The tract on which it is situated is known locally as the Simmons property.

Sample from vein in open cut, $7.44 per ton. Sample from ore pile, $4.15 per ton.

Piedmont Mine—This mine, on Lot 304, 7th district, is situated about two miles west of Buford. From approximately eighty tons of ore, milled when the mine was in operation, about $605.00 worth of gold was obtained.

Placer Deposits of Richland Creek and Tributaries—Considerable valley land on Richland Creek, close to the Piedmont mine, is reported as being auriferous. At the edge of this tract, along a tributary branch, the Richland Gold Mining Company worked an acre or two of placer deposits a number of years ago. It was not learned what success attended these operations.

A little higher up the branch just mentioned considerable placer work has been done in the past years. The strip of valley land along the upper course of this branch is very narrow, but it is reported that a good many thousands of dollars worth of gold were obtained. At the upper end of the old workings it is claimed that a small vein occurs known as the "Nugget" vein, numerous nuggets having been obtained at that point.

Owens Mine—The Owens mine, on Lot 349, 7th district, is three miles west of Buford. No mining operations have been carried on at the locality for some years.

To our knowledge, there is but one deposit of molding sand located in Gwinnett County. It is one mile west of Duluth.

Sand deposits are located in Lawrenceville, one and one-half miles southeast of Lawrenceville, on Shoal Creek; and one which is located one mile north of Duluth, and another located on Suwanee Creek, one and a half miles east of Suwanee.

Granite is located at the following places in Gwinnett County:
The Sawyer Quarry, three-fourths mile northwest of Snellville.
The Snell Quarry, two miles south of Snellville.
The Turner Quarry, five miles southeast of Lawrenceville.
The Ewing property, one and one-half miles southwest of Lawrenceville.
The Cates Quarry, one-half mile northwest of Lawrenceville post office.
The Tribble Quarry, three-fourths mile north of Grayson post office.
The Langley Quarry, two miles south of Grayson post office.
The Mayfield property, one-half mile north of Rosebud.

The Lawrenceville Quarry, at Lawrenceville.

The McElvaney Shoals property, three miles northeast of Loganville.

A number of diamonds have been reported at various times in a number of counties in the State, Gwinnett County being one of the counties noted in which one or more have been found. The list has been compiled from old books, and the reports of individuals. Gwinnett County is not listed as being among those in which a specific find is noted. Most of the finds lack satisfactory verification, and in some instances one is led to suspect that pure deception has been practiced, and that in still other cases other minerals, as very clear quartz crystals have been honestly mistaken for diamonds. However, there are a few well authenticated finds, which place the existence of diamond-bearing rocks in Georgia not beyond the bounds of a probability.

Gneisses are located at the following places in Gwinnett County:

The Sawyer Quarry, Land Lot 25, 5th district, three-fourths mile northwest from Snellville.

Granite gneiss also occurs on Land Lots 37, 38, 39, 5th district, one and one-half miles northeast of Snellville.

The Snell Quarry, two miles south from Snellville.

Dr. M. A. Born's place, two miles east of Lawrenceville.

The Turner Quarry, five miles southeast of Lawrenceville.

The Ewing property, at Ewing's mill, one and one-half miles southwest of Lawrenceville.

The G. W. Cates Quarry, one-half mile northwest of Grayson post office.

The Tribble and Bennett property, three-fourths mile north of Grayson post office.

Mr. Thomas Langley's Quarry, two miles south of Grayson post office.

Mr. E. W. Mayfield property, one-fourth mile north of Rosebud post office.

Lawrenceville Quarry, just outside the town of Lawrenceville.

The McElvaney Shoals property, eight miles east from Lawrenceville, three and one-half miles southeast from Grayson post office.

There are two soapstone deposits located in Gwinnett county, one on Mr. Thomas Doss' property, five miles south of Buford, and another, one hundred and fifty yards south of Norcross depot.

Gold in Gwinnett County is found on the following properties:

A. W. Amphlett, Lot 289, Buford, Georgia, Simmons Mine, three miles southwest of Buford, one mile southwest of Sugar Hill.

Level Creek Mining Company, Suwanee Mine, Buford.

J. A. Thompson, Buford, Ga.

Old Shelley property, three and one-half miles southwest of Buford, Ga.

The geology of Gwinnett County is complicated. That county lies in the upper middle section of the great area of crystalline rocks. The rocks consist in large part, of granite and mica schist. There is a considerable amount of granite in Gwinnett County although at present not much is being quarried. Granite of the Lithonia type is common in the county. Gneiss of the Lithonia type is common around Lilburn and Gloster, along the Seaboard Airline Railroad. At least half or more of the county is underlaid by granite. In the northwestern part of the county along the Southern Railway, there is an extensive occurrence of Brevard schist. This is a fine grained muscovite schist which contains more or less graphite and deposits of graphite schist which may occur in this belt. All of these rocks are of great geologic age and are usually ascribed to that first period of geologic time known as the Pre-Cambrian.

Flora and Fauna

Primeval forests, timber as fine as could be found east of the Mississippi, covered this territory. On every lot stood pine, hickory, poplar, maple, walnut, sycamore, black gum, sweet gum, chestnut, oak, dogwood, cedar, elm, ash.

Animal life was plentiful: Turkey, bear, deer, beaver, fox, squirrel, wolf, panther, mink, coon, opossum, quail, pigeon. The creeks and rivers were alive with fish: Sucker, jack, cat, eel, perch, trout. Geese and ducks rode all the water courses, and birds common to this climate swarmed over the country side. The eagle pitched its nest atop the forest pine and the beaver built its home deep in the bank of every stream. Millions of wild pigeons darkened the sky in their flight and the trees groaned under their weight as they settled down to roost. The Indian roasted his turkey and deer over the coals in his wigwam and the owl made its breakfast on the quivering flesh of the dying rabbit.

This land was a goodly heritage. Nature was lavish in its gifts. Temperate climate, fertile soil, grand forest, abundant streams, ample rainfall, a hunter's paradise—all these and more were here when the Indians moved out and the white man came in.

Chapter IV

CREATION OF GWINNETT COUNTY

Name

THE county bears the illustrious name of Button Gwinnett. In the registry of the church of St. Peter, at Wolverhampton, Staffordshire, England, Button Gwinnett and Ann Bourn signed the following document: "Button Gwinnett of this parish, bachelor, aged 22 years and upwards, and Ann Bourn of the same, spinster, aged 22 years, were married in this church by license from Prerogative Court of Canterbury this nineteenth day of April in the year one thousand, seven hundred and fifty-seven, by me. John Kaye, clerk." Gwinnett was the son of Rev. Samuel Gwinnett, of Gloucestershire, a minister of the Church of England. A friend of his mother, named Button, willed him 100 pounds, hence the name Button Gwinnett. The name was first spelled Gwynnedd, then Gwynett, then Gwinnett. He was in the grocery trade with his father-in-law for some time. From 1759 to 1762 he carried on an extensive exporting business. In 1765 he had established a store in Savannah which he soon disposed of and bought St. Catherine's Island from Thomas Bosomworth, and became one of the largest land owners in the colony. He was a Justice of the Peace in 1767, commissioner to regulate pilotage in 1768, a member of the assembly in 1869. In 1776 Gwinnett was elected as one of the delegates to the Continental Congress and on August 2, 1776, signed the Declaration of Independence. He was speaker of the assembly that drafted the first constitution of Georgia. It is generally agreed that to him belongs the distinction of having done the major portion of the work of drafting this important document. On March 4, 1777, he was elected Governor and served several months. May 15, 1777, Lachlan McIntosh called Gwinnett "A scoundrel and a lying rascal." Gwinnett challenged McIntosh to a duel. They met May 16th, stood twelve feet apart, and at the count of three fired at each other. Both were injured. Gwinnett died on May 19th, and lies in an unknown grave in Savannah.

Creation of the County

The territory included within the boundaries of this county has played an interesting and important part in the history of our state and nation from the time of the founding of the colony of South Carolina and the colony of Georgia down to the day of this writing. A large part of the territory included in this state was a part of the colony of South Carolina. The charter granted by the king of

England to Oglethorpe and his associates described the boundaries of the colony of Georgia in the following words: "Do give and grant to said corporation all those lands, countries and territories situate, lying and being in that part of South Carolina which lies from the most northern part of a stream or river, commonly called the Savannah, all along the seacoast to the southward, unto the most southern stream of a certain other great water or river, called the Altamaha, and westerly from the heads of the said rivers, respectively, in direct line to the South Seas."

The colony of Georgia included the territory lying between the Savannah and Altamaha rivers and between two lines from the heads of said rivers westerly to the Mississippi River. The head of the Savannah River is the Kiowee River, and the head of the Altamaha River is Yellow River, which rises near Rockspring Methodist Church in Hog Mountain district. The colony of Georgia, therefore, included that part of Gwinnett County east of the Yellow River as well as that part between the Chattahoochee River and a line running west from a spring at Rockspring Methodist Church to the DeKalb County line.

Franklin County was created in 1784, and extended to the Appalachee River. Jackson County was created in 1796 out of Franklin, and its western boundary was the Appalachee. Gwinnett County was created in 1818; its western boundary being the Hightower Indian trail, and its eastern boundary the Appalachee River, thence a line northeast to the Hall County line. This act was signed by Benjamin Williams, speaker of the house of representatives; Mathew Talbot, president of the senate, and William Rabun, governor. Four days after the passage of this act another act was passed adding a part of Jackson County to Gwinnett, and providing legal machinery for organizing the county and starting it on its career.

That part of Jackson added to Gwinnett extended from the Appalachee River on the line of Walton County to the Hog Mountain road at Jug Tavern, thence up the Okoloco Indian trail or road by the home of Jesse Osborn at Cedar Hill, County Line Academy, Bethabra Baptist Church, Thompson's Mill to the Mulberry fork of the Oconee River, thence a direct line to the corner of Gwinnett County on top of the Chattahoochee ridge, near Hog Mountain.

All militia officers and justices of the peace living in that part of Jackson County that was added to Gwinnett were to hold and exercise their respective offices in this county in like manner as if commissioned for this county.

Until a suitable courthouse could be erected, it was provided that all courts and elections should be held at the house of Elisha Winn, who lived one mile east of the Appalachee River. After giving twenty days' notice, two justices of the peace were required to hold and superintend an election for five justices of the Inferior Court, and these five justices were then required to hold an election for clerks of the Superior and Inferior Courts, sheriff, county surveyor, coroner, and other county officials. The justices of the Inferior Court were appointed commissioners of the courthouse and jail and vested with authority to select a site for the location of public buildings and enter into contracts for building a suitable courthouse and jail.

Provision was made to lay off the county into company districts and for electing two justices of the peace and militia officers in said several company districts. The militia became a part of the second brigade of the Fourth Division of the Militia of Georgia.

Gwinnett County was added to the Western Judicial Circuit and Superior Courts were to be held on the third Mondays in March and August. The justices of the Inferior Court were authorized to select persons for jurors and proceed to draw grand and petit jurors at such time and place that was most convenient.

The first elections were held as the act provided at the house of Elisha Winn, one mile east of the Appalachee River, and the first Superior Court was held in Judge Winn's barn, Judge John M. Dooly, of the Western Circuit, presiding.

The first county officers elected were William Blake, sheriff, who was commissioned by the governor March 25, 1819; James Wardlaw, clerk Superior Court, commissioned March 25, 1819; Thomas A. Dobbs, clerk Inferior Court; James Loughridge, tax collector, commissioned March 30, 1819; John W. Beauchamp, tax receiver, commissioned March 30, 1819; John Wynn, coroner, commissioned March 25, 1819; James C. Reed, surveyor, commissioned March 25, 1819. The clerk of the Inferior Court was made treasurer.

The first five judges of the Inferior Court were George Reid, Samuel Reid, John Cupp, William Towers, and Joseph Morgan, all of whom were commissioned February 2, 1819. Elisha Winn was commissioned July 21, 1820, succeeding, apparently, Samuel Reid.

John Treadwell was the county's first representative, and George Reid its first state senator, both of whom attended the 44th session of the General Assembly in 1819.

Created December 15, 1818, the county had a full set of officials within three months, duly elected and commissioned. Up to this time, however, the county had not been surveyed nor the land distributed by lottery. Nevertheless, the official machinery of the county was operating in perfect order. Capable men had been chosen for county officials, taxes levied, jurors selected, courts held, captain's districts laid out, militia organized, plans for public buildings outlined, and order maintained.

The act requiring all courts and elections be held at the house of Elisha Winn was amended in December, 1819, giving the Inferior Court authority to erect a temporary courthouse and at the same time prohibiting the court from selecting a permanent site until the land had been distributed by lottery and the center of the county ascertained. In conformity with this act, the justices of the Inferior Court decided to erect a temporary courthouse one mile west of the present location of the courthouse, a site that appeared to be near the center of the county. Isham Williams built this temporary courthouse early in the year 1820, for the court at its March session in 1820 directed the clerk of the court to pay the contractor, Isham Williams, fifty-six dollars. This temporary courthouse was erected on lot number 143. This lot was drawn by Nehemiah Posey, of Pulaski County. William Wardlaw came into possession of this lot and agreed to donate ten acres for the county town or county site. He later repudiated the agreement, which made it necessary for the court to select another site. After the distribution of the land by lottery, it was learned that an adjoining lot, number 146, had been drawn by John Breedlove, of Hancock County. Accordingly, Elisha Winn, a land trader who had been a prominent citizen of Jackson County and a member of the Inferior Court of that county, and who was at that time a justice of the Inferior Court of this county, was selected by the court to buy one of three lots for the county town: Lot 145, 146, or 147, in the fifth land district, this lot being as near the center of the county as any other lot that was then for sale. Winn met Breedlove at Milledgeville on March 4, 1821, and paid him $200 for this lot of 250 acres. Breedlove made the deed to Winn, who paid the fee for placing the deed on record. On his return to Lawrenceville, Winn reported the details of the transaction to the Inferior Court, the Court immediately ratified the same, and then Winn made the deed over to the Inferior Court, thus placing the title to the property in the members of the court and their successors.

With 250 acres in their possession, it then became the duty of the justices of the Inferior Court to select a site for the courthouse square around which the county town would be located. The five justices probably walked over the entire lot, then covered in primeval forest, and finally decided on the spot where the courthouse should be erected.

William Towers was employed to survey the lot for the courthouse and lay out the four streets bordering the courthouse square, and then to survey and mark out the adjacent lots and streets. For this work, he was paid $23.00. Lots on the four streets adjacent to the square were sold at public outcry and soon the noise of hammer and saw was heard there for the first time. The county officials began to buy lots on which to erect homes; prospective merchants attended the auction sales and stores, built with logs, were constructed around the square. A lawyer came along and looked for a place to hang out his shingle. A boarding house, among the first dwellings erected, did a rushing business. William Maltbie, who had been operating a store at Hog Mountain since 1814, moved to the new village and became its first postmaster. He was the second clerk of the Inferior Court, a position he held for more than twenty years. Dr. Philo Hall, Maltbie's brother-in-law, came from Connecticut and practiced his profession here until his death. About this time a young lawyer, N. L. Hutchins, located in Lawrenceville.

A temporary courthouse was quickly constructed and a jail was built out of logs on the lot south of the courthouse square. People from older counties, as well as from older and more populous states, flocked into the new county. On foot, on horseback, in ox carts and wagons they came in increasing numbers, and log cabins sprang up in all directions.

The county officials, all inexperienced in public affairs perhaps, faced their tasks of organizing the new county with commendable zeal. It was more than two years after the creation of the county before a permanent site for the county town could be selected by reason of the fact that the county had to be divided into land districts and lots and distributed by lottery. During this period the business of the county was conducted in an orderly and efficient manner by those who had been chosen to organize and set up the county government.

The site chosen by the justices of the Inferior Court on which to erect the public buildings and around which the town would be developed did not meet with popular favor. Both the northern and the southern parts of the lot appeared more suitable for such a purpose, there being a hill in the center of the site selected. The site chosen forms a watershed separating the basin of the Yellow River from the basin of the Alcova River. In those early days people looking for a place to erect a dwelling or a rude cabin selected a site near springs, not regarding its location and fitness for a permanent home. To be near a bold, free-flowing spring was the deciding factor in selecting a site to erect a dwelling. The justices of the Inferior Court, all residing in sparsely settled rural communities and actuated, perhaps, by a desire to follow this old custom, determined on locating the courthouse and the county seat town where the county officials and inhabitants of the village would have access to several bold springs. The first and last chores of the day the man of the house would be called upon to do would be to walk down to the spring, a hundred yards or more, and carry two buckets of fresh water to his home. The sheriff and other county officials, the doctor, the lawyer, and the merchants in the new village enjoyed the happy privilege of walking a quarter of a mile to one of the several springs within the corporate limits of the county town and supplying their offices and stores with buckets of the refreshing fluid.

There were several clear, bold springs on the site selected for the county town. The high estimate placed in springs by the authorities of the new town is shown by an order of the Inferior Court appointing John Brewster, John Appling, Benjamin Ivie, James Wardlaw and James McClure commissioners "to superintend and keep in order the springs belonging to the town of Lawrenceville, and that they be authorized to enforce such regulations as they may think calculated for the benefit of such springs." George Grace was paid forty dollars to fix one spring, and William Crawn received twenty-five dollars to fix another.

William Maltbie suggested the name for the new town. The people were fond of bestowing names of heroes on towns and counties. Gwinnett County took its name from Button Gwinnett, a signer of the Declaration of Independence; Lawrenceville was named in honor of Captain James Lawrence, a gallant naval officer. The four streets bordering the courthouse square bear the names of Commodore Perry, another great naval officer; Zebulon Montgomery Pike, explorer and soldier; George Croghan, famous soldier in the War of 1812; and Augustin Smith Clayton, one time judge of the Western circuit, and congressman.

While the county was being organized, surveyors began to divide the territory into land districts and the districts into land lots. The surveyors met with some trouble with the few remaining Indians who loitered here and there in the county; and an anonymous writer viewed with great alarm the fate of those pioneers who ventured to settle within the limits of the newly established county. Said this writer: "Nor let me be told about the counties of Gwinnett and other new counties lately laid off upon lands bought from the Indians. Shall these sterile spots be called acquisitions? After all the vaporings to make them appear to be acquisitions of some consequence, it is now known that in a few years they will become barren heaths, incapable of supporting even a vagabond, half-starved race."

While this anonymous writer complained and viewed with alarm, many of the well-to-do citizens of Gwinnett and Walton drove down to Eatonton and paid fifty cents to take a look at "The greatest natural curiosity now exhibited in America," which was an elephant that weighed four thousand pounds and was eighteen feet long from the end of the trunk to that of the tail. And the housewives of the two counties read with considerable amusement the advertisement of Billy Woodlief in a Milledgeville paper in which he stated that he had just received from the North a general "Assortment of the articles used in his profession, viz: perfumes, oils, soaps, brushes, razors, oranges, almonds, raisins, cocoa nuts, preserves. Suppers prepared at shortest notice. Dum vivimus vivamus. Has an elegant assortment of convoluted curls, spiral ringlets, and corsets for gentlemen. Those who have had the misfortune not to have been made in nature's choicest molds and who are desirous of an inimitable contour of form are particularly recommended to make use of the gentlemen's corsets."

Much of the merchandise mentioned in the preceding paragraph was on the shelves of Maltbie's store and Bogan's store at Hog Mountain and soon to be offered to the public in the stores in Lawrenceville. And other merchandise on display at Bogan's and Maltbie's stores at Hog Mountain included such household goods as corded bedsteads, feather beds, walnut sideboards, windsor chairs, candlesticks, spinning wheels, looms, reels, looking glasses, pewter basins, sitting chairs, copper stills, Dutch ovens, iron spiders, tea-kettles, cedar piggins, jugs, decanters, London window glass, wine glasses, dueling pistols, shot, powder horns, gunpowder, hand-made saw-gins, Swede iron, saddles, gigs, harness, corsets for men, tin trunks, bombazetts, osnaburgs, saddlebags. Among the groceries sold were muscovado sugar, Jamaica and Antigua rum, Spanish brandy, Philadelphia, rye whiskey, Teneriffe wine, claret, Holland gin, Malaga wine, London porter, Spanish "segars."

There were no sewing machines and no cooking stoves advertised for sale when this county was created and organized. They were not on the market in those days. The housewife cooked in the open fireplace and the spinning wheel and loom were indispensable necessities in the economy of every home. Clothing for the family was homemade, and provisions came from the cultivated farms and from forests and rivers. The fastest mode of travel was by horseback. There was not a match to start the morning fire and borrowing a live coal from a neighbor was a common practice among the early settlers. Then electricity was a dream and the candle was the only means of lighting the home and store. There was not even a postage stamp or envelope, and a letter was folded and addressed and the postage was often paid by the party receiving the message.

With the early settlers came the land trader and the slave speculator. The former knew that many who drew lots in the county would not become permanent residents and would sell their holdings for a song, and the speculator in slaves had a virgin territory in which to ply his trade. Both prospered.

The first advertisement of a sheriff's sale of a slave in the county appeared in a paper at Milledgeville, September 14, 1819. William Blake was the sheriff, the first to hold that office. The slave was a six-year-old boy, Isham, owned by James H. Kidd, who lived in the vicinity of Hog Mountain. The sale took place at the home of Elisha Winn, the place designated in the act creating the county where courts, elections and sheriff's sales should be held until a permanent location for the courthouse was selected.

John C. Eastman, Adjutant General of the State, ordered militia reviews for inspection in all the counties on July 10, 1819. The first review and inspection of the militia of this county was held on Monday, October 25, 1819.

John W. Beauchamp, first tax receiver, commissioned as such March 30, 1819, promptly made a digest of the property subject to taxation, and James Loughridge, first tax collector, published in the fall of 1819 a list of those who had not settled their tax bills. This list is used here for the purpose of preserving their names as among the first settlers and first taxpayers in the county. It is interesting to note also that the names of the districts appear for the first time. The new county was divided into company districts, each district having enough men to form a company of militia, and each district was referred to by the name of the man who was chosen as captain of the company. Hamilton's District included the territory in which a company of militia was organized with a captain by the name of Hamilton. It was called Hamilton's District. When a new captain took charge of the company, it was no longer Hamilton's District, but usually took the name of the new officer or captain. This method continued for many years.

HAMILTON'S DISTRICT—Stephen Brooks, Joshua Hill, Jesse Horn, James Jordan, Murdock Martin, James Rouin, David Spence, Wm. Stewart, Henry Thompson, Zachariah Thompson, Edward Wade, Sr.

GADDIS' DISTRICT—John Allen, —— Avory, Samuel Bloice, Thomas Dossett, Wm. Garner, Hiram Hall, John Johnston, Josiah Johnston, —— McColum, Wm. McCullers, John Mires, John Moss, Bud Mullins, Frederick McGuire, Benjamin Plaster, George Reid, Septimus Taylor, Jacob Thomas, Michael Thomas, David Powell, Wm. Wiley, Alexander Wright.

CARLISLE'S DISTRICT—James Askin, John Babb, James Baker, Samuel Baker, James Brown, David Corley, Jesse Dobbs, John Dobbs, Thomas Elrod, Obediah Glasgore, Notly Gillam, Thomas Holmes, John Howard, James Hunt, Mandfield Jinkins, James H. Kidd, Jeremiah Morgan, Jourdan Odum, Daniel Pittman, —— Stapleton, James Spuggins, Joseph Turner, Daniel Wester, Joseph White, Reuben Wilkinson.

CAPTAIN POOL'S DISTRICT—John Allen, Wm. Almon, Allen Burch, M. Caldwell, Martin Childers, Robert Caldwell, Wm. Copelin, Micajah Hendrick, Lazarus Jones, John Kite, Robert McGrady, Henry Mitchell, Hubbard Mitchell, Jerry Nesbit, Stephen Parker, B. Price, John Price, Clayton Steen.

CAPTAIN CUPP'S DISTRICT—Joshua Ballard, Arther Barefield, Isaac Bently, James Bonds, Jacob Bournes, Samuel Bournes, Wm. Brewster, Edward Browning, John Burnett, Robert Coker, Solomon Coker, Cheedle Cochran, Merril Collier, Samuel Dennis,

Moses Ellison, Wm. Ellison, John Evans, John Garner, ―― Garrett, Alexander Gustin, George Hagins, Edward Hill, James Hill, John Holyfield, Benjamin Lasiter, Thomas Laurens, John Rutledge, Thomas Minchew, Thomas Mulikin, Sr., Thomas Mulikin, Jr., John Oakly, Hugh Polk, Berry Ragsdale, Joseph Reid, John Seagers, Sr., John Seagers, Jr., Moses Smith, Thomas Throer, Elisha Turner, John Wall, Charles Weeks, John Wood.

CAPTAIN ELLISON'S DISTRICT—James Allen, John Austin, E. Austin, George Burnes, Abner Camp, William Camp, John Clarke, William Clayton, Hiram J. Gills, Joshua Howel, James Killgore, Wm. Killgore, Thomas Kirk, Beverly Perkerson, Joel Perkerson, Gallant Renolds, Ellis Wright, Paul Patrick.

CAPTAIN AUSTIN'S DISTRICT—Robert Adair, Levi Dempsey, Smith Kite, Wm. Malone.

Census of 1820

The census of 1820, two years after the county was created, shows who were the pioneers that settled in Gwinnett County. Of the 689 families in the county at that time, a woman was the head of 46. Of a total white population of 4,741, the males were 2,748 and the females 1,993.

David Dixon and Wilson Strickland were the largest slave owners, each having 14. George Reed, Sr., owned 10; Daniel Pittman, 4, and John Woodall, 5.

Twenty-one of the men who were heads of families were veterans of the Revolutionary War. Here these old veterans came to spend their declining years and here they did their part in planting deep in the fertile soil of the county's early social order the principles of industry, liberty, education and religion. These veterans were: Owen Andrews, Christopher Baker, Enoch Benson, James Camp, Sam C. Caruthers, Abner Coleman, William Copelin, Joseph Couey, Thomas Cox, Nathaniel Dobbs, Joseph Downey, Stephen Harris, Reubin Higgins, Edward Jackson, John Lawrence, William Liddell, John Mattox, Job Red, John Rutledge, Charles Walls, William Wardlaw.

The 1820 census gives the names of the heads of the families in the county, the number of other males and females of each family and the number of slaves, if any, owned by the head of each family. Many of these early settlers have descendants in the county at the present time.

Gwinnett Census of 1820

Head of Family	Other Males	Females	Slaves
Barton Abbott	2	1	
William Abbott	2	3	
Robert S. Adair	3	3	1

Head of Family	Other Males	Females	Slaves
John Adams	4	4	
William Adams			
Christopher Addison	1	2	1
John Agnew	8	4	
James Allen	7	4	
John Allen	3	3	8
William Anderson	1	2	
David Andrews	1	2	
Owen Andrews	3	4	
William Andrews	1	3	
Catherine Arrington		3	
Berry Atwood	3	3	
Jesse Austin	1	2	2
William Babb	5	8	
Crawford Bagwell	5	2	
Frederick Bagwell	1	2	1
Benjamin Baker			
Christopher Baker, Sr.	2	1	5
Green Baker	1		
Honor Baker			
Polly Baker			
William Baker			
Joshua Ballard	4	2	1
Sarah Bankston	2	4	
William Bankston	3	2	
Jesse Barker	1	1	
William Barkins	3	1	
John Barnet	4	3	
Jonathan Barnet	2	2	
Robert Barnhill	2	2	
William Barrett	4	7	
Mathias Bates			
William Baty	2	2	
Henrietta Baxley	5	2	
Dorcas Beam	2	3	
May Beam		1	
John Beasley	4	5	3
William Beasley	1	1	
William M. Beasley	2	2	
John W. Beauchamp	5	3	
Levi Beauchamp			
William Beauchamp	1		2
John Beauford	2	4	
Harman W. Bozeman	3	3	
James Bradberry			

Benjamin Brand	5	2	
Solomon Bridges	5	3	
Wiley Bridges	8	5	
George Brogdon	4	3	1
Jacob R. Brooks	2	1	
Paschal Brooks	1	1	
Ephraim Brown	1	1	
Fanning Brown	1	4	
Isaac Brown	3	5	
James Brown	7	3	
John Brown	5	3	
Joseph Brown	5	4	
Josiah Brown	3	5	
Thomas Brown	4	2	
Wiley Brown	1	1	
Edward Brumbalo	2	2	
Isaac Brumbalo	5	5	
Allen Burch	4	2	1
John Burgess	1	1	
Mary Burgis	2	2	3
John Burnett	1	2	1
Curtis Caldwell	6	5	1
James Caldwell	5	5	
John Caldwell	2	2	1
William Calhoun			
Abner Camp	4	4	5
Andrew Camp	3	4	
James Camp	5	1	
John Camp	7	4	
John Camp, Jr.	1	2	2
Robert B. Camp	4	1	
Solomon Camp	1	8	
William Campbell	3	1	
John Canaday	4	2	1
John N. Cargil	1	6	
Thomas Cargil	1	3	
Benjamin Carrell	1	1	
James H. Carrell	3	2	
Peter Carrell	1	4	
Thomas Carrell	4	4	1
David Carrimore	6	3	1
John Carrimore	1	1	1
Clement Carroll			
John Carter	3	1	5
James Caruthers	3		
Sam C. Caruthers	5	3	
David Castleberry	1	2	

Head of Family	Other Males	Females	Slaves
David Castleberry, Sr.	2	2	3
James Castleberry	3	2	1
Thomas Castleberry	1	4	
Joseph Cavender	3	8	1
Washington Chamberlain	1	7	1
Abraham Chandler	3	3	1
Douglas Childers	4	2	
Jonathan Chiles	2	4	
John Clark	5	5	
Henrietta Cleaton			
Middleton Cleaton			
Sam C. Cleaton			
William Cleaton	1	4	
Andrew Clements	3	4	
Charles Clements	6	4	
James Clements	1	1	5
William Clements	3	2	
Cheadle Cockrum	4	2	2
Abner Coleman			
Hezekiah Coleman	2	4	
Philip Coleman	3	4	1
Meredith Collier	7	4	
Merrill Collier	2	4	
Joseph Collins	3	5	
Joseph Colton	2	3	
Simeon Conger			
John Cook	2	2	
Thomas Copelin	2	1	
William Copelin	1	7	
Elisha Copland	3	1	
James Copland	6	3	
Thomas Cordery	2	1	
James Corlee	2	3	
Martha Corlee	3	4	
William Corlee, Jr.	3	1	
William Corlee, Sr.	3	3	
Curtis Corley	5	6	1
Joseph Couey	4	3	
Isaac Cowan	6	2	3
John Cox	2	6	2
Thomas Cox	4	6	2
Willie Cox	2	2	
Elijah Crawford	1	3	
James Crawford	5	2	2
Joseph Crockett	3	1	5
Celia Culberson	1	1	

Head of Family	Other Males	Females	Slaves
Henry Cupp	6	4	3
John Cupp	5	3	5
William Cupp	1	1	
Henry Curbow	5	8	1
Henry Curtis	1	2	
Elias Davis	3	1	1
Zacchariah Day	4	2	
John Defoor	6	8	5
Henson Dempsey	1	1	
Jesse Dempsey	6	6	
Lazarus Dempsey	2	3	
Levi Dempsey	4	4	
James Diamond	5	1	1
David Dixon	4	2	14
William H. Dixon	3	3	1
William Dobb	3	4	
Austin Dobbs	3	2	
Jesse Dobbs	4	1	2
John Dobbs	2	3	
Mormon Dobbs	1	3	
Nathaniel Dobbs, Sr.	3	5	1
Nathaniel Dobbs, Jr.	2	1	
Silas Dobbs	2	3	
Thomas A. Dobbs	3	3	
William Dobbs	2	2	1
Joseph Downey			
Patrick L. Dunlap	3	1	1
Joshua Easters			
Miles Easters			
William Easters	2	2	
Elizabeth Echols		2	4
William Echols	2	4	
James Edmundson	4	9	
Joseph Edmundson	1		
Charity Ellison		1	
Francis Ellison	1	2	
Moses Ellison	1	2	
Polly Ellison			
Robert Ellison	6	3	
Samuel Ellison	1	2	
Watson Ellison	3	2	1
William Ellison	1	5	
Lindsey Elsberry	1	1	
John Evans	3	1	1
William Evans	7	3	
Margaret Ezard	1	3	

Head of Family	Other Males	Females	Slaves
William Ezard	8	5	
James Farmer	2	2	
James Farmer	4	3	
John Farmer	2	2	
Morgan Fields	2	2	
William Fields	4	9	
Josiah Fincher	3	5	1
George Flanigan	5	4	
Polly Fowler	6	3	
Mary Fry	3	1	
Benjamin Fuller	6	5	
Henry Funderberg	3	5	2
William Fuqua	1	3	
John Gaddis, Sr.	3	5	
John Gaddis, Jr.	4	2	
John Gailor			
Margaret Gailor	2	5	
James Garrett	5	7	
John Gasaway	1	2	1
John Gay	1	2	
Joshua Gay	2	6	
James Gibson	2	4	
James Gilbert	2	1	4
Thomas Y. Gill	1	2	
Isaac Goodwin	3	5	
John Goodwin	6	2	
Neely Goodwin	1	1	
Isaac Gray	4	4	
Jonathan Gray	6	2	
Larkin Green	2	4	
Robert Green	4	4	
Benjamin Green	6	6	
William Green	5	1	1
William Greesom	3	2	
George M. Gresham	3	1	4
John Greson	1	2	
Jofe Griswell	3	4	
Wiley Gross	1		
William Guffin	2	2	1
Frederick M. Guin	3	2	
Peter Hairston	6	8	1
William Hairston	2	2	
John D. Hall			
William Hall	5	6	
James M. Hambleton	3	1	
Samuel Hambleton	4	1	2

Head of Family	Other Males	Females	Slaves
Joseph Hambrick	5	3	2
Mary Hamby	2	6	
Andrew Hamilton	6	14	4
Archy Hamilton	6	4	1
Joseph Hamilton	7	3	
Lewis Hamilton			
William A. Hamilton	2	1	
Hugh Hammel	5	7	1
Robert Hancock	3	4	1
Byos Haney	3	4	
William Haney			
Henry Harebuck	4	6	
Cyrus Harrington	1	2	
Benjamin Harris	6	5	
Buckner Harris	2	1	
Charles C. Harris	5	3	
Daniel Harris	4	3	
Elizabeth Harris	8	1	
Hiram C. Harris	3	1	
Jesse Harris	9	8	2
Stephen Harris	1	2	
Thompson Harris	4	3	
Josephus Harrison	7	3	
John Harrold	4	5	
Frederick Hart	2	5	
Peggy Hart		1	
William Hart	1		
James Harvil	4	2	
James Hayes	2	1	1
G. B. Haynes	3	1	3
Lewis Hays	2	1	
Andrew Hayslett	3	2	4
John Hearstile	4	8	
Micajah Hendrick	3	3	2
John Henry	2	1	1
William Henry	7	4	2
George Herd	2	3	
John Hewett	1		
James Hicks	4	3	2
Mathew Hicks	2	3	
Benjamin Higgins	2	4	
Joel Higgins	1	2	
Joseph Higgins	1	3	
Reuben Higgins			
Edward Hill	3	2	
James Hill	2	6	

Head of Family	Other Males	Females	Slaves
John Hill	2	3	
John Hill, Jr.	1	2	
Joseph Hill	3	3	
Joshua Hill	6	2	
William Hill	3	5	
John Holderfield	3	2	
Sally Holebrooks		2	
Richard Holt	2	2	3
Jess Horn	9	7	2
Stephen Horton	3	4	
Clayborn House	5	6	
Burdig Howell	1	1	
William Huckaby	3	3	
John Hudman	1	1	4
William Hudman	3	4	
Hezekiah Hudman	4	1	
Jennings Hulsey	1	1	2
John Humphrey	5	9	
George Humphries	6	2	
Shadrack Humphries	10	2	
Benjamin Ivy	4	3	
Benjamin Jackson	3	5	
David Jackson	1	6	
Edward Jackson	7	3	
John Jackson	5	6	1
William Jackson	2	1	
Tresso Jarman	4	4	
Joseph Jenkins	2	1	2
Miles Jennings	2	3	
James Jett	4	2	
Stephen Jett	3	4	
Nathan Jinkins	3	3	
Western Jinks	1		
William Jinks	2	5	
Willis Jinks	2	2	
Jourdan Jinn	4		
Josiah Johnson	2	4	
Thomas Johnson	3	4	
Elvira Jones			
Jinney Jones	1	1	
Joal Jones	4	2	
Joel Jones	4	3	3
Lazarus Jones	2	2	
Nancy Jones		1	
Samuel Jones	5	4	1
Thomas Jones	5	4	

Head of Family	Other Males	Females	Slaves
Thomas Jones	3	8	
Thomas Jones	3	2	6
Charles Jourdan	3	1	
James Jourdan	2	2	
Samuel Jourdan	3	1	
Drury Kelly			
Nancy Kelly	2	2	
Rachel Kelly		2	
James Kenady	1	3	
Samuel Key	2	1	
Sarah Key	1	3	
James H. Kidd	4	2	2
David Kight	1	4	
Henry Kight	1	4	
John Kight	2	3	1
North Kight	1	4	
Samuel Kight	2	2	
Thomas Kile	5	3	
James Kilgo	7	1	
William Kilgo	1	2	
John King	4	1	
Catherine Kirk		3	
George Kirk	2	2	
Isaac Knight	4	5	
Presley Knight	6	3	
Jeremiah Lambert	1	1	
Thomas B. Lanear	4	5	2
William Laney	4	3	
Ivy Larson	2	3	
Benjamin N. Lassiter	4	6	2
George Lathrum	1	1	
James Lawrence	1	1	
John Lawrence	5	2	
Sarah Lawson	2	4	
Edward Lee	3	2	
Henry Lee	2	3	
James Lee	1	1	
Samuel Lee	3	3	
John Leverett	5	1	1
Mich. H. Leverett	2	4	
William Liddle	1	1	3
John Liles	3	3	
John Linville	2	3	1
Francis Lock	1	1	
John Lock	3	3	
Elizabeth Loughridge		1	

Head of Family	Other Males	Females	Slaves
James Loughridge	3	5	
Wm. Loughridge	3	2	1
Christopher Lowrey	6	5	
Henry Lowrey	1		
Ephraim Mabry	4	4	2
John Maddox	1	2	
Hamlin D. Maddox	2	2	
William Malone	2		2
William Maltbie	2	2	1
Samuel Manders	5	2	
Thomas Mann	5	5	
Abraham Martin	5	6	1
George Martin	3	5	
Murdock Martin	4	4	
Samuel Martin	1	3	
William Martin	2	3	
William Mathews	5	8	
Ezekiel Matthews	3	4	2
Henry Matthews	2	2	
Thomas Matthews	3	3	
William Matthews	5	2	
John Mattox	1	6	2
Zacchariah Mattox	2	2	
Abagail Mayfield	3	1	
Battle Mayfield	3		
William Mays	1	2	
Thomas McAdams	1	3	2
James McBride	5	5	
John McCoy	1		
William McCulluh	3		
Richard McDuff	4	2	1
James H. McEwen	3	3	
Robert McEwen	2	5	
James McGinnis	1	1	
Silare McGrady	5	4	
Ephraim McLain	10	5	3
Thomas McLelon	3	2	
Sam C. B. McLure	3	2	
James McNeeley	1	2	
James McRight			
William Medford	4	4	
Isham Medlock	5	2	
James Mehathy	1	2	
Thomas Mehathy	4	3	1
Samuel C. Maloney	7	3	
Benjamin Merrill	1	2	1

Head of Family	Other Males	Females	Slaves
John Miars	1	1	
Robert Milford	3	4	
John Mills	4	2	
Nicholas Miner	4	3	1
William Minyard	3	2	
Henry Mitchell	2	2	
Ledford Mobley	3	5	
Benjamin Mankos	2	4	
Elizabeth Mankos	2	4	1
Asa Moore	4	3	
George Moore	6	3	
Willis Moore	4	6	
Jeremiah Morgan	2	3	
Joseph Morgan	4	7	
Austin Morris	1	1	
Shadrack Morris	4	5	
Thomas Morris	2	6	
Nineon Mulican	5	4	
Thomas Mulican	3	2	
John M. Mullen	2	1	
James Murphy	1	3	1
William Myrich	2	2	
Jeremiah Nesbit	1	1	2
William Nesbit	4	6	1
Ambrose Nichols	3	1	
Archibald Nichols	2	2	
Thomas Nichols	3	4	
Sally Nobles	1	2	
George Noland	5	3	2
Isaac Noland	1		
James Noland	6	5	1
Stephen Noland	3	5	
William Noland	1		
James Nolen	3	2	
Elijah Nunn	4	3	
Joseph O'Neal	3	2	1
Britain Osburn	3	3	1
Michael Osteen	2	2	
William J. Osteen	4	2	
Isaac Pace	6	5	2
George P. Parker			
Isaiah Parker	1	2	1
Stephen Parker	4	5	
Axom Pearce	2	1	
Edmund Pearce	2	3	
Gadwell Pearce	2	3	

HISTORY OF GWINNETT COUNTY, GEORGIA

Head of Family	Other Males	Females	Slaves
James Pearce	2	3	1
John Pearce	1	2	
Sion Pearce			
Susanna Pearce			
Wiley Pearce	5	5	1
William Pearce	2	1	3
Ruth Pearson	1	3	
Nimtod Pendley	4	3	
John Pepper	5	1	
Parker Peppers	3	3	
Sam G. Peppers	3	2	
Beverly Perkerson	3	3	
Dempsey Perkerson	5	5	
Joel Perkerson	2	3	
Robert Phillips	3	3	
Daniel C. N. Pittman	3		4
Benjamin Plaster	4	5	
Silas Pool	4	2	1
John Pounds	2	5	
Mary Pounds	1	4	2
Senate Powers	3	2	
Benjamin Price	1	2	
John Price, Sr.	2	1	1
John Price, Jr.	1	1	2
Joel Prickett	5	3	
Joshua Pritchett	7	4	
Benjamin Pruitt	1	1	
John Puckett	2	4	
Richard Puckett	9	3	
Green Pullen	2	3	
John W. Ragsdale	3	2	
Larkin Ragsdale	5	6	
William Rakestraw	3	4	
Charles Randolph	5	7	
Redding Reamus	2	1	
Frederick Reaves	1	1	
Isaac Reaves	3	2	
John Reaves	6	3	
Jonathan Reaves	3	3	
Loftin Reaves	1	1	
Malachi Reaves	9	2	
James Red	3	3	
Job Red	3	3	
Reuben Red	1	2	
Burges Reeves	2	4	
Asa Reid	1	2	

Head of Family	Other Males	Females	Slaves
George Reid, Sr.	1		10
George Reid, Jr.	7	6	1
Joseph Reid	2	2	2
Rhesa Reid	1	1	
Sam C. Reid	1	4	
Samuel Reid	1	1	8
Richard Respass	2	5	
Gallant Reynolds	1	1	1
Jemima Reynolds	5	4	4
David Richardson	5	1	
James Riggs	1	3	
Mathew M. Right	1	3	
Stephen Roberts	4	2	
Luke Robinson	3	4	2
James Rodgers	3	3	
Thompson Roever	1	3	
John Rogers	1	7	
Davis Rollins	4	2	
Willis Rowland	5	3	
James Royals	5	2	3
James F. Ruck	3	6	
William Ruck	4	3	
Mary Rushton	1	2	
David Rutherford	5	4	
John Rutledge	1	4	2
Ephraim Salmonds	4	4	
Grover Salmonds	2	4	1
Howell Sammonds	2	3	
William Scott	1	1	2
John Seagars	1	1	
John Seagars	1	2	
Mary Seagars	1	4	
Southard Seagars	5	4	
Rebecca Shaw	2	3	
Riley W. Shelton	3	1	
William Sikes	6	6	2
Drury Silvy	4	4	
Jesse Simmons	7	3	
Benjamin S. Smith	4	2	
James Smith	5	3	
Moses Smith	4	3	
Redick Smith	1	1	
Thomas Smith	5	7	
Thomas A. Smith	1		
William Smith	5	2	
Mark Snow	3	3	

Head of Family	Other Males	Females	Slaves
Green Sorrell	4	4	2
Jeremiah Sparks	6	7	
David Spence	4	3	
William Spencer	2	3	
Amos Spillars	5	3	
Moses Stamps	6	4	
James Standley	3	3	
John Steele	3	5	1
James Steem	4	4	2
Absalom Stewart	6	4	
William Stewart	2	1	
James Stone	5	3	
Edmund Strange	4	3	1
Jane Strawn		2	
Drury Strickland	8	4	
Simeon Strickland	1	2	
Wilson Strickland	1	2	14
James Sword	1	1	
Gideon Tanner	4	2	4
Hezekiah Tanner	5	1	
John Taylor	8	3	
Septimus Taylor	3	4	
Thomas Terry	1	1	
William Terry	5	1	1
Elizabeth Thomas			
Joseph Thomas	1	2	
Esther Thompson	1	4	
John Thompson	4	3	
Joseph Thompson	7	6	
Martha Thompson	1	5	
Ranson Thompson	10	4	
Zacchariah Thompson	2	2	
Thomas Thrower	5	3	
Sarah Thurmond	1	4	
William Thurmond	1	5	5
Elizabeth Tidwell	1	1	
Vincent D. Tins	3	6	
John L. Tippin	3		1
John Torrence	6	4	
Isaac Towers	1	4	
William Towers	6	3	
Solomon Townsend	4	4	2
John Treadwell	5	3	
Joseph Trimble			
William Tumblin	5	4	
Edward Turner	6	3	

Head of Family	Other Males	Females	Slaves
John W. Turner	1	2	2
Thomas B. Turner	6	7	1
Elijah Tutton	2	4	
Aaron Underwood	2	5	
William S. Underwood	1		
Jehu Vining	1	1	
David Vowel	1	1	
Reichel Vowel		1	
Asa Wade	5	2	
Edward Wade, Sr.	1	1	
Edward Wade, Jr.	1	3	
James Wade	2	6	
John Wade	4	4	
Loudy Walker	7	4	
Peter Wallis	2	5	3
Adam Walls	2	3	
Arthur Walls	5	2	
Charles Walls	3	3	
Hannah Ward	1	2	
Ivy Ward	3	3	3
James Wardlaw	2	2	1
William Wardlaw	12	5	2
William Warren			
James Wates	2	2	2
David Watson	4	4	2
Joseph Watson	2	2	
Thomas Watson	6	3	1
Hope H. Watts	3	3	
Richard J. Watts	3	4	1
Clinton Webb	8	2	
Edward Wester	6	3	
John Wester	4	5	2
Archy Whatley	5	7	1
Alexander White	6	2	3
James White	2	2	1
James White	5	3	
William White	2	5	
Benjamin Whitehead	2	5	2
Thomas Wilkins	1	1	
Isham Williams	5	4	2
Jesse Williams	2	5	1
William Williams	1	3	
John P. Williamson	5	6	
William Williamson	4	3	
Elisha Winn	5	4	6
Francis Winn	1	3	

Head of Family	Other Males	Females	Slaves
John Winn	5	5	2
Thomas Wood	2	6	
John Woodall	7	3	5
William Woodall	1	3	
Catherine Woods	2	2	
Isabella Woods		1	
Thomas Worthy	4	5	2
William Worthy	5	1	1
Alexander Wright	6	1	
John Wright			
Charles Yancey	5	2	
Ezekiel Yancey	3	1	
Wesley Yancy	3	4	
Augustus Young	1		3
Warren Young	4	3	
Peter Youngblood	4	4	

Chapter V

COUNTY SURVEYED—DISTRIBUTED BY LOTTERY

SOON after the creation of the county, plans were made to have it surveyed. The following letter shows this to be true:

SURVEYOR GENERAL'S OFFICE
Milledgeville, Georgia
March 23, 1819

To District Surveyors:

The districts in the counties of Gwinnett, Walton, Hall, and Habersham being now nearly completed and the United States Commissioner expected to pass through Milledgeville in the course of the current week on his way to run the line which is to divide this state and the Province of East Florida, it is deemed advisable to carry into effect as speedily as possible so much of the act for making distribution of the late acquired territory as appertains to your duty. I do, therefore, with the approbation of his Excellency, the Governor, require you to attend punctually at this office on Thursday, the 15th of April, to make choice of your districts, to deposit your bonds and to qualify yourselves in other respects for the discharge of the trust reposed in and duties required of you by said act.

DANIEL STURGES,
Surveyor General.

County Divided Into Four Districts

Surveyors were accordingly sent into the county to lay it out in land lots. There are four land districts numbered 4, 5, 6, and 7. District 4 is a part of a district in an adjoining county that extends into the southern part of Gwinnett. The surveyors began on the northeastern corner of lot 246 in the 4th district and ran a line west to the northwestern corner of lot 351 in the same district on the Hightower Trail. Land district four lies south of this line and contains thirty-six lots and parts of lots.

Beginning at the northeastern corner of lot 319 in district four, a line was run north to the Chattahoochee River, just beyond Duluth. All lots west of this line are in the sixth land district and the lots are numbered from 1 to 367. Lot one is at the southern point of this line and the numbers run to the left, then to the right, until the last lot is reached on the Chattahoochee.

Beginning at the northeast corner of lot 153, in the sixth district, a line runs east just north of Lawrenceville to the southeastern corner of lot 20 in the seventh district on the Appalachee River. All lots south of this line are in the fifth land district, and the lots are numbered from 1 to 362; lot one being on the boundary line of district four, counting up, then down. All lots north of the line mentioned above are in the seventh land district and the lots are numbered from lot 1 to 390. The corner lot of the dividing lines is number one, counting then to the right, then to the left, the last lot resting on the Chattahoochee River.

These lots contained 250 acres of land. Later surveys show that some of the lots have less than that number and some more.

That part of the county as originally established that was a part of Franklin County and later of Jackson was distributed under the head-rights system. Under this plan each head of a family was given 220 acres of his own selection and fifty additional acres for each dependent. But all the land of the county that was once in Franklin and Jackson had been distributed by the head-rights system before Gwinnett County was created.

The surveyors in this county completed their work in the summer of 1820, and immediate steps were then taken to dispose of the land by lottery.

LAND DISTRIBUTED BY LOTTERY

The opening of Gwinnett County for settlement created a great deal of interest throughout the state. A chance to win a lot of virgin land, covered with a primeval forest, attracted hundreds of anxious Georgians. The Governor announced in September, 1820, that printed lists of the names of those who drew lots would be provided weekly to the clerks of the Inferior Courts of the respective counties for the inspection of all concerned and that grants or deeds would be issued by the Executive as rapidly as applied for by those who drew lots.

The lottery began Friday, September 1, 1820, and continued into December. The method was simple. District surveyors reported the number of lots in each district. The number of each lot, the land district in which it was situated and the county were written on blank slips of paper. These slips of paper were then placed in a box. A list of names of those entitled to participate in the lottery was furnished. When a name was called, a slip of paper was drawn from the box and the lot and district written on the paper indicated the prize that party had received.

The lottery was conducted under the supervision of five managers. Successful drawers received deeds bearing the signature of the Governor, attested by the great seal of the state, stamped on a wax pendant, and attached to the deed by a ribbon. Each drawer was required to pay into the state treasury a small fee to pay for the expenses of the lottery. Failure to comply with this regulation resulted in a forfeiture of titles to the land.

Lots 10 and 100 in each district were reserved for school purposes.

GWINNETT CITIZENS WHO DREW LOTS

The land in Gwinnett, Walton, Hall and Habersham counties was distributed in this lottery and at the same time. Citizens of Gwinnett were entitled to participate in the lottery and the following drew lots in this territory: A. Spiller, J. Gibson's orphans, John W. Ragsdale, T. R. Spurgeon, Christopher Baker, Sr., Job Biner, Wilson Strickland, John Gilliam, Silas Lawrence, Wm. Wiley, Ivy Lawson, Wm. Hathorn, Andrew Creathers, J. Cladwell, Wm. Bennett, Andrew McRide, Dennis Tippins, A. Hamley's orphans, Thomas Banier, John Goodwin, Moses Ellison, Mary Hamby, Mark Snow, Bird Culberson's orphans, Wm. McCollock, Edmond Strange, John Bullock, Elijah Dorsett, Jas. M. Hosey, Wm. Baker, Jr., Jas. Wilkins, D. Richardson, John Evans, James Camp, S. Strickland, John Minyard, B. Reid, Wm. Coplin, John Holderfield, Thompson Morris, S. Jurdon, Jr., M. Clayton, A. Martin, Sr., S. Pool, J. R. Brooks, T. Austin, J. Cooney, R. H. Leverett, W. Baily's orphans, John Leverett, T. McLendon, R. Johnson, D. Webster, J. James, John Clark, F. Winn, Sr., J. Thrower, Stephen Parker, J. N. Cargal, B. Baker, John Law, James Ridge, S. Key, R. Phillips, L. Walker, D. Spence, F. Bagwell, I. Fuller, W. Ellison, T. B. Turner, Wm. Almond, J. D. Clarke, R. Burnell, W. Huckbee.

In the following tables are given the names of those who drew lots in Gwinnett County. The tables show the land district, the lot, the drawer and the county where the drawer lived.

FOURTH LAND DISTRICT

Lot No.	Name	County of Residence	Lot No.	Name	County of Residence
246	William Batchelor	Putnam	302	Asa Powell	Clarke
247	Westly Night	Burke	317	Charles Lucas	Morgan
272	Burrell Lea	Clarke	318	Youn F. Gresham	Greene
273	James Wiggins	Burke	319	Beachum Owens	Putnam
274	Daniel George	Laurens	320	Rebeckah Simmons (orphan)	Laurens
275	Samuel Clary (orphan)	Effingham	321	William Page	Elbert
298	John McUlah	Screven	322	John H. Pope	Wilkes
299	Enos Barnes	Jasper	323	Zachariah Mize	Franklin
300	Moses Andrews	Hancock	333	George Carter, Sr.	Tattnall
301	Cattrupt Freeman (Rev. Sol.)	Clarke	334	Gilbert Shearer	Richmond

Lot No.	Name	County of Residence
335	Solomon Thompson	Wilkinson
336	John Thompson	Morgan
337	John Hodges	Twiggs
338	William Hill	Jackson
339	William Harkins	Jones
340	John Webb	Wilkes
341	Randal Burney	Fraction lot
343		
344	John Morris	Fraction lot
345	John Gresham	Walton
346	John Herrington (Frac.)	Burke
347	Isham Thornton	Hancock
348	Edmund Reaves (Frac.)	Gwinnett
349	William Hendley (Frac.)	Gwinnett
350	William Terry (Frac.)	Gwinnett
351	Thomas McGuire (Frac.)	

Fifth Land District

Lot No.	Name	County of Residence
1	Margaret Saph	Emanuel
2	Presley A. Tharp, Sr.	Pulaski
3	Amos Corley	Richmond
4	Robert Atkins	Twiggs
5	William Moxley	Burke
6	Nicholas Willis	Jackson
7	Green Waldon	Twiggs
8	Abner Yotty's orphans	Greene
9	Charles Stewart	Effingham
10	Reserved for school purposes	
11	John B. Childers	Hancock
12	Wylie Scogin	Oglethorpe
13	Sampson Lanier	Morgan
14	John Camron	Clarke
15	Richard Magor	Jackson
16	Judith Hill	Baldwin
17	Burket Davenport	Morgan
18	Noah Ford	Jasper
19	John Moreland	Jasper
20	Richard Tullos	Tattnall
21	Joseph White	Jasper
22	Lewis Tanner	Jones
23	Josiah Godson	Bryan
24	John Davis	Morgan
25	William Cooper	Baldwin
26	Antonine Picquet	Richmond
27	Spencer Runnells	Wilkes
28	Henry Overteen	Jasper
29	John J. Smith	Putnam
30	Aristarchus Newton	Jasper
31	Jesse Tennison	Burke
32	John Wingfield	Morgan
33	John Harden	Putnam
34	William Huckaby	Jones
35	Abner Whatley	Putnam
36	Herod Thornton, Jr.	Oglethorpe
37	William Norman	Lincoln
38	James Williams	Bryan
39	Richard Folds	Richmond
40	Mathew Clements	Baldwin
41	Robert Lassiter	Columbia
42	Abner Guthrie	Warren
43	Henry Smith	Twiggs
44	John Killam	Emanuel
45	Minor M. Stephens	Oglethorpe
46	Zachariah Johns	Putnam
47	William Akridge	Baldwin
48	John Bryant	Jefferson
49	Edward Ware, Sr.	Madison
50	Abner Veasey	Putnam
51	William Barker, Jr.	Wilkinson
52	Daniel R. Waller	Putnam
53	Lewis D. Yancy	Jasper
54	Richard Gray	Jasper
55	Lewis Dorch	Franklin

Lot No.	Name	County of Residence
56	Elijah Wade	Screven
57	James Camp	Gwinnett
58	Thomas Camp	Jackson
59	James Wilson	Columbia
60	Hampton Harris	Bryan
61	Thomas Newberry	Columbia
62	Larkin L. Elliot	Hall
63	Mary Carruth	Madison
64	Daniel L. Marshall	Columbia
65	William Leard	Morgan
66	Joseph Sentell	Jasper
67	Leroy Finnell	Columbia
68	John Williby	Twiggs
69	Phillip Young	Chatham
70	Mathew Jordon	Oglethorpe
71	Joshua Parker	Morgan
72	Sarah Savage	Chatham
73	William Ruckner, Sr.	Elbert
74	Uriah Richards	Greene
75	Joseph Gaunt	Lincoln
76	Milly Canady	Lincoln
77	William Greer, Jr.	Greene
78	William Can	Warren
79	James R. McClesky	Jackson
80	Thomas Mann	Bryan
81	Rufus Christian	Elbert
82	Joshua More	Greene
83	Stephen Thompson	Warren
84	George Hampton	Putnam
85	Meredith Walker	Twiggs
86	John A. Rhodes	Richmond
87	Benjamin Fannin	Elbert
88	Mark Adison	Liberty
89	Richard H. Thomas	Pulaski
90	Nathias Taylor's orphans	Elbert
91	Thomas Johnson	Jasper
92	Alexander E. Beall	Columbia
93	Lewis Ezell's orphans	Twiggs
94	Burwell Waller	Twiggs
95	Nancy Hendry	Morgan
96	Coleman Jennings	Jackson
97	Henry English	Oglethorpe
98	Henry Chambers	Bryan
99	Margarett Lanier	Bulloch
100	Reserved for school purposes	
101	Abraham Kelly	Screven
102	Richard Harvey, Jr.	Bryan
103	Dempsey Phillips	Jasper
104	William Jenkins	Screven
105	William Sheppard	Baldwin
106	Jane Tatom's orphans	Lincoln
107	Noah Griffin	Montgomery
108	George W. Bailey	Putnam
109	William Stoy	Richmond
110	Sara Gordon	Putnam
111	Lodwick Rollins	Jasper
112	McKinney Howell	Hancock
113	Henry Dunn, Sr.	Hancock
114	John D. Overstreet	Wilkes
115	James Hendrix	Bulloch
116	Allen Wood	Warren
117	Isaac Roberts	Greene
118	Levi Patric	Bulloch
119	William Geeslin	Warren
120	Blake Morgan	Jackson
121	Williamson Nix	Elbert
122	Elisha B. Dubose	Jones
123	Joshua Foulley	Camden
124	Jesse Kirkland	Wilkes
125	Wm. Corley's orphans	Morgan
126	Sarah Sims' orphans	Burke
127	Livi T. Wellborn	Morgan
128	Henry Swinney	Madison
129	Wm. N. Griggs	Wilkinson
130	Davis Smith	Laurens
131	Alexander Lambert	Jackson
132	Eason Drake	Richmond
133	Wright Manning	Pulaski
134	Gilbert Nayland's orphans	Burke
135	Elizabeth M. Turner	Elbert
136	Luke Landers	Putnam
137	Ezra Morrison	Elbert
138	Joseph Tarpley	Elbert
139	Russell Jones, Sr.	Franklin

HISTORY OF GWINNETT COUNTY, GEORGIA

Lot No.	Name	County of Residence
140	Henry Chance, Sr.	Burke
141	James More	Camden
142	Thomas Stewart	Clarke
143	Nehemish Posey	Pulaski
144	George Allen's orphans	Hancock
145	Allen Davison	Wilkinson
146	John Breedlove, Jr.	Hancock
147	Reddick Thornton	Bulloch
148	Nancy Wommock, widow	Hancock
149	Lewis Holt's orphans	Hancock
150	Abraham Miles	Washington
151	Elijah Abbott	Richmond
152	Alfred Wellborn	Wilkes
153	Thomas Thomerson	Jasper
154	Harley Attaway, Jr.	Burke
155	Samuel Rembert	Elbert
156	John Scarbrough	Laurens
157	John A. Hall	Telfair
158	Samuel Brown	Clarke
159	Thomas H. Penn, Jr.	Elbert
160	Moses Sutton	Wilkes
161	Abisha Andrews	Twiggs
162	Robert Walters	Franklin
163	Robert McLellon	Morgan
164	Jones Levingston	Laurens
165	John Fatch	Bulloch
166	Julia Campagnac	Chatham
167	James Morriss	Walton
168	Thomas Greer	Jasper
169	Dart's orphans	Glynn
170	Thomas Loyd	Jasper
171	Garrett Newman	Wilkes
172	Thomas Miles	Baldwin
173	Johnathan Battellee	Chatham
174	Samuel Harwell	Jasper
175	Zephania Atha's orphans	Columbia
176	James Cooper	Hancock
177	James Lanier	Morgan
178	William Little	Wilkes
179	James Dobbins	Franklin
180	Josiah Brunson	Richmond
181	Charles Culpepper	Wilkinson
182	Michael Douglass	Tattnall
183	Tandy Glaze	Lincoln
184	John Nash	Columbia
185	James Walker	Camden
186	William McClendon	Jones
187	William Latimer	Warren
188	James Overton	Walton
189	Luke Mizell	Screven
190	Bryant Baleman	Washington
191	Simon Wilkinson	Jasper
192	Reuben Thornton	Elberton
193	Josiah Sterling	Oglethorpe
194	Gibson Collins	Wilkes
195	Ely Bradley	Liberty
196	William Johnston	Morgan
197	John Shuffield's orphans	Warren
198	George Kirk	Jackson
199	Edward Crossbey's orphans	Greene
200	John H. Ash	Chatham
201	Reuben Cole	Jones
202	David Woods	Jefferson
203	James Sims' orphans	Wilkinson
204	Hugh Thomas	Laurens
205	Samuel Fowler	Elbert
206	Solomon and Mary Melton's orphans	Camden
207	William Jenkins' orphans	Morgan
208	Oliver Dalton	Putnam
209	John Green	Burke
210	Roderick McDonald's orphans	Putnam
211	Richard S. Booth	Richmond
212	Robert Bryant	Jones
213	Robert F. Kent	Columbia
214	David Frazer	Lincoln
215	William Pruett, Sr.	Jones
216	Garrett Demott	Camden

Lot No.	Name	County of Residence
217	Thomas Smith	Clarke
218	John R. Skaggs	Putnam
219	Abraham Irby	Greene
220	Robert Allison	Oglethorpe
221	Blake Baker	Washington
222	Jesse Foster	Morgan
223	John Griffis	Emanuel
224	Alexander Faircloth	Emanuel
225	Edward Harden	Chatham
226	James Martin, Sr.	Franklin
227	Thomas R. Asbury	Greene
228	Elizabeth Young, widow	Jefferson
229	Margaret Ann Hinely	Effingham
230	William Hannah	Jefferson
231	Anthony Nowlan	Wilkes
232	John Lacy	Oglethorpe
233	Mathew Jones, Jr.	Bulloch
234	William Jones	Jasper
235	Jesse Trawick's orphans	Washington
236	Richard Davis	Jefferson
237	Jeremiah Phillips	Jasper
238	William Mitcham	Jones
239	Mary Wilder, widow	Jones
240	Jacob Sikes	Bryan
241	William Glenn	Putnam
242	William Thornton, Jr.	Jasper
243	Julius Alford, Sr.	Greene
244	Richard Bradford	Wilkes
245	John Smith	Greene
246	James Bush, Sr.	Pulaski
247	William Adams	Wilkinson
248	William Wright, Sr.	Lincoln
249	Alexander Journigen	Twiggs
250	John Burson	Warren
251	Peter Kemp	Tattnall
252	Elias Wester's orphans	Tattnall
253	Richard W. Whitworth	Madison
254	Stephen Veasey	Hancock
255	Archibald Campbell	Laurens
256	Major Griffin	Wilkinson
257	Samuel Ford	Jefferson
258	Frederick Holley	Franklin
259	Mark Polson	Jasper
260	Stephen Horton	Jackson
261	Eli Tolason	Hall
262	Solomon Willey	Jefferson
263	Young Johnson	Twiggs
264	John W. Tommey	Putnam
265	John Sholdson	Putnam
266	Nancy Harris	Lincoln
267	George W. Wheeler	Jefferson
268	Esucas Fountain	Laurens
269	Thomas Terry	Elbert
270	Thomas Kilgore	Clarke
271	Abraham Venable	Oglethorpe
272	Samuel Webb	Washington
273	Alford Tillery	Putnam
274	Sherrod McCall	Bulloch
275	Elijah Morthan, Sr.	Washington
276	Richard Baugh	Hancock
277	Ann W. Todd	Greene
278	Samuel Maines	Wilkinson
279	Daniel McIntosh	Jasper
280	Joseph Owens	Columbia
281	Daniel Shipp	Lincoln
282	John M. Pope	Chatham
283	William Whorton	Walton
284	Fanny Trammel	Jasper
285	Mary Campbell	Chatham
286	John Peavy	Warren
287	Edmund Hodge	Twiggs
288	John Head	Glynn
289	James Dunn	Franklin
290	Benjamin Allen	Jones
291	Joel Hulsey	Hall
292	John Lea	Clarke
293	John D. Kendrick	Lincoln
294	Nathaniel Harris	Wilkes

Lot No.	Name	County of Residence
295	Robert M. Gower	Clarke
296	Hugh Bryant	Jackson
297	Catherine Patten	Madison
298	Robt. Westmoreland	Jasper
299	Amos Lathan	Glynn
300	Stoddard Bointon	Jones
301	Cyprian Mays	Wilkinson
302	David Brunson	Screven
303	Thomas Long	Morgan
304	John W. Butler	Wilkes
305	Part of lot on Appalachee not drawn.	
306	Hampton Lucas	Wilkinson
307	Frederick Mitts	Washington
308	Jesse Woodyard	Morgan
309	Josiah P. Stephens	Wilkinson
310	Alexander G. Raiford	Jefferson
311	Samuel Godwin, Sr.	Burke
312	William Johnson	Emanuel
313	Reuben Coal	Jones
314	Arthur Sikes	Burke
315	Thomas Jones	Hancock
316	Levina Hadaway, widow	Putnam
317	Levy Galloway	Oglethorpe
318	Ezekial Wimberly, Jr.	Twiggs
319	John Buzbin	Oglethorpe
320	Peter Jones	Franklin
321	John Reynolds	Warren
322	John Waldens	Effingham
323	John Doomine	Wilkinson
324	Wm. F. A. Morgan	Hancock
325	M. L. White	Chatham
326	Jesse Robinson	Jefferson
327	John D. Reeves	Wilkes
328	William Moore	Wayne
329	Stokelly Evins	Clarke
330	Archibald Johnson	Tattnall
331	Moses Manly	Franklin
332	James Thomas	Putnam
333	Henry Turner, Jr.	Hancock
334	Allen Bird	Hancock
335	Part of lot on Appalachee not drawn.	
336	Part of lot on Appalachee not drawn.	
337	Joseph Wright	Jasper
338	John Whittington, Sr.	Hancock
339	Leonard Griffins, orphan	Twiggs
340	Sion Hood	Washington
341	David Henderson	Twiggs
342	Jesse Hodges	Jones
343	Alexander Irwin	Washington
344	Johnathon Simmons' orphans	Jones
345	Robert Williams	Franklin
346	Isaac Harvey	Jones
347	Edward Wilder	Jones
348	Mathew Goss	Twiggs
349	Jonathan Tailor's orphans	Telfair
350	Obediah Owens	Wilkes
351	Joseph Rogers	Jefferson
352	Sara Swilly, widow	Liberty
353	John Johnson	Jones
354	Thomas McDaniel	Richmond
355	Thomas Everingham	Richmond
356	John F. Johnson	Jackson
357	Allen Hester	Montgomery
358	Part of lot on Appalachee not drawn.	
359	Part of lot on Appalachee not drawn.	
360	Part of lot on Appalachee not drawn.	
361	Part of lot on Appalachee not drawn.	
362	Ezekiah Bailey	Elbert

History of Gwinnett County, Georgia

Sixth Land District

Lot No.	Name	County of Residence
1	Taylor Mitchel	Montgomery
2	Thomas Howell	Pulaski
3	Silas Moseley	Twiggs
4	Stephen Boyet, Jr.	Screven
5	Henry L. Coon	Twiggs
6	Henry Dunn, Sr.	Hancock
7	Fraction undrawn.	
8	Fraction undrawn.	
9	Fraction undrawn.	
10	Reserved for school purposes	
11	David Dunn, Jr.	Twiggs
12	Stephen H. Oliver	Richmond
13	John Meazell	Camden
14	Elizabeth Bryant, orphan	Hancock
15	Archibald Perkins, Jr.	Morgan
16	Mary Roberts, widow	Emanuel
17	Daniel Allgood	Laurens
18	Charles Beall	Richmond
19	William Tilly, Sr.	Richmond
20	Obediah Phillips	Richmond
21	Sneed's orphans	Richmond
22	Lewis Williams, Jr.	Franklin
23	John B. Milner	Wilkes
24	Fraction undrawn.	
25	Fraction undrawn.	
26	Elizabeth Johnson	Burke
27	William McElveen	Bryan
28	John West, Jr.	Greene
29	Jeremiah Corley	Jones
30	Elijah Brewer	Richmond
31	John Skelton	Elbert
32	Benjamin R. Jones	Columbia
33	Patrick M. Thomas	Early
34	Robert Cole	Jasper
35	Richard Pucket	Jackson
36	Erasmus Harden	Columbia
37	Isabel Martin, widow	Liberty
38	Thomas Posey	Elbert
39	Moses Handberry	Burke
40	Fraction undrawn.	
41	Fraction undrawn.	
42	Fraction undrawn.	
43	John Benson, Sr.	Putnam
44	James Blackman	Screven
45	Jackey B. Dorsey	Baldwin
46	John Haze	Pulaski
47	Thomas B. Carrol	Twiggs
48	Samuel Bothwell, Jr.	Jefferson
49	John Turner	Burke
50	Thos. Jefferson, Esq.	Jones
51	Wm. G. Springer	Hancock
52	John T. Brooks	Hancock
53	Richard Miller	Jackson
54	Alexander McLeod	Telfair
55	Allen H. Jones	Columbia
56	Eli Whaley	Jackson
57	Tabitha Houghton	Greene
58	James Paulk	Laurens
59	Fraction undrawn.	
60	Fraction undrawn.	
61	William Morgan	Liberty
62	Thomas Moore	Burke
63	Archibald Fraser	Screven
64	Wm. H. Kimbrough	Jasper
65	Job Wilkins	Clarke
66	James F. Turner	Jasper
67	Nathaniel Pritchard's orphans	Baldwin
68	William Morrison's orphans	Telfair
69	Robert Cone	Richmond
70	Elija Russell	Columbia
71	James McCamron	Lincoln
72	Joshua Clarke's orphans	Montgomery
73	Bradley Garner	Columbia
74	Martin East	Clarke
75	John Welch's orphans	Morgan
76	John Wilkes, Jr.	Oglethorpe

HISTORY OF GWINNETT COUNTY, GEORGIA 57

Lot No.	Name	County of Residence
77	Fraction undrawn.	
78	Fraction undrawn.	
79	Hull Sims	Franklin
80	James Clarke, Jr.	Greene
81	Ansel Parish	Bulloch
82	Burrell Lea	Clarke
83	William Doster	Greene
84	George Dawson	Greene
85	Jesse H. Veasey	Jones
86	Robert Stanford	Twiggs
87	Claryann Russell	Lincoln
88	Zilphy Thornton	Burke
89	Margaret Story, widow	Camden
90	Sarah Butts	Putnam
91	Prudence Story	Jackson
92	John Inger	Jackson
93	Hannah Thomas, widow	Emanuel
94	Robert McKnight's orphans	Greene
95	Fraction undrawn.	
96	Fraction undrawn.	
97	Fraction undrawn.	
98	Thomas Knowles, Jr.	Greene
99	William Rhew	Jasper
100	Reserved for school purposes	
101	James Hale	Clarke
102	Elizabeth Lamar	Hancock
103	William A. Brown	Elbert
104	James Barefield	Warren
105	Joseph C. Glenn	Oglethorpe
106	Samuel Rowe	Wilkes
107	Ratliff Boon	Wilkinson
108	Reps Mitchell	Baldwin
109	John Tinley, Jr.	Richmond
110	Richard Rees	Warren
111	Robert C. Graves	Wilkes
112	James Young	Bulloch
113	Joseph Brawner	Elbert
114	William Barnes' orphans	Hancock
115	William Cloud	Twiggs
116	Fraction undrawn.	
117	Fraction undrawn.	
118	Fraction undrawn.	
119	Davis Rhoads	Jones
120	Eliza, Mary, Sara and John Cooper, orphans	Chatham
121	Levi Bright	Washington
122	Allen I. Davis	Jones
123	John T. Patterson	Jones
124	Davis Clements	Glynn
125	William M. Baker	Chatham
126	Aaron Scarborough, Jr.	Pulaski
127	Benjamin B. Smith	Twiggs
128	James Beall	Richmond
129	Warren Barrow	Putnam
130	Hardy Deloach	Liberty
131	Allason Culpepper	Jackson
132	John H. Richardson	Clarke
133	Amos Dow	Chatham
134	Joseph Smith	Elbert
135	Jacob Ogburn	Wilkinson
136	Isaac Harington	Washington
137	John Bailey	Washington
138	Owen O. Daniel	Twiggs
139	Fraction undrawn.	
140	Fraction undrawn.	
141	Fraction undrawn.	
142	Fraction undrawn.	
143	John Varnado	Laurens
144	Joseph P. Johnston	Wilkes
145	Josiah Lewis	Burke
146	Joseph Stile	Morgan
147	Mary Hughes	Wilkes
148	Archibald McCrimon	Montgomery
149	Yirby Strowd	Jasper
150	Stafford A. Somarsall	Liberty
151	Alexander McGowen	Screven
152	John Higgins	Franklin
153	Cornelius Bachelor	Wilkinson
154	Michael Spann	Richmond
155	Henry McGee	Screven

Lot No.	Name	County of Residence
156	Greenberry McCanon	Morgan
157	Moses Hamilton	Morgan
158	Susannah Burnsides	Chatham
159	Moses Mulkey	Burke
160	James Wood	Jackson
161	John Dunn	Screven
162	Richard Evans, Sr.	Burke
163	John Calhoon	Jones
164	Thomas Norwood	Jones
165	Elias Neel	Emanuel
166	Fraction undrawn.	
167	Fraction undrawn.	
168	Edwin Teat	Putnam
169	Richard Myrick	Warren
170	Joseph Reid's orphans	Telfair
171	George Childres	Jones
172	Isham Loyd	Jones
173	William Inge	Warren
174	William Pricker	Richmond
175	James Hardin	Greene
176	John Mullins	Jackson
177	Humphrey D. Landers	Elbert
178	Major Wall	Twiggs
179	William Croose	Wilkes
180	Mathew Stewart	Greene
181	Rebecca Hadaway	Jones
182	Zebulon Veasey	Jones
183	John Speer	Jasper
184	John Williams	Wilkes
185	Elizabeth Paradise	Lincoln
186	Jeremiah Smith	Laurens
187	Wm. G. Brooks	Washington
188	Solomon Guann, Sr.	Effingham
189	Robert C. Parham	Warren
190	Lewis Thomas	Franklin
191	Robert Skelton	Franklin
192	Fraction undrawn.	
193	Fraction undrawn.	
194	William Kindall	Jasper
195	William Dunkin	Wilkes
196	Wm. Partridge	Washington
197	Curtin Green	Jackson
198	Samuel Tedders	Jasper
199	Thomas Ray	Walton
200	Samuel Huey	Jones
201	Levin Collins	Burke
202	James Bullock	Columbia
203	John Kemp, Sr.	Wayne
204	Francis Smith	Lincoln
205	Thomas Cousins	Clarke
206	James Lee	Gwinnett
207	Peter Gent	Baldwin
208	John O'Brannon	Wilkinson
209	John Richards	Burke
210	Edward H. Evans	Putnam
211	Ganaway Martin	Wilkes
212	William F. Barnes	Screven
213	Johnathon Parish	Jones
214	James Jones	Putnam
215	Stephen Hickman	Laurens
216	Robert Still's orphans	Morgan
217	Richard Weathington	Elbert
218	Fraction undrawn.	
219	Fraction undrawn.	
220	Fraction undrawn.	
221	Mathew Bedgood	Burke
222	John Coyler	Franklin
223	Richard Clifton	Morgan
224	John Jordan	Lincoln
225	David Wilson	Chatham
226	Nathaniel Barksdale	Putnam
227	Nathan Isler	Wilkinson
228	Nelson Cash	Elbert
229	Thomas D. Jordan	Franklin
230	Frederick Johnston	Greene
231	David A. Reese	Elbert
232	Thomas K. Wilson	Hancock
233	Phoeba Hudson	Hancock
234	Thomas Burford	Greene
235	William Allen	Clarke
236	Henry McSwain	Columbia
237	Samuel M. Harrell	Jasper

Lot No.	Name	County of Residence	Lot No.	Name	County of Residence
238	Benjamin Mosley	Morgan	277	Samuel C. Wyche	Elbert
239	John Cole	Habersham	278		
240	Edward Cowart	Wilkinson	279		
241	Arthur Rawls	Laurens	280	Thomas Worthy's orphans	Washington
242	Anderson Nix	Madison			
243	Hugh Hogg	Greene	281	Bennet Crawford	Jasper
244	James Waldrobe	Jasper	282	Stephen Williams	Tattnall
245	Memory House	Oglethorpe	283	James Allen, Jr.	Putnam
246	Lyddall Bacon	Jones	284	Isham Hogan	Baldwin
247	Fraction undrawn		285	Sampson Nayle	Chatham
248	Fraction undrawn and added to DeKalb County in 1829.		286	James Caruthers	Jackson
			287	Isham Thompson	Richmond
249	Fraction undrawn.		288	Robert Tucker	Columbia
250	Leonard Dozier's orphans	Warren	289	Benjamin Meadows	Jones
			290	John I. Bulloch	Chatham
251	Jason Watkins	Richmond	291	George McGruder	Richmond
252	Lockey Edwards	Jones	292	James McLeod	Montgomery
253	Lodewick Ashley	Telfair	293	Joab Ferris	Liberty
254	John Higginbotham's orphans	Morgan	294	Samuel Willingham	Jackson
			295	Sarah Raines, widow	Laurens
255	Vines Favour	Putnam			
256	Jesse Duke	Jasper	296	Simeon Ellington	Laurens
257	Pleasant Jackson	Clarke	297	John Proctor, Sr.	Wilkinson
258	Elizabeth Maund	Burke	298	Alexander B. Linton	Greene
259	Robert Venible	Jackson	299	John McKenney	Screven
260	Richard Winn's orphans	Pulaski	300	Joseph Bagby	Jackson
			301	William Roberts	Franklin
261	Hall's orphans	Richmond	302	Mathew Levritt	Lincoln
262	Peter I. Williams	Greene	303	Levin E. Culver	Hancock
263	John White	Greene	304	Daniel McMurphy, Jr.	Richmond
264	Thomas Leveritt	Jasper			
265	Cary Johnson	Warren	305	John Bassett	Morgan
266	Israel Chapman	Burke	306	Isaac Farmer, Jr.	Burke
267	Leroy Gilley	Montgomery	307	Hardy G. Pitts	Chatham
268	Samuel L. Patterson	Wilkinson		—Added to DeKalb County in 1829.	
269	Willis Webb	Jackson	308		
270	John Dailey	Elbert	309		
271	William Miller	Jackson	310		
272	Ann H. Martin, widow	Jackson	311	John Hamilton, Jr.	Putnam
			312	Kurby Langford's orphans	Morgan
273	Samuel Fleming, Jr.	Warren			
274	Burton Crabb	Jones	313	Wilson Bates	Warren
275	Sampson McGill	Pulaski	314	Rebecca Burge, widow	Jones
276	Robert Dickerson	Elbert			

Lot No.	Name	County of Residence
315	Isham Morgan, Jr.	Elbert
316	Mary Fletcher, widow	Morgan
317	Edmund Green	Morgan
318	Jesse Youn	Laurens
319		
320		
321	George Wayne	Wilkinson
322	Green Shell	Hancock
323	Jesse Daniel	Washington
324	Robert M. Barnwell	Franklin
325	Bradley Berry	Oglethorpe
326		
327		
328		
329		
330	Charles Lowry	Jackson
331	John Kelly's orphans	Hancock
332	Jesse Parmer	Jasper
333	William Harbin	Elbert
334	Thomas Humphrey	Hancock
335		
336	Samuel Lark	Richmond
337	Robert Northcut	Laurens
338	Thomas King	Washington
339		
340		
341		
342	Lewis Clark	Jackson
343	Arthur Foster	Columbia
344		
345		
346		
347	Joseph Mimms	Tattnall
348		
349		
350		
351	Michael Watson	Jefferson
352	David W. Waggoner	Warren
353		
354		
355		
356	William Dixon	Wilkinson
357	John Hammet, Sr.	Jefferson
358		
359		
360		
361	Robert Brown	Lincoln
362		
363		
364	George Clower	Wilkinson
365	Sion Perry	Franklin
366	Drucilla McCormack	Montgomery
367	Cranford's orphans	McIntosh

Seventh Land District

Lot No.	Name	County of Residence
1	John Millen	McIntosh
2	James Chitty	Twiggs
3	Jesse Pipkin's orphans	Pulaski
4	Jacob Blockee	Tattnall
5	Rev. William Twidwell	Franklin
6	Thomas Humphries, Sr.	Baldwin
7	Josiah C. Burke	Jasper
8	Mary Channing	Glynn
9	John Nelson	Pulaski
10	Reserved for school purposes	
11	Barnabas Thomas	Hall
12	Grey Tanner	Emanuel
13	Stephen H. Gilmore	Morgan
14	George Dawson, Jr.	Greene
15	John Lawless	Oglethorpe
16	Daniel Evans, Sr.	Burke
17	West Ward	Twiggs
18	David McLaughlin	Oglethorpe

Lot No.	Name	County of Residence
19	John Hill	Jasper
20		
21	Daniel McMurphy	Richmond
22	Tarpley Holt	Putnam
23	Hackett Webb	Walton
24	John McGill	Jefferson
25	Daniel Picket	Chatham
26	Josiah Canty	McIntosh
27	Levi Lowry	Jackson
28	Redmond B. Mason	Pulaski
29	John Adison	Franklin
30	Elias Miller	Jackson
31	Leonard Pratt	Warren
32	John Powers	Greene
33	Abijah Holliman	Columbia
34	Syntha Moore	Laurens
35	William Edmonson	Greene
36	Henry Dykes	Pulaski
37	Joseph Collins	Morgan
38	John Donaldson	Jasper
39	William Simpler	Warren
40	Aaron B. Puckett	Pulaski
41	Samuel McKinzee	Greene
42	Anne Leverett	Wilkes
43	James B. Stripling	Tattnall
44	Daniel B. Lowe	Jefferson
45	Thomas Stephenson	Clarke
46	Benj. H. Johnston	Morgan
47	Lewis Hardy	Jackson
48	Gideon Brantley	Washington
49	Benjamin Brantley	Laurens
50	Richard Ryan	Warren
51	Asa Smith	Twiggs
52	William Ethridge	Jones
53	Hopkins Daniel	Jasper
54	John Wade	Franklin
55	Elizabeth B. Johnston	Elbert
56	James P. Stewart	Camden
57	Jesse Bowers	Baldwin
58	Henry Johnson	Putnam
59		
60	Stephen Murray	Burke
61	Samuel Carter	Twiggs
62	James McMurray	Greene
63	Robert Hill, Sr.	Warren
64	Alexander Kemp	Screven
65	Mary Ann Thorn	Laurens
66	James French	Warren
67	John Brantley	Jones
68	John Bruce	Clarke
69	Abraham Anderson	Columbia
70	Redding Paramore, Sr.	Telfair
71	James Carver's orphans	Telfair
72	Chas. M. Brown	Oglethorpe
73	James Billingsley	Jasper
74	Thomas Nelms	Greene
75	John Dodds	Elbert
76	Leonard B. Gholston	Madison
77	Meriman Herndon	Clarke
78	Lewis Phipps	Elbert
79	John L. Wingfield	Wilkes
80	Daniel Moore	Effingham
81	Charnice Self	Bulloch
82	Jameroon Malone's orphans	Morgan
83	George Low	Hancock
84	James Henderson	Jasper
85	Thomas Elliott	Early
86	James Williams	Telfair
87	John Sudduth	Lincoln
88	Drury Williams	Wilkinson
89	Caleb McKinney's orphans	Twiggs
90	James Hardin	Columbia
91	Young Moore	Greene
92	Mary Webb, widow	Greene
93	Mary Elliott, widow	Hancock
94	Richard Holeman	Jones
95		
96		
97		
98		
99		

Lot No.	Name	County of Residence
100		
101	Martin Willcox	Richmond
102	Richard Hamblin	Jones
103	Elijah Vickers	Jasper
104	Drury Pate	Warren
105	Nathan Pearson	Wilkinson
106	Clem Powers	Effingham
107	Simeon Felts	Putnam
108	Moses Hatcher, Sr.	Wayne
109	Clement Allen	Greene
110	Rachel and Martha Clubb, orphans	Camden
111	Joseph Tailor	Wilkes
112	Isham Williams	Jackson
113	Milton Amos	Jasper
114	Thomas Kinnon	Morgan
115	John Owens	Burke
116	John Griffin, Sr.	Hancock
117	John Champion, Jr.	Warren
118	Morris Martin	Baldwin
119	Nathan Twilley	Jasper
120	Benjamin Blanton	Oglethorpe
121	Robert Jackson	Morgan
122	Aaron Johnston	Clarke
123	Thomas N. Morel	Chatham
124	Randal McDonald	Burke
125	James C. Watson	Baldwin
126	William Formby	Wilkes
127	Enoch Reach	Morgan
128	William P. Taylor	Jasper
129	Lewis Irons	Elbert
130	Jacob Moon	Madison
131	Lewis D. Yancey	Jasper
132	Mary Ann McClaine	Chatham
133	James Wilson	Jasper
134	Daniel C. Heard	Wilkes
135	Isaac Cohen	Chatham
136	Thomas Stamps, Sr.	Clarke
137	Nathan Holt	Jefferson
138	John Moxley	Burke
139		
140		
141	William Simmons	Morgan
142	Joseph Braddy's orphans	Twiggs
143	Marshall Legon	Jefferson
144	William Jones	Hancock
145	William Price's orphans	Greene
146	Chesley Marshall	Jones
147	John Meeds	Screven
148	Samuel Mangum	Oglethorpe
149	Joseph Gromett	Jasper
150	Robert Tucker	Jasper
151	Joel Norris	Warren
152	Mary Bridges	Oglethorpe
153	William O. Wagnon	Walton
154	Elizabeth and Mary McDonald, orphans	Chatham
155	Charlotte Irions	Elbert
156	Elisha Evans' orphans	Greene
157	Jesse Deas	Wilkinson
158	John Hawthorn	Twiggs
159	Joseph More	Morgan
160	Samuel Duke	Burke
161	Wright Murphy	Jones
162	John Hayes	Early
163	John Worsham	Jasper
164	William Armstrong	Jasper
165	James T. Dent	Columbia
166	Eli Cooper	Jasper
167	Richard Mitchell	Jasper
168	John Lamar	Columbia
169	Thos. Willingham	Columbia
170	William Wiggins	Burke
171	John Bartlett	Hancock
172	George Harris, Jr.	Morgan
173	George H. Hughs	Wilkes
174	Staffard A. Somarsett	Liberty
175	Stephen Tullis	Chatham
176	Joab Collins	Tattnall
177	Stephen Gilmore	Wilkinson
178	William Etherage	Jones
179	Archimedes G. S. L. Zachary	Columbia
180	Samuel Brown	Clarke

Lot No.	Name	County of Residence
181		
182		
183	William Branham's orphans	Jackson
184	Daniel orphans	Burke
185	David Jones	Wilkinson
186	Wright Montgomery	Jefferson
187	Phinehas Mathews	Franklin
188	John Knight's orphans	Twiggs
189	James Johnson	Emanuel
190	Young D. Allen	Greene
191	George Herndon	Hall
192	Thompson Bird	Baldwin
193	John Williamson	Screven
194	Elijah Garner	Clarke
195	William Hawkins	Washington
196	Bethany Night	Emanuel
197	John C. Dodson	Wilkes
198	Wm. Freeman	Oglethorpe
199	Isaac Weldon	Jasper
200	Daniel M. C. Johnson	Elbert
201	Benjamin Merrett	Jasper
202	Benjamin Camp	Walton
203	Needham Lee	Jefferson
204	John Brewton	Twiggs
205	John Allmond	Burke
206	John Harper's orphans	Jones
207	John Blackson	Jefferson
208	Bennet King	Wilkinson
209	Shadrack Kite	Laurens
210	Adam Carson	Jones
211	Archelaus Waller	Jasper
212	James Sadler	Putnam
213	Robert S. Sayre	Elbert
214	Elijah Hutchinson	Hancock
215	Randol Bennett	Twiggs
216	Thomas Davis	Jones
217	Michael Robertson	Jones
218	John Rogers	Twiggs
219	Edmund Jiner	Washington
220	George Base	Burke
221	James Ashley	Putnam
222	David Shepherd	Jasper
223		
224		
225	Arthur Lott	Jefferson
226	Wiley Jones	Morgan
227	Redding F. Hunter	Irwin
228	James Ray's orphans	Columbia
229	John Coleman, Sr.	Morgan
230	Samuel Brooks	Jones
231	John D. Brown	Wilkes
232	Benjamin Reynolds	Greene
233	Thomas King	Camden
234	William G. Smith	Jasper
235	John Gilbert	Oglethorpe
236	Thomas Gilleland	Jasper
237	Thomas Durror	Morgan
238	Jacob Lunsford	Wilkes
239	William Martin, Jr.	Madison
240	Lucy Mounger	Greene
241		
242	Jacob Woolbright, Sr.	Wilkes
243	Alexander B. Bowling	Oglethorpe
244	Joseph Melton	Columbia
245	Joseph Ross	Wilkinson
246		
247		
248		
249		
250	Joseph J. Bracewell	Pulaski
251	Mathew Cannon	Pulaski
252	John St. John	Jasper
253	David Mattox	Elbert
254	Jonathan Kennedy	Greene
255	William Abbott	Warren
256	Robert Blair	Baldwin
257	Lavender's orphans	Chatham
258	Patrick Garland	Putnam
259	Patsy Moore	Columbia
260	John Sermon	Pulaski
261	James S. Clements	Jefferson

Lot No.	Name	County of Residence	Lot No.	Name	County of Residence
262	Lewis Burton	Jones	305	James Gibson's orphans	Warren
263	Joseph H. Barnett	Greene	306	William Tankisley	Clarke
264			307	Elizabeth Hemphill	Morgan
265			308	John Farmer's orphans	Emanuel
266	Elijah N. Hascall	Jasper	309	Humphrey K. Guin	Jackson
267	John Rice	Franklin	310	David Burson	Jones
268	William Brown	Columbia	311	David McVay	Washington
269	Hugh Logan's orphans	Baldwin	312	John Thompson	Jackson
270	William Richardson	Putnam	313	Henry Bagley, Jr.	Franklin
271	John Higgs	Tattnall	314		
272	Lewis Gerdine	Clarke	315		
273	Asa Mathews	Wilkinson	316	William Thutmon	Jackson
274	Thomas Eden	Chatham	317	Josiah Hickman	Hall
275	John Russel	Baldwin	318	Frederick and Ester Millen, orphans	Chatham
276	William Harrison	Jones	319	Isaac Russell	Chatham
277	Avorit Taylor	Wilkinson	320	James B. Langston	Jackson
278	Elizabeth Collum	Jasper	321	Preston Glover	Jackson
279	Joseph B. Cofer	Wilkes	322	Joseph Steel's orphans	Baldwin
280			323	John Little's orphans	Baldwin
281			324	Ann and Margaret McLanen, orphans	Chatham
282			325	Edmund Shackelford	Putnam
283			326	Samuel Brooks	Baldwin
284	Amos Cofman	Jasper	327	William N. Elder	Putnam
285	John Swinney	Putnam	328	James Rice	Greene
286	William Norris	Jasper	329		
287	Jonathan Hooks	Wilkinson	330		
288	John Randolph	Jackson	331	Charles Murrah	Lincoln
289	Moses Gunn	Jones	332	Robert Boyle	Jackson
290	Elijah Fenn	Laurens	333	John Hardy	Washington
291	Rhoda Boler	Lincoln	334	James Ransom	Greene
292	Joshua Miles	Greene	335	Cador Harrill	Warren
293	Daniel Garner	Morgan	336	William Scott	Screven
294	Joseph Hampton	Jackson	337	Gibson Evers	Wilkinson
295	William S. Howard	Wilkes	338	Absalom Kidd	Oglethorpe
296	Elijah Brown	Jefferson	339	Felix G. Gibson	Richmond
297	Thomas Thrasher	Franklin	340	John Hart's orphans	Liberty
298			341	Thomas Jinson	Chatham
299			342		
300	Levan Pullen	Hancock			
301	John Burnsides	Bryan			
302	William Curry	Effingham			
303	John Stevenson	Greene			
304	Elizabeth Chalmers	Franklin			

Lot No.	Name	County of Residence	Lot No.	Name	County of Residence
343			366	William Freeman's orphans	Wayne
344					
345			367		
346	Amos Fokes	Jefferson	368		
347	Isaac Mullen	Jefferson	369	Asa Daggett's orphans	Columbia
348	Paton Randolph	Jackson	370	Archibald Nichols	Jackson
349	William Caliway's orphans	Putnam	371	Jethro Holland	Twiggs
350	John Cardin	Jasper	372	Parker Calloway	Wilkes
351	George Buchannon	Jasper	373	Lazarus W. Battle	Warren
352	Simeon Banks	Emanuel	374	Charles McArthur	Telfair
353	Mary Ann Peterson	Pulaski	375	Judy White	Washington
354	Mary Bird	Bulloch	376	Galbry Mathews	Warren
355	Dennis Williams	Washington	377		
356			378		
357			379	Jonas Driggers	Bulloch
358	Thomas Wilson	Elbert	380	Eli Horne	Pulaski
359	Thomas England	Oglethorpe	381	Rachel Hamby	Morgan
360	Robert Carter	Oglethorpe	382	Rial Potter	Jasper
361	Malcom McDuffee	Washington	383	Joseph Bond, Sr.	Franklin
362	Jehu Dickerson	Laurens	384		
363	Mathew Carter	McIntosh	385		
364	John Kemp, Sr.	Wayne	386		
365	James Fleming	Warren	387		
			388	William Rye	Laurens
			389	Joseph Guyton	Laurens
			390	Rowland Parham	Baldwin

By an act of the General Assembly in 1829 lot 307 and fractions of lots 308 and 248 in district 6 were added to DeKalb County.

Revolutionary Soldiers drew the following land lots in this county: Fifth land district—James Camp, who lived in Gwinnett; Amos Latham, Glynn; David Brunson, Screven; Thomas Jones, Hancock; W. F. A. Morgan, Hancock; Thomas McDaniel, Richmond. Sixth land district—Robert Stanford, Twiggs; John Inzer, Jackson; Thomas Norwood, Jones; Robert Skelton, Franklin; John Kemp, Sr., Wayne; Richard Weathington, Elbert; Sion Perry, Franklin. Seventh land district—Thomas Humphries, Baldwin; Daniel Mc-Murphy, Richmond; Joseph Collins, Morgan; Thomas Elliett, Early; John Griffen, Sr., Hancock; Robert Jackson, Morgan; Thomas Stamps, Clark; John Hawthorne, Twiggs; John Kemp, Sr., Wayne; Elias Hester orphans, Tattnall; Elijah Hutchinson, Hancock.

Citizens of this county who were Revolutionary soldiers or widows of such whose pensions were granted as Virginia militiamen: James Barber, Enoch Benson, Thomas Cox, John McDade, Charles Gates,

Sr., John Maddox, Mary Loyd, John Bowen, Samuel Carithers, Elizabeth Haney, Abel Gower, Celia Lewis, Hannah Holbrook, Mary Spence.

In 1838 two Revolutionary soldiers lived in Gwinnett: Richard Simmons and Isaac Horton. Three widows of Revolutionary soldiers lived in the county: Mary Rutherford, Sarah Cheshire and Sarah Alexander.

James H. Kidd, a Revolutionary soldier, settled in this county soon after its creation. He was a native of Mecklenburg County, Va., and entered the army at the age of 14.

Nathan Doobs, of North Carolina, was granted a pension in Gwinnett County in 1831 at the age of 74. He was a Revolutionary soldier.

List of Grantees in the Tenth District
Monroe County

Lot No.	Name of Drawer	County	Date of Grant
15	Rody Gardner	Gwinnett	Dec. 23, 1825
44	William Reaves	Gwinnett	Nov. 4, 1823
81	William Reaves	Gwinnett	March 20, 1822

List of Grantees in the Fifteenth District
Monroe County

Lot No.	Name of Drawer	County	Date of Grant
14	Allen Burch	Gwinnett	March 9, 1826
19	David Jackson	Gwinnett	Dec. 6, 1836
85	Green W. Baker	Gwinnett	Sept. 14, 1825
123	James Garrett	Gwinnett	Nov. 10, 1823
130	William Rucks, Jr.	Gwinnett	Dec. 19, 1823

List of Grantees in First District
Houston County

Lot No.	Name of Drawer	County	Date of Grant
83	Bentley Red	Gwinnett	Dec. 15, 1821
198	Robert Barnwell	Gwinnett	Nov. 17, 1825
319	Robert Atkinson	Gwinnett	Feb. 5, 1830

List of Grantees in Sixteenth District
Houston County

Lot No.	Name of Drawer	County	Date of Grant
41	James H. Kidd	Gwinnett	Feb. 20, 1823
173	Martha Thompson	Gwinnett	March 5, 1829

List of Grantees in Eleventh District
Monroe County

Lot No.	Name of Drawer	County	Date of Grant
56	Wm. Brumbelow	Gwinnett	Apr. 24, 1822
69	Elias Hollis	Gwinnett	Jan. 10, 1823
87	Philip Blunchet	Gwinnett	Jan. 14, 1823
182	Valentine Brumbelow	Gwinnett	May 3, 1823
229	Elijah Horn	Gwinnett	Jan. 14, 1824
268	Thomas Minchew	Gwinnett	Jan. 31, 1825

Lots Sold at Auction

During the 1820 session of the General Assembly a law was enacted authorizing the sale of the fractional lots not drawn for in late land lottery, the sale to be held at Jefferson on the first Monday in August, 1821, and the days following until all lots were sold, and John Loving, Samuel Jackson and F. F. Adrian were appointed commissioners to conduct the sale. The commissioners should not sell any fractional lot in Gwinnett County on dry lines for less than one dollar per acre and on water courses for less than two dollars per acre. At this sale 688 lots were put up and 240 were sold. The sales amounted to $64,561, of which $21,933 was in cash. These fractional lots were in Gwinnett, Walton, Hall, Habersham and Rabun counties, and the proceeds were deposited in the state treasury to pay for the surveying and the distribution of the land.

Chapter VI

EARLY EVENTS OF THE COUNTY

THE new county faced the future with courage. An unbroken forest extended from the Appalachee River to the Hightower Trail. To move in, clear the land, erect homes, construct roads, build bridges, establish schools, organize churches, maintain law and order, and "promote the general welfare" of the pioneer settlers of the county—all these objectives were to be met and accomplished. The county was fortunate in having men of courage, intelligence and ability to carry the work forward.

Elisha Winn bulks large in those early days. The first courts and elections were held at his house. He negotiated the purchase of the lot to locate the county site; he was among the first justices of the Inferior Court, and for years was one of the most active public officials as well as influential citizens of the county.

William Maltbie, a native of Connecticut, contributed his skill to the public welfare. He was the second clerk of the Inferior Court and served in this capacity for many years. He married Philadelphia Winn, daughter of Elisha Winn. She, too, like her father and her husband, was a useful member of the early social life of the community. It is related that she walked into a barroom in Lawrenceville on one occasion and asked the owner not to sell any of his goods to a certain member of her family. When the son returned home in an inebriated condition some days later, she picked up her husband's heavy walking stick, in the handle of which was embedded a long knife blade, and walked into the barroom again. She reminded the barkeeper of her request that he sell no more of his goods to her son; she told him he was engaged in a sorry business, that he was the cause of her son's ruin and disgrace, all of which was breaking her heart. Then she raised that heavy walking stick and knocked every bottle of whiskey from the shelf near her. Another stroke sent a second shelf to the floor. A third stroke scattered broken bottles in all directions. The barkeeper was astonished, frightened, maddened. He attempted to take the stick from her. She looked into his face and told him that if he dared to place his dirty hands on her, she would run him through with the knife blade that was then pointing perilously near him. He backed away, and she continued to use the stick until every bottle in the barroom was smashed.

Another man who left his impress on the early history of the county was Asahel R. Smith, a native of Vermont. He was a school teacher in his young days. He came to Lawrenceville soon after the location of the county site. He was a successful merchant, postmaster for more than twenty years, justice of the Inferior Court, prominent church man and outstanding citizen.

Philip Alston, the first lawyer to locate in Lawrenceville, was soon followed by N. L. Hutchins who became one of the leading lawyers of the state. Hutchins served as judge of the Superior Court of the Western Circuit, represented the county in the legislature, and accumulated a large estate.

Dr. Philo Hall was an early settler in Lawrenceville, coming in 1820 or 1821. He married a sister of Wm. Maltbie in Connecticut, of which state he was a native. He had an extensive practice, riding horseback over the trails and newly opened roads.

In 1824 there came to Lawrenceville a minister and teacher who for twenty years led the forces of temperance, morality, education and religion to great achievements. The Reverend Dr. John S. Wilson took charge of the Lawrenceville Academy in 1826 and was its rector or superintendent for twelve years. This was the first school that was established in the town of Lawrenceville and among the first in the county. Its students came from the best families, as tuition was charged, there being no public schools at that time. Dr. Wilson was pastor of Fairview Presbyterian Church during these years, a church with several hundred members, and the outstanding church in the county. Dr. Wilson was pastor of Goshen Church for ten years.

James Wardlaw, first clerk of the Superior Court, Thomas A. Dobbs, first clerk of the Inferior Court, Edward Featherstone, merchant and justice of the Inferior Court, John Brewster, John Appling, Benjamin Ivey, William Towers, H. B. Greenwood, Edmond Strange, Joseph Morgan, Thomas Monk, William Nesbit, Isham Williams, and William Green were among the first settlers in the new county. They were men of character and ability and gave their time and means to promote the public weal.

Jesse Osborn, Hosea Camp, Ansalem Anthony, John Flanigan, John P. Elder, Bolin Blakey, Manin Cain, and Billy Morgan were some of the early planters and useful citizens in the eastern part of the county. The Dunlaps, the Pools, Shadrack Bogan, the Berry family, the Cupps, Mathias Bates, the Burels settled along the Peachtree ridge west of the Mulberry River as far as Bogan Road. Down the Chattahoochee and along Peachtree Road settled the Stricklands, Silas King, George Brogdon, Wylie Wilson, Joseph E. Teague, William Sudderth, John Rogers, the Brandons, George M. Waters, Evan Howell, James Wheeler, Thomas Lenoir, Samuel Knox, John Pittman, Adam Hoyle, John F. Martin, and Thomas H. Jones. All these men were early settlers and successful farmers. They cleared the land, established churches, organized schools, and were towers of strength in the early life of the new county.

To the western part of the county came Samuel Hopkins, John Beasley, the Montgomerys, the Borings, Moses Liddell, William Mc-

Daniel, Richard Holt, Lazarus Minor, Jackey Pounds, William Jordan, Amos Kelley, David Phillips, James Garner and others, all of whom served their day and generation faithfully and well.

There is now (1942) a sycamore tree not far from Camp Creek Primitive Baptist Church, near Lilburn, that was the riding switch of a young lady, the switch having been brought by her from Barnwell District, South Carolina, and stuck up in the ground near a spring, where the group camped for the night upon their arrival in Gwinnett County in 1821. The young lady left her riding switch sticking up in the ground, and when warm weather came it lived and grew and is now a large and beautiful tree.

In the above mentioned group was William McDaniel, who settled at or near where Liberty Baptist Church stands and in whose home the church was organized. Soon after his arrival in that community, McDaniel heard an ax to the north of his home and upon investigation found Solomon Hopkins erecting his home about two miles north of the present estate of William T. Burns. The fourth generation of the Hopkins family own part or all of the farm of Samuel Hopkins.

In the southern part of the county the early settlers were Daniel Clower, John Rutledge, Levi Loveless, Jesse Rambo, Berry Nash, Young Moore, Levi Cooper, Pittman Williams, James Hawthorne, John Harbin, Robert Craig, William Baugh, and the ancestors of the present generation of Tanners, Camps, Knights, Wages, McConnell, Jacobs, Brownlee, Britts, Lees, Masons, and others, whose upright lives and material achievements have been a benediction to their descendants throughout the years.

Many who drew lots moved here from other parts of the state. Many others came from the Carolinas, Virginia, New England and some from Europe. In every captain's or militia district farms were bought and dwellings constructed by these immigrants, who came seeking new homes on fertile soil, a new chance to find contentment, happiness and a competency.

The pioneers were for the most part of English descent. Some were Irish. The Burels, the Frachiseurs, the Juhans, and the DeSchamps (DeShongs) are French. The Bosses are Dutch. The Anglo-Saxon was the predominant race and remains so to this day. Practically no foreigners live in the county.

The first jail was a log building with iron bars to each room. The room for debtors was above and the dungeon for felons below. It is "Ordered that the clerk of the Inferior Court pay the undertakers of the jail of Gwinnett County four hundred dollars. This 14th July, 1821." This jail was burned in 1830 when two prisoners in the lower room tried to burn a hole in the wall. A prisoner in the room above gave the alarm. Doors were opened, prisoners rescued, but the building was destroyed.

"Ordered that the permanent site for the jail of this county be located on that part of lot No. 22 in the town of Lawrenceville which was on the 4th instant purchased by the Inferior Court of Hudson H. Allan for that purpose. January 5th, 1831." The second jail was erected by Henry Fitzsimmons in 1832. It cost a large sum of money and was built of square blocks of granite with double walls and the blocks doweled together with iron doors and huge locks. This jail is linked with the tragic story of Elleck, perhaps the only slave, but one, ever tried and convicted and sentenced to be hanged by the Inferior Court of this county. Elleck killed his owner. He surrendered and acknowledged he had killed his master, but acted in self defense, he claimed, as his master had chased him up in the loft of his shanty and was striking at him with his sword. The day of the trial came, counsel was assigned for his defense. The case was submitted to the jury which returned a verdict of guilty. The chief justice, or president, of the Inferior Court sentenced Elleck to be executed. He heard the sentence of death unmoved. A short time before the sentence was to be executed, he tried to escape by knocking a hole in the wall of the jail. His blows were heard by someone who gave the alarm in time to prevent his escape. To prevent any further attempt to escape, he was chained down on his back in the center of the dungeon. The poor wretch implored piteously to be spared this punishment. While awaiting the day of execution, Elleck composed a verse which he sang in sad and doleful strains, full of tenderness if not of hope, the chorus of which was

"O Betsy, will you meet me,
Will you meet me, will you meet me;
O Betsy, will you meet me
In heaven above."

On the day of execution the sheriff placed the negro in a wagon with a coffin for a seat, drove to the gallows, placed a rope around his neck, and Elleck dropped into eternity.

"Ordered that the old courthouse be sold to the highest bidder, payable on the first Monday in March next, the purchaser giving bond and security, said building to be removed off the public square in ten days from this day. Inferior Court, December term, 1823." The bricks for the new courthouse were made and furnished by Geo. M. Gresham and David L. Knox, and Major George Grace erected the building in 1824 at the cost of $4,000. Major Grace came from Greenville, South Carolina, and lived here for thirty years. He brought with him an elegant team of horses, a four-horse team, and a fine blue wagon, and Solomon, a big mulatto man, was his driver. The first loaded wagon to pass over the road from Lawrenceville in the direction of Stone Mountain when that road was opened was this team with Solomon as driver. In that day, and for several years after, cotton was hauled from this county to Augusta. Solomon made frequent trips, hauling as many as twenty bales at a time. Starting on these trips, requiring from fifteen to twenty days, his horses in fine trim and handsomely caparisoned with gaudy trappings, he would mount gracefully into the saddle, crack his whip, and move off grandly, singing,

"Gee, wohy, Dobbin,
Gee up and gee wo;
From Lawrenceville we come,
To Augusta we go."

The first regular hotel was opened in Lawrenceville on the top of the hill on Clayton Street by Benjamin Ivie. The house was small and unpretentious. Edward Featherstone built the second hotel, which was larger than the one kept by Ivie. This hotel was kept by Laban P. Pool, then by George Gresham, then by Holmes until it was destroyed by fire. Later another was operated in the southern part of the town by Mr. Mitchell, then by John F. Martin, then by S. F. Alexander, then by Captain Born.

ROADS

With the county organized and people arriving in increasing numbers, one of the big problems that faced the Inferior Court was the laying out and the construction of public roads, building bridges and establishing ferries across the Chattahoochee River. The Inferior Court had jurisdiction over these matters. The justices attacked these problems vigorously as will be seen from the transcription of orders from the court's minutes. Up to this time only one road had been opened west of the Appalachee River and that was Peachtree Road from Fort Daniel, near Hog Mountain, to the Standing Peachtree thirty miles down the Chattahoochee River, a road surveyed and constructed in 1813, during the War of 1812. East of the Appalachee roads were numerous, as that part of the county had been a part of Franklin County twelve years and then a part of Jackson County for twenty-two years.

The first reference to roads in the court's minutes is dated May, 1820, and, together with other orders of the court, finds a place in this record of the court's transactions:

Ordered by the honorable the Court of Ordinary, May term, 1820, that Joseph Hamilton, Esqr., Thomas Johnson and Hugh Dixon be commissioners of roads in Captain Austin's district.

On December 22, 1820, the legislature passed an act to make it unlawful for any person to obstruct or cause to be obstructed more than one-third part of the Chattahoochee River by dams, fish traps or other obstructions, and the main current of said river should at all times be kept open for the passage of fish and boats. No person or persons, under a penalty of $20 per day, should dam, stop or obstruct the said Chattahoochee River from the lower shallow ford in Gwinnett County to the upper line of Habersham County, and Wilson Strickland, Benjamin Plaster and David Dixon were appointed commissioners for Gwinnett County with complete authority to survey and view any obstructions in said river; and should obstructions be found, they had the right to remove or cause to be removed said obstructions by calling to their aid any number of the citizens of the county. At least one-third of the river was declared a free passage for fish and boats.

JUNE TERM, 1821—Ordered that Edmond Strange, David Watson and Daniel Harris be commissioners to lay out and mark a road the nearest and best way from Gwinnett County courthouse to Wm. Jackson's on the Hightower Trail.

JUNE TERM, 1821—Ordered that Wm. Baskin, Mathias Bates, Silas Dobbs, Meredith Collins and James Laughridge or any three of them be commissioners to lay out and mark a road from Gwinnett County courthouse the nearest and best way to Jackson courthouse so as to intersect any of the public roads leading on towards Gwinnett courthouse.

JUNE TERM, 1821—Ordered that Asa Wade, Henry Cupp and John McMillain be commissioners to lay out and mark a road from Gwinnett courthouse to intersect with the Walton road near Heffton's.

JULY TERM, 1821—Ordered that Shadrack Bogan, John Winn and Patrick L. Dunlap be commissioners to lay out and mark a road the nearest and best way from Gwinnett courthouse to the Hall County courthouse as far as the county line.

JULY TERM, 1821—Ordered that Wm. Green, Levi Dempsey, Jacob R. Brooks, John Woodall and Thomas Worthy be commissioners to lay out and mark a road leading from Gwinnett courthouse to the Shallow Ford on the Chattahoochee.

JULY TERM, 1821—Ordered that J. H. Beauchamp, George P. Parker, Thomas Watson, Willis Rowland and Isaac Cowan or any three of them be commissioners to lay out and mark a road the nearest and best way to the county line in the direction to Watkinsville in Clarke County.

DECEMBER TERM, 1821—Ordered that Robert Montgomery, James C. Reed, Wm. Brandon, Wm. Nesbitt and John Suddeth be commissioners to lay out and mark a road leading from Lawrenceville to the Island Ford on the Chattahoochee near the mouth of Richland Creek.

MARCH TERM, 1822—Ordered that the commissioners in the different districts do have the road opened from Price's bridge (Jackson County) on by way of Bogan's store and continue on the old Peachtree Road to the dividing line between the county aforesaid and Henry County.

MARCH TERM, 1822—Ordered that Geo. M. Gresham, David C. Knox, Harmon W. Boseman, Joseph Hamilton and John Hesterly be commissioners to lay out and mark a road from Lawrenceville to Boseman's ferry on the Chattahoochee.

MAY TERM, 1822—Ordered that ground be reviewed for a road commencing at Langston's Mill on the Mulberry River and continuing till it intersects the Hog Mountain road about half a mile west of the plantation of Samuel Reed, Esq., and that Joseph Thompson, John King, Washington Chambley and Nathaniel Dobbs be commissioners to mark out said road.

MAY TERM, 1822—Ordered that Henry Cupp, Wm. Bangston, Joseph Edmondson, Abraham Martin and Richard Watts be commissioners to lay out and mark a road the most direct route from Lawrenceville to Henry County line in the nearest direction to the house of Absolom Stewart.

MAY TERM, 1822—Ordered that Jesse Dempsey, James Jackson, Ely Massey, Hezekiah Hudman and Curtis Cawley be commissioners to mark out a road from Lawrenceville the nearest and best way to Ezekiel Mathews' bridge, and thence to the plantation of William Nesbitt, Esq.

JANUARY TERM, 1823—Ordered that the road leading from Lawrenceville, opened by Mathias Bates to his mill, be a permanent road.

MAY TERM, 1823—Ordered that petition be allowed to alter the road from Hill's old cabin to the high shoals on the Alcova River to the head of Indian Creek.

JUNE TERM, 1823—Ordered that Wm. Lord, Reubin McClung and Asa Wade be commissioners to lay out a road the nearest and best way to the Walton County line, having for its object to meet a road from Covington towards Lawrenceville.

JUNE TERM, 1823—Ordered that Samuel Lee, David Rutherford, Elijah Nunn, Wm. Hall and Chas. McEver be appointed to review and lay out a road leading from Tanner's ford on the Appalachee on a direction to Vann's or Winn's ferry on the Chattahoochee.

SEPTEMBER TERM, 1823—Ordered that a road be marked leading from the DeKalb County line by Choice's Store and Colonel Featherstone's to Lawrenceville, and that John Boring, Jas. Jackson and Thos. Johnson be commissioners to lay out said road.

DECEMBER TERM, 1823—Ordered that Wm. Abbott, Samuel Reed and Enock Benson be appointed to view and mark a road from Lawrenceville to Richardson's mill.

MAY TERM, 1824—Ordered that Gabrial Pool, Wm. Bennett, and Chas. Gordon be commissioners to mark out a road from Lawrenceville to the Rock bridge on Yellow River, and that they mark out a road from Camp's old house to intersect the road leading from Lawrenceville to Covington.

JUNE TERM, 1824—Ordered that James McDill, James McGinnis and Wm. Brandon be commissioners to view and mark a road from Lawrenceville to strike the Chattahoochee at James Gilbert's.

JUNE TERM, 1824—Ordered that the report of a road made by the commissioners running in a direct line from the Rock bridge to George Gordon's, thence the old trail to Charles Gordon's, thence the old trail to Richard Watt's, crossing Pew's Creek between John Wade's and William Bennett's, thence to Jesse Rambo's and to Lawrenceville, be accepted.

JUNE TERM, 1824—Ordered that Henry B. Wadkins, William Hill and William Page be authorized to lay out and mark a road from the Rock bridge in this county to a point in the county line between Gwinnett and Walton counties in the direction of Ellison's mill in Walton County.

JUNE TERM, 1824—Ordered that the road commencing at Richardson's mill and on, by or near, Mr. Green's and on to Monk's mill and from thence to the courthouse, coming in the street that passes the jail, called Croghan Street, with the exception of going through Lewis Cooper's field, and also McWhorter's field, be accepted.

JUNE TERM, 1824—Ordered that Robert Smith, Esq., Robert Ware, Richmond Baker, Thomas Woods and Isham Medlock be commissioners to view the ground and mark a road from Gate's ferry on the Chattahoochee River to the Rock bridge on the Yellow River.

JUNE TERM, 1824—Ordered that Elisha Winn, Joseph Thompson, Enock Benson, Wm. Baskin and Richard Holman be commissioners to view the grounds and mark a road from Lawrenceville to Price's bridge (Jackson county) by Elisha Winn's.

DECEMBER TERM, 1824—Ordered that the commissioners mark out a road from the ford on Henry Bagley's plantation on the Chattahoochee River to intersect the Hog Mountain road at or near the plantation of Joseph Morgan, Esq.

DECEMBER TERM, 1824—Ordered that the old road, commonly called the fiddler's trail road, be, and the same is hereby declared to be, a public road, and to be kept open from Bogan's old store to James Laughridge's and from thence to the Jug Tavern.

MARCH TERM, 1825—Ordered that Richard Plunket, Aaron Brown and William Gordon be commissioners to mark out a road from the high shoals of the Alcova River to Lawrenceville.

NOVEMBER TERM, 1825—Ordered that the commissioners of every district in the county of Gwinnett be notified by the clerk of the Inferior Court to strictly attend to their duty in their respective districts and have the roads well cleared out and put in good condition by the next court or they will be dealt with as the law directs.

NOVEMBER TERM, 1825—Ordered that George Brogdon, Robert Montgomery and Wm. Fields be appointed commissioners to view the ground and mark a road the nearest and best way from Mathew McRight's ferry on the Chattahoochee to the Hog Mountain.

NOVEMBER TERM, 1825—Ordered that Joshua Ballard, Elijah Nunn, Richard H. Leverett and Richard Watts be commissioners to mark out a road from Lawrenceville to Lewis William's bridge on the Yellow River, and thence a direct course to Henry County courthouse.

NOVEMBER TERM, 1825—Ordered that David Garrison, John Vineyard and Walton Bridges be commissioners to mark a road from Beauchamp's shoals on the Appalachee River to the Walton line.

NOVEMBER TERM, 1825—Ordered that Willis Rowland, Thomas Watson and Benjamin Smith be appointed commissioners to mark a road from the Walton line at, or near, Bolin Whitlow's, crossing the Alcova at Garrison's bridge, on to the Jug Tavern or to intersect the Gwinnett road leading on to said Jug Tavern, about or near Jenks' old mill.

JANUARY TERM, 1826—Ordered that Samuel Bolt, Richard J. Watts and John Brewster be appointed commissioners to let out the building of a bridge at or near Whatley's, on Yellow River, and that the said commissioners be required to take bond and good security in quadruple the amount the said bridge be bid off at, to construct a good and sufficient one in the space of six months from the date of the contract, and keep the same in good repair for the safe passage of carriages for the space of five years from the time same is received by the commissioners. Also ordered that the said commissioners do select the site for said bridge and when the said bridge is completed agreeable to contract, the amount of said contract shall be paid to said contractor out of the county tax for the year 1826 on his presenting the certificate of the commissioners that the work has been faithfully executed.

JUNE TERM, 1827—Ordered that forty dollars be appropriated to build a bridge across Sweetwater on the main road from Lawrenceville to Decatur, said bridge to be kept in good repair for five years, and that Thomas Winn, Wm. Nesbit, John Boring, Ezekiel Mathews and John F. Dodds be appointed commissioners to superintend the same.

MARCH TERM, 1828—Ordered that that part of the Jefferson road that crosses the little Mulberry above Anthony's mill be annulled, say from the fork that leads to the said Anthony's mill to the Jackson County line, and the road in future be turned by said Anthony's mill, the same to be cleared out by him, the said Anthony. And it is further ordered that the said Anthony receive out of the county treasurer for the building of a bridge across his mill dam the sum of twenty dollars, which bridge said Anthony is to keep in good repair five years.

MARCH TERM, 1828—Ordered that Robert Craig, John Stewart, Simeon Stricklin and Nathaniel Austin be appointed commissioners to lay off and run out a road agreeably to the petition within, leaving the Decatur road at the lower end of James Austin's plantation and to intersect the Whatley ford near Pew's Creek, and that the overseer, R. Craig, do immediately proceed to open and cut out the same when marked out by the said commissioners. And it is further ordered that the Whatley ford road, from the point where it leaves the Rock Bridge road to Pew's Creek, be discontinued.

MARCH TERM, 1828—Ordered that Allen Walker, Allen Jenks and George Buchanan be and they are hereby appointed commissioners to examine into the practicability and, if found practicable, to lay off and mark a public road from Brewster's bridge in the direction of Monroe, Walton County, so far as this county line, said commissioners to act in concert with such as may be appointed on the part of Walton County as regards the place of crossing the county line. Also ordered that the said commissioners report their proceedings herein to this court with the least possible delay. Said commissioners are appointed in room of Robert Day, Zachariah Cauley and Thomas Johnson, who have refused to serve.

SEPTEMBER TERM, 1828—It is ordered that the public roads in this county be opened 20 feet wide and ditched where necessary; the bed of the road made 12 feet wide, grubbed; the stumps cut as near even the earth as possible; the roots taken up, the washes turned into a ditch or ditches, the swamps, branches and mud holes to be cause-wayed and covered with bushes and dirt; the necessary bridges and abutments to be made of timber laid close; the roads to be measured and posted from the courthouse; a signboard of direction to be put up at each fork of the road. And it is further ordered that one copy of this order be furnished to each district. And lastly it is further ordered that this court adjourn to the second Tuesday in December next when a rule absolute will positively pass against all defaulters failing to comply with this order.

DECEMBER TERM, 1828—Ordered that the path leading from the Hog Mountain road at or near old Mr. Barker's old place, then near Esq. Tanner's and David Rutherford's and Joseph Thompson's and John Ezzard's and into the road at, or near, Maffett's be granted on condition that the petitioners for same will open and keep open said path as a public path.

DECEMBER TERM, 1828—Ordered that the Shallow Ford road be laid out straight and in a direct line from the turn near Daniel Killians and leading from Pike Street (Lawrenceville) to Mrs. Allen's, or at the most convenient point near her house, to suit the general course of the road, and that the same, when opened, be permanent; and that said alteration be done under the supervision of James Wardlaw and John Brewster and Edmond Thompson, who are hereby authorized to lay out and mark the same agreeably to this order, provided the road be first opened without a legal call on the hands liable to work on public roads.

DECEMBER TERM, 1828—Ordered that the following commissioners of roads be fined $20 each for not attending to their duty as commissioners aforesaid, which fines, however, may be remitted by a proper and satisfactory showing by said commissioners on or before the first Tuesday in January next to this court that the roads under their especial care are in good condition agreeably to a former order furnished them. Names of commissioners fined: Young Moore, Thomas Chambers, James Edmondson, Thos. W. Alexander, John Mills, Simeon Stricklin, Richard H. Leverett, John S. Anderson and Lewis Williams.

OCTOBER TERM, 1830—Ordered that Alston Boyd, Daniel Williams and William Montgomery be appointed to view and mark out a road from Lawrenceville to Fairview meeting house to be taken from the west end of Pike Street, and that the clerk notify each of the men appointed and that they report the same as early as possible.

JANUARY TERM, 1831—Ordered that $50 be appropriated to build a bridge at Montgomery's mill, the undertaker to give bond and security to keep it in repair for five years, and that Moses Liddell, Thos. W. Alexander and George M. Gresham be appointed commissioners to let out and superintend the same.

SEPTEMBER TERM, 1831—Ordered that the petition to open a road from McAdam's ford in Harkness' field on the Chattahoochee River to Sugar Hill at Samuel Born's be accepted, provided the petitioners will keep the road in repair, and that Thomas McAdams, Thomas Rutherford and Thompson Moore be appointed commissioners to lay off said road.

JUNE TERM, 1832—Ordered that the report of the commissioners laying off a road beginning at or near E. Thompson's on the Peachtree road and on by Evan Howell's, thence to D. Miller's, crossing Suwanee Creek at Stricklin's fish trap, thence to James McGinness', thence to Wiley Brogdon's, thence to Sugar Hill, and thence on as far as the county line at, or near, William Doster's, be and the same is hereby accepted.

SEPTEMBER TERM, 1832—Ordered that Robert Hamilton, John Steel and William Nunn be and they are hereby appointed to examine the Peachtree Road and report at the next term of this court what alterations are required, if any, in the route of said road as it now runs, having due regard to the convenience and interest of persons resident on said road, provided such private interest does not materially conflict with that of the public; and also that they examine and report in like manner on the road usually called Hoyles Road.

FEBRUARY TERM, 1833—On application of Evan Howell showing to the Court that it will be for the public good to establish a public road from the Chattahoochee River in said county from the bank of said river over the land of said Evan to intersect the road leading from Lawrenceville to Warsaw on said river where said Warsaw road crosses the old Peachtree Road, and to grant to said Evan the right to establish and keep up a ferry at the place first above mentioned. And the Court after duly examining the same have come to the conclusion that it will promote the public good by affording additional facilities to travelers, passengers and others. Therefore, ordered that Evan Howell be and he is authorized to establish a ferry at the above place across the Chattahoochee River on his own land, and that he be authorized to charge and receive the following rates of toll for ferrage, to wit: For each road wagon, 25 cents; each two-horse wagon or carriage, 18¾ cents; each cart or two-wheel carriage, 12½ cents; each man and horse, 6¼ cents; each footman, 6¼ cents; for horses and cattle, 3 cents a head; sheep, goats and hogs, 1½ cents per head; and for all others not mentioned, the usual rates of toll across said river. And it is further ordered that the said Evan enter into bond with good security in the sum of five hundred dollars and be accountable and liable for all accidents to persons and property crossing at said ferry occasioned by negligence or improper conduct on his part or by his agents and servants. And be it further ordered that the commissioners of roads in the 406th district be and they are hereby ordered and directed, to lay and mark the place for the road leading from the ferry to intersect the Warsaw Road where it crosses the Peachtree Road, or such other place as they may think best for the public good, and that they report their proceedings to this court on the first Monday in March next.

Entered by order of the Court.

WM. MALTBIE, Clerk.

JANUARY TERM, 1835—Ordered that the Mayo or new road to Walton County be altered as follows: To leave the present road about fifty yards from Isham Bradford's field fence and to run by the side of said fence to the river and there to cross said river; from thence to near Mayo's still-house, thence across the still-house branch, thence following the line of Mayo's fence to the corner, thence from the corner to intersect an old road leading to the head of Mayo's lane, and thence to intersect the old road.

JULY TERM, 1835—Ordered that Hiram K. Williams, Alfred Williams and James Bracewell be commissioners to let out to the lowest bidder the covering and banistering of Williams' bridge on the road to Decatur, and that Elias Green, Wm. Gordon and James Stanley be commissioners to let out to the lowest bidder the covering and repairing of the bridge on the Alcova at Brandon's Mill.

ROAD COMMISSIONERS

JUNE TERM, 1836—
407 District—B. H. Lamkin, T. W. Alexander, Wm. Gordon.

Green's District—Jas. McGinnis, Newton McDill, Wm. Montgomery.
408 District—Daniel Sanford, Silas Lawrence, James Hawthorne.
474 District—Newton Bramblett, James Stanley, Robt. M. Gower.
316 District—Wm. Rakestraw, Reubin Manning, Samuel McClung.
Choice's District—Lot Rowden, William Nesbit, Ezekiah Mathis.
Green's District—John Baker, Robert Hamilton, Hyram Pitman.
Sugar Hill District—John Anglin, George Brogdon, Samuel Burton.
Morgan's District—John Horn, Joseph Morgan, Wm. A. Hamilton.
Hog Mountain District—Joseph A. Thompson, William White, Wm. Garmany.
Rock Bridge District—Jas. M. Flowers, Thomas Maguire, William Page.
Caruthers' District—John Cooper, Samuel Martin, John Clower.

JUNE TERM, 1843—It is ordered that Jesse Murphy be appointed to attend and keep in repair the railings around the courthouse square and keep the trees and grass in said square from being injured by stock from this date until the second Monday in June, 1844.

SEPTEMBER TERM, 1845—Ordered that the justices of the peace in the several districts of Gwinnett County be and they are hereby required to ascertain the number of indigent children in their respective districts who are entitled to a participation in the poor school fund and report to this court on the first Tuesday in October.

NOVEMBER TERM, 1845—Ordered that Robert Craig, John Bankston and Thomas P. Hudson be commissioners to view, alter and mark out the road leading from Lawrenceville to the road cut out by DeKalb from the depot near Stone Mountain to the Gwinnett line. Also from the depot to Hudson's storehouse.

AUGUST TERM, 1846—Ordered that the road commissioners be fined twenty dollars each, but the above fine may be remitted by their having all the public roads in their respective districts put in good order as the law directs by the first Monday in September next, and report the same on that date, or the fine will be collected forthwith.

MAY TERM, 1847—Ordered that his Excellency, George W. Crawford, Governor of said state, be and he is hereby respectfully requested to pay to William Maltbie, clerk and treasurer of the poor school fund of said county, the amount of said funds due said county up to this date.

DECEMBER TERM, 1847—Mathew Crawford, Samuel Alexander and A. R. Smith having failed to attend the court as jurors to try a case of lunacy this day to be tried, ordered by the court that they each pay a fine of five dollars.

JUNE TERM, 1849—It appearing that the line of what is usually known as Ben Smith's district is subject to dispute, it is ordered that Robert Anthony, Samuel H. McClung and George Reed, citizens of that and the two adjoining districts, be commissioners to cause the lines of the district to be defined and, if necessary, so altered, as to conduce to the convenience of its citizens.

Court adjourned till court in course.

SEPTEMBER TERM, 1849—In 1821 the legislature authorized William Terry to ask, demand and receive toll for the use of his bridge, known as Rockbridge, across Yellow River, and in 1849 Few Gordon, Francis P. Juhan and David Anderson were appointed to represent the county, and Mathew Henry, Thomas Maguire and Levi Stancil to represent the owner, to appraise the value of the bridge at its true worth. The appraisers valued the bridge at $45.00. The Court then passed the following order: "Ordered that the above report be received and adopted and that the said bridge become immediately a public one; and it is further ordered that the county treasurer pay to Levi Stancil or his order forty-five dollars, the reported value of said bridge, out of any moneys in the treasury not otherwise appropriated."

JUNE TERM, 1850—Whereas, Edward H. Chambers, a minor, was apprenticed to Job W. Harris to learn the tailor's trade and for other purposes and considerations, and the said Harris having given bond and security to perform various duties on his part; and he having prayed the court to be discharged from said bond on the grounds that he can not control his apprentice or perform his duties in consequence thereof, it is ordered that said bond be delivered up and cancelled and that said Harris and his securities be and are discharged from all liability on said bond.

RATES OF CHARGES AT TAVERNS

In the early years of the county the Inferior Court had jurisdiction over ferries and inns or taverns. The court fixed the rates that the owner or operator of a ferry or a tavern was allowed to collect.

Single meal, each	$ .37
Persons traveling in public conveyances, each meal	.50
Man or woman, per day	1.25
Man and horse, per night	1.50
Horse, per day	.75
Board, man, per week	5.00
Board, horse, per week	3.00
Board, man, per month	15.00
Board, horse, per month	10.00
Board, man, per year	150.00

Sheriff's Activities

The following paragraphs indicate that a great deal of litigation occupied the attention of the courts of the county in its early history.

Wm. Nesbit, sheriff, advertised in January, 1821, the sale of land lot 230 in the sixth district, property of Frederick Johnson. Johnson lived in Greene County and drew the lot a short while before in the land lottery. Also at the same time were advertised for sale 335 acres on Marberry Creek, joining Humphry Gwinn; 50 acres on the same creek, joining Thomas Watson and Ciah Tanner, and 80 acres on the same creek, joining Wm. Hill. In May the sheriff advertised the sale of two negroes, seven horses, two bridles, three halters, the property of James Steen, in favor of John Rogers; also land lot 364 in the sixth district, property of George Clower, in favor of James Morrison. Clower drew the lot in the recent land lottery and lived in Wilkinson County. Thomas A. Dobbs, clerk, advertised a bay mare taken up by Jack Still, a half-breed Indian.

William Towers, Elisha Winn and John Cupp, justices of the Inferior Court gave notice that on Tuesday, June 12, 1821, twelve lots fronting the public square, in the town of Lawrenceville, would be sold to the highest bidder. "Lawrenceville," said the Justices, "is one of the healthiest parts of the State, handsome and well watered."

Robert Kent, of Columbia County, drew land lot 213 in the fifth district and in the fall of 1820 Sheriff Nesbit advertised it for sale; and Eli Tolison, of Hall County, drew lot 261 and Martin Kolb had it levied on and advertised for sale; and 120 acres on Rocky Creek where Richard Leveret lived were to go the same way to satisfy a claim of Shadrack Bogan; and the 130 acres on Marberry Creek belonging to Wm. Camp was sold to settle a claim of Josephus Harrison. In July, August and September, 1821, Sheriff Nesbit advertised various lands for taxes given in by John Free and John Bently; 50 acres on the Appalachee adjoining Wm. Adams, property of Levi Beauchamp, favor of Andrew Boyd; 300 acres on Appalachee with grist mill and saw mill, property of Willis Jinks, in favor of Andrew Boyd; 300 acres "improved with houses of all sorts, the best in the up country, it being the well-known place called Hog Mountain;" lot 175 in 7th district on the Chattahoochee with excellent mill shoal on same, the property of Shadrack Bogan; lot 149 in 7th district, property of Joseph Gromett, of Jasper County. Claibourn Houze's gray mare was knocked off for the benefit of Samuel Bryant. Gwinnett lost a good citizen when lot 226, in the 6th district, was sold to satisfy a debt owed by Nathaniel Barksdale, of Putnam County, to Jesse Hollis. Thomas Mann, who drew lot 80 in the 5th district, lived in Bryan County but it is not known whether he came to Gwinnett County for his lot was sold to settle an obligation to John Jenkins and John Mars. Dennis Williams, of Washington County, drew lot 355 in the 7th district, and it was sold. John Dunn, of Screven County, won lot 161 in the 6th district, but Jas. Poythress and R. D. Wilkison had it sold. Zachariah Johns, of Putnam County, drew lot 46 in the 5th district, which lay in the bend of Yellow River, three or four miles west of Lawrenceville, but it was presumed that he did not settle there for the lot was advertised for sale.

Among sheriff's sales during October, November and December, 1821, were a negro man named Nelson, woman named Chaney, her child, Mat, boy, Dick, a Jersey wagon, bay horse, bay mare and colt, two feather beds, furniture, papers and accounts of Seaborn Maddox, property of John and Seaborn Maddox, in favor of Charles D. Stewart and George Hargraves; 50 acres of land granted to Edward Doss, next to Willis Rowland, on Appalachee, property of Thomas B. Lannear, in favor of J. W. Beauchamp; 100 acres, next to Ephraim Barker, on Mulberry fork of Oconee River, property of Wm. Corie, Jr., and in favor of Enoch Benson; 45 acres of Wesley Yancy adjoining Samuel Reed; 100 acres on Appalachee belonging to John W. Beauchamp, next to Willis Rowland, in favor of Wm. Pearce; 3 negroes, Paul, Martha, and Molly, cattle, wagon, horses, harness, and lot 75 in the 7th district, with sawmill, property of Shadrack Bogan, in favor of James Thompson; 4-wheel carriage, property of James B. Kidd, in favor of Willis Jinks; lot 116 in the 5th district, drawn by Allen Wood, of Warren County; lot 217, in the 7th district, drawn in the lottery by Michael Roberson, of Jones County. Tarpley Holt, who drew lot 22 in the 7th district, and who lived near Eatonton, would sell or barter the lot for land in Monroe County; 50-gallon still, 12 stands, 2 small kegs, 1 barrel, property of Philip Colman, in favor of Frederick Bagwell; a stray horse with about a dollar-and-half bell tied on with a leather collar.

OTHER COURT RECORDS

The activities of the Inferior Court are indicated from the following transcriptions from its minutes. It will be remembered that the court consisted of five justices who were chosen at popular elections. They were not lawyers, but were farmers, merchants and physicians. The progress and growth of the county can be seen in the court's proceedings.

IMPRISONED FOR DEBT

Imprisonment for debt was the law during these years. Many were placed in jail under this statute. In 1820 the legislature passed an Act to extend to all persons imprisoned for debt the privilege of prison bounds. The law directed the sheriff of the counties to lay off, or cause to be laid off, around the jails in such manner as they may deem most convenient and proper, ten acres which limits should be held and considered as prison bounds. Any person confined in jail under civil process had a right to give a bond for double the amount of the debt and which permitted the prisoner the free use of the prison bounds. He was not confined in the jail, but was at liberty to go anywhere on the territory designated as prison bounds. Should he leave the prison bounds, or pass beyond the boundaries as defined as prison bounds, such passage or departure was taken and considered as an escape and forfeiture of his bond.

At the June term of the Inferior Court in 1823 the Sheriff was authorized to alter the prison bounds so as to include the house of Benjamin Ivy, who was then the county jailor. In 1855 the prison bounds were extended to include ninety-nine and one-half acres.

The law permitting imprisonment for debt shocks one's sensibilities in this enlightened age. However, the records of the court of this county are crowded with such cases. A owed B one dollar, for instance. B secured a judgment in the justice court. The court then issued a warrant for A's arrest; and if A did not settle the account, or give bond, he was placed in jail. An instance may illustrate the legal process here. Instead of the name of the debtor, the name John Doe is used.

"State of Georgia, Gwinnett County. To all and singular the constables of this state: We command you that you take the body of John Doe, if to be found in your district, and him safely keep so that you have his body before the justice court to be held at Pinkneyville in and for the 406th district, G. M., said county and state on the fourth Saturday in April, 1858, then and there to satisfy R. B. Martin the sum of thirteen dollars and 23¾ cents principal and interest, from the 27th day of February, 1858, which was adjudged against him at our said court. And also the further sum of one dollar and 95 cents, our cost thereon, whereof the said John Doe is convicted and liable as to us appears of record besides your fees for this service hereon. Fail not and have you then and there this writ. Witness my hand and official signature this April 7, 1858.

"John A. Jenkins, J. P."

"The cost paid by plaintiff, $1.95. April 7, 1858. J. A. Jenkins, J. P. The defendant, John Doe, superseded the necessity of arrest by giving bond and security in terms of the law. This 8th day of April, 1858. John Duncan, L. C."

If "A" settled the account, he was liberated. If he failed, his bondsman was liable. The debtor could file a schedule of his property before the Inferior Court. If he had no more than was exempted by law, the case was dismissed and he could not be held in prison.

Here are appended a number of orders of the Inferior Court taken from the court's minutes. They are selected at random and cover a period of years from 1820 to the year the court was abolished.

JANUARY TERM, 1820—Ordered that the tax collector of said county shall collect an additional sum on state tax for county purposes to the amount of twenty per cent, and this shall be his authority for the same.

JANUARY TERM, 1820—Ordered that James Wardlaw shall receive out of the county funds nine dollars and fifty cents as compensation for designating the county line, and two dollars for a jury box furnished by him for the Superior Court.

MARCH TERM, 1820—Ordered that Isham Williams shall receive out of the county funds fifty-six dollars, whenever that amount is collected for county purposes, for the building of a temporary courthouse for said county.

March the 5th, 1820. Received payment in full for the above.

MAY TERM, 1820—Ordered that Thomas Johnson shall receive out of the county fund eight dollars and eighty-seven and one-half cents for building a grand jury room for said county.

ORDERED that the clerk of the Inferior Court pay the undertakers of the jail of Gwinnett County four hundred dollars, and make a minute of the same in this office. This 14th of July, 1821.

ORDERED that John Beauchamp do receive out of the county funds five dollars for his service in crying the sale of the lots in the town of Lawrenceville, and letting out the jail and well, and the same to be entered on the minutes of the Inferior Court. July 14, 1821.

ORDERED that Ezekial Yancy do receive out of the county funds the sum of twenty-five dollars for digging and fixing the public well. September, 1821.

DECEMBER TERM, 1821—Ordered that James McBride do receive out of the county funds the sum of twelve dollars and fifty cents for services rendered by him as coroner holding an inquest over the body of Mrs. Leveret.

DECEMBER TERM, 1821—Ordered that Wm. Towers receive out of the county funds the sum of twenty-three dollars for laying off the lots in the town of Lawrenceville.

JANUARY TERM, 1822—Ordered that John Cupp receive out of the county funds four hundred and fifty dollars, and the bond given to the Inferior Court, for building the jail be given up by the clerk to said Cupp.

JUNE TERM, 1822—Ordered that John Cupp receive out of the county funds fifty-one dollars and thirty-two cents for extra work done on the jail.

ORDERED that John Lock receive out of the county funds fifteen dollars and seventy-five cents for work done on the public square.

DECEMBER TERM, 1822—Ordered that the clerk of this court be authorized to contract with the county surveyor or some other fit and proper person to lay out and plainly mark off ten acres of land on the hill northwest of the present plan of the town of Lawrenceville and that the same be set apart and reserved for seat of the county academy.

SEPTEMBER TERM, 1822—Ordered that Geo. M. Gresham and David L. Knox receive out of the county funds one hundred dollars in part payment of their contract with the court for brick.

DECEMBER TERM, 1822—Ordered that the clerk be authorized to employ the county surveyor to lay out a street twenty feet wide on the back of every square of the present plan of the town and then a range of lots of one acre each on every square; then a row of five-acre lots on every square, and the balance of the lands belonging to the public lot be surveyed and laid out in ten-acre lots as near as practicable. And further to post and number every lot and observe the extending of the main streets of the town through the whole plan; that the surveying be completed in twenty days and the clerk pay the surveyor $45 for his services. And it is further ordered that the clerk advertise in the Georgia Journal the sale of all the remaining lots in the town of Lawrenceville on the first Monday in February next.

JANUARY TERM, 1823—Ordered that the clerk of this court cause to be advertised in the Georgia Journal that the building of the courthouse will be knocked off to the lowest bidder on the first Tuesday in March next.

JUNE TERM, 1823—Ordered that John Brewster, John Appling, Benjamin Ivy, James Wardlaw and James McClure be appointed a board of commissioners to superintend and keep in order the springs belonging to the town of Lawrenceville and that they be authorized to enforce such rules and regulations as they may think calculated for the benefit of said springs.

JUNE TERM, 1823—Ordered that John Blalock be an overseer of the poor in Captain Brandon's district; Thomas Jones be overseer of the poor in Captain Ware's district; Nicholas Miner be overseer of the poor in Captain Garmany's district; John McMillan be overseer of the poor in Captain Bailey's district; Charles McEwen be overseer of the poor in Captain Dunlap's district; Reubin McClung be overseer of the poor in Captain Ellison's district; and Elisha Winn be overseer of the poor for Captain Pearce's district.

JUNE TERM, 1823—Ordered that all lots sold at the last sale of lots in the town of Lawrenceville which have not been complied with in the first condition do revert back to the county after the 20th day of this month.

SEPTEMBER TERM, 1823—Ordered that the sum of two hundred dollars be appropriated in part payment for brick for the courthouse, and the same be paid by the clerk to George M. Gresham and David L. Knox.

MARCH TERM, 1827—Ordered that Hines Holt be paid twenty-five dollars for digging up and clearing out and removing the stumps in the public square in Lawrenceville.

DECEMBER TERM, 1828—Ordered that two hundred dollars be appropriated agreeably to the petition of the trustees of the Lawrenceville Academy, and the clerk is hereby ordered to pay over the same to the treasurer of the board.

OCTOBER TERM, 1829—To the Inferior Court: You will accept my resignation of the office of sheriff of the County of Gwinnett and tender through you to the citizens generally my warmest thanks for the confidence so often reposed in me.

WM. NESBIT.

ORDERED that Wm. Martin be and he is hereby appointed to fill the vacancy of sheriff occasioned by the resignation of Wm. Nesbit, Esq., until an election can be had to fill said vacancy.

MARCH TERM, 1830—Ordered that John Peeples have one hundred and fifty dollars for work done in the courthouse.

JANUARY TERM, 1830—The State vs. A Woman—There appearing no legal cause of imprisonment, the prisoner is discharged from her confinement and ordered to go her way and sin no more.

J. WARDLAW, J.I.C.,
REUBEN McCLUNG, J:I:C:,
ASAHEL R. SMITH, J.I.C.

JULY TERM, 1830—Asahel R. Smith vs. John Moseley. Attachment. On motion showing that said attachment has been levied on an old negro woman slave by the name of Phillis, and that the property is of a perishable nature, it is ordered that the sheriff do proceed to sell the said negro woman as perishable property on the first Tuesday in September next at the courthouse in said county according to the statute in such case made and provided. Given under our hands and seals at chambers this 26th day of July, 1830.

JOHN BREWSTER, J.I.C.,
JAMES WARDLAW, J.I.C.

DECEMBER TERM, 1830—Charles S. Simonton vs. John Roper, W. F. Roper, claimant. We, the jury, find the wagon and gear and gray mare subject to the fi. fa.

WM. GORDON, Foreman.

DECEMBER TERM, 1831—Ambrose Harnage & Co. vs. Schonadachee, a Cherokee Indian. We, the jury, find for the plaintiff seventy dollars, forty-three and three-fourths cents, with cost of suit.

R. H. LESTER, Foreman.

DECEMBER TERM, 1831—Ambrose Harnage & Co. vs. Nootarhitah, a Cherokee Indian. Settled at defendant's cost.

JUNE TERM, 1831—Ordered that the clerk of the Inferior Court, or county treasurer, do pay to Henry Fitzsimmons three hundred and ninety-five dollars out of any money in his hands belonging to the county, and take his receipt therefor as part payment of his contract for building the jail in said county.

JUNE TERM, 1831—Thomas Beaty, Jr., having acted in gross contempt of the court, now sitting, by boisterous and disorderly conduct in the courthouse while in the custody of the sheriff, it is ordered that he be fined in the sum of ten dollars and that he stand committed until said fine be paid.

Later—Ordered that the fine on Thomas Beaty of ten dollars be remitted.

The State vs. Thomas Pettit: Murder—Habeas Corpus, July 5th, 1831. The prisoner having been brought before the court and arguments had in the matter, it is the opinion of the court that the courts of the United States had not at the alleged time of committing the offence, or at the present time, any jurisdiction in the matter, and that the courts of the state had not at the time by the laws of the state any jurisdiction over offences committed by or against citizens of the Nation. It is, therefore, ordered that the prisoner be forthwith discharged and that all and singular his property, taken for the purpose of answering cost, be forthwith delivered up to him.

The State vs. Samuel A. Worchester, Elizur Butler, Dickerson McLeode, James J. Trott, Samuel Mays, James Proctor: For residing in the Cherokee Nation without a license and digging gold. July 28, 1831. Ordered that the sheriff in obedience to the several commitments accompanying the returns do forthwith, under a competent guard, convey the prisoners to the keeper of the common jail of the county of Walton, there being no sufficient jail in said county of Gwinnett. Or that each of the said prisoners give bond with good and sufficient security in the sum of five hundred dollars for their appearance at the next Superior Court of said county of Gwinnett, then and there to answer to the several charges made against them in the papers submitted.

Georgia, Gwinnett County: Habeas Corpus Court, August 18, 1831.

The State vs. Edward Deloegur, Austin Copeland: Residing in the Cherokee Nation without a license. The prisoners having given bail for their appearance at the next Superior Court, ordered that they be discharged from confinement.

JANUARY TERM, 1832—Wm. Brewster took the oath as sheriff of the county, and the latter part of the oath was as follows: "And I do further solemnly swear in the presence of Almighty God that I have not since the first day of January, 1829, been engaged in a duel either directly or indirectly as principal or second, nor have I given or accepted or knowingly carried or delivered a challenge, either verbally or in writing, to fight the person of another in the State of Georgia or elsewhere at sword, pistol, or other deadly weapon. So help me, God."

APRIL TERM, 1833—Ordered that the report of the committee to examine the work done by Henry Fitzsimmons in building the jail and to settle the amount due him for extra work be agreed to and the jail be received by the court as fully completed by said Fitzsimmons in compliance with his contract for the building of the same, and that said Fitzsimmons be and he is hereby released from further liability on said contract.

MARCH TERM, 1837—Ordered that Thomas M. Alexander, N. L. Hutchins, Isham Williams, John M. Thompson and James P. Simmons be appointed a committee to select a farm for the purpose of establishing a poor house for the county and that they be authorized to make a contract for the same and make report to the Court as early as practicable.

MARCH TERM, 1839—Ordered that John Mills be appointed the agent of this court to employ counsel to defend them in the case of Lucy Breedlove on application for her right of dower to lot No. 146 in the 5th district of Gwinnett County. (Note by author: John Breedlove drew lot 146 in the distribution of the territory in Gwinnett County by lottery in 1820. It is probable that Lucy Breedlove was his widow. Breedlove sold this lot to Elisha Winn, agent for the Inferior Court, for $200.00. Winn then transferred the lot to the Inferior Court.)

John Gray Takes Oath of Allegiance

JUNE TERM, 1842—We, the undersigned citizens of Gwinnett County, in the State of Georgia, do certify that we have been acquainted with John Gray, whose name appears to the above petition, for several years; that he has resided in said county three years previous to the first day of June, 1842, and has at all times given evidence of his attachment to the Constitution of the United

States and her institutions, and that he is a gentleman of good moral character and correct deportment.

    Nathan L. Hutchins, John Mills, Vivion Holmes, N. J. Ormberg, P. A. Sterling, John Richardson, Asahel R. Smith, John Smith, S. T. Austin, Henry P. Thomas.

 Personally appeared in open court John Gray, who, being duly sworn, saith that it is his bonafide intention to become a citizen of the United States, and to renounce forever all allegiance and fidelity to any foreign prince, potentate, state or sovereignty whatever, and particularly to Victoria, queen of Great Britain and Ireland, whereof he is a subject. Sworn to in open court this 13th of June, 1842.

                  JOHN GRAY.

 JUNE TERM, 1844—I, John Gray, do swear that I will support the Constitution of the United States and that I do absolutely and entirely renounce and abjure all allegiance and fidelity to every foreign prince, potentate, state, or sovereignty whatsoever, and particularly to Victoria, queen of Great Britain and Ireland, whereof I was a subject, so help me God.

                  JOHN GRAY.

 COURT MET SEPTEMBER 21, 1861, for the purpose of appointing committees in the districts to attend to the needy women and children who are wives and orphans of the soldiers now in service.

 Cates: Lewis Nash, J. W. Plummer, W. P. Williams. Berkshire: G. H. Hopkins, R. D. Pounds, Charles McKinney. Martins: E. J. McDaniel, J. W. N. Williams, C. Couch. Pinkneyville: Thomas H. Jones, L. B. Jackson, J. O. Medlock. Goodwins: James Wheeler, S. W. Knox, M. B. Montgomery. Rockbridge: Jesse Bryan, J. H. Weaver, M. M. Mason. Sugar Hill: Burton Cloud, Wyatt Wilson. Hog Mountain: J. C. Dunlap, W. I. Woodward, Wm. Wheeler. Cains: W. A. Cain, Adam Pool, Elijah Maddox. Ben Smith's: James Polk, Samuel Dillard, B. A. Blakey. Harbins: J. S. McElvany, Merit Camp, F. Hamilton. Lawrenceville: A. W. Bates, John E. Craig, M. L. Adair.

 The relief committee reported that on October 8, 1861, there were 45 totally destitute families with 99 children, and 45 partially destitute families with 120 children. On November 7 the committees reported ten additional totally destitute families with 25 children and ten partially destitute families with 21 children.

 On February 5, 1862, the Inferior Court authorized J. M. Mills, clerk, to distribute 25 sacks of salt to the families of soldiers.

 On June 9, Enoch Steadman, agent of the Gwinnett Manufacturing Co., agreed to sell yarns to the families of soldiers at fifty cents less per bundle than the regular price. On September 2 the court levied a tax of 150 per cent on state tax for the benefit of the families of deceased soldiers and families of soldiers in the war. On November 4 the court appointed Merit Camp to buy corn for the poor; corn to be turned over to the court. On November 8 the court ordered John Mills, clerk, to borrow $2,000 to buy corn for the families of soldiers and others in need.

On January 5, 1863, the court ordered the clerk to send for Dr. DeLaPerriere, of Jackson County, to attend to those who had smallpox. On February 3 the court employed Dr. Johnson Mathews to attend on cases of smallpox. W. B. Bracewell, a member of the court, was appointed an agent to buy provisions in the southern part of the State and was allowed $2.50 a day and expenses.

ROAD COMMISSIONERS

The Inferior Court on June 8, 1863, appointed the following road commissioners to serve until June, 1865:
Pinkneyville—Hiram Dean, L. A. McAfee, L. B. Jackson.
Goodwins—G. B. Morgan, A. C. Jackson, J. P. Brandon.
Martins—W. E. Atkinson, T. W. Brown, Sam Paden.
Rockbridge—W. H. Duran, G. H. Weaver, Jefferson Britt.
Harbins—Isaac Bradford, J. A. Nunnally, Merit Camp.
Cains—Manning Cain, Charles McConnell, Levi Deaton.
Sugar Hill—J. T. Douglas, Wyatt Wilson, W. C. Harris.
Berkshire—W. A. Jordan, Charles McKinney, Wm. Garner.
Cates—T. E. Kennerly, Andrew Ford, W. P. Williams.
Ben Smiths—B. A. Blakey, James Polk, David Ethridge.
Hog Mountain—B. F. McHugh, J. D. Hood, W. F. Mitchel.
Lawrenceville—J. W. Glenn, A. J. Shaffer, J. S. Mills.

PATROL COMMISSIONERS

The following were appointed patrol commissioners to serve until November 1, 1863:
Hog Mountain—J. C. Dunlap, Wm. Jackson, W. Sexton.
Lawrenceville—John E. Craig, G. T. Rakestraw, J. S. Wilson.
Ben Smiths—W. W. Parks, James Patillo, M. R. Adams.
Cates—Thomas Jacobs, Levi Loveless, James Flowers.
Berkshire—R. D. Pounds, John Cain, J. Walker Nash.
Sugar Hill—Burton Cloud, John Bailey, D. D. Born.
Cains—W. A. Cain, W. W. Duncan, Adam Pool.
Rockbridge—F. P. Hudson, Alez. Gordon, Nathaniel Juhan.
Pinkneyville—Henly Harris, M. Boyce, Lewis Medlock.
Harbins—Merit Camp, J. B. Coffee, R. H. Bradford.
Martins—Thomas Mutchell, Chancy Couch, Wash. Mills.
Goodwins—M. B. Montgomery, A. W. Cole, James Brown.

The court on June 14, 1864, issued an order directing the clerks of the Inferior and Superior Courts to remove all books and records of the past ten years to some safe place; and the ordinary to remove all records of past twenty years, so that such books and records be safe from the public enemy then invading the county.

April 8, 1865. The State vs. A Still. We, the jury, find that said still is being operated illegally and therefore is a public nuisance, and that said still be sold and money paid into the court.

Posse Comitatus

May 6, 1865.—Court met today. In obedience to the resolution adopted by a meeting of the citizens of the county this day, it is ordered that the sheriff, or his deputy, summons or organize immediately a posse of twelve men to act as a mounted and armed police force, whose duty it shall be to patrol the county and preserve peace and enforce civil authority therein as is contemplated by the resolution at said meeting and authorized by law. Said posse as organized shall be subject to the approval of the court and while in service subject to the order of the sheriff or his deputy. And it is further ordered that said posse shall receive reasonable compensation for their services which shall last for three months or until further order of the court.

Script Issued

Funds were exhausted when the court convened March 23, 1866, and an order was passed authorizing the county treasurer to issue script for $1,000 to meet current obligations.

May 5, 1868—Inferior Court, Gwinnett County, to W. H. Harvey, Dr. To eight days' service as patrol in and about the town of Lawrenceville, Georgia, by order of Major General Meade directed to the sheriff of said county, commencing the 18th day of April, 1868, and ending on the 27th of said month, at $2.50 per day—$20.00.

It is ordered by the court that the above account be allowed and paid by the county treasurer of said county.

WILSON L. VAUGHAN, J.I.C.,
JOHN MILLS, J.I.C.,
JAMES W. PLUMMER, J.I.C.

Similar orders by the court were issued to Cyrus A. Allen, W. J. D. Skelton, Thomas P. Townley, M. A. Mallock and William S. Wright.

Schools

In 1821 an act to provide commissioners or trustees for a county academy was passed by the general assembly, although at that time no academy had been organized nor had any school buildings been erected. Wm. Towers, Wm. Turner, Wm. Maltbie, Thomas Worthy and Jacob R. Brooks were named commissioners for the academy soon to be organized or established. At the December term of the Inferior Court in 1822, it was "Ordered that the clerk of this court be authorized to contract with the county surveyor or some other fit and proper person to lay out and plainly mark off ten acres of land on the hill northwest of the present plan of the town of Lawrenceville and that the same be set apart and reserved for the seat of the county academy." The county academy was incorporated by an act of the general assembly in 1824, and the next year the act was amended and the board of trustees increased by adding James Blackmon, Elisha W. Chester, Philo Hall, Wm. Montgomery, Wm. Green and Joseph Morgan.

The trustees of the academy had no funds to erect a building except what had been appropriated by the state. This fund was inadequate and the trustees appealed to the Inferior Court in the following communication:

Georgia, Gwinnett County.

To the honorable the Inferior Court for said County:

The petition of the subscribers, trustees of the academy of said county, respectfully showeth: That your petitioners, anxious to cooperate with your Honors in contributing to the happiness and welfare of their fellow citizens and the reputation of their county and unwilling that counties of the same age and much more whose soil bore only the print of savage footsteps when the political existence of this county commenced should be before them in establishing seminaries of learning, are desirous, without delay, of commencing a building for the county academy on a scale in some degree proportionate to the population and prospects of the county; but having received only the sum of five hundred dollars from the treasury of the state and being disappointed in their just and reasonable expectations of aid from the legislature, must now look to your Honors for that aid without which the citizens of Gwinnett must for some time remain the humble tributaries of older counties and dependent on them not only for a classical education of their sons and daughters, but also for instructors of primary schools. Under these circumstances your petitioners most respectfully pray that your Honors in the exercise of the powers vested in you by an act of the last legislature will grant to your petitioners in their capacity of trustees of said academy that portion of the state tax which, by the said act, your Honors are authorized to appropriate to such purposes as to you may seem fit; and on such appropriation being made, your petitioners are ready to pledge themselves immediately to commence the said building and to have it in readiness in the course of the present year. And your petitioners will ever pray, etc.

>WM. MALTBIE,
>THOMAS WORTHY,
>G. M. GRESHAM,
>JOHN W. TURNER.

January 5, 1824.
ELISHA W. CHESTER,
  Secretary of the Board.

Whereupon it is ordered that the said petition be granted and that the said board of trustees of the Gwinnett County Academy are hereby fully authorized and empowered to draw on the clerk of this court for the full amount of the state tax paid to him for county purposes by virtue of an act passed at the last session of the legislature entitled "An Act to raise a tax for the support of the government for the political year 1824 which may accrue and become due within the term and space of two years."

>THOMAS MONK,
>WM. GREEN,
>JOSEPH MORGAN,
>EDWARD FEATHERSTONE,
> Justices of the Inferior Court.

The building was erected on the ten-acre lot set apart for that purpose and the Reverend Dr. John S. Wilson was chosen as rector or superintendent. The academy opened for the reception of pupils on January 1, 1826, offering instruction in orthography, reading, writing, arithmetic, surveying, English grammar, geography, the Latin and Greek languages, natural and moral philosophy, rhetoric. The scholastic year was divided into two sessions, the first ending in June, and the second in December, with two vacations of three weeks each. The rates of tuition were: Orthography, reading, writing, $10 per annum; English grammar and the sciences, $16; Latin and Greek, $24; board, $70 to $80 per year. By an act of the legislature in 1828 the trustees were granted authority to raise $5,000 by lottery for the use and benefit of the school. Wm. Maltbie, Wm. Richardson, Elisha Winn, Asahel R. Smith, Thomas W. Alexander and James Wardlaw were named commissioners to superintend and conduct the lottery; and all money raised in this manner, after paying expenses, was to be paid to the trustees for the benefit of the academy.

Washington Academy was incorporated in 1827, with Charles Gates, Wm. Green, David Burge, Samuel Maloney and Henry Dunn as trustees. Next year John Baker and Thomas Morgan were added to the board of trustees. This academy was located near the Chattahoochee River, in Pinkneyville district, where Shiloh Baptist Church now stands. That church was organized in the academy building and continued to use the building until 1885. This academy was patronized by the wealthy farmers who lived along the Chattahoochee River. In 1835 Washington Academy received $260.56 from the state, and had an attendance of 72 males and 31 females as students. Total receipts from the state and from tuition were $455.12 and the expenditures were $313.80, leaving a balance of $141.32.

The Gwinnett Manual Labor Institute, a school fostered by the Presbyterians, was incorporated in 1835 with John S. Wilson, James Gamble, R. Chamberlain, James Stratton, T. Y. Alexander, Thos. W. Alexander, A. R. Smith, Washington Poe, Mathew Robertson, Joseph Cunningham and Levi Willard as trustees. The school was located on a farm of two hundred fifty or more acres, near Fairview Presbyterian Church, the farm now owned by the Sam Craig estate.

An academy for the education of females only was incorporated in 1837, with John S. Wilson, N. L. Hutchins, R. S. Norton, Jas. P. Simmons, B. S. Pendleton, Mathew Crawford, B. M. Powell, John B. Tripp and Henry P. Thomas as trustees. A commodious two-story brick building was erected. It still stands and is being used as a Masonic lodge.

Center Academy was incorporated in 1839 with Geo. W. Jones, Wm. McDaniel, Thos. J. Watkins, J. W. Still and Humphrey D. Landers as trustees. This academy was located in Berkshire district, up the road a mile or so beyond the Henry Young farm and north of the Atlanta highway.

The funds appropriated by the state for school purposes were designated as academic funds and poor school funds. The academic funds went to the incorporated academies to supplement the funds raised by tuition, while the poor school funds were used to operate schools for the poor, those unable to hire teachers or to contribute to the support of the schools by paying tuition. These two classes of schools continued with very little change in name and operation until the common school system of instruction was inaugurated in 1871.

In 1826 Gwinnett's representatives put through an act to establish a system of free schools in the county. It provided a change in the method of handling the funds without any apparent benefit or improvement in the system. The act is given for information:

An Act to Establish Free Schools in County of Gwinnett

Be it enacted by the Senate and House of Representatives of the State of Georgia in General Assembly met and it is hereby enacted by the authority of the same, That from and after the passing of this act George M. Gresham, Isam Williams, Wm. J.

Russell, Thomas McLure, Robt. S. Adair and Reuben McClung be and they are hereby appointed a board of trustees for the establishment and government of free schools in the county of Gwinnett and they are vested with powers to fill all vacancies that may occur in their board from time to time; Provided that the concurrence of a majority of said board shall be necessary for the transaction of any business.

Sec. 2.—And be it further enacted, That each of the trustees of the free schools for the county aforesaid shall, before they enter on the duties of the office, give bond and security to be approved by the clerk of the Superior Court for said county in the penal sum of one thousand dollars each and payable to his Excellency, the Governor, for the time being and his successors in office, conditioned that they discharge their duties faithfully as may be ascertained by law and as may seem in their judgment most conducive to the education of the youths of the county.

Sec. 3.—And be it further enacted, That the trustees of said free schools be and they are hereby authorized and required to receive from the board of trustees for the poor schools of said county all sums of money drawn by said board of trustees for the poor schools in said county from the state for the use of said poor schools and not actually disbursed in the education of said poor children, and on failure or neglect to account for and pay over all sums of money that may be in their hands, the trustees of the free schools for said county are hereby empowered and required to cause suit to be instituted on the bonds of the said trustees of the poor schools and said suit or suits shall be prosecuted in the name of the trustees of the free schools for the county of Gwinnett, and the money recovered or paid over by said board of trustees of the poor schools shall go to and form a part of the free school fund.

Sec. 4.—And be it further enacted, That the trustees of the free schools for the County of Gwinnett shall be entitled to all the privileges and benefits that the trustees of the poor schools were entitled to under the several acts establishing and regulating said poor schools and they are authorized and required to draw on the Governor of said state for the time being and his successors in office at such times as may be needed the amount of money that the trustees of the poor schools would have been entitled.

Sec. 5.—And be it further enacted, That the trustees of the free schools be, and they are, authorized to adopt such measures as they may deem best calculated for the education of the youths in the County of Gwinnett; and they are hereby empowered to use all lawful means to carry this act into effect.

Sec. 6.—And be it further enacted, That all laws and parts of laws militating against this act be and the same are repealed, any law to the contrary notwithstanding.

Assented to December 23, 1826.

The population of the county in 1820 was 4,589, and increased to 13,289 in 1830, a gain of 8,700 in the ten-year period. In 1840 the population dropped to 10,804 and never did it reach the 1830 mark until after 1870. The county was rapidly settled between 1820 and 1830. The people at that time were migratory; and the opening up of new and fresh land to the west caused many to leave the county during those years. The settlers came, built a hut or log cabin, cleared a few acres, hunted and fished a great deal, and hearing of better lands elsewhere, sold their farms for what they could get, loaded their families and furniture in a wagon drawn by mules, and often by oxen, and drove on from day to day until they arrived in the new country where they began life again. With the departure of the first owners of the land, the farms of the county went into the hands of large landowners and the plantation replaced the farm. These plantations were cultivated by slaves and there was developed a landed aristocracy that grew in power, wealth and influence until it was destroyed by the Civil War.

Chapter VII
PROSPEROUS YEARS—1830-1860

FARMING was the principal industry during this period. The farmers were the well-to-do class. Land was cheap and the mode of living simple. Each community had its church, school and store. The people were friendly and neighborly. When a field was cleared, there was a log-rolling; when a barn was to be erected, there was a house-raising; when the corn was gathered, there was a cornshucking. Post offices were located here and there and mail was received every two weeks, then once a week, and later still, twice a week. Travel was by horseback and wagon. At every home and church there was a block of wood for women to mount or alight from their horses. Hand cards, spinning wheels and looms were in all the homes. Most of the clothing was homemade and every farm was self-sustaining. The fertile soil responded to diligent labor, and peace, contentment and plenty prevailed throughout the county.

The basis of the county's prosperity and wealth during these years seems to have been the institution of slavery. While less than twenty-five per cent of the farmers owned slaves, the fact remains that the slave owners were the wealthy class. Their plantations were in all sections of the county and perhaps could not be cultivated without slave labor. There was John F. Martin, who owned 2,500 acres of fertile land on the Chattahoochee River at Jones' bridge, near Norcross. At his death he owned 80 slaves. They were sold for $55,000, while his large farm and personal property, including twenty-five horses and eighty-eight cows, brought only $9,000.

There was Robert Craig, the first. He was one of the most successful planters that ever lived in the county. He and his wife, both young, came from South Carolina in an ox cart, perhaps about 1821, two or three years after the county was created, and settled on the old Stone Mountain road, three miles west of Lawrenceville. He worked hard, lived frugally, accumulated a competency, and left a large estate to his sons and daughters. It was not unusual for him to gather one hundred four-horse loads of corn on his plantation that extended eight or ten miles across the county. He owned many slaves and treated them humanely. His home and farm were called Egypt, for he was the banker, and his barn the grainery for that section. At his death there were 300 bales of cotton in his yard, 4,000 bushels of corn in his cribs, and 2,000 bushels of wheat in his bins. The woods were full of his cattle, sheep and hogs; and in a small chest where he kept his cash there was the snug sum of $16,500.

As rapidly as the plantation supplanted the farm the demand for slaves increased and farming became an attractive and lucrative business. The small farmers cultivated their own fields and gathered their own crops. They were not able to purchase healthy, young negroes at a price ranging from $800 to $1,500. A young negro man or woman was worth as much as a two-hundred acre farm for many years after the organization of the county. The farmer in meager circumstances preferred the luxury of owning his smaller acreage and reaping the harvest produced by his own labor. He had virgin soil, abundant timber, and a "happy hunting ground," for the woods abounded in game and the streams in fish.

The man who farmed on a large scale on his plantation used slaves. As his plantation increased in size and more land was cleared, he bought more negroes. If he was kind and humane, as most of the slave owners were, his negroes worked long and hard at their jobs. Every consideration of self interest as well as humanity prompted the landed proprietor to treat his slaves with kindness. A contented, well-fed and happy negro made a good farm hand. "Old Massa" and "Old Missus" were respected and loved by their slaves; and the "Big House," set far back in the grove and enclosed by a fence constructed of pales, was the seat of justice as well as the source of plenty to the scores of the sons and daughters of Ham, who ate and slept in the neat cabins nearby.

Many laws were enacted by the general assembly relative to the regulation of the slave traffic. Some of these laws seem strange to a people who know nothing of slavery. A few acts of the legislature, dealing with conditions during this period, are copied from Prince's Digest of the Laws of Georgia, published by the author in 1837 by authority of the General Assembly of this State.

The General Assembly in 1821 in an act to alter and amend the several laws for the trial of slaves provided:

"108. Sec. II. Whenever a slave or free person of color is brought before the Inferior Court to be tried for an offence deemed capital, it shall be the duty of said court to pass such sentence as may be pointed out by law for the offence of which such slave or free person of color may be guilty; and in case of a verdict of manslaughter shall be found by the jury, the punishment shall be by whipping, at the discretion of the court, and branded on the cheek with the letter 'M'."

An act approved December 22, 1829, to amend the several laws regulating the conduct of the owners of slaves reads as follows:

"132. Sec. I. If any slave, negro, or free person of color, or any white person, shall teach any other slave, negro, or free person of color, to read or write either written or printed characters, the said free person of color or slave shall be punished by fine and whipping, or fine, or whipping, at the discretion of the court; and if a white person so offending, he, she, or they shall be punished with fine not exceeding five hundred dollars, and imprisonment in the common jail at the discretion of the court before whom said offender is tried."

An act concerning free persons of color, their guardians, and colored preachers, approved December 23, 1833:

"153. Sec. III. No person of color, whether free or slave, shall be allowed to preach to, exhort or join in any religious exercise with any person of color, either free or slave, there being more than seven persons of color present. They shall first obtain a written certificate from three ordained ministers of the Gospel of their own order, in which certificate shall be set forth the good, moral character of the applicant, his pious deportment, and his ability to teach the Gospel; having due respect to the character of those persons to whom he is to be licensed to preach, said ministers to be members of the conference, presbytery, synod, or association to which the churches belong in which said colored preachers may be so licensed to preach, and also the written permission of the justices of the Inferior Court of the county, and in counties in which the county town is incorporated, in addition thereto, the permission of the mayor, or chief officer, or commissioners of such incorporations, such license not to be for a longer term than six months, and to be revocable at any time by the persons granting it. Any free person of color offending against this provision to be liable on conviction, for the first offence, to imprisonment at the discretion of the court, and to a penalty not exceeding five hundred dollars, to be levied on the property of the person of color, and if this is insufficient, he shall be sentenced to be whipped and imprisoned at the discretion of the court: Provided, such imprisonment shall not exceed six months, and no whipping shall exceed thirty-nine lashes."

The penal laws of the state in force in 1834 had the following provision relative to peddlers and itinerant traders dealing with slaves:

"306. Sec. XX. If any peddler or itinerant trader, whether carrying his goods, wares and merchandise in a wagon or otherwise, shall at any time either buy from or sell to or otherwise trade with any slave or slaves, unless it be with the permission and in the presence of the owner, overseer, or other person having charge of such slave or slaves, such peddler or itinerant trader shall be guilty of a misdemeanor, and on indictment and conviction thereof, shall be fined in the sum not exceeding one thousand dollars, one-half to the use of the prosecutor, and the other half to the use of the county where the crime was committed, and the defendant shall stand committed until the fine is paid; and a copy of this section shall be annexed to all licenses granted peddlers."

LOCAL LAWS AFFECTING THE COUNTY FROM 1818 TO 1837

Prince's Digest of Laws of Georgia was approved by the General Assembly in 1836 and published the following year. His summary of local laws affecting this county is reproduced here.

GWINNETT COUNTY

Laid out under the Lottery Act, 1818, vol. iii, 418—Part taken from Jackson, 1818, vol. iii, 226—Lines between Gwinnett and Jackson and between Gwinnett and Hall, 1819, vol. iii, 231—Line defined between Gwinnett and Walton, 1820, vol. iv, 117—No alteration of roads to vary the line between Gwinnett and Jackson, 1820, iv, 118—Part set off to DeKalb, 1822, vol. iv, 121—Part of the unlocated territory added to Gwinnett, 1822, vol. iv, 124—A lot and fraction added to DeKalb, 1828, iv, 138—Another fraction added to DeKalb, 1829, vol. iv, 140.

Public site and buildings, 1819, vol. iii, 234—Lawrenceville declared the public site, 1821, vol. iv, 435—Prison bounds to be adapted to the new jail, 1830, vol. iv, 140.

Organized, 1818, vol. iii, 226; 1819, vol. iii, 234.

Academies and free schools. County academy incorporated, 1821, vol. iv, 9—Lawrenceville Academy incorporated, 1824, vol. iv, 21—Last Act amended and more trustees appointed, 1825, vol. iv, 29—Free schools established, 1826, vol. iv, 36—More trustees to Lawrenceville Academy, 1827, vol. iv, 48—Washington Academy incorporated, 1827, vol. iv, 49—Lottery to raise $5,000 for Lawrenceville Academy, 1828, vol. iv, 52—More trustees to Washington Academy, 1828, vol. iv, 55—All fines, forfeitures, etc., accruing in the county to be vested in the trustees of the poor school fund, 1835, pam. 100—Manual Labor Institute incorporated, 1835, pam. 116.

Disposal by the State of fractions and of lots No. 10 and 100, vol. iv, 244; 1821, vol. iv, 250; 1823, vol. iv, 274; 1825, vol. iv, 328; 1826, vol. iv, 262; 1827, vol. iv, 337; 1828, vol. iv, 271, 272.

Prison fees and officers' costs on criminal cases in the new territory, 1830, pam. 53.

Sheriffs and all other county officers required to advertise in the Southern Banner at Athens, 1834, pam. 221;

advertisements in Milledgeville made valid, 1822, vol. iv, 403. Allowed to advertise in any paper in the Western Circuit or in Milledgeville, 1836, pam. 97.

Extra tax, 1819, vol. iii, 929.

Tax on shows, 1835, pam. 285.

Prison bounds, 1830, pam. 61.

Mistakes in drawers' names corrected, 1820, vol. iv, 273.

Election districts and elections, 1819, vol. iii, 234. Elections to be held at Lawrenceville; at James Laughbridge's; at John Humphries'; at William Green's; and at William Terry's, 1823, vol. iv, 158. At Charles Gordon's instead of William Terry's, 1824, vol. iv, 160. County officers elective at the election districts, 1825, vol. iv, 162. Established at the house of David Watkins in Woodruff's district, and at the house of Samuel Borne, the place of justices' courts in Captain Strong's district, 1827, vol. iv, 173. Elections at Watkins', in Woodruff's district, abolished and one established at the house of John Choice & Co., the place of justices' courts in Captain Everett's district, 1828, vol. iv, 177. Elections to be superintended by one or more justices of the Inferior Court or of the peace and two freeholders; their oath; if no constable the justices may appoint, 1830, pam. 100. Elections established at the house of Thomas MaGuire instead of Charles Gordon's, 1834, pam. 107. Pay of $1 per day for carrying up the precinct returns, 1834, pam. 111. Elections established at the house of Jas. Gordon, 1835, pam. 82. Removed from James Laughbridge to William A. Hamilton's, 1836, pam. 121.

Colonels and majors to be elected at the several election precincts, 1834, pam. 101.

Asylum for the poor and for lunatics may be established by the Inferior Court, 1835, pam. 23.

Roads shall be at least 20 and causeways 12 feet wide, 1828, vol. iv, 397. Inferior Court authorized to grant settlement roads and cartways, 1832, pam. 161.

Inferior Court authorized to sign land warrants, 1820, vol. iv, 116.

Sheriff required to reside and keep his office within a mile of the courthouse, 1828, vol. iv, 407.

Acts of James C. Martin, deputy clerk, legalized, 1831, pam. 131.

Census to be perfected, 1831, pam. 56.

Terry's bridge across Yellow river, 1821, vol. iv, 366.

Bozeman's ferry across the Chattahoochee, 1822, vol. iv, 376.

McWright's ferry across the Chattahoochee, 1824, vol. iv, 385.

Garner's milldam in the Chattahoochee, 1824, vol. iv, 354.

Gate's ferry across the Chattahoochee, 1827, vol. iv, 395.

McAfee's bridge over the Chattahoochee, 1834, pam. 47.

Pitman's ferry over the Chattahoochee, 1834, pam. 123.

Lawrenceville incorporated and made the county site, 1821, vol. iv, 435. Duties and powers of the commissioners defined, 1823, vol. iv, 445. Act amended, 1829, vol. iv, 484. Election of commissioners, 1833, pam. 323.

The Trial of the Missionaries

A case that attracted national attention was tried in the Superior Court at Lawrenceville, September 15, 1831. Augustin S. Clayton was judge of the Superior Courts of the Western Circuit at that time, and Turner H. Trippe, solicitor general. Great interest centered in the trial of eleven men who were under bond for violation of the law relative to illegal residence in the Cherokee Nation without subscribing to the oath of allegiance to the state. Prominence was given to this case because several of the accused were well-known ministers of the Gospel who had spent many years among the Indians as missionaries and teachers.

Under treaties made with the Cherokee Nation the United States claimed the right to enforce the intercourse laws with the Indians, which prohibited anyone from settling on Indian territory or trading with them without first securing a special license from the proper authority. Any violations of these laws were in the jurisdiction of the United States courts.

The Cherokees had set up an independent state within the limits of Georgia, claiming exclusive ownership of and jurisdiction over the territory included within the boundaries of their nation.

In the meantime the General Assembly of Georgia extended its jurisdiction over all the territory occupied by the Cherokee Nation. This meant that the Indians were subject to the laws of the state. At the same time it was enacted that anyone living on Cherokee property within the limits of the state without having taken the oath of allegiance to the state, and obtained a license from the governor or his agent, should be imprisoned in the penitentiary for four years.

These three contentions could not be harmonized. Georgia took the view that a sovereign Indian republic within the state's limits was unthinkable and intolerable. However much the people of Georgia wished to see the continuing and increasing progress of the Indians within its borders, they could not tolerate a situation of this kind. The Indians must become citizens of the state and subject to its laws and obedient to its statutes, or they must seek a home and security elsewhere.

On December 19, 1829, the Cherokee territory was added to the several counties that lay on its southern boundary. Section three of that act reads as follows:

"Section 8.—And be it further enacted that all that part of the said territory lying north of the last mentioned line and south of a line commencing at the mouth of Baldridge's Creek; thence to where the Federal Road crosses the Hightower; thence with said road to the Tennessee line, be, and the same is, hereby added to and shall become part of the county of Gwinnett."

This act extended Gwinnett County from the Chattahoochee to the line of Tennessee, and the Indians living within that added territory became subject to the laws of the state and in the jurisdiction of Gwinnett County. This explains why the missionaries were tried in Lawrenceville.

The oath of allegiance required of whites living in the Indian territory, and which some of the missionaries refused to take, was short and simple. It was couched in the following words:

"I, A. B., do solemnly swear (or affirm as the case may be) that I will support and defend the Constitution and laws of the State of Georgia and uprightly demean myself as a citizen thereof, so help me God."

Repeated efforts had been made to induce the Cherokees to exchange the territory claimed by them in this state for a country west of the Mississippi River, but with no success. William Lumpkin, in 1827, then a member of Congress from Georgia, introduced the following resolution: "Resolved, That the Committee on Indian Affairs be instructed to inquire into the expediency of providing by law for the removal of the various tribes of Indians who have located within the states or territories of the United States to some eligible situation west of the Mississippi." The resolution was adopted, the bill was prepared and introduced and passed and many Indians from different states emigrated to the West, but only about 700 Cherokees consented to go.

The Georgia delegation in Congress entertained the opinion that little, if anything, could be accomplished relative to the removal of the Indians during the administration of John Quincy Adams, the then president of the United States, and who opposed any legislation looking to the settling of the Indians in the West. Adams was defeated for the presidency in 1828 by Andrew Jackson, and Jackson had little love for the Indians. He had fought and defeated them at Horseshoe Bend and in Florida.

In his first annual message to the Congress President Jackson referred to the trouble in Georgia as follows: "The condition and destiny of the Indian tribes within the limits of some of our States have become objects of much interest and importance. A portion of the southern tribes have lately attempted to erect an independent government within the limits of Georgia and Alabama. These states have extended their laws over the Indians, which induced the latter to call upon the United States for protection. Under these circumstances the question presented was whether the General Government had a right to sustain those people in their pretentions. The Constitution declares that 'no new State shall be formed or erected within the jurisdiction of any other state' without the consent of its legislature. If the General Government is not permitted to tolerate the erection of a confederate state within the territory of one of the members of this Union against her consent, much less could it allow a foreign and independent government to establish itself there. Georgia became a member of the Confederacy which eventuated in our Federal Union as a sovereign State, always asserting her claim to certain limits, which, having been originally defined in her colonial charter and subsequently recognized in the treaty of peace, she has ever since continued to enjoy, except as they have been circumscribed by her own voluntary transfer of a portion of her territory to the United States in the articles of cession of 1802. Alabama was admitted into the Union on the same footing with the original states, with boundaries which were prescribed by Congress. There is no constitutional, conventional or legal provision which allows them less power over the Indians within their borders than is possessed by Maine or New York. Would the people of Maine permit the Penobscot tribe to erect an independent government within their state? Would the people of New York permit each remnant of the Six Nations within her borders to declare itself an independent people under the protection of the United States? Could the Indians establish a separate republic on each of their reservations in Ohio? And if they were so disposed, would it be the duty of this government to protect them in the attempt? If the principle involved in the obvious answer to these questions be abandoned, it will follow that the objects of this Government are reversed, and that it has become a part of its duty to aid in destroying the States which it was established to protect. Actuated by this view of the subject, I informed the Indians inhabiting parts of Georgia and Alabama that their attempt to establish an independent government would not be countenanced by the Executive of the United States, and advised them to emigrate beyond the Mississippi or submit to the laws of those States."

Having passed laws extending her jurisdiction over the Cherokee territory and requiring all white men residing in the Cherokee Nation to take the oath of allegiance to the state and obtain a license from the Governor or his agent, the State took steps to enforce its laws and execute its statutes. Copies of the law were sent to the missionaries stationed in the Indian territory.

John Ross, chief of the Cherokee Nation, filed in the Supreme Court of the United States a bill of injunction to restrain the State of Georgia from executing its laws within the territory of the Cherokee Nation. Notice was served on the Governor and the Attorney General of Georgia that the case would be heard by the Supreme Court on March 5, 1831. Attorneys William Wirt and John Sergeant appeared for Ross and the Cherokee Nation. Georgia was not represented. The injunction was denied, Chief Justice John Marshall and Justices Johnson and Baldwin voting against granting it, while Justices Story and Thompson voted in favor of it.

Missionaries and teachers had worked among the Indians for years. Churches were organized and schools established. Other white men had settled among the Indians and intermarried with them and a few Indians married white women. The missionaries, however, were charged with using their influence in directing opposition to the laws of the State and hindering a peaceful settlement of the difficulties between the Indians and the State. On December 29, 1830, the missionaries assembled at New Echota, the capital of the Indian Nation, and passed the following resolution:

"The frequent insinuation which has been publicly made that the missionaries have used their influence in directing the political affairs of the Indian Nation demands from us an implicit and public disavowal of the charge; and we, therefore, solemnly affirm that, in regard to ourselves at least, every insinuation is entirely unfounded. It is our opinion, however, that the extension or establishment of the jurisdiction of Georgia over the Cherokee Nation, against their will, will be an immense and irreparable injury."

The resolution speaks for itself and the views of the missionaries served to inflame the people of the State against them, and their determination to disregard and defy the laws of Georgia brought immediate and disastrous results to them.

In March, 1831, Dr. Samuel A. Worcester, Isaac Proctor and John Thompson were arrested and brought by a writ of habeas corpus to Lawrenceville charged with refusing to take the oath of allegiance to the State and to take out a permit from the Governor or his agent. Counsel for the missionaries moved before Judge A. S. Clayton for their release on the ground that the law was unconstitutional and void. Judge Clayton promptly overruled this motion, but ordered the missionaries released on the ground that Worcester was the postmaster at New Echota and the missionaries had been employed in expending funds for civilizing the Indians and were in some sense agents for the general government and, therefore, the law did not apply to them.

Governor Gilmer addressed a letter to the Secretary of War asking if the missionaries were considered as agents of the government. The answer was no. The Governor then wrote the missionaries, informing them of the statement of the Secretary of War and advising them at the same time to comply with the laws of Georgia or leave the State. Worcester and Butler replied that they would not obey the law that they claimed was enacted for the purpose of securing their removal from the State.

Three of the missionaries, Messrs. Butrick, Proctor and Thompson, complied with the statute and moved their families from the State.

Later, during the summer of 1831, Butler, Worcester and several others were arrested and brought to Lawrenceville. They were carried before the Justices of the Inferior Court for a preliminary hearing to be released, committed to jail, or permitted to give bond.

On Saturday, July 23, 1831, the Inferior Court was called in session to hear this case, as the following transcript from the court's minutes shows:

Georgia, Gwinnett County.: Habeas Corpus Court, 23d July, 1831.

Present their honors, Reubin McClung, James Wardlaw and Clifford Woodruff, Esqrs.

The State vs. Samuel A. Worcester, Elizur Butler, Dickerson McLeode, James J. Trott, Samuel Mays, James Proctor. For residing in the Cherokee Nation without a license and digging gold.

Ordered that the sheriff in obedience to the several commitments accompanying the return do forthwith, under a competent guard, convey the prisoners to the keeper of the common jail of county of Walton, there being no sufficient jail in the said county of Gwinnett, or that each of the said prisoners give bond with good and sufficient security in the sum of five hundred dollars for their appearance at the next Superior Court of said county of Gwinnett, then and there to answer to the several charges made against them in the papers submitted.

On August 18th, Edward DeLoezue and Austin Copeland made bond and were released from imprisonment.

The September term of the Superior Court convened with the following citizens acting as grand jurors: John S. Wilson, well known minister and school teacher, foreman; Isaac Gilbert, James Wells, Jr., Benjamin S. Smith, James W. Moore, Robert Craig, John M. Thompson, Hamilton Garmany, Amos Wellborn, William Green, Buckner Harris, William Rakestraw, Jones Douglas, Wiley Brogdon, B. F. Johnson, Wilson Strickland, Richard J. Watts, John White.

This grand jury brought in an indictment in the following words: "Georgia, Gwinnett County.

"The grand jurors sworn, chosen and selected for the county of Gwinnett, in the name and behalf of the citizens of Georgia, charge and accuse Elizur Butler, Samuel A. Worcester, James Trott, Samuel

Mays, Surry Eaton, Austin Copeland and Edward D. Losure, white persons of said county, with the offence of residing within the limits of the Cherokee Nation without a license: For that the said Elizur Butler, Samuel A. Worcester, James Trott, Samuel Mays, Surry Eaton, Austin Copeland and Edward D. Losure, white persons, as aforesaid, on the 15th day of July, 1831, did reside in that part of the Cherokee Nation attached by the laws of said State to the said county, and in the county aforesaid, without a license or permit from his excellency, the Governor of said State, or from any agent authorized by his excellency, the Governor aforesaid, to grant such permit or license, and without having taken the oath to support and defend the constitution and laws of said State of Georgia and uprightly to demean themselves as citizens thereof, contrary to the laws of said State, the good order, peace and dignity thereof."

James J. Trott, Samuel A. Worcester, and Elizur Butler were the missionaries, the other defendants being white men who resided in the territory of the Cherokee Nation and who had married Indian women.

In addition to Solicitor General T. H. Trippe, the prosecution was represented by N. L. Hutchins and Hines Holt, of the Lawrenceville bar. The defendants were represented by Elisha W. Chester, Judge Underwood, and the law firm of Hardin & Harris. The bill of indictment named John W. A. Sanford as prosecutor.

The attorneys for the defendants charged that the arresting officers had abused and mistreated the missionaries and others under arrest. Judge Clayton called the attention of the grand jury to this charge and directed them to investigate the matter thoroughly, stating that the arresting officers were civil officials and should obey the law themselves; and if they had mistreated their prisoners as charged, they should be brought before the bar of justice in like manner as other violators of the statutes. The grand jury made an investigation, but no presentments or bills were returned against the officers.

Samuel A. Worcester, through his attorneys, replied to the charges made against him and said that he was a citizen of Vermont, residing at New Echota in the Cherokee Nation, under the authority of the president of the United States as an authorized missionary of the American Board of Commissioners for Foreign Missions and engaged in preaching the Gospel to the Cherokee Nation and translating the sacred Scriptures into their language; that the court of Gwinnett County had no jurisdiction over the territory of the Cherokee Nation, nor over the people residing therein, that the law under which he and his colleagues were indicted was unconstitutional and void, in conflict with the laws and the Constitution of the United States as well as in conflict with the treaties made between the Cherokees and the United States.

Judge Clayton overruled this plea. The defendants were then arraigned and they entered a plea of not guilty. The jurors chosen to try the case were James H. Gilreath, foreman, Benjamin Towers, Joseph Bolton, Thomas Weems, John Maffett, Wade Peavy, John L. Tippins, Thomas Burge, Eli Elkins, Wm. M. Downs, Mathew Brown, Geo. W. Edwards.

The State used as witnesses Charles H. Nelson, Moses Cantrell, William Wood, Jacob R. Brooks, John W. A. Sanford, John F. Cox, William Tippins and Hubbard Barker.

Deliberating fifteen minutes, the jury returned a verdict of guilty. Before passing sentence, Judge Clayton asked if any one or all of them had anything to say. Dr. Worcester arose and addressed the court in the following statement: "May it please your Honor, if I am guilty of all or any of these crimes which have been made to my charge in the argument before this court but which are not charged in the bill of indictment, then I have nothing to say why sentence should not be passed against me; but if I am not guilty of all or any of them, which I solemnly aver before this court and before my God that I am not, then I have to say what I have already said that this court ought not to proceed to pronounce sentence against me because the act charged in the bill of indictment was not committed within the rightful jurisdiction of this court."

The court then sentenced the eleven men to serve four years in the penitentiary, but recommended executive clemency if they would agree to take the oath of allegiance or leave the state.

The eleven men who were now carried to Milledgeville by the sheriff were Dr. Samuel A. Worcester, Dr. Elizur Butler, Rev. J. J. Trott, J. F. Wheeler, printer Cherokee Phoenix, Samuel Mays, Surry Eaton, Austin Copeland, Edward D. Lozure, Thomas Gann, Benjamin Thompson and James A. Thompson. Prior to the sheriff's arrival, the inspectors of the penitentiary had received the following letter from Governor George Gilmer:

EXECUTIVE OFFICE
Sept. 22, 1831.

Gentlemen:

I understand that a number of persons have been lately convicted in Gwinnett County for illegal residence in the territory occupied by the Cherokees within the State and will soon be placed in the penitentiary unless they should be considered proper subjects for the exercise of executive clemency. As it is possible that some of these persons may have committed the offence of which they have been convicted under mistaken opinions of their duty or the powers of the government, I am desirous of pardoning such of them as may have thus acted and will now give assurances that they will not violate the laws of the State, if they should be found worthy of such clemency.

You are, therefore, required to see each of the prisoners and converse with them alone and ascertain from them whether they are disposed to promise not again to offend the laws, if they should be pardoned. You are also requested to ascertain as accurately as you can what have been the motives which have influenced them in their opposition to the State.

The result of your inquiry and conversation you will oblige me by communicating with me as early as convenient.

Respectfully yours,
GEORGE R. GILMER.

Messrs. James Carmack,
    Benjamin White,
    Tomlinson Fort,
      Inspectors of the Penitentiary.

The inspectors of the penitentiary answered the Governor's letter in the following communication:

PENITENTIARY
Sept. 22, 1831

Sir:

In compliance with your request of this date, we met at the penitentiary and investigated the cases of each of the individuals brought from Gwinnett County separately. Enclosed we send statements of James Trott, Samuel Mays, Edward Delusier, Surry Eaton, Thomas Gann and A. Copeland. You will also find a written petition from Samuel Mays.

We have personally examined Benjamin Thompson, James A. Thompson and John Wheeler. The above persons all request your clemency on condition that they will not again violate the law of the State. They are stated by Mr. Troot and Mr. Butler to be respectable and honest citizen.

With regard to Mr. Butler, he authorized us to state he could not take the oath without perjuring himself as he views the case. He can not consent to a change of residence with his present feelings.

Mr. Worcester states that he has taken the course he has pursued from a firm conviction of duty. If he had been disposed to submit, he would not have proceeded so far. He has applied to the Supreme Court of the United States and expects to hear from his application.

Mr. Wheeler states that his family is within the chartered

limits and he intends to return there, but will not subject himself to another arrest.

Respectfully, your obedient servants.
BENJAMIN A. WHITE,
JAMES CARMACK,
TOMLINSON FORT,
Inspectors.

Nine of the prisoners accepted the terms proposed by the Governor and were promptly pardoned. However, Dr. Butler and Dr. Worcester refused to accede to the terms proposed by the Governor and they were, therefore, placed in the penitentiary. They carried their case, by appeal, directly to the Supreme Court of the United States. In March, 1832, the case was called and Attorneys William Wirt and John Sargeant appeared for the prisoners. The State of Georgia was not represented at the hearing.

On the third day of March, Chief Justice John Marshall announced the decision of the court in favor of the missionaries, declaring the laws of Georgia extending her jurisdiction over the Cherokee Nation to be repugnant to the Constitution, treaties and laws of the United States and, therefore, null and void. The Supreme Court then issued the following mandate:

"To the honorable Judge of the Superior Court for the County of Gwinnett in the State of Georgia:

"Greeting.

"Whereas, lately in the Superior Court for the County of Gwinnett, in the State of Georgia, before you in a case between the State of Georgia, plaintiff, and Samuel A. Worcester, defendant on an indictment for residing in the Cherokee Nation, without license, the judgement of the said Superior Court was in the following words, viz: 'The defendant in this case shall be kept in close custody by the Sheriff of this County until he can be transported to the penitentiary of this State, and the keeper thereof is hereby directed to receive him in his custody and keep him at hard labor in said penitentiary for and during the term of four years,' as by the inspection of the transcript of the record of the said Superior Court, which was brought into the Supreme Court of the United States by virtue of a Writ of Error, agreeably to the act of Congress in such a case made and provided, fully and at large appears. And, whereas, in the present term of January, in the year of our Lord one thousand eight hundred and thirty-two, the said cause came on to be heard before the said Supreme Court on the said transcript of the record and was argued by counsel, on consideration whereof, it is the opinion of this Court that the act of the legislature of the State of Georgia, upon which the indictment in this case is founded, is contrary to the Constitution, treaties, and laws of the United States, and that the special plea in bar, pleaded by the said Samuel

A. Worcester in the manner aforesaid, and relying upon the Constitution, treaties and laws of the United States aforesaid, is a good bar and defense to the said indictment by the said Samuel A. Worcester, and as such ought to have been allowed and admitted by the said Superior Court for the County of Gwinnett, in the State of Georgia, before which the said indictment was pending and tried, and that there was an error in the said Superior Court of the State of Georgia in overruling the plea so pleaded as aforesaid: It is, therefore, ordered and adjudged that the judgment rendered in the premises by the said Superior Court of Georgia, upon the verdict upon the plea of not guilty afterwards pleaded by the said Samuel A. Worcester, whereby the said Samuel A. Worcester is sentenced to hard labor in the penitentiary of the State of Georgia, ought to be reversed and annulled, and this Court proceeding to render such judgment as the said Superior Court of the State of Georgia should have rendered, it is further ordered and adjudged that the said judgment of the said Superior Court be, and the same is hereby reversed and annulled, and that the judgment be, and hereby is awarded that the special plea in bar as aforesaid pleaded is a good and sufficient plea in bar in law to the indictment aforesaid, and that all proceedings on the said indictment do forever surcease, and that the said Samuel A. Worcester be, and hereby is, henceforth, dismissed therefrom, and that he go thereof, quit without day, and that a special mandate do go from this Court to the said Superior Court to carry this judgment into execution;

"You, therefore, are hereby commanded that such other proceedings be had in said cause in conformity with the judgment of said Supreme Court of the United States, as according to right and justice and the laws of the United States ought to be had, the said writ of error notwithstanding.

"Witness, the Honorable John Marshall, Chief Justice of said Supreme Court, the second Monday of January, in the year of our Lord one thousand eight hundred and thirty-two.

"WILLIAM THOMAS CARROLL,
"Clerk of the Supreme Court
of the United States."

When President Andrew Jackson heard about the decision of the Supreme Court, he is said to have made the following comment: "Now that John Marshall has made his decision, let him enforce it."

In a few days after the decision, attorneys for Worcester moved in the Superior Court of Gwinnett County that the mandate of the Supreme Court of the United States be recorded and the prisoners discharged. The court refused to obey the mandate. An appeal was then made to the Governor and he, too, refused to discharge the prisoners.

Later the missionaries were advised to change their course.

They, accordingly, instructed their attorneys not to prosecute their case any further. The missionaries informed the Governor of their decision and stated in their letter to him that they had not been led to the adoption of this course by any change of views in regard to the principles on which they had acted. The Governor thought this communication disrespectful and remarked that as long as they regarded the principles on which they acted so highly they could stand by them in the penitentiary. When informed of what the Governor decided to do in the matter, they asked Colonel Cuthbert to request the Governor to permit them to withdraw the communication in order to correct its objectionable parts. Of course the Governor refused to grant the request, whereupon they addressed to him a note as follows:

PENITENTIARY
Milledgeville, Ga.
January 9, 1833.

To His Excellency Wilson Lumpkin,
Governor of Georgia:
Sir:

We are sorry to be informed that some expressions in our communication of yesterday were regarded by your Excellency as an indignity offered to the State or its authorities. Nothing could be further from our design. In the course we have now taken, it has been our intention simply to forbear the prosecution of our case and to leave the question of the continuance in confinement to the magnanimity of the State.

We are respectfully yours,
S. A. WORCESTER,
ELIZUR BUTLER.

Governor Lumpkin immediately issued a pardon for the two missionaries.

THE CREEK INDIAN WAR

The Creek Indians at one time occupied the territory now included in Gwinnett County. In 1802 Georgia ceded to the United States all its territory west of its present boundary and extending to the Mississippi River, and the United States agreed to extinguish all Indian titles to lands within this state. The United States neglected to carry out this agreement so far as the Creek Nation was concerned until 1826, when a treaty was made with that nation in which all Creek territory was ceded to the federal government and the Indians were required to move across the Chattahoochee. Perhaps most of the Indians opposed this treaty, but there was nothing they could do about it. In 1836 the Creeks began to make forays into Georgia near Columbus. They burned Roanoke, a village of several hundred people, in Stewart County. So serious did the situation become that Governor William Schley called for volunteers. Three companies were quickly organized in Gwinnett County, two of which were immediately ordered to report for service in what is generally called the Creek Indian War.

Lawrenceville

At an election held in the Town of Lawrenceville on the 24th of May, 1836, for the election of officers to command the Company of mounted Infantry raised by volunteering in the 45th Regiment of Georgia Militia, we the managers of said election, certify that we managed the election agreeable to law, and that Hamilton Garmany was elected Captain; John N. Reeves, First Lieutenant; Henry P. Thomas, Second Lieutenant, and Isaac S. Lacy, Ensign. Done by order of Col. James Austin.

JOHN N. ALEXANDER, J. P.,
THOS. W. ALEXANDER,
C. HOWELL,
Managers.

Georgia, Gwinnett County.
To His Excellency, Wm. Schley.
Dear Sir:

In obedience to your general order of the 13th May, a volunteer Company of Mounted Infantry was attempted to be raised on Friday the 20th, inst., there not being a sufficient number who volunteered to form a full company I thought proper to call out the Regiment to meet at Lawrenceville on Tuesday, the 24th, inst., to make the attempt to complete the Company of Mounted Infantry, and after the men had been formed into line the express from you arrived with your orders to raise every tenth man. The order was then given for volunteers to fill out the Company of Mounted Infantry which was immediately done. I then ordered those from the line who would volunteer for a Company of Infantry would step out, when a company was immediately raised. These two companies constitute as near as I can ascertain every tenth man in my Regiment. The returns of the election of officers, their names and the number of the officers and men is herein enclosed. I hope their commissions will be forwarded to Columbus to them as soon as possible, as I have this day started both companies to that place and directed the officers to report themselves to General Lowe immediately on their arrival at that place. I have furnished them with baggage and baggage wagons and all the necessary implements for their accommodation, and money to buy provisions for themselves and horses on their march. The officers have, and will have, all the necessary vouchers to show the expenditure, and I hope your Excellency will order the wagoners to be paid, as they were promised their pay on their arrival there. I have thought proper as this is a case that requires immediate action and that it is very important that the officers should be immediately commissioned, to send this return by express and hope you will pay him for his services. The papers herein inclosed will show the names of the officers and of the men attached to the different companies—all of which is respectfully submitted to your Excellency.

JAMES AUSTIN, Colonel,
Comd. 45th Regiment, G. M.

Captain Garmany's Mounted Volunteers

Hammond Garmany, Captain; John N. Reeves, First Lieutenant; Henry P. Thomas, Second Lieutenant; Isaac S. Lacy, Ensign; James C. Martin, Henry B. Thompson, Viveon Holmes, Washington Holmes, Edwin Rice, James T. Mcdade [sic], Henry W. Peden, Thos. W. Hunt, J. A. V. Tate, Wm. V. Hacket, Benjn. Couch, Samuel M. Robinson, Chaney Couch, Robt. M. Pucket, Wm. Wardlaw, Robt. T. Holland, James M. Allen, Robert G. Hackett, Saml. M. Ship, Valentine A. Harris, James H. Holland, James R. McAster, James Gorden, Miles Culver, Benj. Laughridge, Raus B. Martin, Wm. E. Atkinson, John L. Foster, James S. Mcdill [sic], James C. Dunlap, Wm. M. Sims, Jesse Wade, James H. Foster, Benj. M. Powel, Theodore D. Doney, Thos. J. Chambers, James Key, Wm. M. Foster, Madison L. Adair, John B. Benson, Thos. P. Nellms, Daniel M. Clower, Saml. Dunn, John Kemp, Wm. C. Orr, Freeman H. Liddle, Patrick M. Scott, David W. Spence, Clark Howell, Capt. Thos. Holland, John R. Alexander, Thos. W. Alexander, Nelson Roberts, John Ezzard, Jeremiah Bateman, B. F. Morgan, A. Pool, John Bowman, Wm. Stapp, Jas. H. Casper, M. T. Hamilton, Thos. Bagby, Jas. Montgomery, Chas. Burton, Meshack Reid, John Strickland, Alfred Penly, Jesse Hunnicut, A. Martin, Drury Peoples, Wm. J. Terry, Perryman Berry.

Reed's Company

George Reed was elected captain of one company. This company was attached to the second regiment of volunteers and ordered into service by Governor Schley. The company was mustered into service at Columbus by Major Kirby, of the United States Army, for three months.

OFFICERS

Captain, George Reed; 1st Lieutenant, Samuel L. Jones; 2nd Lieutenant, John C. Sammons; Ensign, John Cain, 1st Sgt., Joel T. Thresher; 2nd Sgt., William Keenan; 3rd Sgt., Thomas T. Langley; 4th Sgt., Jesse Thompson; 1st Cpl., John Harbin; 2nd Cpl., William Couch; 3rd Cpl., Jeremiah McClung; 4th Cpl., Joseph Terry; Drummer, William T. Gray; Fifer, John Osborn.

PRIVATES

Anderson Arnold, Henderson Arnold, E. C. Atha, John F. Adkins, John W. Austin, John L. Baugh, William P. Brown, Merrell C. Bennett, John G. Bennett, Mahlon Bennett, Jonus Congo, Israel Chandler, Ransom Chandler, James Caloway, Richard Couch, Samuel M. C. Drummond, Pierce Dickens, James W. Davis, Charles Dodson, Turner L. Evans, James J. Ethridge, Jesse Fountain, Thomas Gray, Nathan S. Goza, Oliver H. P. Goza, John Garner, Johnson S. Griswell, Richard G. Harbin, Benjamin M. Harbin, Samuel Hamby, Elisha Holcomb, James Horton, Humphrey Hurst.

Soloman Hopkins, Claiburn Jackson, Soloman H. Jackson, Thomas Jinks, L. B. Jackson, William Jenkins, Johnson Kemp, Stanmore Kilcrease, James Kilcrease, Jeptha V. Langley, Miles Langley, Robert Miller, Joseph Mills, William Nelson, Bartly Parnell, John Pendley, Asa G. Rhodes, Aaron Shadwick, Henry Smith, Joseph Stephens, Burton M. South, Allen Smith, Jefferson Singleton, Dennis Singleton, Martin H. Taylor, William Tutton, Hamilton Trammell, John Y. Terry, Henry M. Taylor, David Taylor, William A. Turley, John Wynn, Thomas Watson.

HOME GUARD

On Tuesday, May 25, 1836, Colonel James Austin, who was at the head of the regiment in Gwinnett County, assembled the entire militia of the county at the courthouse for the purpose of organizing for the Creek War then raging in the vicinity of Columbus. Just as they assembled a messenger arrived from the Governor with orders directed to Colonel Austin to raise men for immediate service by voluntary enlistment or by draft. A call was made for volunteers to form a company for the protection of the citizens of the county and adjoining counties. About 90 men formed a line. Notice was given that on Friday, the 27th, the company would be organized at the courthouse when the following citizens met and organized by electing:

OFFICERS

Benjamin Gholston, Captain; George Oran, First Lieutenant; W. Isham Williams, Second Lieutenant; Ezekiel Mathews, Ensign.

The company was called The Gwinnett Grays.

PRIVATES

Elisha Winn, James D. Peden, J. Barnett, D. Bradford, John Sammon, William Gordon, Asa Wade, M. Mays, Newton Bramblett, R. Halcome, Hugh Baker, J. Mauldin, D. Spence, W. Bennett, J. B. Turner, Wm. Montgomery, M. McKenney, J. Rambo, D. P. Allen, Wm. Tumlin, Charles Lavender, Z. Brooks, John Brooks, Joseph Morgan, A. Clark, Jas. Hood, Wm. Robinson, E. Wilson, Henry

Glassgo, Benjamin Smith, P. Mauldin, Wm. Morrow, George M. Gresham, Fred Hart, T. Langford, Simeon Perry, J. Baker, John Bankston, Few Gordon, Thomas Robinson, Sterling Callahan, H. M. Skaggs, A. Taylor, R. D. Johnson, John Peden, Robert Brown, John Stuart, John Foster, Samuel Austin, E. Jennings, George Atha, Jas. Stanley, Wm. Baugh, A. Brown, Benjamin Higgins, E. Griswold, Joshua Hill, Wm. Richardson, Archibald Harris, Thomas Kircus, Jas. Lanier, John Perry, Jacob Taylor, Wm. L. Dodd, Thompson C. Strickland, John Underwood, Wm. Laughridge, Hugh Mills, Thomas Carter.

Captain James Garmany's Company

The names of the officers and privates in Captain James Garmany's company of volunteers from Gwinnett County are as follows:

OFFICERS

Captain, James Garmany; 1st Lieutenant, T. W. Alexander; 2nd Lieutenant, R. B. Martin; 1st Sergeant, W. B. Byrd; 2nd Sergeant, Lott Rowden; 3rd Sergeant, J. N. Alexander; 4th Sergeant, William Jenkins; 1st Corporal, Chaney Couch; 2nd Corporal, D. P. Clower; 3rd Corporal, Austin Lamar; Ensign, J. S. McGill.

PRIVATES

D. H. Alexander, Jackson Acres, Leroy Adair, Robert Anthony, John Baskin, Edward Brown, John L. Baugh, A. J. Brown, Robert Brown, Pettyman Berry, Jope J. Brogdon, James Brown, J. A. Brown, A. Brown, James W. Brown, N. A. Cody, Thomas Carroll, Thomas Cooper, J. R. Cooper, D. H. Clower, John Carroll, B. P. Couch, Joel Davis, Elias Davis, Jesse Davis, James Davis, G. R. Davis, Thomas Estes, Zadoc Ford, E. C. Gresham, A. C. Gholston, O. H. P. Goza, James Gordon.

James Garmany, John C. Harris, Dillard Haney, E. Y. Hunnicutt, Joshua Hall, Thomas Hunt, R. G. Hackett, P. G. Lamar, Benjamin H. Lampkin, M. McDill, Newton McDill, B. F. Morgan, John W. Maltbie, Ab Martin, Afinicias Massey, Washington Mills, W. C. Mathis, J. D. Morgan, Winship A. Massey, J. W. Martin, Thomas Nichols, H. W. Nance, James Patillo, William Parker, Drewey Peeples, Daniel Paden, William M. Puckett, Nelson Roberts, R. W. Richardson, William Saye, B. E. Strickland, Chaney Stone, David W. Spence, Jackson Smith, John B. Trippe, Jesse Wade, William Wood, W. N. Wood, E. Wilson, Thomas M. Wynn, William S. Wynn, George W. Wiley.

Arrives at Shepherd's Plantation

Captain Hammond Garmany and his mounted volunteers left Lawrenceville on May 26, 1836, and arrived at Columbus on June 3rd. His company was mustered into service and armed and then it continued down the river and arrived at Shepherd's Plantation on the afternoon of June 6. Shepherd's Plantation is about forty miles south of Columbus, in Stewart County, and on arrival there the company pitched its camp about the barn and nearby cabins.

By request Captain Garmany sent twenty-five of his men to guard a fort situated on the river not far away. In the meantime he contacted Captain Jernigan, who was in charge of the local militia, and each agreed to go to each other's assistance in the event of a battle with the Indians.

Between two and three o'clock on June 9th, while Captain Garmany's men were eating their dinner, a firing was heard about half a mile from the place he occupied. Supposing that Major Jernigan and his force were attacked, Garmany ordered his men to leave their dinner and parade immediately. The horses were left, and indeed everything else, except the clothes which the men had on, and the force repaired to the direction where the firing was heard; and having marched about half a mile, found the Indians prepared for battle. When within some one hundred yards of the Indians, Garmany's men fired and six or seven of the enemy fell. The Indians then retreated a short distance and formed a line. Garmany gave them another fire, the savages returning it in regular manner and again retreated. Garmany discovered that every time they retreated they were reinforced to the number of at least 250. As long as they could be kept in front, they were repulsed; but becoming so numerous, and Captain Garmany's company consisting of only forty-two men in line at the time, the Indians began to flank them. A retreat was ordered and the men were commanded to fire on the retreat. Half of them were ordered to face to the right and the other half to the left, and to fire upon their flanks in order to keep the Indians from surrounding them. After having retreated and firing in this way about half a mile, a small field was reached and the fence was used as a breastwork until two rounds were fired. By this time the enemy had succeeded in dividing the party. By firing on the flank, Captain Garmany and about ten men succeeded in getting possession of the yard; and at the time they entered the gate, the enemy had succeeded in getting the opposite side of the yard, but were driven from their position. They then fled to the ginhouse. A position was then taken and an opportunity watched to shoot as they passed around the houses. The troops were directed not to fire until they could be certain to kill, which order was obeyed. Garmany took a position behind two trees so situated that he could not be seen and from that place he was certain that he killed an Indian who was attempting to get one of the horses over the fence. When he fell another Indian attempted to get the same horse, and before he succeeded in getting the animal, he was shot and fell within three feet of the other. Garmany then loaded again, and just at this moment three other Indians passed around the corner of a small house forty yards distant, when they were fired at, and two of them stopped; the other shot Garmany through the thigh, which caused him to fall. The Indian drew his knife and made towards him. Garmany raised up and shot the Indian, bringing him to the ground. At this time a panic was produced among Garmany's men who were present and who cried out that their captain was killed. But he called to them, saying that he was not dead and that they must fight on. Dispatching the Indian after he was wounded, Garmany drew his pocket pistol, determined still to defend himself, and called to his men to turn the horses out of the lot, which they did. Those of his corps that were near continued to fight; and during the whole time, the men on the other flank of the enemy maintained the action with vigor and energy.

Just at this moment Major Jernigan, of Stewart County, who was at Fort Jones, three miles below the battleground, arrived with a small detachment of men, not exceeding thirty, and charged upon the Indians, which diverted them from Garmany and enabled him to make his escape. One of his men, seeing that he was wounded, brought him a horse, took him up behind him, and carried him to Fort Jones.

About this time a body of men who had been sent to Fort McCreary, and had heard the firing, came and charged through the ranks of the enemy, but they were too late to render much assistance. Four of Garmany's company had been left sick at Fort Ingersoll with two others to wait on them, and two or three had gone to the shop to get their horses shod. These things account for the few men he had in the action. Those of his company who were in the engagement acted with great bravery and firmness. Every man stood firm until ordered to retreat.

Ample testimony was borne to the courage and bravery of Major Jernigan and his men who went to the assistance of Garmany. In Garmany's company eight were killed and four wounded. Of Major Jernigan's men, four were killed and three wounded. Those of Garmany's men killed were Ensign J. S. Lacy, Orderly-Sergeant Jas. C. Martin, James H. Holland, Robert T. Holland, James M. Allen, William M. Sims, J. A. V. Tate, and Henry W. Paden. The wounded were Captain Hammond Garmany, John R. Alexander, Thomas W. Hunt, and William Stapp. It was thought that there were from twenty-five to thirty Indians killed, but Colonel Gibson, who afterwards visited the battleground, was clearly of the opinion that the loss of the Indians must have been much greater.

Those of the Stewart Company who fell in the battle were David Delk, Jared Irwin, Captain Robert Billups, and a young man by the name of Hunter. They were all gentlemen of the first standing. Mr. Delk was a member of the bar and occupied a very respectable station in his profession. Mr. Irwin was clerk of the Inferior Court of Stewart County.

At Newnan

On its return the company stopped at Newnan. The *Newnan Palladium* made the following statement about this event:

> Early on the morning of Tuesday, 26th ult., our citizens were apprised of the approach of a company of our chivalrous up-country volunteers; we at once thought it to be our own, but when they approached, who should it be but the gallant Captain Garmany with a part of his command. They were received with enthusiasm by our citizens, and were compelled by urgent solicitation to partake of a breakfast with us, after which the ladies and gentlemen of the town and its vicinity repaired to the courthouse to welcome this heroic band. Col. W. D. Speer was called to the chair; and after making a few pertinent remarks suitable to the occasion, the following song was, after proper intervals, sung thrice with weeping eyes and great applause:

CAPTAIN GARMANY'S FIGHT

See the Chattahoochee flow
By Roanoke descending low;
There our soldiers met the foe
Fierce as panthers prowling.

God! Was not Thy presence nigh
When to Thee, with trusting eye,
Looked our soldiers, while the cry
Burst like wild wolves howling?

Hear our Captain's cheerful tone—
'Courage, soldiers, soldiers, on!
Let no craven fear be shown,
Here no aid can find us!

'Who a home or loved one hath,
Fight like whirlwinds in their wrath;
Fight, there lies no middle path—
Wreath or shade must bind us.

'Should the God of battles smile,
Blessings wait to crown our toil;
Many a lis'ner we'll beguile
With this day's bold story.

'Should we fall, we leave a name
Ages will be proud to claim;
Death upon the soldier's fame
Stamps the seal of glory.'

Garmany, such thy counsels bold,
Now in song thy name's enrolled,
And thy gallant deeds are told
While thousands throng applauding.

Bravery makes thy field her shrine,
Beauty's grateful tear is thine;
Who but would his life resign
Such the meed rewarding?

After the singing had ceased, Captain Garmany arose and spoke as follows:

"Mr. Chairman, I beg leave to respond by offering my thanks, both for myself and in behalf of my company, for the honor conferred upon us. It is true we have encountered hardships, difficulty, great danger, some suffering, and the loss of some of our best men; yet we have done no more than our duty which every man should at all times be ready to discharge. You, dear females, I with pleasure behold here in peace and under the protection of the good and virtuous, while my bosom burns at the thought that I have seen the places where many of your sex have been butchered by those bloodthirsty savages, too cruel to relate. Yes, so cruel and heart rending that my life has almost been my terror."

Tears flowed from the eyes of all in the house which created an inexpressible feeling, and we could not trace him further but can say that he spoke the sentiments of a warm and patriotic heart. The citizens wished to retain them as guests until tomorrow, but the anxiety of the heroes to see and embrace their wives, daughters and sisters was such that we had to succumb.

Bodies of Eight Buried in Courthouse Square

Early in 1837 at a mass meeting held in Lawrenceville, attended by a large number of the leading citizens of the county, it was decided to have the bodies of the eight young men who lost their lives in the battle of Shepherd's Plantation brought back to their home county.

At a second meeting of a portion of the people of Gwinnett County, the committee appointed at a previous meeting for that purpose, made the following report:

"The committee appointed for that purpose beg leave to report that they appointed Captain H. Garmany, Ensign M. T. Hamilton, and Privates Thomas Hunt and Elias Green to bring the remains of Ensign J. S. Lacy, Orderly Sergeant James C. Martin, and Privates J. A. V. Tate, Robert T. Holland, James H. Holland, James M. Allen, Henry W. Paden and William M. Sims, who fell in the battle of Shepherd's Plantation and who belonged to Captain Garmany's Company; that the remains have been carefully disinterred, placed in coffins and boxes, have been brought to this place, and are now in a room in the courthouse, ready for interment.

"Your committee respectfully recommend that they be interred near the northwest corner of the courthouse yard and that a suitable monument be erected to commemorate them for their gallantry and bravery. To this end your committee recommend the adoption of the following resolution:

"RESOLVED, That the remains of the said deceased be interred on Friday, February 17th, 1837, in the northwest corner of the courthouse yard at the hour of 1 o'clock P. M., with military honors, and that a suitable monument be erected in a convenient time to their memory.

"After this report was read, Colonel N. L. Hutchins offered the following as an amendment to the report:

"AND WHEREAS, Our townsman, Captain James C. Winn, who, at the first call to arms, flew to the assistance of the Texans, who were warring for liberty and independence against their oppressors, and his early companion, Anthony Bates, who went with him to share his perils, fight in the same holy cause and to suffer the same sad fate, were both inhumanly butchered in cold blood in Fannin's devoted band;

"AND WHEREAS, by their bravery and devotion to the cause they had espoused, the first was promoted to a Captain, and the latter to Orderly, in a very short time after they entered the service and served with honor to themselves and usefulness to the cause, until they were taken, bravely fighting, and in cold blood butchered by a savage band of Mexicans by order of their still more savage commander; therefore,

"RESOLVED, That Captain James C. Winn and Orderly Sergeant Anthony Bates share the honors bestowed on our other lamented volunteers, and that their names, with suitable inscription, be engraved upon the monument to be erected in the public square.

"This amendment was adopted, and then both preamble and resolution were unanimously adopted.

"On motion of Col. N. L. Hutchins, a committee consisting of himself, Captain H. Garmany, Lieutenant M. T. Hamilton, Colonel H. P. Thomas, A. R. Smith, J. B. Trippe, Esq., T. W. Alexander, John S. Wilson, Wm. Montgomery, and Captain George Reid, was appointed to take order for the interment.

"On motion of T. W. Alexander, a committee consisting of himself, J. W. Thompson, M. Crawford, and William Gordon, was appointed to prepare a vault for this purpose.

"The meeting then adjourned to meet at 10 o'clock on Friday, the 17th of February."

On Friday, February 17th, at 10 o'clock, the day set apart for the interment, the committee appointed for that purpose met and reported as follows:

"The committee appointed for that purpose beg leave to report the following order for the interment of the remains of Ensign Lacy, Orderly Martin, Privates Tate, R. T. Holland, J. H. Holland, Allen, Paden, and Sims, and in honor of Captain Winn and Orderly Bates.

"ORDER FOR INTERMENT—The procession will form in front of Dr. Hall's, in the following order: 1st, The Committee on Arrangement. 2nd, Pallbearers. 3rd, Relatives of the dead as mourners. 4th, The clergy. 5th, The military. 6th, The judges and officers of the courts. 7th, The corporate authorities of the town. 8th, The citizens.

"The procession will march around the public square and enter the inclosure at the east side.

"The pallbearers, under the direction of the Committee on Arrangements, will receive the remains at the east door of the courthouse and proceed to the vault. The remains to be then deposited; the Committee having taken station on the right, the pallbearers on the left, the mourners and clergy on the west side of the vault, and the military to approach the east end of the vault.

"The military will be formed and ordered by Captain Garmany into platoons. Rounds fired in honor of each as follows: 1st, Captain Winn. 2nd, Ensign Lacy. 3rd, Orderlies Martin and Bates. 4th, Privates Tate, Allen, Sims, Paden, R. T. Holland, J. H. Holland. Vault to be filled. The procession will then disperse. The Committee recommend the appointment of a marshal with power to regulate the procession and have agreed on Dr. Thomas W. Alexander as a suitable person."

On February 17, 1837, the bodies of these eight young men were buried in one common grave. A vast concourse of people gathered to witness the solemn and impressive ceremony.

Funds were soon collected by public subscription to place a

monument on this grave. On the east face of the monument is the following inscription:

LONGSWAMP CHEROKEE MARBLE
ERECTED BY HENRY FITZSIMMONS
A. D. 1840

It is probable that this is the first monument ever erected in the State of Georgia out of Georgia marble. Henry Fitzsimmons, who completed the jail in Lawrenceville in 1833, received the contract to erect the monument. He probably was given the order soon after the interment, and it is known that he began to work the marble quarry about that time.

On the south face of the monument is the following inscription:

"To the memory of Ensign Isaac Lacy, Sergeant James C. Martin, and Privates William M. Sims, John A. V. Tate, Robert T. Holland, James H. Holland, brothers, Henry W. Paden, James M. Allen, members of the Gwinnett Company of mounted volunteers, under the command of Captain Hammond Garmany, who were slain in battle with a party of Creek Indians at Shepherd's Plantation, in Stewart County, June 9, 1836. Their remains rest beneath this monument."

Georgia marble was used for the first time in this monument which was erected in 1840 in the courthouse square in Lawrenceville by Henry Fitzsimmons. Betty Harper points to the large ball on top.

A Private's Experience at the Battle of Shepherd's Plantation

James C. Key, who joined Captain Garmany's Company and who participated in the Battle of Shepherd's Plantation, gave an account of his experience on that dreadful occasion in four letters that were published in a Lawrenceville paper in 1898. These letters find a place in this narrative. Mr. Key lived in Texas at the time these letters were written.

Letter One

The State of Georgia, claiming lands originally known as the Mississippi Territory, in 1802 relinquished that claim in favor of the general government, the latter agreeing to purchase for the state all the lands belonging to the Creek Nation within her borders. The United States did not fulfill her part of this contract until 1826, when a cession of the Creek lands was obtained and that people agreed to remove beyond the Mississippi.

The removal, however, did not take place as agreed, and when the Seminole War broke out in 1835, the Creeks became restless and evidently had an understanding of alliance with the Indians of Florida.

When Van Buren became President in 1836, the war was renewed with great vigor, and the Creeks in Georgia and Eastern Alabama armed and made open war against the settlers.

At this time I was going to school in Gwinnett County, Georgia, and being the sixth child and first son, I was on this account much petted, considerably spoiled, and consequently not well calculated to bear the restraints of school life. Therefore, when my father sent me to a Manual Labor School in Gwinnett County in the early part of this latter year, I found the situation anything but pleasing, for heretofore I had been accustomed to having my own way about most things. The steward of the school was to my youthful and perhaps wilful mind a very despot. He ordered me about in a manner that no youth of spirit, and especially one who had been petted as I had been, could possibly bear. At last I positively refused to obey him, and it became evident that one or the other of us must yield. Perhaps I should have been expelled from the school had I remained long enough, but this was not to be.

About this time volunteers were being enrolled all over the state to fight the Indians, who were murdering defenseless whites along the borders of Alabama and Georgia. A company of volunteers was formed in our little village. Everything was excitement. Indignant groups could be seen here and there discussing and condemning with unmeasured disapproval the atrocious butcheries in which the red warriors seemed to delight. Stories were repeated from mouth to mouth, describing in all their sickening details the indiscriminate and merciless slaying of gray-haired fathers and mothers, beautiful young girls just blooming into womanhood, and innocent babes at their mothers' breasts.

Together with many of my companions at school I fell into the whirlpool of excitement. My young heart was stirred to its very depths by the merciless cruelty of the savages. While these stories of butchery after butchery of defenseless women and children aroused within me a natural feeling of revenge, I must confess that the pomp and glitter of war had its effect upon my young mind.

"A soldier's life and a soldier's glory for me!" I cried, and I was only prevented from joining the company immediately by learning of the great grief and anxiety of my dear fond parents. This deterred me for a while, but when the second call for recruits was made I could resist no longer, and together with four of my companions I was duly enlisted as a volunteer.

The organization of a company was completed in a week, a Mr. Garmany was elected captain, and other officers chosen and appointed. During this week my mother's grief was almost more than she could bear, and it so worked upon my father's feelings that he procured a substitute for me, not heeding my remonstrances.

Having once taken the step, my pride was wounded at the very thought of receding from my position. I loved my father and mother, oh so dearly, and my heart was sorely troubled at their grief, but my mind was fixed and settled—I must go! When my mother saw that my resolution could not be shaken and all persuasion was useless, she yielded. My parents unwilling to exert their authority by using force to detain me, my substitute was left at home and I rejoined the company. My mother, brave, truehearted woman that she was, gave me her blessing, bade me not to falter, but do my whole duty, repeating as we parted those heroic words, "Rather would I mourn a fallen hero than clasp a coward in my embrace."

As near as my recollection serves me, we started on the 25th day of May, 1836, for the Creek Nation. I, like most of the youthful soldiers in the command, did not realize the gravity of the situation. To me that day, as we marched away with flags flying, horses prancing, uniforms glittering and sparkling in the sunlight as our officers dashed hither and thither, all to the strains of martial music, was the happiest day of my life. How bright and glorious everything seemed! With what tireless energy I pealed forth note after note from that dear old bugle! Had I been measured on that occasion by the standard of my own feelings, I surely must have reached the full stature of manhood, and giant manhood at that!

At Decatur the citizens received us with open arms, extended to us every hospitality, feeding and lodging us for the night, and next morning cheered us with kindly wishes for our success against the foe, and a safe and speedy return to our homes.

On the 3rd day of June we crossed the Chattahoochee at Columbus, were mustered into the service, armed with muskets, and next morning recrossed the river, our Captain declaring that he came to find and to fight Indians. We then marched down as far as the Cowigees and there camped for the night.

The next morning we experienced our first alarm. Our guard, mistaking for Indians several gentlemen who were traveling from Irwinton to their plantations, fired at them across the river, severely but not dangerously wounding one of the party. This false alarm had a good effect upon the command, for although gaiety was the order of the day and death the last thing thought of, we became somewhat more cautious. In the afternoon we started back for Shepherd's Plantation, which lay between Roanoke and Fort McCrary, arriving there shortly after noon of the next day. Here we camped for many days, and Captain Garmany having been ordered to furnish a detail from his company to help garrison the fort, selected twenty-five of our best men, which was nearly half of our little command. Captain Jeragan being out on a scouting expedition, made us a short visit next morning, and he and Captain Garmany pledged themselves to aid each other if possible, should either party engage the Indians.

When we took our departure from Columbus I left all my clothing there except the suit I wore. It now became necessary for me to renovate these by brushing and washing; I therefore borrowed a suit from one of my comrades, which was several sizes too large, and having cleaned my own and hung them out to dry, I busied myself about the camp fire, preparing dinner for my mess. We occupied some of the huts formerly used for negro cabins, and my comrades were enjoying themselves laughing and talking, and some were bantering others for a trivial bet, when we were startled by the quick "Bang! Bang!" of small arms in the near distance. The next thing we heard was our Captain's voice as he cried, "Parade! Parade, boys!" The company was soon in line and moving away from camp. We had gone but a short distance when I discovered that I had left my ammunition behind. Of course I could be of little or no service without that, so I hastened back to camp, got it, and by hard running, overtook the command. We had marched about a mile in the direction of the firing when suddenly fifteen or twenty Indians rose right up before us from the tall grass, gave us a volley and ran away.

Proceeding a few yards further, some forty or fifty savages emerged from their concealment and yelling like demons gave us another volley. In a moment of time, it seemed to me, the whole wood was alive with a legion of devils; for never in my life before, nor since, heard I such wild vicious whoops and screams as came from those savage throats as they showered their leaden hail upon us. Our little company was taken completely by surprise, for we expected to have met Captain Jernigan's company and acted in concert with him against the foe, but here we were only thirty-nine in number to stand against three or four hundred Indians, who fought, not like men, but like fiends incarnate. Above the din of yelling and firing arose the voice of Captain Garmany. "Each man to a tree, boys! Fight them in their own style!" We each gained a tree and then we heard our captain again: "Pick your man to fire at, boys! Load and fire as fast as you can, and give them back yell for yell!" I can not describe my feelings as I stood behind that tall naked pine tree, when I heard our captain shout: "Each man to a tree!" I gave up all for lost. I only had presence of mind enough to get behind a tree, load, peep out, present my gun in the direction of the Indians, give a big whoop, fire and jump back again.

As the others began to yell, I joined so heartily in the deafening chorus that my spirits soon arose again. I became calm enough to take deliberate aim and finally almost exulted in the perilous situation. The tree behind which I stood was fairly peppered with bullets, and whenever my head and shoulders were exposed in order to fire, this maneuver on my part never failed to bring a number of hissing bullets, filling the air with anything but charming music.

Every incident of that unequal fight is impressed as vividly upon my memory today, as in that long time agone.

Once in loading I dropped my ramrod and endeavored to catch it upon my knee, but my hand missed it, and striking against my knee it flew several feet from the tree. I could do nothing without it, for in those old days the modern breech-loader was a thing not even dreamed of.

Springing toward the ramrod, I fell flat on my face to the ground. A shower of bullets passed harmlessly over my head. I grasped my truant rammer and crawled as flat to the ground as I could, regaining the cover of the tree again. I had been firing directly in front, little dreaming of danger behind, when happening to turn my head, I saw a tall grim-looking old warrior rise and point his gun directly at me. "I am gone now," I thought, for I had often heard of the excellent marksmanship of the Indians. I straightened myself and turned squarely toward him, a fair target for his bullet, but, luckily for me, he proved a poor shot, for his ball whistled by me, leaving me unhurt.

The battle raged furiously for a while, but the odds were too great against us, and Captain Garmany, seeing that we could not hold our position in the open pine woods against such overwhelming numbers, ordered a retreat. Under the circumstances this was a dangerous movement and required as much bravery as it did to face the foe. The order contemplated our falling back to camp, where we would have the advantage of the cabins for a cover. Unfortunately some fifteen of us in the confusion misunderstood the order and retreated to a fence east of us. When we gained this fence, instead of climbing or leaping it, in my hurry I fell over all in a heap. Looking down the line I saw that most of my companions had surmounted the obstacle in very much the same manner.

It is strange that often in moments of supreme danger a sense of the ludicrous will triumph. So it did in this instance, although bullets were flying about us thick and fast, I could not repress a hearty laugh at our awkward situation.

Just as we began the retreat, I heard one of my schoolmates, named Allen, cry out: "Captain, I am wounded!" The peculiar stress of his broken accents, rather than the words themselves, caused me to turn my head in that direction. Never shall I forget his countenance—such agony as it portrayed. Every feature of his noble face was stamped with the hue of death. I thought as I looked upon him that he had but a few moments to live, but three days afterward he was found some two miles from the scene of action, on his knees, dead, as if prayer had been the last act of his life.

Believing that we were to make a stand at the fence, I spread my feet and took a position ready for the approaching Indians. Looking around I saw that my companions had not halted, but were running for dear life. My momentary delay nearly proved fatal. My companions were now some distance beyond me, and I turned in the direction of the camp, only to see quite as many of the enemy in that direction as we had left behind us. There was nothing left for me but flight in the same course taken by my fleeing comrades. Grasping my musket with a tight grip I left the cover of the fence and began my ever-to-be-remembered race for life. I soon came to a shallow pond around which my comrades had turned in their flight. I dashed straight through the water, and by this means overtook the greater part of them. There was one young fellow among them quite seven feet high. As I emerged from the pond he gave a glance backward and then darted away like a bird on the wing. Running was hard work for most of us, but to this long-legged man it seemed but play. Oh, how beautifully he ran—his feet touched the ground so lightly! Ah, what would I not have given to have been able to cope with his fleetness? One of my comrades gave out early in the race, and falling behind a log, lay perfectly motionless as though dead. The pursuers evidently thought so, and did not stop to scalp him. When they were well out of sight he arose and escaped, thus proving that delicacy of constitution does not always work to one's detriment, and that "the race is not to the strong alone."

Letter Two

This man told us, when we met a few days afterwards, that he saw Ensign Lacy wounded; but turning like a wild beast hunted to his lair, he fought his foe until death palsied his hand and closed his eyes forever.

There were two brothers named Holland with us, and as we left the pond one of them was shot and killed. Indeed, it is a great wonder to me that many more of us were not killed just along here, for the Indians kept up a constant firing at us as we ran, some loading while others did the shooting. Our headlong flight soon brought us to a field, and quitting the meagre shelter of the open woods we jumped the fence and continued our race across the opening. I was now running along side by side with J. C. Dunlap, but a ball whizzed between us and tore a piece from an old stump not three yards before us. Dunlap ran off to the right while I turned to the left. He told me afterwards that the Indians did not follow him, but it seemed to me fresh numbers gathered on my trail, for the green blades of corn were popping and flying about the air in every direction, and the balls striking the loose dirt on the ground made miniature clouds of dust. I soon got to a fodder stack and stopped behind it to rest, being very tired and almost exhausted. A moment's reflection showed me the folly of remaining there or attempting to secrete myself in such a place from these lynx-eyed savages, so I plucked up courage and ran on. The wisdom of this conclusion became apparent a few days afterwards when we found the elder Holland, who, stopping there, was discovered and murdered. My clothes, which it will be remembered, was a borrowed suit and several sizes too large, were wet and heavy, greatly impeding my flight. My bayonet and cartridge box I had already thrown away. I now stripped myself of pants and shirt and in a state of perfect nudity ran along, only encumbered by my musket and about $140 in money. I soon hid the money at the root of a tree, so that the savages might not profit by it should they succeed in overtaking me. With nothing in my way but the musket, to which I clung I know not why, I soon overtook my comrades, and it was apparent that we were outrunning the Indians. This, perhaps, because fear was a greater incentive to action on our part than the thirst for blood on the part of the savages.

I was very thirsty and fast becoming exhausted for want of water, when we came upon a dirty little puddle. Dropping on my knees I scooped it up with my hands and drank. My God, such water! So sweet! So delicious! Filthy as it was, the water from that dirty puddle was to me as ambrosial nectar to the gods, for it revived me, restored my wasting energies, and I started again with renewed hope in that race which, if won, was life, and which, if lost, was certain death.

I soon came up with those of my friends whom I had not outrun. We now ran nearly a quarter of a mile on level ground, which brought us to the foot of a long gradual slant. I had climbed about half of this ascent when I became exhausted again. Stopping, I turned and could see no Indians, but could still faintly hear their yells and whoops in the distance. Seeing a clump of blackgum bushes a few yards to my left, I concealed myself in them. After resting a few moments I became uneasy and started on again. This proved to be as fortunate after-thought as my leaving the fodder stack, for when we returned afterwards to bury our dead we found our comrade, James Martin, pinned to the ground with his own bayonet in this clump of bushes. Just as we gained the top of the hill I fell prostrate. In vain did I call on my comrades not to desert me; every man was for himself, and they were heedless of my agonizing cry.

Lying prone upon the earth, I gave up all hope and expected there to die. Every scene of my life was enacted again before my very eyes. I thought of my parents' grief—my mother's cry for her lost son, my sisters' wild lamentation—and all the bright, joyous days of my boyhood so soon to end forever. Alas! the friends who knew and loved me would soon know me no more, and that love be but the shadowy memory of the dead. A soft sleepy languor was stealing over me, and I closed my eyes to resign myself to my fate, with a last silent prayer to Him who is more merciful than the vengeful creatures of His hand, when hark! I hear again those savage cries and yells, as if all the direful spirits of the lower world were loose to ravage and destroy this fair world of ours. Those cries infuse new life into my being, where only despair a moment before had been. My sluggish blood quickens again, leaping and coursing through all my veins. In a moment I am upon my bleeding feet, and as I turn to fly my eyes fall upon my poor comrade, Sims, already beyond the pale of earthly fear. Our good God was too merciful to let those demon yells disturb him as he lay breathing his last, and panting his ebbing life away.

Looking back I saw the Indians not more than four hundred yards behind me, brandishing their war clubs and their guns glistening in the sun. I ran on down the hill with hope, it is true, but oh, so little! At the foot of the hill and somewhat to the left, I saw a small piney woods swamp. I made my calculation to run as far to the left as this swamp reached and conceal myself in it before the Indians could get to the top of the hill. I succeeded in reaching the farther end of the swamp and hid myself as effectually as possible. I remained here but a very little while, and becoming uneasy, pushed on, coming out into the great open piney woods. Greatly perplexed, for a moment I knew not what to do. The Indians were already at the top of the hill where I had left poor Sims, and I saw that whatever I did must be done quickly. Seeing a small swamp connected with the one I had just left, I plunged into the thickest part of it and buried myself in the mud, leaving only my head above the water. I still clung to my musket, which, although it greatly impeded my progress, I could not relinquish. I was determined that should I be overtaken and unable to escape, I would take at least one of my dusky murderers with me to the unknown world.

I had scarcely hidden myself in the mud before I heard the report of a single gun, followed by the triumphant yelling of the savages. That lone shot sent poor Peden to his long home. But I did not know it then. My feelings at this time were simply awful. Alone in a strange country, buried up to my neck in mud, with relentless savages stalking silently to and fro seeking my life. They gave vent to no war-whoops nor demon screams now, treading lightly with moccasined feet, searching here and there, expressing fierce gesticulations, and gutteral at their disappointment at finding no more "pale-faces" to slack their thirst for blood. At times they were not more than fifteen paces from me. Every moment I expected to be discovered, and I held my musket ready to make my last shot a sure one.

Hope was fast fading away again and death seemed inevitable, when I was startled by a volley of musketry. The Indians, with heads thrown forward and nostrils distended, paused a moment, listened and stared before them in the direction of the ominous sound, and then all simultaneously joined in a loud prolonged howl, which reminded me of the noise of a pack of hungry wolves. In a few moments they were all gone and their sudden departure, which then seemed to me a direct interposition of Providence in my behalf, I afterwards learned was caused by an attack made by Captain Jernigan's men. This captain, true to his promise to aid his friend, Captain Garmany, had appeared upon the scene of action as speedily as possible, but having only twenty men, was forced to retire. Nor would he have succeeded in making good his retreat, had not the twenty-five men left by Captain Garmany at Fort McCrary heard the firing and hastened to his relief.

When the Indians were gone I crawled out of the mud, and making my way out of the swamp with great caution succeeded in reaching an oat-field, and lay there concealed in the tall oats until night threw her sable mantle over friend and foe. Here, though hidden from the savage Indians, I was thoroughly chilled and greatly exhausted. The change, however, from the wet mud of the swamp to the dry ground of the field was, to say the least of it, encouraging, and I firmly resolved not to relax my efforts to escape until the last spark of life was gone. Oh, how lonely and still all nature around me! The pale silvery moon seemed to look down with sadness on man—God's last and most perfect work—that they who were "created but little lower than the angels," thus should war against each other. I cast myself upon the mercy of that God who had shielded me thus far and could protect me to the end.

About an hour after night I resolved to make my way, if possible, to Lumpkin, believing that the Indians had killed nearly all of my comrades, for out of fifteen or sixteen I only knew of about four who had outrun me. As to Captain Garmany and the men who had followed him, I believed them also to have been killed, because the force of Indians in that direction was even greater than that which followed us.

Soon after leaving the oat patch I came to a corn-field. I got over the fence and followed the corn rows until I came to the opposite string of fence. Climbing upon this I saw that it skirted the edge of a swamp, and that some distance away were several camp-fires; these I took to be Indian camp-fires, and believing myself to be near an encampment of the savages, I hastily retreated back some two or three hundred yards into the field and stopped to rest, leaning against an old dead tree. My heart beat quick and fast as I thought of the perils and narrow escapes of the day, and I mentally prayed heaven that I might not be taken after all. While leaning against the tree and drawn close to it, I heard a rustling in the corn and saw a man with his gun brought forward in his hands advancing straight toward me. I silently cocked my gun and raised it and pointed it toward the intruder upon my solitude, determined to kill him if I could, and then run for my life. My good angel, I know not what else, caused me to hail him. Judge of my joyous astonishment on hearing in good English the words, "A friend!" Almost doubting my senses I cried, "Come nearer and give me your name."

"Ship," was his answer.

All doubt and hesitation was now gone, and I sprang forward, clasping him by the hand, for I recognized him as one of the company.

Ship was greatly bewildered by my appearance. Naked and covered with mud, he was loath to believe me a white man. After I had told him time and time again my name he still seemed in doubt.

"Yes, yes," said he, "I know you are white, but surely your name can't be Key, for I saw him lying dead, with his head split open."

"You must have seen someone else, Mr. Ship, for although I am without clothes and covered with mud, I am James C. Key, of Captain Garmany's Company—at least what there is left of him."

"Well, well," he said, after dropping his head forward a moment in thoughtful silence, "you must be yourself, but you don't look like anybody I ever saw before, sure. Alas! then the poor fellow I saw dead must have been Tate."

"Have you been out to the fence?" I asked.

"No, have you?"

"Yes," I replied, "and I saw camp-fires out there by the edge of the swamp, and I believe they are Indians."

"We must get out of this then, my boy," he said, "and whatever may happen, here's my hand on it, that we stick together even unto death!"

"It's a bargain," I said, grasping his generous hand.

We quit the field and entered the swamp half a mile lower down than the place from which I first saw the lights. Floundering through the swamp for some distance we came to a small dry hillock and concluded to stop to rest awhile. I quenched my thirst from a stagnant pool, and it is scarcely an exaggeration to say that I strained the water, thick with green slime, through my teeth, yet to me it was cool and refreshing, and I considered it at the time a very God-send.

Having given me his drawers, tied his handkerchief over my sore and blistered shoulders, and put his socks on my worn and bleeding feet, Ship said: "Now, lie down and try to sleep."

"Not until you have told me about your escape," I replied.

"If you will have it so," he said. "My story is soon told. After we got over the fence on our retreat and just after the race for life began, I got separated from the rest of you. At first several Indians started after me, but soon they all turned in another direction, except the two nearest me. These got pretty close and both fired. I raised my gun and shot at one of them. When the smoke cleared away I saw that I had one foe less to contend with. It was a lucky shot, but my hope almost died away when I saw that my flint had broken in two and fallen to the ground. My motto is, 'Never give up,' so I ran into a small clump of bushes and succeeded in getting another flint from my cartridge box, and had just finished loading when the remaining Indian ran up, fired, and missed me. He then turned to run, and as he fled I fired, wounding him so that he was unable to follow. I never expected to escape, but thank God I am still alive and not wounded or hurt as yet. I wandered this way and that, not knowing where I was nor whither I was going until Providence threw you into my path. I see that you can not travel as you are, and you must now go to sleep and refresh yourself for a new effort. I can not afford to lose you after meeting you thus. I will keep watch for Indians and wild beasts. I think I heard the growling of a bear; he may have scented the blood from your feet."

Letter Three

Oh, how sweet was that sleep to me; but alas, it ended too soon. I had not slept long when Ship aroused me, saying: "We must leave this place; I don't like the signs I see around here."

We wandered about the swamp an hour or more, which seemed to me an age, before we reached the high ground on the opposite side from where we entered. Having made up our minds to try to reach Fort Jones we followed a small trail which we hoped might lead in that direction. The trail brought us to a ford on a small creek and we thought we would soon arrive at the Fort, being confident that it was on the same side of the creek upon which we were traveling. From the ford we followed a half beaten trail, but soon lost it, wandered around confusedly in the woods, and at last found ourselves back at the ford. We almost believed ourselves irretrievably lost, but it would never do to sit down with folded hands and wait for morning, for daylight might bring the dreaded foe upon us again. Starting out again, we tramped around a long time in the woods, challenging every black stump that we saw, and at last, almost in despair, came back once more to the ford on the creek. It seemed like fate was against us, but in the midst of our despair we heard the clear ringing notes of a chanticleer, not far away, proclaiming to men that day was breaking. I never heard a sound in my life that cheered me more than that old rooster's crow.

Going in that direction we soon came to a plantation and houses deserted by the owner. Everything was in confusion, as if the family had barely escaped with their lives. We went in at the open door of the largest house, and hanging on the post of the bedstead I saw a large shirt. This I appropriated and immediately put on. It suited me exactly, for it was long enough to serve a double purpose of shirt and pants. It was now day, and I lay down and slept while Ship stood sentinel nearby.

When he waked me the sun was shining brightly; but, oh how sad and lonely everything seemed in that deserted home! Our hearts were heavy indeed, for we were alone in an almost uninhabited country, knowing not which way to go to find our friends or to avoid our enemies.

There was a rough road running parallel with the house. We took the north end of it and had not gone far before we came in sight of a big smoke, which we afterwards learned was the burning of Shepherd's Plantation. I thought it was the Fort, and in the joy of the moment fired off my gun, expecting every moment to be hailed by my comrades and be welcomed to a place of safety and rest. Happening to cast my eyes downward I was almost chilled with horror at seeing, almost under my feet, a cap with a handkerchief and a lock of hair, all matted and gory with blood. While looking at these sad evidences of a struggle fatal to some white man, and trying to conjecture as to which one of our comrades they might have belonged, we heard horses running at the bottom of the hill on which we stood, and aparently coming toward us.

Running back toward the farmhouse, and as we came in sight of it, we saw the horses going in the same direction. The barn lot was open, and the animals, which proved to be a noble sorrel horse and three colts, ran into it. Here was luck for us indeed! Now my poor bleeding feet would get a rest. Without difficulty we caught the horse, which proved to be the property of one of our comrades. Searching in an outhouse I found a headstall and a pair of old-fashioned curb bits. To these Ship added his musket strap for reins, and although the headstall was too small and could only be drawn over one ear, we were but too happy with our outfit. I rode before to guide the horse and Ship, who was much taller, rode behind to keep a lookout for the Indians. Thus mounted we crossed the road in front of the house and took to the woods.

After entering the woods we traveled awhile in my direction, and then Ship undertook to steer the way. We proceeded in this manner some three hours, and then came to a broad plain road. We followed this some distance, coming to a lane nearly a quarter of a mile long, and had gone almost through it when Ship pressed my arm and said: "Stop, there are Indians ahead!" I looked ahead and saw four Indians, with their guns brightly gleaming, ready to fire at us as we passed. I wheeled the horse instantly and we went back at a full run, expecting every moment to be shot at by a hidden foe. Our horse was beginning to show signs of fatigue when we arrived at the only place we had seen that day that was familiar, and that was the ford on the creek, to which we had so often wandered the night before. This time we did not stop to deliberate, but crossed over and dashed onward. On, on we went, our noble horse running at his best speed. He needed no whip nor spur, for instinct taught him that danger was near. Soon we came in sight of men and horses. We approached very cautiously, for we had lately been in too many close places to run heedlessly into danger now. They seemed to be white men, but still we waited and watched until I espied our Captain's "old gray" and exclaimed: "Ah, we can risk that crowd."

In a few moments we were in the midst of our friends, who were just getting ready to hunt for those who had not found their way to camp. Never have I experienced such intense joy. Aye, such rapture of delight as when surrounded by my friends and comrades in that camp, all rejoicing at our escape as though we had been their brothers. Some were profuse in their expression of delight; others plied us with questions, and others still silently clasped our hands with a mute pressure, while glistening tears spoke volumes of tenderness and love that no words could but fail to express.

Having been conducted to the tent where our wounded lay, we found several of our comrades stretched upon beds of pain. For a moment these seemed to forget their wounds, and pressed us to tell the story of our escapes.

The excitement of our reception over, I began to feel the effect of my many bruises and I was soon prostrated, experiencing the most excruciating pain I have ever felt. My legs were drawn into knots. My greatly swollen feet looked as if they had been haggled with a saw, and every toe sawed apart into my feet. But such kind attentions as my rough looking, noble hearted comrades rendered me! Woman's hand could not have been more gentle, nor woman's voice more soothing and kind. This great joy at our reunion can be better understood when it is known that our company was made up entirely in Gwinnett County; that most of us were neighbors, life-long friends, and many related by the ties of blood and marriage.

I soon learned from the boys what had befallen that part of the company which followed Captain Garmany after the retreat was ordered. They retreated to the lot of the camp, hard pressed by overwhelming numbers. Our brave captain fought hand to hand with his foes until he was brought to his knees by a shot from an Indian, and seeing the savage whirling his tomahawk above his head for the fatal blow, he raised his gun quickly, fired, and his would-be murderer fell to the earth mortally wounded.

When Captain Garmany fell most of his men were panic-stricken, and one called out lustily, "Our captain is killed!" "No, no," replied the brave man, "I am not killed, but only wounded. Stand firm, boys! Help me to my horse and we will try to escape." This was quickly done, and though weak and faint from loss of blood, this brave man succeeded in keeping the greater part of his men together and guiding them safely away from the yelling mob of Indians, reached shelter at Fort Jones.

I remained in camp two days to allow my tired limbs to rest and my bruised and swollen feet time to heal enough to permit me to walk. On the third day we returned to the battle ground, and following the trail of our terrible race for life, began the search for our missing comrades. We went about our mournful task sadly enough, for oh! too well we knew what ghastly sights awaited our view.

Our first discovery was the dead body of Holland, lying near the fodder stack behind which I halted a moment on that fatal day. Martin we found lying in the clump of blackgum bushes where I had also halted. Sims lay where I had seen him last, about a quarter of a mile farther on. About three hundred yards farther on, near the foot of the hill, we found poor Peden. This was near the point where I had concealed myself in the swamp, and becoming uneasy afterwards, moved farther on to where I had concealed myself in the mud. I had been greatly affected as I had gazed upon one after another of the ghastly faces of my murdered companions, but now as I looked on Peden, calm in death as if only asleep, my heart was filled with emotion and my cheeks were wet with tears. As my eyes rested upon the silent dead, my mind ran rapidly over the startling incidents of my desperate race for life, while the reflection forced itself upon me that at each place where I had started to hide myself and upon second thought continued my flight, one of my companions lay dead, and I silently turned my heart in thanks to God for what seemed to me His direct providential care. It is not unnatural to suppose that one placed in the extreme peril I have described should have taken but little heed of the many objects met by him in such a headlong flight. This, however, is not so. Every tree, every stump, bush, fence or field, in fact every topographical feature of the ground over which I ran was so vividly and permanently photographed upon my mind in all of its minutest details, that I have never forgotten a single one. As we trudged along that fatal route, I readily pointed out each feature connected with my flight.

Coming to the great towering pine, behind which I had paused a moment—just a little moment—and thus lessened the exultation of my murderous foes should they overtake me, I found my $140 safe under the pine straw. The recovery of my little treasure was a matter of some satisfaction to me, considering the fact that I was without clothing, except a few articles supplied by my comrades, but barely enough to cover my bruised and lacerated body.

Procuring a hoe, we dug holes in the earth as best we could, silently buried our dead comrades where they had fallen, and sorrowfully returned to the fort. Here I remained until about the 18th, when, being sufficiently recovered to travel further, I received a furlough and made my way to Columbus.

A few hours after I left the fort, the Indians were reported to be crossing the Chattahoochee close by. Reinforcements were sent to the point, who were instructed to fall back slowly, and by skirmishing endeavor to draw the enemy toward the fort. In this they succeeded. The Indians, elated over their recent victory, made several efforts to storm the fort, but the garrison was fully alive to the danger, and by rapid and accurate firing never failed to drive them back. The siege was a short one, and the baffled Indians soon departed—not, however, until many feats of individual bravery had been performed, one of which I shall mention.

Letter Four

There was a fine saddle horse hitched just at the wall of the fort when the Indians made their attack. One old warrior, more daring than the rest, came boldly up, mounted the steed and was making off with the prize, when Thomas Chambers, firing from the top of the fort, brought him to the ground. The horse seemed to know the difference between civilized men and savages, and turned and ran back unhurt to the fort. Soon after this occurrence the Indians recrossed the river and Chambers, in accordance with the barbarous custom of that day borrowed from the cruel savages, secured the fallen warrior's scalp, retaining it as a grim trophy of victory.

When I reached Columbus I found that General Winfield Scott had arrived from Florida, assumed command of all our forces, and was putting the army in motion to quell the savages. The company in which I belonged, having lost many men and horses, was left at Columbus to recruit and guard the commissary stores gathered there.

The Creeks of Alabama were evidently in alliance with the Seminoles, and their every effort was directed toward crossing the Chattahoochee and entering Florida. To prevent this, General Scott moved rapidly down the river, strengthening all the forts on the line. General Jessup was suppressing them in the west and Colonel Wilborn fast closing up from the south. Thus these ferocious warriors found themselves completely surrounded and their plan frustrated, and in a few days great numbers of them hastened to General Jessup, surrendered, and requested to be sent to the Arkansas reservation. These brought with them many captured horses, among which was found my own and others belonging to members of the company, but how unlike the sleek fat steeds of only a few weeks ago! Now they were gaunt and lean, the mane roached close to the neck and only the foretop left long to resemble the fantastic head-dress of the warriors.

At this time there was a line of stages between Columbus and Montgomery, traversing what was known as the old Federal Road. The stages from these respective points, each bearing the United States Mail, usually met about half-way on the route.

The stage from Columbus, driven by Mr. Green, was attacked by the Indians about twenty miles west of Columbus, the driver and horses slain and the coach robbed. The stage from Montgomery was also attacked a short distance from the scene of the catastrophe just mentioned. This stage contained, besides the driver, Sam Hardaway and a Mr. Kingsbury. Hardaway was returning to his home at Columbus from Texas, where he had participated in the famous battle of San Jacinto, and was well armed. When the firing began the driver laid whip to the frightened horses and dashed wildly along the road with every prospect of a successful escape. This, however, was not to be easily accomplished. Suddenly they came upon the Columbus stage, which, together with the dead horses and driver, blockaded the road. The horses became unmanageable, and turning into the woods, upset the stage. The driver quickly detaching one of the horses mounted his back and made good his escape into Columbus. Springing out of the overturned coach, Hardaway took refuge in a canebrake near by, and here lying upon the ground with arms in readiness, prepared to sell his life as dearly as possible. The Indians were not long in following their intended victim. Hardaway, being an old soldier, was used to the cunning of the dusky foes, and quietly awaited their coming. At last he heard a gentle rustling sound and saw a tall warrior with a gun in his right hand, parting the cane with his left, and cautiously approaching. A shot from Hardaway brought him to the ground dead. A moment of ominous silence followed and the savages, knowing that their companion had paid the forfeit of his daring with his life, gave a yell of disappointment and fled. Hardaway remained concealed in the cane until night and then made his way to Columbus.

It was never positively known what became of Kingsbury, but it was generally believed that, having been captured, he was carried to an Indian camp a few miles below the scene of disaster on the Big Ochee Creek and there murdered. This belief was confirmed after the termination of the war by finding at that place the skull of a white man, from which the eye teeth were gone, and it was said by his friends that Kingsbury had lost those teeth.

Many arrests were made among the Indians on account of these depredations, and the prisoners were held under the double charge of murder and robbing the United States Mail.

Soon afterwards our company was ordered to General Jessup's camp at Sand Foot to bring these prisoners to Columbus. We took with us the surviving stage driver carrying the United States Mail, and were the first white men to pass through the hostile territory after the robbery. When we arrived at Sand Foot we found that General Jessup had moved into Tuskegee, taking his prisoner with him. Coming to this place, we learned that General Jessup had continued his march to Montgomery.

My horse being jaded, I was left at Tuskegee and the company moved on to overtake General Jessup. This accomplished, they returned, bringing with them a chief, Jim Henry, and two noted warriors, charged with the murder of Green and with robbing the mail. These we conducted back to Columbus and turned over to the authorities.

A few days later we were mustered out of the service, and with a glad heart and fully satisfied with my share of the glories of warfare, in company with two of my companions, Chambers and Wardlaw, I hastened home, to be clasped again in my mother's loving arms. Chambers insisted on carrying his Indian scalp to his dear wife, Betty, but I can not say that the ghastly trophy was appreciated, false hair not being so much prized in those primitive days as in this progressive age.

The chief, Jim Henry, was subsequently tried, acquitted and returned to the Nation. The others were not so fortunate, but being convicted, were hanged at Girard, just across the river from Columbus. When being led to the gallows, these two braves, undaunted by the early prospect of death, paused at a burnt pine stump and smeared their faces and bodies with smut, in lieu of paint, sang their death song, and when on the gallows raised the war whoop, dying as they had lived—without fear.

It was never positively known how many Indians were killed in the battle at Shepherd's Plantation, since they were left masters of the ground, but the belief generally obtained at the time was that their loss amounted to about forty killed and twelve more who afterwards died of their wounds. This is not at all unlikely, considering the fact that our men were each protected by a tree, while their great number precluded this advantage, leaving many exposed to our fire. Their arms were also very inferior, being mostly rifles of small bore. These they loaded hurriedly, chewing the bullets in order to expand them so that they could load without patching. The balls thus roughened and shapeless made their aim less accurate. On the other hand we were armed with muskets, and loaded quickly with cartridges containing one one-ounce ball and three large buckshot. Every shot from one of our guns therefore sent four bullets to our Indians' one. Our company lost eight men killed and six wounded, while Captain Jernigan's loss was four men killed: Robert Billups, David Delk, Ewing and Hunter.

The citizens of Gwinnett County, Georgia, gathered up our dead and buried them in the courthouse yard at Lawrenceville, where a suitable monument was afterwards erected, inscribed with their names, together with the names of Captain James C. Winn and Anthony Bates, two of Gwinnett County's sons who fell at the Alamo (Goliad is correct), in defense of Texas liberty.

Monument Unveiled

On June 9th, 1936, the Roanoke Chapter, Daughters of the American Revolution, of Stewart County, Mrs. Wm. A. Fitzgerald, regent, sponsored the program incident to the unveiling of a monument erected on Shepherd's Plantation near the spot where the battle was fought. By invitation a delegation from Gwinnett County attended this unveiling ceremony, the delegation consisting of Judge

R. B. Whitworth, Jesse Whitworth, George Maughon, T. L. Harris, W. R. Hurst, Paul Dover and J. C. Flanigan. Mr. Flanigan appeared on the program and delivered an historical address.

JAMES C. WINN AND ANTHONY BATES

On the west side of the monument in the courthouse square is the following inscription:

"This monument is erected by their friends to the memory of Captain James C. Winn and Sergeant Anthony Bates, Texan volunteers, of this village, who were taken in honorable combat at Goliad, Texas, and shot by order of the Mexican commander, March 27, 1836."

Captain Jas. C. Winn and Orderly Sergeant Anthony Bates, whose names are inscribed on the west side of this monument, were two young men of this county who joined Fannin's company and went to Texas during the Texas-Mexican War. They, with four hundred others, were captured near Goliad, Texas; and though by the articles of surrender, they were to be liberated at a certain time, yet Santa Anna, the commander-in-chief of the Mexican army, ordered that all the prisoners should be shot. At daylight, guarded by a file of armed soldiers on either side, the whole body of prisoners was marched out some distance from the fort without any knowledge of their impending fate. When they arrived at the place selected for their execution, the double file of Mexican soldiers withdrew to one side and fired upon the prisoners at close range, loading and firing again and again until all were dead. Then their bodies were thrown into heaps with wood and brush and burned.

A Mexican witness of the scene describes it in these words:

"This day, Palm Sunday, March 27, 1836, has been to me a day of heartfelt sorrow. At six in the morning, the execution of four hundred and twelve American prisoners was commenced and continued until eight, when the last of the number was shot. At eleven commenced the operation of burning their bodies. But what an awful scene did the field present, when the prisoners were executed and fell dead in heaps! And what spectator could view it without horror! They were all young, the oldest not over thirty, and of fine florid complexions. When the unfortunate youths were brought to the place of death, their lamentations, and the appeals which they uttered to heaven in their language, with extended arms, kneeling or prostrate on earth, were such as might have caused the very stones to cry out in compassion."

James C. Winn, one of those captured and executed at Goliad, Texas, and whose name is inscribed on the monument in the courthouse square, was the son of Elisha Winn. Richard D. Winn, a brother, writes of his brother's romance and the cause of his leaving his home as follows: "My brother, James Cochran Winn, named for his grandfather, was next in succession, the first man child of the family after four daughters. He was the pride of his father and the hope of his mother. When grown he was of medium height, blue eyes, fair skin, auburn hair, good looking and talented. He was brought up in Lawrenceville. In early life, he formed an attachment for Isabella Hammond, a handsome young lady, much against the wishes of my mother, whose only objection probably was that she was poor. My mother had a weakness about the marriage of her children, looking to their marrying rich rather than to other considerations of much more importance. This opposition interposed by her drove him into dissipation; but finally he cut loose from his profligate associates; and he, with his early friend, Anthony Bates, joined the Georgia regiment then forming in Macon, commanded by Colonel Fannin, and went to Texas to assist that republic to throw off the yoke of Mexican tyranny. Upon the organization of the regiment, he was elected captain of one company and he, with the whole command, was slaughtered in cold blood after their surrender, and in violation of the terms agreed upon, near Goliad, Texas, in March, 1836. He was brave and fearless to a fault. This terrible and cowardly event is a matter of history. His was a tragic fate and his bones have bleached long ago upon the distant plains of a distant state, not having the benefit of a sepulcher."

Of Anthony Bates, whose name is also inscribed on the monument, Judge Winn writes: "I cannot refrain at this point from giving a passing tribute to Anthony Bates. He was a clever young fellow of good humor and genial temperament. He sacrificed his young life in the cause of Texas' independence. He fell with Fannin and his devoted band, near Goliad, in their massacre ordered by Santa Anna in 1836. Alas! Poor Anthony! I knew him well, a fellow of infinite jest!"

Removal of the Cherokees

The Cherokee Indians, who claimed all the territory north of the Chattahoochee River, and who had set up an independent nation similar to the United States, finally were induced to sign a treaty and agree to go to an assigned territory beyond the Mississippi. Their removal in 1838 was an event of national importance. It was a costly undertaking, requiring a vast expenditure of money, time and labor. The Indian population was about 15,000, and to the United States army was given the job of directing the migration from Georgia to their western home. Much suffering and many hardships were the inevitable experience of many. The old, the young, the sick, the well, all had to go. And it is claimed that as many as four thousand died on the way.

Gwinnett County was required to furnish two companies of

volunteers to assist in guarding and protecting the Indians as well as the inhabitants along the line of the migrating throng. Captain Mathew T. Hamilton and Captain James Tuggle were in charge of the two companies as will appear from the following record:

HAMILTON'S COMPANY

Roll of the company of Captain Mathew T. Hamilton was dated at New Echota, Ga., May 16, 1838, and the company was ordered into service by requisition of Major General Winfield Scott for three months, unless sooner discharged, and mustered into service May 16, 1838, by Major M. M. Payne.

OFFICERS

Captain, Mathew J. Hamilton; 1st Lieutenant, James McGinnis; 2nd Lieutenant, Thomas Maguire; 1st Sergeant, Robert Scott; 2nd Sergeant, Burton M. South; 3rd Sergeant, Bennett Lee; 4th Sergeant, John Garner; 1st Corporal, Archibald A. Dunlap; 2nd Corporal, Joseph W. Thompson; 3rd Corporal, Elijah Foster; 4th Corporal, David R. Brown; Drummer, Lewis R. Willis; Fifer, Wilson Camp.

PRIVATES

Jesse Alred, Albert J. Atkinson, David Anderson, Elijah C. Athey, Pinckney Alred, Blewford Bailey, Daniel D. Born, Jefferson Britt, Robert R. Brown, Martin Brooks, Dennis S. Brown, David S. Brandon, Thomas Cockrum, Perry Compton, Joseph Christopher, Ira W. Cates, Moses N. Cruse, Rubin T. Conner, James Cobb, Abednigo Dempsey, Hardy Dover, William W. Duck, Joseph W. Dodd, Newton M. Drummond, Hezekiah W. Donaldson, Richard Davis, James Garner, John J. Glover, William Gordon, David Harris, Daniel Horton, Hardiman Hughes, Early Harris, Minard Harris, John Jones.

Hugh Johnson, William I. Keenum, William Kirk, Benjamin Knight, Thomas Kile, Robert A. Louthridge, William Langley, Hamilton Maffett, Howell Mangum, David Montgomery, James McGinnis, Joseph Mills, Jackson A. Monroe, Josiah J. Morgan, Elijah Osburn, James Parks, Sion Phillips, Daniel N. Pittman, Daniel Parker, Samuel Phillips, Benjamin Prewett, George Powell, Daniel W. Ross, James Sell, Silas Strickland, Joshua Teague, Middleton Taylor, Francis Taylor, Archy Terry, James Vaughn, Charles H. Whitworth, Stephen B. Westbrooks.

TUGGLE'S COMPANY

The company of Captain James Tuggle was enrolled in Gwinnett County March 8, 1838, and ordered into service of the United States by requisition of the Secretary of War for twelve months unless sooner discharged. It was mustered into service at New Echota, Georgia, after traveling 115 miles, on March 22, 1838, by Major M. M. Payne.

OFFICERS

Captain, James Tuggle; 1st Lieutenant, A. D. Chandler; 2nd Lieutenant, John Cain; 1st Sergeant, John Tuggle; 2nd Sergeant, Enoch Lott; 3rd Sergeant, Edward Brown; 4th Sergeant, Jeremiah Skelton; 1st Corporal, James Wallis; 2nd Corporal, Edward Harrison; 3rd Corporal, Roger Gideon; 4th Corporal, John Ezzell.

PRIVATES

Moses Anderson, Jacob Adams, N. B. Banks, Allen Banks, Stephen O. Bryant, James Boyd, Wm. N. Brimer, Henry T. Brantley, Levi G. Brantley, James Butler, Armstead M. Bryant, Gaines Bryant, Henry Bradford, Ruben Bowler, Eli Bailey, Bartley Boyd, Henry Campbell, Wilson Cantrell, John Campbell, Asa Clements, G. W. Crenshaw, Anderson Cook, John Daniel, Samuel Estes, John Evans, James N. Estes, A. J. Fielder, Joseph T. Forester, Samuel Fraser, John Gideon, Stephen Hill, W. H. W. Hall, Lovick Horn, Thomas Kircus.

John Kilpatrick, W. A. Kircus, Green Kennedy, Thomas E. Lancaster, Zaza D. Lemons, Tyrrel Mauldin, Berry W. Martin, A. J. McDaniel, Wm. Murphy, Jr., Wm. Murphy, Sr., James Mackey, William Mackey, Seaborn Maddox, Samuel Otwell, James Pearce, George W. Pirkle, William R. Pirkle, Ambrose Pirkle, Daniel C. Pearce, Charles Rogers, William Redmon, William Sandford, Obadiah Sanders, James B. Tuggle, Martin Thurmond, Michael Winningham, William Wallis, Solomon Wigley, James Wadsworth, Abel Winningham, John C. Wood.

Georgia, Gwinnett County,
February 7th, 1838.

To your Excelency, George R. Gilmer.

Sir: I Received on yesterday your letter which informed me that your Excelency have the offer of the two Infantry Companies to fill the Call of Col. Lindsey and on this day had a muster and while on perade informed the Company the contents of your letter to which the Company all agreed to stand in Readiness agreeable to your request, the objection they had against standing in Readiness was that they wished to Join the Company which would be first Rec'd into service which objection now appears to be entirely removed by believeing that this company by being in Readiness would be as soon Received as any other mounted Company we therefore forward this information to your Excelency and submit the Case.

I am yours most obedient
JAMES TUGGLE.

(Original letter on file in office of Georgia Department of Archives.)

Georgia, Gwinnett County,
February 7th, 1838.

To your Excelency, George R. Gilmer.

Sir our Capt. James Tuggle Received your letter Dated 30th January 1838 on yesterday and on this day had a muster and we the members of said Company receiving information that probably an additional force will in a short time be Called for by Col Lindsey and upon reconsidering the matter we unanimously agree to hold our selves in readiniss as a mounted Volunteer Company to aid and assist in defence of our neighbouring Cherokee Counties should the Indians become hostile and hoping that when your Excelency should be call'd on for a company of mounted Volunteers to go into United States service in said Cherokee nation that your Excelency will give us an opportunity to fill the Call should it be immediately We pray the opportunity and also we request your Excelency to organize our Company in the Commissioning of our officers according to the return of the former Election and we the members of said Company think it entirely unnessessary to furnish your Excelency with a roll of our names to this agreement as your Excelency has already a roll of said members with the Exception of a few additional names

We remain your Humble Subjects
from members of Capt. Tuggles Company

(Original letter on file in office of Georgia Department of Archives.)

Rock Bridge Gwinnett Co. Feby 8th 1838.

His Excelency G. R. Gilmer

Sir I think I can make up a company of Mounted Volunteers by the first of March Next out of the Counties of Newton & Gwinnett in that case please let me know by return Mail if Conveynient if we will be received and if funds will be furnished and how. and all other information which you think necessary touching the organization of said Company your answer directed to Rock Bridge Post office Gwinnett Co will be thankfully Received

your obedient Servant
JOSEPH WELLS

(Original letter on file in office of Georgia Department of Archives.)

Cherokee Land Lottery

The Cherokee Indians were moved out of Georgia and the territory north of the Chattahoochee River was surveyed and distributed by lottery, and the following citizens of Gwinnett County drew lots in this territory; the lot drawn, the name of the drawer, and the district in Gwinnett County where he lived being given:

FIRST DISTRICT—1st Section: 91, Elias Green, Reid's; 68, Robert Cates, Loveless'; 118, John Nix, Reid's; 135, Jas. W. Plummer, Loveless'; 264, Willis Collins, Loveless'; 282, Henry Lee, Hamilton's; 304, Lewis Coffey, Baker's; 306, John Tims, Hamilton's; 318, Samuel Morris' orphans, Hargrove's; 311, Samuel Pearson, Reid's; 418, Sara Stegall, widow, 404; 429, Larkin Brown, Winn's; 481, John Morrow, Town; 487, James Hall, Sr., Bridges'.

SECOND DISTRICT—1st Section: 40, A. L. Anthony, Hamilton's; 117, David Pruett, Reid's; 122, Itliai Bryam, Loveless'; 204, Joshua Estes, Bridges; 229, Mark Waits, 406; 237, John Booth, 404; 266, Absolom Baumgarner, 406; 269, Benjamin Rawlins, Loveless'; 338, Malone Cox, 406; 382, Wm. Brown, Hamilton's; 420, John Stapp, Barker's; 462, Jesse Downs, Reid's; 511, Asa Plummer, Loveless'; 538, Josiah Reynolds, Maguire's; 575, George R. Adair, Chambers'; 578, Littleberry Duke, 406; 602, Martha Hunter, widow, Reid's; 733, Andrew Clemants, Barker's; 795, E. C. Estes, Bridges'; 811, Jas. Ford, Maguire's; 822, John Nash, Winn's; 828, Noah Strong, Barker's; 906, Wm. Edes, Barker's; 908, Thos. G. Garrison, Reid's; 920, Pleasant H. Turner, 406; 948, Hiram M. Gober, Winn's; 969, Kinchin Rambo, Chambers'; 993, Hines Holt, Jr., Chambers'; 1015, John Grubbs, Brisges'; 1037, Vivian Holmes, Loveless'; 1069, Thomas McEver, Hamilton's; 1074, Sampson Lanier, Loveless'; 1088, Catherine Kirk, widow, Reid's; 1146, Wm. G. Hamilton, 406; 1151, David Liddell, Towers'; 1187, Moses Blake, Chambers'; 1241, Willis Rowland, Reid's; 1242, James Brown, 404; 1249, Curtis Corley, 406; 1272, Jas. S. Phillips, Davis'.

THIRD DISTRICT—1st Section: 45, Wm. F. Wigley, Hamilton's; 51, James Boyd, Reid's; 79, Fanny Branham, widow, 404; 110, John M. Born, Maguire's; 134, Robert Cates, Loveless'; 155, Nicholas Rawlins, Loveless'; 214, Randal Baggett, 406; 218, Wm. Johnson, Barker's; 220, John B. Benson, 404; 229, Wm. R. Cole, Winn's; 256, Wm. Lewis, Towers'; 272, Vinson Bowman, 406; 299, Jas. M. Brown, Hamilton's; 330, Arch Harris, Barker's; 370, John L. Doyal, Reid's; 399, Wm. Harris, Hamilton's; 422, David Blackwell, 404; 429, J. M. N. B. Nix, Reid's; 474, Wm. D. Hunt, Chambers'; 502, John Norton, Chambers'; 516, Jas. Hayle, Winn's; 543, Jas. Owen, 404; 585, Bailus A. Jett, 406; 623, Solomon Kemp, 404; 633, Theodore D. Doney, Chambers'; 642, Henry Baglet, Sr., Barker's; 691, Richard Glover, 406; 755, Jas. Wheeler, Barker's; 765, Robert Montgomery, Barker's; 781, Wm. Bennett, 404; 787, Thos. H. Jones, 406; 859, John T. Ezzard, Hamilton's; 905, David Jenkins, Chambers'; 947, Jas. Lawrence, Loveless; 962, Waid H. Bowman, Hamilton's; 988, James Alred, Davis'; 1066, Jas. White, Towers'; 1085, Wm. Vinyard, Reid's; 1098, Nathaniel Burkes, Winn's; 1151, Wm. Baugh, Loveless'; 1210, T. Strickland, Baker's; 1232, Simon Berry, Davis'; 1240, Pleasant Chitwood, Chambers.

HISTORY OF GWINNETT COUNTY, GEORGIA

FOURTH DISTRICT—1st Section: 58, James Brimer, Hamilton's; 74, Henry Bagley, Jr., Barker's; 84, Nathaniel Burge, 404; 86, Humphrey Hurst, Loveless; 98, Joshua Ballard, Maguire's; 105, Elijah Wade, Davis'; 126, Gilly Griffin, 404; 130, James Collins, 404; 152, Bird Pruett, Maguire's; 195, Wm. Spruce, Barker's; 232, Nimrod Vinson, Loveless'; 275, Washington Allen, Chambers'; 278, John Waits, 406; 286, Russell Talley, 406; 340, Edmond Coffey, Barker's; 351, George Maddox, Loveless'; 421, John Bates, 404; 452, John Rutledge, Sr., Loveless'; 456, Hermon Bagley, Barker's; 471, Austin Estes, Bridges'; 472, Elisha Rainey, 406; 473, Frances Allen, widow, Barker's; 477, John Gilliam, Chambers'; 564, Hardy Hart, Chambers'; 575, Erasmus Riddlespurger, Maguire's; 591, Jeptha Whorton, Reid's; 653, Jas. Reid, Wynn's; 677, Capt. John Baker, 406; 718, Elizabeth Harrell, Bridges'; 771, Sylvester Nelson, Bridges'; 824, Isaac Pendley, Barker's; 825, Aaron Godfrey, Reid's; 836, Elijah Anderson, McGinnis'; 841, Thos. M. Bagby, Barker's; 849, Sion Pearce, Bridges'; 871, John Mathews, Wynn's; 885, Dawson Davis, Loveless'; 908, Isaac Steel, Wynn's; 938, Edmond Coffey, Barker's; 945, Jas. Patillo, Chambers; 997, Levi M. Cooper, Loveless'; 1074, Amos Kelley, Wynn's; 1091, John M. Fowler, Barker's; 1120, B. H. Lumpkin, Chambers'; 1126, John Smith, Wynn's; 1128, John Smith, Wynn's; 1178, Roe Seamore, Bridges; 1201, Dennis Sharpton, Bridges; 1203, Joseph S. E. Spears, Wynn's.

FIFTH DISTRICT—1st Section: 91, Solomon H. Jackson, Hamilton's; 109, Joshua Welch, Mangum's; 138, D. P. Perryman, Chamber's; 164, Jas. Kilcrease, Bridges'; 172, Wm. Lee, Hamilton's; 177, Wm. Simmons, Maguire's; 185, Jas. Johnson, 404; 227, George Buchanan, Loveless'; 299, Isabella Stewart, widow, Wynn's; 311, John Steadman, Towers'; 313, Wm. Stone, 404; 332, John Maffett, Davis'; 401, John Whorton, Reid's; 408, Eli Massey, Chambers; 425, Sam M. Wardlaw, Town; 468, Norphlet D. Pope, Loveless; 517, Sara Mackin, widow, Chambers'; 527 Mathew Coffer, Loveless; 566, Zack Conger, Davis'; 610, Wm. S. Harris, Bridges'; 675, Nathan G. Goodwin, Maguire's; 704, Henry B. Watkins, Maguire's; 758, Wm. Haney, Wynn's; 792, Martin Beliles, Hamilton's; 801, Samuel Maloney, 406; 837, Christopher Rutledge, Bridges'; 935, Jane McCulley, widow, Wynn's; 1036, Silas Pool, Wynn's; 1139, David P. Roberts, Maguire's; 1168, Sampson Lanier, Loveless'; 1192, John Anglin, Barker's; 1201, Miles Bramlett, Reid's.

ELEVENTH DISTRICT—1st Section: 10, Archibald Hamilton, Hamilton's; 95, Nicholas Crosnore, Baker's; 131, Jane Compton, widow, Barker's; 187, David Delk, Jr., 404; 210, Thos. M. King's orphans, Bridges; 236, Burton M. South, Chambers'; 253, Joseph Everett, Wynn's; 290, Anderson Wheeler, Loveless; 316, Jackson A. Monroe, Maguire's; 385, Robt. M. Gower, Reid's; 437, Mathew Brown, 404; 476, John Carroll, Wynn's; 503, John M. Gardner, 406;

541, Stephen McPherson, Reid's; 557, John Higgins, Sr., Reid's; 573, Eleanor Tippen, widow, 404; 641, Efford A. Cargill, 406; 687, Sam Parker's orphans, Barker's; 830, Isaac Strickland, 404; 839, Elizabeth York, widow, Wynn's; 873, John L. Moore, Towers; 894, John M. Born, Maguire's; 895, Sherwood Stroud, 404; 913, Nehemiah Summerlin, Loveless'; 955, Nathaniel Burks, Wynn's; 932, Josiah Chadwick, Bridges'; 959, Jacob Crotwell, 404; 1011, John Burns, Wynn's; 1055, Wm. Garner, 404; 1062, L. Yancey, Hamilton's; 1086, Thomas Gaines, Towers'; 1110, Joseph Shippey, 406; 1112, Thos. W. Wilson, Wynn's; 1169, Joseph C. Spencer, Chambers'; 1216, Robt. D. Johnson, Wynn's; 1220, Joseph Bolton, 406; 1233, Rich Lanier, Chambers; 1271, Tilman B. Bobo, Towers'.

TWENTY-THIRD DISTRICT—2nd Section: 33, Hugh Mills, Loveless'; 70, Thomas Taylor's orphans, Maguire's; 102, Biddy Proctor, widow, 406.

TWENTY-FOURTH DISTRICT—2nd Section: 147, Jane Cannon, Davis'; 179, Matilda Cannon, Davis'; 181, Ezekiel P. Ware, 406; 217, Wm. B. Woodruff, 406; 219, Esau Brooks, Towers'; 258, Kinchin Rambo, Chambers; 297, Sinah Williams, widow, Barker's.

SIXTH DISTRICT—3rd Section: 8, Amalia Ramey, widow, Chambers'; 34, Joseph Tary, Chambers; 99, Jeremiah Dean's orphans, Maguire's; 125, Lewis Jenkins, orphan, Loveless'; 227, Robert Brooks, Barker's; 232, Wm. Fowler, Chambers; 285, John Green, Chambers.

SEVENTH DISTRICT—3rd Section: 35, Wm. Tims, Bridges; 61, Nathan Spence, Sr., Loveless'; 67, John Fountain, Davis'; 84, Levi Yancy, Hamilton's; 99, Lewis Coffey, Barker's; 153, Wm. W. Williams, Maguire's; 169, Giles C. Hays, Barker's; 269, Sion Pearce, soldier, Bridges'; 288, Reuben Bramblett, Reid's; 312, Wm. H. Royal, Hamilton's.

EIGHTH DISTRICT—3rd Section: 284, James Bracewell, soldier, Towers'; 298, John Barker, Barker's.

THIRTEENTH DISTRICT—3rd Section: 276, Jas. McBride, Barker's; 285, Richard Simmons, 404; 289, Wm. Ewing, Reid's; 291, Christopher Coleman, Davis'.

FOURTEENTH DISTRICT—3rd Section: 9, Daniel Drummond, Wynn's; 21, Rucker Mouldin, 406; 40, John Mattox, Revolutionary soldier, 404; 133, Wm. Smith, Wynn's; 139, Jas. Rogers, Hamilton's; 151, Nancy Vaughan, widow, 404; 179, Thomas Robinson, Chambers'; 193, Abraham Garrett, Loveless'; 223, Hamilton Garmany, 404; 231, Benjamin Cochrane, Wynn's; 249, Anderson Owens, 406; 254, Benjamin Gholston, soldier, Towers'; 262, John Bolton, 406; 320, Thornton Meade, Maguire's; 322, Wm. Williams, Barker's.

FIFTEENTH DISTRICT—3rd Section: 26, Jas. Tollison, Maguire's; 30, John Middleton, 404; 32, Mary Loyd, widow of Revolutionary soldier, 404; 113, Edmond W. Reynolds, 406; 125, Sarah

Mackin, widow, Chambers'; 146, Bird Puckett, Maguire's; 188, John Manders, Bridges'.

TWENTY-FOURTH DISTRICT—3rd Section: 144, Joseph Miller, 404.

TWENTY-FIFTH DISTRICT—3rd Section: 89, Jas. McGill, Chambers'; 93, Charles Rogers, Chambers'; 163, John Medlock, 406; 166, Wm. Hall's orphans, Hamilton's; 274, Abner Yeager, 404.

TWELFTH DISTRICT—1st Section: 111, Jeremiah Bussell, Davis'; 245, Williams' orphans; 289, Elias C. Downs, Towers'; 311, Humphrey D. Sanders, Towers'; 318, Elizabeth McGuire, Davis'; 321, Thomas Nelms, Towers'; 366, Young Moore, Towers'; 394, Wiley T. Rigsby, Loveless'; 397, Willis Prewit, Bridges'; 419, James Roberts, Towers'; 421, Allen Coleman, Davis'; 426, Stephen C. Taylor, 404; 449, Eliz. Bagley, Barker's; 452, Ellison Cobb, Hamilton's; 454, Hugh Montgomery, 404; 471, Wm. Campbell, Hamilton's; 527, Samuel Day, Loveless'; 560, Jas. H. Brock, Maguire's; 565, John H. McElvaney, Reid's; 605, Ransom Strawhorn, Wynn's; 636, M. Thomas' orphans, Barker's; 671, Ellison Cobb, Hamilton's; 679, C. Montgomery, Hamilton's; 695, John B. Mitchell, Barker's; 708, E. Warbington, 406; 712, Mitchael Redwine, 404; 723, John Choice, Wynn's; 733, John Strayhorn, Davis'; 757, John Green, Chambers'; 763, Daniel Clower, 404; 813, Susannah Jester, Loveless'; 817, Nancy Pearce, Bridges'; 903, John M. Venable, Barker's; 919, Solomon Manning, Bridges'; 954, John Warren, Barker's; 984, Wm. Blanks, Chambers'; 990, H. H. Rowden, Wynn's; 1005, Jas. Echols, Barker's; 1062, Stephen Harris, 404; 1064, Jonathon Stone, 404; 1081, John B. Puckett, Maguire's; 1142, Charles Walls, Hamilton's; 1222, John Chambers, Maguire's.

THIRTEENTH DISTRICT—1st Section, North: 46, Sarah Powell, Chambers'; 52, Mathew Samples, Barker's; 82, Wm. White, Davis'; 146, Wm. L. Caldwell, Wynn's; 166, Jesse R. Hunnicutt, 404; 168, Joel H. Casper, Barker's; 207, John Brand, Loveless'; 206, George James, 404; 214, Samuel Crow, Barker's; 256, Barnabus A. Baker, 406; 330, Abagail Hamilton, 406; 381, Wm. Moore, Hamilton's; 387, Sarah King, Wynn's; 403, Milza Strickland, Davis; 508, George Row, Wynn's; 513, Burnett Tankersly, 406; 523, Moses Strawhon, Wynn's.

THIRTEENTH DISTRICT—1st Section, South: 1, Samuel Boon, Barker's; 56, Zachariah Bailey, Towers'; 65, Henry Dunn, Jr., 406; 113, Thomas H. Jones, 406; 128, Eliz. Osborn, Bridges'; 174, Absolon Baily, 406; 290, Thomas Kircus, Hamilton's; 386, Robert Walker, Maguire's; 434, Moses Kemp, Jr., Bridges'; 470, Wiley Bagley, Barker's; 473, John Butler's orphans, Reid's; 507, Matilda Cannon, Davis; 510, George R. Edwards, Reid's; 534, James Winburn, Barker's; 551, Benjamin Benson, Davis'.

FOURTEENTH DISTRICT—1st Section: 28, Wiley Brogdon,

Barker's; 44, Thompson Dickerson, Wynn's; 45, David Holly, Towers; 56, Appling's orphans, 404; 151, Elias Barker, 406; 166, Samuel McRight, Bridges'; 178, Ambrose George, Reid's; 198, Abel Gower, Revolutionary soldier, Reid's; 309, Wm. F. Roper, Loveless'; 404, Wm. DeFresse, Barker's; 555, Melzer Bumgarner, 406; 605, John Montgomery, 404; 666, Joshua Stevens, Hamilton's; 680, Henry Morgan, Sr., Hamilton's; 691, Joseph Curbo, Sr., Barker's; 699, Fielding Thurmond, Hamilton's; 711, Thomas Mulliken, Loveless'; 719, Wm. P. Brown, Hamilton's; 723, Richard Morris' orphans, Davis'; 725, Joseph R. Thompson, Davis'; 768, Obedience Sterling, Wynn's; 818, Wm. Middleton, 404; 845, Radford M. Carr, Hamilton's; 847, Wm. W. Chesser, 404; 852, Wm. Bailey, Loveless'; 867, Dreury Green, Chambers'; 913, Wm. M. Roberts, Chambers'; 827, Lewis Williams, 404; 937, Joshua Huckins, Bridges'; 970, Wm. N. Flinn, Barker's; 979, Wiley Browning, 406; 980, Henry C. Butler, Bridges'; 1000, Wm. Jackson, Reid's; 1003, Samuel M. Wardlaw, Towers'; 1045, Joseph Foster, Barker's; 1074, Duett Ethridge, Maguire's; 1093, Wm. Bond's orphans, Reid's; 1229, Richard H. Turner, Towers'; 1284, Moses Blake, Chambers'; 1409, Noah Strong, Barker's.

FIFTEENTH DISTRICT—1st Section: 10, Giles C. Hays, Barker's; 110, Manuel Fernandez, Barker's; 111, Thomas Carter, 404; 206, Burwell Cegraves, Davis'; 224, John P. McRight, Hamilton's; 409, Thos. W. Connally, Barker's; 471, Ezekiel T. Harris, Hamilton's; 486, Reuben Warren, Hamilton's; 487, Simon B. Hurst, Loveless'; 488, Moses Care, Hamilton's; 492, Peter Kilgore, Reid's.

FIRST DISTRICT—2nd Section: 15, Wm. Jeffries, Barker's; 21, Wm. Goodwin, Bridges'; 49, Harris Hannah, Maguire's; 113, Geo. W. Morgan, Hamilton's; 134, Miles Fowler, Loveless'; 145, Moses Camp, Sr., Reid's; 148, Solomon Hopkins, Towers'; 258, Jas. Edmondson, Jr., Barker's; 263, Booker I. Jackson, Loveless'; 346, Wm. H. Foster, Chambers'; 435, George S. Foyle, 406; 480, Alex. A. Puckett, Maguire's; 506, Rachel Stanton, Bridges'; 586, Riol Fowler, Loveless'; 614, Wm. N. Bruner, Hamilton's; 621, John S. Moore, Loveless'; 635, Simeon Sheardon, 406; 668, Jas. Dillard, Bridges'; 681, Shadrack Green, Barker's; 709, Nathan Williams, Sr., Hamilton's; 731, Wyatt Chandler, Reid's; 811, Lewis Bridges, 404; 819, Edward Kent, Barker's; 833, Wm. Sterling's orphans, Chamber's; 871, Hessey Mann's orphans, Loveless'; 917, Alec Gillam, Chambers'.

SECOND DISTRICT—2nd Section: 79, Sarah Moore, Reid's; 120, Jas. Tollison, Maguire's; 124, Samuel Phillips' orphans, 404; 280, Hope H. Watts, Towers'; 481, Mary Mitchell, Barker's; 545, Wm. Lard, Maguire's; 563, Wiley T. Rigsby, Loveless'; 589, John Johnson, 406; 618, Wm. Taylor, Loveless'; 707, Hesekiah Plummer, Loveless'; 765, Wm. Simmons, Maguire's; 792, Hilliary Moore, Chambers'; 820, Lloyd Brooks, Loveless; 927, Jeremiah Dean's orphans, Maguire's;

937, Isaac Mayfield, Barker; 946, Thos. Morgan, 406; 951, Elias Fincher, Barker's; 966, George Thrasher, Davis'; 1011, Jas. Boring, Towers'; 1050, Willis Bobo, 406; 1114, Thos. Hawks, Towers'; 1130, Ethelred Wilder, Bridges'; 1246, Sarah Bridges, Bridges'; 1251, Wm. R. Wiley, 404; 1273, Jonathan Fincher, Jr., Reid's.

THIRD DISTRICT—2nd Section: 24, Sara E. Pearce's orphans, Bridges'; 34, Richard Saye, Towers'; 61, Wm. Burnett, 404; 218, Roe Seamore, Bridges'; 246, Richard Wallis, Wynn's; 358, Wm. Garner, Wynn's; 373, Hiram M. Shaw, Towers'; 428, Elisha Vinson, Reid's; 442, Benj. Duncan, Loveless'; 559, Joseph A. Dunbar, Chambers'; 624, Asa Wade, Sr., Chambers'; 653, Joel Higgins, Chambers'; 687, Owen Andrews, Wynn's; 695, John Hughs, Sr., Hamilton's; 698, Thos. A. Pittman, 406; 811, Adeline E. Cox's orphans, 406; 892, Vining Cooper's orphans, Chambers'; 969, Radford Gunn, 406; 1027, Jas. Wardlaw, Chambers'; 1071, Thos. Bennett, 404; 1075, Wm. Burnett, Chambers; 1087, Stephen C. Naylor, 404; 1124, David W. Hames, Bridges'; 1125, Wm. L. Dodd, Bridges'; 1170, Daniel Martin's orphans, Reid's; 1291, John H. Hammond, Chambers'.

FIFTEENTH DISTRICT—2nd Section: 3, Thos. S. Foster, 404; 14, Wm. Buchelow, Baker's; 33, Joseph Defrees, Baker's; 34, Jesse Andrum, Wynn's; 99, Chainey Hamby, Reid's; 163, Barsheba Alred, Davis; 175, Mary Massey, Chambers'; 241, Starling T. Austin, Chambers'; 242, Hilary Atkins, Chambers'; 402, Wm. McDaniel, Wynn's; 447, Nancy Bridges, Bridges'; 510, Joseph Brown, Davis'; 528, Wm. A. Cochran, 406; 532, Richard Hutchinson, Loveless'; 534, Jacob A. Moore, Towers'; 551, Jesse Thomas, Baker's; 590, Ephraim Lee, Loveless; 602, Henry Nicks, Wynn's; 611, Thos. I. Norton, Loveless; 648, Edward Gilbert, Maguire's; 670, Mary Parker, Baker's; 702, Benj. F. Johnson, 404; 706, N. Hutchinson's orphans, Loveless'; 745, Appleton Hagood, Towers'; 763, W. G. Doster, Barker's; 799, Wm. Arnold, Chambers'; 867, James Garner, Wynn's; 887, Reuben Pendley, Barker's; 893, Jas. Harrell, Towers'; 902, Vaughan's orphans, 404; 908, Larkin R. Brown, Hamilton's; 913, Arthur Fowler, Towers'; 944, Wm. *H. Lowery, 404; 955, Jonathan Barnett, 404; 1031, W. G. Brewster, Chambers'; 1049, Wade H. Peevy, Reid's; 1096, Wm. Garner, Wynn's; 1125, Jonathan McLendon, Chambers'; 1143, Hardy Youngblood's orphans, 406; 1160, Jas. P. Hardin, 404; 1161, Preston Giles, Davis'; 1277, Jonas Conger, Barker's.

SIXTEENTH DISTRICT—2nd Section: 44, Jas. McDaniel, Wynn's; 105, Ephraim Sizemore, Hamilton's; 144, Samuel Rawlins, Sr., Loveless'; 206, Jas. H. Pogue, 406; 212, John Whorton, Reid's; 232, Walter Austin, Loveless'; 258, Littleton Baker, 406; 259, Wm. Morrow, Baker's; 272, Richard Pace, 404; 283, Lucinda Moore, Barker's; 288, John Brewster, 406; 310, Reubin Mullins, Griffin's; 328, Wm. Hires, Reid's; 337, Gilbert P. Williams, Towers'; 362, Lott Rowden, Wynn's; 363, Peter Lanton, Chambers'; 383, Thomas Ma-

guire, Maguire's; 385, Jas. Taylor, Maguire's; 412, John W. Moore,
404; 422, Thomas McEver, Hamilton's; 449, John Hamilton, Sr., 406;
587, David Delk, 404; 607, Martha Thompson, Hamilton's; 629,
Frederick Lamb, Barker's; 654, Wm. Cochran, Wynn's; 684, Jesse
Horton, Barker's; 698, Pleasant R. Loyd, 406; 716, Jas. C. Reed, 404;
746, Claraca Leach, Davis'; 777, Cashwell Brand, Loveless'; 787,
Isaac Brown's orphans, Barker's; 797, Wm. H. Cooper, Chambers;
829, Richard J. Jones, Loveless'; 933, Thomas Rutherford, Barker's;
943, Jas. S. Russell, Towers'; 1007, Randolph Dalton, 406; 1076,
Robert A. Adair, Chambers'; 1093, Wm. R. Brandon, 404; 1137, John
Roberts, Towers'; 1226, John B. Hawry, Wynn's; 1251, Wm. Nesbit,
Wynn's.

SEVENTEENTH DISTRICT—2nd Section: 71, Winnie D. Davis,
Loveless'; 91, Edward Hill, Bridges'; 119, Thomas Pruett, Barker's;
120, Enoch Benson, Reid's; 130, Carnelius Roberts, Davis; 149,
Richard Glover, 406; 170, Wm. Ashley, Barker's; 230, Abner Willingham, 406; 287, Wm. McGinnis, 406; 318, Richard Cruce, Towers';
328, Sarah Rawlins, Loveless'; 340, William Williams, Barker's;
393, Hasberry F. Comer, Towers'; 431, Christopher Coleman, Davis';
455, Charles Lavender, Chambers'; 513, Thomas Higgins, Reid's;
523, Amos Welborn, Perkins'; 536, Daniel N. Pittman, 406; 540,
Abram Harris, Towers'; 576, Jacob Cain, Hamilton's; 593, Wm. W.
McClung, Reid's; 626, William Ezzell, Reid's; 633, Jas. Roberts,
Towers'; 824, Jas. D. Peden, Chambers'; 849, Pleasant A. Sterling,
Chambers'; 1074, Jonathan Barnett, 404.

EIGHTEENTH DISTRICT—2nd Section: 13, Solomon Lowery,
404; 22, Joseph Rutledge, Maguire's; 79, Isaac N. Young, Chambers';
119, Esau Brooks, Towers'; 133, Littleton W. Holt, Davis'; 156,
Michael Willingham, Hamilton's; 229, Samuel Caruthers, Towers';
259, James Waits, 406; 351, Edmond Lowery, 404; 393, Wm. Castleberry, Reid's; 396, Claiborn Vaughan, Loveless'; 460, John Wright,
Loveless'; 476, Benj. Manning, Bridges'; 477, Jarrell Hicker, Bridges';
652, John Stuart, Chambers'; 729, Jas. C. Reid, 404; 746, Elizabeth
Haney, Wynn's; 793, Thos. B. Gordan, Maguire's; 843, Wm. M.
Puckett, Towers'; 912, Josiah Moore, Reid's; 913, Jas. Hoyle, Wynn's.

NINETEENTH DISTRICT—2nd Section: 18, Jas. Roberts,
Barker's; 51, Wiley W. Goss, 406; 116, John Bryant, Maguire's; 164,
—. —. Mayfield, 406; 173, John W. Turner's orphans, Loveless';
259, Richard Hutchinson, Loveless'; 276, Wm. Winburn, Barker's;
323, Adam Robinson, Bridges'; 343, David R. Phillips, 404; 347,
Samuel Day, Loveless'; 350, Thomas Jones, Wynn's; 524, Thomas
J. Chambers, Wynn's; 543, Allen Hancock, Chambers'; 623, Robert
Hamilton, 406; 665, Wm. Winburn, Barker's; 712, Peter Welden,
404; 725, Jesse Compton, Barker's; 757, Jeremiah Moore, 406;
764, James Sexton, Maguire's; 815, J. H. Hollingsworth, Chambers';
859, Burrell Higgins, Chambers'; 932, Jesse Osburn, Bridges'; 934,

John Harris, Loveless'; 965, Wm. Atkins, Wynn's; 1020, James Mathis, Hamilton's; 1056, Dreury Green, Chambers'; 1095, Horation N. B. Nunnally, Reid's; 1122, Jacob Bowers, Bridges'; 1124, Thos. C. Butler, Bridges'; 1133, Richard Manning, Maguire's; 1162, Jesse Thrasher, Barker's; 1295, Thos. T. Langley, Loveless'; 1298, Davis Spence, 1301, Isaac N. Young, Chambers'.

TWENTY-FIRST DISTRICT—2nd Section: 5, Wm. Smith, Sr., Bridges'; 73, John C. Chandler, Maguire's; 104, Mitchell Barnett, Chambers'; 172, Henry Fitzsimmons, Chambers'; 179, Nelson Roberts, Loveless'; 322, Joshua Bradford, Bridges'; 331, Jones Douglas, Barker's; 355, Andrew J. Morrow, Barker's; 357, Thomas Deaton, Hamilton's; 369, Wm. Pinder, Barker's; 385, Chas. Dupree, Barker's; 389, Benj. Conger, Barker's; 407, Elias Davis, Hamilton's; 454, Nathan Hall, Bridges'; 459, Chas. Morgan, Maguire's; 484, Wm. A. Tate, 406; 557, Shadrack Bogan, Davis'; 558, Thomas Kile, Barker's; 623, Jas. Highsaw, Loveless'; 657, Wm. Hill, Maguire's; 667, John Brawner, Winn's; 743, Rachael Banks, Hamilton's; 880, Elijah Horn, Loveless'; 924, Wm. Arnold, Bridges'; 940, Wm. C. Thompson, Reid's; 977, Levi Dempsey, Loveless'; 1009, Tabitha Gentry, Chambers'; 1058, John Lowery, 404; 1092, Alexander Brown, Towers'; 1126, Nathan Clark, Bridges'; 1136, Wm. Brewster, Chambers'; 1216, Elijah Nunn, Maguire's.

FIRST DISTRICT—3rd Section: 30, David Pruett, Reid's; 113, Sion Pearce, Jr., Chambers'; 138, John Howell, Reid's; 255, Robt. B. Camp, Reid's; 327, Chas. Roper, Reid's; 441, Reuben Pendley, Barker's; 447, John Barker, Barker's; 520, Aaron Chadwick, Bridges'; 582, Wiley Bracewell, Towers'; 616, Thomas Deaton, Hamilton's; 640, Dudley Maddox, Hamilton's; 698, Jonas Brand, Reid's; 706, Wm. H. Brown, 404; 709, Elijah Moore, Towers'; 711, Hiram Whitworth, Reid's.

SECOND DISTRICT—3rd Section: 47, John B. Malony, Winn's; 151, George Brogdon, Barker's; 231, Sarah Terrell, Chambers'; 255, Wm. Chambers, Winn's; 338, Jesse Compton, Barker's; 348, Zachariah Thompson, Hamilton's; 435, Amos Barnett, 404; 531, S. Bromley, Wynn's; 534, Moses Snell, Towers'; 550, Wiley Pearce, Bridges; 568, E. T. Harris, Hamilton's; 614, Andrew Johnson, Wynn's; 630, James Steele, 506; 561, Thos. J. Mathews, Wynn's; 688, Elijah Lee, Loveless'; 707, David B. Driskell, Barker's; 714, Mitchell Bowman, Bridges'; 734, Jacob Delk, Loveless'; 742, Walter Austin, Loveless'; 777, Thos. H. Spaggins, Bridges'; 909, I. Pendley, Barker's; 917, John McMillan, Reid's; 926, J. R. Williamson, Loveless'; 936, Jeremiah Bateman's orphans, Davis; 941, Nathan Watson, 406; 1120, Wm. Rogers, Hamilton's; 1139, John Brown, Bridges'; 1203, Rice B. Green, 406; 1227, Abner Yeager, 404; 1264, Hope K. Brogdon, Barker's.

THIRD DISTRICT—3rd Section: 7, Reuben Manning, Bridges';

17, Joel Johnson, Loveless'; 123, Stephen Nolen, Hamilton's; 167, George J. Dradd, Barker's; 304, Allen Burch, Wynn's; 355, Richard H. Lererett, Maguire's; 377, Mary Ann Dickey's orphans, 404; 386, Thomas Wynn, Wynn's; 434, Jonathon Johnson, Sr., Towers'; 453, Joshua Bolton, Reid's; 479, David Daniel, Davis'; 523, Jas. Venable, Barker's; 527, George Barker, 406; 559, Geo. R. Edwards, Reid's; 565, George Sizemore, Hamilton's; 570, Stephen Harris, 404; 667, Daniel Herring, Reid's; 687, Isabella Black, Barker's; 702, Isaac Brumbelow, 406; 710, John Bankston, Loveless'; 742, John Furgerson's orphans, Wynn's; 812, Hezekiah Jones, Wynn's; 827, J. S. V. Conger, Barker's; 905, Moses Ellison, Chambers'; 921, Joshua Hill, Bridges'; 929, Larkin Bagwell, 406; 978, George Buchanan, Loveless'; 979, A. D. Brown, Hamilton's; 990, Wm. Sizemore, Hamilton's; 1011, Hardy Hart, Chambers'; 1000, Solomon P. Wood, Towers'; 1126, Edmond Bagby, Barker's; 1135, Robert Craig, Chambers'; 1137, John Osburn, Reid's; 1144, Shadrack Lowry, 404; 1165, B. Ivy, Chambers'; 1199, John J. Austin, Towers'; 1292, John Boozer, Sr., 404.

FOURTH DISTRICT—3rd Section: 30, Wm. Fulton, Chambers'; 86, Samuel Crow, Barker's; 92, David Curbow, Davis'; 99, Samuel Hollis, Maguire's; 115, Joel M. Bryan, Towers'; 117, Wm. J. Nash, Wynn's; 162, John Brawner, Wynn's; 179, John Tuderwood, Towers'; 261, Russell Stovers, Davis'; 343, Hamilton Garmany, 404; 362, Henry E. White, Baker's; 370, John Anglin, Barker's; 429, Lewis Williams, Maguire's; 466, Ira W. Cates, Loveless'; 487, John D. Peden, Chambers'; 533, Wm. Fincher, Barker's; 548, Nathaniel Austin, Jr., Chambers'; 566, H. B. Watkins, Maguire's; 573, W. Yancy, 404; 595, John Freeman, Barker's; 619, Isaac Towers, Towers'; 656, Jas. T. McAfee, 406; 670, Robt. S. Foster, 404; 724, Henry Powell, 404; 749, George Hopkins, Towers'; 753, Elijah Horn, Loveless'; 766, G. A. Gordon, Maguire's; 811, John D. Spence, Barker's; 827, David Abbott, Loveless'; 856, Joel Estes, Sr., Bridges'; 910, John Puckett, Hamilton's; 953, Jas. Bond, Maguire's; 973, John Roberts, Jr., 406; 978, Reuben Donaldson, Maguire's; 981, Proctor's orphans, 406; 1128, Elias Burton, Barker's; 1141, Clem A. Wynn, Chambers'; 1197, W. R. Laughridge, Bridges; 1206, Mathew Tanner, Hamilton's; 1293, Elizabeth Higgins, Reid's.

SEVENTEENTH DISTRICT—3rd Section: 60, John Bryant, Maguire's; 171, Stephen King, Wynn's; 180, Chas. H. Rice, Maguire's; 181, Jas. Berry, Loveless'; 187, Sara M. Griffeth, Maguire's; 228, John Nash, Wynn's; 270, Wm. Shamblee, Wynn's; 414, E. Mathis, Wynn's; 437, Jno. W. Richardson, Chambers'; 462, Thos. Ellison, Davis; 484, Wm. Bailey, Loveless; 504, Robt. A. Camp, Reid's; 633, Luke Pannell, Reid's; 702, Wm. Warren, Barker's; 728, Mark Miller, Wynn's; 763, Chas. Davenport, Barker's; 798, Joseph R. Haney, Wynn's; 840, Robt. Alexander, Barker's; 887, Silas Higgins, Reid's; 924, Richard Beasley, Maguire's; 998, Jas. McDaniel, Wynn's;

1012, Abner Phillips, Barker's; 1022, Jas. L. V. Conger, Barker's; 1024, John Lawrence, Sr., Loveless'; 1038, Daniel Maddock, Hamilton's; 1059, Abner Garrett, Loveless'; 1101, John Pendley, Jr., Barker's; 1270, John R. Townley, Bridges'; 1292, Andrew Owen, 406; 1293, Joel Highshaw, Loveless'.

EIGHTEENTH DISTRICT—3rd Section: 16, Wm. Martin, Sr., Reid's; 29, J. Stanton's orphans, Bridges'; 66, Benj. Johnson, Reid's; 104, Nancy Mason, Davis'; 143, Joseph Everett, Wynn's; 165, John A. Stephens, Chambers'; 214, Isham Medlock, 416; 245, John Leitch, Wynn's; 272, Samuel Wood, 404; 318, Branham's orphans, 404; 392, Miles Langley, Loveless'; 412, Geo. W. Tumlin, 404; 444, F. Mathews, Wynn's; 473, Wm. Robertson, Reid's; 475, Benj. Jackson, Loveless'; 548, Bird Puckett, Maguire's; 553, Jas. Weatherford, Davis'; 561, John D. Peden, Chambers'; 573, Mary Wheeler, Loveless'; 601, John Hamilton, Bridges'; 611, Clairborn H. Thompson, Davis'; 630, William Maltbie, Chambers'; 669, Wm. Tollison, Maguire's; 739, Jas. R. Skinner, Reid's; 786, Daniel Mattox, 434; 799, John T. Bailey, Barker's; 837, T. E. Mathis, Wynn's; 937, James Crampton, 404; 1082, Alfred Glover, Barker's; 1097, Thomas Humphrey, Barker's; 1131, Barney Lee, Wynn's; 1202, David Hamilton, Reid's; 1277, Charity Mathews, Wynn's; 1288, Andrew B. Bond, Maguire's.

NINETEENTH DISTRICT—3rd Section: 2, Nathan L. Hutchins, Chambers'; 32, Cheney M. Lindsey, Loveless'; 38, Enoch B. Duncan, Davis'; 61, Ambrose McGinnis, 406; 119, Luke Johnson, Maguire's; 159, A. Massey, Chambers'; 162, R. B. Harris, Wynn's; 180, Clark Howell, 406; 200, Thomas Maughan, 404; 369, James Noel, 404; 371, Harrison Bryan, Maguire's; 492, Samuel Maffett, Bridges'; 497, Sarah Key, Loveless'; 503, Rucker Mauldin, 406; 514, John Roberts, Towers'; 527, Lewis Jenkins, 406; 682, P. Coleman, 406; 697, S. W. Otwell, Barker's; 700, R. B. Robinson, Reid's; 743, R. Trammell, Towers'; 761, J. T. Wasson, Chambers'; 800, Britten Brewer, 406; 810, Williams' orphans, 404; 878, Radford Gunn, 406; 901, Hugh Mills, Loveless'; 911, Wm. Thompson, Wynn's; 1018, John Miller, 404; 1091, David Turner, Hamilton's; 1157, Oswell Langley, Loveless'; 1169, T. S. Cole, Wynn's; 1195, Elijah Tippen, 404; 1204, Wm. Robinson, Bridges'; 1229, M. C. Malone, Reid's.

TWENTIETH DISTRICT — 3rd Section — 10, Jas. Blackman, Wynn's; 11, J. G. Roberts, Loveless; 14, Elisha Deloney's orphans, Reid's; 29, Wm. Green, 406; 93, Archibald Hamilton, 406; 54, Tillman Nesbit, Maguire's; 57, Wm. Dodd, Towers'; 63, Howell Mangum, Barker's; 92, Wm. S. Ivie, Chambers'; 161, Wright Lee, Wynn's; 176, Elisha Winn, Chambers'; 191, Absalum Bailey, 404; 200, G. H. Harris, Chambers'; 203, Lewis Corley, Loveless'; 256, Riley Medlin, Towers'; 270, Wm. Timms, Bridges'; 273, Edward Dodson, Bridges'; 288, Hardy Burrell, 404; 350, J. J. McJunkin, 406; 403, Lovic Pearce, Bridges'; 450, Obel Waldrip, Davis'; 497, Thos. T. Kilgore,

Reid's; 558, Joshua Hill, Bridges'; 585, John Jones, Hamilton's; 645, John G. Park, Chambers'; 673, James Westmoreland, 404; 735, Nicholas Rawlins, Loveless; 756, Richard Nolan, Hamilton's; 838, Andrew M. Hamilton, 406; 845, James Mathews, Barker's; 953, Ira Camp, Maguire's; 995, John Ellison, Reid's; 1015, Mathew Henry, Maguire's; 1024, Wm. Morrow, Baker's; 1026, Abner Willingham, 406; 1037, Merriman Cape, 404; 1130, Chas. Estes, Reid's; 1148, Joel Higgins, Chambers'; 1224, Thomas Burge, 404.

TWENTY-FIRST DISTRICT—3rd Section: 48, John Pounds, Wynn's; 78, Thos. W. Brandon, 404; 88, Isham Lee, Loveless; 122, Joseph R. Thompson, Davis'; 185, Susannah Martin, 404; 228, Thomas Ezzell, Reid's; 256, H. M. Barker, Hamilton's; 311, R. Brewer, 406; 342, Baily G. Lard, Maguire's; 360, John Peeples, Chambers; 453, Robert Alexander, Barker's; 467, Elijah Holcomb, Reid's; 539, Henry Glasgow, Chambers'; 545, John Pevy's orphans, Reid's; 579, Jas. McGinnis, 404; 639, John H. Leverton, Wynn's; 646, John Boland, Maguire's; 704, John Wynn, Towers'; 713, John H. Coxley, 406; 747, J. Alexander's orphans, Chambers'; 766, Elias Norton, Chambers'; 766, Hannah Holbrook, Towers'; 804, E. P. Ware, 406; 806, James McGill, Chambers'; 808, John Brunly, Wynn's; 869, D. A. Coker's orphans, Loveless; 873, J. Autry, Sr., R. S., 404; 907, James Brown, Bridges'; 933, Arbin Moore, Barker's; 968, Wm. P. Brown, Bridges'; 980, Obediah Miller, 404; 1005, Absolon Duncan, 404; 1039, John Mailer, 404; 1061, John Ivie, Chambers'; 1114, Thos. Ballard, Bridges'; 1184, Laban Bowden, Wynn's; 1213, William Boyd, Reid's; 1247, Edward Brumbelow, 406; 1257, Allen Clark, Bridges'; 1279, E. Barker, Hamilton's; 1295, ——. ——. Smith, Chambers'; 1297, Wm. Morris, Hamilton's.

FIRST DISTRICT—4th Section: 4, Benjamin Manning, Bridges'; 189, Wm. Medford, Towers'; 190, Jason Harrison, Bridges; 198, Green B. Harris, Chambers'; 217, Joseph Turner, Towers'; 237, Hiram Bowen, 404; 311, Wm. Lambert, Chambers'; 329, John P. Mcright, Hamilton's; 335, B. M. Powell, Hamilton's; 345, Joseph Mims, 406; 354, Jesse Broadwell, Hamilton's; 369, Elijah Keheley, Bridges'; 463, Wm. Armstrong, Barker's; 554, Wiley Browning, 406; 572, B. Upchurch, Towers'; 575, Jas. B. Head, Loveless; 590, Thos. Taylor's orphans, Maguire's; 648, Lucinda Fowler, Loveless'; 693, Wm. Tumlin, 404; 708, Thos. Mathews, Jr., Wynn's; 730, Richard Bowen, Reid's; 752, Martin Ayers, 404; 765, N. Austin, Sr., Chambers'; 793, J. W. F. Thompson, Barker's; 809, Jas. McGill, Chambers'; 804, Thos. W. Bacon, 406; 896, Isaac Blount, 404; 906, Richard Davis, Reid's.

SECOND DISTRICT—4th Section: 179, John Calaway, Barker's; 192, James Cates, Loveless'; 299, John Strayhorn, Davis'; 440, John T. L. Cain, Hamilton's; 448, Elias Pruett, Barker's; 493, Mark Snow, 404; 503, Wm. King, Wynn's; 532, Lott Powden, Wynn's;

HISTORY OF GWINNETT COUNTY, GEORGIA

535, W. S. Maloney, 406; 565, B. Cochran, Maguire's; 617, Jas. S. Porter, Reid's; 660, Thomas Johnson, Wynn's; 665, Dorcas Beam, Bridges; 715, W. Puckett, Maguire's; 745, Jas. Calaway, Barker's; 753, Henry Dunn, Jr., 406; 757, Jas. McBride, Barker's; 759, Wiley B. Rucks, Davis; 762, Benj. F. Morgan, Hamilton's; 765, Jesse Herring, Sr., Reid's; 779, Enoch J. Moore, Reid's; 804, Jas. Defoor, 404; 810, David Hitchcock, 404; 826, Jas. Robertson, Bridges'; 905, Luke Pannell, Reid's; 967, Jas. W. Moore, Reid's; 979, N. Johnson, Maguire's; 1040, David Halley, Towers'; 1089, Samuel Burton, Barker's; 1118, Z. M. Samples, Barker's; 1194, Few Gordon, Maguire's; 1231, Samuel Duncan, Davis'; 1254, William Brown, Hamilton's.

THIRD DISTRICT—4th Section: 7, Sara Smith, Chambers'; 20, Elias Carroll, 406; 57, Wm. Cruce, Towers'; 75, Mary Rutherford, Barker's; 94, H. H. Corley's orphans, 406; 153, Elias Wells, Maguire's; 197, Jesse Dickerson, 406; 212, Isham Williams, Chambers'; 220, John F. Perdue, 406; 244, Clairborn Osburn, Loveless'; 370, Young P. Pool, Barker's; 357, Joseph B. Mills, Loveless'; 374, Wells Thompson, Chambers'; 393, Margaret Echols, Hamilton's; 417, Dennis Chadwick, Bridges'; 421, Wash Bougs, Reid's; 439, Elias Keller, Wynn's; 446, David Jackson, Loveless; 448, James Roberts, Barker's; 455, Benj. Brewer, 406; 467, Samuel Maffett, Bridges'; 491, H. Mouger, Chambers'; 518, Jesse Burrell, 604; 536, Thos. W. Wilson, Wynn's; 665, Adam Crotwell, 404; 795, L. Bankston, Chambers; 822, Tilman Nesbit, Maguire's; 857, Asa Wade, Loveless; 866, A. D. Brown, Hamilton's; 881, Wm. H. Boyd, Hamilton's; 919, James Gibson, 416; 942, John Higgins, Sr., Reid's; 1010, B. J. Bridges, Bridges'; 1050, John Davany, Sr., 404; 1087, M. Hall, Wynn's; 1108, Richard Bostic, Jr., 406; 1142, Robert McEwin, Maguire's; 1148, J. W. Dunbar, Loveless'; 1169, J. Kinny's orphans, Chambers'; 1177, Benjamin Brand, Maguire's; 1182, Clinton Webb, 406; 1241, Henry Wade, Barker's; 1283, John Rainey, Hamilton's; 1292, C. Bromley, Hamilton's.

SIXTEENTH DISTRICT—4th Section: 79, William Mathews, 404; 95, James Sea's orphans, Wynn's; 108, James Hood, Chambers'; 111, John R. Medlock, 406; 124, H. H. Allen, Chambers'; 170, Edward Williams, 406; 267, David Rawlins, Maguire's; 293, Samuel Coney, Towers'; 305, Richard Hays, Barker's; 335, Jason Fain, Barker's; 405, Robert Chamblee, Wynn's; 417, Jane Doss, Bridges'; 421, James Bracewell, Towers'; 435, Geo. M. Gresham, Chambers'; 519, Patrick Bailey, 404; 527, James Rogers, Hamilton's.

SEVENTEENTH DISTRICT—4th Section: 42, Wm. McGinnis, 406; 93, J. H. Holbrook, 406; 133, Jas. M. Brown, Hamilton's; 144, L. J. Pearce, Bridges'; 191, John Huff, Chambers'; 224, E. Chamberlain, Hamilton's.

Gwinnett's Pensioners—1835

James Baber, John Bagby, Enoch Benson, Hugh Brewster, Elias Baker, John Bowen, Daniel Clower, Joseph Curbow, Thomas Cox, John Davis, Nathan Dobbs, Wm. Gunnell, Abel Gower, Littleton Hunt, Stephen Harris, Jesse Herring, Isaac Horton, Phillip Iseley, Lewis Jenkins, Jonathan Johnson, Edward Jackson, Christopher Kehela, William Liddell, William Morris, Sr., John McDade, John Roper, George Thrasher, Charles Walls, William Wardlaw, Leonard Wills, John Lawrence.

List of 1840

Owen Andrews, Reuben Bramblett, Enoch Benson, Ben Conger, Daniel Clower, Joseph Curbow, John Davis, Nathan Dobbs, Adel Gowers, Isaac Horton, Stephen Harris, Littleton Hunt, Joseph Herrington, Phillip Iseley, Edward Jackson, John Lawrence, Wm. McRight, John McDade, Robert Patterson, George Thrasher, Nathan Williams.

Strange Transaction

One of the most singular transactions perhaps ever made in this state was the one for erecting and keeping a fence around the courthouse square in Lawrenceville. Fence after fence had been erected by the justices of the Inferior Court during the years. The fence was maintained for the purpose of keeping cattle, sheep, goats and other animals that ran at large out of the public square. Keeping up this fence was a real problem in those early years. Stock laws had not been thought of and cattle, goats and hogs ran at large, and rail fences were erected to prevent them damaging public property. Cows could jump a fence; boys could let the fence down; gates were left open. Any of these things could happen while cattle walked in and parked themselves in the courthouse square. And the neighbors' goats, bewhiskered and with flags flying, could easily climb over the styles and spend the night in the halls of the courthouse to the annoyance and disgust of the justices of the court and county officials. For thirty years the justices of the Inferior Court had been annoyed and bedeviled with the courthouse fence problem. Finally the chief justice of the court called the other four associate justices into an extraordinary session and informed his colleagues that he had a plan to settle the fence question. "The town is full of smart lawyers," said the chief justice to his colleagues, "who are used to settling other people's troubles. Let's give them the job of settling the fence question. My idea is to give four of these lawyers the corner lots of the courthouse square with the explicit understanding that they keep a good substantial fence around the square. And as a further inducement we can permit them to construct brick office buildings on these lots." The four associate justices immediately agreed to the plan as suggested by the chief justice. Four prominent lawyers thought the plan a good one and entered into formal contracts with the justices of the Inferior Court. The southeast lot went to Charles H. Smith, a young attorney, who in later years became famous as a writer under the name of Bill Arp. The deed was made to him on November 28, 1849, and he erected the building during the following eighteen months. The southwest corner was deeded to N. L. Hutchins; the northwest corner to James P. Simmons, and the northeast corner to T. W. Alexander.

The deeds provided that the title to these lots should vest in the owners of the office buildings so long only as the occupants and owners maintained a good and substantial fence around the courthouse square. Should they fail at any time to maintain and keep up this fence, then the lots, including the office buildings, would revert to the justices of the Inferior Court, or to the county. Failure on the part of the owners to maintain the fence gave the justices of the court the right, after a sixty days' notice, to take over the property, declaring that "this conveyance shall cease, determine and be void and the privilege hereby conveyed shall revert to and revest in the justices of the Inferior Court of said county, and the house shall be subject to the occupancy and control for the use of said county."

The four deeds are worded substantially alike. The deed to N. L. Hutchins reads as follows:

Georgia, Gwinnett County.

Justices of the Inferior Court

To N. L. Hutchins:

Know all men by these presents that we, William Maltbie, Richard D. Winn, James M. Gordon, Jesse Lowe, and John Mills, justices of the Inferior Court of said county, do by these presents bargain, sell and convey unto Nathan L. Hutchins, his heirs and assigns, the southwest quarter of the public square in the town of Lawrenceville in said county for the following considerations and under the restrictions hereafter mentioned: That this conveyance is to give to said Hutchins, his heirs and assigns, the right to build a stone or brick house on the southwest corner of said square which shall be of at least sufficient size for a commodious and comfortable office, the size and form to be determined on by himself, with the above provisions, the same to be done in a good workman-like manner, and to be completed within eighteen months from this date; that the southwest quarter of the said public square is duly conveyed to vest in said Hutchins, his heirs and assigns, possessory rights to enable him and them to keep the same in good order for the use of the public, except the house and a sufficient yard which is to be for his or their own private use. And the said Hutchins, his heirs and assigns, are to keep a good substantial railing from the south style to the west style, including the enclosure of the said square. And it is further provided that should the said Hutchins, his heirs and assigns, fail to build and complete said house within the time above specified, or should at any time fail or neglect to keep up a good and sufficient railing around the outside of the said southwest quarter of said public square, then and in that event this conveyance shall cease, determine and be void; and the privilege hereby conveyed shall revert to and revest in the Justices of the Inferior Court of said county, and the house shall be subject to the occupancy and control for the use of said county, provided, nevertheless, this forfeiture shall not occur until said Hutchins, his heirs or assigns, shall have sixty days' notice of the day the forfeiture will be declared; and if the work is done and completed and in order within that time, no right is forfeited, but this conveyance to be and remain binding and effectual between the parties.

In witness whereof we, the Justices aforesaid, have hereunto signed our hands and affixed our seals, this the 28th day of December, 1849.

In the presence of   RICHARD D. WINN, J. I. C. (Seal)
  B. C. Strickland,   JAMES M. GORDON, J.I.C. (Seal)
  Jesse Murphy, J. P.   JESSE LOWE, J.I.C. (Seal)
                                WILLIAM MALTBIE, J.I.C. (Seal)
                                JOHN MILLS, J.I.C. (Seal)

The new owners of the four lots erected a rail fence eight feet high around the courthouse square and styles instead of gates were used for crossing over the fence. Styles were little bridges of stair-steps that led over the top of the fence and there was one at the middle of each side of the square. The task of maintaining the fence was shifted from the justices of the Inferior Court to the owners of the corner lots and they soon had difficulties enough to worry even the lawyers who were now in possession of them. Chestnut rails made good fire wood. The fence slowly lost its height. A fence of pales was constructed and yet there was trouble in keeping cattle and goats out. At the June term of the Inferior Court in 1865 the following warning was issued by the court:

"Court met pursuant to adjournment. Present their honors, John Mills, W. W. Brand, Daniel M. Byrd, and W. B. Bracewell. On motion it is ordered by the court that the sheriff or his deputy is hereby required to notify the owners of goats about town that no goat shall be permitted to come inside of the courthouse square after the 25th instant; and if any goat shall be found therein after that time, that said sheriff or his deputy shall kill all that may be so found."

At the term of the court held on December 11, 1865, the

following order was passed directed to the owners of the buildings on the courthouse square:

"It is ordered that the owners of the buildings on the corners of the courthouse square suffered the fencing inclosing the same to go down and become useless so that the square is open and the public buildings and shade trees are subject to damage from trespassers; it is, therefore, ordered by the court that the clerk of this court serve each of said parties, to wit: J. P. Simmons, N. L. Hutchins, Sr., N. L. Hutchins, Jr., and T. M. Peeples, with a notice requiring them and each of them to repair the inclosure belonging to their respective corners according to their several agreements with this court, the inclosure to correspond to the present inclosure except that four rails are to be used instead of five."

When the stock law became effective there was no need for a fence for the purpose of keeping cattle from the square. The owners of the lots neglected, therefore, to maintain a decent fence. It leaned here and was down there. It became an eye-sore. Finally, with the assistance of the board of county commissioners, the present granite and iron fence was constructed. Bill Terry furnished the granite posts. They were set up around the square and iron pipes bolted firmly in the posts.

A Most Unusual Case

One of the most interesting and unusual cases ever tried in the Superior Courts of Gwinnett County was the Waters will case. Judge James Jackson, a man of outstanding ability as attorney and judge, presided at the trial, which was held during the September term of the court in 1855. The ablest talent of the Georgia bar was employed on both sides. N. L. Hutchins, an able and successful practitioner of the Lawrenceville bar, and Thomas R. R. Cobb represented the executors of the Waters estate, while Charles J. McDonald, a former governor of Georgia, and the law firm of Howell Cobb and William Hope Hull appeared for the heirs of the estate under the will.

The prominence of the interested parties, the verdict of the jury, the suggestive comments of the chief justice of the Supreme Court in writing the decision, the importance of the question at issue, together with the events that followed, give this case a unique and important place in the history of jurisprudence in this county.

George M. Waters, according to the census of 1840, owned 100 slaves. His monument in the cemetery at Fairview Presbyterian Church shows that he was born in 1777 and died in 1852. He left a will disposing of a large estate. Item three of his will reads as follows:

"Thirdly. Whereas, I own and hold in possession the undernamed slaves, to-wit: Rory, Queen, his wife; her children, William and Rose; Mary's brothers, Pompey and Tom; Mary's sister Caroline, and Caroline's daughter, Dinah, (with the exception of Pompey, the above people are at present in Bryan County in this state). Also the following slaves in Gwinnett County, state aforesaid, to-wit: Polly, her children, James, Morgan; Jefferson, Cherokee, John, Elizabeth, boy Swimmer, George, girl Polly, Peggy, sister to Polly; her children, Charles, Bowling, Betsey; Betsey's children, young Peggy, Catherine, Willey, Georgia, Thomas, infant girl, Josephine; Jenney, sister to Betsey; Jenney's children, to-wit: Sarah, Harriet, Hughes, Henry Clay and infant boy, Clark; Lydia, sister to Jenney; Lydia's children, Hannah, Josey and infant boy; Susan, alias Sukey, sister to Lydia; Sucky, infant girl, Caroline; Prudence, sister to Peggy, and Polly, Prudence's daughter, Cynthia. On account of the faithful services of my body servant, William (the husband of Peggy) I will and desire his emancipation or freedom, with the future issue and increase of all the females mentioned in this term of my will. If it is incompatible with the humanity, etc., of the authorities of the State of Georgia, I direct my qualified executors to send the said slaves out of the State of Georgia to such place as they may select; and their expenses to such place shall be paid by my executors out of my estate; and that the whole of this proceeding be conducted according to the laws and decisions of the State of Georgia, I having no desire or intention to violate the spirit or intention or policy of such laws; and I do further direct that if any person to whom any bequeath or disposition contained in this item offers any impediment to its being carried into execution, he or she shall in no event receive any part of my said estate, but my executors are enjoined to withhold from the person so opposing any share or portion herein devised and bequeathed to him or her and distribute the share so forfeited among my other heirs, per stirpes and not per capita. I desire that the said slaves, if compelled, may select their residence out of the State of Georgia and in any part of the world."

The concluding part of the will follows: "I appoint Asahel R. Smith, William Rogers, of Forsyth County, and my son, Thomas J. Waters, my executors to this, my last will and testament. And in witness whereof I have hereunto set my hand and seal this 12th day of March in the year of our Lord one thousand eight hundred and fifty-one (1851). Signed, sealed and declared by the testator as his last will and testament in the presence of us, who, in his presence and at his request and in the presence of each other, have hereunto subscribed our names in witness thereto.

"GEORGE M. WATERS.

"Attest: Joseph W. Baxter, B. E. Strickland, John Smith."

The executors of the will filed a bill in the Superior Court of the county asking the court by the verdict of a jury for an interpretation of the third item of the will. The executors seemed to take the view that all the slaves mentioned in the third item of the will were emancipated, while some of the heirs of the deceased claimed that only William, the body servant of the testator, and the future increase of the females, were manumitted. The heirs, by their attorney, Charles J. McDonald, filed a demurrer and for grounds of demurrer alleged:

"The demurrer of Williamina C. Cleland, Archibald Howell and his wife, Catherine E. Howell; George W. Cleland and Leticia Pooler, the two last minors by their guardian ad litem, Archibald Howell; Harriet Fitts and Catherine Fitts by their guardian ad litem, W. H. Fitts; Sarah M. Charlton and Thomas J. Charlton; and Sarah E. Charlton, a minor, by her guardian ad litem, Archibald Howell, defendants to the bill of complaint of Thomas J. Waters, Asahel R. Smith and William Rogers, the only qualified executors of George M. Waters, complainants.

"These defendants by protestations and confessing any or all of the matters and things in the said bill of complainants to be true in such manner and form as the same are therein set forth and alleged do demur to the said bill and for cause of said demurrer show: That it appears in and by the complainants' bill of complaint and the exhibit thereto attached and made a part thereof that the said George M. Waters, the complainants' testator, did not in and by the third item of his will, or by any legal and proper contention of said will, emancipate and set free all the slaves mentioned in the said third item of the said will, but only a part thereof, to-wit: The body servant of the testator, William, and the future increase of the females mentioned in the third item in said will, and any discovery which can be made by these defendants or any of them touching the matters complained of in said bill or any of them can not be of any avail to said complainants for any of the purposes for which a discovery is sought against these defendants by the said bill. Wherefore, and for divers other good causes of demurrer appearing in the said bill, these defendants do demur thereto and they pray the judgment of this Honorable Court whether they shall be compelled to make any further or other answer to the said bill, and they humbly pray to be dismissed with their reasonable costs and this demurrer sustained."

Judge James Jackson overruled the demurrer. The case was tried at the September term of Gwinnett Superior Court, 1855. The jury brought in the following verdict:

"We, the jury, find and decree in favor of the complainants, that it was the will and intention of the testator in and by the third item of the will to manumit and set free all the slaves and the future increase or issue of all the females therein mentioned that might be born after the making of said will, that it was his intention and so willed that his executors should apply to the legislature for an act of emancipation and that if such act was refused, then it is the duty of the executors to remove the said slaves out of the state of Georgia and to any part of the world, where they can be free and enjoy their freedom. We further find and decree that the provisions of said will providing for the emancipation of said slaves are legal and not in conflict with the laws of Georgia. September 14, 1855.

"THOS. H. JONES, For."

The case was then carried, by appeal, to the Supreme Court of the State which held in a lengthy decision, written by the able chief justice, that the intention of the testator was to emancipate all the slaves mentioned in the third item of his will.

Under the law at that time slave owners could not emancipate or set free their slaves. But Waters, in his will, stated that certain of his slaves should be given their liberty at his death. The courts had ruled that all the slaves mentioned were entitled to be emancipated. It then became the duty of the executors to carry out the mandate of the court. The executors could apply to the General Assembly for an act of emancipation, or they could send the slaves out of the state. The second method was used to solve the difficulty.

Thirty-seven of the slaves agreed to leave the state and go to a foreign country. They were sent to Savannah, turned over to the African Colonization Society and transported to Liberia, a small negro republic on the western coast of central Africa. Before leaving, each slave was furnished suitable clothing and $100 in gold, a total cash expenditure of $3,700. And their transportation expenses were also paid, making a total of several thousand dollars, all of which was paid out of the estate of George M. Waters.

The hot climate of Liberia, however, was not as conducive to their physical comfort and health as the milder seasons to which they were accustomed on the Waters plantation in Gwinnett County. The songs of freedom of their black brothers and the national anthem of the Republic of Liberia were not nearly so sweet as the "Song of the Chattahoochee," a famous river on whose banks they had cultivated and gathered lengthening fields of corn and cotton and from whose turbid waters they had, on countless occasions, pulled many a loggerhead turtle and slithery eel.

The record shows that thirty of these emancipated negroes died in Liberia within twelve months. The surviving seven found passage on a merchant vessel which landed them, moneyless and friendless, in Philadelphia. Their plight came to the attention of Howell Cobb and Alexander H. Stephens, who furnished them the means to return to Georgia.

The Waters plantation was on the Chattahoochee River near Duluth, at Abbott's bridge, the Craig sisters now owning a part of it. There the seven negroes returned, preferring to be laborers or slaves on this Chattahoochee plantation than citizens of the African republic across the seas.

Owners of Slaves in 1820

Robert S. Adair	1	Isaac Cowan	3
John Agnew	1	John Cox	2
John Allen	8	Thomas Cox	2
Jesse Austin	2	James Crawford	2
Frederick Bagwell	1	Joseph Crockett	5
Christopher Baker	5	Henry Cupp	3
Joshua Ballard	1	John Cupp	5
John Beasley	3	Henry Curbow	1
William Beauchamp	2	Elias Davis	1
John F. Beavers	2	John De Foor	5
James Berry	1	James Diamond	1
William Blake	3	David Dixon	14
John Blaylock	3	W. H. Dixon	1
James Bonds	1	Jesse Dobbs	2
Smith Bonner	1	Nathaniel Dobbs	1
George Brogdon	1	William Dobbs	1
Allen Burch	1	Patrick L. Dunlap	1
Mary Burges	3	Elizabeth Echols	4
John Burnett	1	Watson Ellison	1
Curtis Caldwell	1	John Evans	1
John Caldwell	1	Josiah Fincher	1
Abner Camp	5	Henry Funderburg	2
John Camp, Jr.	2	John Gazaway	1
John Canady	1	James Gilbert	4
Thomas Carroll	1	William Green	1
David Carrimore	1	George M. Gresham	4
John Carrimore	1	William Guffin	1
John Carter	5	Peter Harrison	1
David Castleberry	3	Samuel Hambleton	2
James Castleberry	1	Joseph Hambrick	2
Joseph Cavender	1	Andrew Hamilton	4
Washington Chamberlin	1	Archy Hamilton	1
Abraham Chandler	1	Hugh Hammel	1
James Clements	5	Robert Hancock	1
Cheadle Cochran	2	Jesse Harris	2
James Cochran	1	James Hayes	1
Philip Coleman	1	G. B. Haynes	3
Curtis Corley	1	Andrew Haslett	4

Micajah Hendrick	2	Silas Pool	1
John Henry	1	Mary Pounds	2
William Henry	2	John Price, Jr.	2
James Hicks	2	John Price, Sr.	1
Richard Holt	3	George Reid, Sr.	10
Jesse Horn	2	George Reid, Jr.	1
John Hudman	4	Joseph Reid	2
Jennings Hulsey	2	Samuel Reid	8
John Jackson	1	Gallant Reynolds	1
Joseph Jenkins	2	Jemima Reynolds	4
Joel Jones	3	Luke Robinson	2
Samuel Jones	1	James Royal	3
Thomas Jones	1	John Rutledge	2
Thomas Jones	6	Grover Salmonds	1
James H. Kidd	2	William Scott	2
John Knight	1	William Sikes	2
Thomas B. Lanier	2	Green Sorrells	2
Benjamin N. Lasiter	2	John Steel	2
John Leverett	1	Edmond Strange	1
William Liddell	3	Wilson Strickland	14
John Limville	1	Gideon Tanner	4
William Loughridge	1	William Terry	1
Ephraim Mabry	2	Wm. Thurmond	5
William Malone	2	John L. Tippin	1
William Maltbie	1	Solom. Townsend	2
Abraham Martin	1	John W. Turner	2
Ezekiel Mathews	2	Thos. B. Turner	1
John Maddox	2	Peter Wallis	3
Thomas McAdams	2	Ivy Ward	3
Richard R. McDuff	1	James Wardlaw	1
Ephram McLain	3	Wm. Wardlaw	2
Thomas Mahaffey	1	James Waits	2
Benjamin Merrill	1	David Watson	2
Nicholas Minor	1	Thomas Watson	1
Elizabeth Monkos	1	R. J. Watts	1
James Murphy	1	John Wesrer	2
Jeremiah Nesbit	2	Archie Whatly	1
William Nesbit	1	Alex. White	3
George Noland	2	James White	1
James Noland	1	Benj. Whitehead	2
Joseph O'Neal	1	Isham Williams	2
Brittain Osburn	1	Jesse Williams	1
Issac Pace	2	Elisha Winn	6
Isaiah Parker	1	John Winn	2
James Pearce	1	John Woodall	5
Wiley Pearce	1	Thomas Worthy	2
William Pearce	3	Wm. Worthy	1
Daniel C. N. Pittman	4	Augustus Young	3

Owners of Slaves in 1830

A. Anderson	1	Robt. Bradford	2
Jas. Alexander	9	John Boring	2
R. S. Adair	2	Hugh Brewster	4
Nat Austin	10	Polly Baker	2
Elijah Anderson	9	Dudly Bonds	10
Isaac Adair	9	Nancy Bryant	3
John Adkinson	4	Ittai Bryant	1
Geo. R. Adair	6	Jas. Blackmon	12
Thos. W. Alexander	14	Allen Burch	7
Sara Alexander	10	John Burns	1
Ansalem Anthony	23	Nancy Burns	9
James Austin	40	Rebecca Bagwell	3
Walter Adair	2	Joshua Baker	5
Thos. B. Adair	3	R. D. Beesom	2
James Allen	1	James Boring	2
A. R. Allen	1	Alex. Brown	6
Thos. A. Allen	11	J. W. Beaty	1
D. P. Allen	2	Thomas Beaty	8
Thomas Allen	1	George Baker	4
John Anglin	10	Edward Brown	2
Wm. Armstrong	5	R. M. Barnwell	7
John Baskin	1	John Bankston	1
Shadwick Bogan	4	Barnabus Baker	1
F. L. Brogdon	1	David Burge	17
George Brogdon	10	Randall Baggett	12
Wm. Brandon	10	James Boyd	9
Thomas Burge	4	James Berry	7
Nancy Baker	4	William D. Byrd	5
Christopher Baker	1	Wiley Brogdon	9
Wm. Brewster	9	Nathaniel Burge	8
Harmon Bowen	1	Thomas Ballard	4
Hugh Brewster	1	Almond Bryant	5
John Bagley	7	Lewis Blackburn	29
Mitchel Bennett	2	Robert Berry	2
J. B. Benson	3	Joshua Buffington	4
Hugh Brewster, Sr.	2	Samuel Barton	1
Enoch Benson	9	Charles Beasley	1
Benj. Benson	1	T. J. Chambers	10
John Brewster	4	T. Connally	5
Benj. Baker	7	John Cain	6
John Berry	1	Thomas Carter	1
Martha Brown	5	George Crotwell	9
Austin Boyd	8	Robert P. Camp	9
Mary Burgess	4	Washington Chamberlin	8
Mathias Bates	3	John Carr	1
Wm. Baskin	4	David Castleberry	6

Curtis Caldwell	1	Margaret Echols	1
Lewis Coffee	1	Eli Elkins	5
Sterling Callahan	2	Thomas Ellison	7
Sara Carroll	5	Thomas Ewing	1
Ann Cowan	6	John Freeman	4
John Canine	1	Elikah Foster	1
H. K. Craig	1	John Foster	2
Robert Cates	8	Patsy Fincher	4
John Chandler, Jr.	11	Elias Fincher	2
John Choice	12	George Y. Glenn	1
Richard Cruce	1	Isaac Gilbert	5
John Carroll	6	Hamilton Garmany	6
Thomas Carroll	5	Aaron Godfrey	1
Charles Caldwell	1	William Gordon	7
Samuel Caruthers	4	Thomas Gaines	1
Stephen Cruce	1	Few Gordon	1
John Clower	1	George Gordon	13
E. W. Chester	2	G. M. Gresham	13
Benjamin Cox	2	Willea Glover	1
Thomas Cox	5	Wm. Y. Gober	2
Alsa Camp	1	Zack Gholston	12
Vining Cooper	3	John Gregg	7
Robert Craig	13	James Gilbert	21
John Chandler, Sr.	12	John Gray	4
Thomas Cordery	1	William Green	7
Maxfield Chambers	4	Charles Gates, Sr.	10
Joseph Crutchfield	2	Chas. Gates, Jr.	22
Thomas Cline	1	James Gordon	1
William Chamblee	1	Tamer Gilbert	1
Absalom Duncan	4	Thomas Gann	5
W. W. Downs	1	Thomas Gast	1
Samuel C. Dunlap	9	Benj. Gholston	8
Allen Dyer	2	Richard B. Green	2
George Doss	2	Daniel George	1
Edmond Dillard, Sr.	2	John Humphrey	1
Richard Davis	1	Buckner Harris	2
Edmond Dillard, Jr.	1	Peter Hairston	2
James S. Deal	1	James Hood	7
John Dodd	1	Vivian Holmes	4
John F. Dodd	5	George Hays	1
Richard Davenport	1	Nathan L. Hutchins	11
Henry Dunn	3	Archibald Hamilton	3
Robert Duncan	5	John Harris	1
David Delk	4	William Hendley	2
John H. Dobbs	4	James Hoyle	2
Jesse Dobbs	4	Ransford Haynes	1
Reuben Daniel	2	Dorcas P. Harkness	13
William Downing	1	L. D. Harris	1

HISTORY OF GWINNETT COUNTY, GEORGIA

Name	Count	Name	Count
John P. Hutchins	1	Jacob Light	1
Philo Hall	2	Meron Lankford	3
John Hamilton	7	William Liddell	13
Andrew Hamilton	8	Tyre Landers	2
Robert Hamilton	6	George W. F. Lamkin	1
Abigail Hamilton	9	David Lowery	4
Joseph Hamilton	6	Thomas Lenoir	13
Thomas Hollingsworth	6	Pleasant R. Lysle	2
Evan Howell	40	George Lamar	5
Adam Hale	18	Zachariah Lee	8
John L. Hamilton	1	H. Lankford	2
Ambrose Harmage	20	John Lay	6
Jane Harmage	1	William Lay	1
George Hartin (Martin?)	11	E. Leach	1
James Humphries	1	James McGill	3
John Ivie	1	Thomas Monroe	3
Benjamin Ivie	3	R. Montgomery	7
Robert Jackson	1	Robert McCaula	2
G. W. Jones	1	James McGinnis, Sr.	9
Benjamin Johnson	1	Stephen McGinnis	2
Janes Jones	2	James McGinnis, Jr.	1
Thomas Jones	1	John Middleton	1
William Jones	1	Christopher Moore	2
Sara Johnson	3	Thomas Morgan	8
Charles C. Jackson	5	John Maffett	2
Thomas H. Jones	2	John P. Moon	1
Jonathan Johnson	2	Joseph Morgan	11
Nathan Johnson	3	John Mills	4
Frank Jones	3	H. T. Morgan	1
W. Johnson	3	William Moore	1
Andrew Johnson	2	John Maddox	7
Robert D. Johnson	5	Rhesa McGreggor	1
William Knox	16	Mathew McRight	3
James Kircus	1	Archibald Meeks	1
Sol Kemp	1	James Mann	9
Amos Kelley	3	Jackson Monroe	1
Hi Kite	1	James P. Maguire	2
Hosea Camp	17	Thomas Maguire	1
Thomas Kile	2	Daniel Mathews	5
H. T. Killian	2	Samuel McKinney	5
Moses Liddell	11	Thomas Mathis, Sr.	7
Daniel Liddell	4	H. T. Mathis	1
John Lowery	1	Ezekiel Mathis	1
Richard H. Lester	3	Thomas Meadows	1
John W. F. Lowery	5	William McDaniel	8
John Langley	1	Elizabeth McDill	2
James Loughridge	6	Abraham Martin	8

Name	Count
James Mills, Sr.	2
Thomas McAdams	8
James Maughon	2
Micajah Mays	11
Hugh Mills	2
Elijah Moore	1
James F. McAfee	2
Battle Mayfield	1
David Miller	2
Merrett McGee	1
William Montgomery	21
Samuel Maffett	2
Benjamin W. Maddox	1
William Moses	1
John W. Medlock	4
Margaret Middleton	3
Richard Minor	3
John F. Martin	32
Abraham Moore	1
William Maltbie	4
Nancy Mason	1
Thompson Moore	7
John Medlock	4
William Mathews	1
Eli McConnell	3
Lucy Martin	12
Samuel May	3
Samuel Means	5
Robert Naylor	1
James Nolan	1
William Nesbit	12
James Nason (Mason?)	1
Stockley T. Nelson	1
Thomas Nelson	9
James Nettles	2
Jesse Osborn	7
Benjamin Pruett	8
Richard Plunkett	1
James S. Porter	2
John Puckett	5
John Peeples	1
John M. W. Pierce	1
Wiley Pierce	4
George Perry	1
Abner Phillips	2
S. D. Peden	2
John Peden	9
James D. Peden	1
Francis Pittman	8
Jeffery Pittman	13
James S. Porter	2
Daniel L. Pittman	35
William Page	3
Thomas Pettit	8
Caty Pettit	4
James D. Pate	1
John G. Park	12
James Pogue	2
Sara Powell	6
Benj. M. Powell	5
Sara H. Puckett	1
James C. Reid	2
William Richardson	6
James S. Russell	3
Jesse Rambo	11
R. B. Robinson	2
Charles W. Rawson	2
Milly Raimy	4
William Robinson	3
William Rakestraw	1
David P. Roberts	5
Richard Richardson	7
Thomas Robertson	2
Hefflin F. Rhodes	1
Samuel Reid	19
Kinchen Rambo	2
William Rogers	5
John Rogers	18
Joseph Rogers	1
Asa Reid	6
Claiborn M. Styles	2
George Still	9
John Sudderth	2
Mathew Strickland	6
John Sammon	8
Samuel Scott	4
Simeon Strickland	4
John L. Sims	2
John Stuart	7
A. R. Smith	1
Daniel N. Smith	1
John Smith	2
William Sudderth	4

John Still	1	A. G. Van Valkingburg	3
John Spence	2	Allen Vinyard	1
John A. Stevens	1	Elisha Vincent	1
Wilson Strickland	25	Isham Williams	15
Samuel Smith	3	A. Wilborn	7
Andrew Scott	1	W. Welborn	2
Joseph Shippy	3	Hiram R. Williams	15
Henry Sparks	1	James Wells	2
Noah Strong	3	Asa Wade	3
John Sparks	1	Gilbert P. Williams	3
Samuel Smith	3	John W. Wright	1
John Sanders	7	E. Warbington	1
Watt Sanders	1	John S. Watson	2
George Still	9	Glowman Winn	2
John H. Spencer	5	John Williamson	2
Hardy Strickland	3	John White	33
Imri Tumlin	1	Thomas Winn	8
Asa A. Turner	1	Alfred Williams	7
John Turner	17	Richard Whitworth	1
David Turner	1	John L. Ward	1
Hiram Trammell	2	Elisha Winn	29
Thomas B. Turner	4	Joshua Welch	1
Zach Thompson	1	William Wardlaw	2
Joseph Thompson	8	Mathew Wynn	6
William Tumlin	2	David Watkins	1
T. B. Turner	4	John Winn	7
J. M. Thompson	7	Richard I. Watts	6
Ephraim Thompson	3	James Wardlaw	16
Sara Terrell	24	Clinton Webb	2
John L. Tippins	1	Thomas Ware	12
Johnson Thompson	7	Thomas Worthy	10
W. I. Tarver	2	John Winn	4
Chas. T. Thomton	6	William Webb	4
Samuel Terrell	1	James Waits	22
Henry Turner	2	Thomas Watson	3
Jesse Thomas	1	John Wright	20
Wells Thompson	50	Mark Waits	1
Thomas Todd	1	Isaac N. Young	4
Aaron Underwood	1		

Owners of Slaves in 1840

Elijah Anderson	14	James Austin	54
Ansalem Anthony	22	George Anderson	4
Robert Anthony	10	S. F. Alexander	14
Thos. Alexander	27	Isaac Adair	15
Elizabeth Anglin	2	Isaac N. Allen	2
Nathaniel Austin	18	Robt. S. Adair	13

Name	Count	Name	Count
John B. Austin	1	Lewis Coffee	1
John Akers	8	Daniel P. Clower	1
Nathaniel Akers	1	John Cooper	4
John Atkinson	8	Hosea Camp	15
Jas. Alexander	6	Jesse Cole	1
John N. Alexander	8	Wm. A. Cain	1
Sara Alexander	9	John Cain	9
James Allen	3	Ranson Cooper	2
Absolem Allen	2	John Collins	1
Lovic P. Allen	19	Mathew Crawford	2
John Bryant	2	Robert Craig	21
Elijah Bagwell	2	Thomas Carroll	8
Nancy Briant	1	Curtis Caldwell	1
William Brooks	1	Wm. Crowell	2
Hope S. Brogdon	2	John Carroll	10
George Brogdon	14	John F. Comer	2
Harrison R. Brogdon	2	Enoch Cobb	2
Samuel Burton	1	Austin W. Cole	1
Balom S. Bridges	2	Wm. Cruse	1
Wiley Brown	5	L. M. Cates	10
Isabella Baskins	4	Levi Cooper	9
Joseph W. Baxter	1	Vining Cooper	5
William Brandon	19	Bennett Cooper	4
Robert Bagwell	2	Robert Cates	7
James Blackmon	41	Robert Camp	6
James Blackman	6	Merrett Camp	2
Joshua Barnett	1	Thomas Cox	2
Miles Barnett	2	Washington Dunbar	1
Ellender Bagley	4	Edward Doss	2
Mary Brown	5	Stephen Douglas	1
Edward Brown	2	David Daniel (free)	5
Henry Brockman	2	Wm. H. Drummond	5
Lewis Brown	4	Jesse Davis	11
David D. Brown	1	Samuel Dunlap	7
Wm. Baugh	1	George R. Davis	1
David D. Byrd	16	John Dodd	5
Samuel Bolling	1	Wm. Drummond	5
Wm. L. Born	1	B. J. Drummond	4
Dudly Bonds	13	Robt. Duncan	2
Berry Bramlett	12	Jesse F. DeShong	1
Britton Brewer	11	Robt. Echols	7
John Bacon	2	Thos. Edwards	2
Richard Bostick	1	Thomas Ellison	8
John A. Brown	2	James Flowers	1
David Burge	22	Reubin Fields	8
Allen Birch	9	Benj. F. Fuller	1
Benjamin Conger	2	Thomas Foster	1

John Foster	3	John Jackson	6
Robt. S. Foster	2	Chas. M. Johnson	3
Elijah Fleming	1	Saml. L. Jones	1
Wm. H. Fitts	6	Geo. W. Jones	4
Wm. S. Fitts	1	W. M. Johnson	3
George Gordon	21	W. H. Jinkins	11
Few Gordon	6	Thos. H. Jones	30
James Gilbert	26	Robt. Johnson	1
Joseph Goodwin	3	Wm. Knox	20
Isaac Gilbert	9	Thomas Kile	2
William Gordon	8	Daniel Killian	1
Hamilton Garmany	14	Amos Kelly	3
Frances Gober	2	George Kirk	1
Elias Green	3	Jackariah Lee	13
William Garmany	4	Alex. Lockridge	1
Thomas Garner	1	Wm. Langley	4
James Garmany	1	John Langley	1
R. J. Goza	4	Thos. Lenoir	17
Vivian Holmes	8	Moses Liddell	16
James Hawthorne	6	G. W. F. Lampkin	3
Mathew Henry	2	A. F. Linky	19
James Highsaw	1	Ben. Lampkin	1
Archibald Hamilton	2	C. C. Lankford	8
M. T. Hamilton	1	Elizabeth Lee	1
Buckner Harris	5	Daniel Liddell	14
James Hood	4	Sara Lord	4
George H. Hopkins	1	Geo. Lamar	4
Soloman Hopkins	5	Anna Little	1
James Hale	3	Fielding Maddox	1
Thompson Hale	2	Daniel Mathis	2
Thomas P. Hudson	2	Thos. Maguire	12
David Holmes	17	Jacob Moulder	6
Arthur G. Holmes	4	John Montgomery	5
James Hutchins	7	Wm. Morris	2
Alex. Holmes	2	Benjamin Manning	9
Hugh Hutchins	6	M. C. Malone	2
Lueding Hamilton	3	M. R. Mitchel	9
Wm. Hunnicutt	1	William Moore	2
Evan Howell	40	Daniel Matton	2
Wm. Holton	1	George W. Morgan	1
Adam Hoyle	27	Charles Montgomery	1
Amelia Hollingsworth	6	William Montgomery	27
Eli Hood	8	James McGinnis	5
N. L. Hutchins	21	Elizabeth McGinnis	2
John T. Iveskil	4	Stephen McGinnis	6
Luke Johnson	3	William Morrow	2
Wm. Johnson	5	Thomas Mills	1

John F. Martin	47	Thomas Pittard	3
John W. Medlin	4	Sara Puckett	1
William Maltbie	7	Elizabeth Pittman	36
Thomas Mathis	3	Daniel N. Pittman	7
Charity Mathis	4	Thos. A. Pittman	7
Mark Miller	4	William Robinson	4
Eli S. McDaniel	1	William Rakestraw	1
Samuel McKinney	8	Nelson Roberts	1
Samuel Martin	2	Wm. M. Roberts	2
Elijah Moore	1	Kinchen Rambo	6
Thomas Mathis	2	Jesse Rambo	19
Absalon Martin	2	Wm. I. Russell	11
William Minor	7	Samuel Ritchie	6
R. B. Martin	1	Jas. S. Russell	5
James McDaniel	1	George Reid	2
Sherod Morris	4	Wm. Robinson	1
John Maffett	1	Samuel Reid	27
Thomas Moore	8	Wm. Richardson	10
Nancy Mason	1	Jas. Sexton	2
Joseph Mims	2	Wilson Strickland	38
Robert McAfee	21	Mathew Strickland	11
John W. Medlock	15	William Sudderth	7
Newton McDill	1	George Sudderth	2
William McDaniel	9	Mehala Sanford	1
William Nesbit	19	Henry Strickland	9
Thomas Nelms	9	Isaac Strickland	9
Willis Norris	1	Pleasant A. Sterling	4
James Orr	2	John Smith	2
Wm. Orr	8	Asahel R. Smith	1
Syree Osborn	10	John Stewart	5
Elizabeth Osborn	5	Milza Strickland	2
Neels G. Ormburg	1	James P. Simmons	5
Daniel Plunkett	1	Orring Smith	1
James C. Patterson	2	Elizabeth Scott	2
Garling Prince	7	John Sammon	5
Isikiah Plummer	1	Jefferson Smith	1
Israel B. Pickins	2	Marion Spraggins	3
Daniel Pearce	2	John Steele	3
Joseph Pulliam	2	Bartlett Thomison	6
James Paden	1	Hiram Taylor	5
Adam Pool	1	Zachariah Thompson	1
James D. Peden	1	John B. Trippe	3
Benjamin Pruitt, Jr.	1	Sara Terrell	29
Benjamin Pruitt, Sr.	18	Moses Tiller	1
John Peden	6	Thomas Turner	8
John Pittard	4	Lucinda Turner	11
Samuel Peden	2	Henry Turner	1

Henry P. Thomas	9	Mary P. Winn	10
Robt. Underwood	6	Hiram Williams	7
Elisha Winn	53	John Winn	5
Thos. Williams	8	Wiley W. Webb	10
Wm. T. Willingham	3	Olsey Wells	3
George M. Waters	100	Richard Whitworth	1
Geo. W. Wright	6	Barbara Winn	6
Richard D. Winn	5	James Vinyard	12
Isham Williams	9	Mary Wright	4
John S. Wilson	4	Mark Waits	9
Thomas Worthy	11	Absolom Waits	3
Thomas Winn	2	Asa Wade	4

OWNERS OF SLAVES IN 1850

Charity Allison	8	Eli J. McDaniel	6
Sara Ackert	10	Samuel McKinny	10
Robt. Bagwell	1	John McKinny	3
James Blackburn	17	Charity Mathews	2
Rhoda Carroll	13	Henry Mathews	2
Curtis Caldwell	1	John Maffett	1
V. L. Corley	2	John W. Nash	1
John W. Chamblee	1	Lewis Nash	1
Nancy Davis	6	Azariah Noel	1
Frances Gober	3	William Nesbit	26
Few Gordon	7	Samuel Peden	1
James B. Head	1	David R. Phillips	2
Rev. James Hale	3	Nancy Allan	1
George H. Hopkins	1	Elizabeth Atkinson	2
Jemes R. Henry	1	Wm. Atkinson	5
Thompson Hale	1	Washington Allen	4
Richard Holt	15	Dudly Bonds	26
Hugh Hutchins	7	Hardy Bennifield	2
Samuel L. Jones	2	John Beasley	3
Robert B. Johnson	3	Newton Bramblett	2
Locke Johnson	2	Lewis Brown	8
Amos Kelly	6	Levi M. Cooper	15
Curtis C. Lankford	3	Walton Camp	1
Aram Lankford	5	Merrett Camp	7
Levi Loveless	2	Robert B. Camp	15
William C. P. Liddell	3	Temperance Crenshaw	3
Mark Miller	5	Mathew P. Cooper	1
Darling R. McDaniel	5	Eleanor Cates	8
Sara McDaniel	4	G. W. F. Craig	19
Daniel Minor	1	W. A. Cain	3
Wm. W. Minor	1	Thos. W. Cunningham	7
Rachel Minor	6	Wm. Drummond	8

Wm. I. Drummond	7	Nathaniel Austin	27
Daniel Dunn	2	Geo. Braswell	1
Reuben Donaldson	1	Starling E. Brown	1
Robert Echols	11	Anthony W. Bates	7
Samuel Echols	2	Daniel M. Byrd	14
Robert Gower	4	Wm. D. Byrd	14
Louiza Hawthorne	12	John C. Copper	2
Wm. Hamilton	1	Robt. L. Caldwell	4
G. B. Hudson	1	John E. Craig	20
Thos. P. Hudson	1	Mathew Crawford	3
John Harbin	3	Robt. M. Cleveland	13
William Hosch	1	Margaret Canine	1
Thomas Jacobs	4	Robert Craig	47
Charles Johnson	4	A. W. Cole	1
George Kirk	3	Elizabeth Dunlap	5
Sherod Morris	4	Joel Davis	1
James McDaniel	4	John L. Davis	3
James M. Moore	2	Dr. James Garmany	8
Miranda Malone	13	Robt. J. Goza	2
D. E. Moore	1	Dr. Jas. M. Gordon	7
Samuel Martin	3	T. G. Horton	4
Thos. E. Mathis	1	W. P. Hunnicutt	2
John McCurdy	3	James Hood	4
Benjamin O'Kelly	2	Nathan L. Hutchins	61
Delila O'Kelly	9	N. L. Hutchins (guardian)	7
Jas. M. Orr	7	Henry Holmes	10
Elijah B. Puckett	1	John P. Hutchins	19
Jas. L. Russell	7	L. E. Jenkins	17
Hiram Stephens	1	Margaret Lanier	6
Henry Strickland	13	William Langley	6
David Thomas	1	Moses Liddell	15
Nemisses Vinyard	7	Wm. Lacount	2
Asa Wade	2	Jesse Lowe	6
Geo. W. Wiley	2	Charles Mason	2
Henry W. Wells	4	Elizabeth Morrow	3
Wiley W. Webb	24	William Maltbie	10
James Wilson	2	John F. Martin	59
Isham Williams	7	Jas. C. Patterson	11
John Winn	2	Dr. R. M. Parks	1
Richard Whitworth	4	Daniel N. Pittman	4
Asa B. Wright	1	Elijah Pittard	6
D. A. Alexander	8	Josiah Patterson	2
Robt. L. Adair, Sr.	2	Wm. Wichardson	2
S. F. Alexander	31	Mary Roberts	5
Thos. W. Alexander	4	Leroy Robinson	2
Martha Alexander	13	Mary Roberts	4

History of Gwinnett County, Georgia

Wm. J. Russell	17	Samuel Knox	4
Jesse Rambo	18	Elleanor Knox	10
Asahel R. Smith	5	Thomas Kyle	4
D. W. Spence	40	T. H. Liddell	2
John Smith	5	Isabella Liddell	12
Bryant E. Strickland	2	Moses W. Liddell	4
James P. Simmons	4	Francis Lenoir	10
P. A. Sterling	10	John W. Lenoir	3
Sara Terrell	16	Thos. Mathis	6
Taylor Tiller	4	Charles McKinney	2
Alfred Williams	20	Stephen McGinnis	8
Elizabeth Williams	1	M. C. B. Montgomery	7
Parthenia Williams	1	C. L. Montgomery	2
Elisha M. Winn	10	Samuel Martin	3
R. D. Winn	11	Elizabeth Norton	4
M. W. Armstrong	3	Isaac N. Strickland	15
Thos. Cox	4	Henry Strickland	14
Charles Carr	11	Keenan Terrell	7
W. H. Caldwell	3	Jesse Thornton	2
Robt. Duncan	5	Geo. M. Waits	61
Jesse F. DeShong	3	Thos. J. Waters	36
Elmina Goodwin	4	Margaret Allison	3
Archibald Hamilton	11	Mary Brown	3
Adam Hoyle	19	Hope J. Brogdon	8
Thos. H. Jones	38	Daniel D. Born	3
Edward W. Musgrove	1	Benj. W. Bagley	1
Jas. J. Medlock	1	George Brogdon	20
John W. Medlock	5	John A. Born	12
Mary McAfee	12	John R. Baker	4
Henry Minor	33	H. R. Brogdon	3
Walton W. Smith	1	Mary Brown	8
Mark Waits	11	John Bankston	9
Chas. N. Woodall	7	Larkin Bagwell	2
Rev. James Williams	2	Joseph W. Baxter	1
Wiley F. Atkinson	1	Mark Camp	1
Jas. Alexander	1	J. W. Chambers	1
Anderson Arnold	1	Burton Cloud	4
John Carroll	22	Lewis Coffee	1
Joel N. Culver	2	Stephen Cruce	1
Lodowich M. Cates	17	Edward Doss	1
Levi Davis	1	Sherod Everett	4
Jas. C. Dunlap	8	Sara Ford	2
Wm. H. Fitts	11	James Flowers	9
Isaac Gilbert	10	Thos. Foster	4
Evan Howell	45	Benjamin Gholston	21
Washington Holmes	1	William Garmany	4
W. Holmes	1		

Jas. A. Hutchins	5
A. G. Holmes	7
H. T. Hill	1
Archibald Hamilton	4
Mathew T. Hamilton	2
Wm. C. Harris	2
Thomas Johnson	2
William Johnson	5
John King	11
Jacob Moulder	8
Thompson Moore	11
Abram Moore	2
Jesse Osburn	13
John Plunkett	1
John Puckett	5
Wiley Pierce	1
Thos. G. Pullian	4
William Scales	17
William Sudderth	12
Leonard Thomas	1
James Wheeler	1
William L. Winn	6
John Young	1
Ansalem Anthony	8
Miles Barnett	5
Nathan Clark	2
John Cain	10
Rebecca Caldwell	1
Hugh Duncan	1
Archibald A. Dunlap	3
Charles Dean	1
Wm. Guffin, Sr.	1
William Hunter	2
M. J. Harrison	3
John A. Huff	1
Newton L. Liddell	1
John Leach	2
Archibald Leach	3
John W. Maltbie	3
Daniel Maddox	2
Adam Pool	5
Robt. A. Reed	1
John L. Reed	4
John Stuart	6
Milza Strickland	2
William Sammon	2
Mary B. Sammon	10
Milton H. Thomas	1
Benjamin Thomas	1
James Tuggle	2
David Anderson	11
James Cates	2
James Highsaw	11
Mathew Henry	5
Rebecca Lee	18
Thomas Maguire	22
Daniel Minor	1
William M. Minor	2
Theophilus Simonton	1
James Sexton	5
Benjamin Weaver	2
Thos. Williams	3
John C. Whitworth	3
Mary Brandon	1
Mary Brandon	5
Elias Cannon	1
William Garmany	3
Hamilton Garmany	8
Elias Green	8
Green B. Harris	1
Buckner Harris	7
Madison R. Mitchell	19
Samuel Ritchie	11
Henry P. Thomas	5
Robert Underwood	10

Owners of Slaves in 1860

Rebecca Ashford	1
M. H. Adams	4
James Brown	3
Mary F. A. Brownlee	8
John A. Born	16
Wm. J. Born	2
Austin W. Cole	4
Joel F. Cash	1
Burton E. Crawford	2
Oliver Cosby	3
James R. Cosby	5
Elias Copeland	1

A. A. Chandler	1	Union Gholston	3
Thomas Dillard	8	Thomas Liddell	3
Elmire Goodwin	9	Nathaniel Reeder	4
Philo H. Gilbert	1	Moses W. Liddell	3
John A. Huff	4	Thomas H. Mitchell	4
James P. M. Harper	3	C. A. Mitchell	1
Wm. Langley	3	C. A. Mitchell (for minors)	19
M. Landley	1	Rachel Minor	6
Jas. L. Lamberth	1	Moses N. Cruse	1
Elmira L. Lewis	1	Eli J. McDaniel	16
Middleton B. Montgomery	17	L. A. McAfee	12
Jesse Osborn	11	Mary McAfee	2
Jesse M. Osborn	3	Charles McKinney	5
D. W. Pentecost	2	Lafayett McDaniel	7
Sara Pentecost	1	W. A. Massey	1
Henry Strickland	23	H. W. Mills	7
Isaac Strickland	24	Alfred Williams	23
Grant Taylor	2	Sara Akers	8
Elizabeth Wardlaw	5	R. M. Brandon	1
F. M. Wardlaw	5	S. S. Kelly	5
Thos. J. Waters	55	C. C. Langford	6
Wm. S. Woodall	1	A. Leitch	9
William Bonds	3	Henry Mathis	3
Ann A. Bonds	1	Charity Mathis	3
Wm. J. Drummond	8	D. P. McDaniel	6
S. H. Freeman	9	Sara McDaniel	6
Ferib (Ferth)	1	William Nesbit	11
Abel Griffin	4	A. C. Nesbit	14
Mary E. George	10	E. Pittard	7
R. M. Gower	9	G. W. Ambrose	9
Thomas Hunter	1	Elizabeth Atkinson	2
John Harbin	8	Meshack Bois	18
A. A. Hollis	1	Hardy Bennifield	5
Zachary Jackson	3	Robt. Bradford	4
Joseph Livsy	4	Wm. Bradford	2
Benjamin Rice	3	Miles Barnett	10
Ansley A. Tribble	6	George Craig	22
Nevias Vinyard	1	Benj. F. Carr	1
John C. Whitworth	7	Charles Carr	8
Mary Whitworth	1	John Carroll	21
W. E. Atkinson	5	Merritt Camp	2
Daniel Dunn	4	Robert Camp	6
J. J. Daniel	13	H. H. Dean	1
John W. Daniel	2	Jas. C. Dunlap	20
Catherine Gholston	9	T. W. Dunbar	2
Benjamin Gholston	2	Robert Goza	2
Philo Gholston	3	Geo. H. Hopkins	9

Evan Howell	72	Jeremiah Cleveland	1
Harvy Harris	7	Robert Craig	65
Henry Harris	9	Eliza Dunlap	5
J. R. Humphry	7	John P. Hutchins	21
J. W. Hamilton	1	W. H. Hardaman	8
James Garner	2	James Hood	4
John A. Jenkins	3	N. L. Hutchins	49
Thos. H. Jones	14	W. S. Harris	1
S. S. Kelly	4	W. F. Kennedy	2
Eli McDaniel	5	Jesse Lowe	1
J. O. Medlock	2	Benj. Lampkin	1
Thos. L. D. Medlock	3	M. L. Lenoir	12
Clara J. Marable	3	Wm. Minor	1
John Morrow	1	Elisha Martin	1
Moses McConnell	1	Tilford McConnell	2
J. A. Nunnally	4	John R. Moore	2
John Steele	2	A. A. Omburg	1
John Smith	1	Mary Nesbit	7
Jas. P. Simmons	7	Mary Orr	3
B. T. Thomas	4	Caroline Orr	1
A. B. Wright	4	Nancy C. Peeples	16
J. W. N. Williams	10	T. M. Peeples	1
John Winn	1	R. M. Parks	1
B. A. Blakey	7	Jesse Rambo	18
C. T. H. Cox	5	G. T. Rakestraw	2
W. P. Hunnicutt	7	Wm. Richardson	3
A. M. Hamilton	6	Wm. J. Russell	20
Robert Jenkins	5	Henrietta Strickland	4
James M. Liddell	4	Mary Stuart	4
Isabella Liddell	12	D. W. Spence	8
Thos. E. Mathews	2	E. D. Sammon	7
R. B. Martin	4	K. T. Terrell	3
Rebecca Massey	6	Wm. C. Wilson	2
James Thrasher	9	Jas. Waiter	1
Newton Waits	3	Brazil Waiter	1
Nathaniel Austin	17	R. D. Winn	17
T. W. Alexander	6	David Anderson	13
H. S. Bonds	1	A. A. Arnold	5
J. O. Bramblett	1	Patsy Adair	1
J. J. Bonds	8	William Adair	4
Anthony Bates	5	D. M. Byrd	10
John Beasley	2	E. L. Braswell	2
Newton Bramblett	3	Robt. Bagwell	7
J. B. Collins	1	Larkin Bagwell	6
Martha Corley	2	John Bankston	14
John E. Craig	25	W. D. Byrd	29
R. M. Cleveland	16	J. M. Cochran	27

Levi Cooper	30	Thos. Nash	1
Mathew Cooper	9	Walker Nash	3
John Carroll	2	John W. Nash	3
Rhoda Carroll	21	Lewis Nash	9
J. C. Carroll	4	T. D. O'Kelly	7
L. M. Cates	21	J. W. Plummer	14
J. W. Chamblee	2	R. D. Pounds	5
Reubin Donaldson	3	John Pounds	1
Seaborn Davis	12	D. R. Phillips	4
John Freeman	2	W. Parr	1
J. M. Flowers	1	Jas. S. Russell	16
James Flowers	13	N. P. Rawlins	4
A. Ford	2	W. B. Roberts	3
James Garner	1	Samuel Rawlins	12
Mathew Henry	9	James Sexton	1
R. H. Hannah	2	E. Steele	2
Perry Hudson	1	David Thomas	2
John Hudson	1	Sara Terrell	18
Thos. Hale	1	A. J. Veal	8
J. R. Henry	2	G. H. Weaver	3
Thos. P. Hudson	13	Geo. W. Wiley	2
A. G. Holmes	7	Mary P. Wisen	6
Mary Hutchins	6	Mrs. Wells	1
W. N. Irwin	3	W. W. Webb	31
Johnson Johnson	2	Washington Allen	6
Robt. Johnson	5	H. H. Andrews	2
Thos. Jacobs	5	A. Beall	10
S. W. Knox	4	John Clark	8
Major Knight	5	Buckner Harris	7
Rebecca Lee	19	J. L. Harrison	2
James Loveless	1	Winnie Horton	2
James Lester	6	J. D. Hood	2
Levi Loveless	4	Wm. Jackson	3
Thos. Maguire	26	Thos. W. Mitchell	1
W. P. Massey	1	W. F. Mitchell	1
Jas. L. Mecox	2	Milza Strickland	6
L. S. Moore	3	Elizabeth Williams	1
G. W. Minor	3	Wyatt Wilson	3
A. J. Minor	2	Wm. Baugh	10
Mark Miller	7	John Carroll	3
Chas. Mason	1	R. B. Echols	17
—. —. McDaniel	8	Delia O'Kelly	10
J. B. Mills	2	Thomas O'Kelly	5
Nathan Morrison	3	Benjamin O'Kelly	1
Daniel Minor	1	R. P. Weaver	3
Thomas Mathews	9	M. A. Armstrong	11
Samuel Martin	3	B. M. Bagby	2

W. F. Brogdon	8	Wm. A. Cain	16
H. G. Brogdon	12	John Cain	1
H. R. Brogdon	5	Joel N. Culver	8
Dan. D. Born	10	Levi Davis	1
W. R. Brogdon	4	L. D. Davis	7
Noah R. Brogdon	2	Hugh Duncan	6
George Brogdon	20	Washington Duncan	2
J. W. Baxter	7	Wm. Hunter	6
J. P. Brandon	12	Wm. Hunt	3
Thos. Carter	1	Archibald Hamilton	4
Burton Cloud	18	Mathew Hamilton	9
Saleta Doss	1	Wm. Jackson	83
J. R. Hargrove	2	Allen Jones	2
Kisiah King	11	Franklin Killian	9
Thos. Kile	5	Gilbert Lynch	5
Jacob Moulder	10	Elijah Maddox	1
Abram Moore	10	John Maddox	5
N. F. McElroy	4	Dudly Maddox	2
Wm. P. Moore	1	Robert Mitchell	4
Toliver Strickland	4	Sara W. Mills	3
Mathew Strickland	26	William Maltbie	10
William Sudderth	21	Milton Osborn	2
Allen Sudderth	1	Adam Pool	17
James R. Spiner	4	John Puckett	5
Adam Williamson	20	Mary B. Sammon	12
James Wheeler	3	Bryant E. Strickland	2
N. L. Adair	4	P. A. Sterling	13
Mary Brown	4	John T. Smith	5
Caroline Blakey	2	Lovic P. Thomas	2
Ira S. Bell	2	Henry P. Thomas	11
Manning Cain	4	James Tuggle	7
Nathan Clark	4	Wm. Wilson	1
Jas. Cain	4	Isaac M. Young	7

The 1850 census gave the following information about Gwinnett County: Dwellings, 1,600; number of families, 1,600; white males, 4,490; white females, 4,454; free colored males, 4; free colored females, 6; total white population, 8,953; total free negroes, 10; number of slaves, 2,294; deaths in county, 110; number of farms, 1,036; manufacturing enterprises, 26; 31 public schools with 31 teachers and an enrollment of 800 pupils; school income from taxation, $556; school income from other sources, $1,700; attendance in all schools, 1,186; illiterates in county, 869 white and 1 free colored; 1,227 working oxen; 2,611 houses; 403 mules; 3,286 milch cows; 6,820 sheep; 26,494 hogs; 108 pounds rice; 5,901 pounds tobacco; 2,531 bales of cotton of 400 pounds; 10,858 pounds of wool; 120 pounds of flax; 8,373 pounds of honey; real estate,

$977,693; total personal property, $1,440,125; 14 Baptist, 16 Methodist, and 3 Presbyterian churches, valued at $9,850, and accommodating 10,050 people.

The public places, not including Lawrenceville, were Auburn, Cains, Orrsville, Suwanee, Pinkneyville, Yellow River, and Choice's Store.

PLANTATIONS OF 500 OR MORE ACRES IN 1860

HARBINS
John T. Bonds	567
R. H. Bradford	600
Henry George	643
Robt. B. Camp	950
Merit Camp	640
W. I. Drummonds	875
R. M. Gower	587
John Harbin	660
Mastin Prewett	500
Asa B. Wright	770
John C. Whitworth	777

BERKSHIRE
Robt. J. Bagwell	600
Rhoda Carroll	915
Wm. Garner	500
G. H. Hopkins	596
Elizabeth Kelley	600
Mark Miller	1000
Thomas Mathews	508
Henry Mathews	500
Wm. F. Mitchell	625
Wm. Nesbit	650
Wm. S. Massey	500
Richard Pound	540
John Chamblee	862

HOG MOUNTAIN
Washington Allen	668
Daniel Born	576
Jas. C. Dunlap	750
N. F. McElroy	583
Abner R. Roberts	675
Wm. Wheeler	680

ROCKBRIDGE
David Anderson	670
Reubin Donaldson	675
Seaborn Davis	611

Mathew Henry	882
Richard Holt	882
Rebecca Lee	760
Thos. Maguire	956
David Rawlins	925
N. W. Rutledge	600

MARTINS
W. F. Atkinson	500
M. N. Cruse	508
Williamson Cruse	632
Jas. M. Liddell	600
E. J. McDaniel	625
W. A. Massey	600
R. R. Turner	517

CATES
J. W. Plummer	725
John Bankston	686
Jas. S. Russell	876
Daniel M. Byrd	1300
W. B. Roberts	850
Wm. Baugh	560
David Thomas	725
W. D. Byrd	680
Wylie W. Webb	2950
Levi Cooper	1750
M. J. Cochran	675
Robt. Echols	1670
Jas. Flowers	923
Thos. P. Hudson	562
A. G. Holmes	1000
Levi Loveless	650
Jas. Lanier	730
Jas. McDaniel	630
Lewis Nash	535
Benj. O'Kelley	725

BEN SMITHS
W. H. Adams	725

Oliver Cosby	500	Joseph P. Brandon	625
Thomas Dillard	700	John Born	2145
W. A. Hamilton	550	J. W. Baxter	625
Jesse Osborn	800	W. C. Jackson	516
John O. Perry	608	S. W. Knox	570
W. W. Pierce	600	M. B. Montgomery	500
W. W. Park	500	Wm. Montgomery	700
Sunberry Peppers	600	John R. Maffett	1200
		Henry Strickland	2118

PINKNEYVILLE

		Isaac Strickland	1754
M. Boyce	500	F. M. Wardlaw, admr.	1723
Miles Barnett	545	T. J. Waters	1300
John Carroll	1147	Jas. Wheeler	625
H. H. Dean	600		
Henly Harris	794	LAWRENCEVILLE	
Evan Howell	3000	P. A. Sterling	670
Thos. H. Jones	840	A. W. Bates	1174
John M. Pittman	500	J. P. Simmons	1300
		Robt. Craig	1600

SUGAR HILL

		John E. Craig	2233
J. R. Skinner	500	Geo. W. F. Craig	2655
George Brogdon	1235	K. T. Terrell	680
Wyatt Wilson	1175	S. H. Freeman	550
H. J. Brogdon	800	Sarah Terrell	1035
Adam Willianson	650	Buckner Harris	820
R. H. Brogdon	980	R. D. Winn	672
John Caloway	579	W. H. Hardman	718
Burton Cloud	650	Alfred Williams	1396
Saleta Doss	800	N. L. Hutchins	2283
Jacob Moulder	1132	M. L. Lenoir	590
Abram Moore	680	Wm. Maltbie	893
Jas. Roberts	665	Tilford McConnell	575
Wm. Sudderth	2922	Adam Robinson	501
Wm. Scales	1911	Jesse Rambo	510
Robt. Strickland	562	W. S. Russell	2700

GOODWINS

Mathew Strickland	1492	Mary B. Sammon	500

Number of Taxpayers and Slave Owners in the County in 1860, by Districts

HARBIN'S DISTRICT—Taxpayers, 162; slave owners, 26; per cent slave owners, 16.

BERKSHIRE DISTRICT—Taxpayers, 176; slave owners, 40; per cent slave owners, 28.

HOG MOUNTAIN DISTRICT—Taxpayers, 177; slave owners, 16; per cent slave owners, 9.

ROCKBRIDGE DISTRICT—Taxpayers, 124; slave owners, 16; per cent slave owners, 13.

MARTIN'S DISTRICT—Taxpayers, 137; slave owners, 29; per cent slave owners, 21.

CATES' DISTRICT—Taxpayers, 216; slave owners, 38; per cent slave owners, 17.

BEN SMITH'S DISTRICT—Taxpayers, 213; owners of slaves, 24; per cent slave owners, 11.

PINKNEYVILLE DISTRICT—Taxpayers, 141; slave owners, 31; per cent slave owners, 22.

SUGAR HILL DISTRICT—Taxpayers, 120; slave owners, 23; per cent slave owners, 19.

GOODWIN'S DISTRICT—Taxpayers, 100; slave owners, 26; per cent slave owners, 26.

LAWRENCEVILLE DISTRICT—Taxpayers, 268; slave owners, 63; per cent slave owners, 23.

Total taxpayers, 1,885; slave owners, 330; per cent slave owners, 17½.

They Paid A Tax of $1 or Less

In 1860 the number of taxpayers who paid a tax of not more than one dollar or less amounted to 927. The number by districts follows: Berkshire, 77; Ben Smith's, 122; Cates, 149; Goodwins, 43; Harbins, 73; Hog Mountain, 66; Lawrenceville, 140; Martin's, 65; Pinkneyville, 62; Rockbridge, 62; Sugar Hill, 62.

Total Property Value in 1860

Polls, 1,672; professions, 29; free negroes, 7; children between 6 and 18, 2,804; acres of land, 309,994; value of land, $1,680,791; value of town property, $78,926; number of slaves, 2,573; value of slaves, $1,782,724; money and solvent debts, $581,158; merchandise, $50,067; stocks and bonds, $50,400; ($50,000 of the former item was the cotton mill known as the Lawrenceville Manufacturing Company returned by Enoch Steadman); household and kitchen furniture, above exemption, $6,525; all other property, $477,744. Total property value, $4,694,404.

Enoch Steadman was the largest land owner, perhaps, that ever lived in Gwinnett County. He lived in Lawrenceville on the lot recently owned by L. M. Brand and for many years the property of the late Judge Sam J. Winn. He was connected with the cotton factory that stood just south of the Sam Craig residence.

In 1864 Enoch Steadman returned for taxation the following farm lands: Gwinnett County, 1,314 acres; Newton, 3,656 acres; Early, 7,664 acres; Carroll, 405 acres; DeKalb 252 acres; Towns, 4,400 acres; Paulding, 40 acres; Taylor, 202 acres; Lumpkin, 120 acres; Muscogee, 202 acres; Irwin, 512 acres; Appling, 409 acres; Dooley, 202 acres; Troup, 7 acres; other counties, 3,007 acres. Total, 22,392 acres.

Chapter VIII

THE CONFEDERATE STATES OF AMERICA

THE institution of slavery brought on the war between the North and the South. The election of Abraham Lincoln to the presidency of the United States was soon followed by the secession of South Carolina. The question of secession was discussed on every stump in Georgia. The legislature in November, 1860, passed a resolution, which was signed by Governor Brown, requiring the people of the state to vote for delegates on the following January 2nd, which delegates from every county in the state would assemble in Milledgeville two weeks later and, as a sovereign body, determine whether Georgia should remain in the Union or withdraw from it. The attention of the people of the county then turned to the election of delegates to this convention. It was a momentous issue that the people were called upon to settle. Gwinnett County elected James P. Simmons, a successful lawyer; Richard D. Winn, for many years a justice of the Inferior Court, and Thomas J. P. Hudson, a successful farmer and business man.

The convention assembled at Milledgeville at the appointed time and the delegates from Gwinnett County were in attendance and participated in its deliberations. Simmons, of Gwinnett, was especially active in all the proceedings of the convention.

Ordinance of Secession

Eugenius A. Nesbit, of Bibb, offered the following ordinance of secession:

"AN ORDINANCE

"To dissolve the union between the State of Georgia and other states united with her under a compact of government entitled 'The Constitution of the United States of America.'

"We, the people of the State of Georgia, in convention assembled, do declare and ordain, and it is hereby declared and ordained: That the ordinance adopted by the people of the State of Georgia in convention on the second day of January, 1788, whereby the Constitution of the United States of America was assented to, ratified and adopted; and also all acts and parts of acts of the General Assembly of this state ratifying and adopting amendments of the said Constitution, are hereby rescinded and abrogated. We do further declare and ordain that the union now subsisting between the State of Georgia and other states under the name of the United States of America is hereby dissolved, and that the State of Georgia is in the full possession and exercise of all those rights of sovereignty which belong and appertain to a free and independent state."

Simmons, Winn and Hudson, of Gwinnett, voted against this resolution or ordinance, but the ordinance was passed by a vote of 208 to 89.

Simmons, of Gwinnett County, offered then the following resolution, or protest, which was ordered spread on the journal of the proceedings of the convention:

"We, the undersigned delegates to the convention of the State of Georgia now in session, while we most solemnly protest against the action of the majority in adopting an ordinance for the immediate and separate secession of this state, and would have preferred the policy of cooperation with our southern sister states, yet as good citizens we yield to the will of a majority of her people as expressed by their representatives; and we hereby pledge 'our lives, our fortunes and our sacred honor' to the defense of Georgia, if necessary, against hostile invasion from any source whatever."

This resolution was signed by Simmons, of Gwinnett; Thomas M. McRae and F. H. Latimer, of Montgomery; Davis Whelchel and P. M. Byrd, of Hall, and James Simmons, of Pickens.

Once at war the county rallied to the call of the newly created Confederate States of America. Volunteers flocked to recruiting stations, donned uniforms, shouldered muskets, and went forward to meet the enemy. Under Morgan, Wheeler, Gordon, Jackson, Johnston, Lee and other great generals, Gwinnett's soldiers gave a good account of themselves and exemplified on many a battlefield that courage and that valor that are the proud possessions of every citizen of the county. County officials took immediate steps to give assistance to the families of soldiers left in destitute circumstances. This assistance was continued during the war as circumstances would permit. The purpose to render all possible aid to the needy was expressed in a resolution and an order of the Inferior Court as follows:

"Pursuant to a call made by several of our prominent and influential citizens, the people assembled at Lawrenceville on Tuesday, 7th of May, for the purpose of organizing a volunteer company, and for providing for the families of those who are called off to defend their county, and it was

"Resolved, That the Inferior Court be requested to borrow of whomsoever they can such sum of money as will in their judgment be sufficient to support the families of such soldiers as have volunteered or may volunteer hereafter in said county in their country's service, or to equip such volunteers as may need assistance for such purpose, provided, nevertheless, said fund shall in all cases be disbursed among such families aforesaid as are dependent for a subsistence upon the daily labor of such volunteers.

"Resolved, That said court be hereby requested to levy a tax for the purpose of paying the sum thus borrowed and that on the failure to borrow the same, they be requested to raise the amount by taxation, the volunteers in either case to be exempt from such taxation.

"Resolved, That said court be requested to appoint such committees as they may deem proper to disburse the sum thus raised.

"Resolved, That our senator and representatives in the next legislature be instructed to have passed an act legalizing said proceedings of the Inferior Court."

The Inferior Court immediately issued the following order:

"In pursuance of the above resolutions, it is ordered by the Court that a tax of fifty per cent be levied for the purposes named in said above resolutions. June 10, 1861."

       ADAM ROBINSON, J.I.C.
       JOHN MILLS, J.I.C.
       DAN'L. M. BYRD, J.I.C.
       W. B. BRACEWELL, J.I.C.
       W. F. KENNEDY, J.I.C.

Many prominent citizens of the county were officers in the Confederate armies. Brigadier-General Gilbert J. Wright was reared in the county. Colonel Lovic P. Thomas was a well known citizen who commanded the 42nd Georgia Regiment in the Battle of Atlanta. Others winning distinction were N. L. Hutchins, W. E. Simmons, S. J. Winn, Benjamin P. Weaver, G. T. Rakestraw, W. W. Parks, T. M. Peeples, J. T. Douglas, J. T. McElvaney, J. H. F. Mattox, T. E. Winn, and Moses Richardson.

COMPANY A, 42ND GEORGIA INFANTRY

Company A, Forty-Second Regiment, Georgia Infantry, was organized in Lawrenceville, March 4, 1862. The names of the officers and privates are given here:

OFFICERS

Captain, Lovic P. Thomas; 1st Lieutenant, Darling P. McDaniel; 2nd Lieutenant, Noah R. Brogdon; 3rd Lieutenant, John O. Medlock; 4th Lieutenant, Benjamin Gholston; 1st Sergeant, John M. Sexton; 2nd Sergeant, Thomas W. Mitchel; 3rd Sergeant, William Davis; 4th Sergeant, Hamilton Goza; 1st Corporal, A. M. Bramblett; 2nd Corporal, C. T. Shelnutt; 3rd Corporal, Erwin Smith; 4th Corporal, Russell Whaley.

PRIVATES

John Q. Allison, Junius H. Armstrong, James H. Arnold, Wiley F. Armstrong, Daniel G. Brogdon, Simon Berry, Shadric G. Brogdon,

Joseph T. Baxter, Charles G. Baker, John F. Baker, Findal Bell, Thomas J. Bennett, Thomas Braziel, John R. Bostwick, Marshall Bolton, Daniel J. Barnett, Stephen Burdett, John K. Barnett, William Burns, Philo Brooks, Larkin K. Bagwell, Samuel J. Burrell, George Burdett, George W. Brown, Sylvester Bolton, William H. Craig, James H. Culver, Mathew W. Culver, William H. Cole, Allen Carr, William M. Carr, C. C. Caldwell, David C. Cole, Bazel W. Davis, William P. Doss, Wilburn S. Defoor, Sanford M. Davis, William Everett, R. P. Forkerson, F. M. Forkerson, Harrison M. Gunter, Henry J. Ginn, William Grogan, James F. Garner, David T. Garner, Union Gholston, Andrew J. Garner, John Garner, John T. Hanson, William G. Haney, Elijah Hunter, William J. Ingraham, William F. Johnson, George H. Jones.

George Jones, Robert D. Jones, J. H. J. Jones, John C. King, Andrew J. King, Silas Kirby, Daniel Kaheley, Amos N. Kelley, Moses Martin, A. P. Martin, John M. Martin, Elijah Martin, Robert H. Munday, J. W. Morgan, Augustus S. Mahaffey, John V. Mewborn, H. M. Mewborn, W. L. McDaniel, F. L. D. Medlock, James R. Noel, G. W. Noel, S. L. Nunnally, Amos Parks, William I. Pruett, Thomas Phillips, John T. Pittard, J. M. Pittman, S. C. Pittman, William C. Ramey, C. G. Rowden, C. E. Ross, Sanford Roberts, Wilson Roberts, L. H. Roberts, J. H. Reynolds, James M. Roberts, Joseph W. Roberts, Carter E. Ross, Geo. M. Stephenson, Joseph Scales, V. K. Stevenson, John M. Singleton, R. C. Stevenson, John C. Smith, J. R. Stevenson, C. J. Shelnutt, J. K. Simmons, Emanuel Sudderth, Hosea C. Stanly, Wiley S. Townley, M. J. Townley, Robert H. Teague, James B. Whitworth, William B. Worsham, J. J. Wiggins, William K. Waldrip, H. F. M. Wilson, Hiram Wilson, Eli H. Whaley.

DEATHS

A. S. Mahaffey, Vicksburg, 6-20-63.
T. J. Bennett, Vicksburg, 7-14-63.
Allen Carr, Vicksburg, 7-17-63.
Mathew T. Culver, Vicksburg, 6-20-63.
Sanford M. Davis, home, 9-7-63.
A. J. Garner, Richmond, 7-30-63.
John T. Pittard, home, 8-18-63.
J. W. D. Ramey, Brookhaven, Miss., 5-12-63.
W. A. Ross, Enterprise, Miss., 5-20-63.
C. T. Shelnutt, Enterprise, Miss., 7-20-63.
M. J. Townley, Vicksburg, 8-5-63.
J. J. Wiggins, Vicksburg, 6-5-63.

COMPANY B, 42ND INFANTRY

This company was organized in Gwinnett County and left Yellow River March 10, 1862, and arrived at Camp McDonald, Georgia, the same day. It left this camp April 16, 1862, and arrived at Knoxville April 17, 1862. It left Knoxville, Tenn., April 23, at noon, and arrived at Cumberland Gap April 28, and was mustered in there May 19th.

Discipline was good. Instruction was defective owing to recent organization. Military appearance tolerably good. Arms, English muskets in good order. Accouterments and clothing good. Shoes issued to some at $2.50 per pair.

The company was mustered in at Vicksburg, Miss., April 30, 1863. Discipline, instruction and military appearance not very good, but improving. Arms, accouterments and clothing in good order.

Mustered in at Dalton, Georgia, December 11, 1863, Lieutenant W. H. Williams in command. Discipline, instruction and military appearance good. Arms and accouterments in good order. Much new clothing needed.

Events: Arrived at Vicksburg December 27, 1862. Engaged the enemy at Chickasaw Bayou December 28 and 29. Marched around and below Vicksburg, thence to Big Black River, thence to Baker's Creek, engaged in a fight on May 16, 1863. Marched from Baker's Creek to Vicksburg, getting back May 17 and remained during the siege and surrendered on July 4th. Paroled and departed, arriving at Mobile July 23. Furloughed home. Afterwards reported at parole camp at Decatur, Ga. Reorganized and left Decatur October 2 and joined Bragg's army at Chickamauga on October 4, then sent to East Tennessee, thence to Chickamauga Valley. Was engaged in the fight on Missionary Ridge, supported Anderson's battery at Rossville.

OFFICERS

Captain, Benjamin P. Weaver; 1st Lieutenant, Andrew Ford; 2nd Lieutenant, Wm. H. Williams; 3rd Lieutenant, Wm. P. Donaldson; 1st Sergeant, Jesse S. Bryan; 2nd Sergeant, James Garner; 3rd Sergeant, Wm. W. Russell; 4th Sergeant, Wm. S. Starr; 1st Corporal, Thomas McCart; 2nd Corporal, J. C. Crow; 3rd Corporal, James M. Henry; 4th Corporal, Joseph A. Hannah.

PRIVATES

John A. Austin, Wm. F. Arnold, Elsberry Andrews, Isaac D. Aderhold, Asa D. Aderhold, D. J. Brand, Ransom Brand, Wm. H. Bailey, I. W. Bennett, J. S. Bennett, John G. Bennett, A. P. Beaver, F. M. Buchanan, Henry H. Bracewell, John A. Betts, Milton Brownlee, John C. Brownlee, John W. Clower, John S. Cain, Elias Cannon, Elbert Collins, Wm. C. Cruse, G. W. Dutton, Leroy Freeman, George W. Freeman, James P. Freeman, James M. Flarity, John M. Franklin, Charles Green, William Gresham, D. J. Gattis, Milton N. Harris, Berry Hollingsworth, John J. Haney, George W. Haney, Stephen S. Haney, James Holt, A. A. Hewett, Wm. P. Hutchins, James G.

Herring, W. B. Jones, W. J. Jackson, Henry T. Johnson, Allen S. Jenkins, Charles King, John E. Kennerly, Wm. P. Kircus, J. L. Long, D. J. Liddell, D. M. Liddell, F. M. Lanier.

Miles J. Langley, S. P. Maughon, S. N. Martin, S. C. Martin, D. M. Martin, R. A. Mills, E. J. Mathews, W. S. Massey, W. V. Moore, Charles G. McGuffey, James L. McGuffey, D. M. McDaniel, John T. Nash, James B. Nash, Wilson D. Nichols, F. C. Okelly, W. S. Paden, S. W. Paden, D. J. Peters, W. S. Parr, W. P. Phillips, H. W. Robinson, John Rawlins, C. H. P. Rawlins, W. C. Richards, G. I. Smith, S. A. Starr, George Smith, J. W. Stapp, R. P. Smith, W. T. Smith, James Tallent, J. T. Williams, James S. White, C. W. Wilson, John W. Wilson, Thomas O. Wilson, George W. Wilson, Thomas Worthy, H. A. Worthy, M. M. Hale, J. R. Hale, D. M. Still, W. B. Mills, J. B. Mills, W. P. Thomason, B. C. Thomason, F. M. Thomason, John E. Craft, R. C. Betts, G. C. Smith, W. L. Pass.

DEATHS

The records show some interesting facts about the fate of the men in this company. The entries are from original documents.

Captain B. P. Weaver was killed in battle, Franklin, Tenn., November 30, 1864.

W. P. Kircus died in Lawrenceville, January 2, 1863. Pay to include August 31, 1862.

John G. Bennett died of wounds at Vicksburg, January 7, 1863. Paid up to August 31, 1862.

John E. Craft died of fever at Vicksburg January 20, 1863. Received no pay.

R. C. Betts died at Vicksburg January 28, 1863. Received no pay.

S. N. Martin died at Vicksburg January 30, 1863. Paid to September 1, 1862.

First Corporal John C. Crow died at Magnolia, Miss., February 10, 1863. Paid to October 31, 1862.

J. R. Hale died at Jackson, Miss., February 12, 1863. Received no pay.

John W. Wilson died at Vicksburg March 15, 1863. Paid to February 28, 1863.

Miles J. Langly died at Vicksburg March 15, 1863. Paid to February 28, 1863.

Thomas C. Brownlee died at Vicksburg March 27, 1862. Paid nothing.

Charles King died at Jackson, Miss., April 7, 1863. Paid to February 28, 1863.

H. W. Robinson died at Vicksburg April 12, 1863. Paid to February 28, 1863.

First Corporal W. P. Thomason died at Vicksburg June 2, 1863. Paid to February 28, 1863.

F. M. Lanier died at Montgomery July 26, 1863. Paid to April 30, 1863.

G. W. Freeman died at Montgomery July 29, 1863. Paid to May 1, 1863.

O. H. P. Rawlins died at Vicksburg July 19, 1863. Paid to May 1, 1863.

G. C. Smith died at Vicksburg July 30, 1863. Paid to May 1, 1863.

James S. White died at Vicksburg July 7, 1863. Paid to May 1, 1863.

Sergeant D. M. Martin died at St. Clair, Ala., August 20, 1863. Paid to May 1, 1863.

J. J. Haney died in Gwinnett County September 2, 1863. Paid to May 1, 1863.

W. P. Phillips died in Gwinnett County September 5, 1863. Paid to October 1, 1862.

G. W. Wilson died at Lawderdale Springs, Miss., August 20, 1863. Paid to March 1, 1863.

Sergeant W. W. Russell died in Gwinnett County November 14, 1863. Paid on hospital descriptive roll.

D. M. Still died at New Orleans hospital August 11, 1863. Paid to May 1, 1863.

W. J. Jackson died at Fort Delaware August 31, 1863. Paid to May 1, 1863.

M. N. Harris died at or near Raymond, Miss., July 22, 1863. Paid to May 1, 1863.

D. M. McDaniel died of fever at Morristown, Tenn., July 9, 1862.

B. F. Phillips died of measles at Strawberry Plaines, La., June 23, 1862.

H. T. Johnson died of typhoid at Beam's Station, Tenn., September 6, 1862.

W. R. Jones died of wounds at Walden's Ridge, Tenn., September 16, 1862.

W. S. Paden died of fever at Danville, Ky., October 6, 1862.

W. E. Cruce died of exposure at Beam's Station, Tenn., November 2, 1862.

C. W. Wilson died of fever at Lenoir's Station, Tenn., November 7, 1862.

J. B. Collins died of fever at Atlanta November 20, 1862.

W. L. Pass died of pneumonia at Atlanta December 10, 1862.

William C. Richards died in battle December 29, 1862.

T. O. Wilson died of fever at Readyville, Tenn., December 21, 1862.

J. W. Brewer left and supposed to be dead October 26, 1862.

John Rawlins was killed in battle December 29, 1862.

M. V. Moore died at Atlanta, of smallpox, January 20, 1864. He received pay up to November 1, 1863.

A. S. Jenkins was killed in battle at New Hope Church, Ga., June 4, 1864, and was paid up to November 1, 1863.

J. G. Herring died at Covington, Ga., June 6, 1864, having been paid up to March 1, 1864.

D. J. Peters died in Gwinnett County June 15, 1864.

B. A. Starr died at Covington, Ga., of fever, June 28, 1864. He received no pay from his enlistment to his death.

J. A. Betts died at Newnan, Ga., of fever, July 10, 1864. He received pay up to July 1, 1863.

J. T. Nash died at his residence in Gwinnett County August 18, 1864, and received pay up to May 1, 1863.

Berry Hollingsworth was killed in battle at Resaca, Ga., May 15, 1864. He had been paid up to November 1, 1863.

Corporal J. M. Henry was killed in battle at Resaca, Ga., May 15, 1864, and was paid up to November 1, 1863.

The book now in the possession of Mrs. May Roberts, daughter of Lieutenant Wm. H. Williams, in which the names of men in the company were kept, also shows the accounts of the soldiers. A few of such accounts are given as information:

D. M. Clower

1864

February 16—to one coat	$14.00
February 28—to one pair shoes	10.00
June 8—to one pair pants	12.00

J. W. Clower

March 13—to one pair drawers	$ 3.00

J. R. Britt

February 9—to one shirt	$ 3.00
February 16—to one pair pants	12.00
January 19—to one hat	2.00
January 25—to one coat	14.00
February 9—to one shirt	3.00
April 19—to one pair pants	12.00
April 19—to one pair drawers	3.00

Thomas McCart

1863

September 26—to one pair shoes	$ 5.00
December 22—to one coat	12.00
December 24—to one shirt	3.00
December 24—to one pair drawers	3.00
December 30—to one coat	12.00
December 30—to one pair pants	9.00

D. J. Liddell

June 2—to one hat	$ 4.75

November 3—to one pair shoes 5.00
December 6—to one coat 12.00

A. P. Beaver

October 13, 1863—to two shirts .... $ 6.00
October 13, 1863—to three pair drawers 9.00
November 3, 1863—to one blanket 10.00
December 10, 1863—to two caps 4.00
December 22, 1863—to one coat 12.00
December 29, 1863—to 1 pair drawers 3.00
December 30, 1863—to 1 pair pants 9.00

J. B. Nash

June 2, 1863—to one pair pants $12.00
November 3, 1863—to one blanket 10.00
December 10, 1863—to one pair pants 9.00
December 22, 1863—to one coat 12.00
December 30, 1863—to one pair shoes 5.00

J. E. Kennerly

December 10, 1863—to one cap .... $ 2.00
December 19, 1863—to one blanket 10.00
December 24, 1863—to one shirt 3.00
December 24, 1863—to one pair drawers 3.00
December 30, 1863—to one coat 12.00
December 30, 1863—to one pair drawers 3.00

COMPANY C, THIRD BATTALION
GEORGIA SHARPSHOOTERS

Company C, Third Battalion, Georgia Sharpshooters, was organized June 8, 1863, from members of older organizations of the Army of Northern Virginia by authority of an act of the Confederate Congress. Some of those named here were perhaps not citizens of Gwinnett County. Composed of veteran soldiers, the company required no preliminary training and plunged into some of the greatest battles of the war as a part of General Wofford's Brigade. It was engaged in the battles of Gettysburg, Chancellorsville, The Wilderness, Spotsylvania Court House, Front Royal, Farmville, Russellville, Tenn., Richmond, and surrendered with General Lee at Appomattox. The company lost heavily in killed, wounded and captured in most of these battles. Major William E. Simmons, of Lawrenceville, was captured August 16, 1864, at Front Royal, Va., sent to Old Capitol Prison, in Washington, and later to Fort Delaware, where he was released July 24, 1865, by order of the President. Lieutenant-Colonel Nathan L. Hutchins, Jr., of Lawrenceville, was captured April 6, 1865, at Sailor's Creek, Va., sent to the military prison at Johnson's Island, Ohio, and released July 25, 1865, upon taking the oath of allegiance.

The muster rolls of the Third Battalion, Georgia Sharpshooters, cover the period from June 8, 1863, to August 31, 1864. Just how many survived until the surrender at Appomattox April 9, 1865, is not known. Names of officers and privates are given here:

OFFICERS

Lieutenant-Colonel, Nathan L. Hutchins, Jr.

Captain, William E. Simmons, June 10, 1863, to October 18, 1863. Appointed Major.

Captain, Charlton H. Strickland, March 15, 1864, to October 22, 1864. Absent, wounded.

1st Lieutenant, Samuel H. Ware, June 10, 1863, to November 24, 1864. Dropped.

1st Lieutenant, William C. Muse, June, 1864, to April 6, 1865. Captured at Sailor's Creek.

2nd Lieutenant, Charlton H. Strickland, June 10, 1863, to March 15, 1864. Appointed Captain.

NON-COMMISSIONED OFFICERS

1st Sergeant, Thomas P. Nelms, May 6, 1864. Absent. Wounded at Wilderness, Va.

2nd Sergeant, Andrew J. Farril, April 9, 1865. Surrendered.

3rd Sergeant, Henry H. Butler, August 16, 1864. Wounded at Front Royal, Va.

4th Sergeant, Daniel H. Witcher, August 9, 1864. Died of wounds at Richmond.

5th Sergeant, Samuel Z. Dyer, April 6, 1865. Captured at Farmville, Va.

1st Corporal, John O. Collins, October 19, 1864. Absent. Wounded at Cedar Creek, Va.

2nd Corporal, James R. Beard, April 6, 1865. Captured at High Bridge, Va.

3rd Corporal, William P. Cosby, May 10, 1864. Absent. Wounded at Spotsylvania, Va.

4th Corporal, James W. Black, April 6, 1865. Captured at Sailor's Creek, Va.

PRIVATES

William M. Adair, July 4, 1865. Killed at Gettysburg.
James H. Braziel, April 6, 1865. Captured at Farmville, Va.
James H. Bullock, August 16, 1864. Captured at Front Royal, Va.
Joseph G. Burson.
John T. Clark, July 4, 1863. Captured at Gettysburg.
Seaborn A. Cone, April 6, 1865. Captured at High Bridge, Va.
Dudly C. Chandler, April 6, 1865. Captured at Farmville, Va.

General W. Davis, May 3, 1863. Absent. Wounded at Chancellorsville.
Samuel Davis, May 6, 1864. Absent. Wounded at Wilderness, Va.
James A. Davidson, July 11, 1863. Killed at Hagerstown, Md.
William Z. A. Doster, April 6, 1865. Captured at Farmville, Va.
James S. Fergurson, May 6, 1864. Absent. Wounded at Wilderness.
Willis W. Gholston, August 16, 1864. Captured at Front Royal.
Isaiah G. Grayham, August 16, 1864. Captured at Front Royal.
John H. Grayham, August 16, 1864. Captured at Front Royal.
William D. Grayham.
Elisha Herring, April 6, 1865. Captured at High Bridge.
Johnathan Johnston, April 6, 1865. Captured at High Bridge.
James W. Kirk, April 9, 1865. Surrendered with company.
Asa McMillan, April 6, 1865. Captured at High Bridge.
Andrew J. McWhirter, April 9, 1865. Surrendered at Appomattox.
William A. Martin, August 16, 1864. Captured at Front Royal.
Robert M. Moon, August 16, 1864. Captured at Front Royal.
George N. Morgan.
Dilmus Morris, August 16, 1864. Captured at Front Royal.
Walter G. Morris, February 15, 1865. Died in prison at Elmira, New York.
William C. Muse, August, 1864. Appointed First Lieutenant.
William B. Owens, May 6, 1864. Absent. Wounded at Wilderness.
Russell J. Porterfield, April 1, 1864. Died.
William S. Self.
Gilford Sartin, August 16, 1864. Captured at Front Royal.
Wade H. Slaton.
Pearson C. Smith, April 9, 1865. Surrendered at Appomattox.
Sanford Smith.
William D. Spence, August 16, 1864. Killed at Front Royal.
James E. Stephens, March 14, 1865. Died in prison at Elmira, New York.
Richard A. Vanderford, April 6, 1865. Captured at High Bridge.
James S. Watson.
William H. Witcher, April 9, 1865. Surrendered at Appomattox.
J. B. Arwood.
J. M. Barrett, June 30, 1864. Discharged as a minor.
John Carter, May 6, 1864. Absent. Wounded at Wilderness.
A. J. Gunnels, August 16, 1864. Captured at Front Royal.
T. R. Huff, December 10, 1863. Died in prison at Middle Brook, Tennessee.
P. R. Hutchins, April 9, 1865. Surrendered at Appomattox.
W. F. Phillips, August 16, 1864. Captured at Front Royal.

TROOP C, 10TH CAVALRY REGIMENT

The Tenth Cavalry Regiment, Georgia State Guards, was mustered into service July 18 to August 1, 1862, to serve six months from

August 1, 1863, in that portion of the State of Georgia from the lower part of Muscogee County on the Chattahoochee River and along the railroad to Macon and thence to the Savannah River at the lower part of Richmond County. Forty cents per day was allowed each soldier for use of his own horse. They were enrolled by Lt. Col. S. B. Wright at Lawrenceville.

OFFICERS

Captain, G. T. Rakestraw, age 46; 1st Lieutenant, E. J. McDaniel, 46; 2nd Lieutenant, B. A. Blakey, 37; 3rd Lieutenant, John Cain, 49; 1st Sergeant, James C. Dunlap, 47; 2nd Sergeant, R. S. Adair, 38; 3rd Sergeant, Wyatt Wilson, 45; 4th Sergeant, William Thrasher, 50; 5th Sergeant, Thomas D. Mathews, 43; 1st Corporal, J. H. Kimbrell, 45; 2nd Corporal, Charles McKinney, 45; 3rd Corporal, James W. Andrews, 29; 4th Corporal, James McDaniel, 51.

PRIVATES

L. J. Adair, age 45; J. F. Barnes, 45; W. J. Brooks, 26; J. W. Bailey, 45; B. J. Bailey, 47; J. J. Bonds, 45; John Boozer, 43; Tandy Brown, 39; E. C. Brown, 17; M. M. Bolton, 41; Jefferson Britt, 47; J. O. Bramblett; James R. Bracewell; Moses N. Cruse, 46; C. C. Caloway, 47; Joel N. Culver, 48; Burton Cloud, 45; Walton Camp, 45; W. W. Duck, 45; Thomas Dillard, 17; W. N. Duran, 39; B. B. Fields, 45; Twigs Forest, 45; Andrew Ford, 40; Joel Gossett, 63; Abel Griffin, 44; J. M. Gower, 17; W. F. Glawson, 45; Daniel Harris; S. B. Hay; Jesse Holden, 48; John Holt, 44.

N. P. Hotchkiss, age 45; Timothy Hanet, 45; T. P. Hudson, 30; John C. Harris, 39; William C. Harris, 34; Williamson Johnson, 47; Kinchin Jenkins, 53; E. B. Jordan, 45; Robert Johnson, 45; Willis E. Kilgore, 43; Elias N. Knight, 45; J. V. Langley, 46; Joseph Livsey, 44; J. J. Lee, 45; Thomas Lee, 22; Jesse McGee, 41; James L. Moore, 42; John Q. Massey, 42; Robert Medlock; R. M. Nash, 58; Richard D. Pounds, 44; Mastin Prewett, 55; John O. Perry, 38; James M. Patterson, 40; James W. Plummer, 52; R. M. Parker, 42; James A. Patillo, 35; William T. Perry, 17; J. M. Pheriby, 44; W. N. Pounds; John T. Rice, 19; W. T. Robinson, 17; H. T. Sells, 17; Manassa Sammon, 42; William Wheeler, 61; Mitchel White, 45; Reubin Wallace, 45; W. T. Yarbrough, 44.

COMPANY C, GWINNETT GUARDS

This company was mustered in at Lawrenceville by Lt. Col. S. B. Wright, August 1, 1863, for six months for duty on line north of Columbus, Macon and Augusta. These soldiers were called to active duty September 5, 1863. It was stationed at Atlanta, Rome and Savannah.

OFFICERS

Captain, Williamson W. Parks; 1st Lieutenant, Benjamin T. Thomas; 2nd Lieutenant, Charles McConnell; 3rd Lieutenant, Francis M. Wages; 1st Sergeant, T. C. Hardigree; 2nd Sergeant, F. L. Hearn; 3rd Sergeant, James H. Polk; 4th Sergeant, Samuel Cox; 5th Sergeant, W. N. Bates; 1st Corporal, John J. Wages; 2nd Corporal, George L. Bagwell; 3rd Corporal, G. W. Seymore; 4th Corporal, J. H. Elder.

PRIVATES

M. H. Adams, Robt. Boyd, Henry T. Betts, E. Boyd, Alfred Beaty, S. A. Clack, J. R. Davis, J. M. Davenport, David Ethridge, S. J. Ethridge, W. G. Edwards, Reuben Fowler, N. O. Gunnin, P. H. B. Gower, John Helton, Samuel Harrison, J. W. Hill, Columbus L. Jones, J. C. Jones, James Kilcrease, A. J. Kilgore, Elias W. Knight, Elijah Knight, Martin L. Knight, J. S. King, John King, Mathew Mobley, A. McDaniel, S. P. Mangum, Milton Osburn, James Polk, W. F. Phillips, —, —. Peavy, A. W. Puckett, Willis Phillips, John Peppers, J. A. Patillo, Sanford Peppers, G. A. Stewart, S. H. Simpson, Gilbert Simpson, G. H. Stewart, George W. Thomas, J. A. Timms, J. W. Timms, Andrew J. Wood, William A. Wilson, Dalton Willard, J. A. Wills, J. N. Wages, James W. Wilson, S. B. Wright.

BATTERY D, NINTH BATTALION GEORGIA ARTILLERY

Battery D, Ninth Georgia Battalion light artillery, known as Gwinnett Artillery, was organized April 23, 1862, and sent to Atlanta to guard government stores, awaiting the arrival of arms and equipment.

OFFICERS

Captain, Tyler M. Peeples; Senior 1st Lieutenant, William J. Born; Junior 1st Lieutenant, Thomas H. Loveless; 2nd Lieutenant, John T. Clower; 3rd Lieutenant, Robt. C. Montgomery, Jr.; 1st Sergeant, William A. Baxter; 2nd Sergeant, George T. Moore; 3rd Sergeant, Daniel A. Brooks; 4th Sergeant, Elsberry Holcomb; 5th Sergeant, Lewis P. Jackson; 1st Corporal, Stephen Ryle; 2nd Corporal, William W. Wilson; 3rd Corporal, Alonzo J. King; 4th Corporal, Andrew J. Abbott.

PRIVATES—149

John S. Atkinson, John T. Adair, James W. Adair, John M. Alexander, John L. Abbott, Mathew B. Abbott, James W. Adams, Joseph G. Barker, John R. Barker, William W. Born, Noah B. Brogdon, William R. Brogdon, Andrew J. Brown, Morgan S. Brown, Caleb A. Blake, W. F. Baily, Shelton Benson, Barton Barton, John H. Benefield, Jesse N. Brooks, Richard T. Brooks, George W. Brooks, Scott L. Baugh, James A. Bennett, Truman F. Barber, George W. Betts,

Daniel S. Cates, Hiram Clark, Archibald Clark, Samson Crumly, Benjamin F. Chesser, James D. Crumpton, George L. Chamblee, Mathew W. Chamblee, Pearson Duveau, Moses H. Duncan, Nelson Dollar, Willard I. Durham, William J. H. Davis, Van Davis, Meredith E. Edmondson, LeRoy Edmondson, William E. Ewing, John Ewing, Robert F. S. Ethridge, William F. Flowers.

R. Clinton Fields, William F. Forister, Norton Fountain, Geo. W. Frazier, Henry H. Frazier, James F. Griswell, Alford T. Green, George W. Green, Jesse A. Horton, Charles W. D. Horton, George R. Horton, Mathew M. Holcomb, Henry P. Holcomb, Elijah S. Holcomb, William B. Hay, Francis M. Hart, William F. Herrington, James I. Herrington, Jesse T. Herrington, George H. Hutchins, Joseph E. Hope, James F. Jackson, Henry M. Jackson, Mitchell H. Jackson, Charles M. Jackson, John Johnson, William T. Johnson, Andrew J. James, John W. James, Sanford M. Kemp, Jasper L. Kyle, Levi J. Loveless, Francis M. Loveless, Edmond I. Lowery, Elyah M. Lowery, Amon Lockridge, Francis M. Lockridge, Thomas N. Lockridge, Hugh B. Moulder, Singleton Moulder, James McConnell, Richard F. Morgan, William P. Moore, William B. Parks, David E. Pruett, Albert G. Pirkle, Andrew J. Pirkle, Richard N. Phillips, Le Roy Robinson.

James P. Sudderth, William H. Sudderth, Joseph E. Sudderth, Allen R. Sudderth, Hardy W. Strickland, Ephram Sizemore, Willia J. Segraves, Anderson G. Samples, Sexton Williams, Willis Venable, John L. Verner, Walton A. Williamson, John L. Wisdom, John D. Wilkenson, George Whitly, Richard Wheeler, James L. Wilson, Martin Leggett, William G. Smith, Pierce M. Wellborn, David W. Young, Christopher C. Young, Robert N. Maffett, John Neighbors, W. B. Payne, Tabner G. Roberts, W. B. Nicholson, Green M. Doss, William T. Craig, James K. Craig, Joseph W. Cox, Francis M. Brooks, James C. Brooks, Richard M. Bennett, William C. T. Read, John T. Edmondson, Gaston Green, John Hill, William R. Johnson, Patrick M. Kircus, Hugh A. Kenedy, Daniel W. Maddox, Henry C. McClung, William A. Mangum, John Murphy, Thomas Pruett, William Payne, Francis M. Robertson, James Ragan, James F. Robertson, Andrew J. Smith, Moses Swafford, William D. Thompson, John Tinney.

COMPANY E, EIGHTH INFANTRY, STATE GUARDS KNOWN AS GWINNETT GREYS

These soldiers were armed with Belgian rifles and swords, and were stationed at Lawrenceville August 1, 1863, and Savannah January 1, 1864.

The Gwinnett Greys were mustered in on August 1, 1863, by Lieut. Col. S. B. Wright at Lawrenceville for six months to serve north of a line from Columbus to Macon and to the Savannah River at the southeast corner of Richmond County.

OFFICERS

Captain, J. T. Douglas; 1st Lieutenant, B. M. Bagley; 2nd Lieutenant, J. M. Mills; 3rd Lieutenant, J. J. Benefield; 1st Sergeant, J. R. Maffett; 2nd Sergeant, T. J. Millican; 3rd Sergeant, R. A. Lockridge; 4th Sergeant, H. Maffett; 5th Sergeant, A. W. Bramblett; 1st Corporal, A. J. Atkinson; 2nd Corporal, J. A. Webb; 3rd Corporal, Willis Benson; 4th Corporal, A. J. Fielder.

PRIVATES

M. W. Armstrong, John Adair, E. F. Bagby, J. T. Benefield, W. H. Benefield, A. D. Braziel, J. H. Bailey, J. G. Brand, Newton Baker, William Bonds, J. A. J. Bailey, John Caloway, G. W. Christian, J. N. Cox, B. F. Carr, W. T. Christian, S. H. Durham, Nelson Dollar, Morgan Fields, W. J. Hay, J. A. Horton, T. W. Horton, S. B. Haney, G. B. Hopkins, J. G. Jackson, A. H. Jackson, Nelson Joyce, William Langley, J. W. Langley, Reuben Long, J. S. Mitchel, Pinkney Mathews, George W. Minor, J. A. Martin, Pittman Martin, Wiley Plunkett, Samuel Pugh, William Pugh, Isaac Petty, W. N. Pounds, James Pruett, J. T. M. Rider, A. B. Roberts, W. B. Roberts, J. J. Townley, J. R. West, G. J. White, Thomas Wright, A. Young.

COMPANY F, 35TH GEORGIA REGIMENT

This company was organized in Gwinnett County September 23, 1861, and became a part of the Thirty-fifth Georgia Regiment. Company H, organized in Gwinnett and Hall, was a unit of the same regiment. There were eight other companies in the regiment, one each from Haralson, Newton, Campbell, Troup, Heard, Walton, Harris and Chattooga counties.

After the regiment was organized it was assigned to the brigade of Brigadier-General French and stationed at Evansport, Va., supporting river batteries until early in March, 1862, when it followed the Army of the Potomac to the line of the Rappahannock and was stationed near Fredericksburg. Here Brigadier General J. J. Pettigrew assumed command of the brigade, participated in the removal to the Peninsula, formed part of the reserve under Major General G. W. Smith, who brought the rear in the retreat from Yorktown. It was engaged in the battle at Seven Pines, May 31, 1862, being part of the force that attacked the right of the enemy forces. Lieutenant Colonel G. A. Bull was killed in this engagement.

This regiment formed part of Brigadier General Anderson's force and under the command of Colonel Edward L. Thomas accompanied that brigade in its charge on the position of the enemy at Mechanicsville, June 26, 1862, maintaining the unequal conflict until night. Adjutant J. H. Ware, Company K, was killed, and Col. Edward L. Thomas and his nephew, Captain Lovic P. Thomas, were among those who were wounded.

In other engagements around Richmond the brigade was commanded by Captain W. L. Groover, of Company I. During the latter part of July, Hill's Division was transferred to Jackson's command and under the command of Major Bolling H. Holt. The rest of the regiment was on the extreme right of the line at the battle of Cedar Run August 9, 1862. This was the first field fight in which the regiment was engaged. It performed its duty nobly and repelled every attempt of the enemy to turn the right flank. This victory was hailed with rejoicings throughout the South.

In Stonewall Jackson's famous campaign following this battle, the regiment accompanied Thomas' brigade to Manassas and witnessed the destruction of trains captured there by General Stewart, marched to Centreville, retraced its steps to Manassas, formed there in line of battle, supported General Ewell's Division in action on August 31, 1862, and on August 29, occupied a position on the railroad, sustained the assault of the enemy in front until late in the evening when the enemy broke through a gap in the line, flanked and forced the brigade to retreat a short distance. The regiment soon rallied and accompanied Pinder in his splendid charge on that day. On the following day it was again in line of action and advanced, driving the enemy from the field.

At Ox Hill the regiment was not engaged. At Harper's Ferry it supported Pinder, who entered the town at once after its surrender. He remained there three days to guard vast quantities of military stores that were captured. It was on guard at Shepherdstown, assisted in destroying the B. & O. Railroad, near Harper's Ferry, picketed at Snickers Gap, then marched to Fredericksburg and took an active part in the repulse of General Burnside's army December 13, 1862.

During this period Colonel Edward L. Thomas was promoted to Brigadier General, Major Holt to Colonel, Captain McCullough to Lieutenant Colonel, and Captain Groves to Major.

The winter was spent at Guinea Station, Va. With the coming of spring, General Hooker crossed the Rappahannock and was fortifying within twelve miles of the Army of Northern Virginia. Such audacity must be punished. On May 3, 1863, Captain Duke took part in the battle of Chancellorsville, charged the enemy, drove them back more than a mile, took their breastworks and captured many prisoners.

After the death of Stonewall Jackson, Major General A. P. Hill succeeded to Jackson's army. Early in June, 1863, Hooker's army crossed to the east bank of the Rappahannock. In the meantime Lee's army was on the march into Pennsylvania and engaged the enemy at Gettysburg. The world knows about this battle. Pickett's charge was the great event of that engagement. On July 5th, the old regiment of Gwinnett volunteers left Pennsylvania and returned to Virginia, and in various engagements sustained itself with honor. In addition to the losses tabulated below, there were many disabled by wounds but not discharged, and many missing, making the total losses more than two-thirds of all who composed the Thirty-fifth Georgia Regiment.

OFFICERS

Captain, J. T. McElvany; 1st Lieutenant, T. J. Davis; 2nd Lieutenant, W. M. Rawlins; 3rd Lieutenant, J. B. Williams; 1st Sergeant, J. J. McDaniel; 2nd Sergeant, J. F. Pruett; 3rd Sergeant, H. J. Coon; 4th Sergeant, W. B. Harbin; 5th Sergeant, J. A. Jordan.

R. M. Rawlins was elected captain of this company at its organization, but his name does not appear in the list of officers or the list of privates. He was killed in the seven days' fighting around Richmond in the latter part of June, 1862, and James T. McElvany was promoted to captain.

PRIVATES

James Allen, Thomas V. Allen, Presley M. Allen, Alfred Brand, David J. Brand, G. W. Brand, Wilson Brand, Jonathon Brand, G. M. Brand, W. M. Brewer, G. W. Brewer, W. H. Brewer, J. A. Brewer, R. D. Benefield, H. J. Benefield, James Benefield, Robert Benefield, G. W. Bailey, W. R. Bond, Phillip A. Brooks, H. F. Herring, William Herring, Thomas Hawkins, William Harris, J. J. W. Herring, D. B. Holt, Wilson Herring, Wm. J. Jones, Warren Jones, W. A. Jones, R. D. Johnson, John A. Jordon, James T. Jordon, A. S. Jenkins, W. J. Knight, T. B. Knight, Thomas J. Knight, Jesse Knight, John T. Knight, Robert Knight, J. H. Knight, J. N. Knight, T. W. Knight, W. R. Knight, G. T. Kirk, George Kirk, Robert T. Livesey, J. H. P. Born, S. B. Boggs, William Boggs.

William T. Brown, Alvin Bryant, James Bryant, Joshua Bradford, George A. Campbell, J. B. Campbell, Joseph D. Campbell, John Cowsart, Robert Camp, Henry Coon, David Cofield, J. G. L. Dutton, James Dutton, Henry Davis, Richard P. Ellis, W. H. Ellis, Jasper Estes, Newton Estes, Cicero Estes, Samuel J. Ewing, James Freeman, R. D. B. Holt, William Holt, Stephen Humphries, Wiley B. Harbin, William Harbin, J. R. Harbin, J. H. Kirk, N. G. Knight, Enoch Langley, Oswell T. Langley.

David S. Lanier, Robert T. Livesey, Marcus M. Minor, A. M. Minor, William Minor, D. Robert McDaniel, John McCart, John J. McDaniel, James McDaniel, William A. McElvaney, J. A. Newson, John Newson, John Nix, Bradley Nash, I. J. Petty, H. J. Price, John F. Pruett, David Pruett, James P. Phillips, John S. Plummer, James Plummer, David S. Rawlins, James A. Rawlins, William J. Rawlins, J. Samuel Rawlins, W. H. Rawlins, S. F. Rawlins, Isham G. Rawlins, J. A. Stevens, James C. Summerlin, Syrenus D. Summerlin, Williamson L. Sexton, J. H. Stevens, Bradley H. Stevens, Samuel

H. Starr, Joseph Smith, George Smith, David Thomas, Henry W. Thomas, Patrick W. Wiley, J. S. Wilder, James O. Whitworth, John C. Whitworth, Daniel Williams, J. J. Wright, S. J. Wright, Harris Wade, John B. Williams.

TABULATION

	Killed	Wounded
Seven Pines	23	50
Mechanicsville	18	61
Battles around Richmond	3	13
Cedar Run	9	17
Second Manassas	18	55
Ox Hill	0	2
Harper's Ferry	0	4
Shephardstown	0	9
Fredericksburg	14	41
Chancellorsville	8	27
Gettysburg	9	53
Mine Run	0	2
Wilderness	4	22
Spotsylvania	10	37
Jerico Ford	10	28
Haynes Shop	2	6
Petersburg	0	3
Total	128	429

Entire losses from deaths, wounds, disease, discharge, transfer and desertions were 660.

COMPANY F, 24TH GEORGIA INFANTRY
THE INDEPENDENT BLUES

G. W. Maffett, clerk of the Inferior Court, placed on record in the minutes of the court immediately following these words: "Recorded 9th October, 1861," the muster roll of the Gwinnett Independent Blues. The muster roll follows just as recorded in Record C of the Inferior Court of Gwinnett County:

OFFICERS

Captain, J. H. F. Mattox; 1st Lieutenant, T. E. Winn; 2nd Lieutenant, A. Robinson; 3rd Lieutenant, W. W. Brand; 1st Sergeant, N. F. McElroy; 2nd Sergeant, James M. Patterson; 3rd Sergeant, G. Harris; 4th Sergeant, T. L. Harris; 1st Corporal, R. W. Martin;

2nd Corporal, A. W. Wardlaw; 3rd Corporal, William Bradberry; 4th Corporal, H. Davis.

PRIVATES

J. A. Adams, R. W. Bradford, I. N. Bramblett, H. G. Brown, William Brown, W. H. Bradford, F. M. Beavers, A. W. Bramblett, S. P. Burnett, E. G. Burnett, H. S. Bonds, Wiley J. Baggett, R. F. Brown, D. P. Cross, Wm. Cofield, David Childers, B. F. Childers, W. C. Cole, W. R. Chandler, J. F. M. Cain, W. S. Durham, J. Dukes, J. B. Davis, John Davis, Levi Daniel, W. D. Deaton, Hugh Duncan, Jr., J. M. Deaton, M. E. Ewing, Thos. A. Ethridge, Joseph Ewing, W. M. Forester, J. M. Gower, John W. Gouge, R. T. Higgins, M. E. Higgins, Jesse Holder, H. Hawkins, Isaac Hamilton, Allen Jacobs, James Kimbro, J. W. Blackburn, A. B. Kilgore.

J. D. Kinnett, John Henry Kemp, R. T. Lowe, J. N. Lowery, R. A. Lamkin, C. W. D. McHugh, J. N. McDaniel, Samuel Morgan, T. K. Mitchell, Q. E. Mattox, S. Massey, J. M. Mitchell, Jas. A. Moulder, J. W. McHugh, George McMillan, A. M. Massey, J. R. Mayne, John P. Mackin, B. C. Pirkle, G. W. Pharr, Thomas Price, W. L. Robinson, J. B. Rice, Thomas Sparks, J. M. Smith, W. M. Stewart, W. B. Sherwood, R. R. Stewart, C. Thompson, J. Tullis, K. T. Terrell, A. M. Winn, S. P. Wardlaw, D. H. G. Wardlaw, J. W. White, J. C. Whitworth, M. D. Whitworth, G. B. Wigley, G. S. Vineyard, E. A. Ivey.

Below follows a more complete muster roll and history of the Independent Blues as gathered from official records in Washington by George W. Jacobs:

The Independent Blues was the third company organized in Gwinnett County, originally commanded by Captain John H. F. Mattox. The company was later designated Company F, 24th Georgia Infantry. This company was organized August 24, 1861, all members being enlisted for the duration of the war, and was stationed at Washington, N. C., October 31, 1861.

The company was commanded successively by Col. Robert McMillan, of Clarkesville, Ga., from August 24, 1861, to January 9, 1864, when he tendered his resignation on account of his failure to be promoted to the position of Brigadier General, and then by Col. C. C. Sanders, of Homer, Ga., from January 9, 1864, to April 6, 1865, when he was captured at Sailor's Creek, Va., and sent to a prison in the North.

Thomas E. Winn represented Gwinnett County on the company's staff as First Lieutenant and Captain of Company F and was then promoted to Major on May 6, 1864, and then to Lieutenant Colonel on September 20, 1864.

Dr. Tandy Key Mitchell, of Lawrenceville, enlisted as a private in this company August 24, 1861, and was at once placed on duty as physician in the Regimental Hospital. He was appointed assistant surgeon of the regiment on January 4, 1862, and continued as such until General Lee surrendered at Appomattox April 9, 1865. Others on the staff from Gwinnett County included Kennan T. Terrell, who was promoted from private in Company F, on September 14, 1861, to Acting Commissary Sergeant with the rank of Captain and continued as such until April 15, 1862, when he resigned. Ensign John C. Whitworth was another officer from Gwinnett County, whose promotion from First Corporal of Company F was recommended June 24, 1864, for having carried the Colors of the Regiment with distinguished gallantry and bravery from May 7, 1864. He was killed in action October 19, 1864, at the battle of Cedar Creek, Va.

This regiment was attached to General Lee's army, known as the Army of Northern Virginia, during the entire war. The Gwinnett soldiers, therefore, were in many of the great battles of the war. The fall and winter of 1861 was spent at Washington, N. C. Then in March, 1862, they were at Suffolk, Va., and at Yorktown a little later. In May they moved on to Richmond. In the early fall General Lee crossed the Potomac River and campaigned in western Maryland. This company lost several men killed, wounded and captured at Crampton's Gap, on South Mountain, and at Antietam September 14th and September 17, respectively, and at Sharpsburg, Md., September 20, 1862. The company recrossed the Potomac at Shepherdstown, W. Va., and remained in the vicinity of Winchester, Va., until October 31, 1862, when it marched to Culpepper, and in three weeks marched to Fredericksburg. The company took part in the battles at Fredericksburg, December 11 and 13, 1862; Chancellorsville, May 3, 1863; Gettysburg, July 3, 1863; Cold Harbor, June 1, 1864; Front Royal, August 16, 1864; Cedar Creek or Strasburg, October 19, 1864. A considerable number from the company were captured in 1865 at Sailor's Creek, Farmville, and Burkesville, Va., and what was left surrendered April 9, 1865, with General Lee at Appomattox Courthouse, Virginia.

It may be of interest to note the salaries the Confederate officers received. Colonels received $195 per month; Lieutenant-Colonels, $170; Majors, $150; Captains, $130; First Lieutenants, $90; Second Lieutenants, $80; First Sergeants, $20; Sergeants, $17; Corporals, $13; Privates, $11.

COMMISSIONED OFFICERS

Captain John H. F. Mattox, August 24, 1861, to August 12, 1862. Resigned.

Captain Thomas E. Winn, August 19, 1862, to May 6, 1864. Promoted to Major.

Captain Edward B. Thomas, May 6, 1864, to April 9, 1865. Surrendered.

1st Lieutenant Tom E. Winn, August 24, 1861, to August 19, 1862. Promoted to Captain.

1st Lieutenant Jas. M. Mitchell, September 5, 1862, to October 15, 1862. Died.

1st Lieutenant Wm. M. Stewart, October 15, 1862, to July 2, 1863. Killed at Gettysburg.

1st Lieutenant Richard W. Martin, August 27, 1863, to November 14, 1864. Dropped.

1st Lieutenant Francis M. Beaver, November 14, 1864, to April 9, 1865. Surrendered.

2nd Lieutenant Adam Robinson, August 24, 1861 to April 1, 1862. Resigned.

2nd Lieutenant Jas. M. Patterson, August 6, 1862, to February 2, 1863. Resigned.

2nd Lieutenant Francis M. Beaver, February 2, 1863, to November 14, 1864. Promoted to 1st Lieutenant.

2nd Lieutenant James M. Deaton, November 14, 1864, to —.

3rd Lieutenant William W. Brand, August 24, 1861, to November 30, 1861. Resigned.

3rd Lieutenant Nathan F. McLeroy, December 1, 1861, to October 26, 1863. Died in prison.

NON-COMMISSIONED OFFICERS

1st Sergeant Nathan F. McLeroy, December 1, 1861. Appointed 3rd Lieutenant.

2nd Sergeant Jas. M. Patterson, August 6, 1862. Appointed 2nd Lieutenant.

3rd Sergeant George W. Harris.

4th Sergeant, Tyre L. Harris.

5th Sergeant George McMillan.

1st Corporal Richard W. Martin, August 27, 1863. Appointed 1st Lieutenant.

2nd Corporal Alfred W. Wardlaw, February 19, 1863. Died of disease at Lynchburg.

3rd Corporal William Bradberry, November 28, 1861. Discharged for disability.

4th Corporal, Harman Davis, December 18, 1861. Discharged for disability.

PRIVATES

John A. Adams, October 31, 1861. Captured and took oath.

Edward G. Burnett, June 1, 1864. Captured at Cold Harbor, Va.

Samuel P. Burnett.

William Brown, September 10, 1861. Rejected.

Hamilton G. Brown, April 6, 1865. Captured at Farmville, Va.

Wm. J. Brown, June 2, 1862. Captured.

Robert F. Brown. Detailed as Regimental Commissary Sergeant.

Robert W. Bradford.

Isaac N. Bramblett.

John W. Blackburn.

Augustus W. Bramblett, August 14, 1862. Discharged for disability.

HISTORY OF GWINNETT COUNTY, GEORGIA

Francis M. Beaver, February 2, 1863. Appointed 2nd Lieutenant.
Hillary S. Bonds.
Wiley J. Baggett, August 8, 1862. Died at Richmond.
Wm. H. Bradford, July 25, 1862. Discharged for disability.
Samuel T. Bracewell, April 13, 1862. Died of disease at home.
Perry G. Bracewell.
William C. Cole, August 1, 1862. Discharged for disability.
Wm. R. Chambly.
John F. M. Cain, October 19, 1864. Captured at Strasburg, Va.
Daniel P. Cross, February 18, 1863. Died at Fredericksburg.
William Cofield, February 1, 1862. Died at Washington, N. C.
David Childers, April 12, 1862. Discharged—over-age.
Benjamin F. Childers, October 14, 1862. Died of wounds at Fredericksburg.
Joel B. Davis, September 14, 1862. Killed at Crampton's Gap, Md.
Levi Daniel, November 29, 1861. Died of disease at Washington, N. C.
Hugh Duncan, July 25, 1862. Discharged for disability.
John M. Davis, June 6, 1864. Killed at Richmond.
Wm. D. Deaton.
James M. Deaton, November 14, 1864. Appointed 2nd Lieutenant.
John Duke, August 16, 1864. Captured at Front Royal, Va.
Wm. S. Durham, March 24, 1862. Discharged for disability.
Joseph Ewing, July 25, 1862. Discharged for disability.
Miles E. Ewing, June 1, 1864. Captured at Cold Harbor, Va.
Thos. A. Ethridge, March 24, 1862. Discharged for disability.
Wm. M. Forrester.
John George.
John M. Gower, October 14, 1864. Retired to Invalid Corps.
Isaac Hamilton, July 7, 1862. Died at Richmond.
David Harris, August 16, 1864. Captured at Front Royal, Va.
Hosea Hawkins, May 6, 1864. Killed at Wilderness, Va.
Marion E. Higgins, July 13, 1862. Died of disease at Petersburg.
Reubin T. Higgins, June 3, 1862. Discharged.
Jesse Holder, April 12, 1862. Discharged for disability.
Edmund A. Ivey.
Allen T. Jacobs, July 27, 1862. Discharged for disability.
John H. Kemp.
Joshua D. Kennett, November 8, 1862. Died of disease at Lawrenceville, Ga.
Berry A. Kilgore, June 1, 1864. Captured at Cold Harbor, Va.
James Kimbro, April 12, 1862. Discharged for disability.
Robt. A. Lampkin.
John N. Lowery.
Richard T. Lowe, June 7, 1864. Died in prison at Rock Island, Ill.
John P. Mackin, July 25, 1862. Died of wounds at Richmond.
Affanacius Massey, April 6, 1865. Captured at Farmville, Va.

Sylvester Massey, June 26, 1864. Died of wounds at Richmond.
Quincy E. Mattox, May 28, 1862. Died of disease at Richmond.
James A. Mauldin, January 8, 1865. Died in prison at Elmira, N. Y.
Jas. R. Mayner, December 18, 1861. Discharged for disability.
James N. McDaniel.
Chas. W. D. McHugh.
John W. McHugh, May 12, 1864. Killed at Petersburg, Va.
Samuel Morgan, July 18, 1863. Died at Hagerstown, Md.
James M. Mitchell, September 5, 1862. Elected 1st Lieutenant.
Tandy K. Mitchell, January 4, 1862. Appointed assistant sergeant.
Chas. T. Parrish.
Benj. C. T. Pirkle, May 11, 1862. Died at Richmond.
George W. Pharr, October 19, 1864. Captured at Strasburg, Va.
Thos. J. Price, September 10, 1861. Rejected.
James B. Rice.
William T. Robinson.
William B. Sherwood.
John M. Smith, December 18, 1861. Discharged for disability.
Thomas Sparks, June 1, 1864. Captured at Cold Harbor, Va.
Robt. R. Stewart, October 10, 1862. Discharged for minority.
Wm. M. Stewart, October 15, 1862. Elected 1st Lieutenant.
Chas. W. Thompson, April 12, 1862. Discharged for disability.
Wm. J. Tullis, July 23, 1862. Died of disease at Richmond.
Geo. S. Vineyard, April 6, 1865. Captured at Farmville, Va.
David H. G. Wardlaw, October 1, 1862. Died of wounds at Burkittsville, Md.
Saml. P. Wardlaw, May 6, 1864. Killed at Wilderness, Va.
James W. White.
John C. Whitworth, June 24, 1864. Appointed Ensign.
Mathew D. Whitworth, May 23, 1862. Died at Richmond of disease.
Green B. Wigley, June 26, 1862. Discharged for disability.
Archibald M. Winn.
Kennan T. Terrell, September 14, 1861. Appointed Captain.
Jonathan Potts, December 18, 1861. Discharged for disability.
A. J. Anderson, July 1, 1862. Killed at Malvern Hill, Va.
Wm. H. Arnold.
Nathaniel Bailey.
Wm. J. Bailey, May 6, 1862. Died at Richmond.
James Bradford, April 9,1865. Surrendered with company.
F. A. Bonds.
John M. Bonds, January 26, 1863. Transferred to G 29th Georgia Infantry.
J. W. Bonds, January 26, 1863. Transferred to G, 29th Georgia Infantry.
William Bonds.

HISTORY OF GWINNETT COUNTY, GEORGIA 211

Joseph Brewer, June, 1864. Died at home.
W. F. Brewer, July 12, 1864. Retired to Invalid Corps.
John A. Brewer, May 16, 1862. Died at Richmond.
Washington Bradford, December 18, 1861. Discharged for disability.
Wm. M. Brown, July 2, 1863. Captured at Gettysburg.
Randal J. Burel.
Cicero C. Cain, August 16, 1864. Captured at Front Royal, Va.
Clinton M. Cain, March 1, 1862. Discharged.
J. H. Camp, April 9, 1865. Surrendered with company.
F. E. Childers, September 14, 1862. Captured at Crampton's Gap, Md.
Ira A. Corbin, April 6, 1865. Captured at Burkville, Va.
James Crenshaw, May 24, 1862. Died in Richmond.
C. C. Cross. Retired to Invalid Corps.
W. H. Cross, June 30, 1863. Died in Hall County, Ga.
Z. N. Cross, March 30, 1865. Retired to Invalid Corps.
G. H. Davis, April 9, 1865. Surrendered with company.
James Davis.
Joel M. Davis.
Samuel Davis, June 2, 1862. Died at Richmond.
Samuel M. Davis, June 15, 1862. Died.
Ely J. Deaton.
McDonald Deaton, August 16, 1864. Captured at Front Royal, Va.
Anderson Delashaw, July 2, 1863. Captured at Gettysburg.
R. H. Duncan.
Samuel Glaze, July 27, 1862. Died of disease at Richmond.
Wm. M. Glover, December 24, 1862. Died of disease at Lynchburg.
W. P. Glover.
John W. Gouge.
Wm. E. Gower, April 6, 1865. Captured at Burkville, Va.
A. W. D. Gower, September 17, 1862. Captured and died at Antietam, Md.
J. B. Gunter.
J. P. M. Hadaway, November 11, 1864. Died in prison at Elmira, N. Y.
W. R. Hadaway, August 16, 1864. Captured at Front Royal, Va.
E. D. Hayes.
David Holman, June 1, 1864. Captured at Cold Harbor, Va.
J. G. Hurst, August 16, 1864. Captured at Front Royal, Va.
Obediah Copeland, April 6, 1865. Captured at Burkville, Va.
H. J. Jackson.
J. C. Jones, April 6, 1865. Captured at Farmville, Va.
Wm. Kimbro, September 29, 1864. Died in prison at Elmira, N. Y.
Harrison Mattox.

Nathan Mattox, September 20, 1862. Died of wounds at Sharpsburg, Md.
S. P. McHugh.
J. N. Pharr, October 19, 1864. Captured at Strasburg, Va.
Andrew S. Puckett, May 14, 1863. Died of wounds at Richmond.
James S. Puckett, April 6, 1865. Captured at Sailor's Creek, Va.
John H. Puckett, November 2, 1862. Died at home.
P. A. Puckett.
S. M. Porter.
Joshua J. Pruett, September 12, 1862. Discharged for disability.
J. R. Ramey.
H. J. Robertson, April 9, 1865. Surrendered with company.
D. B. Stanford, April 9, 1865. Surrendered with company.
H. S. Stanford, August 16, 1864. Captured at Front Royal, Va.
A. N. Stephens, September 14, 1862. Killed at Crampton's Gap, Maryland.
Joseph A. Stephens.
George Sparks, April 9, 1865. Surrendered with company.
M. C. Stone.
C. N. Segraves, August 16, 1864. Captured at Front Royal, Va.
Wm. T. Mauldin, May 22, 1862. Died at Richmond.
S. F. Taylor, September 2, 1864. Retired to Invalid Corps.
William Tinney, August 9, 1862. Died of disease at Richmond.
S. P. Vineyard, September 14, 1862. Left in battle, Crampton's Gap, Md.
W. M. McDaniel, June 3, 1864. Captured.
J. A. Whiteby, June 3, 1864. Captured at Cold Harbor, Va.
John Williams, May 3, 1863. Killed at Chancellorsville, Va.
Linsey Williams.
J. P. Sindon.
J. H. Green.
H. T. Gurnsey.
W. F. Gunning.
Sanford McDaniel.
D. McDonald.
Tliver M. McHugh.
John Morgan.
James A. O'Neill.
James Ramsey.
W. R. Stephens.
G. W. Whicker.

Company H, 16th Georgia Infantry
The Flint Hill Greys

This company was recruited by Captain Moses Richardson, being the second military organization raised in the county during the war. Many, if not most, of the company lived in the Flint Hill community, in the immediate vicinity of the old Flint Hill Campground, long since abandoned, not far from Norcross. However, many of the company lived in other sections of the county. The Sixteenth Georgia Infantry was composed of ten companies, two of which were from Gwinnett County—the Flint Hill Greys and the Hutchins Guards. The company's commanders were Colonels Howell Cobb, Goode Bryan, Henry P. Thomas and James S. Gholston.

Company H was mustered in on August 11, 1861, and was sent at once by rail from Stone Mountain to Richmond. Captain Moses Richardson resigned September 3, 1861, being succeeded by Captain Benjamin Gholston, who resigned September 23, 1861. Private Nathaniel Reeder was then chosen Captain. Military training followed and by October 18th the soldiers were furnished with Enfield muskets, bayonets, leather slings, bayonet scabbards, leather belts and cartridge boxes. Each man had his mess-kit and blanket roll and was furnished twelve pounds of straw a month for a bed on the ground. Privates were paid $12 per month.

On October 9, 1861, the company marched with the regiment to Yorktown, Va., and Camp Bryan was established near Upper Grafton, York County, named in honor of Lieutenant-Colonel Goode Bryan. From November, 1861, to February, 1862, the company and regiment were stationed at Camp Lamar, near Wynne's Mill, York County, Virginia, and on April 16, 1862, engaged in the first serious battle with the enemy at Dam No. 1, Warwick Creek, near Yorktown. Private S. F. Gassaway, who was killed in this battle, appears to have been the first man of the company killed in action, though several had died of disease. The regiment was at Bivouac Sallie Twiggs May 1, and at Drewry's Bluff, near Richmond, May 21, 1862. Near this point was established Bivouac Ella Duncan, supposed to be named for the wife, mother or girl-friend of one of the officers. July 1st brought on an engagement near Richmond where a number of casualties occurred. On August 9th the company was camped at Bottom's Landing on the James River. The next major engagement was the battle of Crampton's Pass, or South Mountain, Md., September 14, 1862. Many were killed and wounded and others captured and carried to prisons in the North. Captain Nathaniel Reeder was shot through the thigh, captured, and taken to the U. S. Hospital at Burkittsville, Md. His leg was amputated and he died September 24, 1862. He was succeeded by First Lieutenant Andrew B. Cain. The company crossed the Potomac and returned to the vicinity of Fredericksburg where the broken ranks were refilled with recruits from Georgia, many of whom were from other counties than Gwinnett. Soon they were in the great battle of Fredericksburg, lasting from December 11 to 13, losing heavily in captured and wounded. The winter was spent in the vicinity, and on May 3, 1863, the company took part in the battle of Chancellorsville. After resting a few days in the camp near Raccoon Ford it marched with Lee's army into Pennsylvania and participated in the great battle at Gettysburg. Major James S. Gholston was among the large number captured there. The company retreated with Lee's army through Virginia. The company on November 28th and 29th was engaged in the battle at Knoxville, Tenn., where Colonel Henry P. Thomas was killed in action. Many were captured and wounded in this engagement.

In February, 1864, occurred a heart-rending example of man's inhumanity to man. On the tenth of that month a large number of soldiers, including many from this company, fell into the hands of the Federal forces at Russellville, Tenn., and soon smallpox broke out among the prisoners. Becoming a burden to their captors, they were abandoned and left behind in the small Lost Creek Baptist Church near Newmarket, Tenn., which had been hastily converted into a hospital, where they died.

Returning to Virginia the company was soon engaged in the midst of the heaviest fighting, taking part in the great battles of Cold Harbor, The Wilderness, Spotsylvania, Front Royal, and Cedar Creek or Strasburg. It was a losing fight and the company was all but wiped out. The last muster roll of the company on file in the War Department, made early in 1865 to cover the period from July 1 to August 31, 1864, shows only two lieutenants, two corporals, and seven privates present for active duty. The last engagement in which the company participated was at Sailor's Creek, Va., April 6, 1865. Three days later it surrendered with Lee's army at Appomattox. The men were at once paroled and allowed to return home. Within a few months most of those confined in Northern prisons had been released upon taking the oath of allegiance, and returned to their homes in Gwinnett County.

OFFICERS

Captain Moses Richardson, August 11, 1861, to September 3, 1861. Resigned.

Captain Benjamin Gholston, September 4, 1861, to September 23, 1861. Resigned.

Captain Nathaniel Reeder, September 24, 1861, to September 24, 1862. Died of wounds.

Captain Andrew B. Cain, September 24, 1862, to August 16, 1864. Captured.

1st Lieutenant E. F. Gober, August 11, 1861, to December 15, 1861. Died of disease.

1st Lieutenant Andrew B. Cain, December 28, 1861, to September 23, 1862. Promoted to Captain.

1st Lieutenant James L. Liddell, September 25, 1862, to April 6, 1865. Captured.

2nd Lieutenant W. T. Smith, August 11, 1861, to November 20, 1861. Resigned.

2nd Lieutenant Andrew B. Cain, November 25, 1861, to December 27, 1861. Promoted to 1st Lieutenant.

2nd Lieutenant James M. Liddell, April, 1862, to September 24, 1862. Promoted to 1st Lieutenant.

2nd Lieutenant John F. Martin, March, 1863, to May 16, 1863. Transferred to Third Battalion, Ga. S. S.

2nd Lieutenant John S. Garner, May 16, 1863, to January 26, 1865. Resigned.

Junior 2nd Lieutenant James L. Liddell, August 11, 1861, to April, 1862. Promoted to 2nd Lieutenant.

Junior 2nd Lieutenant John F. Martin, April, 1862, to March, 1863. Promoted to 2nd Lieutenant.

Junior 2nd Lieutenant John F. Wallis, June 28, 1863, to April 9, 1865. Surrendered with Company.

NON-COMMISSIONED OFFICERS

1st Sergeant Thomas L. D. Medlock. Discharged for disability December 14, 1862.

2nd Sergeant E. M. McDaniel, June 1, 1864. Captured at Cold Harbor.

3rd Sergeant Moses L. Herrington, April 7, 1862. Died at Suffolk, Va.

4th Sergeant Samuel B. Couey, October 17, 1861. Died at Richmond, Va.

1st Corporal, Elbert Daniel, May 18, 1863. Died at Richmond, Va., of wounds.

2nd Corporal Thomas R. Wood.

3rd Corporal Green B. Rabern, October 1, 1864. Discharged, over-age.

4th Corporal W. E. Franklin, October 4, 1861. Discharged for disability.

PRIVATES

Geo. W. Atkinson, May 30, 1862. Died at Richmond, Va., of fever.

F. M. Beardon, July 17, 1862. Discharged for disability.

Robert T. Bolton.

Joel H. Braswell, August 16, 1864. Captured at Front Royal, Va.

James T. Beatey, April 9, 1865. Surrendered with company.

Isaac D. Bradberry, February 22, 1863. Died of disease in Gwinnett County.

S. D. Brewer, April 9, 1865. Surrendered with company.

James L. Brewer, August 28, 1863. Captured at Knoxville, Tenn.

Oscar Benson.

Thomas P. Cofer, February 10, 1864. Captured at Russellville, Tennessee.

C. N. J. Cole, October 23, 1863. Died in prison, Ft. Delaware.

William D. Cruse, November 11, 1862. Died of disease at home.
W. H. DeShong, July 2, 1862. Died of disease, Richmond, Va.
John R. Davis, April 22, 1864. Died at Montgomery Springs, Va.
Newton J. Daniel, May 3, 1863. Killed at Chancellorsville, Va.
William J. Dyer, May 6, 1864. Killed at Wilderness, Va.
Robert H. Dunn, January 31, 1863. Died at Richmond, Va.
John D. Dickerson, June 4, 1862. Died at Petersburg, Va.
W. H. Dickerson, March 27, 1862. Died at Goldsboro, N. C.
G. W. Davis, April 6, 1865. Captured at Sailor's Creek, Va.
W. H. Ellis.
George W. Flowers, April 3, 1865. Wounded and captured at Richmond, Va.
Washington N. Franklin, November 28, 1863. Captured at Knoxville, Tenn.
Benjamin Gholston, September 4, 1861. Elected Captain September 23, 1861. Resigned.
S. F. Gassaway, April 16, 1862. Killed at Dam No. 1, Warwick Creek.
John S. Garner, May 16, 1863. Appointed 2nd Lieutenant.
D. W. Haney, June 1, 1864. Captured at Cold Harbor, Va.
Wm. M. Hunnicutt, December 5, 1863. Captured at Knoxville, Tennessee.
Green B. Hamby, September 14, 1862. Killed at Crampton's Pass, Md.
David H. Johnson, December 14, 1863. Died of disease, Gwinnett County.
G. W. Jackson, October 16, 1862. Died of wounds, Burkittsville, Maryland.
Wm. H. Johnston, August 21, 1862. Discharged for minority.
John T. Kircus, November 29, 1863. Killed at Knoxville.
Eli P. Landers, December 7, 1863. Died of disease, Gwinnett County.
Daniel P. Leopard, May 3, 1863. Killed at Chancellorsville, Va.
Willis S. Langley, August 16, 1864. Killed at Front Royal, Va.
G. T. Littleton.
John A. Long, March 16, 1864. Died of disease, Newmarket, Tenn.
Wm. Mayfield, March 11, 1864. Died of disease, Newmarket.
Benjamin Mathews, September 14, 1862. Died of wounds, Burkittsville, Md.
Jas. A. Mathews, May 5, 1863. Died of wounds, Fredericksburg, Virginia.
S. E. Massey, February 18, 1865. Died in prison, Elmira, N. Y.
W. M. Newborn.
A. W. McDaniel, September 14, 1863. Captured at Crompton's Gap, Md.
Wm. T. Mathews, March 1, 1864. Discharged for disability.
Willard P. Mason, November 27, 1862. Died at Burkittsville, Md.

HISTORY OF GWINNETT COUNTY, GEORGIA

R. N. Miner.
D. B. J. McGinnis.
T. W. Massey.
Wm. Massey, May 9, 1862. Died of disease, Petersburg, Va.
A. M. Nash.
Thos. H. B. Nichols, July 5, 1863. Died of wounds, Gettysburg, Pa.
John H. Owens, December 31, 1862. Died of disease, Richmond.
A. J. Odum, June 1, 1864. Captured at Cold Harbor, Va.
H. J. Odum, July 3, 1863. Captured at Gettysburg, Pa.
E. N. Payne.
John M. Paden, October 19, 1864. Wounded and captured, Cedar Creek, Va.
Nathaniel Reeder, September 24, 1861. Elected Captain. Died September 24, 1862.
M. J. Rutledge, February 10, 1864. Captured, Russellville, Tenn.
J. E. Rutledge, March 11, 1864. Died of disease, Newmarket, Tennessee.
Jos. M. Rutledge, August 16, 1864. Captured at Front Royal, Va.
John A. Rutledge.
Jas. R. Scott, February 1, 1865. Discharged for disability.
Lindsey Smith, August 16, 1864. Captured at Front Royal, Va.
Newton A. Smith, April 30, 1863. Died of disease at camp.
Jas. M. Stansell, December 17, 1863. Died of disease at LaGrange, Georgia.
Thos. N. Sanders, October 6, 1861. Died of disease at Richmond, Virginia.
W. L. Traynham.
Thos. F. Todd, February 15, 1864. Died of disease, Louisville, Ky.
John F. Wallis, June 28, 1863. Elected Junior 2nd Lieutenant.
J. W. White, March 18, 1862. Died. No details given.
Asa Wright.
W. L. Wommock, May 10, 1863. Died. No details given.
T. W. Weathers.
Miles Bennett, February 1, 1862. Transferred to 23rd Georgia Infantry.
Marion Bradfield, November 28, 1863. Captured, Knoxville.
E. P. Brooks, August 16, 1864. Captured Front Royal, Va.
Andrew B. Cain, November 25, 1861. Elected 2nd Lieutenant.
D. T. Cain, April 9, 1865. Surrendered with Company.
John Cobb.
Wm. C. Cofer.
Joseph A. Couey.
Thomas Drewry.
W. N. Garner.
Thomas N. Gassaway, July 2, 1863. Captured, Gettysburg.
Alfred J. Ginn, October 11, 1861. Died of disease at Richmond.

Geo. W. Givens.
George Guess.
Green B. Harper.
G. N. Herrington. Wounded, and blacksmith.
Jeremiah R. Langley, August 16, 1864. Captured, Front Royal, Virginia.
Green McKerley, December 25, 1863. Died in Gwinnett County.
Robert McKerley, June 1, 1864. Killed at Cold Harbor.
Benjamin F. Plaster, February 22, 1864. Died at Montgomery Springs, Va.
Seborn Rowe.
David S. Rutledge, April 9, 1865. Surrendered with company.
John D. Sanders, October 8, 1861. Died of disease, Richmond.
James A. Smith, June 19, 1864. Died of wounds, Washington, D. C.
Hiram Wavaster, December 19, 1863. Died of disease, Knoxville.
Josiah H. White, April 15, 1865. Surrendered at Lynchburg.
H. C. Yarbrough.
John D. Yarbrough, April 6, 1865. Wounded and captured at Sailor's Creek, Va.
James N. Yarbrough.
T. A. Barnes, Wm. T. Massey, J. A. Nuseman, J. Rush, James Welch, F. M. Gregory, T. Mathews, Joseph H. Prichard, J. Rutherford, J. C. Hard, J. W. McDaniel, J. C. Rogers, H. Sanksley, S. Hardy, J. M. Monsett, J. Rowell, W. B. Slaughter.

TROOP H, 10TH CAVALRY, STATE GUARDS

These soldiers were mustered in by Lieut. Col. S. B. Wright at Lawrenceville for six months at various dates from July 18 to August 4, 1863. They took the following oath: "You and each of you do solemnly swear that you will bear true faith and allegiance to the Confederate States of America, resist all her enemies, and do duty in her services for state defense for the term of six months from August 1, 1863. So help you, God." Forty cents per day was allowed for the use and risk for horses. Ages are given here.

OFFICERS

Captain, William A. Cain, 45; 1st Lieutenant, Daniel M. Byrd, 37; 2nd Lieutenant, Thomas H. Mitchel, 33; 3rd Lieutenant, Robert Hope, 40; 1st Sergeant, Bryant E. Strickland, 45; 2nd Sergeant, Manning Cain, 37; 3rd Sergeant, W. C. Harris, 38; 4th Sergeant, James D. Hood, 38; 5th Sergeant, Robert H. Allen, 21; 1st Corporal, A. G. Harris, 30; 2nd Corporal, William Jackson, 37; 3rd Corporal, H. W. Sexton, 38; 4th Corporal, B. E. Crawford, 53.

PRIVATES

George W. Ambrose, 40; Jacob M. Ambrose, 37; William M.

Brand, 42; John R. Craig, 41; George W. F. Craig, 44; James E. Cruce, 45; S. W. Davis, 45; L. B. Davis, 21; Chandler Dutton, 37; J. G. Everett, 38; Joshua N. Glenn, 36; P. H. Gholston, 26; J. A. Huff, 42; Sannah Hannah, 45; J. R. Henry, 54; J. P. Hutchins, 66; J. W. H. Hamilton, 38; S. B. Hay, 47; F. M. Jordan, 37; Thomas H. Liddell, 44; J. H. F. Mattox, 39; Elijah Mattox, 48; Johnson Mathis, 32; Robert Medlock, 30; A. C. Nesbit, 40; A. A. Omburg, 45; G. W. Russell, 45; W. B. Smith, 30; Eldridge Strickland, 16; J. M. Skinner, 16; A. J. Shaffen, 37; W. M. Strickland; Charles S. Thomas, 16; J. W. Tuggle, 37; Toliver Tuggle, 36; S. B. Wright, 42; J. S. Wilson, 39; J. W. F. Williams, 31.

This troop was stationed at Lawrenceville August 1, 1863, and at Rome, January 1, 1864. Privates received $12 per month. Corporals and Sergeants received from $13 to $20 per month.

COMPANY H, 35TH INFANTRY

This company was organized at Hog Mountain September 24, 1861, from Gwinnett and Hall counties.

OFFICERS

Captain, Aaron K. Richardson; 1st Lieutenant, Charles M. Tuggle; 2nd Lieutenant, James M. Roberts; 3rd Lieutenant, John Wheeler; 4th Lieutenant, Ezekiel M. Roberts; 5th Lieutenant, Thomas B. Jones; 1st Sergeant, Thomas B. Jones; 2nd Sergeant, Henry H. Beard; 3rd Sergeant, George M. Tuggle; 4th Sergeant, William Swafford; 1st Corporal, Adam G. Tuggle; 2nd Corporal, John W. Cross; 3rd Corporal, William McKinney; 4th Corporal, Obediah N. Wheeler.

PRIVATES

Henry D. Anglin, Martin V. Bailey, Elijah P. Bailey, John L. Black, Jasper L. Black, Eli Bailey, Newton J. Bailey, Benajah H. Bragg, Jonathon W. Crow, Richard M. Cook, Alfred M. Crow, Charles A. Cash, James Campbell, Joseph T. Carlisle, John W. Cash, William M. Collier, Andrew J. Deaton, Benjamin F. Duncan, William B. Duren, John Devite, Levi J. Deaton, John M. Fox, James Fox, John M. Frazier, Joseph A. Frazier, Bluford H. Fields, Elijah S. Gresham, Harris Gresham, John Herron, William Herron, William Hendrix, Edward Harrison, James Huckaby, Clark M. Harris, Thomas C. Harris, Hiram R. Holmes, James J. Johnson, Joseph T. Johnson, Isaac A. Jones, Thomas S. Jones, George W. McKinsey, James Mickler.

Dolpham T. McKimsey, Absolem Martin, James McCutchins, William Overby, Mathew Parker, George T. Puckett, Warren C. Payne, Richard Phillips, William G. Puckett, Elias Puckett, William B. J. Payne, David H. Puckett, Milas W. Rainey, Albert C. Roberts, Carnelius H. Roberts, Martin V. B. Roberts, Ezekiel M. Roberts, Hardin Roberts, William E. Roebuck, Christopher Rainey, Ephriam

E. Sizemore, Seaborn J. M. Sizemore, Andrew J. Swofford, Isaac Swofford, Russel A. Tuggle, Manning J. Tuggle, Anderson Tuggle, Sanford Tuggle, Henry H. Tuggle, Spenser Tillison, Francis M. Thomas, Thomas W. Wayne, James P. Wood, Robert W. Williams, Nathan G. Williams, Permenus Williams, Robert P. West, Isaac D. Wiley, Andrew J. Whitley, William C. Williams, Andrew F. Young.

This company was stationed at the following places: Evansport, Va., January 27, February 15, February 28, 1862; Fredericksburg, Va., November 31, 1862.

The company participated in the following battles: Seven Pines, May 31; Mechanicsville, June 26; Game's Mill, June 27; Frazier's Farm, June 30; Malvern Hill, July 1, all in 1862.

The company was then transferred to General Stonewall Jackson's command and engaged in battles at Cedar Run August 9, and Second Manassas, August 28, 29, 30, 1862. The army crossed the Potomac and marched to Frederick, Md., and was present at the surrender of Harper's Ferry September 15, 1862. On September 20 it was in an engagement at Shepherdstown, and participated in the fighting near Fredericksburg, December 11, 12, 13, 1862.

COMPANY I, 55TH INFANTRY

This company was organized in Lawrenceville in May, 1862.

OFFICERS

Captain, David E. Lee; 1st Lieutenant, William Hardman; 2nd Lieutenant, Sanford A. Scales; 3rd Lieutenant, Robert Ethridge; 1st Sergeant, Wallace R. Russell; 2nd Sergeant, R. B. Moore; 3rd Sergeant, D. J. Austin; 4th Sergeant, Enoch V. Pool; 5th Sergeant, W. A. Perry; 1st Corporal, John H. Freeman; 2nd Corporal, W. R. Hunnicutt; 3rd Corporal, J. C. Brown; 4th Corporal, Henry Hinton.

PRIVATES

J. J. Adams, Willis M. Bowen, G. W. Bilew, A. J. Bilew, S. S. Bowen, J. D. Bradberry, W. J. Bradberry, J. L. Brown, S. C. Brown, J. T. Burel, J. N. Bagwell, J. T. Cain, Hiram Clark, C. W. Cheatham, Ichabod Cowser, J. C. Corbin, E. H. Chambers, J. P. Crawford, G. M. Cox, S. N. Davis, Jesse Davis, B. M. DeLong, A. J. Dodd, W. R. Dodd, A. H. Dodd, A. P. Everett, J. M. Ellison, J. Ethridge, R. Ethridge, J. J. Farr, D. A. Farr, J. N. Terrell, A. L. Freeman, J. S. Freeman, J. T. Freeman, J. H. Freeman, William Freer, H. G. Gibson, W. W. Garner, A. J. Garner, J. H. Gresham, J. H. Gouge, M. W. Hargrove, M. J. Harrison, J. F. Harris, H. Hall, B. B. Herring, A. B. Higgins, J. J. Higgins, W. T. Hunt, W. A. Hamilton, Z. L. Hamilton, A. H. Jackson, J. W. Jennings, W. D. Jenks, E. W. Jones, Castleberry Johnson, Caloway Johnson, John N. Jackson, W. T. Jiles, S. Kennerly, A. Kirby, G. M. Knight.

J. Mayne, R. M. Mays, A. McDaniel, J. H. Mitchel, E. Mauldin, John C. Nix, J. O'Shields, M. H. Osburn, G. W. Osburn, H. L. Payne, J. M. Perry, J. M. Peppers, J. R. Peavy, Benjamin Y. Pharr, Caleb V. Pool, Allen Ridgway, J. S. Rowbuck, J. P. Rowbuck, J. W. Rutledge, J. N. Rutledge, B. C. Scales, Richard Sharpton, J. B. Sammon, O. A. Stone, J. B. Smith, G. W. Sweat, J. Tanner, P. T. Toler, D. J. Wallace, W. W. Webb, W. H. Webb, J. W. Willis, Elisha C. Wilburn, A. J. Willbanks, Andrew J. Whitworth, W. S. Wood, G. L. Young, W. McElroy, N. A. Perkins, William Adams, B. S. Barton, J. W. B. Carroll, J. Tims, J. Moore, P. T. Taylor, C. C. Morgan, J. W. Moon, J. G. Bowen, J. M. Bowen, W. H. Britt, W. B. Burel, David Daniel, G. W. McElduff, Rutherford Mobley, Robert E. Oliver, J. S. Boozer, R. R. Berry, C. B. Williams.

COMPANY I, 16TH GEORGIA INFANTRY
THE HUTCHINS GUARDS

Company I, Sixteenth Georgia Infantry, designated at its organization as the Hutchins Guards, was the first one organized in Gwinnett County for service in the Confederate Army. Officers of the company were elected March 6, 1861. Its organization was completed July 16, 1861, when the company was enlisted for the duration of the war by Regimental Adjutant James Barrow. The company arrived at Richmond, Va., July 23, where the regiment to which it was assigned assembled at Camp Cobb under the command of Colonel Howell Cobb, later a Major General in the Confederate Army. There, August 16, 1861, Captain Henry P. Thomas was promoted to the position of Major; First Lieutenant Nathan L. Hutchins to Captain; Second Lieutenant William E. Simmons to First Lieutenant, and First Sergeant Julius S. Boring was elected Second Lieutenant. The company was drilled and equipped with Enfield rifles and all necessary accouterments. It was stationed at the same places and was in the same battles as Company H until the close of the war. The company surrendered at Appomattox with General Lee's army April 9, 1865.

OFFICERS

Captain Henry P. Thomas, July 16, 1861 to August 16, 1861. Appointed Major.

Captain Nathan L. Hutchins, Jr., August 16, 1861 to June 10, 1863. Appointed Lieutenant Colonel.

Captain Nicholas A. Moss, July 20, 1863 to April 9, 1865. Surrendered.

1st Lieutenant N. L. Hutchins, Jr., July 16, 1861 to August 16, 1861. Appointed Captain.

1st Lieutenant William E. Simmons, August 16, 1861, to June 10, 1863. Appointed Captain Third Battalion, Ga. S. S.

1st Lieutenant Edward B. Thomas, July 20, 1863, to May 22, 1864. Promoted to Captain Company F, 24th Infantry.

2nd Lieutenant Julius S. Boring, August 16, 1861, to December 13, 1862. Killed at Fredericksburg.

2nd Lieutenant Joseph H. Brogdon, September 1, 1863, to June 1, 1864. Captured at Cold Harbor.

Junior 2nd Lieutenant John A. Mitchell, July 19, 1861, to August 2, 1862. Died of disease.

Junior 2nd Lieutenant Edward B. Thomas, April 22, 1863, to July 20, 1863. Promoted to 1st Lieutenant.

Junior 2nd Lieutenant Isaac M. Young, May 21, 1864, to April 9, 1865. Surrendered.

NON-COMMISSIONED OFFICERS

1st Sergeant Julius S. Boring, August 16, 1861. Appointed 2nd Lieutenant.

2nd Sergeant Robert M. Hughes, April 28, 1863. Detailed as tanner—Ordnance Department.

3rd Sergeant Wm. H. Robinson, July 19, 1862. Discharged for disability.

4th Sergeant John F. McElvaney, January 21, 1863. Died of disease at Fredericksburg.

1st Corporal Elisha W. Maltbie, March 16, 1863. Died.

2nd Corporal John M. Light.

3rd Corporal Joseph H. Brogdon, September 1, 1863. Elected 2nd Lieutenant.

4th Corporal, Hilliard J. Wilson, June 16, 1863. Discharged for disability.

PRIVATES

Wm. M. Adair.

Andrew J. Ambrose, December 11, 1862. Killed at Fredericksburg.

W. L. Andrews, November 16, 1861. Discharged for disability.

James R. Atkinson, July 2, 1863. Captured at Gettysburg.

Jesse A. Atkinson, November 4, 1862. Died of disease at Winchester, Va.

Osborn E. Bailey, November 17, 1861. Died of disease at Camp Bryan, Va.

John T. Bankston, July 14, 1862. Discharged for disability.

Ira H. Betts, January 27, 1865. Died in prison at Elmira, N. Y.

Wm. H. Boring, September 14, 1862. Killed at Crompton's Pass, Maryland.

Joshua Bradberry, September 14, 1861. Died of disease at Richmond.

R. M. Braden, July 2, 1863. Captured at Gettysburg.

R. W. Bradford.

James H. Braziel.

Henry M. Britt, June 14, 1862. Died of disease at Richmond.
Berry Broadwell, July 18, 1862. Killed near Richmond.
Jesse Broadwell, October 19, 1864. Killed at Cedar Creek, Va.
Thomas J. Brown, August 27, 1861. Discharged for disability.
Wilborn T. Camp, September 21, 1861. Died of disease at Richmond.
David Carter, April 9, 1865. Surrendered with company.
Benjamin R. Cash.
John T. Clark.
Nathan B. Clark, December 14, 1862. Discharged for disability.
Osborn Cole, May 5, 1863. Killed at Chancellorsville, Va.
Richard Cox, December 10, 1861. Discharged for disability.
Wm. C. Cox.
Zebulon B. Craig.
General W. Davis.
Samuel Z. Dyer.
John Ethridge, July 14, 1862. Died of disease at Everettsville, Ala.
A. J. Fewell.
Lewis A. Glossom, May 3, 1863. Died from wounds at Fredericksburg.
J. J. Glover, June 1, 1864. Captured at Cold Harbor, Va.
Newman Green, April 9, 1865. Surrendered with company.
Geo. W. Hardigree, December 29, 1862. Died of wounds at Richmond.
Wm. J. Hardigree, July 12, 1864. Retired to Invalids Corps.
Robert C. Harris.
Hayden C. Haslett, April 22, 1863. Discharged for disability.
Thomas H. Holt.
Henry C. Horton, July 4, 1863. Captured at Gettysburg.
John Hughes, August 22, 1861. Discharged for disability.
Thomas B. Hutchins, August 26, 1862. Discharged for disability.
John S. Hutchinson, October 5, 1861. Discharged.
Silas Kadle.
Joseph W. Kirlin, October 24, 1861. Died of disease at Yorktown, Virginia.
Wm. B. Kimbro, December 28, 1861. Discharged for disability.
N. W. LaFoy, November 29, 1863. Captured at Knoxville.
James L. Light, October 7, 1862. Died of wounds at Burkittsville, Md.
Laban Mauldin.
Wm. J. McCune, September 14, 1862. Killed at Crampton's Pass, Md.
Samuel J. McElvany, January 1, 1863. Died of disease at Fredericksburg, Va.
Asa McMillan.

John F. Martin. Transferred to Company H and appointed 2nd Lieutenant.
James R. Mitchel, May 1, 1862. Discharged for disability.
S. J. Mitchell.
John J. Miller, November 22, 1861. Discharged for disability.
George N. Morgan.
Nicholas A. Moss, August 11, 1862. Appointed Junior 2nd Lieutenant.
R. S. Myers, June 1, 1864. Captured at Cold Harbor, Va.
Henry C. Nash.
Lewis M. Nash, June 12, 1862. Died of disease, Richmond.
Thomas P. Nelms.
Wm. M. Orr, April 9, 1865. Surrendered with company.
Asa H. Pittman, April 2, 1862. Died of disease at Goldsboro, N. C.
J. G. Pittman, October 19, 1864. Captured at Cedar Creek, Va.
John Porter.
Joseph F. Russell, March 4, 1863. Detailed as tailor, Richmond.
J. F. Russell.
Nathan Russell.
J. A. Singleton.
P. V. Singleton, August 16, 1864. Captured at Front Royal, Va.
Joel J. Skinner, January 1, 1865. Died in prison, Elmira, N. Y.
J. M. Snead.
John C. Snead.
H. S. Stanley, August 16, 1864. Captured at Front Royal, Va.
Charlton H. Strickland, June 1, 1863. Appointed 2nd Lieutenant, Company C, 3rd Battalion, Ga. S. S.
E. W. Strickland. Appointed Sergeant Major 3rd Battalion, Ga. S. S.
Edward B. Thomas, April 22, 1863. Elected Junior 2nd Lieutenant.
E. A. Thornhill, March 18, 1865. Retired in Invalid's Corps.
John H. Underwood, 1863. Died at Richmond.
Thomas J. Vaughan, August 19, 1863. Detailed to QMC, Saltville, Virginia.
N. R. Wheeler.
W. H. Wilson.
Samuel B. Wright.
Isaac M. Young, May 21, 1864. Appointed Junior 2nd Lieutenant.
James M. Bagley, May 10, 1863. Died of wounds at Richmond.
J. W. Bagley, July 28, 1863. Disability discharge.
J. P. Barnett, June 1, 1864. Captured at Cold Harbor, Va.
J. F. M. Beddingfield, June 24, 1863. Died of disease, Richmond, Virginia.
G. W. Bradford.
Obediah Copeland.
R. F. Cox, July 2, 1863. Captured at Gettysburg.

James Glosson, April 9, 1865. Surrendered with company.
D. S. Gower, August 16, 1864. Captured at Front Royal, Va.
Thomas C. Greeson.
W. C. Greeson.
L. W. Griswold.
D. H. Hamilton.
N. H. Hamilton.
Emesah W. Hannah, April 9, 1865. Surrendered with company.
B. J. Harris.
Benjamin A. Holmes, October 19, 1864. Captured at Cedar Creek, Virginia.
John R. Hood, May, 1864. Died of wounds at place unknown.
James E. Ivey, July 6, 1862. Died of disease at Farmville, Va.
M. M. Johnston, February 2, 1863. Died at Richmond, Va.
Francis M. Leopard, May 12, 1864. Killed at Spotsylvania, Va.
Wm. P. Leopard, August 16, 1864. Captured at Front Royal, Va.
Waddt T. Lewis, August 26, 1862. Disability discharge.
James A. Mackin, April 9, 1865. Surrendered with company.
Drayton McDaniel.
D. M. McDaniel.
S. J. Moncrief.
Washington McDaniel, September 24, 1862. Died of wounds at Sharpsburg, Md.
J. C. Myers.
Milas M. Nicholson, April 29, 1863. In Ordnance Department at Atlanta.
W. J. Nunnally, June 1, 1864. Captured at Cold Harbor, Va.
John R. Parks, April 9, 1865. Surrendered with company.
Wm. T. Pittman, June 1, 1864. Captured at Cold Harbor, Va.
John R. Robinson, June 1, 1864. Captured at Cold Harbor, Va.
Job Smith, June 1, 1864. Captured at Cold Harbor, Va.
G. W. Thomas, June 1, 1864. Captured at Cold Harbor, Va.
Wm. J. Portor.
A. N. Robinson.
Jas. A. Robinson, July 4, 1863. Captured at Gettysburg.
R. N. Robinson.
William J. Robinson.
Willis F. Scales, November 29, 1863. Captured at Knoxville, Tenn.
Joseph Simonton, August 16, 1864. Captured at Front Royal, Va.
Wm. S. Summerlin, December 24, 1862. Died of disease at Richmond, Virginia.
Jas. H. Westbrooks, August 12, 1864. Discharged.
B. T. Cox, J. Curtis, Cy Dickenson, H. J. Ferrill, Alexander Galwood, W. B. Wright, B. J. Haines, H. C. Harling, J. A. Harris, B. C. Haynie, B. Hixer, Jas. M. Hughes, I. Ivey, J. M. Karr, J. Lower, J. McKinsey, James Moore, Ira S. Myers, C. Nash, N. H. Nicholson,

J. Putten, E. D. Sammon, W. S. Self, J. R. Shaw, W. H. Tansell, Saml. M. Whitworth.

The records show that First Sergeants were paid $20 per month; the Sergeants, $17 per month; the Corporals, $13 per month, and the privates, $11 per month.

TROOP I, 16TH BATTALION, GEORGIA CAVALRY
LATER 13TH GEORGIA CAVALRY

Troop I was composed of those who were over and under the conscription age or were otherwise exempt from service. It was mustered in at Bethany, Ga. This company was made up from the counties of Jackson, Gwinnett, Hall and Fulton. Jackson furnished five Sergeants, four Corporals and forty Privates. There were three Privates from Hall, and one from Fulton.

The Privates from Gwinnett County were enlisted by Lieutenant John M. Martin, February 10, 1864.

OFFICERS

Captain, James A. Strange, Jackson County; 1st Lieutenant, Joseph C. Holiday, Jackson County; 2nd Lieutenant, John M. Martin, Gwinnett County; 3rd Lieutenant, John Nixon.

GWINNETT PRIVATES

D. L. Born, J. L. Burel, J. J. Bonds, William Bonds, John O. Bramblett, J. M. Clark, Arnold Clark, Mathew Davis, Thomas Dillard, Samuel Dillard, L. L. Davis, H. J. Duncan, Henry F. Ethridge, Jones H. Ewing, Joseph T. Forester, W. J. Freeman, Abel Griffin, G. W. Gunnion, W. C. Harris, Samuel Hutton, J. M. Johnson, William Kimbrough, Seaborn Knight, W. S. Knight, Elias W. Knight, Martin Knight, Elijah Knight, James Kilgore, Thomas J. Mewborn, James Mitchel, Joseph W. Mitchel, J. A. Noel, H. T. Peavy, George Price, Fielding Rutherford, J. T. Rice, J. W. Rice, H. F. Sells, J. G. Stanley, Isaac Teagle, H. T. Teagle, J. W. Tallent, J. W. Watson.

COMPANY K, 36TH GEORGIA INFANTRY

This company was organized in Gwinnett County May 13, 1862, for the duration of the war. It was stationed at Camp Big Creek Gap, Tennessee.

OFFICERS

Captain, A. A. Dyer; 1st Lieutenant, James C. Carroll; 2nd Lieutenant, T. J. Cruse; 3rd Lieutenant, N. L. Wallace; 1st Sergeant, E. G. Nash; 2nd Sergeant, William A. Carroll; 3rd Sergeant, Tandy Y. Nash; 4th Sergeant, George W. Minor; 5th Sergeant, M. N. Bankston; 1st Corporal, T. H. Dyer; 2nd Corporal, G. B. Lee; 3rd Corporal, G. K. Nash; 4th Corporal, W. M. B. Langley.

PRIVATES

Louis Barton, G. A. Barton, John T. Butler, E. P. Brooks, J. M. Bagwell, W. L. Chamblee, Thomas M. Criswell, M. Dutton, John Dutton, James Driver, R. S. Franklin, T. S. Franklin, O. P. Ford, W. P. Franklin, W. C. Green, William Groves, Moten Hutchins, Thomas Hutchins, J. R. Hambrick, M. D. Hopkins, G. T. Hopkins, W. M. Hopkins, W. G. Hamilton, I. L. Johnson, W. L. Kelley, N. B. Landers, H. B. Lancaster, Alfred Langley, W. A. Lietch, W. S. Lanier, M. T. Mathews, W. D. Massey, Thomas McKinney, William R. Minor, J. H. Maloney, W. H. Mathews, W. J. R. Mathews, W. W. Mason, M. McDaniel, E. W. Nash, S. C. New, John Parks, W. H. Peevey, S. H. Pickens, Thomas Payne, J. W. Ray, P. H. Ross, J. K. Roberts, C. A. Rowden, John A. Reeves, William J. Veal, T. G. Wallace, T. H. Dyer, Daniel Minor, Wilson McKinney, W. S. King.

TROOP K, 16TH BATTALION, GEORGIA CAVALRY
LATER 13TH GEORGIA CAVALRY

Those enrolled in this battalion from Gwinnett County follow:

OFFICERS

Captain, W. Scott Thomas; 1st Lieutenant, J. C. Whitehead; 2nd Lieutenant, H. J. Randolph; 3rd Lieutenant, C. W. Shackelford; 1st Sergeant, W. S. Maltbie; 2nd Sergeant, C. W. Strickland; 3rd Sergeant, Albin Ormberg; 4th Sergeant, Edward L. Wright; 1st Corporal, Robert H. Allen; 2nd Corporal, J. H. F. Maddox; 3rd Corporal, C. S. Thomas; 4th Corporal, D. C. Spence.

PRIVATES

Charles Ambrose, Jacob M. Ambrose, Napolean B. Allen, A. W. Bramblett, J. Crow, T. Crow, David Ethridge, ——. ——. Holcomb, J. D. Hood, J. G. Johnson, J. Kirby, C. Knight, E. Knight, Hiram O. Mackin, L. S. Moon, J. M. Moon, W. Mitchel, Edward Mackin, R. W. Martin, J. T. Pruett, J. T. Rice, T. Sells, D. W. Thompson, N. Tullis, A. Tullis, J. Worthan, William M. Winn.

CAMP'S COMPANY
COMPANY D, 16TH GEORGIA VOLUNTEER CAVALRY

Company D, Sixteenth Georgia Volunteer Cavalry, was made up of men from Gwinnett and Jackson counties who lived on and near the county line.

MUSTER ROLL

Vard Allen, C. C. Bell, Lafayette Bell, Tyler Bell, Marion Bell, A. E. Brooks, Harrison Bridges, Marion Blankinship, Hutch Blankin-

228 HISTORY OF GWINNETT COUNTY, GEORGIA

ship, Joseph Brown, Wm. Brock, D. A. Camp, L. H. Cronic, John Cato, Thomas Cato, Monroe Cato, James Cooper, James Clark, Wm. Davenport, W. H. Duncan, N. B. Duncan, J. T. Duncan, L. G. Duncan, George Duncan, Thomas Deaton, Joshua Elder, Wm. Elsbury, James M. Flanigan, Elijah Flanigan, Jasper N. Flanigan, C. S. Freeman, Eli Garner, Francis Hudgins, Jeptha Hudgins, Jas. Holland, Sanford Holland, James Harvil, G. W. Irwin, John Kerbo, Thomas Kinney, Tillman Lancaster, Wm. Lancaster, Jordan Lott, Ezra Lyle, J. B. Lyle, J. A. Lyle, John Major, Middleton Mangum, —. —. McKinney, John Maddox, Seaborn Maddox, M. M. Mauldin, George Manus, Ephraim Matthews, G. W. Mahaffey, Joseph McEver, Andrew McEver, John M. McEver, Green Osborn, W. L. Pike, J. M. Pool, John Park, L. Park, Wm. Pierce, Elijah Queen, John Smith, Pendleton Wallace, T. W. White.

YANKEES OVERRUN GWINNETT

Gwinnett County was overrun by Union soldiers during 1864 when Sherman captured Atlanta. No engagements of major importance took place in the county, but several skirmishes occurred in different communities. There was one at Auburn; one at Jug Tavern, and one at King's Tanyard on the road from Jug Tavern to the County Line school on the Pentecost farm. The Confederate cavalry surprised the Union soldiers at King's Tanyard, killed several and put the enemy to flight, capturing a portion of them.

Foraging expeditions of the Union soldiers into the county met with some resistance. An occasional enemy was killed. The farms were stripped and homes were looted.

Bands of men, passed the age for service in the army, and boys, too young, were organized to protect the county from the foragers of Sherman's army. These were called scouts, or home guards, or rangers, while Sherman's foragers were called bummers. There were numerous skirmishes in the western part of the county between these two groups of soldiers. The home guards prided themselves on their marksmanship and it was their proud boast that a lighted candle on the roadside could be snuffed out with their pistols as they galloped by at full speed. The practice grounds for one group of rangers were near the store of Thomas P. Hudson at Five Forks. One of the foraging expeditions came as far as Killian Hill, where shots were fired by both groups. The rangers burned the bridge across Yellow River to prevent the enemy from crossing.

A group of the enemy passed along the Rockbridge Road by Trickum and as they approached a dwelling, later the home place of James W. Andrews, the crackle of a rifle gave notice that danger lurked nearby. Another shot brought the second enemy to the ground. In all, five Yankees were killed. A man by the name of Goldsmith had concealed himself in a log smokehouse and he it was who shot the foragers. The enemy soon located the smokehouse, set fire to it, and Goldsmith met a horrible death.

Lewis Nash owned a number of slaves, two of whom were Green and Nelse. Nash, like everyone in that part of the county, hid his cattle, stock and hogs in the swamps, hoping the foragers would not find them. As the Yankees were pillaging the Yellow River section, they went to Green's house and told him that he was free and advised him to quit working for his master and to join them in Atlanta. That sounded well to Green. In the meantime he informed the Yankees where he had helped Nash conceal all his property. Green left with the Yankees and after remaining with them for a week, he returned to make ready to move on with the army as it passed by Stone Mountain. The rangers heard of Green's return, took charge of him, carried him to the east bank of Yellow River, some distance below the bridge, and the negro was never seen again.

Nelse, the other negro belonging to Nash, was persuaded to leave and go with the foragers. After three trips to the enemy's camps, they decided that Nelse could not be trusted. They tied his hands behind him and lashed a live sheep to his back, in which condition he returned home, a distance of three miles.

In the section around Holt's mill and on beyond, where Richard Holt, David Anderson and Thomas MaGuire lived, a great deal of foraging was done by the Yankees as will be seen from reports made by the officers commanding the foraging expeditions. It is said that several Yankee soldiers were killed by two of the MaGuire boys, then only twelve and fourteen years old. On the farm of Billie Jordan a skirmish occurred between the rangers and the foragers and three of the latter were killed and buried on the Jordan farm. Twenty years later the bodies were removed to a national cemetery.

Wiley Webb, a large landowner who lived in the Rosebud community, lost all his stock, cattle, hogs and sheep. He had 300 bales of cotton. The Yankee soldiers burned it.

The following reports of federal officers show what their foraging expeditions did in this county:

HEADQUARTERS SECOND DIVISION
TWENTIETH ARMY CORPS
ATLANTA, GA.

October 31, 1864.

Colonel:

I have the honor to submit the following report of the foraging expedition made in compliance with orders from Major-General Slocum:

At 6 o'clock on the morning of the 26th instant the following troops and wagons reported to me on the Decatur road: Third

Brigade, First Division, numbering 1,200 men, under command of Colonel Robinson; Third Brigade, Second Division, numbering 945 men, under command of Lieutenant-Colonel Van Voorhis; Second Brigade, Third Division, numbering 642 men, under command of Major Brant; two batteries of artillery, under command of Captain Bainbridge, and 450 cavalry of the Army of the Ohio, under Colonel Garrard. Wagons as follows: Headquarters Twentieth Corps, 42; First Division, Twentieth Corps, 83; Second Division, Twentieth Corps, 100; Third Division, Twentieth Corps, 87; Fourteenth Army Corps, 130; Captain Hade, post quartermaster, 21; ordnance train, Department of the Cumberlain, 54; medical supply train, 20; batteries and outside detachments, 115; making the total number of wagons 652, which, with the addition of 20 small wagons, made the entire train consist of 672 wagons. At 7 o'clock I moved toward Decatur which I reached, without incidents of note, about 10 o'clock. At this place I learned from inhabitants that there was a force of the enemy, variously estimated as numbering from 2,000 to 4,000, between Stone Mountain and Lawrenceville. I also learned that detachments from this force had been in Decatur on the previous day. These reports of the whereabouts of the enemy, varying only in the estimates of force, confirmed by intelligence received from the scouts of Colonel Garrard's cavalry, induced me to ask General Slocum for reenforcements of artillery and infantry. To guard against any attack on my train from the right and towards Stone Mountain, I detached the main force of cavalry, 700 infantry under Lieutenant-Colonel Van Voorhis, and a section of artillery, the whole under command of Colonel Garrard, to move to Stone Mountain direct and hold the roads and passes at that place.

With the remainder of my command, and with the train, I moved from Decatur on the Lawrenceville road. I moved on this road about six miles, where I passed to the right over a wood road, and struck the main road to Stone Mountain about two miles from that place. At the mountain I was joined by Colonel Garrard. Leaving a strong cavalry guard to hold the village, I moved on the Stone Mountain and Lawrenceville road to Trickum's Crossroads, near which I parked the train and camped the troops on the farm of Mr. Bracewell. About 9 o'clock in the evening an aide reported that the Second Brigade of my division, under Colonel Mindil, and one section of artillery were four miles beyond Stone Mountain. I ordered Colonel Mindil to push as near the mountain as possible during the night and to join me on the following morning. Reports of the inhabitants in the vicinity of my camp confirmed those already received at Decatur. During the morning several attacks were made upon the pickets and outposts by rebel cavalry, in one of which one of my men was killed and another severely wounded. I remained in camp all day, sending out detachments of the train under strong guards and succeeded in loading about 300 wagons. In the afternoon Lieutenant-Colonel Way, commanding a regiment of cavalry, reported he had met the enemy near Yellow River, about 400 strong, and that the inhabitants stated that a force of 4,000 was near Lawrenceville. Soon after he reported, the former party had retreated across the river and destroyed the bridge. I immediately ordered him to follow and push toward Lawrenceville to ascertain, if possible, the whereabouts of the enemy. He moved to Lawrenceville and, charging furiously upon the town, drove the enemy through it in great disorder, scattering them in all directions. From reports from my cavalry, I learned it would be impossible to load the remainder of my train west of the river and learning that an abundance of forage could be procured east of it, I resolved to cross and forage there.

Accordingly on the morning of the 28th, I sent 250 wagons with a guard of 1,500 infantry, a regiment of cavalry and a section of artillery, the whole under command of Colonel Robinson, with orders to cross the river and load in the fields just beyond. The remaining empty wagons I sent with a guard of 400 infantry and a section of artillery to report to Colonel Garrard, who was encamped on the Rockbridge road about three miles distant from the main camp and eastward from the mountain. At three o'clock I learned that the wagons under charge of Colonels Robinson and Garrard had been loaded and were ready for the returning march. Desiring to move as rapidly as possible toward Atlanta, I sent orders to Colonel Garrard to move with his trains on the road leading south of the mountain and to the village at its base, and knowing Colonel Robinson's command would readily reach the camp before all the wagons there had moved out, I started at 4 o'clock with the Second Brigades of the Second and Third Divisions as advance guards, leaving a picket at every road and important point along the line of march, with orders to remain until the rear of the entire train had passed. I marched two miles beyond Stone Mountain and commenced parking my trains for the night, at 7 o'clock, on the farm of Mr. Johnson on the Decatur road. The wagons laden by Colonel Garrard commenced coming in about 11:30 o'clock and I was joined by that officer about 1 on the morning of the 29th.

All my troops and wagons having reached my camp by 1 o'clock, I commenced moving toward Atlanta at 7. Dividing the train into sections, and interposing between each a strong guard of infantry, I moved with the advance, posting as on the previous night a picket at every road and commanding position to remain until the entire train passed. My advance reached Decatur at 11:30 a. m., where I found the First Brigade of the First Division, which had been sent out to meet and, if necessary, to assist me. After halting for some time at Decatur to close up my train, I again resumed the march, leaving the brigade just mentioned to bring up the rear. I reached

Atlanta without incident at 3 p. m., where the troops and train were ordered to rejoin their respective commands.

My quartermaster reports the amount of corn procured to be 9,300 bushels, besides were brought in 5 loads of wheat and 4 bales of cotton, and about 100 head of cattle, which were distributed among the several commands. I take great pleasure in commending the officers and men under my command for the hearty cooperation yielded me during the labors of the expedition. My thanks are eminently due to Colonel Garrard, his officers and men, for the activity and zeal manifested and for information obtained. I regret to except from my commendation of the officers and men the lieutenant in command of the exterior picket captured on 27th instant. Armed with Spencer rifles, captured in broad daylight without firing a shot, by a force scarce more than its equal, this picket was undoubtedly guilty of gross neglect. No words of reproach can be too strong for an officer who, allowing care for personal ease to exceed his zeal for duty, permits himself and command to be ignominiously captured.

Subjoined is a list of the prisoners captured from the enemy.*

I am, sir, very respectfully, your obedient servant,

JNO. W. GEARY,
Brigadier-General U. S. Volunteers.

Lieutenant-Colonel H. W. Perkins,
Assistant Adjutant-General.

Lieut.-Col. Edward Bloodgood, 22nd Wis. Inf.

September 2, 1864, the regiment took an active part in the occupation of Atlanta. Nothing of note took place until October 16 when the regiment, with a brigade, commanded by myself, accompanied a large foraging expedition, being absent four days, penetrating some 30 miles into the enemy's country, and loading some 800 wagons with corn and forage. A similar expedition started October 26, not going so far, however, but meeting with the same success, and without finding any considerable force of the rebels.

Col. Jas. S. Robinson, 82nd O. Inf.

On the 25th, I received an order to join with my brigade a foraging expedition to be sent on the following day under command of Brig.-Gen. Geary. According to directions, my command reported to General Geary on the Decatur road at 6 a. m. on the 26th, and was assigned, in connection with a battery of artillery, to the duty of covering the rear of the column. Passing through Decatur at 11 a. m. my command reached Stone Mountain at 9:30 p. m. Early on the 27th, by General Geary's direction, I sent out two regiments to assist in loading wagons with corn. They returned to camp

---

* List shows 12 men taken prisoners.

at 6:30 p. m., having succeeded, in spite of the very inclement weather and prowling detachments of hostile cavalry, in loading 196 wagons. On the 28th, by direction of General Geary, I proceeded with my brigade, a section of artillery, a battalion of cavalry and about 300 wagons across Yellow River in the direction of Lawrenceville. I found here a productive country and had no difficulty in loading the entire train. My command returned toward Berkshire at 3 p. m., crossing Yellow River upon a bridge which, though partly burned by the enemy the day previous, was nevertheless easily rendered passable for the train. The column reached Berkshire at sundown and pushed forward, following the remainder of the expedition which had already preceded us on its return march. Reached Stone Mountain at 10:30 p. m. and encamped three miles beyond Stone Mountain station about midnight. On the following day my brigade formed the vanguard of the expedition and returned without incident to its encampment at Atlanta. During this expedition my brigade secured about 6,000 bushels of corn, besides the usual amount of provisions and other promiscuous articles.

YANKEE OFFICER HANGS NEGRO

After Lee and Johnston had surrendered and the war at last came to an end, a detachment of Union soldiers was encamped at Lawrenceville. Captain A. E. Hunter, of the 15th Ohio Cavalry, was in command of the company. Mart McConnell, a former slave of Tilford McConnell's, had assaulted a white woman. Bailiff Joshua S. Wilson had a warrant for the negro who fled to Lawrenceville and sought protection in the camp of the Yankee soldiers. The following colloquy occurred in the national house of representatives January 18, 1922, between Congressman Charles H. Brand, of Georgia, and Congressman Hamilton Fish, of New York:

Mr. Brand: Will the gentleman yield.

Mr. Fish: I will.

Mr. Brand: Has the gentleman any information in regard to the first lynching that occurred in Georgia?

Mr. Fish: There have been lynchings there for 50 years.

Mr. Brand: Has the gentleman any information as to when the first lynching occurred in Georgia?

Mr. Fish: I do not know when the first occurred.

Mr. Brand: The first lynching which ever occurred in Georgia, so far as I can gather, was in 1865. A negro man criminally assaulted a white woman in Gwinnett County. He fled for protection to Lawrenceville where a company of Federal soldiers was stationed. When learning the facts, they took him in custody and hanged him in the courthouse square. The lynchers were partly from your own state and other states north of the Mason and Dixon line.

Congressman Brand in his discussion of the anti-lynching bill then under consideration in the congress, made the following additional statement in reference to this incident:

"As I stated on the floor the other day in a brief colloquy with the congressman from New York, Georgia never began or initiated the lynching business, but a company of Yankee soldiers did, which was the first lynching in Georgia and probably in the south. A negro man had committed a criminal assault upon a white woman, near Lawrenceville, Georgia, and after committing the act he fled to Lawrenceville, thinking that these soldiers would protect him from violence by the family and friends of the outraged woman. When his pursuers arrived in Lawrenceville, the officer in charge of the company was told what the negro had done. The officer therefore took the negro in custody, purchased a rope and had it tied around the negro's neck. He called upon an old negro man who was present with a wagon and yoke of oxen. The accused was placed in this wagon and the old negro man was ordered to drive under a certain tree in the courthouse square. One of the soldiers climbed the tree, hung the rope over a limb and the negro driver was ordered to drive on. He hesitated, but at the point of a bayonet he finally moved and left the negro swinging to the limb until he died."

PENSIONS FOR SOLDIERS

No provision was made for aid to Confederate soldiers before 1879. The state constitution was amended authorizing the General Assembly to appropriate funds to buy artificial limbs for Confederate soldiers and to pension soldiers and their widows. Pensions were not granted until 1890 and only to maimed soldiers; the pensions ranging from $5.00 to $150.00, depending on the extent of the injuries received during the war. Later, in 1891, Confederate widows, married at the time of service, were given pensions, and later still, all widows of Confederate soldiers were placed on the pension list.

At this writing not a veteran of the war survives in this county. With the death of T. A. Barker, of Buford, early in 1941, passed the last soldier of the Lost Cause. His was the experience of many. The close of the war left him in Virginia. Bare-footed and without a dime, he turned his face towards his home near Suwanee and after many days of continual walking, reached his native hills and began life again.

The records show the following veterans were on the pension list: H. D. Anglin, E. W. Atha, W. M. Arnold, P. M. Allen, T. G. Anglin, Wm. Athey, J. W. Abner, L. A. Adams, W. L. Andrews, J. T. Atkinson, J. M. Archer, J. R. Adams, E. L. Andrews.

I. W. Bennett, W. D. Broadnax, Joshua Brown, F. Bramblet, Milton Brownlee, G. G. Bowman, W. E. Boyd, W. J. Born, W. D.

Burtchaell, J. F. Blissett, E. P. Brooks, Cooper Bennett, A. J. S. Brooks, J. J. Barnes, G. W. Braswell, J. A. Blake, J. N. Bullock, J. W. Bennett, C. C. Brewer, J. M. Burnett, J. R. Britt, David Bradford, J. F. Barnes, U. Q. Baggett, T. C. Bowles, Elijah Beam, Jas. Bradford, D. P. Brandon, J. J. Bachelor, J. A. Boggs, R. N. Boggs, J. T. C. Brown, H. C. Branan, J. M. Browning, J. B. Burnett, C. D. Burnett, J. L. Broadwell, J. H. Bailey, John H. Bailey, J. P. Biggers, A. M. Brown, J. N. Baker, G. B. Bennett, W. J. Baggett, J. T. Born, T. A. Barker, D. J. Barnett, M. V. Black, J. L. Burel, J. M. Bonds, D. J. Brand, O. H. Brooks, H. J. Bedingfield, W. J. Bradberry.

J. F. M. Cain, W. H. Carlisle, W. C. Cofer, I. A. Corbin, W. J. Craig, J. H. Cook, E. C. Cook, J. C. Clack, J. F. Coggins, G. W. M. Chandler, John Childs, David Carter, W. E. Cole, G. L. Craft, T. Cannon, J. M. Creel, J. A. Coker, R. W. Chapin, Jones Cain, J. T. Carlisle, W. J. Cox, Z. N. Cross, N. B. Caldwell, E. W. Casey, J. M. Carroll, W. A. Couey, W. C. Cole, S. J. Crow, G. A. Clemant, C. C. Cross, E. C. Clark, Francis Castleberry, J. A. Cain, C. B. Cook, C. A. Conway, D. M. Clower, W. A. Carroll, W. T. Craig, J. W. Cates, W. A. Copeland.

J. P. Davis, James Dollar, J. S. Duran, J. M. Dodd, S. Dillard, J. F. Daniel, J. W. Dalton, J. C. Davenport, J. S. Davis, G. H. Davies, H. Z. Day, J. J. Duran, J. C. Dutton, A. H. Dodd, T. B. Daricott, M. L. K. Durham, A. C. Dickert, J. M. Deaton, John Deaton, J. G. Dunn, A. J. Dodd, V. C. Dalton, W. H. Dollar, I. W. Duncan, B. W. Davis, R. H. Duncan, L. J. Deaton, W. M. Daniel, L. C. Davenport.

J. C. Edwards, M. A. Edwards, S. D. Edwards, S. J. Ewing, J. L. Ewing, J. L. English, Joseph Ewing, E. B. Evans, H. T. Ethridge, R. H. Elrod, Robert Ethridge, S. A. Edmonds.

W. R. Fields, H. P. Fagans, R. S. Franklin, H. R. Findley, R. P. Furgerson, D. A. Farr, S. A. Freeman, E. E. Freeman, J. J. Farr, J. P. Freeman, W. J. Forester, A. J. Furgerson, Wm. Fountain, W. N. Franklin, H. F. Freeman, J. W. Farr, H. M. Freeman, A. J. Garner, G. W. Garner, J. J. Griffeth, W. B. Gossett, S. W. Gresham, W. E. Gower, H. W. Gregg, W. M. Grogan, J. W. Griffin, T. Grimes, H. H. Grissom, W. M. Greenway, J. F. Greeson, R. M. Gower, John L. Goolsby.

M. C. Hale, J. F. Harrison, G. F. Harris, D. C. Hawthorne, H. F. Herring, J. W. Genry, M. C. Hale, J. F. Henderson, A. H. Holland, W. H. Howell, W. M. Hunnicutt, John Hays, L. W. Hays, David Hamilton, T. J. Hawkins, S. A. Hagood, T. G. Haynes, W. B. Harbin, W. M. Hamby, L. J. Hamilton, Wm. Harris, T. J. Harbin, W. J. Hay, J. A. Hall, W. H. Hosch, N. B. Hardy, Y. A. Houston, J. D. Herrington, S. D. Holmes, A. J. Haywood, F. M. Hardy, M. B. Howington, F. P. Hudson, R. M. Helton, A. A. Hayes, G. N. Herrington, J. I. Hudgins, H. H. Hinton, T. G. Holbrook, A. J. Hill, Isaac

Hill, T. C. Holt, J. J. Hinton, Peter Hester, W. N. Henderson, E. M. Henderson, W. H. Harris, T. W. Hay, G. M. Higgins, W. K. Hudlow, W. B. Hay, E. W. Hannah, D. M. Holman, J. A. Hall, T. L. Harris, A. A. Hewatt, Thos. Holbrook, J. L. Hunnicutt, J. W. Hamilton, G. W. Hopkins, John Hall, W. A. Hays,

W. D. Irwin, J. W. Jones, J. B. Johnson, T. H. Johnson, A. B. Jones, W. J. Jones, W. W. Johnson, David Johnson, J. A. Johnson, M. C. Jackson, H. M. Jackson, A. H. Jackson, O. W. Jones, W. G. Jones, T. G. Jones, Geo. H. Jones, Wilburn Jones, L. A. Juhan, W. E. Jones, R. D. Johnson.

R. Knight, A. L. King, A. J. King, Thomas Knight, C. W. Knight, Elijah Knight, W. C. Knight, A. B. Kilgore, W. E. Kilgore, John Kennedy, W. F. Kirkpatrick, J. M. Kent, J. R. Kerlin, T. J. Kilgore, G. L. Knight, W. E. Hendricks.

J. T. Lamkin, Richard Ledbetter, J. W. Lewis, P. H. Lindsey, W. R. Lawhorn, J. C. Lowery, Eli Landers, W. A. Lyle, Mathew Landers, T. J. Lamb, L. Lawson, J. M. Lawson, D. W. Lupo, G. W. Lee, W. L. Lott, J. T. Lewis, J. C. Langston, D. A. Liles, G. W. Lyle, J. M. Lindsey, J. S. Langford, J. B. Lankford, A. Lockridge, E. C. Lanford, C. P. Lively, J. W. Langley.

J. W. Mitchell, T. K. Mitchell, G. T. McMillan, H. K. McKenzie, Moses Martin, A. J. Minor, J. J. McDaniel, D. R. McDaniel, A. J. McDoniel, L. Mauldin, S. T. McElroy, D. D. McElroy, David McElroy, J. L. McGuffey, S. P. McHugh, C. W. D. McHugh, N. A. Moss, Wm. Massey, T. J. Mitchell, W. D. Massey, G. W. Mills, W. B. Moore, W. S. Mitchell, H. Maddox, D. W. Maddox, J. B. Masters, Geo. McMillan, D. H. Mobley, J. J. Moore, Thos. Morris, J. T. McElvaney, J. B. Mills, H. J. McAdams, R. N. Maffett, J. M. Medlock, J. W. McWright, ——. ——. McCart, A. C. Mitchell, Pleasant Murrow, R. F. Morgan, P. G. Maddox, G. W. McDaniel, D. McDaniel, E. V. W. Mahaffey, J. M. Mills, J. D. Mayson, Wm. McElroy, H. K. McKnight, R. P. Mitchell, E. C. Mauldin, J. M. Martin, H. B. Mathews, J. W. McCart, F. M. Mills, J. V. Montgomery, W. G. Mitchell, W. F. Maxcy, Joseph Moulder, M. M. Minor, J. F. Mathews, J. R. Mc-Kelvey, R. A. Mayfield.

W. J. Nunnally, W. D. Nichols, T. O. Norris, W. H. Neese, M. H. Neese, A. F. Norton, W. T. Nix, W. T. Nash.

Solomon Puckett, W. A. Patrick, J. M. Peters, H. Plunkett, J. M. Partain, B. F. Pugh, G. N. Pratt, David Pugh, T. J. Pass, W. W. Phillips, W. A. Patrick, S. H. Pickens, H. L. Payne, A. J. Parks, M. C. Penn, J. S. Porter, Kelly Peppers, G. H. Peppers, W. N. Pounds, S. A. Pate, J. D. Pittman, T. L. Poss, A. Parting, J. M. Peppers, J. G. Power, J. N. Pharr, J. M. Pittman, S. A. Patrick, W. M. Phillips, E. A. Puckett, H. T. Peavey, R. C. Pressley, J. P. Peavey, S. C. Poe, Nash Pirkle, W. M. Pitts, W. M. Power, J. M. Phillips, C. B. Pool.

P. H. Reese, A. J. Reese, W. W. Reynolds, R. N. Robinson, S. W. Robinson, W. E. Roebuck, Nathan Russell, T. J. Rowe, G. W. Revier, D. R. Ray, W. T. Ray, E. W. Riden, J. W. Ray, R. J. Ross, J. B. Ryler, J. F. Rutledge, C. J. Rider, C. A. Rowden, J. W. Reynolds, W. H. H. Rogers, W. J. Robinson, J. E. Robinson, J. W. Roberts, J. M. Rutledge, C. R. Ross, A. L. Rogers.

W. R. Stilwell, W. H. Smith, B. H. Stevens, W. B. Stephens, J. H. Stephens, E. Sudderth, Lewis Swords, Jas. Spicer, J. W. Shoemaker, R. N. Smith, Lindsey Smith, Britton Smith, L. R. Smith, W. H. Slaton, P. V. Singleton, Joshua Sweat, J. R. Stringer, C. C. Stone, Wm. Swafford, D. F. Spruell, N. J. Strickland, A. L. Smith, A. J. Smith, J. H. Smith, G. A. Seay, A. P. Sudderth, S. J. Stapp, D. C. Simpson, H. J. Stevenson, J. S. Spivey, A. P. Singleton, G. W. Sims, R. J. Saterfield, W. H. Sudderth, J. E. Sudderth, W. A. Sanders.

E. M. B. Taylor, J. A. Thomas, J. B. F. Dodd, Uriah Taylor, W. H. Tate, J. B. Thomas, G. W. Tatum, N. V. Tweedy, R. Thornton, H. L. Totty, G. P. Trout, G. W. Turner, J. N. Tullis, Jas. Tippins, P. S. Vandiver.

J. H. Wilson, J. O. Whitworth, J. B. Williams, J. M. Wiley, A. M. Winn, J. L. Wisdom, W. T. Wood, J. S. Wright, H. T. Wallace, J. W. Woodruff, A. J. Wages, Jas. Weathers, J. I. Wages, M. Waits, W. H. Wigley, T. A. Williams, J. W. Whitehead, M. M. Waits, W. F. Wilson, D. J. Wallace, G. W. Wright, W. A. Windsor, J. N. Worthy, W. M. Whitlock, W. J. Warbington, P. W. Whiten, W. H. White, J. B. Wright, T. V. Wheeler, J. H. Worsham, G. J. Weathers, G. J. Williams, S. G. Wiley, Asa Wright, W. J. Wootem, H. W. West, N. J. Wallace, T. F. Worthy, W. B. Williams, P. O. Whiting, J. B. Whitworth, W. M. Winant, W. W. Wilson, J. P. Webb, A. J. Webb, W. H. Wilson, W. T. Yarbrough, F. L. Yancey, D. W. Young.

WIDOWS OF CONFEDERATE SOLDIERS
WHO DREW PENSIONS

Laura F. Adams, Roxiane E. Atha, L. C. Adams, Martha Armstead, Naomi Allen, R. A. Anglin, Elizabeth Aderhold, Susan Anderson, S. C. Arnold, Mary Anglin, Mary Andrews, Margaret Anderson, Elizabeth Jane Adams.

Tremilza Brown, Eliza Brown, Margaret Bailey, Martha Boozer, Eugene Brown, Artemus Bryant, Seleta Braziel, Mary Butler, Mary Bagley, Eliza Bagwell, S. M. Bagwell, Stacy Bailey, Margaret Barnes, Matilda Brand, Susan Breedlove, Mary Brock, Elizabeth Burger, Elizabeth Burel, Martha Byrd, Parthenia Burns, Eunice Baxter, Victoria Biggers, Armitta Bailey, Rilla Brannon, Missouri Batchelor, Sara Brown, M. A. Brannon, Hattie Bolton, Malissa Bennett, Nancy Black, Ellen Beam, Frances Bennett, Mary Bass, Eliz. Brownlee,

Emily Brand, Mary Bradford, M. C. Bowen, Catherine Boner, Lucy Bowles, Delilah Brooks, F. Z. Burkhart, Eliz. Brock.

Sara Childers, Samantha Chriswell, Frances Cofer, Harriet Carroll, Permenia Coker, Mary Chapman, Nancy Corbin, Mary Criswell, Rebecca Cofield, Louisa Camp, E. A. Chastain, Amanda Churchill, R. F. Cook, Eliz. Coon, Sara Cross, Luvinia Crow, M. L. Crumpton, Nancy Crow, Sara Camp, Carrie Clark, Nancy Carter, S. A. Cole, Sara Clark, Edna Caloway, M. M. Carlisle, Martha Coggins, Mary Campbell, Eliz. Cole, Susan Casey, Julia Couey, Martha Collins, Josephine Clemant, Sara Cain.

Pollie Day, Margaret Davenport, Susan Dillard, Parthenia Davis, Sara Dodd, Martha Duncan, Frances Daniel, Mary Dutton, Eliz. Duran, Sara C. Dodd, Sytha Donaldson, Linda Dial, L. A. Deaton, Sara Downs, S. A. Dutton, Mary Douglas, S. A. Dalton, L. F. Duncan, Sara Davis, Mary Durham, Caroline Dickens.

Jane Ewing, Lina Evans, Polly Ethridge, Mary Ethridge, M. J. Ethridge, Susan Ethridge, Charity Ethridge, Mary Ewing, Phoebe Edmondson, Sara Edwards, Mary Fountain, Eliz. Freeman, Elizabeth F. Freeman, Frances Freeman, R. M. Fagans, Katie Fields, Eliz. E. Freeman, M. E. Giles, M. E. Ginn, S. S. Gower, Nancy Greeson, Samantha Glaze, M. M. Gibson, Sara Garner, Mary Grogan, Julia Green, Martha Gresham.

Percilla Holman, Nancy Hawthorns, Margaret Huston, Margaret Hix, Jane Head, Mary Haslett, M. M. Horton, Nancy Harris, Caroline Hutchins, N. A. Hill, Sarah Hadaway, Elizabeth Hale, Frances Hamilton, Laira Hunnicutt, M. M. Harrison, M. P. Haney, M. J. Holcomb, Anna Higgins, Margaret Higgins, M. J. Hunnicutt, Martha Hogan, F. A. Holbrook, L. M. Holbrook, Beaddy Holman, Mary Hosch, Margaret Hosch, Rebecca Hill, Elizabeth Holmes, Mary Hester, Sara Herring, Alice Hunnicutt, Mary Hester, Rebecca Howell, Alice Hinton, L. M. Hopkins, Elizabeth Hannah, Margaret Hill, Lula Hinton.

Harriet Jordan, Lucinda Jones, S. F. Jones, Sara Jordan, Sara S. Jordan, Julia Knight, Angelina Jackson, Elizabeth Jett, Emiline Johnson, Leddie Johnson, Nancy Johnson, Elizabeth Johnson, V. E. Johnson, Elizabeth Jones, Arabella Johnson, Georgia Jackson, Nancy Juhan, Emily Jones, Lucinda Jordan, Georgia Juhan, Amelia Jones.

S. C. Kelley, E. D. King, E. J. King, Nancy King, Mary Knight, Julia Knight, Martha Keady, Sallie Kent.

Nancy Lee, Sara Leaverett, Nancy Langford, Elizabeth Langley, Sara Langley, Elizabeth Lee, Mary Langston, S. A. Legg, Mandy Lewis, Sara Lott, Mattie Light, Julia Little, Cyntha Lockridge, Evaline Lawson, Clara Lankford, Annie Langford, Mary C. Lanford.

Sidney E. Moore, Martha McMillan, L. A. Mason, E. J. McDaniel, Mary F. McDaniel, Sara McHugh, Mary McKinney, Mary Maddox,

Allivia Mathews, S. E. Morris, Elizabeth Mooney, Mary McDonald, Mary McKerley, Elizabeth Morgan, Frances Morgan, Martha Mann, Georgia Martin, Amanda Massey, Martha Mayfield, Mary Mathews, E. M. Melton, Harriett Minor, Rebecca Mize, Susan Massey, Nancy McCurley, Louisa Mobley, Seny McDaniel, Kissiah McDaniel, Sidney E. Moore, Elizabeth McFarland, Susan Martin, Sara Montgomery, Mary Mann, Eliz. H. Martin, Eliz. Medlock, Mary Moon, Sara Moore, Roda Maddox, Emma Mitchell, Susan Martin, Margaret McCart, Athelia Mitchell, Emiline Moss, Sara McCart.

Nancy Nash, M. S. Nix, Lucinda New, Sena Newson, Rachel Nuckoll, Mary A. Nash, Margaret E. Nix, Dora H. Nash, Sara Overby, Mary Oakes, Catherine O'Kelley.

Mahala Phillips, Mary A. Peeples, Joanna Paden, Winnie Puckett, M. E. Phillips, Lucinda Peters, Martha Plunkett, R. E. Puckett, Julia Partain, S. E. Patrick, Anna Penden, M. S. Perry, Mary Phillips, Amanda Pittard, S. M. Powers, Eliz. Pruitt, L. C. Puckett, Milly Pounds, Mary Puckett, Eliz. Pugh, Mary Pugh, Mary Peavy, Sara Peavy, F. E. Peppers, Anna Pickens, Julia Parker, Mary J. Peppers, Emilne Price.

A. B. Russell, Fannie Robinson, Mary Reeves, Ritta Rutledge, Elizabeth Rawlins, A. J. Roberts, Permelia Robuck, E. E. Roquemore, Frances Rutledge, Isabella Rutledge, L. Roberts, Mary Ross, Jantha Roberts, Vianna Rogers, Frances Robinson.

C. F. Still, Margaret F. Smith, M. J. Smith, Easter Smith, Bitha Stovall, Margaret Spruell, Caledonia Sargeant, Nancy Sweat, M. M. Sims, Susan Still, A. A. Swoffard, Martha Smith, Sara Smith, E. W. Shelnutt, Amanda Stapp, Elizabeth Stanford, Eliz. Shelnutt, Eliz. Sudderth, Nancy Stephenson, Bertha Stovall, Mary Steel, Mrs. W. E. Simmons.

Susan Tapp, Sara Tucker, M. R. Turner, Rachel Taylor, Julia Thomoson, Levina Tate, Matilda Turner, Sara Trout, Ella Thurmond, Martha Upchurch, Nancy Upchurch, Eliz. Vaughan, Mary Verner, Sara Vaughan.

Hester Williams, Eliz. Williams, L. C. Wynn, Mary Wilkins, Martha Wiley, D. F. Worthy, Margaret Wages, Amanda Waiter, Salenia Waits, Mary Wall, S. A. Watson, Sara Wheeler, Rebecca Wacaster, Mary Wiggins, Mary Willard, F. C. Wood, S. A. Worthy, Lucy Webb, Matilda Whitworth, Amanda Whitworth, Mary Ward, Adelia Walton, M. C. Wise, Nancy Wade, C. E. Westbrooks, Annie White, S. F. Winn, Eliza Wells, M. J. Wisdom, Sara Worthy, Syntha Wright, Rebecca R. Winn, Martha Whitworth, Susan Wages, Abbie Wheeler, Lou F. Whiting, Mary Webb, Mrs. E. J. Whitehead, Nancy A. Young.

A Soldier's Life in Civil War

Captain Benjamin P. Weaver lived in Rockbridge district and his popularity and ability were shown by his being chosen captain of Company B, 42nd Georgia Volunteers in the Civil War. His letters to his family make interesting reading. His wife was the daughter of Thomas MaGuire.

Knoxville, Tenn., April 22, 1862.
Tuesday Evening, 4 O'clock.

Mr. Thomas MaGuire,
Dear Sir:

I write this evening to let you know how Captain B. P. Weaver is at this time. He thinks he is better and I think so, too. I wrote for you to come and see him this morning, but this evening he says he thinks he will be able in a few days to come home, if he can get a furlough, and for you not to come. I am trying to make arrangements for John W. Clower to stay and wait on him. Col. R. J. Henderson says he will do all he can for the Captain. The boys are cooking two days' rations for us to march on. We will leave here in the morning for the Cumberland Gap which, they say, is about 75 miles, which will wear me out. I am sorry the Captain is sick and I have to leave him. I remain

Your friend,
LT. ANDREW FORD,
For Capt. B. P. Weaver.

Camp Walnut Ridge, Tenn.,
December 8th, 1862.

Dear Wife and Children:

Having stopped to rest I will spend the time in writing you a line. We left our camp near Manchester yesterday morning at 9 o'clock and had a hard day's march as I ever made. The ground was covered about one inch with snow and had frozen, but thawed a little today. We made 14 miles by sunset. Camped where the snow was about four inches deep. Scratched around old logs and then piled in fence rails to lay on and make a fire. It is against orders to burn rails, but we had to do that or freeze. We burned about 500 panels during the night. We are marching in a northwest direction from Manchester. I don't know where we are going to, reports say to Murphreesborough. It looks hard to march good men in such weather. Some of my men are barefooted. I could see the tears trickling down some of their faces this morning, caused by the pain from cold, but not a murmur escaped them. I think we are seeing some hardships that will equal those of our forefathers in the old revolution; but if we can liberate our country and once more see it free, we will be satisfied to endure still more. We have marched about eight miles today and are waiting for the ground to freeze again, as it has thawed enough today to cause it to be so slick that we get lots of hard falls. My feet and ankles have been so stiff that I have but little use of myself. I have taken several hard falls today that hurt me a little. This country here is very mountainous and rough; but few inhabitants living here, no roads. My health is much better than it has been.

I would like to hear from home very much, but we will get no mail until we stop again. I wrote to you and your Pa acknowledging and giving the acct. of two letters from you. I hope Mary is well before this. I slept but little last night, it was so very cold that I could not sleep. My men are lying around me on the snow fast asleep while I write. I can't help feeling sorry for them, when I look on their toil-worn faces as they lie unconscious. Mr. Crolley gave out this morning on the road and has not come up yet. I must close.

Goodbye, my dear wife and children,

B. P. WEAVER.

(Last letter written by Captain Benj. P. Weaver to his wife before he was killed in Franklin, Tenn., November 30, 1864.)

Camp Near Florence, Ala.,
November 13th, 1864.

Dear Jenny:

This being Sunday and I at leisure I will write to you again, but have little hope of it reaching you as our communication is in a bad condition at this time. I have received but two letters from you since I left home. They were dated October 15th and 20th, and were of great satisfaction to me; but I am anxious to hear from you, not knowing what may be your situation. We have no news from Georgia that is reliable. The best information we can get is the enemy is still in Atlanta and foraging our country. I did hope that when we moved around here they would be obliged to leave that place, but it seems our best hopes are always thwarted. My general health is good at this time, though I still suffer with rheumatism in my back and hips. We suffer with cold here as we have no tents and but few blankets. We will not remain here many days longer; where we will go I cannot tell, but think we will go towards Nashville. We have done a great deal of hard marching since I overtook the army. As I have nothing else to write, I will give you a description of my trip from home to this place.

As you recollect I left you on the 8th day of October. That day we marched 2 miles, passed Conyers. Next day we marched 13 miles and camped near McDonough. The 10th we marched 15 miles and camped near Fayetteville. The 11th marched to Palmetto and reported to General Iverson. He ordered me to report to General Tyler at West Point, got to that place at time set, the 13th reported to General Tyler. He ordered me to take the next train for Montgomery. We did not get a train 'till next day at 7 a. m., the 14th. We got to Montgomery at 7 o'clock p. m., then took the Beat Toney for Selma; had a fine ride and got to Selma at daylight the 15th, and was ordered to Blue Mountain Station. Took the train at 8 o'clock a. m., got to Blue Mountain at 12 midnight, remained until day. We were now 140 miles from Selma. Set out at sun-up to march to Jacksonville, 10 miles, got to that place at 10 p. m., was put in Camp Direction October 21st. Set out again on the march in direction of Cave Springs. Marched 13 miles; found our brigade was going in the direction of Gadsden, so we turned across the mountain and marched all night and got to Gadsden at sunrise. Crossed the Coosa River which took over half a day. While waiting here I came up with your Uncle David's Ely. The captain he was with said if I did not take him he would leave him. So I took him in the hope of having a chance to send him home soon. We marched 8 miles that day. We then marched at an average of 20 miles a day for two days and a half on Sand Mountain which is a strange country. Some places level and rich. Crossed one large river, the Black Warrior, on the mountain. The people on the mountain are generally tories and poor ignorant creatures. We got to the Tennessee River at 4 p. m., the 30th, commenced shelling the enemy across the river while our men were crossing in small boats. The cowardly scamps run without firing a gun. So we marched up in town without opposition. The ladies shouting and crying in turns. This town is a nice place of about 1500 inhabitants and I expect a business place in good times. We camped in town until the 10th when we moved about two miles out north of town. We have done but little duty except build breastworks since we have been here. Our rations quite short. Cornbread and jerked beef is all we get except as we forage in the country. We can get a goat or mutton occasionally and if we could hear from home we would do pretty well.

Health of my company pretty good. Sent one man to hospital yesterday, S. C. Martin. Doctor said he had pneumonia. Say to Uncle Dave I will send Ely home by the first one that is passing. He is in good health and anxious to get home. He is of good service to me to make fires, wash, cook, etc. If you have a chance, send word to Lieutenant Williams' folks he is well and anxious to hear from them. I hope to hear from you soon. I would be so glad to hear the acursed Yanks had left Atlanta. Give my best love to all the children. Kiss Put for me. My respects to Pa and family. Tell him I would like to hear from him. So I must close my long and uninteresting letter. May God bless you, my dearest wife and little ones. Goodbye for this time.

As ever, your loving husband,
B. P. WEAVER.

Chickamauga, Tennessee,
October 20, 1863.

Dear Son:

I take my pen this morning to let you all know that I am not right well. I have got a bad cold. I have stood in the rain three days and nights, ankle deep. I am better this morning. I hope these lines will find you all well.

We are now on the road to Charleston, Tenn., they say, but I don't know where they will go to. They had a fight about Chattanooga. We whipped them bad. I can hear the cannons roaring every day.

Nicholas, be a good boy. It will make a man of you. Tell the truth and stand to it, let what will come.

Bill, you do so, too. Bill, I think I will come home again. You work good and I will bring you and Daniel and Charley a purty some day.

Rachel, can E. P. walk yet? I would like to see you all, but it is 100 miles from you all. I would like to be there to eat potatoes. I haven't had any but once and I hooked them then.

It is cold at night and I stand cold when on guard and lie cold sometimes in a mud hole. It is bad.

It is clear now. I have dried all my things. I think I can sleep tonight, if we don't travel. Daniel, Eli Landers says he wants to see you all. He could tell you a heap. Poor fellow! He sees hard times. This water does not agree with him, nor Bob, neither. When I get a letter from home, you can let me know how they are a faring and where they are.

H. C. Minor, a few lines to you. Would like to see you. I could tell you a heap that I can't write, but I am here and you are there. It may be that we will meet at home again. I want you to keep the children from cursing, if you can. I want you to tell Mama I want her to keep out of the cold as much as she can. Tell her not to be uneasy about me. I will do the best I can for myself. Go to bed and sleep, if she can.

Harriet, I don't like your Berkshire mail, but you know my reason. I don't like the direction. I want you to tell Joe Nash I want him to write.

I must close. So I remain
Father 'till death,
DANIEL MINOR.

(This was the last letter Mr. Minor wrote, having died from pneumonia in Tennessee.)

THE SIMMONS DIARY

Major Wm. E. Simmons was captured near the close of the Civil War and sent to Fort Delaware, Del., and his diary bears the date of June 5, 1865. It contains several war poems and the names of many of his fellow prisoners with their rank and address. A few are given here:

Your sincere friend, Raiford Bell, Major, 12th Miss. Regt., Infantry, Sataria, Yazoo Co., Miss.

Isaac Hardeman, Lieutenant Colonel, 12th Ga. Inft. Reg. A. N. Va., Clinton, Ga.

A. W. Gibson, Major, 45th Ga. Regt., Knoxville, Ga.

James Strawbridge, Colonel, 1st La. Inf. Regulars, New Orleans, Louisiana.

Very truly yours, James W. Hinton, Colonel, 68th Reg. No. C. L., Elizabeth City, N. C.

Thomas W. Hooper, Colonel, 21st Ga., Rome, Ga.

Houston Hall, Major, 62nd Va. Regt., Staunton, Va.

J. C. McDonald, Major, 4th Ga. Cav., Waynesville, Ga.

Geo. W. Bartlett, Captain; Brig. Gen. Irenus Staff, Wheeler's Corps, Monticello, Ga.

J. N. Harrell, Lieutenant Colonel, 1st N. C. Regt., Murfreesboro, North Carolina.

T. D. Love, Major, 24th N. C. Troops, St. Pauls, N. C.

John T. Gregory, Adjutant, 12th N. C. Inft., Halifax, N. C.

I. G. W. Steadman, Colonel, 1st Regt. Cav. Vol., Allenton, Ala.

A. S. Talley, 1st Lieutenant, Co. A, 9th Ga. Bat., Atlanta, Ga.

J. T. Morehead, Jr., Colonel, 53rd N. C. Inft., Greensboro, N. C.

W. H. Bennett, Captain, and A. C. S. Benning's Brig. A. N. Va., Columbus, Ga.

R. A. Brown, Lieutenant and Ordnance Officer, Staff General Gardner, P. A. C. T., New Orleans, La.

Richard T. Watts, Adjutant, 35 Batt. Va. Cav., Selma, Ala.

P. W. Armington, Adjutant, 30th N. C. Regt., Jackson, N. C.

P. A. McMichael, Lieutenant-Colonel, 20th S. C. Regt., Orangeburg C. H., S. C.

W. L. DePass, Captain, Lt. Batt. S. C. V. P. A. C. S., Camden, South Carolina.

W. Cosby Shame, A. D. C., P. A. C. S., Morgan's Cavalry, Breckinridge, Texas.

Wm. L. Platt, Adjutant, 7th Regt., Georgia Cavalry, Augusta, Ga.

Chas. H. Landers, Captain, Co. A, Cobb's Legion, Covington, Ga.

Captain R. T. Thorn, C. S. A., A. Inspr. General, Montgomery, Ala.

Julian P. Lee, Captain, C. S. A., Buckhead, Prince Williams County, Va.

C. S. Jenkins, Captain, Co. K, 64th Ga. Regt., Dallas, Ga.

Esquire S. Mitchell, Lieutenant, Co. F, 45th Ga. Inf., Clinton, Ga.

Delona Bunt, Lieutenant, Co. D, 3rd Ga. Bat. S. S., Lithonia, Ga.

M. F. Crumley, Captain, Co. A, 3rd Btn., Ga. S. S., Augusta, Ga.

John E. Shelton, Lieutenant, Co. E, 3rd Btn., Ga. S. S., Acworth, Georgia.

C. S. Porter, Adjutant, Cobb's Legion, Madison, Ga.

John F. Martin, Captain, Co. E, 3rd Btn., Ga. S. S., Lawrenceville, Ga.

C. M. Baldwin, Captain, Co. G, Cobb's Legion, Madison, Ga.

Henry G. Lewis, Major, 32nd N. C. Inf. A. N. V., Scuppernong, North Carolina.

Ladies were allowed to visit relatives in the prison. Major Simmons asked one of his fellow prisoners to introduce him to a young lady as his cousin, which he did. The Major asked the lady to come again and instructed her to tell her lady friends to call with the admonition that they should be sure to call for Cousin William. They did so and soon he had a continuous stream of 'cousins' calling on him. He introduced his 'cousins' to his fellow prisoners and in this manner made prison life more pleasant. His diary carries many names of these ladies, written by their own hand, a few of which are as follows:

Miss Julia Jefferson, New Castle, Del.; Mary A. Timberlake, Box 36, Norfolk, Va.; Miss Bessie Barney, New Castle, Del.; Miss Lettie Spotwood, New Castle, Del.; Marion G. Howard, Baltimore, Md.; Miss Beula S. Reese, Alexandria, Va.; Miss Julia Ogle, New Castle, Del.; Miss Virginia Harrison, Alexandria, Va.

Chapter IX

THE NEW ERA
1870 - 1900

HALF of the wealth of the county was lost by the Civil War. The plantation gave way to the small farm. The impoverished soldier had to begin life anew. For several years he was bedeviled with alien military rule. The Freedmen's Bureau, an agency set up by the Federal Government, took the freed negro in charge, supervised his work with white people, furnished him food and clothing and acted as a relief organization for the colored race. As long as it confined its work to these ends it received the respect and support of the white population; but when it attempted to give the negro a social and political standing equal to the white race, bitter opposition was met on every hand. Adam Robinson, Phillip D. Claibourne and H. C. Flournoy were agents for Bureau in Gwinnett.

Federal soldiers were stationed in the county. They supervised the elections, but their presence and activities generally were resented by the people. This opposition expressed itself in an organization calling itself the Ku Klux Klan. The Klan had its origin in Tennessee and soon spread over the entire South. With the removal of Federal soldiers from the state, with the restoration of order and with the county government in control of the white people, the Klan gradually disintegrated and passed out of existence.

The Inferior Court was abolished in 1868. The Court of Ordinary in 1852 took over all matters of estates and the board of county commissioners, created in 1872, began to function in 1873, and all other matters originally in the court's jurisdiction were handled by this body.

With the increase in population, more land was cleared and put in cultivation. Cattle, hogs and sheep ran at large. All cultivated land was fenced, usually with chestnut rails. Splitting rails, building and keeping up fences required much time and labor. The range, too, was gradually disappearing. Agitation began for a no-fence or a livestock law, which meant that stock should be placed in pastures and not be allowed to run at large. Elections were had, district by district, and in several years the livestock law prevailed over the county.

The Superior Court of Gwinnett County met in regular two weeks' session on the first Monday in September, 1871. It was then, as it is now, the custom to call the civil docket the first week, and the criminal docket the second week. The first week's session had closed and on Monday of the second week the criminal docket would be called.

The courthouse burned on Sunday night, September 10, 1871, the night prior to the time of calling the criminal docket. All the court records were destroyed in the fire except some of the records of the old Inferior Court and the Court of Ordinary.

The grand jury had been in session during the week before the burning. All business was suspended by the court except the convening of the Grand Jury for the purpose of assisting in planning the erection of a new courthouse. Prior to its abolition in 1868, the Inferior Court had charge of county affairs. The office of Ordinary was created in 1851 and this work now came under the Ordinary's jurisdiction.

The grand jury met and recommended that the Ordinary appoint a committee to cooperate with him in building a new courthouse. The Court of Ordinary met immediately, and in compliance with the recommendations of the grand jury, Ordinary James T. Lamkin appointed the following committee: R. D. Winn, James P. Simmons, M. B. Montgomery, James D. Spence and Dr. John R. Moore.

The jury expressed the belief that the burning was the work of an incendiary and recommended that the Ordinary offer a reward of $500.00 for the apprehension of the guilty party or parties with evidence to convict. This request was complied with and the reward was advertised in the Gwinnett Atlas, the immediate predecessor of the Gwinnett Herald.

At the March term of the Superior Court, 1872, the grand jury recommended that R. M. Cole be paid $50 for saving some of the records of the Court of Ordinary.

To rebuild the courthouse, bonds were issued which were purchased by the citizens of the county. On March 25, 1872, Judge Lamkin, ordinary, collected the following payments from parties who had purchased the bonds:

Name	Bonds	Price	Amount
Mary E. Moore	6 bonds	@ 92	$ 552.00
John R. Moore	4 bonds	@ 92	368.00
W. L. Vaughan	11 bonds	@ 95	1,045.00
M. W. Armstrong	12 bonds	@ 90	1,080.00
W. T. Scales	5 bonds	@ 90	450.00
G. & J. Hillyer	9 bonds	@ 90	810.00
George Hillyer	10 bonds	@ 90	900.00
J. W. Baxter	10 bonds	@ 90	900.00
W. T. Scales	2 bonds	@ 90	180.00
Joseph H. Williams	2 bonds	@ 90	180.00
John A. Born	2 bonds	@ 90	180.00

Twenty-one of the bonds became due January 1, 1873, and twenty-six on January 1, 1874, and the same number on January 1, 1875.

The completion of what is now the Southern Railroad through the county in 1871 was an event of major importance. For fifty years Lawrenceville was the only town in the county, but with the opening up of this road, Norcross, Duluth, Suwanee and Buford were founded and became live commercial centers. In 1881 a branch road was completed from Suwanee to Lawrenceville.

The Seaboard Air Line Railroad was completed through the center of the county in 1891-92 and a branch road to Loganville was built in 1898. Along this road were located the towns of Carl, Auburn, Dacula, Gloster, Luxomni, Lilburn, Grayson and Lawrenceville.

The Lawrenceville Manufacturing Company, a cotton mill, was operated in Lawrenceville during the eighteen fifties. It stood in the western part of the town in block three, between Pike and Croghan streets. J. P. Simmons was president of this company, and its successful operation for years was no doubt due to his executive ability. Enoch Steadman, a man of large estate and wide experience, was superintendent of the enterprise. The property was destroyed by fire in 1864 and Sherman's soldiers get credit for applying the torch. It was a serious loss to the business life of the community.

A cotton mill was organized and erected in Lawrenceville in 1900. For several years this plant was in continuous operation and gave employment to a large number of people. In 1940 this property was purchased by the General Shoe Company, one of the large shoe manufacturing corporations in the United States, with a dozen or more plants located in various sections of the southern states. This plant manufactures ladies' shoes exclusively, and several hundred young men and women find remunerative employment there.

One of the largest industries in the state is located at Buford. Bona Allen, Inc., manufacturers of shoes, harness, horse collars, etc., gives employment to perhaps two thousand people, and its finished products go to every part of the world. The Allens are natives of the county, and their success is a splendid illustration of what can be accomplished by work, sound business sense and unfailing integrity.

After the civil and political affairs of the county had been freed from the slimy regime of the carpetbaggers, the men who fought in the war took charge of the county and progress was the order of the day. These soldiers became the leading citizens of the county. They, for the most part, owned their homes, supported the schools and churches, kept up the public roads, sat on the petit and grand juries, served as justices of the peace, filled all positions of public trust and were as a class as fine a group of men as ever lived in the county. They pointed out the way of life from the pulpit, administered impartial justice from the bench, sought equal rights to all in legislative halls and promoted the general welfare by loving their neighbors as themselves.

Dr. Jesse Boring, noted Methodist minister, one of the family of that name that settled at Bethesda, established on April 26, 1871, a home for orphan children at Norcross at the former residence of Thomas H. Jones. Dr. Thomas Boring was placed in charge of the home and one year after the home was opened thirty-seven children were enjoying its benefits. Not long thereafter the home was moved to Decatur.

A general improvement in agriculture was noticeable throughout the county from year to year. The farmer worked hard, economized and lived simply, but it was with great difficulty that he made enough to meet his obligations and lay aside a little for a rainy day, especially so when he had to sell his cotton at five to eight cents per pound and his corn for fifty cents per bushel. In the middle eighties, this unrest began to show itself in an organization under the name of The Farmers Alliance.

THE FARMERS ALLIANCE

The movement to organize the farmers met hearty response in this county. Every community had its lodge which was a branch of the county alliance. The county alliance sent delegates to the state alliance, and the state alliance was represented in the national alliance. It was a large, live and militant organization, an agrarian revolution, county, state and nation wide in its operations and influence. The alliance won the support of a majority of the farmers and business men of the county. The merchants sought their trade and the politicians courted their influence and vote.

Two minutes of the county alliance, copied from original records, are used here. The order finally plunged headlong into politics in 1890. It placed candidates in the race for representatives and nominated its president for congress. Excitement ran high during the campaign. Tom Watson, the leader of the agrarian revolution in the state, spoke to five thousand people in Lawrenceville and the alliance candidates were swept into office. Out of the Farmers Alliance came the Populist Party.

LAWRENCEVILLE, GA., OCTOBER 24, 1888

Pursuant to adjournment the Gwinnett County Farmers Alliance met at the Baptist Church instead of at the courthouse, Col. Thomas E. Winn, president, in the chair. The sergeant-at-arms being absent, the president appointed John B. Hill for the day. The alliance was opened in regular order. The names of the several alliances were called and the delegates elected for the present quarter were enrolled as follows:

1. New Hope—A. M. Bramblett, F. M. Wages.
2. Chinquepin Grove—J. H. Freeman, W. J. H. Davis, A. J Wood, S. A. Edmonds.

3. Sweetgum Grove—L. C. Brand, J. D. Pittman, T. M. Jordan, S. M. Knight.
4. Oakland—D. S. Williams, J. D. Bagwell, A. P. Brooks, J. F. Wilson.
5. Pleasant Hill—E. M. McDaniel, J. P. Brockman, J. N. Corley, J. S. Wright.
6. Sweetwater—R. T. Upchurch, Darling Brown, H. H. Bracewell.
7. Trippe Academy—J. P. McConnell, B. B. Herring, J. F. Johnson, J. D. Williams, J. E. Kennerly.
8. Snellville—Thos. J. Cooper, T. A. Pate, E. M. Crow, A. A. Hewatt, W. H. Williams, E. T. Nix, J. B. Gresham.
9. Yellow River—E. W. Lee, W. W. Jordan, W. D. Irwin.
10. Jackson's Creek—E. C. McDaniel, Nathan Russell, T. P. Cofer, R. C. Harmon, W. L. Singleton.
11. Centreville—W. L. Livesay, S. P. Williams, G. M. Brown, F. J. Livesay.
12. Rockspring—M. C. Tanner, J. J. Hinton, J. C. Johnson, J. T. McMillan.
13. Lowery—W. S. Wages, J. C. Lowery, H. N. Mulkey.
14. Ben Smith—M. S. Brown, John Helton.
15. White Plains—Isaac Hill, John Hill, J. W. Morgan, John B. Hill.
16. Zion Hill—A. J. Pirkle, W. T. Wallace, A. J. Hadaway, S. M. Puckett, J. B. Smith, W. L. Andrews.
17. Hog Mountain—T. J. Cooper, R. M. Bural, A. F. Guthrie.
18. Gunter's—N. B. Bates, H. J. Stevenson, A. J. Abbott, G. W. Roberts, C. L. McHugh, C. D. Gunter.
19. Ivy—A. G. Beaty, J. H. Braziel, J. B. Gunter.
20. Sugar Hill—W. H. Brogdon, B. M. Garner, W. M. Shelley, W. F. Scales.
21. Smith's Grove—A. S. Street, R. L. Phillips, J. N. Verner, W. S. Moore.
22. Level Creek—A. W. Moore, J. L. Kennedy, J. H. Hawkins.
23. Farmer's Academy—M. C. Mewborn, T. W. Liddell, J. R. Noel, J. W. Langley.
24. Suwanee—J. S. Bennett, D. M. Born, A. M. Baxter.
25. Refuge—G. T. Sparks, H. L. Collins, G. B. Bennett, T. N. Smith.
26. Duluth—Daniel Windsor, Eli M. Pittard, W. M. Mewborn.
27. Norcross—A. M. Green, W. R. Simpson.
28. Shiloh—M. B. Boyce, G. W. Jackson, C. I. Flowers, G. W. Mills.
29. Beaver Ruin—J. P. Phillips, G. L. Buchanan, S. C. Martin, R. N. Holt.
30. Duncan's Creek—W. L. K. Durham, S. A. Patrick.
31. Allum Cave—W. J. Rawlins, B. F. Knight, J. A. Cox.

32. Gravel Springs—J. G. Robinson, C. B. Cross, Thomas Ramsden.

The enrolling of delegates having been completed, the president read an interesting communication from a cotton factor on trusts, after which he made some good and wholesome remarks, urging the members to stand shoulder to shoulder and make one grand effort to save the farmers and success was surely ours. The president then appointed an executive committee as follows: J. S. Dobbins, W. J. Born, F. M. Wages. The minutes of the last meeting were read and adopted. A recess of one hour was taken for dinner.

The alliance met at one o'clock. The president was asked to give his opinion in regard to ginners who are members wrapping cotton for customers who are not members in jute bagging. This he did briefly. A motion was made to add to the resolution passed at the last meeting to use anti-trust sheeting or any other material as bagging. This carried.

A motion was made and carried to require the treasurer of this alliance to enter into a bond with good and sufficient security in the sum of $500, payable to the president of this alliance and his successors in office. A motion was made to elect a trade agent by ballot, which carried. The following names were put in nomination: J. S. Dobbins, Bliss Woodward, M. C. Mewborn, A. P. Brooks, and W. J. Born. After the first ballot the names of A. P. Brooks and M. C. Mewborn were withdrawn. After the second ballot the name of Bliss Woodward was withdrawn. J. S. Dobbins was then elected.

A motion was made and carried to elect a trade committee of five for the county. Bliss Woodward, M. C. Mewborn, W. J. Born, J. W. Morgan and Thos. A. Pate were elected.

A motion was made and carried to allow the secretary to draw upon the treasurer for money to scour the church.

Upon motion the secretary is requested to tender the thanks of this body to the members of this church for the use of the building at this meeting. A motion to adjourn to meet on Wednesday after the first Tuesday in December was made and carried. This alliance then closed in regular order.

THOMAS E. WINN, President,
D. T. CAIN, Secretary.

LAWRENCEVILLE, GEORGIA, APRIL 3, 1890

The Gwinnett County Farmers Alliance met this day in the courthouse at 10 o'clock A. M., and was called to order by the president. Prayer by the chaplain. The committee on credentials submitted the following list of names as the delegates composing the body for the present quarter:

1. Sugar Hill—W. A. Brogdon, W. H. Brogdon, John Owens, J. H. Brown.
2. Smith's Grove—N. L. Pirkle, M. C. Benson.

3. Rocksprings—N. G. Pharr, S. M. Davis.
4. White Plains—John Hill, W. T. Blakey, W. S. Fowler.
5. Beaver Ruin—J. C. McDaniel, J. R. Cain, J. L. Mills, T. W. Mills.
6. Lowery's—T. B. F. Todd, Thomas Knight, J. H. L. Woodruff, W. B. Edwards.
7. Farmers Academy—J. R. Noel, M. C. Mewborn, T. W. Liddell, W. J. Langley, D. J. Langley.
8. Hog Mountain—T. J. Kennerly, H. H. Holland, J. H. Burel.
9. Gunter's Hall—I. J. Tims, J. R. Davis.
10. Sweetgum—T. M. Jordan, J. S. Davis.
11. Refuge—J. W. Roberts, H. L. Collins, W. M. Langley, W. A. Sewell.
12. Ben Smith—L. F. Maxey, J. M. Wages, W. J. Ethridge.
13. Chinquepin Grove—J. D. Hood, J. M. Newton, W. J. H. Davis, M. L. Sammon.
14. Mulberry—W. B. Stevens, W. M. Ethridge, G. W. Masters.
15. Jackson's Creek—J. C. Carroll, E. C. McDaniel, Thos. Singleton.
16. Yellow River—J. C. Cole, W. J. Jinnings, S. D. Pittard, H. B. Johnson.
17. New Hope—J. C. Johnson, T. L. Harris, J. A. Pate.
18. Duncan's Creek—J. Y. Hays, S. A. Patrick, P. H. Reese.
19. Ivy—
20. Norcross—G. H. Jones, A. M. Greer.
21. Button Gwinnett—W. N. Garner, A. Y. Pounds, H. R. Wells.
22. Zion Hill—W. A. Hays, S. M. Cross, F. L. Hamilton, J. O. Johnson, John Hamilton.
23. Suwanee—A. G. Harris, A. M. Baxter, W. L. Andrews.
24. Sweetwater—R. T. Upchurch.
25. Midway—W. G. Jacobs, A. D. Johnson.
26. Gravel Springs—H. J. Stevenson, J. P. Pharr.
27. Shiloh—M. B. Boyce, W. H. Bolton.
28. Level Creek—D. W. Andrews, A. W. Moore.
29. Centerville—J. T. Campbell, J. M. Guess, Thos. McCart.
30. Pleasant Hill—S. Z. Dyer, Daniel Windsor.
31. Mulberry 2—J. M. Deaton.
32. Alum Grove—J. H. Cox.
33. Bay Creek—G. H. Johnson, J. W. McElvaney.
34. Snellville—A. J. Harris, W. H. Williams, T. A. Pate, W. D. Sims.
35. Oakland—S. W. Paden, W. S. A. Keown.
36. Trippe—
37. Duluth—G. W. Magnus, W. F. Herrington.
38. Lawrenceville—T. K. Mitchell, N. B. Bates.

The roll was called and absentees marked. The minutes of

the last meeting of the 11th of January were read and approved. On motion the minutes of the convention of delegates who were elected by the several alliances and appointed by the president of the county alliance and who met in the courthouse on the first Tuesday in February were read and approved; but as that was not a meeting of the county alliance, the proceedings were not to be recorded on the minutes. The committee appointed to investigate the rumor as to the Buford alliance having ignored and disregarded the action of the state alliance as to using jute bagging as a covering for cotton reported that the same was true and requested that charges ought to be brought against that lodge. A motion that charges be brought against the Buford alliance was made and carried.

The president read a letter from the secretary of the DeKalb County alliance requesting the cooperation of the Gwinnett County alliance in erecting a guano factory, a cotton bagging factory, and a cotton seed oil mill in this county at the place known as the J. E. Maguire's mill. In this connection J. L. Mills offered the following resolution:

"Resolved, That the county alliance of Gwinnett County heartily endorses and approves the movement inaugurated in the DeKalb County alliance looking to the cooperation of the order of the two counties on the subject of factories, education, legislation and prices of our products and that the president appoint a committee of five to meet and act with the committees of DeKalb and Henry counties at such time and place as may be designated and that the secretary notify Col. W. G. Whitley of this action together with the names of our committee and their post offices."

The resolution was approved.

A. L. Sammon offered the following resolution, to wit:

"Resolved, That the Gwinnett County alliance urge every member to use means available to keep posted on the objects and purposes of the order and especially on the sub-treasury plan formulated by the supreme council and also the position the order has taken on the subject of railroad manipulation in this state with a view of casting their votes intelligently when candidates for the legislature and candidates for congress in this district shall ask for our suffrage. Resolved, That we know of no better way of keeping ourselves informed on these questions than taking and reading the National Economist, our national organ, and the Southern Alliance Farmer, our state organ, and we recognize them as able and zealous advocates of our righteous cause.

"Resolved, That these resolutions be published in the Southern Alliance Farmer."

This resolution was adopted.

T. B. F. Todd offered the following resolution:

"Whereas, The Exchange of Georgia is the creature of the state alliances and depends upon them for life and support in its fight against monopolies and trusts; and whereas,

"It is the duty of all true alliance men for the benefit of themselves and their families to aid in this matter so that the Exchange shall prosper and live; therefore be it

"Resolved, That we, the Gwinnett County Alliance, do recommend and endorse to the State Alliance of Georgia that the money hereafter to be raised for the Exchange shall be placed as quarterage or annual dues, say ten cents, or an amount additional on the quarter, to be applied to the Exchange, on all alliance men until the amount needed or required for the Exchange is collected so that the burden will be equal on all, and every alliance man will likewise be a member of the Exchange, and the State Alliance is requested so to act."

This resolution was adopted.

E. C. McDaniel offered the following resolution:

"Resolved, That the Gwinnett County Alliance hereby ratifies the action of the Supreme Council in the adoption of the use of cotton bagging and we urge every member to continue its use as a permanent cover for cotton provided it be of standard weight and width; that we take no step backward in this righteous warfare on the jute monopoly, but we will continue to fight it as long as this enemy is before us and we confidently expect that a satisfactory adjustment of the tare question will be arranged this year so that we will not lose anything by the use of the lighter covering."

This resolution was adopted. The alliance adjourned for dinner.

AFTERNOON SESSION

T. B. F. Todd offered the following resolution which was adopted:

"Resolved, That the Gwinnett County Alliance does most emphatically recommend and require that whosoever becomes a candidate for the legislature and wishes the support of the members of this order to pledge himself or themselves to work for retrenchment, reform and economy in the discharge of state affairs and the legislature; that he should strive to pass a bill to pay members of the legislature not more than four dollars per day for the first forty days and actual railroad mileage, and if the term should exceed the constitutional limit of forty days, the members shall receive no pay therefor. And we recommend further that our law makers work for legislation beneficial to farmers and working men and oppose monopoly in all its forms."

George H. Jones offered the following resolution which was adopted:

"Whereas, at the regular meeting of the County Alliance held on the second day of January, a convention of delegates from the several alliances was called to meet at the courthouse on the first Tuesday in February to take into consideration the policy of the alliance in politics; and whereas, said convention of delegates, elected by the several alliances, met on said first Tuesday in February and while in convention assembled nominated Col. Thomas E. Winn as the choice of the convention for representative to congress from the Ninth Congressional district of Georgia; now be it therefore

"Resolved, That we, the county alliance of Gwinnett County now assembled do heartily endorse and hereby ratify the action of said convention and most heartily recommend him to the brethren of the alliance in the said ninth district as being sound in the faith of the alliance cause and a staunch Democrat, and one in whom we can safely trust our cause."

A motion to ask the Democratic executive committee of Gwinnett County to call a primary election not later than June 15th to nominate a candidate for congress from the Ninth Congressional district was carried.

W. W. Wilson and D. T. Cain were elected delegates to the state alliance meeting in August next.

The president appointed Nathan Russell, A. W. Moore and J. C. Johnson to act as the committee on credentials. He also appointed J. T. McElvaney, N. B. Bates, G. H. Jones, W. T. Nesbit and T. W. Davis as a committee to meet with committees from Henry and DeKalb counties relative to factories, education and legislation.

The executive committee made its report, which was adopted. The report follows: "There has been paid to the secretary for the quarter ending January 1st last as fees and dues from the various alliances the total sum of $133.30
Paid to treasurer .... $ 67.30
Paid to state secretary 65.80
                                                                              ———
                                                                              133.10

                                                                              $ .20
Balance last report 27.10

Balance in secretary's hands .... $ 27.30
Received by treasurer... 67.30
Balance in hands treasurer last report....................... 98.86

Total on hand $166.16
Paid by treasurer to J. E. Cloud, business agent........$100.00

Paid doorkeeper and marshal 6.00
$106.00

$ 60.16
In hands secretary 27.30

Balance on hand .... $ 87.46

The committee has no instructions in regard to paying county business agent, J. E. Cloud, and refer the matter to your body."

J. R. Cain offered the following resolution:

"Resolved, That the County Alliance favors holding a primary election in every militia district to nominate candidates for the General Assembly and for delegates to the next congressional convention as well as to the convention to nominate a candidate for governor. This will give every voter an equal chance to express his choice for candidates. We do not believe that a courthouse caucus at this time will be satisfactory to the people and we ask the Democratic executive committee to order a primary election for governor, state house officers, commissioner of agriculture, congressman and members of the legislature, said primary to be held not later than June 15."

This resolution was adopted.

W. T. Timms, of Mulberry Alliance No. 1,490, lost his home by fire and each alliance was asked to contribute something for his relief.

A motion was adopted requiring each alliance to pay the county lecturer a reasonable sum when called on to visit an alliance.

A motion was adopted requiring an alliance buying guano through the business agent to pay him for his services.

A motion was adopted to have a meeting of the alliance the first Tuesday in June for the purpose of nominating candidates for the legislature.

There being no other business the alliance closed in regular order.

THOMAS E. WINN, President,
D. T. CAIN, Secretary.

The alliance met again on June 3, 1890, for the purpose of nominating candidates for the legislature, a candidate for congress and a candidate for governor and other state house officers. H. B. Johnson moved that the alliance proceed to nominate candidates for the legislature first. The following names were presented as candidates: Nathen Bennett, W. T. Nesbit, J. C. Carroll, J. M. Williams, J. M. Pool, H. L. Peeples, R. L. C. Weaver, J. H. Braziel, Dr. S. L. Hinton, Rev. A. H. Holland. H. L. Peeples received a majority of the votes on the first ballot. Nathen Bennett received a majority of the votes on the second ballot. Messrs. H. L. Peeples and Nathen Bennett were, therefore, declared the choice of the Gwinnett County Farmers Alliance as candidates for the legislature.

The alliance then proceeded to express its choice for governor. The names of L. F. Livingston and W. J. Northen were presented. Livingston received 46 votes and Northen 33. Livingston was therefore declared the choice for governor.

H. B. Johnson nominated Thomas E. Winn for congress. President Winn retired from the room and Vice-President H. L. Peeples put the question. Mr. Winn was the unanimous choice of this body to make the race for congress from the Ninth district.

In the general election of 1890 H. L. Peeples, of Goodwin's district, and Nathen Bennett, of Bay Creek district, were elected to represent Gwinnett County in the legislature. Thomas E. Winn also was duly chosen a representative in congress from the Ninth Congressional district. W. J. Northen was nominated and elected governor of Georgia.

COTTON BAGGING WEDDING

At the Atlanta Exposition in the fall of 1890, one day was given over to the farmers. October 29 was designated as Farmers Alliance Day and the city and the exposition grounds were overrun with tens of thousands of farmers from every section of the state. The main attraction for Farmers Alliance Day was a widely publicized cotton bagging wedding in which four couples, dressed in cotton bagging, were married at the exposition grounds in the presence of a vast throng of fun loving people. Both brides and grooms were dressed in white bagging. The dresses of the brides were made up in the style of the day by a leading Atlanta dressmaker, and the bridegrooms were supplied with suits of the same material. All were paid for by the Exposition, and each couple received $50 in gold and enough furniture to set up housekeeping. As the four couples arrived in the city, they were met by a reception committee, rushed to the shop of the tailor and dressmaker, loaded in carriages, and paraded through Whitehall and Peachtree streets to the exposition grounds between cheering throngs lining the sidewalks. Atlanta's leading citizens were in the parade.

Gwinnett County furnished one bride and one groom. The bride was Antoinette Petty and the groom George W. Stovall, both of whom lived near Grayson. The bride was 15 years old and the groom 24. Mr. Stovall died in 1906 and later Mrs. Stovall married Mr. A. V. Moon and they now reside near Grayson. In company with Dr. A. D. Williams, the author called on Mrs. Moon during the latter part of the summer of 1940. She recalled the day when she went to Atlanta and married George W. Stovall at the exposition grounds. Asked who read the marriage ceremony, she quickly replied that Sam Jones, the famous Georgia evangelist, performed the ceremony. Dr. James W. Lee, a famous Methodist preacher, who was born and reared at Centerville, married one of the couples.

"We went down to Atlanta on the 'shoo-fly' train," said she, "and it was just jammed and everybody was excited over our being the ones to get married at the fair. There was a big crowd at the depot. I went right to Mrs. Adair's millinery establishment on Whitehall Street and they fixed the dress made for me. My husband had a suit of clothes made out of that soft bagging and a new black hat. The ladies in that store fixed me up nice and I was so proud of the long skirt and pretty dress and my nice hat had lace on it, and they gave me such long white kid gloves and every one of the ladies made such a fuss over me. Well, they fixed us up nice and we got in that open carriage and it had long pieces of cotton bagging tied on it and the driver had a high hat, too. The three other couples were in carriages and so the bands struck up with lively music and we paraded through the streets and got to the fair grounds. People cheered and waved at us all along the streets. We got married on a platform out there and so did the other three couples. I never heard such a racket of yelling as the ceremony ended, and we were so happy and I was scared. Everybody was shaking our hands and telling us good luck and congratulations and all that sort of thing that goes with happy weddings. The bands played loud and the nice people of Atlanta who were our attendants were so kind and thoughtful and pleasant to us."

Spanish - American War

The Spanish-American War of 1898 attracted a number of volunteers from this county. None lost their lives in battle. John P. McDaniel died of disease February 8, 1899, at Guantanamo, Cuba, and was buried at Camp Lawton, Cuba. Several saw service in Cuba and the Philippines, but most of them served only at Camp Northen, Griffin, Ga.

Robert L. Allen—Company K, 3rd Georgia Infantry.
Robert A. Ambrose—Company A, 2nd Georgia Infantry.
William E. Aycock—Company A, 3rd Georgia Infantry.
William Bradley—Company K, 1st Georgia Infantry.
William B. Brand—Battery E, 2nd U. S. Artillery.
William E. Bryson—Company D, 2nd Georgia Infantry.
Russell A. Cain—Company F, 3rd Georgia Infantry.
Joseph A. Carter—Company G, 2nd Georgia Infantry.
Homer M. Chamblee—Company G, 2nd Georgia Infantry.
Reuben R. Cofer—Battery F, 5th U. S. Artillery; Battery B, 2nd U. S. Artillery; 13th Company Coast Artillery.

Robert L. Cole—Company I, 2nd Georgia Infantry.
Jesse P. Cooper—Company B, 7th U. S. Infantry.
Mark E. Cooper—Battery E, 2nd U. S. Artillery.
Virgil M. Copeland—Company L, 29th U. S. Vol. Infantry.
Dave C. Dean—Company L, 3rd Georgia Infantry.
Andrew J. Flowers—Company D, 3rd U. S. Vol. Infantry.
Joseph M. Gilbert—Company E, 3rd Georgia Infantry.
Bruce D. Gill—Hospital Corps, U. S. A.
Paul Hall—Company G, 2nd Georgia Infantry.
Robert A. Harmon—Battery A, Georgia Light Artillery.
William M. Harmon—61st U. S. Coast Artillery.
Ira D. Haynie—Company C, 29th U. S. Vol. Infantry.
James M. Henry—Company A, 3rd Georgia Infantry.
W. Bartow Higgins—Company A, 2nd Georgia Infantry.
Dr. Thomas E. Hill—Company H, 5th U. S. Inf. and Hospital Corps.
Arnold S. Invester—Battery A, Georgia Light Artillery, and Company G, 29th U. S. Vol. Infantry.
J. Wilburn Johns—Company M, 3rd Georgia Infantry.
James K. Johnston—Company F, 3rd Georgia Infantry.
James R. Jones—Company G, 2nd Georgia Infantry.
William S. Kemp—Company F, 29th U. S. Vol. Infantry.
Ham E. Knight—Company A, 29th U. S. Vol. Infantry.
Henry McDaniel—Troop A, 3rd U. S. Cavalry.
John P. McDaniel—Company D, 3rd U. S. Vol. Infantry.
Robert A. McDaniel—Company I, 2nd Georgia Infantry.
William Millwood—Company M, 3rd Georgia Infantry.
William Nesbit—Company L, 3rd Georgia Infantry.
Thomas O'Shields—13th Battery, U. S. Field Artillery.
Charles E. Pharr—Company E, 3rd U. S. Vol. Infantry.
Cicero E. Pharr—Company D, 2nd Georgia Infantry.
John F. T. Price—Troop G, 2nd U. S. Cavalry.
Hartwell M. Ramsey—Company B, 1st Georgia Infantry.
Joseph B. Reynolds—Company D, 3rd U. S. Vol. Infantry.
Robert Russell—Company D, 3rd U. S. Vol. Infantry.
John E. St. John—Company F, 2nd Georgia Infantry.
Abner A. Smith—Company F, 3rd Georgia Infantry.
Charles B. Spicer—Company K, 3rd Georgia Infantry.
Edward L. Thomas—Company F, 3rd Georgia Infantry.
Edgar T. Turner—Company F, 3rd Georgia Infantry and Companies D and G, 5th U. S. Infantry.
Chelsey B. Wilson—Company I, 2nd Georgia Infantry.
Homer E. Wilson—Company C, 29th U. S. Vol. Infantry.
James A. Yarbray—Battery E, 2nd U. S. Artillery.
Oscar E. Johnson—Company D, 2nd Georgia Infantry and Company I, 1st U. S. Infantry.

CHAPTER X

THE MULTIPLYING YEARS
1900 - 1943

THE horse-and-buggy age reached its highest development by nineteen hundred. In the roaring nineties a rubber-tired buggy and a fast-trotting horse indicated prominence, social standing and often romance. Rural life was simple, natural and moral. The farmer worked five or five and a half days each week, went to mill or town on Saturday afternoon, attended preaching services once a month and knew all his neighbors for a distance of four or five miles in all directions. Village life differed very little from rural life, for the villager was a farmer moved to town. He perhaps went to church twice a month, wore patent leather shoes, discarded his celluloid collar for one of linen, and began to eat post toasties and baker's bread. And at the county seat, the Georgia colonel ventured forth with a topper and a gold-headed cain; the judge drove to divine services in a two-horse carriage; the boys about town began to smoke cigarettes; mothers and daughters parked their hoopskirts and bustles in the garret, and an atmosphere of ease and courtesy and elegance permeated the social and professional life of each urban and rural community.

Electricity and the gasoline engine have changed the way of life. When a Buford citizen purchased the first car and drove it out towards Strickland's bridge, by Level Creek Methodist Church to Suwanee and back to Buford, he was from that day an enthusiastic advocate of better roads. And when the second car, a coal burner, snorting and puffing, made its initial run from Lawrenceville to Loganville, putting to flight countless herds of cows, its owner began to preach better roads even louder than the locomotive-like noise of his Franklin car. To meet the increasing clamor for better roads, the county commissioners began using convicts on the highways in 1909. The winter rains turned the roads into quagmires. The riding public now called for soiled and paved highways.

The first paving project was the Lawrenceville road to the DeKalb County line, near Tucker, completed in 1924. Since then three major highways have been paved, each extending through the county. At this writing (1943) there is a total of 96½ miles of paved roads in Gwinnett County. In addition to the paved roads, fifty-two miles of other roads have been taken over by the State Highway Department. The public roads of the county, paved and unpaved, are as good, if not better, than those of any other rural county in the state. And this progressive improvement of the roads has been financed without any material increase in the tax rate and without floating bonds. The county owes no debts and operates on a cash basis.

Modern road building is expensive. Nearly three million dollars have been paid to construct the ninety six and a half miles of paved roads in this county. It cost $10,000 a mile to grade the road from the DeKalb line through Lawrenceville to the Barrow County line, and $20,000 a mile to pave it; a total cost of $30,000 per mile. The grading and paving on the Norcross-Buford road cost $35,000 a mile.

GWINNETT'S PAVED HIGHWAYS

	Grading	Construction	Total
No. 8—23 miles— DeKalb to Barrow	$230,000	$460,000	$690,000
No. 13—25 miles— Norcross-Buford	375,000	500,000	875,000
No. 10—20 miles— Stone Mtn.-Loganville	300,000	400,000	700,000
No. 20—12 miles— L'ville-Buford	120,000	192,000	312,000
No. 20—4 miles— Buford-Cumming	32,000	64,000	96,000
No. —2½ miles— Norcross-Cumming	15,000	20,000	35,000
No. —10 miles— L'ville-Duluth	100,000	50,000	150,000
Total—96½ miles	$1,172,000	$1,686,000	$2,858,000

UNPAVED ROADS IN HIGHWAY SYSTEM

Snellville-Lithonia, 7½ miles; Lawrenceville-Snellville, 7½ miles; Norcross-Cumming, 5 miles; Hog Mountain to Barrow, 12 miles; Buford-Cumming, 6 miles; Lawrenceville-Loganville, 10 miles; Grayson-Snellville, 4 miles. This gives 52 miles of unpaved roads that are kept up by the state. On the Snellville-Lithonia road $10,000 have been spent; on the Lawrenceville-Snellville road, $112,000; and on the Lawrenceville-Loganville road, $70,000. The other roads under the state system are unimproved.

There are about 1,400 miles of roads that are kept up by the board of county commissioners. The board, at this writing, includes T. L. Harris, W. R. Hurst and Paul Dover. Mr. Dover lives at Buford, is serving his third term, works hard at his job and is a capable commissioner. Mr. Hurst lived in Garner district, but has made Lawrenceville his home since his election to the position of commissioner in 1929, an office he fills with credit to himself and satisfaction to the people of the county. Mr. Harris grew up on a farm near Snellville, became a school teacher, a rural mail carrier and for more than twenty years has served on the board of county commissioners. John N. Holder, for years chairman of the State Highway Board, spoke of Mr. Harris as being one of the most competent commissioners and road builders in the state.

M. L. Shadburn, son of the late T. C. Shadburn, was until recently state highway engineer. He was reared at Buford and honored his native county in the important position he filled. Sam Allison, division engineer, lives at Lawrenceville and has thirty-six counties under his jurisdiction.

THE WORLD WAR

During the World War, which the United States entered in 1917, there were 5,327 young men registered in Gwinnett County, 626 of whom were inducted into service. Many of them were included in the expeditionary forces and sent to France. They participated in some of the great battles that drove the enemy to defeat and surrender. The following list of officers and private soldiers has been furnished the compiler.

OFFICERS

William A. Abbott, Clara Bennett, Russell L. Boutell, Howard Huggins Buice, Alonzo Clifton Evans, Howard P. Garner, Albert Lee Hinton, Chalmers Hinton, William Jackson Hutchins, Guy Randolph Jones, Thomas H. Jones, Daniel Claud Kelley, Byrd Little, Losco LaFayette McDaniel, Irad Roland Moore, Frances Clifford Nesbit, Noye Harland Nesbit, Calvin McCluny Parsons, Jr., Maude Simpson Ramsey, James Clarence Rogers, Gladstone McClendon Rowe, Morris Luther Shadburn, Lewis Eugene Singleton, Newton H. Strickland, Lyman Dean Turner.

WORLD WAR VETERANS

James Adams, James H. Adams, Carl K. Alford, Marshall Blanchard Allen, Charlie Andrews, Silas Anglin, Howard Lester Anglin, Millard J. Arnold, Sidney E. Arnold, John R. Askew, William R. Atchison, Lonnie A. Atkinson, Melvin P. Atkinson, Noah A. Atkinson, Willie R. Atkinson, Lester Auston (col.).

Henry G. Bagley, Clifford Bailey (col.), Clifford F. Bailey, John L. Bailey, Louis Chandler Bailey, Noah Bailey, Thomas A. Bailey, Truman H. Bailey, William O. Bailey, Willie Baker, Noah Ballard (col.), Berry B. Banghcum, James C. Barker, Harry Barker, John H. Barnett, Henry A. Beard, James W. Beard (col.), Simp Benjamin (col.), Guy B. Benefield, John William Benefield, Hosea E.

HISTORY OF GWINNETT COUNTY, GEORGIA 263

Bennett, Loyd A. Bennett, Raymond L. Bennett, Richmond H. Bennett, Walter Bennett (col.), Bud B. Bentley, Geo. L. Bentley, Reuben Bentley, Clarence Reneau Beutell, James O. W. Biggers, Paul Bird, John F. Bishop, Frank N. Blair, William J. Blair, Atkinson Blake (col.), James S. Blake, Virgil D. Blake (col.), Hubert Blankenship, Robert L. Blankenship, John W. Blankenship, Grady Lee Blount, Atha Boozer, Sterling Boss, William A. Boss, Frank W. Bowden, George W. Bowen, Erman R. Bradford, Quill Bramblett, Calvin D. Brand, Perry C. Brand, Reuben A. Braswell, Carl Braziel, Burl Braziel, Clyde Braziel, Darling Britt, Walter T. Britt, William C. Britt, Will Brock (col.).

Clower Brogdon, Bonnie R. Brogdon, Ernest P. Brogdon (col.), Maze Brogdon (col.), Geo. Louis Brogdon, Jr., Guy Wilson Brogdon, Ken Brogdon (col.), Kyle W. Brogdon, Louis Warren Brogdon, William L(ester) Brogdon, Clarence S. Brooks, George Brooks, Norman C. Brooks, Truman A. Brooks, Victor Hugo Brooks, Clifford Brown, Earl A. Brown, Geo. H. Brown, James W. Brown, James H. Brown, Lawrence A. Brown, Rogers Dixon Brown, William P. Brown (col.), Bice Brownlee, Oliver Lane Brumbelow, Charley L. Bryan, Jamie N. Bryan, William H. Bryant, William J. Bryan, Grady S. Buchanan, Basker N. Burell, Howard Burnett, Alvin E. Burnett, John A. Burns, John H. Burson (col.), Albert C. Burton, Joseph H. Butler, Goodwin Brooks.

Clyde T. Cain, Collie E. Cain, Elbert Cain, Fred W. Cain, L(athan) A(ndrew) Cain, Charlie J. W. Camp, George P. Camp, Wilburn F. Camp, Albert Cantrell (col.), Roy Edward Carlyle, Amos R. Carroll, Rufus Carroll, William Glad Carroll, John A. Casey, Woodie G. Cassity, Jamie L. Cates, John M. Caylor, Dawson Chandler (col.), Bennie L. Cheek, Grady Cheek, Simon R. Cheek, Ervin C. Chesser, Luther R. Chesser, Carl J. Clack, Jewell H. Clack, Clarence Clark (col.), Robert W. Cofer, Lewis Cole, Edward C. Collins, Hines Collins, Belva Combs (col.), Quinlan B. Comfort, Jesse Cook (col.), Robert Cook (col.), Lemmie Cooper (col.), Willie M. Cooper, Floyd A. Corbin, Frank G. Craig, Raymond Craig (col.), John F. Crane, Early T. Crow, Emory Harris Crow, Love N. Crow, Nathan B. Crow, William C. Crow, John Crow Cruce, Leonard Cunningham (col.), Roy Henry Cunningham.

Henry Dailey (col.), Cliff Dalton, James Daniel (col.), Lafayette Daniel, Jones A. Davenport, Arthur D. Davis, Clyde W. Davis, Floyd Davis, Fred Iverson Davis, Guy E. Davis, Guy Z. Davis, Hoyt Davis, John L. Davis, Otis H. Davis, Sidney Harlen Davis, William C. Davis, William I. Davis, William M. Davis, James H. Deaton, Henry G. Deaton, Herbert G. Deaton, Lester Deaton, Lance G. Dean, Lawrence I. Dean, N. M. DeJarnette, John B. Dixon (col.), James Clifford Doby, Jack Dodgen, Arthur L. Dodd, Emery W. Dodd, James W. Dodd, Wiley M. D●dd, Henry V. Dollar, William H. Dowis, Ester

Dunagan (col.), James V. Dunagan, Sylvester Dunbar (col.), Calip H. Duncan, Corvin Duncan, John S. Duncan, Samuel Dunham (col.), Ezra F. Durham, Joseph J. Dutton, John Dye (col.).

Cornelius Echols (col.), Thomas S. Echols (col.), Samuel N. Edmonds, Coner Edmondson, Norman B. Edwards, Troy C. Edwards, Paul S. Elder (col.), William Elder (col.), Walter J. Ellis, George R. Ethridge, Howell R. Ethridge, Ottis Robert Ethridge, William C. Ethridge, Clark O. Eubanks, Oliver B. Everson (col.), Henry G. Evans, Paul R. Evans, Erza L. Ewing, Lorenzo Dow Ewing.

Philip Few (col.), James L. Fields, Millard H. Fincher, Lee B. Findley, Doyle Lanier Ford, John H. Ford, Milton Fortson (col.), Joseph D. Fountain, Thomas J. Fountain, Homer L. Fowler, Lewie Fowler, Marion Fowler, Guy L. Freeman (col.), Otis Freeman, Pleamon T. Freeman.

New Dock Gamble (col.), Sanders Gamble (col.), Lee Garmon, Carlus Andrew Garner, Horace B. Garner, Robert A. Garner, Thomas F. Garner, William H. Garner, William S. Garner, Jr., Will Garrison (col.), Paul T. Gary, James G. Gazaway, James M. George, Glenn H. Gilstrop, Ural Graham, Johan Grant (col.), Clarence Edward Green, Henry J. Green, James C. Green, Joseph C. Green, Samuel Green, Early T. Greeson, Henry C. Greeson, John Greeson, Willie H. Greeson, Carl I. Gresham, Lannie S. Gresham, Homer Griswell, Dee C. Gunter, Harl E. Gunter, Edwin C. Guthrie, Jessie T. Guthrie.

Arthur H. Hadaway, William E. Hall, Walter L. Hall, Claud R. Halloway, Henry G. Hambrick, Uzell Johnson Hambrick, Byron W. Hamilton, Frank I. Hamilton, Robert D. Hamilton, Daniel H. Haney, George D. Haney, Easter M. Hansard, Will G. Hardy, Arthur W. Harrington, Cliff Harris (col.), Earnest E. Harris, Ernest Harris (col.), Golden Harris (col.), John Harris (col.), Emanuel Harrison, John W. Harrison, Thomas A. Haslett, Jr., Ben Hays, Lubie T. Haynes, Loyd D. Head, Curtis (W.) Henderson, Clyde Jackson Herring, Alfred T. Herrington, Earnest Herrington, Alexander Higgins, Raymond M. Higgins, L. O. Hinton, Elery C. Hogan, George C. Holbrook, Henry D. Holbrook, James F. Holbrook, Russell B. Holbrook, Plennie Wayne Holland, Hugh L. Holt, Richard S. Holt, William G. Holt, George M. Honea, John C. Houston, Tyler P. Houston, Hillie Howell (col.), Leo Howell (col.), Toney Howell (col.), Collon J. Huff, Thomas L. Huff, Clifford Dylan Hughes, Louis E. Hughes, Ernest Noble Humphries, Joseph R. Hunt, Arthur Hush (col.), Samuel P. Hutchins, Samuel S. Hutchins, William R. Hutchins.

Grover N. Ivester, Harold Ivester, Calvin Sarims Ivey, Alonzo G. Ivy, Clifford N. Ivy.

Barney L. Jackson, George Jackson (col.), George Jackson, Henry B. Jackson, John A. Jackson, Luther Jackson, Pennel E. Jackson, Eugene L. Jenkins (col.), Albert S. Johnson, Collie M. Johnson, Joseph A. Johnson, Joe D. Johnson, Miles M. Johnson, Oady

Johnson, Quillan Alexander Johnston, Vannoy R. Johnson (col.), William C. Johnson, Asher Jones (col.), George W. Jones, Henry G. Jones, John Jones, Lemiel I(saac) Jones, Mack H. Jones (col.), Roy S. Jones, Tom Jones (col.), Usher Jones (col.), Grady B. Jordan, Robert Marvin Kellett, Herman M. Kelley, John I. Kelley, Otis S. Kelley, Paul V. Kelley, William A. Kelley, Oliver Kenedy, Ernest L. Keown, Leslie Earnest Kidd, Jackson F. Kilgore (col.), Roy King, James F. Knight.

Luther L. Landress, Summey L. Lanford, William Thomas Lane, Horace F. Lawson, Donnell Lee (col.), Henry Lewis (col.), Roy Lewis (col.), Frank Liddell (col.), Floyd P. Lietch, Frank Y. Light, James E. Long, John Long, Clifford Lott (col.), Cuthbert C. Lowe, Buran E. Lowry, Guy O. Lowry, Waymond Lucas (col.).

Claud McCarty, John Newton McClure, Claud S. McDaniel, Fred McDaniel, James McDaniel, James T. McElreath, Arthur B. McElroy, Leonard Frank McElroy, Orval A. McGee, Robert Ritchard McGee, Dewey S. McHugh, Clark J. McKerley, Will W. McKerley, William C. McKerley, Warren McKinney (col.), Will McKinney, Olen E. McNabb.

Herman Mabry, David A. Maddox, George Lester Maddox, James S. Maddox, John L. Maddox, Bliss E. Maffett, William Florence Maffett, Alston Martin, Virgil E. Martin, Clifford M. Mason, Bernard Victor Maughon, Arthur L. Maxey, Robert David Medlock, T(homas) E(dwin) Medlock, Willis Hugh Medlock, John Raymond Merritt, Barto Middlebrooks (col.), Clarence Miller, Reps Miller, Joseph P. Milligan, Marion Mills, Henry L. Mitchell, William L. Mitchell, Dock Moody, George L. Moon, Robert Moon, Gilbert Moore, Patrick E. Moran, Henry G. Morgan, Fletcher W. Mosley (col.), Earnest Moulder, Talmage D. Murdock, Ernest E. Murphy, Forrest Murphy.

Jewitt Nance (col.), Ed Nash (col.), Emmett Nash (col.), Ethel Eli Nash, Garner H. Nash (col.), Jewell T. Nash, John Nash (col.), Roy T. Nash, Cliston Neal (col.), Miller Neal (col.), Charles P. Nelson, Barney J. Nesbit (col.), Eddie M. New, Roy C. New, Willis T. Newman, Paul W. Nichols, Carl A. Nix, Charley G. Norton, Thomas O. Nuckles.

James R. Oakes, Julius C. Oakes, Walter Patrick O'Rourke, Willie Orr (col.), James T. O'Shields, Floyd R. Otweld, George L. Owens, Roy F. Owens.

George A. Paden, Joe Parks, Calvin M. Parsons, Jr., Fred M. Parsons (col.), Gamaliel Parsons (col.), David N. Partee, F(rank) S. Partridge, George S. Partridge, Bothwell Pass, Joseph C. Pass, Atticus H. Pattillo, Leonard Booker Pattillo, Elmer B. Pearson, James W. Perkins, Enos Windell Petty, Cecil S. Pharr, Otis N. Pharr, James A. Phillips, William E. Phillips, William Phillips (col.), William T. Pickens, R. P. Pickens, Grover Pipkins, William L. Pirkle, Willie S. Pittard, Lonnie L. Pitman, Moses Poole (col.), Louy S. Pounds,

Chalmers Powell, Arthur W. Powers (col.), Andrew O. Pratt, Middleton P. Pratt, Ernest G. Pruett, Pickett W. Pruett, James T. Puckett, Zealous H. Puckett, Alvin Pugh, Wesley Pugh. Edwin Herbert Quinn.

Joseph A. Rabern, Lynton F. Ramsey, Clyde Z. Rawlins, Hugh Livingston Ray, George Reese, Hoyt W. Reese, Floyd L. Reeves, Winfred James Reeves, Robert Reid, George Reynolds, Lewis K. Rhodes, Hollie J. Riley, Andrew Roberts, Corris Boston Roberts (col.), Elbert J. Roberts, James P. Roberts, John A. Roberts, Quinton Henry Roberts, Rollie William Roberts, William W. Roberts, Frank Robertson, William David Robertson, Claude E. Robinson, Hardy G. Robinson, Joe Rogers (col.), Robert C. Rogers, Joe J. Rolader, John H. Rooks, Spartan E. Roper, Walter Roper, Sidney Adolphus Ross, Wiley I. Ross, Erskine P. Rowe, Hope Russell, Israel D. Rutledge, Ronzo Dewy Rutledge.

Guy Samples, Benjamin F. Sapp, John Die Satterfield, Fred I. Sears, Thesta Settle, Toy Eugene Settle, George L. Shadburn, Jr., Fred W. Shellnut, John C. Shelnut, Claude W. Sheubert, Daniel L. Shell, L. W. Sikes, Alonzo L. Simonton, Jonah Simonton, John R. Simonton, Richard C. Simonton, Robert C. Simonton, Johnie Sims, Roger Sims (col.), Vaughnam A. Sims, Benjamin F. Simpson, Oliver Orion Simpson, Alvert I. Singleton, John H. Sizemore, Frank Skinner, Early Smith (col.), Enlo E. Smith, Isiah Smith (col.), James T. Smith, Jesse Smith (col.), John Calhoun Smith (col.), John D. Smith, Lewis Smith, Oscar E. Smith, Winslow W. Smith, Robert Sorrels (col.), Maury A(lexander) Sprayberry, Judson Lowe Stanley, Clyde W. Stephens, Albert R. Stewart, William G. Stewart, John B. Stone, Frank C. Street, James H. Street, Artie C. Streetie (col.), Charlie Edward Strickland, Millard Strickland (col.), Wiley Strickland, Walter L. Strickland, Miles Strong (col.), Alvin A. Sudderth, Lovic C. Sudderth, Hilluer (Hillyer?) M. Summerlin, Benjamin F. Summerour, Charles W. Summerour, Jr., Arthur Summey, Golden Sweat.

Walter C. Tankersley, Harrison T. Tanner, John P. Tanner, Mat Tanner (col.), William Maynard Tanner, Lewis C. Tatum, Darling R. Taylor, Elmer E. Taylor, Amos A. Teague, Walter O. Teague, John E. Terrell (col.), Howard H. Terry, Luther Thornhill, Charles A. Thomas (col.), Frank Thomas (col.), Lonnie F. Thomas (col.), John W. Thompson, Willie Thompson (col.), Leno Wiley Thornton (col.), Scott Thornton (col.), Charles W. Tisdale, Marion Towler, George J. Towler, Dallas T. Townley, Earl D. Townley, Howard T. Townley, John Tribble (col.), Arthur J. Tuck, E(a)rnest U. Tuck, George S. Tuck, Hugh E. Tuck, Jesse D. Tuggle, Clarence W. Turner, James H. Twitty.

William Henry Vandeford, Edgar Allen Vance, Robert G. Vance, Jessie Varner (col.), Alexander Vines (col.).

Henry Walker (col.), Buel H. Wallace, Russ Warbington (col.), William A. Warbington, Otto Ward (col.), Henry B. Waters (col.), James C. Waters, Malone Waters (col.), Doctor D. Watkins, Asberry Weathers, Norman A. Weathers, Obie Weaver (col.), Almand C. Webb, Glynn C. Webb, William A. Webb, Lem O. Webb, Theron V. Webb, Edward Weeden, Charles N. West, Woodfin West, Samuel G. Westbrook, Albert Wheat (col.), Emory White, Henry G. White, James A. White, Norman White, Amos Whitehead (col.), John H. Wilbanks, Robert Cloy Wilbanks, John Alfred Williams, John W. Williams (col.), Joseph Wilmot (col.), David C. Wilson, Doff Wilson, Jonah Wilson (col.), Luther Odus Wilson, Roy C. Wilson, William Witherspoon (col.), Henry Witt (col.), George Woodcliff (col.), Grover Wofford (col.), Moses Clifford Wofford, Robert P. Wood, Marvin O. Worthy, Gordon L. Wright, Thomas Wright (col.), Virgil E. Wright.

Arthur P. Young, Calvin D. Young, Fred Young, George Young (col.), John Q. Youngblood.

DECEASED

Homer D. Brooks, George Harold Byrd, Charlie Clack, Virgil G(uerry) Craig, William I. Hannah, Charles E. Hawthorne, Charles W. Holbrook, Rubie L. Johnson, Willie Kinchen (col.), James R. King, Paul H. Marchman, Willie Mathews (col.), Sampson Melton (col.), Clarence R. Morgan, Clyde Y. Nix, Lloyd C. O'Kelly, Dee Phillips (col.), John C. Reeves, Robert L. Roberts, James P. Samples, Clarence B. Tumlin, Zed Tye (col.), Lewis Webb, Leroy White (col.), Ivory W. Woodward, Arthur C. Wylie, Lee Frank Youngblood.

NAVY

Samuel Knox Abbott, James Arthur Alford, John Inzer Alford, James Lewis Bennett, Clifford Hugh Britt, Charles Frederick Brown, Calvin Marion Cain, John Rufus Cain, Troy Lee Carroll, Henry Bern Coffman, Weyman Wesley Cooper, Joseph Daniel Cross, Walter Winn Davis, James Reed Gouge, Ernest Floyd Green, William Ivie Hagood, Frank Meadows Haygood, William Vernis Hays, Jesse Herrington, Henry Grady Hewatt, John Hubert Higgins, Claude Hinton, Olin Jackson Holland, James Hoyt Holt, Fred Rick Humphries, Frank Johnson, James Lee Johnson, Ollie Lee Johnson, Robert Plinnie Johnston, James Thomas Jordan, Logan Harrison Kelley, Ernest Kent, Earnest Harrison King, Thomas Leonard Lanford, Jeter Schuylar Ledford, Thomas Aubury McClung, Tom Wilkes McDaniel, Luther Franklin McKelvey.

Charles Tillman Martin, Lovic Brogdon Martin, Marvin Clarence Mauldin, Maurice Marl Nesbit, Robert Lee Norton, Clarence Nicely Oakes, Tandy Mitchell Patterson, Alfred Lamar Philyaw, Raleigh Hobart Pierce, Harry Douglas Power, John Wiley Reese, Raymond Reed Roberts, Bonnie Gordon Rowe, Thomas Eson Sams, John

Williams Seay, Joseph Ernest Shafer, James Franklin Simpson, Glenn Beauregard Strickland, James Henry Strickland, Leonard Sudderth, Albert Griffie Summers, John Borton Thrasher, Emory Austell Thompson, Charles Armon Turner, David Leonard Venable, Newton Jackson Waits, Richard Tillman Waits, Cliff Henry Webb, Frank Harold Webb, George Franklin Wilson, Absolom Holbrook Wingo, Jr., Elmer Spergeon Wright, Ned Ebraska Yearwood.

Robert Lee Voyles (died September 28, 1919).

DISTINGUISHED SERVICE CROSS

Awarded for Extraordinary Heroism in Action to Natives of Gwinnett County Who Served in the Army During the World War

KELLEY, HENRY G.—Place of birth, Buford. Private, Company G, 119th Inf., 30th Division. Near Bellicourt, France, September 20, 1918, voluntarily advancing alone against a machine-gun nest which was causing heavy casualties in his platoon, he bombed the enemy position, killing five of the crew and capturing the remaining three.

MAHAFFEY, EMORY.—Cantigne, France, May 28-29, 1918. Private, 1st Class, Medical Detachment, 28th Inf., 1st Division. He did more than his duty under violent fire in the open to relieve the sufferings of the wounded. On his way to a machine-gun emplacement to succor men who had been injured there, he stopped to give first aid to Private Jay L. Antes who lay mortally wounded and exposed to machine-gun fire and while performing this heroic aid was killed. Posthumously awarded. Medal presented to his mother, Mrs. Victoria Mahaffey. Was a native of Gwinnett County but lived in Atlanta.

DISTINGUISHED SERVICE CROSS

Awarded for Exceptionally Meritorious and Distinguished Service

JONES, CLIFFORD.—G. O. No. 56 W. D. Lived at Norcross. Colonel (Coast Artillery Corps), General Staff Corps, United States Army. In the office of the executive office of the Chief of Staff during the World War and the following demobilization period, his tactfulness and initiative in meeting the varied situations presented and sound judgment in passing upon many matters of the highest importance contributed materially to the successful functioning of that office during the war. During demobilization his conception and organization of the emergency discharge section of the office not only protected the War Department from imposition but served in a marked degree to preserve the morale of the civilian population during that trying period.

WOUNDED U. S. MARINES WHO LIVED OR WERE BORN IN GWINNETT COUNTY

ANGLIN, HOWARD L.—Private, Org., 74th Co., 6th Regiment. Gassed April 13, 1918.

IVESTER, HAROLD.—Private, Org., 74th Co., 6th Regiment. Gassed April 13, 1918.

SYKES, JOHN D.—Born in Gwinnett. Private, Org., 80th Co., 6th Regiment. Wounded July 19, 1918. Died later of disease.

UNITED STATES SHIP CYCLOPS

Cyclops, a Navy Collier, tonnage 19,360, left the Barbados, West Indies, March 4, 1918, and was never heard of again. On June 14, 1918, the Navy Department officially announced the death of all on board this ship. It has been said that the Navy Department was advised in 1930 that the Cyclops was sunk by an explosion of bombs placed in the engine room by German agents. There were 309 men on the ship, all of whom were lost. Among the lost was Orth Stanley, son of R. L. Stanley, who lives three miles east of Lawrenceville.

NURSES IN WORLD WAR

Of the 238 Georgia women who were commissioned in the Army Nurse Corps during the World War, two were from Gwinnett County. They were Cleo Booth, daughter of Frank Booth, Centerville, and Edith A. Pirkle, of Norcross.

OTRANTO WENT DOWN

The British ship, Otranto, with 701 American soldiers, sailed from Hoboken, N. J., September 25, 1918. The greater number of these soldiers were trained in coast artillery tactics at Fort Screven, Ga. The ship was struck by another British ship during a storm off the coast of Scotland on October 6th and was sunk, and 369 American boys lost their lives. Of this number, one hundred and forty were native and adopted Georgians.

Raymond R. Knight, a native of Gwinnett County, was one of the lost.

DIED OF DISEASE WHILE IN U. S.

ALLEN, THOS. M.—Born in Gwinnett; Org., Co. A, 122nd Infantry. Died July 8, 1918.

CRAIG, VIRGIL G.—Private, Org., SATC University of Georgia. Died October 7, 1918.

O'KELLEY, LLOYD C.—Born in Gwinnett; Corporal, Org., Supply Co., 27th Infantry. Died November 4, 1918.

TUMLIN, CLARENCE B.—Born in Kentucky, residence in Gwinnett; Private, Org., Company B, 122nd Infantry. Died September 20, 1918.

YOUNGBLOOD, LEE F.—Private, Org., Company C, 106th F. Sig. Bn. Died January 5, 1918.

Wounded in World War While Serving in United States Army

OFFICERS

WARD, THOS. F.—First Lieutenant, Org., 106th Inf., 27th Division, at Bony, France. Degree, severe. Awarded Distinguished Service Cross.

PRIVATES

ASKEW, JOHN R.—Org., Co. H, 28th Inf. Degree, severe; October 6, 1918. Awarded a citation.

ATKINSON, LONNIE A.—Org., Co. H., 6th Inf. Severe, November 4, 1918.

BLAKE, JAS. S.—1st Cl., Org., Co. B, 102nd MG. Bn. Slight, October 23, 1918.

BLANKINSHIP, JOHN W.—Org., Co. I, 28th Inf. Severe, October 17, 1918.

BROOKS, TRUMAN A.—Org., Co. L, 326th Inf. Severe, October 17, 1918.

BROWN, FLOYD—Org., Co. M, 327th Inf. Slight, September 12, 1918.

COFER, ROBT. W.—1st Cl., Org., Co. M, 327th Inf. Severe, October 8, 1918.

ENGLISH, BYRD P.—1st Cl., Org., Co. E, 327 Inf. Slight, September 17, 1918.

GUNTER, LEON O.—Org., Co. B, 151st MG Bn. Severe, July 27, 1918.

HAYNES, LUBIE T.—Org., Co. B, 131st Inf. Slight, October 12, 1918.

HOGAN, ELERY C.—Corporal, Org., Co. C, 307th F. Sig. Bn. Severe, October 12, 1918.

HOLBROOK, HENRY D.—Sergeant, Org., Co. I, 26th Inf. Severe, October 10, 1918.

HUGHES, LOUIS E.—1st Cl., Org., Co. I, 26th Inf. Severe, September 12, 1918.

LANDRESS, CHANCY H.—Org., Co. D, 23rd Inf. Slight, October 6, 1918.

MADDOX, GEO. L.—Org., Co. F, 23rd Inf. Slight, October 6, 1918.

PHARR, WENDAL W.—Org., Co. D, 309th Am Tn. Untdt. October 14, 1918.

PRUETT, ERNEST G.—1st Cl., Org., 13th Amb. Co., 1st San Tn. Slight, April 28, 1918—Slight, October 9, 1918.

ROBINSON, CLAUD E.—Org., Co. M, 126 Inf. Severe, October 2, 1918.

RUSSELL, HOPE—1st Cl., Org., Co. H, 9th Inf. Severe, October 7, 1918.

TAYLOR, DARLING R.—Org., Co. H, 9th Inf. Severe, October 3, 1918.

TAYLOR, ELMER E.—Org., Co. H, 9th Inf. Severe, October 3, 1918.

TERRY, HOWARD H.—Org., Co. F, 131st Inf. Slight, October 17, 1918.

TOWNLEY, DALLAS T.—Org., Co. B, 110th Am. Tn. Slight, September 26, 1918.

WEBB, GLYNN C.—Hostler, Org., Co. C, 8th F. Sig. Bn. Slight, September 30, 1918.

WILSON, DAVID.—Org., Co. K, 11th Inf. Severe, September 12, 1918.

WILSON, Wm. R.—Org., Co. B, 9th Inf. Severe, October 3, 1918.

Heroic Sons of Gwinnett County Who Made the Supreme Sacrifice in the Cause of Humanity in the World War

LIEUTENANT GEORGE HAROLD BYRD, Lawrenceville, Ga.

Lieutenant Byrd entered the Officers Training Camp at Fort McPherson, Ga., August 15, 1917. After receiving his commission he was attached to 327th Infantry, 82nd Division, Camp Gordon, Ga. He embarked for overseas April 25, 1918. Lieutenant Byrd was killed in action by a high explosive shell fragment October 11, 1918, Argonne, France. His body was returned and lies by the side of his parents, Mr. and Mrs. J. P. Byrd, in Shadowlawn Cemetery, Lawrenceville.

JOHN COLEMAN REEVES, Lawrenceville, Ga.

Private Reeves entered service May 29, 1918. After receiving his military training he was attached to Company B, 47th Infantry, and embarked for oversea service July 26, 1918. Private Reeves was engaged in active service when killed in the battle of the Argonne Forest, France, October 7, 1918.

CLYDE YATES NIX, Grayson, Ga.

Corporal Nix entered the service in November, 1917. He received his military training in local camps and was attached to Machine Gun Company, 327th Infantry, 82nd Division, with which unit he embarked for oversea service and was killed in action in the Argonne Forest sector by a machine gun bullet, October 13, 1918.

HOMER D. BROOKS, Norcross, Ga.

Private Brooks entered the service May 29, 1918. He was attached to Company L, 102nd Infantry, 26th Division, Camp Gordon, Atlanta, Georgia, and embarked for oversea service with this unit. He was killed in action at Bois de Ormont, France, October 25, 1918.

CLARENCE RAINEY MORGAN, Norcross, Ga.

Private Morgan entered service September 7, 1918. He was attached to Company "I," 5th Replacement Battalion, 161st Regiment, Unassigned Division. He embarked for overseas October 18, 1918. He contracted pneumonia, which resulted in his death at St. Aignan, France, November 28, 1918.

JAMES R. KING, Lawrenceville, Ga.

After a short period of military training in local camps, Private King was attached to Company C, 163rd Infantry, American Expeditionary Forces, and with this unit embarked for overseas. After arriving in France he contracted pneumonia which resulted in his death September 14, 1918, in an American Base Hospital.

CHARLIE E. HAWTHORNE, Grayson, Ga.

After receiving his preliminary training in local camps, Private Hawthorne was attached to Company B, 30th Infantry, First Division, and with this unit embarked for overseas. Private Hawthorne served in the front line trenches in several battles before he was killed in action October 10, 1918, at Meuse-Argonne, France.

WILLIAM I. HANNAH, Buford, Ga.

Private Hannah entered the service August 26, 1918. He was attached to Company A, 2nd Infantry Replacement Regiment, Camp Gordon, Atlanta, Ga. After a short period of training, he embarked for overseas. He contracted measles, which later developed into pneumonia, resulting in his death at Le Mans, France, December 2, 1918.

CHARLES CLACK, Lawrenceville, Ga.

Private Clack entered service September 7, 1918. He was attached to 17th Company, September Automatic Replacement Draft, Camp Gordon, Atlanta, Ga., and embarked for overseas with this unit. Upon his arrival at Winchester, England, he contracted pneumonia, which resulted in his death at Morn Hill, England, November 14, 1918.

ARTHUR CLINTON WYLIE, Buford, Ga.

Private Wylie entered the service as a member of the Georgia National Guard, and was attached to Company K, 5th Georgia Infantry. After a short period of training in local camps, he embarked for oversea service. He was stationed in the front line trenches when killed in action, July 18, 1918.

IVORY W. WOODWARD, Buford, Ga.

Private Woodward entered service April 1, 1917. He was in training at Fort Oglethorpe, Georgia, for about nine months. He served also on the Mexican border. He was attached to Company B, 6th Infantry, 10th Division. He embarked for overseas April 12, 1918, and was killed in action at St. Mihiel, France, September 14, 1918.

LEWIS WEBB, Lawrenceville, Ga.

Private Webb entered service August 15, 1918. He was attached to the 22nd Company, September Automatic Replacement Draft, Camp Gordon, Ga. He was later transferred to Camp Merritt, N. J., from which point he embarked overseas. Upon his arrival in England he contracted pneumonia, which resulted in his death in Paignton Hospital, England, September 30, 1918.

JAMES PRESSLY SAMPLES, Lawrenceville, Ga.

Corporal Samples entered service May 29, 1918, at Camp Gordon, Ga., and was later transferred to Camp Merritt, N. J., from where he embarked for overseas August 14, 1918. He was attached to Company D, 39th Infantry, 4th Division. He was wounded in action on the Argonne-Meuse front, dying as a result of his wounds in Evacuation Hospital No. 8, October 13, 1918.

RUBIE JOHNSON

Home, Gwinnett; private, Org., Co. E, 17th Inf. Killed in action November 7, 1918, Meuse-Argonne, France.

PAUL H. MARCHMAN

Residence, Gwinnett; private, Org., Co. G, 165th Infantry. Killed in action July 15, 1918, Aubrive, France.

THE AMERICAN LEGION

The American Legion includes in its membership veterans of the World War. There are two posts in Gwinnett County, the Hugh Holt Post at Lawrenceville, and the Ivy Woodward Post at Buford.

PREAMBLE OF THE CONSTITUTION OF THE AMERICAN LEGION

"For God and country, we associate ourselves together for the following purposes: to uphold and defend the Constitution of the United States of America; to maintain law and order; to foster and perpetuate a one hundred per cent Americanism; to preserve the memories and incidents of our association in the Great War;

to inculcate a sense of individual obligation to the community, state and nation; to combat the autocracy of both the classes and the masses; to make right the master of might; to promote peace and good will on earth; to safeguard and transmit to posterity the principles of justice, freedom and democracy; to consecrate and sanctify our comradeship by our devotion to mutual helpfulness."

AMERICAN LEGION AUXILIARY

The American Legion Auxiliary is a civil organization of the wives, mothers, daughters and sisters of the members of the American Legion, and of the wives, mothers, daughters and sisters of the men and women who were in the military or naval service of the United States between April 6, 1917, and November 11, 1918, and died in line of duty or after honorable discharge; and of those women who of their own right are eligible to membership in the American Legion. The preamble of its constitution and by-laws is the same as that of the American Legion with the exception of one clause which reads as follows: 'To participate in and to contribute to the accomplishment of the aims and purposes of the American Legion.'

THE NEW DEAL

Several agencies of the State and Federal governments operate in the county for the benefit of the people. The county health department, with its full-time physician and two trained nurses, gives aid to many. This is a valuable service that needs to be supported and developed. A county hospital is needed.

The United States Department of Agriculture, through its extension service, has done a vast amount of good in educating the farmers in the science of agriculture. This service operates through a county agent. Soil improvement, pure bred stock, cattle, hogs and poultry; diversification and rotation of crops—these and other problems are being solved through this department.

The Agricultural Adjustment Administration, known as the triple AAA, is administered by the farmers themselves. The government pays certain sums to farmers to limit production of staple crops—cotton here—and allows benefits for food and soil building crops.

The Farm Security Administration finances worthy persons to operate their farms. Loans are advanced in instances where credit can not be secured from banks or individuals. A farmer can also purchase land on long time and pay the loan over a period of thirty or more years. There are in Gwinnett County 17 farmers who have purchased land under this arrangement.

The Soil Conservation Service should prove vastly beneficial to the farmers. Its main object is to conserve the soil and stop erosion. This is done in part by proper ditching and terracing, as well as by planting such root crops as will prevent or lessen erosion.

The home demonstration agent makes a strong bid for public favor. She operates among all classes, rural homes receiving special attention. Home life, with its garden and flower yard, its balanced budget and the intricate problems of home economics, the rearing and education of children, is a question that challenges the attention of all housewives.

The Department of Public Welfare seeks employment for those who need work. Pensions are granted to those who come within the requirements of the law. The blind are aided, the illiterate are taught to read and write, and other classes receive aid from a benevolent government.

Diversification of crops and placing every farm family on a self-sustaining basis should be, and is, the goal of the various agencies that operate in the county. A healthy, well fed, well housed, well clothed and well educated family, with an income from the farm equal to that of the family engaged in industry or employed in labor, is the hope of the country and it is not asking too much of those in authority to work and legislate to that end.

The dairy industry is a growing business in the county. Modern, sanitary dairies, equipped with every modern device, are located in various communities and find a ready market in near-by towns and in Atlanta. There is a noticeable increase also in truck farming and the poultry industry.

A desire that farmers of the county be provided with home-grown seed led to the organization of a cooperative seed-cleaning plant at Lawrenceville. Not only are the farmers assured of clean seed, but the plant is designed to be a place where seed can be exchanged from one farmer to another. A farmer, for instance, has fifty bushels of oats for sale. He takes them to the plant, has them graded and cleaned, and leaves them. Most farmers in the county are learning that this plant is the place to go when they want to buy seed. The machine which was bought cooperatively by farmers of the county cleans every kind of seed. Not only has it served its purpose in turning out quality small grains, but farmers have brought their turnip and collard seed to be cleaned and these, in turn, have been sold to local merchants at a good price. The seed-cleaning machine is said to be the best of its kind made in America. The seed pass over or through four screens, 36 by 48 inches, and the machine is also equipped with a suction. This gives a separation both as to size and weight of the seed. It not only removes all kinds of weed seed but small, weak seed grain.

SALUTE TO GWINNETT COUNTY

On December 20, 1941, The Atlanta Journal's radio station, WSB, broadcast over a nation-wide hookup from the Colonial

Theater in Lawrenceville a salute to Gwinnett County. The program included vocal and instrumental music and three-minute talks by the county historian, the county superintendent of schools and the county home demonstration agent. The county historian said:

"The General Assembly of this state passed a resolution creating Gwinnett County December 15, 1818. The county was named for Button Gwinnett, a representative in the continental congress, signer of the Declaration of Independence and governor of this state. William Maltbie named the new county seat town for Captain James Lawrence, famous officer in the American navy. At the same time the four streets bordering the courthouse square were named for Zebulon Pike, Commodore Perry, George W. Croghan and Augustin S. Clayton, famous American soldiers and statesmen. Settled by many of the veterans of the Revolutionary War and of the War of 1812 and by the descendants of those who founded this great state on the principles of wisdom, justice and moderation, it is needless to say that in all of our wars the people of this county have exemplified on countless battlefields that courage and that chivalry that are common heritage and the personal possession of every patriotic citizen who fights his country's battles. And in the great conflict in which our country is now engaged, this county stands one hundred per cent behind our President and our soldier boys and not one of us will be satisfied until victory crowns American arms and Hitlerism is swept from the face of this earth.

"Two years after the creation of the county, its population was 4,700. Ten years later its population was more than 13,000. Here they came by hundreds and thousands from older counties and older states. Here came Elisha Winn and William Maltbie, N. L. Hutchins and Asahel R. Smith, Isham Williams and William Nesbit, Robert Craig and John S. Wilson; here came Thomas H. Jones, whose grandson, a native of Norcross, is today a brigadier general in the United States Army; here came Evan Howell whose descendants have been the publishers of an Atlanta daily paper; here came John Rogers, of the same family that gave to the world the famous Will Rogers, of Oklahoma; here came John Alexander, one of whose grandsons is the present chief justice of the Supreme Court of Texas. Here all these and thousands more came, seeking new homes and an opportunity to begin life again.

"Gwinnett County lies between Atlanta and Athens. It has an area of 440 square miles and a population of 30,000, ninety per cent of whom are Anglo-Saxons. There are ten incorporated towns in the county. Two great railroads pass through the county. Three paved highways traverse the county from east to west. One hundred miles of its roads have been paved at a cost of about three million dollars. One of the largest industries in the South is located at Buford and has a payroll of $1,250,000. The General Shoe Company, of Lawrenceville, has a payroll of $400,000, and the Henson

Pants Factory has a payroll of $100,000. These three great industries, together with many other smaller enterprises, pay their employees around $2,000,000 a year.

"If you wish to engage in farming, come to Gwinnett. Atlanta stands at our front door and will buy every product of the farm. If you wish to establish a new industry, come to Gwinnett. Competent and intelligent labor is plentiful. If you wish to build a new home, come to Gwinnett. We are a friendly people. Our homes and our institutions send forth brilliant young men and divinely beautiful young women. Young men? Yes, and they are men of honor, men of character, men of intelligence, men who love their country and obey its laws. Young women? Yes, for they are beautiful beyond words, gracious to a fault, maintaining homes of culture and refinement and living up to the splendid traditions of southern womanhood that has always been, and is today, the pride and the glory of our county. Come, come to Gwinnett."

County school superintendent, Howard Pool, said:

"Gwinnett County had sixty-six white schools in 1933; today we have eighteen white schools and twelve colored schools in the county system. In addition to the county system we have two independent systems, Buford and Lawrenceville, with excellent schools, fully accredited by the Southern Association of Secondary Schools and Colleges.

"The county system has seven accredited 4-year high schools, Bethesda, Dacula, Duluth, Grayson, Norcross, Snellville and Sugar Hill.

"Transportation is one of the major problems of the Board of Education with 1,369 miles of bus routes and forty-one buses. The board employed a Transportation Supervisor, Mr. O. D. Cain, at the beginning of this fiscal year. This act was commended by the Grand Jury as a forward step in the interest of better transportation for less money.

"The board is out of debt and pays all bills promptly.

"The county has a principals' association that meets once a month which is attended by the superintendents of Buford and Lawrenceville as active members. It is the purpose of this association to improve the schools of the county by united efforts of all concerned. One of the projects now being planned is a reading clinic for the entire county.

"The primary teachers, the Home Economics, and Vocational Agriculture teachers' organizations meet monthly.

"We have Vocational Agriculture and Home Economics in all the accredited High Schools of the county system. Also, commercial courses in all accredited high schools, in addition to the courses offered in Buford and Lawrenceville. The ten Vocational Agriculture teachers instruct 260 all day boys and 135 day unit boys. Two hundred and seventy-two boys are members of the FFA. There are 480 evening class members. These teachers have supervised twenty-three defense courses with an enrollment of 453. They have used nine WPA assistants during the past year and served 742 families in shop work.

"We have a county library jointly sponsored by the Gwinnett County Board of Education and County Commissioners with a Book-Mobile that serves every school and community.

"We have lunch rooms in most schools.

"The Home Demonstration Agent, Miss Dora Perkerson, works in cooperation with the board of education and extension service. There are 883 4-H club girls enrolled in projects, and 326 women organized in Home Demonstration Clubs. Four thousand, two hundred and eighty-eight mattresses and 1,000 comforters have been made under her supervision this year.

"Every school in the county has volunteered to do anything in the fight for freedom that it is officially called upon to do. The teachers have organized the civilian defense of the county and handled the registration of volunteers.

"Along with the schools we have plenty of churches, 91 in number. In addition to these churches for white people, there are 20 churches for the colored population."

Miss Dora Perkerson, home demonstration agent, spoke as follows:

"Hello! Everyone:

"My interest is in the agricultural development in Gwinnett County. Agricultural agencies have been striving for years to assist Gwinnett County farm families to strike a balance of a better living and a better income from their farms.

"If the complex problem which faces agriculture today is to be eventually solved, the individual one-, two- and three-horse farm will need to find a way to make that farm a self-supporting enterprise, geared to meet market consumption and each farm's own reasonable needs. Many of our agricultural economists say that the family size farm will never be a money maker for the operator. Therefore, we should place emphasis on the good life, and less on commercial agriculture. This means that we should not deal only with purely local conditions such as soil and kitchen sinks. There must be a broader knowledge of state, national and world conditions, but with local implication, stated as clearly as possible and studied by methods which are developing in adult education.

"This new situation calls for greater understanding and cooperating with other federal and state aided agencies with similar interests.

"Gwinnett County is one of the largest counties in Georgia,

containing 281,600 acres of land devoted to the production of crops, permanent pastures and forest. It lies northeast of Atlanta and is crossed by three main paved highways leading from the city of Atlanta to eastern points. This makes it possible for the farmers to drive into Atlanta in a few minutes, with their truck crops, dairy and poultry products. We also have two leading railroads.

"Gwinnett county has 3,811 small farms. The farm land is gently rolling, productive and responds rapidly to soil-building practices. Considerable progress has been made in soil-building, as indicated by the increased yield in lint cotton per acre of 50 pounds over the old average. It was one of the first counties in the state to start growing Kobe lespedeza, and it has become one of our leading soil-building and hay crops.

"The principal crops of the county are cotton, corn, wheat, oats, rye, barley and truck crops. The county produces a considerable amount of lumber and lumber products.

"Gwinnett County has the only cooperative seed cleaning and grading plant in the South. This plant has cleaned, graded and treated more than a half million pounds of seed.

"For two years there has been a land use planning group and nutrition council working with leading farmers of the county, and representatives of all other agencies, namely: vocational teachers, Soil Conservation, Farm Security, Agricultural Adjustment Administration, and County and Home Agents. These groups have given much time and thought to planning a program that has provided service agencies for sound practical practices for the farmers that will make far more ideal living conditions; instead of the one-crop system which has been in practice for years.

"Gwinnett county was the first county to start community cooperative canning as a part of a live-at-home program. One plant was established by a vocational teacher and another by the Extension Service. A Commercial Concern supplied 51,800 cans for the project. The farmer filled the cans and took 60 per cent for his part and 40 per cent went to the community chest. More than 100,000 cans were filled that season by these two pressure cookers. Now the county has six well equipped canning plants under the supervision of Vocational teachers of consolidated schools where thousands of cans are filled annually.

"Gwinnett county farms are operated by a very intelligent, loyal group of people who love the American Way of Living more than life itself. Many farm boys have already gone to the defense of our American Way of Life, and they will continue to go as they are needed. They will do their part in the patriotic American way. We are proud of these boys and will produce the hams, eggs, dairy products, vegetables and all other products they can use to keep them physically fit. As one farmer said, "We have more to fight for than any people in the world, and we will feed the boys the best regardless of what it takes." We are doing our part at home by having a Citizens Defense Group, County Defense Corps, and Gwinnett County will defend our country 100 per cent."

INDUSTRIES IN THE COUNTY

The 1820 census shows the following industries in the county:

3 Hatmakers using 250 pounds of fur and 200 pounds of wool	$ 330.00
2 Saddlers using 74 sides of leather valued at	122.74
1 Shoemaker using 33 hides of leather valued at	100.00
5 Blacksmiths using 8,500 pounds of iron and 500 pounds of steel	819.25
1 Spinning wheel shop using timber valued at	10.00
Total 12	$1,381.99

Industries in 1845: Wool carding mills, 2; sawmills, 9; gristmills, 26; merchant mills, 3; distilleries, 9.

INDUSTRIES IN 1854

Lawrenceville Manufacturing Company, situated at Lawrenceville, has a capital of $90,000. The building is of granite, 220 feet long, 50 feet wide, and four stories high. Spindles, 3,050; looms, 36; operatives, 80. Connected with this establishment is a flour and grist mill, the whole propelled by steam. The 1850 census shows Gwinnett County had 1,610 dwellings, 1,600 families, 4,499 white males, 4,454 white females, 4 free negro males, 6 free female negroes. Total free population, 8,963; slaves, 2,294. Total population, 11,267. There were 1,036 farms, 26 manufacturing establishments, total value of real estate, $977,693; personal property, $1,440,125.

ALLEN MANUFACTURING COMPANY

The Allen Manufacturing Company, makers of cotton horse collars, was established in Lawrenceville in 1906. The owners were L. R. Martin, Clarence Allen and Wilse Martin. The sole owner at this writing is L. R. Martin. Fifteen to twenty hands are employed.

CHAS. W. HENSON GARMENT MFG. CO., INC.

The Chas. W. Henson Garment Manufacturing Co., Inc., established its factory in Lawrenceville in 1939 and has been in constant operation since. About 135 people find employment there. This company manufactures the Red Fox Brand of cotton pants and shirts, supplying the trade throughout the southern states.

The pay roll amounts to more than $100,000 per year, and the yearly output of merchandise is over $300,000.

GENERAL SHOE COMPANY

The General Shoe Company operates twelve plants at this writing. It bought the vacant cotton mill building in Lawrenceville in 1939 and work began in the fall of that year. Approximately 6,000 people find employment in the twelve plants, and produce in round numbers 42,000 pairs of shoes every day, with a weekly pay roll of $100,000.

The Lawrenceville plant in August, 1941, had about 370 on its pay roll and expects to increase this number from time to time to 500. The monthly pay check amounts to $26,000, or a yearly pay roll of $312,000. All employees live in the county, most of whom are high school graduates. In personnel, the employees compare favorably with those of any other company in the nation.

In equipment, sanitation, working conditions, wages and supervision, the Lawrenceville branch of the General Shoe Corporation bears the reputation of being the best shoe factory in the United States.

SOBECO TANNERIES, INC.

The Sobeco Tanneries, located at Norcross, do a remunerative business and employ several workmen. It is a substantial concern with years of continuous service.

FURNITURE

J. V. Attaway, Dacula, manufactures furniture and finds a ready market for his products.

C. M. Moore, Five Forks, also makes furniture.

MACON COOPERAGE COMPANY

The Macon Cooperage Company, Suwanee, manufactures material for making barrels.

PLOW FACTORY

Alford Brothers, chain store merchants, operate a plow factory at Gloster.

WOOL CARDING MILL

Charles P. Jackson has owned and operated a wool carding enterprise for many years. It is located at his home in Goodwin's district. Clips from the flock are shipped to him from far and near.

BONA ALLEN, INC.

Bona Allen, Incorporated, has been for years one of the largest industries in the South. It is located at Buford. The several departments included a shoe factory, tannery, horse collar factory, saddle factory, and a harness factory. About two thousand people were employed and the pay roll was about one and a quarter million dollars. The shoe factory was discontinued the latter part of 1941.

VITAL STATISTICS
BIRTHS

Year	1933	1934	1935	1936	1937
Live	606	618	665	668	605
Still	25	27	26	22	26
Total	631	645	691	690	631

DEATHS

	1933	1934	1935	1936	1937
All causes	220	248	242	294	233
Most Common Causes:					
Heart Diseases	38	27	32	46	34
Cerebral Hemorrhage	12	20	19	33	23
Pneumonia	17	20	23	30	16
Nephritis	22	17	16	29	21
Accidents	12	17	15	20	23
Malformation	17	15	16	10	22
Influenza	18	17	15	15	13
Cancer	8	13	16	18	12
Tuberculosis	14	11	6	5	7
Total	158	157	158	206	171
Infant Mortality	33	39	45	37	35
Medical practitioners					15
Dentists					6

DENTAL STATUS OF SCHOOL CHILDREN
1937 - 1938

Average daily attendance	5,563
Total number	
Inspected	4,654
Tabulated	4,645
Been to dentist	2,180
Been to dentist within last year	1,445
With cavities	4,151
Having one toothbrush	3,943
Total apparent malocclusions	109
Total prophylaxis needed	4,489
Total cavities in permanent teeth	10,378
Total cavities in permanent and deciduous teeth	18,524

Public Assistance Statistics
Gwinnett County for
January, 1939

OLD AGE ASSISTANCE

Recipients: Number, 468; amount, $3,316.50; average, $7.09; applications pending, 540.

AID TO THE NEEDY BLIND

Recipients: Number, 3; amount, $36.50; average, $12.17; applications pending, 10.

AID TO DEPENDENT CHILDREN

Recipients: Families, 47; children, 105; amount, $794.00; average per child, $7.56; applications pending, children, 139.

GENERAL RELIEF

	Cases	Persons	Obligations	Average Obligation
Family	11	37	$ 52.64	$4.79
Single Persons	13	13	83.40	6.42
Total	24	50	$136.04	$5.67

SERVICE TO CRIPPLED CHILDREN

Approved: For registration, 5; for registration and treatment, 15; not treated, 12; total examined, 21; total treated, 3.

ALMSHOUSE POPULATION

There is no almshouse in Gwinnett County at the present time. Summary benefits received during January, 1939: Old Age, Blind, and Dependent Children, $4,147.00; Surplus Commodities, $2,827.33; C. C. C., $2,222.00; General Relief, $136.04; Total, $9,332.37.

AGE COMPARISON OF PERSONS ON RELIEF ROLLS

Census population 1930	27,853
Number persons on relief 1935	2,631
Residual	2,227
Age 65 and over, 1930 census	1,220
Relief rolls 1935	167
Number per 1,000 aged population	137
Children 16 and under, 1930 census	10,905
Relief rolls 1935	237
Number dependent children per 1,000 under 16	22

COUNTY AND MUNICIPAL FUNDS FOR RELIEF EXPENSE AND ALMSHOUSE

Total	$13,672.83
(a) County poor funds for general relief	10,140.06
Almshouses	2,232.77
(b) Municipalities	1,300.00

AGRICULTURAL STATISTICS FOR GWINNETT COUNTY, 1935

FARM AND FARM OPERATIONS

Number of farms in county	3,811
Farm operators by color:	
White	3,572
Colored	239
Farm operators by tenure:	
Full owners	1,132
Part owners	136
Managers	3
Tenants	2,540

FARM ACREAGE, VALUE AND LAND AREA IN 1935 EXPRESSED IN ACRES

Approximate land area	281,600
Average size of farms	63.3
All land in farms	241,357
By color of farm operators:	
White	227,377
Colored	13,980
By tenure of farm operators:	
Full owners	73,976
Part owners	9,029
Managers	2,067
Tenants	155,725

VALUE OF FARMS, LAND AND BUILDINGS IN 1935

Expressed in Dollars	5,018,316
Average value per farm	1,317
Average value per acre	20.79
By color of farm operator:	
White	4,772,602
Colored	245,714
By tenure of farm operator:	
Full owners	1,727,720
Part owners	213,790

Managers	95,000
Tenants	2,891,806

CROP LAND, IDLE OR FALLOW, EXPRESSED IN ACRES

By tenure of operator:

Full owners	5,023
Part owners	368
Managers	578
Tenants	10,886

School Statistics 1937-1938

School census	8,191
Total number enrolled	7,999
Prior enrollment	762
Net enrollment	7,237
Number not enrolled	954
Average daily attendance	5,457
Children lost in daily average attendance	1,780
Total loss due to non-attendance	2,734
Teachers lost	91
Teachers assigned to county by State Department of Education	232
Teachers' salaries lost, $70 per month	$44,590

4-H Clubs

Total number enrolled in 1938	605
Number members completing projects in 1938	467

Marketing Analysis, Population, Agriculture, Industries in Gwinnett County

Land area in square miles	440
Population in 1930	27,853
Urban	3,357
Negro	3,343
Illiterate	1,257

Agriculture in 1930:

People engaged in farming	5,762
Number of farms	3,925
Land in farms, acres	232,298
Value of crops	$3,202,160
Value of dairy products	119,452
Value of livestock	911,986

Industries in 1935:
 People engaged in manufacturing 1,563
 Number of establishments 12
 Value of manufactured products $4,885,911
 People engaged in mining in 1930 6
 People engaged in forestry and fishing in 1930 1
Electrification:
 Number of domestic meters 1,026
Income:
 Number personal federal income tax returns 1936 141

RETAIL SALES AND KIND OF STORES IN 1935

	Stores	Sales
Total	286	$2,952,000
Food stores	79	514,000
Eating places	21	60,000
General food stores	46	655,000
General merchandise	9	269,000
Apparel stores	3	63,000
Automotive stores	13	601,000
Filling stations	71	334,000
Furniture, household and radio	9	91,000
Hardware, lumber and building	7	60,000
Drug stores	8	96,000
Other stores	20	209,000

JAILS

According to a classification of county jails in 1937 by the State Department of Public Welfare, Gwinnett County has one of the 35 county jails in the state classified as fair.

PATIENTS AT MILLEDGEVILLE

Gwinnett County had 214 lunacy cases from January 26, 1928, to June 16, 1941.

NYA STATISTICS IN GWINNETT COUNTY

Number of youths assigned to NYA work projects September, 1938:

 White 122
 Negro 0

 Total 122
Average earnings per month for 12 months $14.00

Youths receiving high school aid in 1937-38:

White	62
Negro	8
Total	70
Average earnings per month for 9 months	$4.00

Number receiving college aid 1937-38:

White	11
Colored	0
Total	11
Average earnings per month for 9 months	$12.00

W. P. A. EMPLOYMENT OCTOBER, 1938

Areas, 6; number of persons, 279.

CHURCH MEMBERSHIP BY DENOMINATIONS 1926

Baptist bodies:

Southern Baptists	7,633
Negro Baptists	1,291
Primitive Baptists	134
Colored Primitive Baptists	83

Methodist bodies:

Methodist Episcopal Church	672
Methodist Episcopal Church, South	3,098
African M. E. Zion Church	522
Presbyterian Church	301
All other bodies	156
Total all denominations	13,890

COUNTY LIBRARY

On August 12, 1936, the Lawrenceville Public Library held its formal opening in the city hall, an attainment realized through the cooperative efforts of the Lawrenceville Parent-Teacher Association, Mrs. R. H. Sams, president, Professor Paul King, Mayor W. G. Holt and council, and the public spirited citizens of Lawrenceville. The Parent-Teacher Association, through the leadership of the library committee, composed of Mrs. T. J. Jackson, Mrs. Margaret Dorris and Miss Mary Stewart, supplied the equipment; the City of Lawrenceville provided the room; Mrs. T. J. Jackson served as the volunteer librarian. The five hundred books placed in circulation were secured through funds provided by one dollar membership subscriptions, individual donations and a book shower.

A few months later the City of Lawrenceville elected Mrs. T. J. Jackson the city librarian at a salary of ten dollars a month.

On November 3, 1936, the Lawrenceville Public Library became the Gwinnett County Library with a W.P.A. librarian in addition to Mrs. T. J. Jackson, supplied by the city, with a board of trustees elected by the county board of education and the City of Lawrenceville composed of Heard Summerour, chairman; T. E. Johnson, treasurer; Marvin Allison, city representative; Mrs. R. H. Sams, secretary, with an additional appropriation of $100.00 a month from the county commissioners and the county board of education.

In February, 1942, the Gwinnett County Library had four W.P.A. workers and a bookmobile, ranking second in service in this regional library district. This library, which has six thousand books and an average monthly circulation of nine thousand, is one of the few in the American Library Association chosen as a center of information in the national defense program.

Other libraries in the county: Norcross, 4,000; Buford, 2,700. School libraries: Buford, 2,140; Lawrenceville 2,000; Duluth, 1,100; Norcross, 1,143; Dacula 4,900; Grayson, 1,300; Snellville, 8,500; Sugar Hill, 1,300; Bethesda, 800.

POPULATION GWINNETT COUNTY

Census	Population	White	Negro
1820	4,589	4,050	539
1830	13,289	10,949	2,340
1840	10,804	8,552	2,252
1850	11,257	8,952	2,305
1860	12,940	10,358	2,582
1870	12,431	10,272	2,159
1880	19,531	16,016	3,515
1890	19,899	16,903	2,996
1900	25,585	21,442	4,143
1910	28,824	24,393	4,431
1920	30,327	26,094	4,233
1930	27,853		
1940	29,087	25,731	3,335

Of the 29,087 people living in the county during 1940 when the census was taken, 14,572 were males and 14,515 females; 25,731 were white and 3,335 colored and 1 another race; only 20 were foreign born. Number in county under 5 years of age, 3,004; from 5 to 24, 12,086; 25 to 54, 12,275; 65 and over 1,722; 21 and over, 16,055.

POPULATION BY DISTRICTS

	1870	1940
404—Goodwins	480	743
405—Berkshire	1,352	1,666
406—Pinkneyville	1,120	2,667
407—Lawrenceville	1,201	3,835
408—Cates	1,201	1,579
444—Hog Mountain	1,006	1,520
478—Harbins	1,050	1,065
544—Martins	1,151	1,522
550—Sugar Hill	847	5,762
571—Rockbridge	851	994
1269—Duluth		1,248
1295—Bay Creek		1,912
1397—Pucketts		575
1564—Dacula		787
1578—Garner		734
1587—Rocky Creek		656
1604—Suwanee		1,216
1749—Duncans		606
562—Cains	874	
316—Ben Smiths	1,298	
Total Population	12,431	29,087

Ben Smiths and Cains districts were lost to Gwinnett County in 1914 when Barrow County was created.

OCCUPIED AND VACANT DWELLINGS IN GWINNETT COUNTY, 1940

Total, 7,171; occupied, 6,822; vacant, 349; per cent vacant, 4.6.

IN BUFORD

Total number of dwellings, 1,013; occupied, 1,000; vacant, 13; population, 4,191.

POPULATION OF TOWNS IN COUNTY

	1940	1930
Buford	4,191	3,357
Dacula	315	304
Duluth	626	608
Grayson	228	245
Lawrenceville	2,223	2,156
Norcross	979	892

Rest Haven	91	
Snellville	204	105
Suwanee	179	214
Sugar Hill	599	
Total	9,635	7,881

Gwinnett is regarded as a rural county. However, the census shows that 9,635 people, or one out of every three, live in the ten incorporated towns in the county.

REGISTERED VOTERS IN 1941

No. 1295—Bay Creek	473
No. 405—Berkshire	561
No. 408—Cates	529
No. 1564—Dacula	266
No. 1263—Duluth	377
No. 1749—Duncans	82
No. 1578—Garner	211
No. 404—Goodwins	131
No. 478—Harbins	191
No. 444—Hog Mountain	256
No. 407—Lawrenceville	1,761
No. 544—Martins	292
No. 406—Pinkneyville	768
No. 1397—Pucketts	264
No. 571—Rockbridge	258
No. 1587—Rocky Creek	125
No. 550—Sugar Hill	2,061
No. 1604—Suwanee	338
Total number registered	8,944

GWINNETT BAR

From the organization of the county to the present time the bar of Gwinnett County has been one of the best in the state. The following names include those who lived in the county. The list may not be complete for the Superior Court records were lost in the fire of 1871. The records of the Inferior Court are the only source for the names of practicing attorneys prior to the destruction of the courthouse. The date after each name indicates the first time the attorney's name appears on the court's minutes.

Philip Alston, 1821; Abraham Baldwin; N. L. Hutchins, 1823; John G. Park, 1823; E. W. Chester, 1825; Green W. Smith, 1825; Hines Holt, 1825; S. W. Blain, 1828; Henry Mounger, 1829; Jas. C.

Martin, 1829; Mat. J. Williams, 1830; R. H. Lester, 1832; J. B. Trippe, 1833; H. P. Thomas, 1836; J. P. Simmons, 1836; J. R. Alexander, 1838; Kinchin Rambo, 1842; W. J. Norton, 1844; T. W. Alexander, 1848; L. F. Wilcox, 1848; Charles H. Smith, 1851; J. J. Diamond, 1851; J. T. Allen, 1853; J. N. Glenn, 1854; Cincinnatus Peoples, 1854; W. J. Peeples, 1854; J. H. Hunter, 1855; J. M. Young, 1855; F. F. Juhan, 1857; M. L. Lenoir, 1858; Luther Easley, 1858; Sam J. Winn, 1858; T. M. Peeples, 1859; W. E. Simmons.

N. L. Hutchins II; N. L. Hutchins III; R. Maltbie; Junius Hillyer; L. F. McDonald; E. S. V. Bryant; R. W. Peeples; Oscar Brown; C. H. Brand; O. A. Nix; J. A. Hunt; John R. Cooper; J. V. Poole; E. W. Born; J. A. Perry; J. C. Flanigan; I. L. Oakes; S. G. Brown; J. O. H. Brown; R. B. Fortune; D. M. Byrd; M. L. Ledford; M. D. Irwin; D. K. Johnston; E. O. Dobbs, Sr; J. C. Houston; J. I. Kelley; W. L. Nix; G. F. Kelley; R. N. Holt; A. G. Liles; P. Cooley; M. A. Allison; E. O. Dobbs, Jr.; E. W. White; C. D. Pittard; Roy Nix; D. B. Phillips; G. R. Roberts; R. F. Duncan; T. O. Davis; Hope Stark; O. N. Pharr; W. E. Orr; W. O. Cooper, Jr.

GWINNETT COUNTY PHYSICIANS

Dr. Lemuel Jackson, Dr. Bangs, Dr. Philo Hall, Dr. Jesse Lowe, Dr. Wideman, Dr. H. B. Johnson, Dr. R. B. Moore, Dr. S. H. Freeman, Dr. S. T. Hinton, Dr. T. A. Fowler, Dr. W. H. Thurman, Dr. John W. Maltbie, Dr. John Moore, Dr. Wm. J. Russell, Dr. T. W. Alexander, Dr. W. P. Cofer, Dr. W. H. McDaniel, Dr. A. G. Carroll, Dr. T. L. Phillips, Dr. Moses Richardson, Dr. J. C. Harris, Dr. L. A. Lee, Dr. J. W. Riley, Dr. W. W. Power, Dr. N. C. Osborn, Dr. John R. Minor, Dr. G. A. Mitchel, Dr. T. B. Bush, Dr. T. K. Mitchel, Dr. T. K. Mitchel, Jr., Dr. M. L. Mahaffey, Dr. John Mathews, Dr. O'Kelley, Dr. J. A. Pirkle, Dr. T. E. Hill, Dr. S. C. Hopkins, Dr. P. F. Dickens, Dr. W. T. Hinton, Dr. B. V. Wilson, Dr. J. T. Wages, Dr. A. M. Winn, Dr. R. J. Bagwell, Dr. M. A. Born, Dr. A. J. Shaffer, Dr. M. T. Johnson, Dr. G. S. Kelley, Dr. C. A. Kelley, Dr. W. P. Ezzard, Dr. A. D. Williams, Dr. J. M. Oliver, Dr. O. B. Tucker, Dr. J. R. DeVore, Dr. N. H. Pierce, Dr. E. D. Little.

Dr. H. T. Smith, Dr. T. M. Lee, Dr. H. D. Lee, Dr. Virgil Nash, Dr. O. O. Simpson, Dr. W. J. Hutchins, Dr. W. C. Pirkle, Dr. Sam Scales, Dr. G. W. Mills, Dr. J. B. Gurley, Dr. D. C. Kelley, Dr. J. C. Orr, Dr. M. S. Archer, Dr. N. L. Pirkle, Dr. J. R. Chastain, Dr. O. D. Hall, Dr. J. W. Quillian, Dr. Joe Woodward, Dr. M. W. Jinks, Dr. W. J. Jinks, Dr. B. D. Rhodes, Dr. H. T. Dickens, Dr. J. M. Guess, Dr. Paul McDonald, Dr. Q. L. Brantley, Dr. W. J. Rowe, Dr. L. A. Williams, Dr. Eli McDaniel, Dr. Tom McDaniel, Dr. Roy Pounds, Dr. Edward Pounds, Dr. M. T. McDaniel, Dr. H. B. Hambrick, Dr. P. J. Brown, Dr. J. C. Harris, Dr. L. P. Pharr, Dr. J. E. Norton,

Dr. A. W. DeVore, Dr. A. H. Wingo, Dr. J. J. Bridges, Dr. Chalmers Hinton, Dr. R. L. Neal, Dr. J. M. Hulsey, Dr. J. S. Cochran, Dr. W. W. Puett, Dr. J. E. Christian, Dr. N. J. Guthrie, Dr. F. P. Hudson, Dr. Sylvester Cain, Dr. S. H. Adams, Dr. W. P. Walker, Dr. A. A. Bagwell, Dr. A. R. Danforth, Dr. C. K. Lewis, Dr. O. D. Woodall, Dr. R. L. Ellison, Dr. C. A. Davenport, Dr. M. M. McGhee, Dr. Daniel D. Reid, Dr. W. H. Rice, Dr. Morman, Dr. Schaffold, Dr. L. E. Roper, Dr. W. C. Bryan, Dr. H. W. Guthrie.

Dentists

Dr. Thomas Jacobs, Dr. John M. Jacobs, Dr. V. G. Hopkins, Dr. H. P. Edmonds, Dr. J. W. Nicholson, Dr. Ben Clements, Dr. L. H. Letson, Dr. Neil Loveless, Dr. B. L. Mumfort, Dr. T. C. Mason, Dr. W. F. Moore, Dr. W. L. Pritchett, Dr. H. K. Bowman, Dr. H. B. Hansard, Dr. M. C. Duncan, Dr. P. L. Barnwell, Dr. John B. Hopkins, Dr. R. H. Truesdell, Dr. S. C. Hopkins.

Chapter XI

PUBLIC SCHOOLS OF GWINNETT COUNTY

THE General Assembly of 1870 provided the legal machinery for a system of public schools in this state. The sum of $175,000 was appropriated to operate the schools the first year; and the legislators, with characteristic self-interest, promptly diverted the fund to their own use, and instead of paying the teachers, the entire school fund was used to pay the salaries of the members of the General Assembly and to satisfy other obligations created by them.

Prompt steps were taken to organize the school system in Gwinnett County. The board of education, the county school commissioner and the teachers were promptly selected and at least a start was made. The first board of education included Thomas MaGuire, J. R. Moore, T. D. Mathews, Samuel Knox and Wm. A. Cain. They were prominent and influential citizens from different sections of the county. They selected J. N. Glenn as the first county school commissioner.

The second board of education was composed of R. D. Winn, president; John R. Moore, Daniel M. Byrd, William I. Woodward and J. T. McElvaney. They began their duties in 1873. R. D. Winn lived two miles west of Lawrenceville and was a man of ability. A chapter in this history contains his literary productions. John R. Moore was a leading physician of Lawrenceville. Daniel M. Byrd was a prominent farmer and owned a large plantation on the Stone Mountain road. Wm. I. Woodward stood high in the estimation of the general public and lived at Woodward's Mill. J. T. McElvaney was a substantial planter and public spirited citizen in the southern part of the county.

J. N. Glenn resigned as school commissioner, and the board elected J. L. King to that important position. Mr. King, commenting on the importance of public schools, said:

"We are informed that the people are taking a deep interest in the establishment of common schools. It is the duty of parents to educate their children. If you can't give them a good education, teach them at least to read and write and the elementary principles of arithmetic. By this means they will be able, if they have the proper ambition, to educate themselves without a teacher. You are compelled to pay your taxes to assist in supporting the common school system, and your interest and duty unite in urging every head of a family to give his children the benefit of at least three months' schooling during the year."

Administration of J. N. Glenn

The first state school commissioner, J. R. Lewis, made his first annual report for 1871 in which he gave the following information about the schools in Gwinnett County:

Number school houses: white, 36; colored, 2.
Number school houses built during the year, 4.
Eight white and 9 colored new school houses needed.
All schools were mixed, ungraded.
Average days taught: white, 48; colored, 60.
Number teachers: white, 39; colored, 2.
Average number months taught: white, 3; colored, 3.
Average salary per month: male, $48.70; female, $36.51.
Number children 6 to 21: 4,189; number enrolled, 2,204.
Number children over 16 years of age, 475.
Average attendance, 1,463; average age of pupils, 12.

Subjects taught in schools:
Webster's Elementary Spelling book;
Webster's dictionaries;
Holme's 1st, 2nd, 3rd, 4th, 5th, 6th readers;
Holme's History of the United States;
Scribner's System of Penmanship, writing books 1 to 12;
Sanford's arithmetics;
Bonnell's Composition;
Harvey's Grammar and Harvey's English;
Cornell's series of Geographies and Maps.

Number taught:

In alphabet, 268; spelling, 1,446;
Reading, 1,055; writing, 814; mental arithmetic, 15;
Written arithmetic, 552; geography, 121;
English grammar, 223; higher branches, 49.

Private schools:
Number private schools: white, 16; colored, 0.
Number private teachers: white, 19; colored, 0.
Number pupils in private schools, 837.
Number months private schools in session, 6.
Average cost of tuition per month in private school, $1.50.

Duties of school commissioner:

(1) Hold teacher's examinations: Applicants: male, 34; female, 9.

(2) Visits of commissioner: Number schools visited, 40; addresses made, 43; number days on official duties, 43.

(3) Granting licenses to teachers; Males: 1 year, 19; 2 years, 6; 3 years, 9. Females: 1 year, 3; 2 years, 3; 3 years, 3.

PAUL DOVER

BOARD OF COUNTY COMMISSIONERS

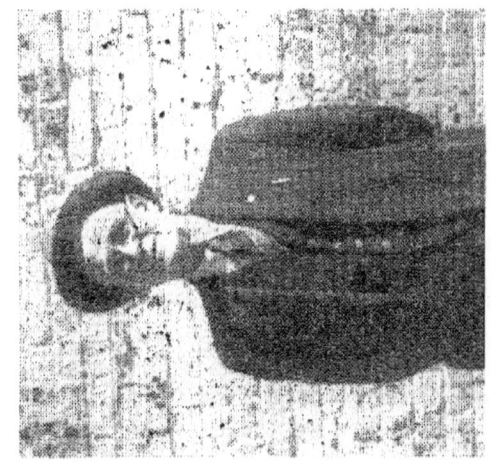
WILLIAM R. HURST

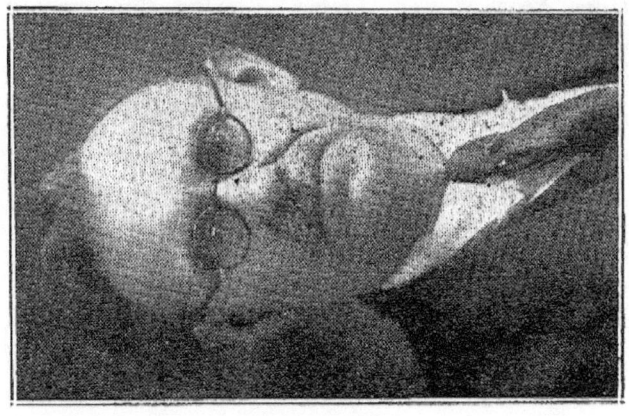
THOMAS L. HARRIS

Administration of J. L. King

The school fund for 1871 was diverted to other purposes and the teachers were not paid. G. J. Orr, who was appointed state school commissioner in January, 1872, reporting to the governor, had this to say:

"I am sorry to be under the necessity of reporting that not a dollar of debt due to teachers and school officials contracted in carrying on the school work of last year has been paid."

Schools were suspended during 1872. No funds were available to operate them. The public school system began to function again in 1873 and the records for that year include all teachers of music, painting, dancing, and drawing, as well as professors in the colleges of the state. The record shows that to every 160 school children there was only one teacher who was actually engaged in teaching the elementary branches.

For the year 1873: Number children between 6 and 18—White, 2,837; colored, 721; total, 3,558. Number schools—White, 31; colored, 3. Number pupils enrolled, 1,695; average attendance, 904. Private schools—White, 14; enrollment, 810. Number months taught, 5 11/14. Subjects taught—Elementary branches and classics. School fund, $3,467; school population, 3,629. Subjects taught—Spelling, reading, writing, grammar, geography, and arithmetic.

A two-story school house with eight rooms was erected at Norcross soon after the railroad was completed. The closing exercises in May, 1873, revealed that two flourishing literary societies were doing fine work in the school. Professor Vincent was in charge and the enrollment went beyond 100. The closing or graduation exercises included the following numbers:

1. Extract, "Mrs. Candies' Lecture," Miss Alice Harrell, Cumming.
2. "Talking." Composition by Miss Nora Strickland, Duluth.
3. "Hidden Flowers and Genis." Composition by Miss Ellen Thrasher, Norcross.
4. Valedictory. Miss Helen Jones, Norcross.

Year 1874: White schools, 44; colored, 4; total, 48. Number between 6 and 18, 4,242, plus Confederate soldiers under 30. Illiterate: White, between 10 and 18, 544; colored, 349; total, 893. Illiterate over 18: White, 663; colored, 603; total, 1,266.

Enrolled, 2,434; average attendance, 317; average cost per pupil, $1.45 per month; paid by state, 90c. Subjects taught: Spelling, reading, writing, grammar, geography, arithmetic.

Private schools: White, 20; colored, none; total, 20. Number teachers, 21; number pupils enrolled, 778; number months, 4½. Branches taught: Elementary; average monthly cost, $1.45.

Winn's Administration

Thomas E. Winn was elected county school commissioner in 1876 and served until October, 1890. He was a member of one of the first families in the county. He resigned this office on his nomination for Congress in this district. He was elected congressman, served one term and was defeated in his second race.

During his administration the school population gradually increased, more children attended school, larger school funds were appropriated, more competent teachers entered the profession, and the common school system grew in public favor.

Of the 4,242 children between 6 and 18 in 1876, the illiterate numbered 693, and there were 1,266 above 18 who were classed as illiterates. Only 3,013 of the 4,242 of school age were enrolled with an average attendance of 1,628. The state paid 74 cents of the monthly cost of $1.24 per pupil. In addition to the public schools, there were private schools to the number of 25 with 30 teachers.

The school fund was $1,643 for 1877, the salary of the commissioner was $150 and he was required to work four months. In 1878 the school fund ran up to $1,637, a gain of $3.00 and the commissioner's salary was increased from $150 to $156. In 1880 the schools opened the first Monday in July and were continued 60 days.

The board of education now adopted school books for a period of three years. The books adopted were Sanford's arithmetics, Derry's history, McGuffey's readers, Eclectic geography, Smith's or Harvey's grammar, and Webster's spelling books. "While a change of books may be objectional to many," said the commissioner, "a beginning had to be made in establishing a uniform system. One of the greatest, and we sometimes think, one of the most unnecessary expenses connected with our school system is the frequent change of text books. Every teacher has his own preference and concludes that the books he studied are the best and every time there is a change of teachers there is another bill for new books. Under the present action, there will be no more changes for at least three years."

In 1880 the high school made its advent in Duluth. Duluth Academy had two teachers and 59 pupils. The school ran for ten months, and R. H. Villard and W. C. Wright, the teachers, instructed their students in mathematics, science and the classics. At Norcross the high school pupils under B. S. Crane studied the classics, mathematics and English at a cost of $2.00 per month.

Summer schools for teachers were called teachers' institutes. In 1880 three such schools were held at Toccoa, Americus and Milledgeville. Four years later one of the three institutes was held at Norcross, W. H. Baker in charge. Addressing a letter to G. J. Orr, state superintendent, Baker said:

"I have the honor herewith to submit my report of the Teachers' Institute held at Norcross during the month of August. From the enclosed list you will find that there was an enrollment of 32 white and 43 colored teachers, making a total of 75. In seeking for the cause of this small number I am induced to believe it was owing to the fact that the public schools in the county were in session during the entire month. If it is thought desirable to keep up these institutes, it will be necessary either to select another month or dismiss the schools. There can be no doubt that if the attendance of teachers can be secured, these institutes will be productive of great good. In no other way can the character of our teachers be so readily improved. I have reason to think that those who were in attendance at Norcross will return to their work with renewed enthusiasm, and the improved methods which were presented to them at the institute will tell you the progress of their scholars. I beg to be allowed to commend the fidelity and efficiency of my colleagues, Messrs. S. C. Caldwell and W. S. Bogart."

The schools increased to 81 in 1883 with an enrollment of 3,911 whites and 809 colored, and the commissioner's salary was increased to $300. The school fund was $6,471 and schools ran three months. Norcross high school had on its roll 105, with N. F. Cooledge, principal.

W. M. Winn and an assistant had charge of the Lawrenceville academy, and W. R. Pool had charge of the Buford academy. Norcross had also another school known as the Georgia School of Languages, Science and Art. T. T. Simmons was principal, charging pupils $3 per month.

Competent teachers were in demand then as now. Peabody College, in Tennessee, gave scholarships to those who would agree to follow teaching as a profession. Such students received free tuition and a sum of money to pay expenses. J. S. Dobbins, in 1880, and W. B. Coffee, in 1883, were appointed from this county.

The school population increased to 6,458 in 1887 and the public school fund was $3,869. This fund, together with a small amount collected as tuition, paid the salaries of 64 white and 20 colored teachers for their school work. With such meager funds, salaries were small and the school term short.

County School Commissioner Winn held an examination on January 29, 30 and 31, 1889, when the following teachers took the test: T. G. Chapman, D. B. Mewborn, J. J. Nash, D. L. Kennedy, Sallie Mathews, A. J. Mayfield, J. B. Scales, J. O. Johnson, Adaline Hill, W. A. Davis, U. G. Sloan, W. T. Hinton, J. C. Cole, J. J.

Jordan, A. M. Brooks, W. T. Johnson, J. E. Jacobs, T. L. Phillips, E. V. W. Mahaffey, Mrs. W. D. Griner, Miss S. A. Donaldson, R. W. Woodall, A. A. Fields.

Rural school buildings were generally shabby structures. Usually they were log cabins or unceiled frame houses with a wide fireplace in one end. Pupils sat on slab benches, solved their arithmetic on slates, played town-ball and marbles for recreation, and walked from one to five miles to school without a complaint.

On Friday afternoons recitations and spelling bees were in order. The small children delighted the teacher and their assembled parents with "Twinkle, Twinkle Little Star," "The Boy Stood On the Burning Deck," and other well known selections, while the larger boys and girls recited "A Psalm of Life," Patrick Henry's famous "Give me liberty or give me death," "The American Flag," and "The Barefoot Boy."

When Friday afternoons were devoted to spelling bees, two of the best spellers would choose sides, selecting the smartest students one by one until all were stood in line. Then the teacher would take Webster's Blue Back spelling book and give out the words. Usually he began with simple words that any child could spell. Then he turned the leaves of his book and announced such words as caoutchouc, ennui, incompressibility, and phthisic, and out went the spellers in rapid order.

Often at the end of the summer term of the school, the closing exercises took on an elaborate program of recitations, dialogues, songs and comics under the name of exhibition. Great preparations were made for these exhibitions. Days were spent in practice. The youth of the neighborhood put on their best clothes and on the night of the exhibition people came from far and near on foot, horseback and in wagons and buggies. A temporary stage was erected on the outside. Sheets were used for curtains and candles and lanterns furnished sufficient light. Recitation followed recitation, dialogue after dialogue, and the exhibition usually closed with a negro sermon delivered by a blackfaced comedian.

In those days it was considered an insult to the school for any man in passing to holler "Schoolbutter." Should this incident occur at the noon recess, the older boys accepted the challenge and immediately set out to catch the offender. John Dough, a young man living near Harmony Grove school, a few miles away, drove by County Line academy in Rocky Creek district and shouted "Schoolbutter" to the boys playing townball at the noon recess. Instantly balls and bats were tossed away, and John Martin, Will Attaway, Bud Doster, Pope Pentecost, Oscar House, Will Robinson, John T. Wright, John Williams, Bart Parker, and others gave chase. The offender was driving a young mule to a light wagon and was two hundred yards down the road when the race started. The mule was soon going at full speed and so were the boys. A half mile down the road there was a short turn. The wagon turned over and the driver went into a ditch. Before he was able to get up, a half dozen boys were on him. They ducked him in a nearby pond. He was made to drive back to the school house. The boys were acclaimed as conquering heroes by the other students as they rode around the house several times. Then the boys made the offender stand on his head five minutes; he was made to put his head between his knees and roll over a score of times; he was made to haul a wagon load of girls up and down the road several times. Then the teacher rapped the side of the house with his cane. That meant books.

RESIDENCE OF MR. AND MRS. ROY SIKES
Located one and a half miles east of Snellville, just off the Atlanta-Athens highway on the estate of the late James Emory Johnson.

Tanner's Administration

T. E. Winn resigned as county school commissioner and on September 27, 1890, the county board of education met to elect his successor. The applicants were W. T. Tanner, J. T. McElvaney, J. E. Cloud, W. E. Jones. Tanner received a majority on the second ballot and was declared elected to fill out Winn's term.

Commenting on his experience as student, teacher and commissioner, Mr. Tanner said:

"I started to school in 1867 just beyond Dacula. My elementary training was in a private school. I attended a private school in Lawrenceville and in Suwanee. Schools then were quite different from what they are now. We talked out loud as we studied. I first studied Webster's blue-back speller and reading. Soon I began simple arithmetic. Punctuation was learned by the time the second reader was completed. We spelled by syllables and had to give vowels without touching the lips together. Each day there was a 'heart lesson' in which the entire school talked out loud and made such a racket that it was almost impossible to hear your own voice. Advancing I studied Latin, Greek and algebra. We were in the school room eight hours a day, and the school ran about three months a year. I attended Emory College one year, and then completed a business course which has been a great help to me. After I finished school, I began to teach, generally in one teacher schools. In one school there were 90 pupils which made it necessary to have an assistant. I had little trouble with discipline and did not whip much.

"I became county school commissioner in 1890 and was in office about ten years. When I first went in office, teachers were paid by the number of days made by the pupils. My salary and all expenses were less than $400.00 per year. The public school fund amounted to $5,623 in 1889 and increased to $16,168.00 in 1900."

RESIDENCE OF GEORGE WESLEY GOUGE
Grayson, Georgia

Teachers 1897

Ronald Johnston and J. A. Bagwell were the experts at the institute for teachers held in Lawrenceville in the month of June, 1897. The group of teachers included Ada Hinton, Mary Loveless, Mattie Hawthorne, Louise DuBose, Sallie Pendergrass, Lula Hays, Mertice Sewell, Cora Holland, Leila Hunnicutt, Angie Maynard, Sallie Jackson, Floy King, Jessie Brown, Bettie Boyd, Mollie Cochran, Sallie Malby, Mrs. Bessie Exum, Mrs. M. G. Howard, Mrs. Clara Mewborn, Mrs. Ellen Houston, W. H. Thomas, J. T. Jones, J. W. Morgan, J. S. Porter, T. S. Garner, T. G. Chapman, S. C. Wood, H. C. Hudson, F. Q. Sammon, W. T. Brooks, J. W. Boss, J. D. Pruett, S. M. Cruce, J. G. Mewborn, A. L. Loveless, F. B. Maddox, E. S. Moore, T. M. Holland, D. L. Kennedy, H. C. Jordan, J. D. Reese, F. T. L. Howard, G. W. Woodruff, W. F. McMillan, J. H. Buchanan, D. H. Hutchins, J. B. Moore, J. R. Wages, A. S. Hopkins, J. H. Queen, D. T. Williams, H. S. Oliver, J. A. Mewborn, W. L. Harris, O. A. Nix, J. A. Pool, J. M. Sewell, J. W. Pierce, W. T. Jones, J. P. Hadaway, W. E. Pool, T. L. Harris, J. F. Weaver, L. C. Davis, R. B. Whitworth, F. B. Brogdon, S. W. Du Bose, J. W. Ford, J. W. Coggins, J. W. McElvany, G. W. Williams, M. B. Sewell, B. H. Jenkins, C. C. Williams, J. C. Flanigan, J. E. Flowers, L. R. Moore, C. C. Dalton, N. D. Meadow, B. H. Meadow, G. M. Brown, J. M. Davis, G. L. Veal.

Commissioner Tanner changed the method of paying teachers from the daily attendance to the salary system. The salary schedule varied according to the grade of license and class A, B and C teachers with first grade licenses received $40, $35 and $30 per month respectively; A, B, and C teachers with second grade licenses received $35, $30 and $25; and A, B, and C teachers with third grade licenses received $30, $25 and $20. However, the salaries of teachers varied from year to year as the school funds increased.

The school fund amounted to $7,318 in 1890, which paid the salaries of the 81 white and 17 colored teachers. In 1891 the schools ran five months and the 97 teachers were paid from a fund of $10,722 and the commissioner made 120 visits. The 101 teachers in 1892 had a fund of $10,908 to operate the schools; an institute was held with E. L. McNabb as expert; and one teacher attended Rock College. There were 103 teachers in 1893, the school fund was $12,084, and subjects taught were orthography, reading, writing, grammar, geography, arithmetic and history. The school fund was $15,344 in 1894; the 110 teachers enrolled 5,990 pupils, and the commissioner made 210 visits to the schools. In 1895 fourteen teachers attended the State Normal School; of the 102 teachers in the same number of schools, 36 had a first grade license, 26 a second grade and 40 a third grade; 3 teachers had normal training; 6,177 pupils were enrolled with an average attendance of 3,118; and the normal trained teacher with a first grade license luxuriated on an average salary of $28 per month, while the teachers with a license of the second and third grades received $24 and $20 respectively.

The records for 1897 show that 102 teachers were employed in the 102 schools, and of these 53 had first grade licenses, 24 second grade and 25 third grade; ten had normal training; 6,556 pupils were enrolled with an average attendance of 3,268; the average salaries were $30, $26 and $23 for first, second and third grade teachers; the commissioner made 192 visits; 85 school houses were valued at $5,500 while buildings in the towns and villages were worth $16,000; school fund $13,280; four private high schools enrolled 200; Lawrenceville had a local system and there was one college, Perry-Rainey College, at Auburn, Prof. J. A. Bagwell, president.

The school census of 1898 revealed that there were 6,309 white and 1,149 colored children between 6 and 18 years; only one building was owned by the county; the commissioner made 180 visits; the school fund was $18,632; and there were 14,481 school books for which the patrons paid $5,950.

The 1899 school term continued 100 days and pupils were allowed to make the time between November 1, 1898, and November 1, 1899. Nine teachers attended the State Normal School. Of the 116 teachers in the county, 60 held a first grade license, 26 second grade and 30 third grade, and 22 had normal training. In the 104 schools, 7,135 pupils were enrolled with an average attendance of 3,590. The school fund was $15,927. First grade teachers were paid $38, while those with a third grade grew rich with a monthly check for $23.04. Teachers with degrees, if females, hastened to accept the first proposals, while teachers of the masculine persuasion looked to other fields of endeavor for a competency. The commissioner made 209 visits. Perry-Rainey College, Auburn, reported a good year with Jas. C. Flanigan, president, and W. H. Maxwell, principal.

In July Commissioner Tanner issued licenses to the following teachers: W. H. Jacobs, Nelly Pickens, Mrs. J. A. Bagwell, John Maynard, C. R. Ware, Angie Maynard, J. A. Waldrop, G. M. Kilgore, W. O. McConnell, J. D. Pruett, O. A. Nix, H. S. Oliver, F. Q. Sammon, T. M. Holland, J. S. Porter, S. H. Lindsey, G. L. Veal, Anna Holland, E. C. Lester, T. S. Garner, Mrs. B. H. Jones, Cleo Medlock, Dora Cain, Lula Wisdom, J. G. Mewborn, L. C. Davis, D. M. Williams, B. B. Johnson, J. A. Bagwell, H. C. Jordan, May Peeples, J. A. Smith, Flora Wilson, Mattie Coggins, Dollie Hawthorne, Leo Adams, Myra Ware, Mrs. Ila Waldrop, Birdie Wood,

Thomas Langley, J. M. Maynard, Jesse Brown, J. S. Cheek, W. M. Jackson, C. C. Williams, F. M. Moore, Ara Parks, J. L. Exum, O. A. Jacobs, E. S. Moore, Sallie Ledford, J. K. Pirkle, D. H. Mobley, M. D. Jacobs, J. L. Green, Lula Hays, Nora Morton, W. B. Whitworth, F. M. Reeves, H. B. Harmon, J. B. Moore, Miss Q. C. Pickens, W. H. Thomas, D. L. Kennedy, Lilla Sewell, B. H. Meadow, H. H. Pharr, R. V. Martin, J. H. Buchanan, W. L. Harris, J. W. Langley, L. P. Cross, Hanes Williams, J. C. Cole, J. S. Brogdon, R. P. Simpson, E. H. Sammon.

HOME OF ED CRAIG
Near Lawrenceville

COMMISSIONER BAGWELL

On February 10, 1900, the board of education met to elect a county school commissioner. The board included Dr. A. M. Winn, chairman; W. P. Cosby, B. L. Patterson, T. C. Shadburn and E. G. McDaniel. James A. Bagwell was chosen. Mr. Bagwell graduated from Mercer University with second honor and was an experienced school man.

Commissioner Bagwell had $16,168 to pay the teachers during 1900; and of the 123 teachers employed, 68 had a first grade license; 29 second grade, and 26 third grade, and of these only 16 had normal training. The enrollment was 6,913, with an average attendance of 3,819. First grade teachers received $37.25; second grade, $31.30, and third grade, $20.15. The institute for teachers was held during the year with W. H. Maxwell as expert.

Commenting on the school situation, Commissioner Bagwell said: "Within the last two years twelve old school houses have been torn down and twelve new ones erected. The standard of teachers has been raised, more than fifty applicants for teachers' licenses having failed to make any grade at all. There used to be private schools in the county, thus showing disloyalty to the public school system. Today there is not a single private school in all the county. But there is much to be done. The board of education at its last session unanimously decided to lay off the county into school districts, and it is now high time that the school territories should be definitely known. When this work is done, the teachers will know where to find their children, the children will know to which school they must go, and the commissioner and board of education will be able to ascertain the reasons for non-attendance in any district in the county."

For several years the school funds, the number of teachers, their salaries and the annual enrollment showed little if any change. Physiology, civics and agriculture were added to the school curriculum.

School districts in 1906 were called Alcova, Bay Creek, Braden, Beaver Ruin, Brown, Buford, Chattahoochee, Concord, Carter, Centerville, Cedar Hill, County Line, Duluth, Duncan's Creek, Dacula, Friendship, Garner, Glenn, Glover, Grayson, Gwinnett Hall, Gravel Springs, Haynes Creek, Harris, Harmony, Hopewell, Lilburn, Loxomni, Lee Academy, Liberty, Lawrenceville, Lenora, Lowery, Level Creek, Mulberry High School, Maddox, Mechanicsville, Midway, Mulberry, Norcross, Nazareth, Ozora, Oak Grove, Oak Shade, Old Suwanee, Old Field, Oakland, Pittman, Pleasant Hill, Pharr's, Prospect and Peachtree, Rock Springs, Roberts, Rosebud, Snellville, Sam Craig, Sweetgum, Sugar Hill, Union, Victory, Walnut Grove, Zion.

Licenses were issued to the following teachers in 1906: T. G. Chapman, Kope Taylor, H. Ben Smith, H. B. Harmon, H. D. Meriwether, Jonnie Thorpe, Annie Perry, Flora Wilson, J. A. Mewborn, W. S. Richburg, Bertie Harmon, W. L. Nix, J. C. Pool, Pauline Petty, Nena Vance, Lillie Tanner, Dollie Hawthorne, Pearl Hutchins, Mattie Williams, Alma Craig, A. C. Tanner, J. Frank Snell, H. P. Oliver, B. B. Crane, C. C. Brooks, Ed Freeman, Bertie Wood, W. D. Watson, Cora Brown, Carfax Baxter, Mamie Duncan, J. M. Skelton, Sallie Ledford, Floy Smith, Theo Sockwell, Dora Pirkle, Cynthia Medlock, Earl Holt, W. S. Burel, May Hadaway, Lena Page.

Ware's Administration

C. R. Ware was elected commissioner to succeed J. A. Bagwell October 5, 1907. He went into office October 9th.

The schools were operated during 1908 for six months, using the same schedule of salaries. There were 36 white and 3 normal trained teachers in the county, and the 88 schools enrolled 7,108 pupils; the six high schools having 390 students. The school fund was $21,893.

The school census of 1908 gave the school population at 7,703. An institute was held in June with J. T. Walker as expert. In the local press it was stated that local taxation seemed to be the only way in which long term schools can be maintained in rural communities.

School expenses for the year were: To white teachers, $22,639; colored, $1,279; commissioner's salary, $900; salary board of education, $135; incidental expenses, $423; total, $25,376. In his report to the grand jury Commissioner Ware said:

"The public schools of this county were authorized to be taught for a period of six months. There are 86 white schools, 34 of which were in operation for the full six months, while the remaining 52 averaged a little less than five months. There were enrolled 6,980 pupils, or about 90 per cent of the school population. The average attendance was 4,527, or about 62 per cent of the enrollment, or about 50 per cent of the school population. These figures furnish conclusive evidence that the people of this county are, as a whole, very indifferent towards educational matters, and that there is a crying need for compulsory educational legislation. And while the school houses as a whole are good, it is to be regretted that so many of them are furnished with inferior desks or no desks at all. There is only one rural school in the county with patent desks, while many of them have only the crudest benches, such as were in use fully 50 years ago."

In 1910 schools ran five months. Commissioner Ware was re-elected for another term. A boy's corn club was organized and prizes were offered for the largest yield of corn on one acre, and prizes were offered to girls on sewing and cooking.

The state paid $3.38 per capita for instruction for children of school age in 1911. Seventeen school districts now had local taxation, most of the houses were comfortable, several put in patent desks, 150 teachers found work in the schools, and the school fund amounted to $26,100.

Local tax districts increased from 17 to 21 in 1912; the salary of the commissioner was increased to $1,200; there were 66 school districts; school houses were classified and salaries of the teachers were regulated by this classification; 29 houses having been classed as good, and 44 bad. During this year the following boys joined the corn club:

Roland Couey, Fred Pass, Hugh Baker, Floyd Branan, Tom Campbell, Raymond Campbell, Moses Davis, Sarge Freeman, Frank Grizzard, Leonard Glaze, Herman Harbin, Berry Langley, Lee Norton, Dewey Rutledge, Herschel Smith, John Henry Mahaffy, Holland Davis, Marvin Wages, Ashley Durham, Willie Harris, A. B. Clack, Clarence Bennett, B. A. Culberson, A. B. Weathers, Oscar Dunagan, Alva Singleton, James Weathers, Anton Pharr, B. A. Roebuck, Adolphus Ford, Colone L. Brown, James Whitehead, Erbie Clack, Sanders Clack, Harold Morrison, Ledford Martin, J. C. Garner, Marvin Harrison, Edmond Hendrix, Floyd Hendrix, Otho Smith, Floyd Smith, Odell White, Raymond Williams, Herschel Williams, Harlin Davis. Girls who belonged to the canning club: Azilee Clack, Cammie Clack, Effie Martin, Belle Morrison, Effie Montgomery, Bessie Montgomery, Bertha Pool, Leila Pool, Lillie Smith, Ola Smith, Adeline Smith, Luella Smith, Ila White, Lena White, Etta Wages, Tinzie Kerr. Girls belonging to the poultry club: May Branan, Sadie Davis, Birdie Evans, Ila McCart, Lena Sexton, Lena Gresham, Lessie McDaniel, Essie McDaniel, Mary Grizzard, Ruby Freeman.

On February 12, 1913, the county board decided not to allow any new schools established and emphasized its position that it was not more schools the county needed but better schools. The public fund was $26,498. The trustees of Midway school asked to be allowed to operate their school two months during the summer, giving as the reason that stringent financial conditions made it difficult to maintain the school, that there were 27 vacant houses in the district, 14 that were occupied had no children of school age, while only 22 homes had children of proper age to attend school. The board borrowed $16,000 during the year to finance the schools.

To pay the salaries of teachers during 1915 a loan of $24,000 was negotiated.

In 1917 the county board determined the number of teachers allowed in any school. An average attendance of 25 pupils authorized the use of one teacher; 45, two teachers; 90, three; 125, four; 160, five; 200, six; 235, seven; 270, eight; 300, nine; 335, ten. The board also adopted for five years the following books for the four high school grades:

EIGHTH GRADE

Arithmetic—Wentworth and Smith, Book 3.

Algebra—Wentworth and Smith Academic.

History—Montgomery's English.

Spelling—Eldridge's Business Speller.

Electives—Choose one: (1) Latin, Pearson's Essentials; (2) Science, Clark's Introduction to Science; (3) English, Lewis and Hosic's Practical English.

NINTH GRADE

Arithmetic—Wentworth and Smith's, Book 2 Review.

Algebra—Wentworth and Smith's Academic.

English—Lewis and Hosic's Practical English in High School.

History—Mayer's Ancient.

Spelling—Eldridge's Business Speller.

Electives—Choose one: (1) Latin, Allen & Greenough's Caesar, Books 1-4; (2) Pearson's Latin Prose Composition based on Caesar; (3) Science, Hunter's Civic Biology.

TENTH GRADE

Geometry—Wentworth and Smith's Plane Geometry.

Algebra—Wentworth and Smith's Academic Review.

English—Long's American Literature.

History—Harding's Medieval and Modern.

Spelling—Eldridge.

Electives—Choose one: (1) Latin, Allen & Greenough—Cicero, 6 orations; (2) Pearson's Prose Composition based on Cicero; (3) Bennett's Latin Grammar; (4) Science, Holligan's Fundamentals of Agriculture; (5) French, Chanderal's Complete French Course.

ELEVENTH GRADE

English—Long's English Literature.

History—Adams and Trent's United States.

Spelling—Eldridge.

Civics—Stickle's Elements of Government.

Science—Millikan & Cales' First Course in Physics.

Electives—Choose one: (1) Latin, Virgil; (2) Math—Solid Geometry, Trigonometry or Review Algebra; (3) French, Luper's French History.

Third Year Classics: Ivanhoe, Silas Marner, Tale of Two Cities, Autobiography Benjamin Franklin, Merchant of Venice.

Fourth Year Classics: Burke on Conciliation, Vicar of Wakefield, Idylls of the Kings, Julius Caesar, Milton's L'Allegro.

J. K. Jackson, a teacher for many years, succeeded J. W. McElvaney in 1918 as a member of the school board. M. T. Verner resigned and J. C. Byrd succeeded him. A board of health was set up with Victor Allen, chairman, and C. R. Ware and Dr. W. H. Hutchins, members.

On August 14, 1919, the board ruled that no teacher would be employed who did not hold a regular certificate. A compulsory attendance law became effective and J. C. Johnson secured the position of attendance officer. The school commissioner now changed his official name to school superintendent and his salary was increased to $1,800. The compulsory attendance law was never enforced. The law required children between 8 and 14 who had not completed the seventh grade to attend their respective schools six months, beginning the first day of the term. There were many in the county over 18 years of age who could not read or write, and the board, following the enactment of a law to establish an illiteracy commission, planned to undertake this work in October, the object of the law being to stamp out adult illiteracy in the county. Illiteracy was not stamped out.

The salaries of the colored teachers were increased to $30 per month by the board in February, 1920. Lenora Gibson, a faithful teacher for thirty years, drew a monthly check for $35. Snellville, Haynes Creek, Pharr's and Oak Shade districts were consolidated to become effective at the beginning of the fall term in 1921. This consolidation was again continued until September, 1922.

GWINNETT COUNTY BOOKMOBILE
John Ramon Gunter, driver, and Mrs. Berthel Sears, librarian (1942).

Meriwether's Administration

On January 1, 1921, H. D. Meriwether became superintendent. His bond was fixed at $20,000. The salary of the superintendent was increased $25 per month to employ aid in his administration of the duties of his office. Just what aid he needed was not stated. The Chattahoochee school was consolidated with Norcross. County-wide taxation for school purposes was fixed at four mills. Treasurers of the local districts were required to give bonds and schools with three teachers were permitted to teach high school courses.

The school term in 1922 was six months. By invitation M. L. Duggan, of the State Department of Education, made a survey of the schools. His findings were published under the title of "Educational Survey of Gwinnett County." He was rather severe in his report. Said he:

"According to the United States census, Gwinnett County shows nearly or quite the greatest percentage of adult illiteracy of any county in Georgia. There are to be found some good schools in the county, but they are not a result of the system, but rather they have been built up by local or individual initiative and in spite of the system. The holding power of the schools is very little, for we find that only 818 remain in school long enough to reach the fourth grade, and only 521 enter the seventh grade."

In 1923 the teachers in the county were:

School	Teachers	No. Pupils	Maintenance
Alcova	Mrs. A. A. Loveless	84	$120 per month
Bay Creek	A. L. Geiger	120	915 per year
	Mary Lou Tuck		
Beaver Ruin	Frank Cain		
	Nora Jones	60	
Bermuda	James W. Stone	40	450 per year.
Bethesda	Jewel Campbell	48	1,050 per year
	Jewell Petty		
Braden	Ella Sue Minor	49	
	Mary Kelley		
Browns	Mrs. J. T. King	28	
Brushy Fork	Mrs. Mamie Oliver	50	825 per year
	Montine Lanford		
Carters	J. B. Dunagan	46	70 per month
Centerville	L. C. Allison	120	1,205 per year
	Mamie Booth		
	Goldie Smith		
Dacula	J. M. Cochran	164	4,000 per year
	Lucile Wilson		
	Daisy Keown		

School	Teachers	No. Pupils	Maintenance
	Una Hinton		
	Cassie Tanner		
Duncan's Creek	F. J. Hendrix	110	900 per year
Duluth	(See elsewhere)		
Five Forks	P. J. Funderburg	66	
	Essie Williams		
Garner	Verlon Kennerly		
	Odessa Moore	49	625 per year
Glenn		46	815 per year
	Mary Lou Pinson		
Glover	R. P. Pickens	172	2,000 per year
	J. G. Stewart		
	Clara Latham		
	Kate Garner		
Grayson	L. F. Herring	200	8,000 per year
	J. F. Reid		
	W. C. Britt		
	W. W. Childs		
	Mrs. W. C. Britt		
	J. B. Dunagan		
	R. L. Herring		
	Mrs. L. F. Herring		
Gravel Springs	Doolie Puckett		
	Mrs. J. C. Barker	84	825 per year
Gwinnett Hall	Tyna Johnson	68	105 per month
	Lessie Keheley		
Harmony	Mrs. G. W. Duncan	80	800 per year
	Ollie Duncan		
Harris	Mrs. J. R. Simonton	128	150 per month
	Oscar Dunagan		
	E. Q. Kennedy		
Haynes Creek	Mrs. N. L. King	55	
	Mattie S. Hannah		
Hog Mountain	A. V. Kimsey	78	115 per month
	Mrs. Fern Oakes		
Ivy Creek	Myrtie Bush	30	500 per year
Jackson's	Ora Hamilton	38	
Lenora	Mrs. J. A. Bryant	137	115 per month
	Orpha Lee		
Level Creek	Mrs. J. R. Hunt	49	500 per year
	Mrs. J. W. Brogdon		
Liberty	Ruth Chapman	104	800 per year
	Desma Bradley		
Lilburn	Alice Kelley	70	200 per month
	Daisy Carter		
	Irma Garner		

School	Teachers	No. Pupils	Maintenance
Lowery	J. W. Knight	70	950 per year
	Jewell Maughon		
Luxomni	C. M. Cain	90	125 per month
	Louise Garner		
McKendree	Roy Mercier		
	Mrs. Roy Mercier	78	
Meadow	Corinne Roberts	84	875 per year
	Ethel Carter		
Mechanicsville	Alma Ramey	87	150 per month
	Lou Burns		
Midway	Pearl Harris	83	900 per year
	Lilla Williams		
Mt. Moriah	Howard Pool	45	455 per year
New Prospect	H. G. Morgan	31	400 per year
Norcross	W. H. Maxwell (See elsewhere)		
Duluth	W. F. Harvey (See elsewhere)		
Oak Grove	Pearl Hudgins	135	180 per month
	Daisy Ethridge		
	Mrs. T. E. McMillan		
Oakland	Mattie Williams	107	1,150 per year
	Gypsy Coursey		
	Mattie Adams		
Oak Shade	P. E. Jackson	87	115 per month
	Lucy Johnson		
Old Field	Mrs. P. Stonecipher	53	
	Eula Mae Whitlock		
Old Suwanee	Gertrude Hays	38	800 per year
Ozora	J. A. Conn		
	Vendetta McElroy	48	850 per year
Peachtree	Grace Brooks	43	60 per month
Pharr's	Gueston Brooks		
	Cadell Brooks	80	135 per month
Pittman	C. F. Fisher	90	
	Rosa Gillespie		
Pleasant Hill	Mrs. S. C. Kilgore	118	975 per year
	Lena Martin		
	Leona Fowler		
Prospect	Beula Davis	48	70 per month
Rabbit Hill	E. A. Hays	32	
Roberts	J. O. Barrett	73	815 per year
	Maephus Ethridge		
Rock Springs	Cassie Turner	28	475 per year
Rocky Branch	T. E. Sherwood	36	420 per year
Rosebud	Mrs. Mamie Oliver	38	750 per year

School	Teachers	No. Pupils	Maintenance
Sam Craig	Annie Laurie Harling	34	625 per year
Snellville	J. D. Bryant	90	180 per month
	Edith Burnett		
	Lillian Harris		
Sugar Hill	F. E. Driskell	68	1,100 per year
	Bessie McDonald		
Sweet Gum	K. E. Taylor	65	
	Mrs. K. E. Taylor		
	A. L. Robertson		
Suwanee	—. —. Swetman		
Trinity	Elizabeth Echols	63	
	Rebecca Winters		
Union	H. H. Britt	75	120 per month
	Mrs. H. C. Peavy		
Vance	Ione D——	38	
Walnut Grove	Elsie Jackson	42	75 per month
Whiteoak	Allie Benson	20	
Yellow River	Alene Hogan	29	450 per year
Zion's Hill	J. T. Swanson	120	1,100 per year
	Mrs. J. T. Swanson		

H. B. Harmon was elected attendance officer and assistant superintendent for the 1923-24 school term at a salary of $500. No holidays were allowed in 1923. Teachers observing holidays had to teach on Saturdays to make up the time. The Board discussed the matter of employing a home demonstration agent at its May meeting, but postponed action. High school principals were paid a salary of $80, and if the high school attendance averaged 25, his salary was $100. Consolidation received the attention of the board of education. White Oak and New Prospect were consolidated. Three one-teacher schools were abolished. Grayson was allotted $1,000 to maintain higher standards of teaching. In March, 1924, it was decided to class a second grade high school certificate equal to first grade elementary license in fixing salaries. The board appropriated $50 to enlarge the county library. The term of the 1923-24 schools was for six and a half months.

At the October meeting of the board, L. F. Herring appeared and asked that the $1,000 high school aid under the Barrett-Rogers Act be allocated to Grayson for the next school year. W. H. Maxwell and J. S. Cochran, of Norcross, did the same, and T. A. Pate and W. C. Britt, of Snellville, asked it for their school. Snellville was given $1,000 and $500 was given to Norcross.

"The first successful consolidations were during my administration," said Superintendent Meriwether. "Some had been attempted but had failed. County-wide taxation for school purposes was first levied by me. Only two schools were accredited when I went in office but in 1924 there were five. Snellville is a splendid example of what consolidation can do for a school."

TAYLOR'S ADMINISTRATION

K. E. Taylor became superintendent in January, 1925. He acted as attendance officer with Mrs. Taylor as assistant.

The board of education agreed to pay a home demonstration agent half her salary provided the county commissioners paid one half. County-wide taxation was fixed at five mills, and salaries of one-teacher schools were $60.

Lucile Wilson was attendance officer for the term of 1925-26 at a salary of $75. Lena Bess Medlock was employed as home demonstration agent February, 1926, and Lucile Wilson was again employed for her same work at a salary of $100.

Lena Bess Medlock continued her work through 1927 and was instructed to reach rural sections in order to contact those who needed home training most.

Reba Prickett was retained as home demonstration agent for 1929, and Mrs. L. O. Hinton as supervisor of primary education. In December the board employed Miss L. Watson as visiting teacher and assistant supervisor at a salary of $1,800.

The common school fund for 1930 was $36,100. The board contributed $200 to the illiteracy fund and levied a five mills tax for school purposes.

In 1931 the board made a rule that the public school term should be uniform and that all schools must start and stop at the same time, summer schools being eliminated. The scale of salaries for teachers was adopted and group one received $90 per month; group two, $88; group three, $70; group four, $65; group five, $60; group six, $50; group seven, $45; group eight, $40. During Taylor's administration some of the schools were operated longer than before; a home demonstration agent was employed for the first time, and salaries of teachers were increased. A primary supervisor was also introduced for the first time and requirements for teachers were slightly raised and monthly meetings of teachers organized.

SIMONTON'S ADMINISTRATION

R. S. Simonton went into office January 1, 1933, and served eight years. During his administration schools were consolidated and better buildings erected. There were 61 white schools when he assumed office and 18 when he retired. Accredited schools were Norcross, Dacula, Duluth, Grayson, Snellville. The school term ending in the spring of 1934 used 147 white and 13 colored elementary teachers; 23 white high school teachers and 7 vocational teachers, making a total of 190 teachers employed in the county schools.

Dacula has three school buildings valued at $30,000 and uses 17 teachers. The progress made in school buildings, equipment and attendance places this school among the best in the county. Grayson consolidated school has four buildings, valued at $15,000, and employs 17 teachers. The teacher personnel compares favorably with any other school in this section. Snellville consolidated has made more progress perhaps than any other school in the county. Its buildings are modern, its equipment first class, and its faculty of 17 rates high. Its buildings are valued at $50,000. Bethesda consolidated school has three buildings valued at $20,000. It uses 16 teachers. In 1931 it was a one-teacher school; in 1938 six teachers were employed; in 1939 twelve teachers were used, and at the beginning of the school year 1940 sixteen were required. A donation of fifty acres of land by Mrs. J. A. Alford insures a well-balanced agricultural program for its students in that vocation. The first class to graduate from this school in 1941 included twenty-five seniors. Rubye Moore won first honor, and Clon Vincent, second. The class roll was Howell Black, D. C. Cooper, Jesse Cruce, Elizabeth Cruce, Hinton Donald, Martha Donald, Donald Ford, Marguerite Hamilton, Milton Hamilton, Grace Harrison, Virginia Harrison, Inez Jordan, Helen Landress, Geneva McAdams, Louise McAdams, Gertrude Nichols, Elnora Smith, Gerald Thompson, Mildred Walker, Doris Britt, Colon Vincent, Marion Corley, Bernice Thompson, Rubye Moore, Commie Blankenship.

Norcross has three buildings valued at $60,000, and uses thirteen teachers. For many years this has been one of the best schools in the county and is accredited first class. Duluth public school is housed in one large building and employs twelve teachers. The school property is valued at $35,000. Competent and well trained teachers are used in this school. Sugar Hill consolidated has five buildings and uses sixteen teachers. Its buildings are valued at $30,000. It is an eleven grade school and has grown rapidly during the past few years. Suwanee has a building about completed at this writing which will cost about $55,000. Eight teachers were used during the term 1940-41. Lilburn was advanced from a junior to a senior high school beginning with the 1941-42 term. Funds are available to erect another building. Sunny Hill, with eleven teachers, was made a senior high school at the beginning of the 1941-42 term. The junior high schools are Centerville with six teachers, Harbins with five teachers, and Harmony with five teachers.

COST OF OPERATING COUNTY SCHOOLS
1939-1940
TOTAL RECEIPTS

County	$186,385.93
Buford	24,796.76
Lawrenceville	21,717.56
Total receipts	$232,900.25

EXPENSES COUNTY BOARD

Salary county superintendent	$ 1,749.90
Expenses county board	254.00
Administration salary	155.55
Clerical help	600.00
Office supplies	446.66
Compulsory attendance	1,617.50
Other expenses	53.73
Total	$ 4,877.36

INSTRUCTIONAL SERVICE

The total instructional service for white schools amounted to $111,889.77; Buford, $15,902.39; Lawrenceville, $14,855.78.

TOTAL EXPENSES

Grand total expenses: $177,707.35. Buford, $22,202.54; Lawrenceville, $21,088.91.

TRANSPORTATION

Transportation expenses	$ 21,234.00
Equipment	6,647.00
Total transportation expenses	$ 27,881.00

From March 5, 1940, to March 5, 1941, transportation expenses reached the sum of $65,000, including the purchase of fifteen busses.

ATTENDANCE

Enrollment by grades: 1st grade, 989; 2nd, 747; 3rd, 666; 4th, 648; 5th, 618; 6th, 505; 7th, 501; 8th, 382; 9th, 321; 10th, 196; 11th, 141. Total, 5,256. Buford, 646; Lawrenceville, 511.

NUMBER OF TEACHERS

Number of teachers, 160. Buford, 20; Lawrenceville, 19.

BUILDINGS

Cement, 1; stone, 3; brick, 8; frame, 19; total, 31. White schools, 18. Value of buildings and land, $297,300. Buford, $98,000; Lawrenceville, $80,000.

LIBRARIES

Number of books in school libraries, 6,405. Buford, 1,650; Lawrenceville, 1,700.

VALUE OF TEXTBOOKS FURNISHED

	1937-38	1938-39	1939-40	Total
County	$16,893.38	$5,007.68	$7,711.12	$29,612.74
Buford	2,356.81	468.36	1,127.33	3,952.50
Lawrenceville	2,452.04	2,167.22	261.40	4,880.66

COLORED SCHOOLS

Enrollment, 545. Buford, 236; Lawrenceville, 140.

Salaries: County, $5,478.75; Buford, $2,561.00; Lawrenceville, $907.00.

Number of teachers: County, 17; Buford, 5; Lawrenceville, 2.

Number of schools: County, 12; Buford, 1; Lawrenceville, 1.

It is heartening to see that the public school system has made marked progress during these multiplying years. The teachers are better qualified and better trained. In 1890 there were about one hundred schools in the county. Now there are eighteen for white pupils and thirteen for the colored. Of the eighteen schools for white children, seven are accredited. Two more were made senior schools at the opening of the 1941 fall term and were accredited in 1942. Forty years ago all children walked to school without a complaint. Now they ride. Then they sat on rough benches in shabby school houses. Now they sit on modern desks in steam heated buildings. Then schools were not graded. Now books are furnished by the state, and tuition is a word no longer used by pupil, patron or teacher. A high school diploma opens the door to positions of importance or admits one to any college in the state.

Lawrenceville and Buford have independent school systems and both schools are on the state and southern accredited lists.

WHITE TEACHERS

1933

Number of teachers with county license	18
Number of teachers with less than 1 year college	60
Number of teachers with 1 year college	26
Number of teachers with 2 years college	40
Number of teachers with degree	31
	175

1940

County license	None
Number of teachers with less than 1 year college	None
Number of teachers with 1 year college	5

Number of teachers with 2 years college 35
Number of teachers with 3 years college 43
Number of teachers with 4 years college 74
Number of teachers with 5 years college 9

166

Pool's Administration

Howard Pool was elected county superintendent in the election of 1940 and took office January 1, 1941. He entered upon his duties with enthusiasm and with every assurance of a successful administration.

Perry-Rainey College

In the early eighteen nineties a movement arose to establish a high school within the boundaries of the Mulberry Baptist Association, an organization with churches in Gwinnett, Jackson and Hall counties. The association sponsored the movement and the school was established at Auburn. J. O. Hawthorne gave ten acres of land for school purposes. The building was erected and the first term began in the fall of 1893, with J. A. Bagwell as superintendent. The school was a success from the beginning, with students registering from many sections of the state. A suggestion that a college be organized met with prompt support. A building to be used as a college went up, and classes matriculated in the fall of 1894. Enough students were enrolled to organize freshman, sophomore and junior classes. Nearly every home in Auburn, Carl and surrounding community became a boarding house to accommodate the increasing flow of students. Two literary societies for boys and one for girls were organized. The Clario-Sophic and Alpha Sigma societies were rivals for membership among the young men, and all the girls joined their society.

J. A. Bagwell, John S. Bagwell, Miss Sallie Pendergrass, Miss Ida Horton, T. J. Kilgore, R. T. Clayton were some of the teachers during the first years. Preachers, educators, lecturers and politicians swarmed down on the school with information, inspiration and advice. Commencements were occasions of unusual importance. A famous preacher delivered the commencement sermon before a crowd that filled the auditorium. The literary address drew a full house. But the event that aroused the most enthusiasm was the annual debate between the Clario-Sophic and the Alpha Sigma literary societies. The three best speakers in each society were chosen to participate in these debates; and it was considered that the greatest honor to be won in the college was to be selected as one of the debaters. And those annual debates would compare favorably with anything heard from the rostrum of any college in the state.

The first class to graduate at Perry-Rainey College consisted of eleven students—six girls and five boys. The class graduated in May, 1896, and included Minnie Perry, Blanche Cosby, Bertha Blakey, Maud Jackson, Bertie Jackson, Pearl Jackson, George N. Bagwell, Justus Blakey, R. Frank Smith, Truman M. Holland and J. C. Flanigan, the last two winning second and first honors, respectively.

J. A. Bagwell continued as president of the college until the end of the term in 1897. W. H. Strickland succeeded him and resigned at the Christmas holidays. A. E. Booth finished the term. J. C. Flanigan was president of the college for two years, 1898-1900. He was succeeded by W. H. Maxwell. Others teaching there were A. J. McCoy, J. B. Brookshire, A. R. Moore, W. L. Ward, L. P. Green, Eugene Talmadge, W. C. Carlton.

The old building was destroyed by fire and rebuilt in 1909. The Baptist Association sold the property to the Christian Denomination and the name was changed to the Southeastern Christian College. Years later the property was bought by the local school district and now houses a junior high school.

Perry-Rainey College was named for Rev. Hiram N. Rainey and William T. Perry, the first a well-known Baptist minister and capitalist, and the latter an outstanding farmer and merchant. The college educated many men and women, and contributed more to the advancement of the moral, educational and religious life of this section of the state than any similar institution or movement. It served its day nobly and left a record to which all can point with pride.

Chapter XII
THE WRITINGS OF JUDGE WINN

MAJOR RICHARD D. WINN

BEGINNING in 1871 and continuing for several years, Judge Richard D. Winn, for years a judge of the Inferior Court, and one of the county's most distinguished citizens, wrote biographical sketches of about fifty men who had lived in the county during its early history. These sketches make interesting reading and are given in this chapter without a change in composition.

The figures above the name of each individual is the year the sketch was written and the reader should keep this in mind as he scans these interesting sketches.

1871
Rev. John S. Wilson, D.D.

Beneath the rugged elms, the yew tree shade,
Where heaves the turf in many a mouldering heap
Many in their narrow cells forever laid
The forefathers of the hamlet sleep.

Far from the maddening crowd's ignoble strife
Their sober wishes never learned to stray;
Along the cool, sequestered vale of life
They kept the noiseless tenor of their way.

I promised some pen and ink sketches of some of the early settlers of Gwinnett County. The scope of these sketches, if I shall be able to continue them, is intended to embrace some of the more useful and prominent men and will be confined mostly to those who have shuffled off mortal coil, with now and then one who may be still in life and who has moved from among us.

I shrink from the task, feeling my inability to do justice to the old fathers, having but little data to aid me and will have to rely mainly upon my memory and recollection of facts and incidents in each case as I may endeavor to present it. Therefore, whatever of facts and circumstances that may be lacking to make these sketches interesting to my readers must be attributable to this fact and to the additional fact that I am not their contemporary and was not in such intimate relations with them as if I had been older.

The first I select is that of the Rev. John S. Wilson, D.D., who was not one of the early settlers of the county; but coming here very soon after the organization of the county, I select his name, though still in life, for my first chapter on account of his long residence among us, for his distinguished character as a Christian gentleman and his great usefulness as a minister and teacher.

He was born in Anderson District, South Carolina, in 1796. His early days were spent on a farm and in farm work. His parents moved to Missouri in his childhood but returned to the South where his education commenced. Besides his English school he spent several years at an academy at a place called Varrennes in his native county. Afterwards he attended a school at Ruckersville in Elbert County under the direction of Mr. McDowell. From there he went to Columbia, S. C., and studied under Dr. Cooper.

He was licensed to preach at Fairview, in Greenville District, South Carolina, in 1819, after which he taught school at Ruckersville four years and from there came to Gwinnett County in 1824 and was a resident here twenty years. He left the county in 1844. During the twenty years he lived here, he was pastor of Fairview church and projected and built up the Presbyterian Church in Lawrenceville, a branch of Fairview Church, and preached alternately at the two churches. The great prosperity of these two churches was due to Dr. Wilson, and the success of Presbyterianism in the county at that time was due to his influence and efforts. After his removal, these declined and I am sorry to say are at a low ebb.

For fifteen years he was rector of the old academy in Lawrenceville and had large and flourishing schools, consisting in large part of grown up young men from different parts of the county and from adjoining counties.

In 1844 he moved to Decatur where he engaged in teaching and was in charge of the Presbyterian Church there for fifteen years. He then moved to Atlanta, his present home, where he has resided twelve to fifteen years as pastor of the First Presbyterian Church in that city.

He has been in the ministry nearly fifty-three years, a teacher twenty-five years, and has educated several hundred boys and girls, more, perhaps, than any other man in Georgia, except the celebrated

Dr. Waddell. The last years of his teaching was confined to female students.

He has had three pastoral charges in forty-five years and all within the space of thirty miles. Some are members of his church now who were members of his first charge at old Fairview. He has been a member of eleven general assemblies of the Presbyterian church and often moderator of the presbytery to which his church is attached.

The honorary title of doctor of divinity was conferred on him by Oglethorpe University in 1856.

My acquaintance with him commenced in 1825, he as teacher, I as pupil, at the old academy in Lawrenceville. My early impressions were that he was stern, inflexible and severe in discipline. He was my teacher for several years. Two occasions do I remember well when he applied to me the birchen rod, the only correction I ever received at school. Of course I thought them unjust and inflicted for his personal gratification. I then resolved on terrible deeds in retaliation when I should become a man; but, like all such determinations, they were, of course, never kept or put in execution. My venerable preceptor will forgive me, if this should meet his eye, when I say that it took me forty years to overcome this early impression and get rid of this prejudice.

As a minister Dr. Wilson classes among the ablest in the state and no one within my knowledge has done more to evangelize the people. The old church at Fairview was indebted to him for her great prosperity in the olden time, her large membership and her spiritual prosperity.

In addition to his great influence as a minister and teacher, he was the great apostle of temperance and the leader of the temperance reform in our county and did more for the furtherance of this good cause than any other citizen. He may have had his foibles. He was stern and somewhat irascible, but strong in his principles and attachments, kindly in his nature and uncompromising in his devotion to the right. But to speak in extenso of this good man would occupy more space than you can give. I regret that I have so little when so much ought to be said.

Dr. Wilson is now far advanced in life and is nearing the octogenarian age; but when I last saw him, he was in robust health, erect and had the same elastic step of other days and bids fair to be spared yet for many years. But a report has reached me since I began this sketch that he is very ill. I quote from a paragraph: "We regret to say that the health of the venerable Dr. Wilson is not as good as his many friends could wish. The Doctor is a type of that noble school of men who have stood the test of time and risen above the popular isms of the day and already bears upon his brow the crown of saintship."

I hope his illness is only temporary and that he will soon be restored to health to still bless the church and country. When such men die the world becomes much poorer for the loss. But a few years more at most and the aged Doctor will be gathered to his fathers, despite the wishes of his numerous friends for his longer stay. Man must die, the fiat has gone forth, it is irrevocable.

> "Oh! a wonderful stream is the river of Time
> As it runs through the realm of tears
> With a faultless rhythm and a musical rhyme
> And a broadening sweep and a surge sublime
> That blend with the ocean of years.
>
> "Oh! remembered for aye be the blessed isle,
> All the long days of our life, till night
> When the evening comes with its beautiful smile
> And our eyes are closing to slumber awhile
> May our greenwood of soul be in sight."

1879

JAMES BRACEWELL

James Bracewell, who was one of the first settlers of Gwinnett County, descended from a long line of ancestors who immigrated to this country from Ireland in the early part of the eighteenth century. The name of the immigrant father is unknown. He settled on Tar River, near Tarsbrough, N. C., and reared only two children, both sons, Richard and Robert. Richard was the great grandfather of James. He reared eight children, all sons, one of whom was Richard, the grandfather of James. This Richard had two wives. By the first he had one child, a son, Robert, who served through the Revolutionary War, during which he made a powder horn upon which he carved his initials and that horn is still in the family.

In the year 1864, or '65, Richard married Agnes Proctor and reared a large family, all boys except one daughter, and her name was Elizabeth. She is said to be the last daughter to be born in the Bracewell family in this country. His family was nearly all born and reared to be nearly grown in North Carolina. Soon after the war he sold out and moved to Georgia and settled on Briar Creek in Burke County. The climate proved to be deleterious to the health of the family and several died. He then moved to Washington County, now Laurens, and settled on the Oconee River when it was the dividing line between the whites and the Indians. In a few years all his children died but three, Richard, Sampson and Elizabeth.

Richard, the father of James, in the year 1793 married Charity Scarborough and their first child, James, was born June 5, 1794, in

Allen's Fort, for the people then had to live in forts to protect themselves from the Indians. Richard had three other sons, Wiley, Richard and William. His wife died in 1804. After many years he married a Miss Carlisle by whom he had two sons, Kindred and Allen. He died in the year 1816, of consumption at about the age of fifty years, leaving his son, James, as executor of his estate. After closing up the estate, James went to Morgan County in the year 1817 on a visit to his relatives and decided to make it his home. He began merchandising in that county in 1818. He did well in his business for a time and his credit was perfectly good. He indorsed for a neighbor by the name of Richardson in the Darien bank for a large sum and had it to pay. This broke him up financially and in the year 1821 the sheriff of Morgan County sold all the property he had to satisfy said debt which left him penniless with a wife and two children looking to him for support. He had married Elizabeth Butler, the daughter of Jesse and Mary Butler, on May 10, 1820, in Morgan County. Soon after his financial trouble, he determined to return to the county of his birth, which he did in the early part of the year 1822, and settled at the mouth of Little Rocky Creek on the Oconee River. There his wife and children soon took chills and fever and remained sick until the latter part of the summer of 1823 when he determined to carry them up to his mother-in-law in Morgan County to see if they would improve in health. While there he heard of Gwinnett County, which was then beginning to be settled, was highly spoken of, and he decided to go up and see it. He and his brother-in-law, William Butler, came up and looked at the lands on Yellow River. They were well pleased and Butler bought the half lot of land upon which Affanicious Massey now lives.

One of his old Morgan County friends, Thomas Robinson, the old wagoner, had already moved and then was living on Yellow River. He returned to Laurens County, wound up his little business and went to Morgan County, got his wife and children, and in a one-horse wagon landed upon the lot of land bought by Butler, in the early part of December, 1823. He remained there some three years, then he and Butler divided the tract of land and he built and settled on his part in the year 1827 or '28, where Mr. Massey now resides. He embraced religion at Boring's campground, now Bethesda, in the year 1824 or '25. He remained on that half lot of land until 1835, when he sold out and bought out Joseph Couey, moved to that place and remained there until 1859, when he sold that and bought land one mile south of Lawrenceville and moved to it in 1862.

Soon after this his wife died and he broke up housekeeping and moved to the home of his son, J. R. Bracewell, four miles north of Stone Mountain. After the death of his wife he lost energy and in a few years showed signs of failing health. In the year of 1875 he complained of shortness of breath and it was soon found out that he had dropsy of the chest which gradually grew worse until death ended his suffering on December 12, 1875.

His mind was good to the last. He straightened himself out and closed his eyes. The fact of his having a good memory was universally admitted. He was politically a Henry Clay Whig, and lived and died opposed to the Democratic party. He never had any political aspirations, but always voted for his party friends. He was strongly opposed to secession and the Southern Confederacy. In religion he was a Methodist to the core. From the best information we have, his ancestors were members of the Episcopal Church, but joined the Methodist Episcopal Church soon after its organization in this country. So the family is almost universally Methodist by instinct.

The removal of the grandfather from North Carolina to Brier Creek gave the family a shock from which it never recovered.

I am indebted to W. B. Bracewell, the oldest living son, for the elaborate history of the ancestors of James Bracewell, the subject of the present sketch. It is complimentary to them that they have kept a history of their family for nearly two centuries. In my task of trying to chronicle the history of the early settlers of Gwinnett County, I found that their descendants generally were lamentably ignorant of their genealogy.

Mr. Bracewell reared eleven children, five sons and six daughters. The oldest son, Richard W., died in Texas at about forty years of age. Samuel T. was a member of the Independent Blues, a company recruited in this county at the beginning of the War Between the States. He was a good soldier and died during the war. William B., James R. and Henry, the surviving sons, still are worthy, respected citizens of this county. I would speak of his daughters, but all of them, except four, have gone from memory. I recall the wife of Mr. Early Harris, and the wife of Mr. Swann Harris, and the wife of Mr. Huff, the wife of Mr. H. O. Nackin, of Lawrenceville, and the wife of Mr. Oliver Mathews of this county.

Mr. Bracewell was a politician in his day. He was well informed on political subjects and the history of political parties from the Federalist and Republican parties, the Troup and the Clark parties in Georgia, the Union and States Rights parties of 1833-35, to the Whig and Democratic and all other parties that divided the people.

He had a retentive memory and could quote from history with great precision and correctness. In his politics he was as steadfast and immovable as the hills and was ready to defend his party's principles by argument and facts. His wonderful memory of public men and political events gave him an advantage over most of his compeers whom he might encounter. I give an anecdote of one of these that is in point.

He had a neighbor who was as strong a Democrat as Mr. Bracewell was a Whig. This neighbor, J. W. S., was a talking man, full of gas, but with him it was fuss and feathers mostly. The gauge of battle had been thrown down by one of them, and it was as promptly taken up by the other. By agreement they were to discuss the questions at issue on a certain day at a certain place and the public was invited. The day came and so did the crowd. Mr. S. opened the discussion, lauded General Jackson as the father of the Democratic party and told of his great deeds as a warrior and of his great victory at New Orleans. He described the march of the British up the Alabama River under Cornwallis to sack the city and how he was repulsed by Old Hickory; and with a flourish of sure triumph and assumed victory, he sat down.

Mr. Bracewell rejoined and opened his speech by saying: "The honorable gentleman has given me some information I have never heard of before about the battle of New Orleans and the British going up the Alabama River to sack the city. Before proceeding to discuss the policies of the two political parties, I will submit this proposition to the gentleman: If he will tell me correctly where New Orleans is and who commanded the British forces at the battle referred to, I will yield the point in question, quit the discussion and vote the Democratic ticket."

Mr. S. in answer said that he was not much of a grammarian, but he thought New Orleans was on the Alabama River and he had always heard that Lord Cornwallis commanded the British forces.

This was a triumph for Mr. Bracewell and he replied by saying: "The gentleman is at fault in this as he is in his politics. I will endeavor to enlighten him by telling him that New Orleans is on the Mississippi River and that Packenham commanded the British and not Cornwallis, who was a British general in the Revolutionary War."

His long opposition to the Democratic party had so engrafted that opposition to his nature that after the war, like thousands of other Whigs in the South, he could not align himself with that party. All his traditions and life-long prejudices forbade it. Had the name been otherwise, he could have changed; but as it was the same old name, he could not do so. No one can make allowances in his case better than the writer. I found it difficult to make the transition, but I did it. Others who had grown grayer in their opposition could not.

Mr. Bracewell was as ardent a Methodist as he was a Whig, as unyielding in the one as the other. He was long a member of the church at Bethesda and at his death was a communicant at her altar.

1871

ISHAM WILLIAMS

This gentleman is eminently entitled to a place in these sketches as one remarkable and very worthy man of his day. He was the early and long friend of my father, the friend of his country and of human kind for which he is entitled to this tribute at my hands. One of the most prominent and distinguishing traits of his character was his benevolence and charity to the needy and destitute. Not only his ear but his purse, corncrib and smokehouse were ever open to the widow and the needs of the orphan. Many a poor woman's can has been supplied with oil and her barrel with meal from his generous munificence.

One incident of many that might be related will illustrate this prominent trait in his character. A poor woman, lately bereft of her husband, in needy circumstances and belonging to the same church with himself, met him in the store of D. W. S. in Lawrenceville. She saluted him as Father Williams and he responded by calling her 'My daughter.' After the usual inquiries as to each other's health, families, etc., she asked if he had any corn to spare, which was answered by an emphatic yes. She stated to him that she had some difficulty in getting bread for her children. He asked her if she could send for it and being informed that she could, he informed her that he would have Charles and Stuart, two of his servants, to shell her ten bushels in the course of two days. She asked what he would charge for it. He replied, "Not a cent, not even thank you." This is one of many similar cases that might be noted in his history.

His generosity was always as the Dutchman's. When a poor distressed woman with her children ragged and destitute were passing, this one was sorry for them, and another was very sorry for them, and still another was terribly sorry. The Dutchman said: "I ish sorry five dollars," and suiting his action to word, gave her the money. Such was always Isham Williams' sorrows. It not merely touched his heart but his pocket, too.

He was a man of strong native intellect, sound discriminative judgment, and with proper early education would have been a man of mark. He had many unique sayings, full of good sense and sound practical import which grew into proverbs with him, such as "The least said is soonest mended"; "If you make a good trade, say nothing about it, and if a bad one, stick the closer to it."

In speaking of boys and their worthlessness generally, he would say: "I would not give a thrip a thousand for boys only it took boys to make men." The soundness and force of his homely sayings I have seen exemplified in a thousand instances.

I was present at the marriage of his youngest daughter, thirty-eight years ago. It was a trying time with the old man to give up his baby girl as it is with all fathers who are devoted to their offspring, especially their tender jewels. On the morning after when she was about ready to leave the home of her father and mother, one of the most trying and affecting incidents in a woman's life, the old gentleman was full to overflowing. The goodbye was to be said, the care and protection of the father and mother were to be exchanged for that of a husband, which is untried and uncertain in most cases. With streaming eyes and choked utterance, he said the goodbye and "God bless you, my daughter! Come to see us when you can, but don't come too often."

A strange speech was it at such a parting, I thought, and I took the liberty to refer to it in a subsequent conversation with him. He replied by saying that he meant for them to come as often as they could when it did not interfere with their business or interest, and it was the advice he gave all his children.

In early life I moved near to his residence and for years enjoyed his friendship, favor and counsel. Our intimacy was as great and cordial as is ever between men, disparity of age being considered. He was kind and affectionate to me as a father could be to a son. In an evil hour the serpent entered the Eden of our friendship and created a breach between us that was never healed until he went down to his grave. This, however, never lessened my regard for the man nor my high appreciation of his noble qualities.

After years of intimate acquaintance and close observation of his character, I take pleasure in bearing testimony that his only material fault was his quick temper. All men, it is said, have their besetting sin. With some it is the love of money; with others, the love of wine; with others, the love of women. None of these beset the life of Mr. Williams. He had a quick, irascible temper which sometimes led him into difficulties and unpleasantness. This was his only fault.

One more incident will further illustrate his character for benevolence. After the battle at Shepherd's Plantation in 1836, in which the Gwinnett Volunteers under Captain Garmany were engaged with the Indians and in which they sustained great disaster, the monument in the courthouse square tells the melancholy tale, a vague rumor of the battle had reached the county but none of the particulars had been learned. All the people were in painful suspense for all had friends and many had relatives in that company. Everybody was in a state of feverish anxiety and excitement and many had come to town expecting to get the facts. A young man, the mail carrier from Madison, from which place we get our mail, arrived with a newspaper containing an account of the battle and the disaster to our boys. The exclamation from many mouths was that it be read aloud that all might hear. The paper was handed to Dr. Alexander who, mounting into the high piazza known as the burnt corner, read it to the anxious crowd as one like the Doctor could do. Ah, me! Martin was killed! Paden, Lacy, Tait, the Holland brothers, Sims and Allen! Captain Garmany was wounded! Ramsey Alexander, Hunt and others, too! Many in the retreat had run for miles, pursued by the savage Indians, losing their clothes and everything. What a time! Tears ran from every eye. The sobs of stern men and the wails of heart-broken women echoed through the streets in wild discord such as was never heard in the old town before nor since. The excitement and distress were terrible.

After the first paroxysms of grief had somewhat subsided, old man Williams stood up. I see him in imagination now as then. Like the old Roman of the elder Cato's time, his marked face all bathed in tears, clad in home jeans of home manufacture, shad-bellied Methodist coat such as he had always worn from the time when I can first recollect him to the day of his death, broad brimmed hat that had seen long service and probably made by Ferrier, the old French hatter who had lived in his neighborhood many years before and whose hats never wore out, and after an effort to control himself he said: "The boys are no doubt in great need and must be helped." Then taking off his hat he drew out his pocketbook and made an emphatic deposit in the old hat, then passing round, such a rush of bankbills and silver flowed in as I never saw before. No grudging that day. No miserly feelings then. No holding back part of the price. All mercenary selfishness had fled and the great and absorbing idea with that crowd was what could they do for their brave boys.

Today I stood by the grave of my old friend, which is on an eminence in front and overlooking his old homestead where he lived so long and which he loved so well. Nearly twenty years have passed with their changing cycles, their sadness and sorrow, their desolations of war and its terrible conflicts, the dissolutions of governments, the fall of civil liberty in the country he loved so much, and the perversion of the good government under which he was born and reared, since his remains were deposited. But all these changes from good to bad 'he recks not.' They all fall unheeded on the 'dull cold ear of death.'

From the grave tablet the eye surveys the former homes of his old friends, William Montgomery, Thomas Morrow and Benjamin Baker, with each of whom he was in cordial fellowship for many years in the long last. With two of these he struck hands, we trust, in the happy land of spirits. The other yet briefly lingers on time's crumbling shores, so soon now to follow after.

Oh, the blessed reunion of friends in the haven of Heaven's

bright abode after the cares, conflicts and sorrows of life's weary pilgrimage are ended.

> "There is a land where death casts not its shade,
> A land where gold-eyed flowers ne'er fall asleep.
> Where o'er life's lyre no more by time's hand played,
> God's living music like a fawn doth leap."

> "There is a land where old friends meet,
> Where shoeless the tired pilgrims findeth rest
> With heads pillowed on an angel's breast."

By his side lies the wife of his youth, the loved of his early as well as of his declining years, the partner of his hopes, the sharer of his sorrows and the joy of his whole life. She was one of the best women I ever knew. To me she was for many years as a good mother and true friend. I was often the recipient of her kind hospitalities and motherly attentions. While the pen endeavors to record this brief and feeble tribute to her memory, the eye fills with a tear as I stand by her grave and remember her great kindness to me and mine in the days of my younger years.

1871

ELISHA W. CHESTER

Mr. Chester was a lawyer and came to Lawrenceville in 1822. He had the house built for a residence where Colonel Juhan now lives. He also erected the building where Colonel Juhan now has his law office. He was a contemporary of Green W. Smith, Abraham Baldwin, P. H. Alston and N. L. Hutchins.

Green Smith, if I recollect right, lived in a house down near the graveyard which was afterward burned. He was at one time solicitor general of the circuit. He was a man of some ability. It has been nearly half a century since I knew him, but I have a distinct recollection of his personal appearance. He was tall and bony, six feet high or more, a Roman nose, face with a red mark as large as a silver dollar on his cheek, and a voice, when addressing a jury, like one of the "Bulls of Basham."

Abe Baldwin had married the widow Greenwood who lived in a house, built after the fashion of a barn, on the corner near the street of Colonel Simmons' lot. He was, as I remember, then of middle age, somewhat seedy in appearance and of not much force of character.

Philip H. Alston was a man of decided character, tall and slender, cadaverous complexion, erratic in disposition, and plucky.

Elisha Winn, who was a violent politician in his day, once had a political quarrel with Luke Robinson on the Troup and Clark question in Lawrenceville, and Philip Alston was present and was in sentiment with Mr. Winn. It terminated in a heated quarrel and Winn twisted Robinson's nose and Alston spat in his face. Robinson took it coolly, did not resent it, but said: "I am bitten by an old dog and slobbered on by the puppy."

Alston and Hutchins had formed a law partnership and were employed by a man charged with bastardy and who wanted to get possession of the child. The case was probably before the Inferior Court on a habeas corpus. Colonel Chester was not in the case, but officially called the attention of the court to a similar decision made some time before which was prejudicial to the side of the case represented by Hutchins and Alston. Chester's action was considered unprofessional and it aroused the ire of Phil Alston. Chester soon left the court room for his office, and Alston, leaving Hutchins to manage the case, followed after him. He picked up a broom straw and, holding it up in a threatening manner, pursued Chester to his office. Afterwards he often laughed and said: "Chester was a coward for I ran him to his office with a broomstraw."

Mr. Chester was considered a lawyer of some ability, but he was a poor speaker. Dr. Hall, after he fell out with him, used to say: "Chester is like Jacob's gourd: he went to bed one night and got up next morning a lawyer."

If I recollect right Junius Hillyer read law with Chester and for a while after his admission to the bar was in partnership with him. I recollect a Mr. Winn, who had been buying land somewhat extensively when this county was new, had purchased some lots from men who had moved to Alabama. Some difficulty arose regarding one of his purchases and it was necessary for him to go to Alabama and take with him a lawyer. He took Hillyer. The journey was made on horseback. A long journey through a wilderness it was and there were many streams to swim. It was a new and fearful business to Hillyer. On coming to a stream, Mr. Winn would say: "We'll have to swim it—come on Hillyer." Mr. Hillyer would hesitate and say: "Conscienciously, Squire Winn, I shall be drowned."

Major Mat Williams also read law with Mr. Chester. He was educated at West Point and his education was thorough, but he never succeeded well at the bar. He was irritable and passionate in his younger days and would pitch into the biggest man, if insulted by him, though he himself was small in stature. Nevertheless, he was a courteous, courtly gentleman, the soul of honor as well as of wit and humor. He would sometimes write poetry for the young fellows. One day he asked me to keep his office for him a few hours. I consented upon condition that he would write me some poetry on his return. He consented, and when he returned he sketched off the following impromptu lines:

>John Rochell and little Mell
>Went out to visit Hannah;
>John flourished high 'tween earth and sky
>His beautiful bandana.
>With toes turned out he blew his snout
>And quite low addressed her:
>"My dearest Miss, just look at this,
>See how my nose does pester."

There were three other stanzas equally pointed, but this is only given as a sample. To understand characters named, these circumstances are necessary to a proper appreciation of the poetry.

Again: Two gentlemen on one occasion were taking an inventory of their stock of goods, and had their doors closed. Major Williams came down and wanted to get in. The junior member agreed to let him in provided he, too, would write him some poetry. The Major consented, the door was opened, and with a pencil he wrote the following on wrapping paper:

>"Here simple Dick and honest Clark
>Get rich by raising high their mark
>In selling cotton goods and flannel
>To Wardlaw's Ike and Downs' Daniel."

Wardlaw's Ike was the meanest negro in town and old Daniel Downs the shabbiest and most dilapidated.

Mr. Chester was a Presbyterian, but took sides against his pastor, John S. Wilson, in the old Academy difficulty between Mr. Wilson and the trustees, Mr. Chester being one of them. This, of course, Mr. Wilson could not brook. He must be dealt with in the church, and a statement Mr. Chester was alleged to have made that Dr. Waddell was opposed to the revival then going on at Franklin College and that Dr. Waddell was not a suitable man to preside over the college was made the basis of the charges preferred against him. He was tried, found guilty and excommunicated. Several years after, he was received back into the church and was dismissed upon his removal from the county.

During the Academy difficulty, my father put me in Mr. Chester's care and he kindly agreed to hear my recitations. He had two slaves, a girl and old Tom. Tom was a man past middle age. He had belonged to Isham Williams. Tom was a good hand to work, but would get drunk and run away. His old master had tried every means to break him, but was not successful. He finally despaired and sold him to Mr. Chester. I was passing one morning by the lot where Tom was at work and he called to me. I halted and he commenced a tale of his grievances. Said he: "I thought my old master was the hardest man in the world. He used to give me the devil, but I deserved it; but I never knew what hell was until I fell into the hands of Chester."

When Mr. Chester left Lawrenceville he went to Cincinnati and edited an abolition paper. I think at any rate he became a sober abolitionist and was bitter in his denunciations of our section on account of the bad treatment of the slaves. If one slaveholder in ten had been so severe on his slaves as I knew Mr. Chester to be to his, I, too, would have been an abolitionist. I have written this sketch of Mr. Chester, not by way of reproach or ridicule, his cruelty to his slaves or his views after leaving here, but because he had many excellent traits of character which I respect and for which I give him credit. He was a native of the land of steady habits where it is said they make wooden nutmegs, horn flints and wooden canvas. He is still in life, I am informed, now residing in the state of New York.

I have made Mr. Chester the text from which I desired to make some reference to some other citizens who were in identification with him and of whom I can not give a separate account, for I shall soon probably have to bring these sketches to a conclusion for the want of time to continue them.

It may be that some sanctimonious churchman may find fault with me and this sketch because I have not made it an exclusive glorification of religious life and because I have interspersed it with some anecdotes that may not comport with their puritanical ideas. I yield to no man in my admiration for the Christian character, for my faith in the truth of the Gospel of Jesus Christ is as steadfast as the eternal hills. I do not believe all that glitters is gold, nor every one who sayeth "Lord, Lord," shall enter into the kingdom of Heaven. Though a man may speak with the tongues of angels and hath not charity he becomes as sounding brass or a tinkling cymbal.

1871

Daniel H. Arnold

Mr. Arnold came to this county in 1823, settling first on Redland Creek and afterwards on Pugh's Creek where he lived for many years. He was born in Providence, R. I., on November 4, 1794. His ancestry is traced back to the Pilgrims who landed at Plymouth Rock in 1620. His father was a sea captain who made a voyage around the world, taking five years. On his next voyage his vessel was wrecked, but all the crew was saved except the captain of the ship. Having fallen overboard in his efforts to regain the wreck, he was assisted by two of his crew when he was attacked by a shark and was lost. His mother was Deborah Hopkins, a daughter of Stephen Hopkins, one of the signers of the Declaration of Independence, and was afterwards governor of Rhode Island.

The Hopkins family was a noted and distinguished one. Easech Hopkins was a commodore in charge of a squadron in the United

States service during Revolution. William Hopkins, another brother, was noted for his talents and valor in the provincial army of the Revolution. Thus it will be seen that our subject was descended from one of the most illustrious of Rhode Island families in her colonial days.

Mr. Arnold was reared and educated in the city of Providence, imbibing the industry and energy of her people and the general characteristics of her early population. In his early manhood he formed an attachment for a young lady who was a member of one of the first families of the city. It proved unfortunate for him; and with disappointed hopes and a lacerated heart, he left his native state, the scene of his youth and the firesides of his kindred, to seek a panacea in the far distant sunny South, relying upon his strong arm, indomitable energy and his skill as a machinist and manufacturer for support in his new home.

He came to the new and fertile district of Greenville, South Carolina, and soon engaged to fit up a cotton factory for a Mr. Perry. This he accomplished, and it was the first ever built in that state. He operated this factory as superintendent for several years; and during this time, he married Mary Dunbar, the daughter of John Dunbar, who subsequently moved to Georgia and settled on Pugh's Creek in this county where he lived and died. Soon Mr. Arnold followed and settled in the same neighborhood, and engaged in farming, as well as the vocations of a machinist and a mechanic.

For a number of years after this he was engaged as a plantation overseer for Robert Craig and others. When not engaged in this, he would work as a day laborer in the fields, making rails, repairing fences, building and repairing houses—anything that came to hand. His theory was: "Work at something; if you can't get a good price, take a less one. Be occupied." And a better or more faithful worker I never knew. For the long years that he resided here, up to old age, he was the most untiring laborer I ever knew, and yet he never prospered in the sense of accumulating wealth.

The cold Saturday in February, 1835, is a memorable day, the coldest in the memory of the oldest inhabitant. So excessive was the cold that all business was suspended and people hovered around their fires to keep from freezing, and yet Mr. Arnold cut briars for Eli Hood. This illustrates his resolution as a worker.

In everything he was resolute and fearless. To have known his mother nothing less would have been expected of him, for she was as dauntless as the historic Nancy Hart, of Revolutionary fame. To illustrate I give the following: At the time to which I refer she lived in the outskirts of North Providence, then sparsely inhabited. She was a widow with several small children, our subject being one of them. A crazy negro, large, powerful and dangerous, had escaped from his confinement and was approaching her house. Hastily thrusting her long-handled shovel into the fire, it was soon heated; and as the negro came to the door, she met him with the shovel and thrust it against his naked breast, saying: "I'll burn you to death, if you come in here." He raised a yell and hastily retreated. But for her heroism and presence of mind, some of her children most likely would have been killed by the enraged maniac.

A singular incident in Mr. Arnold's life occurred years ago. He was miller for John Wright on Pugh's Creek. It was a small mill with a large patronage and often he would run the mill until late at night. On one occasion he worked till midnight and he was alone with a bright pine knot fire on an old mill rock. A female figure entered the door at the opposite end of the house, passed in a short distance, crossed the room and disappeared. He at once recognized it as his sister, Joanna, whom he left in Rhode Island and had not seen in twenty years. To his mind it was evidently an apparition. A short time afterwards, he received a letter from his mother telling him of her death, and it occurred at midnight on the night he had seen the figure enter the mill house.

Mr. Arnold had no respect nor patience with wife beaters. While at Perry's factory a distant relative of his also came on from the North and was engaged in the factory. This relative had brought with him his wife who was a docile, quiet little Yankee. He was sometimes guilty of using his whip on her. His conduct came to Mr. Arnold's knowledge and he said to him: "Shubel, if you whip your wife again while I am here, you will have me to whip, too." Not many days later, while Mr. Arnold was engaged in the picker room, the little wife came rushing in with her head bleeding from a blow by her husband and who was following her with a loaded whip. Mr. Arnold at once met him in a threatening manner. A blow from the whip was dodged by Mr. Arnold, who in a lick with his ponderous fist knocked down the wife beater and administered to him a sound castigation. The offender begged for mercy which was granted upon the promise that he would never whip his wife again. He kept his word.

Another case: When Mr. Arnold lived on Pugh's Creek in this county, in passing near a neighbor's house, he heard the cries of a woman. Hastening to the house, he found it was a case of wife beating. Interfering at once he was struck by the husband. Arnold returned the blow and the husband was knocked down. The wife grabbed the firestick and gave Mr. Arnold a severe blow. Releasing his hold at once, Arnold said to her: "You are a darned heifer—your husband ought to whip you every day."

I have spoken of Mr. Arnold's resoluteness. Great fortitude was another characteristic. I give this incident: Many years ago he was employed to cover the dwelling of John Stuart. It was the custom then to joint the shingles before putting them on. During the job, Saturday night and Sunday intervened and Joe, whose business it was to do the joining, went on a bust and was not on his post Monday morning. Mr. Arnold immediately took his place and in the operation cut his finger. Applying to Dr. Wildman, he decided that amputation was necessary. The doctor said it would be a painful operation and that he must submit to being tied. "I'll not be tied," said Mr. Arnold. "Then my young men will have to hold you," said the good Doctor. "I'll not submit to that either. I can bear it." So clasping the chair with his well hand and clinching his teeth, his hand was extended, the finger taken off at the first joint, the diseased flesh scooped out and not a muscle moved. Dr. Wildman said it was the most remarkable case of fortitude he had ever witnessed.

In his later years his health was poor. I visited him on one occasion and inquired about his health. "It is very poor," he said. "How is your appetite?", I inquired. "It is very good. If it were not for what I eat, I could not live." "It is just so with me," I remarked, "and with most people, I believe." He took the joke and enjoyed it.

He was a man of brittle temper, but quite congenial as a companion and a good laugher. In politics he was an inordinate Whig and died in the old faith. He was violently opposed to secession and was never reconciled to it. It was natural when we consider the place of his nativity.

He died May 11, 1868, in the 75th year of his age, and was buried at Roswell, in Cobb County, near which place he had lived for ten years.

1871

William Maltbie

The subject of this sketch was born in Fairfield, Connecticut, April 9, 1783, and died at his home in Lawrenceville September 24, 1865. He was the son of Captain Jonathon Maltbie who held a commission in the United States Navy. He was commander of a revenue cutter during the Revolutionary War and was highly esteemed as a brave and active officer. Under the undaunted Brewster he engaged in one of the most sanguinary battles of the Revolution and in a hand-to-hand fight on Long Island Sound with a vastly superior force of British soldiers and seamen defeated the enemy.

In early life William Maltbie engaged in the mercantile business with a Mr. Morgan, who came south and opened a store near Hog Mountain at the home of John Winn for the purpose of trading with the Indians. On Mr. Morgan's return north to buy goods, he was taken sick and died. It became necessary, therefore, for his partner, Mr. Maltbie, to come to Georgia to look after the business. This was about 1815 or 1816, and at that early date he became a citizen of this section.

In 1817 he married Philadelphia Winn, daughter of Elisha Winn. He continued to sell goods at the head of the Appalachee River until Gwinnett County was organized. He then moved to his residence one-half mile north of Lawrenceville. He was elected the first clerk of the Inferior Court and clerk of the Court of Ordinary and served as such for nearly thirty-five years.

The contract to build the first courthouse in Lawrenceville was let by him by the authority of Elisha Winn, a justice of the Inferior Court.

Lawrenceville was named by Mr. Maltbie in honor of Captain James Lawrence who was commander of the boat Chesapeake in the War of 1812, and who immortalized his name by his heroic services in the navy of the United States. After being wounded several times in the engagement with the Shannon, he exclaimed to his men on being carried below: "Don't give up the ship." These words of the dying Lawrence will never be forgotten while American liberty has a votary or the United States has a ship roaming the sea.

Mr. Maltbie was a man of fine practical sense and business talent. He did as much or more in organizing the county than any man connected with its past history.

As citizen and public officer he contributed more to the county's organization and starting its internal machinery than any man living or dead. Even before he became a member of a church, his deportment was upright, his morals correct, and his daily walk and conversation were above reproach. A long and intimate acquaintance with him in numerous business transactions enables one to say that he was truthful, conscientious and strictly honest.

The words of Pope, "An honest man is the noblest work of God," were fully exemplified in his character. In all the relations of life as husband, father, brother, friend, neighbor and citizen, he was kind, affectionate and dutiful, more so than any man I have ever known.

Reared a Presbyterian, he had great respect for the quiet order and impressive method of worship of that venerable church. However, he joined the Methodist Church and was the main pillar of the Lawrenceville Church for more than a quarter of a century. It was a great loss to the church when he died.

His obituary appeared in The Christian Advocate a short time after his death and reproduced here:

"William Maltbie, Esq., died in Lawrenceville, Georgia, September 24, 1865, in the 82nd year of his age. He was a native of Fairfield, Conn., but for more than forty years he was a citizen of Lawrenceville and one of the pioneers of Gwinnett County. I knew him from my earliest childhood and during my manhood and call him my friend. He was a friend above reproach. He was in the full sense of the term a friend to the poor. Many a poor individual's cruse has been filled with oil and the barrel with meal from his generous munificence. He filled for nearly half a century various offices of trust in his adopted county with honor to himself and benefit to the people. For years he made application for pensions for the surviving soldiers of the Revolutionary War and collected them for the veterans, doing all this without any compensation. Innumerable services of a like nature were rendered by him to the poor and destitute without reward or the hope thereof. In all relations of life, he was circumspect and faithful. Such was his character that none knew him but to love him, none named him but to praise him. And above all he was a Christian gentleman without reproach. For more than forty years he adorned the faith of his Christianity by a pious walk and a Godly conversation. For more than a quarter of a century he was the pillar of his church. He has gone to his reward in a green old age. Like a shock of corn fully ripe, he has been gathered to his Father. All that was mortal of my old friend sleeps in the old graveyard near which he worshipped. It is a sacred spot, the eternal home of so good a man. Farewell, my friend and brother, but in the impressive language of his partner at his interment, 'Not forever'."

He was the best friend the writer ever had. Whatever commendable traits of character I may possess, if any, are attributable to the counsels of my old friend and to his good examples and brotherly attentions to me when I was treading the slippery pathways of youth's giddy rounds. I have a grateful memory of him, his gentle, kindly face, his soft voice and his fatherly counsels and admonitions as well as the prayers offered up by him in my behalf. A thousand thanks go up from my heart as I pen these lines to his memory that I had so kind and so good a brother-in-law to guide my wayward footsteps.

How near and dear are the many old friends I have. I was young when I first knew them, but autumn days are coming upon me rapidly now. I have endeavored to turn back the volume of time, to read over again the record of past days and make memories once more realities as they once were. It has been a pleasant yet a melancholy one. I have to some extent lived my life over again. Then the sad reality is upon me that nearly all my old friends are gone. I, too, feel that I am hastening to the brink of the 'Dark River.'

Oft in the stilly night
E'er slumber's chain has bound me,
The smiles, the tears, of boyhood years,
The words of love then spoken,
The eyes that shone, now dimmed and gone,
The faithful hearts now broken,
When I remember all
The friends so linked together
I've seen around me fall
Like leaves in winter weather.

1871

James S. Russell

The announcement of the death of Mr. Russell impresses me sadly. On account of his advanced age it was not unexpected. Yet he passed so suddenly that the news fell upon me like a pall. 'Dust thou art and unto dust shalt thou return.' This is an edict long since enunciated and from which there is no appeal. The varying cycles of ninety winters served at last to carry him to the grave.

Fifty-five years and more I knew him, he a man of mature years, I a youth of ten. Since then I knew him well.

In early times he lived on Beaver Ruin Creek in the western part of the county and resided there until the death of John Lamar, when he bought a farm on Pugh's Creek, moved to it, remodeled the mills and added a wool factory made by his own hands and did a prosperous business with both.

He was a natural mechanic and became a skilled workman and millwright, house builder and an adept in any mechanism that required edged tools, was master of his trade and yet served no apprenticeship.

The old Fairview Church now standing for sixty years was built by him, in the shadow of which after long years he finds his last resting place. Later the Presbyterian Church in Lawrenceville was the outcome of his skill in architecture, both of which will be monuments to his memory until destroyed by the corroding tooth of time. From my earliest acquaintance with him, he was an ardent Presbyterian, being a member first at Fairview, then at Goshen when it was constituted, he being one of the original founders and the builder of the church edifice.

In politics, he was a Whig and as steadfast well nigh in the support of that party as in his Presbyterianism.

Abstemious in his habits, he never used tobacco and the intoxicating bowl never touched his lips during his long lifetime, hence perhaps his life's prolongation to the great age to which he was spared.

If the world was like him the jails would be tenantless, criminal dockets without cases, grand juries would have no bills of indictment to find, and locksmith's occupation would be gone.

For many years he was the compeer and intimate friend of William Montgomery, Moses and Daniel Liddell, Richard Saye, William Knox, John Mills, A. R. Smith, Dr. Alexander and Thomas H. Jones, and though these formed a galaxy of great and good men, James Russell was as good as the best of them.

Much more might be said of the exalted good qualities of Mr. Russell, but let this suffice for me. It is intended as a brief tribute to a good man whose whole life was worthy of emulation and who was my friend for back in the shadowy long past.

1871

Rev. Ansalem Anthony

This venerable man lived in the eastern part of Gwinnett County, near the line of Jackson County, from my earliest recollection until a few years ago when he moved to Meriwether County to live with one of his sons. He died there. I have no means of ascertaining when he was born or where, but would say that he was born not far from 1780, and I think in Georgia, probably Wilkes County.

He was a Baptist preacher, but I do not know whether he was identified with the old organization or with the missionary church. I think he was a kind of go-between, holding to some of the doctrines of the old side and to some of the missionary church. He advocated some of the benevolent institutions of the day such as Bible societies and temperance movements. But he condemned Free Masonry and was an uncompromising opponent of this ancient order.

I remember in 1845 staying at his home all night and enjoying his hospitality, which was a liberal and generous one; and we sat up until past midnight, our principal conversation being the denunciation of Masonry. I had recently read Morgan's Disclosures and was in high vein for it. I afterwards renounced my anti-Masonry, while my old friend held out against it until his dying day. He had a deep-seated prejudice against the order, arising no doubt from the want of proper knowledge of the institution and its benevolent and moral teachings. He never knew that Clay and Jackson, Few and Longstreet, Franklin and Washington, and tens of thousands of the best and most enlightened, both of church and state, were its votaries. I accord to him honesty and sincerity in his opposition; and in his denunciation, he thought he was doing God's service as much as to denounce the brothel or the grog shop.

In the temperance reform of his day, he was zealous and indefatigable and was a co-worker with J. S. Wilson, Dr. Alexander, Hosea Camp, Moses Liddell, William Montgomery and others of the old fathers, and was as uncompromising in his opposition to the liquor traffic as the strictest of the sect. An anecdote will illustrate his character and his strong opposition to drinking whiskey under any and all circumstances. Arriving in our village early one morning, having tarried the previous night not far off, he called in at the store of one of our merchants who had known him all his life, and after the usual salutations, he complained of not feeling well and asked for some water, remarking that he had not had the opportunity of taking his morning dram. His friend, Mr. S., was greatly astonished at this as he had supposed he could not be induced to take even a morning dram under any circumstances; and his countenance betrayed to the old gentleman that astonishment. He at once explained in his soft, slow and measured words that he did not mean that stinking, debasing, poisonous stuff called whiskey that runs men mad, that poisons their life blood, that fills our jails and poor houses, that breaks the hearts of women and makes beggars of children, but he meant that sparkling, health-giving beverage, the best temporal gift of God to man, water; that his habit for years had been, upon his rising every morning, to repair first to his spring and take large drafts of water, which aided digestion, improved the health and prolonged a man's life.

Mr. Anthony was never a great preacher in the common acceptation of the term. He was not fluent or animated, but he was profound as a theologian. His voice was soft and low, his enunciation slow and measured, his ideas always sensible and scriptural, and he fulfilled his mission as acceptably and as faithfully as any of his contemporaries; and in eternity, his crown will be adorned and bedecked with many bright jewels of souls saved through his instrumentality.

In personal appearance Mr. Anthony was of the Roman type, six feet two or three in height, large frame but no surplus flesh, calm dark face, bespeaking a quiet, benevolent heart, all indicating reverence for God, charity to man and universal goodwill to his race.

Blessed old man! Had the world been filled with such, peace would have had universal reign and the blessedness of millennial glory would have blessed the earth for a thousand years.

Note of Editor: Mr. Anthony lived on the road from Harmony Grove Church to Bethabra Baptist Church. The Anthony farm was well known to the public in that section of Gwinnett County. The late William Elijah Flanigan, who died there in January, 1940, owned part of the farm for more than sixty years. Mr. Anthony was the founder of Bethabra Baptist Church and its pastor from its organization to 1856, more than thirty years. His remains, together with several of his family, lie in the churchyard there.

The minutes of the Inferior Court held December 2, 1856, show that Mr. Anthony was given a judgment against the Lawrenceville Manufacturing Company for $1,437.00. That was the cotton mill then located in the western part of Lawrenceville before the War Between the States.

1871

Rev. Hosea Camp

Hosea Camp was a local Methodist preacher and was born in South Carolina about the year 1774 and removed in early life to Georgia and settled on the Mulbury River near the present residence of Mr. D. R. Lyle, in Jackson County, where he resided for some time and afterwards removed eight to ten miles farther west to what is now known as his old home place, some thirteen or fourteen miles east of Lawrenceville, the present residence of William Jackson, where he resided until 1847. He was distinguished for his quiet and unobtrusive deportment, never engaging in controversies either of politics or religion, though firm and decided in both. He was a firm and unwavering Whig on politics and a staunch and unyielding Methodist in religion; but being strictly honest in his principles himself, accorded the same honesty to those with whom he disagreed. This was a commendable trait in the character of our old friend and let us commend this spirit to the readers of this sketch as an illustrious example to be followed by them.

Men generally have too little charity for those with whom they differ in politics and more especially with those who differ with them in religion. This illiberality and uncharitableness among men professing to be the followers of our Savior is, to my mind, the most unreasonable and inconsistent spirit that pervades the human mind, all professing to serve the same Lord whose law is charity and love; striving for the same heaven and yet falling out and quarreling by the way. If heaven be pure and holy, the soul must be purified from all this base material before it can ever enter its blessed portals. Such was not of our old friend. With him his neighbor might be a Democrat and a patriot, a Presbyterian or a Baptist and a Christian.

As a minister he classed respectably. His sermons were plain and yet forcible; and while the opening was somewhat tame, generally his perorations were striking and touching. He was the neighbor and compeer of Samuel Anthony and with him was a co-worker in the salvation of souls. Wherein they differed, "they agreed to disagree" without controversy.

Mr. Camp was happy in his domestic relations, rearing twelve children and all of them taking honorable positions in their communities, and were useful and respected citizens, following in his footsteps and governed by his example. In social life he was pleasant and agreeable in his manners, soft and gentle and somewhat mirthful. He was a good laugher, not a smiler such as we sometimes see, and such as I always suspect of deceit and treachery; nor such as was Shakespear's Iago "Smile and smile and yet a villain," but his was the ringing, pealing laughter from an honest, cheerful heart that makes digestion good and draws nails from the coffin, of the "laugh and grow fat" specimen.

Save me from the smiler. So obsequious, "so happy to see you" with the "how are you, my brother" and then strike you under the fifth rib. After a somewhat long experience and some observation of men's character, I never knew such a one but, if not a scoundrel, was a hypocrite.

Another beautiful trait in his character was that he never spoke evil of his neighbor. He had not the tongue of the back-biter nor the slime of the slanderer so prevalent in the present day. If it was my prerogative to speak of it, I would say it is one of the greatest evils of the age, the most damnable and diabolical.

"Who steals my purse steals trash; this something-nothing, 'twas mine, 'tis his and has been slave to thousands. But he that filches from me my good name, robs me of that which not enriches him and makes me poor indeed."

Oh, the slanderer! the defamer! the back-biter! "If thou hast no other name to be known by, let us call thee DEVIL."

We commend especially this beautiful trait in Hosea Camp's character to all who may read these lines and let them try and profit by his example.

He removed from Gwinnett to Polk County, having been a citizen here for forty years and one of the best of the old fathers.

He died in 1859 or 1860, aged 86 years, exceeding the Psalmist's limit by 16 years.

"The days of our years are three score and ten; and if by reason of strength they be four score years, there is strength, labor and sorrow, for it is soon cut off and we fly away."

The prolongation of this good man's life was one of the rewards vouchsafed from heaven for his godly upright life. And in his advanced age he was translated from earth to heaven with but little of the pangs of dissolution.

"My buried friends, can I forget
Or must the grave forever sever?
They linger in my memory yet
And in my heart they'll live forever.

"I fain would weep, but what of tears?
Not tears of mine could e'er recall them;
Nor would I wish that groveling cares,
Cares like mine should e'er befall them.

"They rest in realms of light and love;
They dwell upon the mount of glory;
They bask in beams of bliss above
And shout to tell the pleasing story."

Notation by Author: The William Jackson farm referred to as the home of Hosea Camp is on the road from Auburn to County Line Consolidated School, now Barrow County.

1871

N. L. Hutchins

" 'Tis hard to venture where our betters failed
Or lend fresh interest to a twice told tale."

So much has been said and written about Judge Hutchins, and so much better than I can say, that I shrink from the task of attempting to give even a sketch of him. But to leave out his name in my sketches of the early settlers of this county would be leaving out a link that would weaken, if not destroy, the whole chain. I therefore, console myself by saying that I only write for the eye of his old friends and neighbors, those who knew him long and well.

Nathan Louis Hutchins was born April 11, 1779, in Pendleton, now Anderson, District, South Carolina, near the confluence of Seneca and Tugalo rivers, the head waters of the Savannah. His father was without means to educate his children. He was permitted to attend school when the weather or the condition of the crops made it unnecessary to work. In this way he finished his pupilage at the end of a three months' course at the old field school.

After learning to read he would pursue his studies and general reading late at night by the light of a pine knot fire. Thrown on his own resources when quite young, he sought employment as a clerk in a country store at Ruckersville or Petersburg, a trading point at the head of the Savannah and soon thereafter went to Elberton. There he was employed by a Mr. Boen, clerk of the Superior Court, to write for him. General John A. Heard, a distinguished lawyer, was much pleased with him as a promising young man. Impressed by his remarkable memory, which he tested by lending him books and then questioning him about them, advised him to study law. The pittance he earned in the clerk's office and the generous kindness extended to him by General Wiley Thompson, government agent for the Cherokee Indians, and his estimable wife, encouraged young Hutchins to accept General Heard's kind offer to use his library and assist him.

He made rapid progress as a student and in due time was admitted to the bar at one of Judge Dooly's courts. Through the advice of Judge Dooly, General Heard and others, he was induced to cast his lot with the men on the frontier, and came to Gwinnett

County, then just organized, in 1822. His attention to business, his industry, soon commended him to the young and hardy community, and his success at the bar marked him as a man of ability.

In 1825 he was elected to the legislature and again in 1827. After this he never held a political office.

In 1829 he married. His wife died in 1851. He remained a widower the balance of his life. After this he devoted himself to his profession and ranked with the remarkable men who made the bar of the Western Circuit so distinguished.

He was not distinguished as an orator. But the comprehensiveness and the analytical power of his mind, his knowledge of human nature and his keen insight into the motives of men, enabled him to lay his cases before juries so that the most illiterate understood him and his success attests his power as a practitioner.

Notwithstanding his defect in his early education, he loved nature, looked into the cause and effect of everything that came under his observation and with judgment and tenacious memory he stored up a fund of information and learning that overcame that defect.

In 1857, Governor Johnson appointed him to a vacancy in the judgeship of the Western Circuit, which position he continued to fill until 1868. He entered again upon the practice of his profession in which the triumphs of his life had been won.

He never professed religion, but was always charitable and liberal towards the Christian churches. His life was guided by stern principles of morality and his precepts always good.

A prominent citizen and lawyer, it is not unnatural that he made enemies. Generally they were soon reconciled, for no one was more prompt than he to make amends; and his long service on the bench, where he knew neither friend nor foe, showed him devoid of malice and few who knew him failed to become his friend.

For two years or more he had been troubled with a heart ailment and had symptoms of paralysis. He had apprehended sudden death and was reluctant to travel alone. But in January, 1870, when in usual good health, he left home on business and also to visit his only daughter at Rome. He had been gone about ten days and on his way to Madison, feeling unwell from having contracted a cold on a hand car from Kingston to Rome a few days before, he stopped to pass the Sabbath at Social Circle. He took to his bed that day. Wednesday he seemed almost well, but that night the disease ran rapidly into pneumonia and on Friday night, February 11, he died. Conscious to the last, he directed matters as if preparing for an ordinary journey with a calmness and composure that awed the two or three at his bedside into silent wonder, then without a struggle quietly breathed his last as if going into a quiet sleep.

My first recollection of Judge Hutchins dates back forty-six years from the time he first came to Lawrenceville. He then boarded with a friend of mine who lived in a house on the street east and a short distance from the present residence of Mrs. Culver. The old house has long since been torn down and removed.

Our people then were plain and unpretending. The sound of the now fashionable dinner bell, "these valleys and rocks had never heard." The harsh and head-splitting gong was a thing unheard of as much as the magnetic telegraph or the mountains in the moon; and if one of these abominable gongs had been let loose in the town, the staid men of that day would have been excited as at the rush of a tornado or the rockings of an earthquake; and the women, too, would have gone into hysterics and fits. The calls to the boarders then were by the plain old fashioned tin trumpet or ox horn.

Judge Hutchins was then regarded by our people as a remarkable man indeed, for he was a lawyer, and lawyers in those days were looked upon as wonders.

I next remember him as a colonel of county militia. I recollect him well upon the parade grounds before the regiment which was armed and equipped as the law directs, some with long sticks, some with polk stalks, some with umbrellas, and a few with old guns without locks in many cases, and with all these, they went through the manual of arms. The Colonel, mounted upon his beautiful sorrel horse, handsomely caparisoned, with long flowing mane, tassels pendant from the headstall and browband of his bridle, fancy housings attached to his saddle, his gilt saber glistening in the sunbeams, he was the admiration of all; and to my young mind, the most 'marvelously proper man' I had ever seen. It aroused the aspirations of my young ambition and I hoped some day that I, too, might be an officer to command and look like him. After a time my young ambition was somewhat gratified by being chosen a Georgia Major, but I could never approach within gunshot distance of what I had considered his elevation.

I hope I shall be pardoned for the above seemingly light and trivial reminiscences. They come upon the memory and cause me to incorporate them in this sketch as incidents in the early history of the old county.

Judge Hutchins was a man of chivalry and high personal courage. Not like the pugilist or bully, but his was a high, manly courage to resent and punish insult and impertinence. I have sometimes witnessed his rencounters with his adversaries, some of them as fearless as himself. In none of them did he ever disclose any other but cool courage and indomitable pluck. In the rencounter with Gordon, when they fought with knives, it was the most dangerous affray that had ever occurred in the town. With Hutchins and Gordon it was 'Greek meets Greek, Then comes the tug of war.' Two more fearless men I have never seen. Both carried the scars of the fight to their graves. They afterwards became friends and remained cordial through life, each having great respect for the satisfactory evidence of the other's pluck.

Judge Hutchins was never properly understood by some of his fellow citizens. By some he was considered selfish, perverse and unfeeling, that he cared for nothing except for himself and his own interest and aggrandizements. This grew out of the fact that the collection of debts was placed in his hands. He prosecuted the claims of his clients with vigor and it may have been sometimes with apparent rigor.

In the courthouse as an attorney he made enemies by the zeal and tact with which he prosecuted his clients' interests, often with apparent harshness to the adverse party. Contrary to this I have been informed by his executor that there are claims, notes, fi. fas., amounting to thousands of dollars now belonging to his estate which might have been collected, but for his indulgence which by way of delay are a total loss.

I state frankly that I have lived under a misapprehension of the man for forty years. I had considered him as caring for neither king nor country and only for himself and his. My opinions, however, have been undergoing a change for some years past and an incident just after the war changed the whole current of my estimate of the man.

At the first court he held in the county after the war, I was the foreman of the grand jury. Society was terribly demoralized. Crime and transgression of the law were rampant and unrestrained. Society was unhinged and the lawlessness of the times was fearful. At that term of the court were found a great many bills of indictment and special presentment by the grand jury. When the jury would enter the courtroom to return their bills his practice was to have the foreman to sit by his side; and one evening while the clerk was calling the jury, he took from my hands the bills and glanced over them. Then turning to me, his eyes full of tears, said: "Oh! What a wretched state the county is now in and what is to become of us, God only knows." The deep solicitude in his face to the conditions of the county, especially the tears in his eyes, changed the whole current of my opinions of the man. I could not mistake him then. The face may deceive but there is truth in a tear.

> "Too oft is a smile
> But the hypocrite wile,
> To mask detestation or fear;
> Give me the soft sigh
> Whilst the soul telling eye
> Is simmed for a time with a tear."

But he is gone to his grave and his old friends feel his loss. I quote from H. P. B. in a letter of condolence to his son shortly after his death: "One by one of our wisest and best men are passing away and their places are being filled by desperate and reckless adventurers, whose counsels and conduct are controlling the destinies of a great, unfortunate and suffering people." Yes, one by one the old fathers of our county are passing away. Nearly all are gone. They were a noble race of men. "We shall never see their like again."

Finally, we quote from a newspaper article of him shortly after his death: "The highest praise that can be awarded to any man is to say of him after his death that his virtues alone are remembered. If he had faults, a grateful people, deeply indebted to him, will never speak of them, but will cherish with pride and affection the memory of his many virtues and of his greatness in private life, at the bar and on the bench."

1871

ELDER JAMES HALE

Mr. Hale became a citizen of Gwinnett County as early as 1821. He settled on a lot that he drew from the state as a soldier of the War of 1812, which is situated in what is known as Berkshire district in the western part of the county. Upon this place was his home from 1821 till May, 1855, the time of his death.

He was born in Johnson County, North Carolina, in 1778, and came to Georgia when a small boy, first living in Oglethorpe, then in Clark and then in Gwinnett.

The date of his conversion was at an early period and he began to preach in 1811. While in the army of the War of 1812, he preached to his comrades and brothers in arms whenever opportunity offered, not as a chaplain but as a fellow soldier, feeling it his duty to preach the Gospel even by the wayside, on the highways and hedges, thereby casting the bread of life upon the waters, hoping that it might be gathered up after many days.

Very soon after he came to this county, old Camp Creek Church was organized, he being one of the founders, and was chosen its first pastor which position he held to the time of his death, a period of 35 years. During that long time he was faithful in his ministerial duties and was always acceptable to that church, they never getting tired of him, nor were they willing to exchange him for another. This was a high compliment to the old man, and it proves him to have been a faithful, conscientious preacher of righteousness, doing his duty before God and man to the best of his ability.

I know of no similar instance of a preacher serving a church so long a time, over a third of a century, and during that long time he had no strife or bickerings or even unkind feelings with his flock.

Men are fond of a change, and a change in nothing more than in preachers as a general thing. Hence it is the policy of some denominations to continue the same minister not longer than a brief period to the same charge. To be able to serve the same people acceptably for thirty-five years is one of the highest encomiums that could have been paid Mr. Hale. They loved the old man and he was to them as a prophet in Israel.

During this time he served other churches, generally four, which embraced all the Sabbaths in the year, working faithfully on his farm and for his family during the week, and as faithfully for his Lord and Master on Saturdays and Sundays. Among them he served Sweetwater fifteen years.

I quote from a letter by an old friend and brother of his which furnishes me some data that assist me in making up this sketch. When Mr. Hale began exercising in public, it is said of him that he could not read a chapter in the Bible or a hymn in the hymnbook, but eventually he became a good reader and was well versed in the Scriptures. He was ever esteemed and loved by the Primitive Baptists and his neighbors always spoke highly of him and had much reverence for him as a man and a Christian.

I have often attended on his ministry, always to my edification, not for any high sounding words or sentence, nor for any display of rhetoric or eloquent declamation, for to none of these did he make any pretensions; but for his plain, practical, unpretending exposition of the words in force and simplicity. His style was of the Primitive Baptist style, peculiar to that church, which the fashionable and fastidious of this day would not probably admire; yet I liked it for its unpretentiousness and its simplicity. "No pent up Utica contracted his powers." He preached to his people as he would have talked to his children.

Often after stating a proposition or a Scriptural theorem, he would say: "Some people would not agree with me on this, but it is the opinion of the old man anyhow." He would often refer to himself as the 'Old Man,' sometimes as the 'Old Hale.'

Many years ago I attended one of his meetings. It was footwashing day. I had been brought up in a church that did not observe this ordinance and that probably did not consider it an ordinance. Curiosity, to some extent, prompted me to attend this meeting to see the foot washing, not simply for amusement or to laugh and make sport, for I never did this at church, not even when a boy, but I had never seen the like and wanted to. In witnessing the ceremony and performance, it changed my mind; for instead of looking foolish, as I had supposed, it was solemn and impressive, and it made a good impression on my mind. However much other churches may object to it, and I don't know that they do, there is an illustrious example for it given in the 13th Chapter of John. When the Savior, after supper, laid aside his garments, he took a towel and girded himself. After that He poured water into a basin and began to wash the feet of the disciples and dried them with the towel with which he was girded. Again, "For if I then your Lord and Master, have washed your feet, ye also ought to wash each other's feet."

Daddy Hale, as he was familiarly called, especially in his old age, 'Hard Shell,' as he was called by some by way of reproach, was one of the most exemplary of the old fathers. There were as few objectionable traits in his character as any of them. Always quiet and kind in his intercourse with his neighbors, having no strife or disagreements with anyone, earning his bread by the sweat of his face, he served his God in his day and generation to the best of his ability and 'fell on sleep' in a green old age at peace with God and his fellow man, in the 77th year, beloved by all who knew him and no doubt saved in Heaven.

The grave now covers his ashes as it does Paul, and as "Abel lying in his blood beneath his altar, and Noah resting where they placed him in the renovated earth fresh from its deluvian baptism; and Abraham with his cherished Sarah, and Isaac with his beloved Rebecca, and Jacob brought up from Egypt to be laid by his Leah, all reposing in death and Hades. And among the sleepers are Paul from the block, Peter from the cross, Polycarp from the stake, and Luther from the rage of Rome and hell." And there, too, are Anthony and Camp and Hale, whose virtues still survive them like the odors of flowers fresh fallen, and many dear companions with whom they walked hand-in-hand along the path of life.

In concluding this brief sketch of Father Hale, I feel that it is very imperfect. I desired to delineate his character and commend his honest, straight-forward life as worthy of imitation. His religious faith I know is objected to by many who will read this article. Of this I have nothing to say. It is not my business nor my purpose to discuss it here.

He was an honest man, honest in his religious faith and everything. His long life was a consistent one. He turned neither to the right nor left in his duty to God and his fellow man. Let none say of him that he was an old 'Hardshell' and can have no fellowship with him. Let none say of Anthony that he was a Missionary and have no confidence in him, nor of Hosea Camp that he was a Methodist and expected to save himself by works, nor of John S. Wilson that he was a Calvinist and preached a partial atonement. A man's religious creed is not the criterion by which he should be judged. His walk, his life is the great test of character. The world is full of error, has been, is now, and will be until the old heaven and the old earth shall have passed away and the new Heaven and the new earth shall be ushered in.

Because we may differ with our fellow man is no evidence that he is wrong and we are right. We all now see as through a glass darkly and the vision is different to many, even from the same standpoint, the Bible. Some are wrong, but who is it?

1871

HENRY P. THOMAS

Colonel Thomas was born in Franklin County, Georgia, May 10, 1810. He was reared on his father's farm and when he was sixteen years of age was sent to school at Salem, Clarke County, Ga. Afterwards he attended Franklin College at Athens. He graduated from that institution along with Howell Cobb, Alexander Stephens and William H. Crawford, Jr., in the class of 1832. After completing his college course he taught school one year at Ruckersville, in Elbert County, and among his scholars was Peter W. Alexander, the celebrated war correspondent in the late war, whose letters were read with so much interest by our people.

In 1835 he began the study of law under Col. Joseph Ligon, of Watkinsville. He was admitted to the bar in 1836 and came to Lawrenceville with the purpose of practicing his profession and did so in partnership with John B. Trippe, who died lately at Milledgeville.

On December 5, 1837, he married Ellen E. Burroughs, who lived in Columbia County in this state, which good lady yet survives him.

He was a lieutenant-colonel of volunteers in the Creek War of 1836 and served under General Scott and part of the time on Scott's staff.

In 1844 Colonel Thomas relinquished the practice of law and moved to his plantation on the headwaters of the Appalachee, where he continued to reside until the date of his death which occurred in Knoxville, Tennessee, November 20, 1863. He fell at the head of his brigade on the parapet of Fort Sanders at the assault on that stronghold pierced by fourteen rifle balls. He had been wounded early in the action in the right arm, but refused to resign his command. He was killed while in command of Cobb's old brigade, Colonel Ruff, of the 18th Georgia, having been killed about five minutes before Colonel Thomas. Colonel Thomas held many positions of honor and trust. He was ordinary of this county, represented his county in the State Senate and House of Representatives and often served as a delegate to political conventions both in his district and the state. He was a member of the celebrated Charleston convention in 1860 and also to its adjourned session at Baltimore a month later, and voted for the nomination of John C. Breckenridge, and died defending the political principles he had always believed to be correct.

Colonel Thomas was a man who showed his faith by his works. He was a strong advocate of the secession of the southern states from the Union, after the election of Lincoln to the presidency. When Georgia and other southern states passed their ordinances of secession and Mr. Lincoln made war upon us, Thomas raised the first company of volunteers from this county, the old Hutchins Guards, and was elected captain, and like Bartow and a thousand of other gallant Georgians, illustrated Georgia on a hundred battlefields. He was in the seven days' battles around Richmond in 1862—at Crampton's Gap, at Fredericksburg, at Chancellorsville, at Sharpsburg, at Gettysburg, at Knoxville, and wherever the battle raged fiercest in defense of his loved South.

I hope I shall be pardoned if I give some personal reminiscences which I feel may bring the writer with too much prominence before the reader. I would gladly disconnect myself from them if I could. I only design to speak of my friend, to point out incidents and reminiscences that I hope and believe will interest his old friends.

Mr. Thomas came to Lawrenceville when a young man only one year out of college and with a classical education and his prospects in life of the most flattering character. The writer of this unpretending memorial was just grown up and six years his junior. Between his father and mine was an enmity as bitter as the grave, growing out of the celebrated Patterson lawsuit. We met, were introduced, I having a prejudice against his name and he probably against mine. His open manly face pleased me. We became friends at once which on my part grew with the years. I had no cause to hold his friendship doubtful and it continued until he fell on the bloody field of Knoxville. We differed in politics from 1840 to 1860, often meeting on the stump at the public places in our county, he on one side, I on the other. No personal animosity or rupture ever occurred between us; and it is attributable solely to his high, noble manliness, and to no virtue of mine. He was a noble, high-toned adversary, never making a political disagreement a matter of personal dislike.

The last time I ever saw him was at his tent in Fredericksburg about the first of 1863. He had a few days before passed through the terrible fight of the 13th of December in which General Tom Cobb was killed. He was in good vein, for the Yankees had met a terrible defeat.

The writer found it important to borrow a horse for half a day to enable him to accomplish a purpose, important to him, in a short space of time to enable him to get back to Richmond by the evening train from Hamilton's Crossing. I applied to Colonel Thomas for his, and it was brought up and saddled for me. I was a little distrustful of his old Ball, for the boys had spoken in my presence of his running away with the Colonel a short time before when on dress parade. When brought up his appearance did not seem to indicate a great deal of spirit, but showed signs of having seen service and privations common to all then and there. I asked the Colonel if I would need a spur and he replied: "Yes, two of them, one in the head and one in the heel and the one in the head will be worth two in the heel." He furnished me both and I found both of much service in enabling me to accomplish my undertaking, more especially the one in my head.

Colonel Thomas may have had his faults. All men have them. Some can see glaringly in others, not in themselves. No mortal man has lived who had them not. Even Abraham, the father of the faithful, lied before God in representing his beautiful Sarah as his sister instead of his wife. Jacob cheated his brother out of his birthright and his father-in-law out of his cattle. David, the sweet singer of Israel, committed murder in the case of Uriah, and then took his wife. Paul was an unrelenting persecutor of the saints of God even unto death. Peter, a beloved disciple, denied his Lord, lied in his throat, profaned the name of his Master whom he professed to serve, and committed mayhem by cutting off the ear of the high priest's servant.

Colonel Thomas was not a religious man, did not claim to be, but was infinitely better than thousands who profess to be such. He was generous, high-toned, chivalrous and manly in the highest sense of the term.

"Let his faults be writ in water,
His good deeds live in brass."

1871

Dr. Philo Hall

I have no means of obtaining any memoranda of this gentleman as he left no relatives among us and I shall have to rely solely on my recollection of him and I can only promise, therefore, a brief outline of his character. That he was in some respects a remarkable man many who yet live and knew him will admit. That he was a man of many redeeming traits of character will be denied by no impartial mind that knew him, however much he may have objected to some of his peculiar characteristics.

He came to Lawrenceville from Weston, Connecticut, about the year 1820, and built the house where Judge James W. Lampkin now resides and occupied the south end of it as a residence and the other as a doctor's shop.

He had married a sister of William Maltbie, in Connecticut, and I suppose he was induced to move here by that gentleman, who had preceded him to this section several years.

He practiced medicine from the time he came here until his death, which embraced a period of more than twenty-five years; and no physician had the confidence of his patrons more fully than he, especially the women and children. During the whole time of his residence here, he was my father's family physician; and the writer, who was a feeble, sickly boy in his earlier years, well remembers that, when often very sick, the coming of the Doctor always reassured him and he felt that he would be cured without a doubt.

He was a warm friend and devotedly attached to all who employed him, but had no good word for those who employed another. He did a large practice and was as successful in his cases as any physician who has lived among us. He kept accounts upon a daybook, never on a ledger, and did not post his accounts. Hence when his customers came to settle, he had to look through his whole book very often to find the items.

It was his boast that he never sued a man in his life or asked his patrons for money. I have heard him relate an incident that illustrates his character for leniency to those who were indebted to him, and it seemed to give him great satisfaction to tell it. A man who lived in Hog Mountain District whose name was Jackson, I believe, had a sickly family and Dr. Hall was his physician. The Doctor had attended this family for a considerable time, the account had run for two or three years for the man was poor and unable to pay. Finally, despairing to be able to make the money where he lived, he concluded to move; but how could he get away without paying Dr. Hall's account? He called in to see the Doctor on the subject, stated to him his condition and his difficulties, his inability to pay him, the improbability that he ever would be if he stayed on his poor little farm and said: "I have concluded to move to Campbell County, if you let me go." Dr. Hall responded at once in his blunt, abrupt way, saying: "Go along, I shall not hinder you. I have not asked you for money." And three years after as the Doctor was sitting in his shop smoking his pipe, to his surprise Mr. Jackson stepped in and greeted the Doctor with a warm shake of the hand, which was warmly returned by the Doctor. After some conversation between them, Mr. Jackson said: "Well, I am now able to pay and have come to do so. Get out my account and count the interest." After a long search the account was made out and paid off, the Doctor saying to him: "You are a fool if you think I would willingly charge such a man as you interest." He told the Doctor that he had done well in his new home, that he had taken it afoot to pay him his money, had two good horses but they were at home plowing in wheat; had plenty of cattle and hogs, a large crib of corn, and had made cotton enough to pay his debt and had fifty dollars left, and did not now owe a cent in the world. He remained till next morning; and when getting ready to start back, the Doctor went to his bureau, took out a case of fine razors, saying: "I want to make you a present. If the razors shave well, you will remember me. If they pull, you will be sure to remember me." I have often heard him say: "As long as Jackson lives, there will be one honest man in the world."

He once had a fight with Alston Boyd on the street near where Harvey's tailor shop now stands. Boyd was a merchant and occupied the house now owned by B. E. Strickland. No one who ever saw Dr. Hall would have taken him for a fighting man. He was a large man and I would as soon have looked for a fight by an old woman. He was returning from the post office one day and had a newspaper open and was reading it as he passed down the street. Boyd came out of his store and attacked him and when the fight was over, the Doctor said: "I whipped the darn rascal and read my paper all the time."

He owned a negro named Ham and he was as black as the ace of spades and as ugly as a baboon. He bought the negro when quite young, petted him a good deal, kept him about his lot to feed his horse, black his shoes, and to do small jobs generally. Ham was a great rascal and would often transgress. The Doctor kept an account against him. When he would fail to black his shoes, he would enter it against him. When he would neglect his horse, he would charge that against him. When he would throw rocks at his chickens and break their legs, he would charge that, and so on. And when his account got large enough for settlement, he would call him up, call over the account item by item, then thrash him and credit the account in full. He kept this up until Ham grew to be a man and then Ham became rebellious. In attempting to settle the bill one day, the Doctor, apprehending some resistance, caught hold of his shirt bosom and commenced the settlement when Ham tore loose from him and ran away, greatly to the chagrin of the Doctor. In speaking of it afterwards and telling of the great strength of the negro, he said: "'Twould have been as easy to hold a thunderbolt with a cotton thread as to have held him by his osnaburg shirt." The Doctor sold him later and he turned out to be a very bad negro and soon went to the bad.

Doctor Hall was no doubt a descendant of the Pilgrim fathers who came to this country in the Mayflower when they landed at Plymouth Rock. He was peculiar in personal appearance and habits. In stature he was six feet two in height, large frame, of considerable embonpoint, black eyes, bald on his crown, the hair brought up from his temples and tied in a knot on the top of his head, fat cheeks and full face. He was the most cleanly man I ever saw and was as punctilious in this respect as an old maid. He shaved every day, and half an inch below the skin, put on a clean shirt every morning when at home, wore low quartered shoes, well polished, and white socks, a drab beaver hat which he always brushed and then smoothed over a silk handkerchief before going out, and in summer always wore a huge long morning gown. As many of my readers never saw such a garment and probably never heard of one, I will try to describe it, although it was a nondescript thing and difficult to describe. The material was of calico or gingham and required fifteen yards or less to make it, extending from his neck to his heels, with large flowing sleeves after the style of the mutton leg worn by ladies thirty years ago; and the gown when inflated by the wind as he walked along the street resembled a balloon just ready to go up but cut half in two. Seeing the Doctor with his morning gown on, I was always reminded of the curt reply' of the boy who went to school with a bad fitting coat, the first coat he had ever had, and on being asked by another boy in derision who cut his coat, replied that it wasn't cut, but was torn out.

But peace to the ashes of the good Doctor. He saved my life, I have no doubt, by his skill, and I love his memory. He was my friend.

All that is mortal of him lies at the old graveyard in Lawrenceville and he sleeps well. I visited his grave yesterday and it brought up many a pleasant reminiscence of Auld Lang Syne. I give the epitaph on his gravestone which is truthful and appropriate:

"In memory of Dr. Philo Hall, who was born in the town of Weston, Connecticut, April 27, 1784, and died in this village March 17, 1839. He was a skillful and humane physician and his memory will be long and gratefully cherished in that community where the success of his professional exertions has been so frequently realized."

1872

JESSE RAMBO

Uncle Jesse Rambo was an odd genius, full of eccentricities and quaint sayings. Everybody knew Jesse Rambo. Those who came to town had seen the old man, heard his queer talk, and went home and told about the strange little man they had seen. Therefore, everybody big, little, old and young, black and white, knew Jesse Rambo.

He was queer in his looks, queer in his talk, queer in his notions, queer in his habits, queer in everything. We miss the old man from our town with his good humor, his anecdotes, his droll sayings and expressions. Twelve years have passed since he died, yet all these are vivid in my mind. The memory of the man, what he used to say, how he used to look, how he used to act, comes back and makes me laugh.

To write properly of him requires a more graphic pen than mine. To portray his idiosyncracies, which were all of him, is an undertaking that I feel incompetent to perform. He was a character such as I never saw before and shall never see again. That he was a man taken all in all we shall never look upon his like again is an aphorism to which all who knew him readily assent. A man of good property, good farm, many slaves, cribs full of corn, smokehouse full of bacon, yet he was always going to starve to death.

He would often speak of his poverty-stricken condition so piteously, and apparently so truthfully, that one was ready to believe it and sympathize with him, though he might know to the contrary.

Once when he was in our town bewailing his poverty and his inexorable fate of starvation, a stranger who was present was touched in his sympathy for the poor old man; and taking out his purse, said: "Old man, I am a poor man myself, but I am able to work and you are not." Thus speaking, he handed him a dollar and continued: "If this will do you any good, you are welcome to it." Mr. Rambo drew back in surprise, and taking off his hat, said: "I thank you, sir; I am mighty poor, but will try to make out without charity."

He was close in his dealings, saving with his money, not much given to bestow charity, but was honest, wanting only his own, but wanted all of that. He was very friendly with Asa Smith. Smith had great confidence in him and generally divided his little trade with him at his store. He would frequently go behind the counter looking about. Smith's brother, John, slipped a ball of shoe thread into the pocket of his long-tailed coat to tease him. I never think of that old blue coat but what I think of "Old Gimes" and the stanza I learned when I was a boy:

> "Old Gimes is dead, that good old man,
> We ne'er see him more;
> He used to wear an old blue coat
> All buttoned down before."

Mr. Rambo did not find out about the shoe thread until he got home and did not know how it got there. He was very much perplexed and troubled. Finally he concluded that John Smith, "that mischiefous rascal," did it. Next morning bright and early he went back to town, much discouraged, and asked John if he put that thread in his pocket. Smith expressed great surprise and greatly astonished that he, Mr. Rambo, should have taken the thread, that he had always thought him honest, had allowed him to go behind the counter when he pleased, had no idea that he would take anything, had missed the ball of thread but had not thought he took it, and would have to watch him thereafter. It was too serious with the old man to make a joke of it, and never while he lived did he forgive John Smith.

Forty-five years ago, the Hunnicutts lived in Lawrenceville and worked at the blacksmith's trade. Buck was then one of the boys and was fond of playing off on Allen Dyer, Jesse Rambo and others. It was summer time and crops were fine. Mr. Rambo had a field of fine corn near his house. Buck conceived the plan and another helped to carry it out. The procured two cowbells and went over to his house about a mile and a half from town. It was night and not far from bedtime. Buck went to one side of the field and his friend on the other side. First one and then the other would rattle his bell. The old man heard them and supposed his cornfield was full of cattle. He was in a great sputter, called up his negroes and they went in great haste to get them out. One bell would stop as they approached that side of the field, and the one on the opposite side would ring, then this one would cease and the other begin. In this way they kept the old man and his negroes two mortal hours running from one side of the field to the other, he dealing out imprecations that the darn cows would destroy all his corn. One of the perpetrators of this joke has long since passed on, but Buck still lives. Let me say to him that was a trick well conceived and executed, but you served the old man mighty bad.

Mr. Rambo, while a splutterer, was an inoffensive man. I never heard of his doing any harm to any one or to their property but once. Robert Craig, who was his neighbor, had a bull that was large and fat and went where it pleased, a twelve rail fence to the contrary notwithstanding. One day Mr. Rambo heard him coming down the lane, bellowing furiously, and visions of destroyed cornfields flitted through his mind. Gathering his old shotgun, he met him up the lane, the bull on the outside, he on the inside. Approaching within a short distance, he fired through the crack of the fence, giving him a full dose of blue pills in his flank, contrary to the dignity and comfort of the bull and the peace and quietude of Mr. Craig. When the animal went home, the owner found that he was shot and soon ascertained that Mr. Rambo did it. Mr. Craig, hot as pepper, went over to see about it. The following colloquy took place:

"Rambo, did you shoot my bull?"
"Yes."
"Was he in your field?"
"No."
"Was he doing any mischief?"
"No."
"Where was he?"
"In my lane."
"Then why did you shoot him?"
"I was sick that morning and in an ill humor."
"Well, sir, the next time you get sick I want you to go to Dr. Russell and get a dose of medicine and not shoot my bull again, and as you are poor, I will pay for it."

He used to say he never bet but once in his life. When he lived in South Carolina, and soon after his marriage, a big, awkward, lightwood-smoked, spraddle-footed piney woodsman, without shoes, his copperas breeches reaching half way from his knees to his ankles, marched up to his cabin with a rifle and took his seat in the yard. He soon began to tell of his exploits as a marksman, the number of deer and turkeys he had killed, and that he would never shoot a squirrel except in the eye. Just at this moment, a rooster walked across the yard. The hunter said he could shoot off his comb without otherwise touching it and that he would bet a dollar on it. Mr. Rambo thought it an impossibility, was sure he could win his money and covered the bet with the first and only money he had ever earned. The man raised his rifle, clucked to the chicken to attract its attention, fired, shaved off its comb as if it had been cut with a knife. Mr. Rambo's dollar was gone. That broke him from gambling.

Mr. Rambo came to this county about 1820. He came from piney woods, not far from Charleston. He had been very poor, but by industry and frugality became well off. He never spent money, except for the education of his only child, Rev. Kinchin Rambo, a Baptist minister, long a citizen of this county, now a resident of Floyd County. He saved his money and was a money lender. His friend, Mr. Cleveland, in whom he had great confidence, once wanted to borrow some money. Mr. Rambo was in town and it was not convenient for him to go home to get it. Mr. Cleveland wanted it right then and said he could write his wife an order for it and he would send and get it. "That would do no good," said Mr. Rambo, "she might think it a forged order." So he sent Perry, Mr. Cleveland's colored man, his old pocket knife, and the $500 were sent.

He was a Baptist when I first knew him and was regular in his attendance at his church at old Redland, complying strictly with all its ordinances, but fell from grace and died out of the church.

In politics, he was a Democrat dyed in the wool both warp and woof. He never split his ticket. He would have considered it worse than sacrilege to have voted for a Whig or any one who was not a Democrat.

I might give many other anecdotes of Jesse Rambo. I might tell of Bob Coker wanting to go home with him from town one day and the old man's many excuses for him not to go. First, his wife was sick and couldn't have company, and of Bob's saying he was a very quiet man and would not be troublesome; that his cook was sick, too, and of Bob saying that he was a first rate cook and would do the cooking; that he had nothing in the world to eat but cowpeas, and Bob saying that he liked cowpeas better than anything in the world; of the old man's evident despair in trying to get rid of him; of Bob finally stepping into the grocery to get another drink to give the old man a chance to run, of how he did run, and how he made tracks over the hill towards home, leaving a blue streak behind him. Further space will not admit of more on this line.

The meanest and most diabolical act I ever knew perpetrated in our county was the robbery of Jesse Rambo. He was a little old man. His family consisted of himself, wife, and negro slaves. It was believed generally that he had money, and he did; but the day before the occurrence, he had taken the most of it and deposited it with Hutchins, Cleveland, or Spence. I have forgotten which. Five or six men went to his house late at night disguised. Two guarded the negro houses to keep them in. The others went into the house and demanded the key to the safe; they blindfolded the old man, hit him with a stick and used violence on Mrs. Rambo by choking her. The old man could hear her gurgling her throat in the effort to breathe, and he begged them to spare her but kill him if they would. I have heard of honor among thieves, of magnanimity of highwaymen, but the attack on Mr. Rambo and the violence to his wife were the most fiendish that ever occurred in the county. It was currently believed that at the time and that opinion is still entertained that the perpetrators of this foul deed were partly at least of our own citizens, men who stood well in general estimation, men who probably often prated their honesty, integrity, uprightness and fair dealing. And if this should meet their eye, let me say: Ye hypocrites, your sins find you out. A day of retribution will come. You will yet call for the rocks and mountains to fall upon you and hide your naked deformities from the presence of an indignant and offended God.

Finally, Jesse Rambo was as queer and unique in personal appearance as he was in sayings and actions. He was about five feet eight inches in height, weighed about one hundred and ten pounds, was erect and fidgety, clad generally in summer in a long-tail blue surtout of homespun manufacture, copperas pants with legs stuck in his stockings, with cow leather shoes tanned in his own trough and made by his negroes, a pair of brass-rimmed spectacles always on, and for many years a high-topped hat of the beegum style given him by Mr. Spence, and a little old blue cotton "umberrill" carried in his left hand when not stretched over him.

I thought I could describe him better when I commenced, but like Dr. Hall's morning gown, he was non de script in all his parts and I have made a failure.

The queer old man is sleeping in his grave and I shall not disturb him. I always liked him for his oddities, his good nature, and his great flow of quaint humor. It was a great freak in nature when he was made. The world has seen but one Jesse Rambo and will never see another.

1872

Hamilton Garmany

Captain Garmany was born in Newberry District, South Carolina, about the year 1798 and came to Gwinnett County in 1823.

He was a Presbyterian, strict in the faith and practice of that church. He helped wih his own hands to build the old church near where the present one now stands at Fairview in 1823-24. The male members and other friends met to begin the work. They did not complete it on the first day. It was a cheap, unpretentious, split-log house. At the close of the day's work, Billy Montgomery, who was the prime mover in the matter, said: "We must come back another day and finish it." All agreed but Mr. Garmany who remarked that charity begins at home and that he was building himself a house to live in and could not come on the day mentioned. He lived in that house which was on the headwaters of Yellow River until a year or two after the organization of the Gwinnett Manual Labor School when he was chosen to the position of farmer in that institution. His business was to oversee the boys in their farm work and succeeded Moses Liddell who held the position from the first.

. I would say, from my knowledge of the two men, that Mr. Garmany was in some respects better qualified for the position than Mr. Liddell, not that he was a better farmer, for I think he was not, nor do I think he had better judgment, but he was not blunt or so strict in discipline. The boys and young men then composing the school were the sons and wards of the wealthier classes from the different parts of the state who had never worked and did not comprehend the dignity of labor and who were adverse to it. Mr. Liddell was for bending them to it. Mr. Garmany was more persuasive and lenient. I have often thought that the trustees were unfortunate in their selection of a farm for boys who were wholly unused to farm work, or any other kind of work for that matter. While the soil was good, it was the rockiest farm in the state and would have discouraged a man of the most energetic will who had been used to plowing and hoeing all his life.

I have no doubt its roughness and difficulties in working it gave to many of the boys an aversion to farm work they never forgot. Labor in the sun on the farm by the sons of the wealthier class was by them considered menial and degrading and should be performed by poor white folks and negroes. Hence the failure of the Manual Labor School. Labor is a noble employment, labor on the farm, turning up the soil, cleared of the heather, to the rays of the sun and dews of heaven, planting the seeds of the harvests to supply the trade of commerce and the wants of man and beast, nursing them into life, vigor and maturity that we may sing "Harvest Home" in summer and autumn. This is in accordance with the behests of the Creator and is the grandest calling of all.

After Captain Garmany severed his connection with the school, he purchased the John Turner plantation, where Mr. George Craig now lives, and lived there a few years. During his residence there the Creek Indian War broke out near Columbus and two companies of volunteers were raised in the county, one of mounted men commanded by Captain Garmany, the other of infantry commanded by Captain Reed. In the early summer of 1836 they took up the line of march for Columbus near the seat of war and not long after their arrival at the place of rendezvous they engaged in a fight with the Indians at Shepherd's Plantation in Stewart County. It was a terrible fight for raw soldiers to encounter, but they maintained it well and covered themselves with honor. Ample testimony was at hand to show the courage and bravery of Captain Garmany and his men.

Eight of his men were killed. Four were wounded. Those killed were Issac S. Lacy, Sergeant J. C. Martin, J. H. Holland, Robt. T. Holland, J. M. Allan, Wm. M. Sims, J. A. V. Tate and Henry W. Paden. Those wounded were Captain Garmany, John R. Alexander, Thomas W. Hunt and Wm. Stapp, none mortally.

Soon the war was closed and our volunteers returned home.

The gallant Captain and nearly all of his brave command have gone to join their dead comrades in the land of the spirits. The event referred to was of comparative recent date, yet nearly all engaged in it are dead. Absolem and Byrd Martin, Doney, Chambers, Hunt, the Captain and others, more than half of them are dead. Oh, Death, thou insatiate monster! Never will your cormorant appetite be stayed until the last man, woman and child of Adam's fallen race become victims of thy fearful rapacity.

After Captain Garmany's return he was greeted with universal applause, and was regarded with a favor amounting to veneration. At the first election after his return, he was a candidate for the Senate and was elected almost by acclamation. At the next election he was again a candidate and was defeated, for in the meantime he had become a gallon law man, and a large number of our people were so sensitive on this question that they have preferred to vote for Beelzebub, if he was sound, than for the Apostle Paul if he were a gallon man.

We were very tenacious of our liberty then. Where is our liberty now? I will let those men answer who were lately arrested without warrants or accusation and imprisoned for several days in Atlanta, soon to be dragged up again before the United States District Court for trying to enjoy a little liberty for the stomach's sake.

The Captain was assistant keeper of the penitentiary the last term of Governor Crawford's administration and moved to Milledgeville and served one year as principal keeper under Governor Towns.

Soon after he returned to Gwinnett, he engaged energetically in the construction as stockholder and director of the Lawrenceville Manufacturing Company. After the failure of this enterprise, he sold out and moved to Walker County. He was one day at his new home hunting birds and had discharged one of the barrels of his gun and in reloading it the other barrel went off, discharging its contents in his side, from which he died in twenty-four hours in the year 1856.

Captain Garmany and the writer were neighbors for some time, and from a good deal of personal intercourse afterwards, I have no scruples in saying that he was a good man, a good neighbor, a good citizen, public spirited, kind in his domestic relations, benevolent, kind hearted and a Christian gentleman.

1872

John and Henry Cupp.

As far back as I can remember John Cupp, the older brother of Henry Cupp, lived in what was then Jackson County, in that part which is now Gwinnett, east of the Appalachee River. After Gwinnett was surveyed, and lotteried with Walton, Hall and Habersham embracing what was known as the four mile purchase, he moved west of said river and settled what is now known as the Chambers place, four miles east of Lawrenceville, where he died. He settled at that place as early as 1819 or 1820. He was a substantial citizen and had some means consisting of negroes and other property. Jerry, the venerable old black man still living here (1879) and known as Jerry Harris, was born as his property. He is respected for his industry and good behavior, taking no part in politics and never expected to get forty acres and a mule.

John Cupp was chosen one of the justices of the Inferior Court of this county at its first organization. He reared four sons and six daughters. Of the sons I propose to speak somewhat in detail. Judge Cupp died many years ago and my personal recollection of him is indistinct.

His sons were William, Michael, John and Rolly. Bill and Mike were frolicsome. John and Rolly were not. Bill was a strong party man and was for "Troup and the treaty" to the death. Then he was a States' Rights man and a nullifier, both warp and woof. I never knew a more devoted party man than Bill Cupp. When his party was successful in the elections, he was happy and would get gentlemanly groggy; but when defeated, he would get drunk as the "fiddler's b--ch." On one occasion, the parties were nearly evenly divided in this county. After a fierce contest in which party zeal was wrought up to its highest pitch, the vote was so close that it required the consolidation of the precincts to determine who were elected. During the consolidation by the managers, the crowd gathered around, some hoping, others despairing, and it was finally announced that Cupp's friends were elected by five majority. To him the good news was overpowering; and, throwing his hat high in the air, he exclaimed, "Hurrah for Troup and the treaty." He got gloriously drunk and was on a bender for a week. He went to Walker County forty years ago and I never saw him after.

Mike was tall and slender, strong and active, and a great worker when not on a "bust." He would cut and split five hundred rails a day. He was a fighting man and to use his own language: "When any fighting is to be done, I am on hand and a full scholar." He settled on Pugh's Creek, four miles south of Lawrenceville in the same neighborhood of Bill Williamson, Tom Williamson, John Mills, Dave Watson, Bill Hooper and others of the same feather, who were noted in early times for their rows and fights, and Mike was equal to the best of them. He went to Coweta County years ago and died there.

But old Henry Cupp is the main objective point in this chapter. He was a character! I remember him distinctly, for when once seen he never could be forgotten. Brusque and burly in size, well nigh dark as an Indian, eyes dark, piercing and full of the lurking devil, in all these I have never seen his counterpart. He lived near Hog Mountain, then near the line of the Cherokees and was a rough and tough backwoodsman. He drank whiskey and was often engaged in brawls and fracases with those with whom he disagreed.

After one of his protracted carousals, drinking mean whiskey for a week, he became dissatisfied with life and decided to hang himself. He had two sons, Warner and Mike. Warner was 16 and like his mother. Mike was 14 and like his father. Procuring a rope, he went to a suitable place, taking care to let his sons know about it, tied the rope around his neck and swung off. Warner cut him down. A few days later he repeated the attempt. The boys were on hand again. Warner hastened to his relief, but Mike interposed and said: "Let the old fool hang awhile and it will learn him some sense." But the other boy cut him down. As soon as he recovered, he gathered a pale and gave Mike a severe beating for wanting him to hang longer. The truth was he did not intend to hang long, for he knew Warren would cut him down in good time.

Men sometimes imagine that they are tired of this world, but when they get sick they send in haste for a doctor. Men sometimes commit suicide, but it is agreed that they are insane. We cling to earth no matter what are our troubles or what our preparation for the world to come.

Judge Colquitt's anecdote of the old negro is in place here and points a moral. Sambo had a hard lot and many troubles and thought he would like to get out of this troublesome world. Every night for a time he would pray that the good Lord would come and take poor Sambo out of this wicked world. His young master heard him and concluded to test his faith and knocked on his door. "Who's dat?" asked Sambo. "It is the good Lord come down to take poor Sambo out of this troublesome world." "Hump! Sambo ain't bin here des three weeks."

Old Henry Cupp had a horse stolen by the Indians, some of whom lived not far from him. With his rifle he gave pursuit and found the horse in possession of an Indian known as Pretty Charley who lived not far from what is now known as Strickland's Ferry. He was abusive to the Indian whose savage nature was excited, and, pulling open the bosom of his hunting shirt, he defiantly dared him to shoot Pretty Charley. At the word it was done and the sharp crack of the rifle sent the spirit of Pretty Charley to new hunting grounds beyond the river.

The wild life and turbulent nature of Henry Cupp finally terminated in a horrible and tragic death. He moved to Cobb County many years ago and was hauling hogs—live hogs—on a slide. His horse became frightened at the noise of the hogs and ran away. One of the traces came loose from the singletree and it was wrapped around one of his legs. The horse was going at full speed. He was dragged a mile or more and was terribly mangled and died in a few hours. Thus ended most horribly the ill-starred life of Henry Cupp.

There are but few descendants of the Cupp family living now, a few of the grandchildren of Judge Cupp, the children of Buckner Harris who married Sallie Cupp.

In my young days I always liked the Cupps, drunk or sober, for they were the fast friends of my people, and I like them yet.

1872

JOHN ROGERS

John Rogers was born in Bullock County, Georgia, in 1774 and spent the early days of his boyhood in his native county. While still a boy, he was discarded by his father and left to take care of himself. Feeling keenly his condition, he bade adieu to his mother with the promise that he would never forget her and sought a home amid the solitudes of unbroken wilderness in what was then the northwestern portion of Georgia; and after wandering for some time, eventually settled one mile below the mouth of Suwanee Creek upon an eminence that overlooked the valley of the Chattahoochee for a considerable distance. This was then Indian territory, but was afterwards embraced in the county of Gwinnett. At and near this place he lived fifty years, rearing and educating a large family.

In many respects he was a remarkable man. Nature had given an indomitable will and a firmness of purpose that no obstacle could deter him from where the path of duty led. He was as true to principle as the needle to the pole. The widow in her bereavement and distress and the orphan in its destitution found comfort and sustenance at his hands. The hospitality of his home was ever open to assuage and relieve their wants.

By energy, industry and sound judgment he prospered in business and amassed a large property, which was not hoarded up with parsimonious niggardness, but was appropriated for the comfort of his family, for the education of his children, for the relief of the poor and needy, and for the advancement of the church of God. Blessed be the memory of John Rogers, for his hospitality, for his benevolence, for his kindness and charities to the poor, for his contributions to the Gospel and his unnumbered good deeds. The memory of such a man should be cherished as a bright spot in a world of darkness and an oasis in a desert of selfishness.

The father who had so unnaturally cast him off from the parental roof when he was a beardless boy became poor and a wanderer in after years, and on his way to the West visited his cast-off son and asked for assistance. The son heaped coals of fire on his head by returning kindness for neglect. He gave him a good horse, saddle, bridle and money. The country beyond the Chattahoochee was an unbroken wilderness and only occupied sparsely by the rude aborigines, with no roads, and with only narrow Indian trails to guide him he passed through this wild and untraveled country. The son conducted the father as far as the Hightower on his way. He then halted and thus addressed him: "You are my father, but I can never forget your casting me off when a poor weak boy. Providence has smiled on me and I could give you more. I have a wife to support and children to rear and educate. I have discharged my duty by giving you what is necessary and my conscience is clear." And turning his horse and with a long goodbye, left him forever.

In the Creek War or the War of 1812 he volunteered as a private and served in the army until the battle of Horseshoe Bend. Such was his promptness in the discharge of his duty that he was recommended to General Jackson as a suitable man to ride as a courier on what was considered a very dangerous express from the seat of war to Monticello, Georgia, through a pathless forest and guided alone by instinct and a knowledge of the direction, he reached his destination in safety. In after years General Jackson with high commendation called him the brave little John Rogers.

During that trip, after riding for several days and nights, he was so worn from exhaustion that it was absolutely necessary for him to rest. To sleep in safety was a doubtful and serious question. After riding nearly all night he found a dense canebreak, and turning into it, he kindled a small fire, cooked and ate some food, tied his horse so he could graze, placed his saddle under his head for a pillow and soon was lost in profound sleep. Upon awaking at early dawn on opening his eyes he saw a tall Indian, who had probably been attracted by the remains of the fire, standing over him. The Indian knew him, had been treated kindly by him and though his tribe was on the warpath, he did not molest him but offered him tokens of friendship.

The first church ever built on the territory of our county was erected mainly through his instrumentality near his residence on the Chattahoochee. I have tried to learn the name of this rude sanctuary of the living God and something of its history, but the story is now numbered with the forgotten things and, like those who used to worship there, has passed away forever. An incident connected with its erection is worthy of mention and worthy of Methodism. On preaching day in the neighborhood by one of the pioneer preachers of Methodism, who, be it said to their honor, always penetrated the outskirts of civilization and erected the altar of God as fast as the "Star of empire westward took its way," the question of building a meeting house was raised, discussed and decided upon. Immediately after the door of the church was opened for any who wished to join. In the congregation was a man who was notoriously wicked, but a man of generous impulse and public spirit. He misapprehended the proposition. He thought it was a call upon those who were willing to build a church to give evidence of it, and he therefore went up and gave his hand to the preacher under this impression. When the congregation was dismissed, Mr. Rogers approached him and asked if he knew what he had done. "Yes, John, I am willing to help build the house as any man here." "But," said Mr. Rogers, "you have joined the church, you are now a member of the Methodist Church on probation." Hanging his head and reflecting for a moment, he replied: "Well, John, if I have, I will never do anything to disgrace it."

This man was Parker Collins, a brother-in-law of John Rogers; and in my early boyhood, I repeatedly heard a gentleman, who knew him intimately and was capable of judging, say: "Parker Collins was the best man I ever knew." "There is a tide in the affairs of men, which, taken at the flood, leads on to fortune." The tide taken that day by Parker Collins led him to Heaven, though taken by misapprehension.

Mr. Rogers was in favor of strict justice to all. If the Indian did wrong, he was for punishing him. He always treated them kindly, and was, therefore, popular with them. The Indian never forgets a kindness, and never forgets or forgives an injury. An incident of his kind treatment to a starving Creek Indian family is worthy of mention. Soon after the war this family came to his house and asked for food, which he gave them and allowed them to stay on his premises for some time. In this family was a small boy. Years after, Mr. Rogers had a horse stolen by the Indians. Following the direction taken by the thief, he pursued him to the line of Alabama. Riding up to an Indian house, he made some inquiry about the stolen horse, giving a description of it. A young Indian, about grown, informed him that, from the description he had given, he knew the horse, that he then owned the horse, that he got it honestly, but he had no doubt it was the property of Mr. Rogers and would give it up. "Get down and stay till I come back and I will bring the horse," stated the Indian. In a short time he returned with the horse. He then asked Mr. Rogers if he did not live near the mouth of Suwanee Creek on the Chattahoochee River, and was informed he did. Then said he: "Do you remember several years ago you fed a Creek family who went to your house in a starving condition and a little boy was one of the family?" "Yes," said Mr. Rogers. "Well, I am that little boy and I could not tell a lie about the horse." Mr. Rogers paid him for the horse and offered a reward of $50.00 for the thief. He was captured and delivered to Mr. Rogers who gave him the choice of being tried under the laws of Georgia or under the laws of the Cherokee nation. He chose the latter. On the trial the same Indian boy appeared as a witness. The thief was convicted and sentenced to receive thirty-nine lashes on his naked back, well laid on. Through the interposition of Mr. Rogers, he was let off with twenty-five. Thanking Mr. Rogers for his kindness, he bade him a friendly goodbye and was never heard of again.

Mr. Rogers reared nine sons and three daughters. With five of his oldest sons I went to school at the Lawrenceville Academy under the tutorship of Rev. John S. Wilson. Robert was the oldest and was a grown young man. He was a noble specimen of a man physically, and mentally was far above mediocrity. His face was very much after the type of Commodore Oliver H. Perry. He became a Methodist preacher and was for a time a member of the Georgia Conference. William was great in many respects: six feet tall, great in moral rectitude for a better and more conscientious man I never knew, great in intellect, and but for his innate modesty would have been a star of first magnitude both in church and state. I need not attempt to give a personal description of him. He is remembered by most of my readers for his manly form, his kind, intellectual face all radiating with love of God, charity to man and beneficence to his race. He was a Methodist preacher for a long time and his memory is held in grateful remembrance.

Johnson was somewhat after the style of William, not quite so tall, probably not quite so intellectual, but far above the average, and something of a model man. He, for thirty years, was agent of the Cherokee Indians and he lived in Washington and died there.

Joseph moved to the West in 1835 and lived for only a few years. He made quite a reputation and was accumulating property rapidly when the end came. He was buried at old Fort Wayne with the honors of war.

Lovely, the fourth son, when I knew him, was just grown up, with pale face and a young man of fine capacity. He now lives in California and is doing well.

George, one of the younger sons, died in the West in the Confederate service.

John moved to the West and is living in the Choctaw Nation. Jackson is in Whitfield County in this state, and Col. Henry C. is living in Milton County on the old homestead of his father.

I never saw any of the daughters except Mary, the oldest. I remember her well when she was just growing up and was just from school. She was a beautiful girl with a lily complexion, glossy black hair and beautiful black eyes. I think she was educated in North Carolina and, to my young mind, was one of the most lovely women I ever saw. The memory of her sweet face haunts me still after these forty long years; and if I had been older, I should have worshipped at her shrine. She married a Mr. McNair and I understand made a good wife to a good husband.

Finally, John Rogers was a good man and a Christian gentleman—a Christian at home and a Christian abroad. At the close of day his prayers went up to Heaven at the family altar. At morning the same devotions were offered up for many years. He reared a large family of sons and several of them were great men, great in manly proportions, great in moral worth, great in Christian virtues and great in intellectual capacity.

> "Lives of great men all remind us
> We can make our lives sublime,
> And departing leave behind us
> Footprints on the sands of time—
> Footprints that perhaps another,
> Sailing o'er life's solemn main,
> A forlorn and shipwrecked brother
> Seeing shall take heart again."

In politics Mr. Rogers was a Whig, but at the same time an admirer of General Jackson, not for his politics, but for his military genius, his patriotism and for his personal kindness to him. He named one of his sons for Jackson.

Mr. Clay was his polar star in politics until his dying day. I have never heard it stated but I think his son, Henry C., was named for the "Gallant Harry of the West." I have great respect for Col. H. C. Rogers for his moral worth and intelligence, and this good opinion is enhanced because I thought he bore the name of Henry Clay, my political idol. Like John Rogers I was a follower of Mr. Clay in my young days and the proudest satisfaction I now have is I was his follower.

1872

THOMAS P. HUDSON

Mr. Hudson's family who survive him are all moved from the county except one son-in-law whom I have been unable to see, and I have no information as to his age, when he was born or the place of his nativity. But this is not material to my purpose. I think he was born in South Carolina, and not far from 1800. I first recollect him when he was a candidate in this county for the legislature on the gallon law ticket some thirty years ago, which ticket was defeated. He had not then been long a citizen of the county. A few years from this time he was a candidate on the democratic ticket, but his party being in the minority in the county at the time and some prejudice still against him on account of his temperance principles formerly entertained, he was again defeated. After this he was a candidate again and again for several times without success, but gaining in his vote each time. His defeats never nonplussed him. He would always express himself as satisfied and would try again. He differed in this from his political friend, H. P. T., who upon being defeated for the senate, denounced in bitter expletives the d--- ignorant, woolhat, copperas-breeches, crack-heeled democracy as not fit to trust.

Mr. Hudson did no such thing as this, but took his defeat kindly, seemed to be as happy as if he had been successful and was as genial and cordial to his friends as if they had put him through. By his course he made many friends, everybody was pleased and admired his resignation and good temper under defeat. Many were sorry that they had not voted for him and voluntarily promised to do so next time. He finally succeeded and was elected several times.

He and the writer differed in politics until 1860 and had many a tilt at the Justice Courts with each other. I always found in him a foeman worthy of his steel. In 1860 he belonged to the cooperation party, was opposed to secession, was nominated by his party and elected from this county to the convention of that year and voted against the ordinance of secession. Nevertheless, he was as true a southern rights man as the straightest of the sect. It was a matter of judgment and expediency with him in opposing it.

I give a private incident that occurred in that convention which may interest some of his old friends. The ordinance was passed by about thirty majority, eighty or ninety of the delegates voting no. It was desirable on the part of the majority that all should sign the ordinance and every appliance was brought to bear to effect this result.

The argument was used that it would immortalize the names of all who signed it, that it would be held as sacred as the Declaration of Independence, that it would be framed and hung up in the museums of the rich and in the cabins of the poor from the mountains to the sea and worshipped as a household god. As a further incentive to this move, A. H. Stephens, leader of the co-operationists in the convention, offered a resolution "That we will all sign the ordinance, those voting against it and those voting for it." A committee, with P. W. A. as chairman, was appointed to have the ordinance engrossed upon parchment for the signatures of the delegates and after a brief period reported that it would be ready by twelve o'clock next morning. The day arrived, the hour, and the secretary commenced in solemn tones to call the counties in alphabetical order, commencing with Appling, and the delegates went up and signed it. And so the roll call proceeded. It was a slow process. As the secretary got down to the G's, Mr. Hudson left his seat and went over to one of his colleagues and with some apparent trepidation, for it was a time that tried men's souls, remarked to that colleague: "What shall we do? Had we not better sign it?" His friend, who was a stubborn, bull-neck man, and who had determined not to be influenced by the mighty pressure brought to bear but whose knees, if he had stood up, would have been somewhat like Belshazzar's, replied to him with some wrath: "You may sign it if you wish: I will not." Mr. Hudson, feeling somewhat the rebuff, returned to his seat and soon Gwinnett was called, but no one answered or moved. Again it was called in a louder tone but there was no response. Mr. Hudson never signed it, but did his whole duty in helping on the cause by equipping the volunteers and helping their families when the war came.

A company was raised mainly through his instrumentality that bore the name of Hudson Guards, and all of that gallant company who survive honor his name.

The same colleague afterwards signed the ordinance of secession when the convention reassembled to adopt the constitution of the Confederate States, and became as hot a war-man as any, losing his love for the Star-Spangled Banner, and became a worshipper of the Bonnie Blue Flag. That song of our flag is a beautiful song and should never be forgotten by the friends of the lost cause.

In passing near a bivouac of a regiment in the early part of the war, his ear was charmed and his soul inspired by this song for the first time. The patriotic Southern sentiments which it breathed as the words came upon his ear:

"We are a band of soldiers and native to the soil
Fighting for our property we've gained by honest toil,
And when our rights were threatened the cry rose
near and far
Hurrah! for the Bonnie Blue Flag that bears a single
star."

And then when the last stanza came floating out on the evening breeze,

"Then cheer, boys, cheer, raise the joyous shout
For Arkansas and North Carolina now have both
gone out;
And let another rousing cheer for Tennessee be
given,
The single star of the Bonnie Blue Flag has grown
to be eleven."

He then and there dedicated his whole soul to the Confederacy. The cause was lost but not the song.

Henry McCarth's name should be immortal for giving us the Bonnie Blue Flag, as is Francis S. Key's for the Star Spangled Banner. But to return. During some of the hard years of the war and while he lived, he did his whole duty in letting the people have supplies, especially the women and children whose husbands and fathers were in the war. He had a store, it will be remembered, and furnished molasses, salt and other necessities to the poor. Great crowds of women and children and old men would flock there to get their supplies. His storehouse was often full of jugs and kegs, too late for the last hogshead but waiting for the next. But for him, it was said at the time often spoken of now, many would have suffered and some would probably have starved. He had enemies as all men do who are worth anything. He had faults. I never knew a man who had none. But he was honorable and high-minded and possessed many of the best principles of human nature.

He was a fine business man with fine sense, fine judgment, a fine scribe, good accountant, and a man far above the average in intelligence. He died during the war and was a member of the legislature at the time.

1872

Moses Liddell

Moses Liddell was a stern man, as stern and inflexible in his principles as Andrew Jackson. Though very stern, and apparently harsh, he was kind in his nature and devoted to his friends. In the days of his early manhood, it was said that he was noted for his bold wickedness, his turbulent disposition and his readiness to engage in broils and fights. But the grace of God upon his heart changed all of these. From the harsh and wicked man, he become a pious, zealous and faithful disciple of his Heavenly Master.

In the year 1822, he embraced religion in Franklin County, Georgia, where he then lived, and joined the Presbyterian Church in South Carolina near where he lived on the border of the state.

He was born in old Pendleton, South Carolina, October 13, 1786, moved to Franklin County in 1814, then to Gwinnett in the latter part of 1825. On the 11th of February, 1826, he presented to the session of Fairview Church a certificate of good standing of himself and his wife, Polly Liddell, expressing a desire to unite with the church and they were accordingly received. On the same day he was chosen a ruling elder of that church and was set apart to the functions of his office on April 22, which office he held till his removal from the county in 1857.

Mr. Liddell was noted for his zeal and strict notions of church duties. He remembered the Sabbath day and kept it holy, in form and spirit, and was faithful in his attentions and observances of all the ordinances of the Church and delighted in them. I am permitted to make an extract from a private letter to the writer from Mr. Liddell's old friend and brother, A. R. S., referring to his great fortitude and Christian resignation under afflictions: "Mr. Liddell was for a long time afflicted with white swelling on the knee, resulting from a kick of a horse, and amputation became necessary to save his life. Dr. Banks attended as surgeon. Mr. Liddell's friends gathered in to sympathize with him in his fearful and painful crisis. He asked them one and all to pray for him in his extremity and seemed prepared for the event, whatever might be the issue. The operation was performed with great skill and success, and he lived many years after to enjoy his attendance on the sanctuary." It may be noted as remarkable if not unprecedented that, though he was a large man and had heavy muscles, such was his great fortitude and Christian resignation to his fate and great power of endurance that during the exceedingly painful operation he made no exclamation of pain except when the surgeon's saw touched the marrow in the thigh bone, and then only one grunt, though no chloroform or other opiates were used in the operation.

One more extract from the same letter: "He scrupulously performed all of his religious duties and seemed intent on making every Sabbath a day's journey towards Heaven. One circumstance impresses me forcibly. It was the practice of the elders and members of Fairview Church to meet on the Sabbath for prayer and exhortation when there was no preaching. As Mr. Liddell was some distance from the postoffice, his letters at times remained on hand and I thought it would do him a favor to take them to him at the church on the Sabbath. I gave him the letters before services commenced. He hardly looked at the superscription, but put them in his pocket, remarking that he would read them tomorrow. And then as if he wished to forget the subject as soon as possible, he would open his hymn book and say to his brethren: 'Let us sing "Oh! For a Closer Walk With God".' This was his favorite hymn. Of course I did not trouble him afterwards with letters on Sunday."

In 1826, he organized a Sabbath school at Fairview, the first one that was established in the county. He was chosen superintendent, and George M. Gresham and wife, Dr. Alexander and wife, Dr. Samuel Means, William Montgomery, David L. Wardlaw, John Mills, and others as teachers. Mr. Saye was appointed moderator on the outside, and he would go around among the outsiders and, in his quiet way, keep them in order. So strict was the discipline that when any of the class wanted water the entire class accompanied him with the teacher to the spring. One of the pupils at the school, a little boy then, an old man now, going with the class to the spring, accompanied by their teacher, David L. Wardlaw, began to whistle as they walked along. His teacher very friendly reminded him that everything must be quiet and orderly in this school.

I give this incident to show how strict and proper everything was conducted in the first Sabbath school organized in our old county with Mr. Liddell as superintendent. A Miss Cooper, whose mother was an Abbott, was a member of the school and walked six miles to attend it. She would often recite a hundred verses of the Bible she had committed to memory during the preceding week. Several who were members of that school went out and were watchmen on the walls of Zion afterwards.

Mr. Liddell moved to Decatur in 1857 and before his death became feeble in mind and died May 10, 1858. His ashes now slumber in the graveyard of his old church at Fairview. He and most of those who used to meet and worship with him at the old church have gone to meet their rewards in Heaven. A few, only a few of them, Wilson, Montgomery, Smith, Mills and Strickland, old, shriveled and gray, still survive, rapidly approaching, with feeble footsteps, the dark river over which they must soon pass to meet their old brethren on the other side. God bless these men in their old age, and may their example be followed by those who come after them.

Among the many good traits of character which Mr. Liddell possessed none were more beautiful and lovely than his tenderness and affection for the female members of his household. Civilization has done a great deal for women and religion has done much more. In the dark ages, and even now, with savage tribes and barbarians, the women were made slaves to their lords and masters and were regarded as no better than menials and beasts of burden. That same disposition of heathendom to regard the female sex as serfs still prevails to a considerable extent in this enlightened age.

Frail, weak woman, who should be regarded as the tender jewel of the household, is often deprived of all privileges and made a beast of burden by a heartless and debased father or husband. A man who thus acts with the wife of his bosom, and the daughters that God has given to him, is a barbarian and a wretch who should be kicked out of the community and spurned by all decent people. Many a good woman has been driven to desperation and dishonor by the brutality of him she must call father, or formed an alliance for life with one she knows to be far beneath her to escape the tyranny of her father. If it were the province of the writer to pass sentence on such a father, I would sentence him to the galleys ball and chain for life, and then consign him to the deepest, darkest, hottest and most dolorous regions of perdition forever. Such was not my old friend, Moses Liddell, and I am rejoiced to record the fact.

I have thus performed a melancholy duty in trying to chronicle and perpetuate the virtues and good deeds of my old friend who was one of the most Godly men I ever knew. Blessed be the memory of the old fathers, and may we never forget their good examples and Christian teachings while life shall last.

1872

WILLIAM NESBIT

William Nesbit was the first sheriff of Gwinnett County and held the office consecutively as sheriff and deputy sheriff for fourteen years. It has been said, and it was universally conceded by the old citizens, that he was the most efficient sheriff the county ever had. As an arresting officer especially, he has had no equal with my knowledge so far as this county is concerned.

In his day as sheriff, the county was new, the population to a great extent wild and lawless, and had within its limits many desperadoes as is common in all new countries. It was said by William Brogdon once that North and South Carolina had boiled over and the scum had run over into the new part of Georgia. Many of these desperate men had at various times resisted successfully the constables, but when Nesbit got after them, if they could not outrun him, they were sure to be taken.

I still remember his clear shrill voice in calling parties and witnesses into court. That clarion voice is still upon my ear as he would open court with his "Oyes! Oyes! Oyes! The Superior Court of Gwinnett County is now opened according to adjournment. God save the state and the honorable court." It was said with as much grace and dignity as it is said in England by one of the high sheriffs of the realm.

Those were my Robin Hood days, the days of the log cabin and the sanded floor, of pewter plates and basins displayed in the sun and to passers-by on a shelf at the front door and to visitors in the cupboard in the principal room in the house; of tinkers with packs on their backs to mend such wares as might be broken, or to mould new ones from the old for the thrifty housewives. Those were the days when the land was fresh from the hand of God. No sedge or old pine fields; and the country was covered with magnificent forests, and the streams were full of fish. If a young man wished to marry, he went on the other side of the spring, or to the other side of his father's virgin soil, built his log cabin, cleared a turnip patch and cowpen, married and went to multiplying and replenishing the earth according to law. Since then, alas! The country is scarred with red gullies and old wornout fields, the forests are gone, and if a young man marries, there is but little assurance but that he will become a profligate and debauchee, and procuring an emigrant ticket, elopes with another woman to the distant West, leaving his wife in wretchedness and his children in want.

Mr. Nesbit served two sessions in the state senate, first in 1829 and again in 1833. He was born in York District, South Carolina, and in early life came to Jackson County and afterwards moved to this county and died June 27, 1863, at the age of 76. He lived for many years near the DeKalb County line on the Hightower trail, the dividing line between the counties of Gwinnett and DeKalb. He was a man of striking appearance, full six feet high, of well-rounded proportions, evincing strength and activity, a remarkable walk indicating independence and resolution. His face was of the finest type, bespeaking manliness but kindness and benevolence.

Upon a recent visit by the writer to his son, Hon. John Nesbit, of Milton County, he showed me a photograph of his father. It was a perfect facsimile of William Nesbit, with his peculiar form, handsome face and determined contour of the mouth that had so often excited my admiration of the original when in life.

It was in his domestic life that the nobler and kinder traits of the man were displayed. When his married daughter would reach that point in married life, woman's greatest extremity, when all the affections of the father are drawn out and his keenest solicitude aroused for the safe passage through the dreaded ordeal, he would be there at the bedside to administer comfort and assurance; and amid all his noble traits of character, this was the noblest and kindest, the best of them all.

Of all the men of whom I have or may write, the subject of this sketch has claims upon me hardly equaled by any. He was for a long series of years the fast friend and companion of my father and the devoted friend of his family, agreeing in all their views, especially in politics in which they were in harmony through a long life with uninterrupted friendship and cordiality. Being of the first settlers of the new county, they went, shoulder to shoulder, in efforts to suppress crime and rascality, thereby contracting an intimacy that terminated only with their lives.

I would that I was competent to pronounce a suitable eulogy of his private life and public services. I feel my inability for the task.

He, with his associates and compeers of early times and history of our county, had their brief day. They have now nearly all 'wrapped the drapery of their couch about them and lain down to pleasant dreams.' It is left to me, in a feeble way, to call up their memories. This task is agreeable but the service is lame.

"I name them over one by one
And weep o'er days forever gone;
O'er friends whose suns of life have set
And voices thrilling memory yet.

"They vanished like a morning beam
Or sunlight on the rippling stream;
And gloom lurks in the web of years
And hope of youth all disappears.

"Now when the moon her chariot drives
And night, the jeweled maid, arrives,
I think upon departed hours
With hush of moon and blush of flowers."

JOHN C. WHITWORTH

Like many of the old settlers of this county, Mr. Whitworth was born in Pendleton, S. C. I have been impressed that so many of those whom I have written were from the same place, Wilson, Hutchins, Garmany, Whitworth and others, all were from that district.

Mr. Whitworth was born in 1800. He came to this county in August, 1823, and lived with his brother, Richard Whitworth, until October of the same year, when his first marriage took place to Isabella Drummond and by whom he had eleven children, eight sons and three daughters. His first wife died in 1847. He lived a widower a year or more and married his second wife, Jane Johnson, by whom he had five children, one son and four daughters. He was, therefore, the father of sixteen children and from his sons and daughters went out several sons to defend the rights of the South against the tyranny of the North in the late war.

His sons were good soldiers, and several of them sacrificed their lives in our struggle for independence. I remember two of them especially who went out with the Independent Blues, John C., named for his father, and Mathew. I have often heard their captain speak of John and Mathew Whitworth as good soldiers, performing their duty both in the camp and on the field of battle, faithfully and gallantly. Mathew, I believe, died and John was killed in battle. Two others, I think, belonged to the Army of North Virginia, and others of the family were in the western army.

Mr. Whitworth was many times honored by the people of this county, first as justice of the peace, justice of the Inferior Court, and a member of the legislature, the latter position he having filled as many as six times. He filled all these positions creditably to himself and to the satisfaction of his constituents. The writer was associated with him for four years on the bench of the Inferior Court. At that time the Inferior Court had the supervision of all county matters and sat every two months for ordinary purposes. Judge Whitworth was always prompt in his attendance and faithful in the discharge of his official duties as one of the court to my knowledge. He was a staunch Democrat of the old school, was popular with his party and always received Whig votes. He was sometimes elected when his party was in the minority. He was never unsuccessful before the people but once and that was for the state convention in 1850. He ran the race on the southern rights ticket and the other party had the then popular cognomen, the Union Party. The latter party succeeded and Mr. Whitworth was defeated for the first time.

Eight or ten years before the death of Mr. Whitworth, which occurred November 18, 1864, he was attacked with palsy or paralysis, from which he never even partially recovered, but continued to grow worse until he became a wreck in mind as well as body. The last time I saw him he was a pitiable object of decrepitude and imbecility. The strong man had become as feeble and helpless as a child, and the strong and vigorous mind was as inactive as the body.

The forcible lines of Johnson referring to the insanity of Swift so frequently quoted by John Randolph in the last years of his life, and which shows us life in its most melancholy form, were applicable to Mr. Whitworth.

> "In life's last scenes what prodigies surprise
> Fears of the brave and follies of the wise;
> From Marlborough's eyes the sheams of dotage flow
> And Swift expires a driveller and a show."

1872

WILLIAM BAUGH

I propose to give a somewhat photographic likeness of Mr. Baugh so far as I may be able to do so, of his many good traits of character, some of his odd notions and some of his marked peculiarities. He differed in many respects from ordinary men and was a character not often seen.

His neighbor, Rambo, as has been shown, had singularities peculiar to himself. Mr. Baugh had his, too, but of a different type altogether. The former was erratic and fidgety, the latter was stern, solid and courageous even to his oddities. He was cool, not at all excitable, but calm and determined in all his purposes, and would resent an insult coming from whatever source it might. To illustrate: Mr. Baugh had a brother that was a bully and had whipped every man with whom he had fought. Some disagreement occurred between them. The brother said to him that if it were not a disgrace for brothers to fight he would give him a whipping. Mr. Baugh replied: "You have got your name up by whipping drunk men and boys. Pull off your coat and try a man." It was no sooner said than done. At it they went and the bully got a terrible licking. This occurred before he came to Gwinnett County, but after he had joined the church.

He was a man of peace, a religious man at heart and soul. He had but few personal difficulties after he came to this county. I remember but one. There was a controversy about the change of a road in which Mr. Baugh was interested. He was on one side of the controversy and Hugh Hutchins on the other. It eventually culminated in a personal rupture and a quarrel—not quarrel, for Mr. Baugh would not quarrel, but an altercation occurred between them, and Mr. Baugh forgot his Methodism and advanced upon Hutchins who considered discretion the better part of valor and beat a hasty retreat. It was well, for if Mr. Baugh had gotten hold of him, he would have remembered it to his dying day.

A somewhat long life has made me acquainted with many men of different types and various caliber. Mr. Baugh differed from all

I have ever known in many particulars. He was a man of cool courage and determination, as fearless of personal danger as Andrew Jackson or the elder Bonaparte.

He was a soldier in the War of 1812 and, I believe, was wounded in the right hand which disabled him to some extent ever after. He received a pension from the government therefor in the latter years of his life. A regiment of such as he would have been unconquerable and irresistible.

He was a solid man in all his plans and ideas. His dwelling, outhouses, his farm, cow houses and everything about his farm and homestead fully demonstrated this. Everything about him was of the most substantial character.

When he came to this county, he bought the farm of Richard Watts who had lived on the place until he thought it was worn out. Mr. Baugh soon renovated it and the whole establishment. He repaired the dwelling, cribs, barns, stables and everything, planted a new orchard, repaired the fences, and soon made more corn and cotton, wheat and oats than Mr. Watts ever did even when the land was fresh. To show how precise and systematic in everything: In planting his orchard he employed a man who was a New Englander to assist him. The rows were marked off as straight as a line and the trees were to be thus planted. One tree seemed to get out of its place and it had to be changed. A second trial was made and still it was not right. Then a third, then a fourth and still it lacked a little. After these repeated trials still another was to be made. The man got out of all patience, refused to take it up again and remarked: "I have taken it up four times and still it doesn't suit you; if you wish, you may try your hand on the d--n thing." Mr. Baugh laughed at his friend's remark, took it in hand himself and eventually got it right.

I remember that orchard with a lively satisfaction. The beautiful, thrifty trees, straight as the line of a compass, attracted the eyes of all passers-by; and I remember it more especially from having partaken of the delicious fruits from its bending boughs and from his wagons on the streets of our town groaning under the weight of its rich production and driven by Mr. Baugh himself.

He was a deadly enemy to whiskies and to masculine long hair. He used to say: "I am always uneasy about my gimlets, augers, pocket knife and hen roost when the whiskered gentry come about my house."

His old friend, Allen Turner, whom he had known and loved for many years and to whose plain and practical sermons he had listened with interest for nearly half a century, was passing from Oxford, where he lived, to Lawrenceville to attend a quarterly meeting. Accompanying him was Mr. Richard Whittick, a gentleman of culture, of fine sense, good morals, a churchman and gentleman.

He wore a long beard. Brother Turner remarked that they would go to Brother Baugh's and spend the night. It was a good place to go. They would get a good supper, a good breakfast next morning, hospitable entertainment for man and beast, provided they did not wear long beards. Mr. Whittick was under the guidance of Brother Turner. Upon their arrival and after an introduction to the strange brother and cordial greetings of old friends, Mr. Baugh brought out his keen razor with a basin of water and a towel and invited Brother Whittick to shave. He declined, saying: "I do not wish to shave." Mr. Baugh insisted and still Mr. Whittick declined. Finally Mr. Baugh said: "You can't stay all night with me unless you shave." Mr. Whittick, a little huffy, left and went over to the home of Mr. Flowers, who did not object to his beard, and there he spent the night.

Of the propriety of Mr. Baugh's course in this matter I propose not to speak. I relate it as one of the peculiar traits in his character of the subject of my present sketch. It occurs to me, however, if my old friend with his prejudices against long beards could look back now upon the sublunary things of this wicked world and see the long and glossy beards worn by some of his immediate offspring, he would turn restlessly in his grave.

Mr. Baugh lost his first wife, who was Elizabeth Lindsay, whom he married in 1815. He lived a widower about a year and concluded to marry again. As soon as he thus decided, he went to see a maiden lady with whom he had long been acquainted and who, he thought, would suit him. At his first visit he informed her that he had come to propose marriage. He made this a matter of business. In his characteristic way he approached the subject abruptly and bluntly. He brought to her none of the swaviter in mode, nor did he adopt the Byronic way of winning a woman, first to pique, then to soothe by turns. He popped the question at once and demanded an answer at once.

Women have their ways; and however fully they have made up their minds, they want time to consider. Time he would not grant. She must answer now or not at all. The result was that he left to return on this business.

His next step was to go to Jackson County, where, I believe, he married his first wife. He knew a lady there who thought would suit him, for he had known her from the time of his first marriage. Thither he bent his way, the agreement was made, and the marriage soon took place. The writer remembers the occasion well. Mr. Baugh on the day fixed for the marriage left in his carriage. Before getting far from home, something about the buggy broke. No time was there to mend it and no time to get another. Returning home, he got another horse, came by town and I sold him a side saddle; and he then started again on his journey, riding one horse and leading another, and arrived on time, was married, and returned next day with his bride. It proved to be a happy union for both. She agreed with him in his religious views, was industrious, kind, affectionate to him and his children, and she was one of the best women I ever knew. I remember to have seen her at church in her younger days. How sweetly she used to sing the songs of Zion! She still lives a mother in Israel, but soon will go to join her husband in the happy land of Caanan.

Thirty-five years or more ago he built a little log meeting house and organized a church there, with himself, his wife and a few of his neighbors as members. About once a month circuit preaching was held on week days and class meetings on Sunday with Mr. Baugh as class leader. A lady friend of mine often spoke to me with lively interest of the meetings she used to attend at that little church. On preaching days she would ply the batten of the loom vigorously until near the hour of preaching; then gliding from the loom bench, she would slip on her clean homespun dress, recomb her hair, put on her little hood, and trip along the pathway to church. Soon Mr. Baugh would begin singing:

"Children of the Heavenly King,
As we journey let us sing."

This was sung to one of the old plaintive tunes that our fathers and mothers used to sing with so much zest and devotion. Or he would select that other old hymn:

"Approach my soul the mercy seat
Where Jesus answers prayer."

I never hear those old songs now, but the eye moistens and the heart becomes mellowed and sad at the memories they bring up. They remind us of the days of our childhood.

On Sunday Mr. Baugh would hold his class meetings here and the heart was made better and the spirit was made glad in the plain and simple worship of the Heavenly Master.

Afterwards he built a new church known as Baugh's Chapel where he worshipped until he was gathered to his fathers.

Mr. Baugh was born in Laurens District, South Carolina, on the 8th day of March, 1792. His father moved from there to Franklin County, Georgia, in 1794. He was married to Elizabeth Lindsay in October, 1815. She was a gentle, pious woman, of quiet turn and remarkable for her industry and domestic habits. She was the mother of four sons and four daughters, and died in May, 1837. He then married Elizabeth Henderson, of Jackson County, in February, 1838, who still survives him. She is the mother of four sons and, I believe, three daughters. He moved to this county in January, 1831, and settled on the Dickey Watts old place on Pughs Creek and lived there until his death in August, 1862.

It was a distinct loss to our old county when he died. His example as a farmer was worth much to our people; his example as a good man and church member was worth much to them; his integrity and fair dealing in all of his transactions taught a good lesson to the rising generation; and although he was singular in many of his notions, I remember no one who was a more valuable member of the community in his day and sphere than William Baugh. The memory of him is embalmed in the hearts of his aged partner, his children and friends, and may his good examples be followed by his offspring and others coming after him!

1872

Dr. James M. Gordon

The subject of this sketch, the son of Few Gordon, was born in Gwinnett County April 21, 1821. After securing the rudiments of an education at such schools as the county at that time afforded, he was sent to the academy at Monroe, where he applied himself diligently to his studies and acquired a good English education. Soon after leaving school, he began the study of medicine under Dr. William J. Russell, of Lawrenceville, and graduated at the Medical College at Augusta. After receiving his degree, he began the practice in partnership with Dr. Russell, and after the dissolution of this partnership, continued the practice until his removal to Savannah in 1854.

Dr. Gordon's rise in his profession was rapid and in a short time his practice was not only extensive but lucrative. On December 24, 1843, he was married in the Presbyterian Church in Lawrenceville by the Rev. James C. Patterson to Miss Elizabeth A. Alexander, daughter of Dr. Thomas W. Alexander. From this union sprang four children, three of whom are still living. The oldest boy, Albert A. Gordon, having at a tender age entered the service of his country during the late war to defend the land that gave him birth, died in a hospital at Mobile February 5, 1865, and his mortal remains now fill a soldier's grave.

Dr. Gordon continued in the practice of his profession in his native county until the spring of 1854, when, wishing to enlarge the sphere of his usefulness and find a more extended field in which to win distinction in his profession, moved to Savannah and entered into the drug business with James H. Carter, a prominent and popular druggist in that city. He, however, devoted his own time and attention to the practice of his profession and in a very short time had taken position among the foremost physicians in that city. Now when his prospects seemed brightest and his hopes and aspirations so fondly cherished for years were about to be realized, the destroyer came. That fell demon, yellow fever, which, like a dark cloud, had been hovering over the devoted city, burst forth in all its fury, and sorrow and distress, sickness and death, followed in their wake. Long will the citizens of Savannah remember the dark days of the fall of 1854. The city was draped in mourning. All, who could, left their business and fled for their lives. Many of the physicians even left their posts of danger and ingloriously fled. There were scarcely enough to attend the sick or bury the dead. Dr. Gordon, soon after the epidemic made its appearance, sent his family away, but remained himself at his post of aid with all the medical skill he possessed dedicated to the relief of the suffering people. The constant and earnest importunities of his friends he heeded not. Although he had been but a few months among that people, he felt that it was cowardly and dishonorable to leave them to their fate. In one of the letters written to his wife, in which he gave a most gloomy and appalling picture of the condition of the people, occurs this noble and self sacrificing language which deserves to go down side by side with the dying sentiments of the patriots and heroes of antiquity: "I have finally concluded to remain and am devoting my whole time and energies to the relief of the sufferers. Should I fall in the epidemic, my friends at least have the gratification to know that I fell in the discharge of my duty." Thus laboring day and night, without taking time to sleep or scarcely to eat, he continued until the epidemic had considerably abated and the dark cloud had begun to show its silver lining when suddenly he was stricken down. He was kindly and tenderly nursed during the five days of his illness by many friends, conspicuously among whom was his brother-in-law, W. W. Alexander, of Augusta, who was with him during the period of his sickness. He felt that his time had come from the first and in the language of one who was very near and dear to him: "He was perfectly conscious to the last moment, calmly made arrangements to cross the dark river, giving such directions as to the disposition of his mortal remains and kindred matters as was consonant with his views, and then sweetly fell asleep."

William King, a gentleman of great wealth and benevolence, who was his constant attendant during his illness, had him buried in his yard so that his grave might not be lost as was frequently the case during those trying times. After the epidemic had ceased, his remains were buried in Laurel Grove Cemetery where a beautiful monument was erected to his memory, bearing the following inscription:

>"To the memory of Dr. James M. Gordon
>who died of yellow fever in this city
>September 18, 1854."

Resolute in his devotion to the call of humanity, he shrank not even from the pestilence, but fell himself a martyr amidst those he sought to save.

The celebrated Dr. Wildman, formerly so well known in this county, also fell in the epidemic and it is not even known where he was buried.

Dr. Gordon died at the age of thirty-three, before he had scarcely reached the meridian of his days and usefulness, but he lived long enough to make for himself a reputation commensurate with the state. After his death, letters of condolence, tributes of respect and testimonials of every kind came pouring in to his family from every quarter, showing the high esteem in which he was held throughout the state.

Devotion to truth, fidelity to his friends, and a sovereign contempt for anything that was mean or dishonorable were the most salient points in his character. He was ambitious for distinction in his profession, but he sought that distinction not by denying merit in others but by exhibiting it in himself. He was a most sincere student all his life and when not professionally engaged would frequently sit up to a late hour at night in reading and study. In this he set an example worthy of imitation by many of our doctors of this day, who deem their education complete when they receive their diploma.

Dr. Gordon, like most of his family, was of an ardent and impetuous disposition, quick to resent an insult or an indignity, and as ready to extend the hand of forgiveness and reconciliation when the olive branch was held forth. Although never indulging in dissipation of any kind, he was eminently social in his disposition and was a most pleasant and agreeable companion.

He was an advocate of education and a patron of learning. He was one of the founders of the Atlanta Medical College, and was elected to one of the professorships, a position however which he declined. He was one of the projectors of the Lawrenceville Manufacturing Company and lost heavily when it failed.

Firm and unyielding in his convictions of what was right and honorable, steadfast in his devotion to principle, constant and faithful in his friendships, he went down to his grave a martyr to the cause of humanity, leaving as many devoted friends and as few enemies as any man occupying his position ever lived in the county.

For a series of years he was the intimate friend of the writer and his family physician. I knew him well and he had my confidence as a man of integrity, of high attainments, literary as well as social and professional. I have read many of the productions of his pen which gave evidence of fine acquirements and splendid abilities. Had he lived he would have become one of the first men of the state.

He never sought office but was chosen one of the justices of the Inferior Court and discharged its duties with fidelity and ability for four years.

He was a member of the Masonic fraternity and was a craftsman good and true, with whom his brethren were proud to be associated within the temple and without. In his death the mystic chain was broken and one of its links gone that can never be replaced.

He was a genial companion, full of life and full of hope. His merry pealing laugh, as it used to well up in the social circle, falls on me still with its enlivening, inspiring tones, never to be forgotten! And what more can I say of Dr. Gordon? This feeble tribute to his memory is but a poor yet sincere offering from his old friend. Not half has been said in commendation of him as might be said.

His old county was proud of him while he lived and still proud of his memory. In speaking of her native born sons who were reared on her soil and went out to do her honor, not one of all the number is spoken of with more pride and satisfaction than Dr. James M. Gordon.

1872

RICHARD SAYE

In several of my former sketches I have referred to Mr. Saye because he was intimately and closely connected with several of whom I have written. A more extended notice is due to him on account of his good standing and excellent character as a citizen and for his exemplary conduct as a religious man.

The old church book at Fairview which was kindly placed in my hands a year ago by the late and lamented John M. Mills, whose mortal remains were yesterday deposited in the grave, mentions the name of Richard Saye for the first time at a session of the church held April 22, 1825. He had been elected a ruling elder and met with the session that day. That old book is to me an interesting relic of the past. In reading it, it revives old memories, brings up old friends whom I knew in my childhood, and chronicles histories and incidents of the church that the cycles of time had obliterated from my memory.

These old minutes were recorded by George M. Gresham, the first clerk, and then by Dr. Thomas W. Alexander, extending from August 9, 1823, the time when Fairview Church was first constituted, to April, 1835, when a new book was opened extending to the present time. Through all these minutes the name of Richard Saye appears as a ruling elder, sometimes as a delegate from that church to Hopewell Presbytery, from April, 1825, to October, 1867, the date of his death.

He was born in Union District, S. C., June, 1777. In his early manhood he moved to Franklin County and settled with the bounds of Hebron congregation, of which the Rev. Thomas New was then pastor. He united with that church and soon was chosen one of the elders and was ordained and set apart to that office in 1819 by the celebrated Dr. Moses Waddell.

In March, 1825, he came to Gwinnett County and was a citizen here for forty-two years. He was not an active man like Dr. Alexander, Moses Liddell and some others of his brethren. His temperament was totally different. He was not excitable under any circumstances, but always calm, quiet and uniform.

I give an extract from a letter I received from an old friend who was long identified with our people and with the members of Fairview Church and who was a member of that church for a long period of years. In speaking of Mr. Saye he says: "Every one who knew him would call him a good man, one of the salt of the earth. When I first knew him, he was called 'good old father Saye.' He had no enemies, for he never engaged in any strife or contention. He mingled with the world but little, but rather silently pursued the even tenor of his way. If he could do no good, he was certain to do no harm; and his example had a good influence and was a safe guide to follow. His natural feelings were not excitable or were easily controlled. He was a good man but not very active. It was not common to see him much excited on any subject, but at one time at a revival his feelings were much stirred up, and he remarked that he held the world as he did his coat, ready to drop it at any time, and he suited the action to the word so fully that he thought he would drop his coat right there."

He had two sons, James H. and John, who were partly educated at the old academy in Lawrenceville. Both of them became Presbyterian ministers and are men of great usefulness and have talents of a high order, especially the first named.

At this point I must digress to say what I have long desired to say, that our old county has done more in sending out men who have become useful and great to honor her than any county in the state. The bench is now graced by two of her sons, the bar by a large number of lawyers of distinguished ability, able and skillful physicians, successful merchants and farmers, and ministers of the Gospel who, for learning, eloquence and usefulness, cannot be surpassed by any, and of the latter the two sons of Mr. Saye are very properly classed. At some future day I propose to give biographical sketches of the native sons of Gwinnett who have gone out to other parts and do honor to their old mother.

Twenty or more years ago I solemnized the marriage of Mr. Saye's youngest daughter, his youngest child, who now lives in one of the far-off states to the southwest. She, as all of his children, like their venerated father, was of quiet, calm and gentle disposition. This is a characteristic of all his children, sensible, quiet, correct in deportment, and religious in practice.

It was said of Mr. Saye what can be said of few others: He had no enemies, none spoke evil or disrespectfully of him, he had the confidence of all who knew him as an honest man and a Christian, and this is his best eulogy.

1872

ASAHEL REID SMITH

The subject of this sketch was born in Springfield, Vermont, in 1794. His youth was spent in toil and hardship, struggling against poverty in an effort to support and educate his younger brothers and sisters. Nine months of the year he worked on neighboring farms and earned enough to provide against want. During the three winter months he attended the free school and acquired the substantial elements of a good education.

At the age of twenty he aspired to the high calling of a teacher and began his career in a small school at Leicester, Massachusetts. By dint of hard study he kept ahead of his pupils and in time acquired a substantial reputation both as a teacher and a disciplinarian.

In 1818 he concluded to make a venture upon an uncertain sea. He had heard such glowing accounts of the demand for and the compensation paid to teachers in Georgia that he emigrated to this state and settled in Montgomery County. He paid his traveling expenses by chartering a sloop, loading it with brick and selling the cargo in Savannah. In Montgomery County he found friends who were willing to entrust the education of their children to a Northerner and he resumed his former vocation. Among those whose acquaintance he made was John A. Jones, then a young man of promise. Judge Jones was some years his senior and was always his warm, personal friend. It was in this county that Caroline Ann Maguire, an orphan, became one of his pupils and later his wife. (This statement differs from that of Charles H. Smith, or Bill Arp, who was the son of Asahel R. Smith.—Editor.)

In 1822 he came to Lawrenceville and began merchandising and lived here for thirty years. In his first venture as a merchant he lost his little capital amounting to $1,000 and found himself in debt a like sum. His creditors did not sue him, but extended to him additional credit and sold him more goods. With this help he began anew, avoiding the errors he had made in the past, and he became a successful and prosperous merchant. For twenty-four years he was postmaster at Lawrenceville, holding the office under both Whig and Democratic administrations.

In 1823 he married Caroline Maguire, his former pupil, a young lady of lovely character and uncommon beauty, and whose history was most tenderly and touchingly romantic. Left an orphan in the city of Charleston when she was seven years old, she was taken to Savannah and placed in an orphan's asylum to avoid the yellow fever epidemic then raging in Charleston. Her parents had died of this dreaded disease. After remaining in the orphan's home for some time, she was selected as a protege by a Mrs. Goulding, the mother of a distinguished Presbyterian divine by that name.

It was most touching to hear her relate her asylum experience. She well remembered how the girls were arrayed in their best clothes and with clean faces and well combed hair were made to stand up in a line around the large hall to be inspected by kind ladies who came to select one for adoption. With what timidity and trembling the children all scrutinized the countenance of each lady who slowly walked around the line and who was to be the mother or the tyrant of one of their number. At last little Caroline was chosen and she left the orphans' home forever.

She had in her childhood remembered that she had a brother a little older than herself, but no clue was found of him or of any of the family in Charleston. After her marriage, she so often urged that another and more diligent search be made. Mr. Smith had inserted in various papers an advertisement for the lost brother by the name of James Maguire who was taken from Charleston during the yellow fever scourge of 1813. In the meantime the brother had grown to man's estate, had prospered, married and was living in Boston, Massachusetts, where he had been taken as a parentless waif at the same time his sister had been taken to Savannah. James Maguire had twice been to Charleston in search of his sister, but could learn nothing of her or his kindred. Providence was overlooking both of them and the advertisement was seen in a Boston paper by a friend of the brother. The story of the reunion of this brother and sister is of such hallowed joy that I will not speak of it. I remember it well and many others wept with joy besides the family.

In 1832 Mr. Smith became a member of Fairview Presbyterian Church. In 1836 he was chosen an elder of the church.

He was a justice of the Inferior Court of Gwinnett County for ten years and was always found foremost in doing his official duties.

As a patron of education no man took more interest in the establishment of schools than he. He was most diligent in securing competent teachers and most liberal in voting them good salaries. Believing in the idea of raising boys to work, he was among the first in our state to urge the adoption of the manual labor system of schools. Mainly by his efforts the Gwinnett Manual Labor School was founded. For a year or two it was successful and prosperous, but it soon broke down. The boys would not work and the system has generally been abandoned as a mistake. Mr. Smith had it so much at heart that he advanced considerable of his individual means to sustain it, which was entirely lost.

In 1853 he moved to Rome where he at this writing still lives in comfort and contentment. His children and grandchildren are all near him to cheer and gladden his heart during his last days. My personal recollection of Mr. Smith dates back to about the year 1826 when I was scarcely ten years old. Then he was selling goods in the old wooden storehouse, made of logs, on the northwest corner of the square in Lawrenceville where the brick store stands and which was built by him. He was a popular merchant with the people of that early day and had the entire confidence of the honest pioneer citizens of our old county.

When a boy I was often impressed with the confidence and cordiality that existed between him and his customers, especially the old men and women who traded with him and who lived in the country. In dealing with his clerks, they were sometimes distrustful perhaps and thought the prices too high, but what Asa said about it was all right. It was not uncommon for many people to think when they came to settle at the end of the year that their accounts were too large and that many goods had been charged to them that they had not bought. During the long time he sold goods in Lawrenceville, I never heard that charge laid to him. Mistakes of this kind were sometimes made by his clerks, but Mr. Smith always made everything satisfactory.

In a conversation with a lady who was reared in this county, now living elsewhere, she remarked that Mr. Smith was the first man ever to offer to sell her goods on a credit. She had just grown up, was proud, handsome, industrious, but poor. It was the custom then for smart girls to make homespun cloth by carding the cotton, spinning the thread and weaving it into cloth for their own dresses as well as to clothe the family. Much of the homemade cloth was sold to the stores and taken up in calico for Sunday dresses, pins, needles and other notions and occasionally a bonnet. This young lady had made and sold to Mr. Smith a considerable quantity during the year; and late in the season brought in a bolt of forty yards, the last in that line for the season. The cloth was measured, entered on the book and Mr. Smith asked her if she did not want a nice dress. Turning to a clerk, he gave him instructions to sell her the finest dress in the store on credit. "We have some fine silk dresses," replied the clerk. "Well, a girl who makes as much cloth as she has sold to us this year is good for even a silk dress or anything else she wants in my store."

In early life the greater portion of his earnings was applied to the education of his brothers and sisters. One by one he paid their way south from Vermont until he got them all near him but two. Those two sisters married in New England.

The first brother to come was Henry. He came in 1826, was 18 years of age, amiable, intelligent and considered the flower of the family. But consumption had marked him for its prey and he soon died and was buried in old Lawrenceville cemetery. This inscription is on his gravestone:

> This monument is dedicated by fraternal affection to perpetuate the memory of Henry Smith, who departed this

life October 31, 1829, aged 21 years. The choicest fruit drops earliest to the ground.

The next one to come was John, then Jacob, then his sister who became Mrs. Norton, and last Daniel. The brothers were all intelligent, business men and respected citizens. His sister was an amiable, interesting girl.

It was a great loss to our community when Mr. Smith moved from among us. His place has never been filled.

When last seen time had dealt gently with him. Still its impress was perceptible in the deepened lines about his face and the imperfection of his hearing. He spoke of his long residence in Lawrenceville with emotion. He said that the happiest days of his life were spent there, and with tears in his eyes remarked: "I shall probably never be permitted to visit the old place again."

This brief memorial of him is but a feeble tribute to this eminently good man. His habits of industry, his inflexible integrity, his honesty, his uprightness in dealing with mankind, his pious life and correct habits are models to be imitated by those who are to come after him.

1873

Captain John Beasley

It is sometimes profitable in our race of life to stop and study human character. Pope said: "The greatest study of mankind is man." While it may be said that human nature is the same the world over, yet it is a fact that there is a wide difference in human character. This is not attributable solely to education and early training, but perhaps to a difference in mental construction.

Human nature may be the same as to passions and prejudices. The hopes and fears common to one may be common to all, yet with less force in some than in others. In point of hope, humor, expectancy, brain and goodness of heart, there is as great a dissimilarity as in face and physiognomy of the human race. Some are cold and phlegmatic, not easily excited by hopes or fears; others are ardent, sanguine and easily elated. Some plod along through life's brief journey with dull and listless indifference to the great aims of life, while others with swift race follow the money gods, distinction and pleasure.

Again, in the race of life there is a fork in the road, one leading to fame and fortune, the other to obscurity, and sometimes to the prison or the gibbet.

The subject of this sketch is peculiar morally, mentally, physically and furnishes a subject that may be studied with interest and profit. With a commanding presence, having the front of a Jove and the crest of a god, a lofty and graceful bearing, and a mental capacity far above the average, his inordinate love of fun and frolic was the incubus that weighed down all his better instincts and caused him to take the wrong fork of the road in "Life's morning march." Had he but taken the other, he might have been the guiding genius of his state and thrilled and startled senates with his eloquence. His tall, erect and graceful figure, the whole contour of his face, his eagle eye, were the facsimile of the great commoner, Henry Clay. With the proper direction in early life, he might have rivaled that matchless orator on the forum or in the senate chamber.

His road was in the wrong direction. The squeaks of the fiddle, the ribald jests and the songs of the bacchanalian revel were his highest enjoyments and they lured him astray. With a good heart, "full of the milk of human kindness," the tenderest and most manly sensibilities, always ready to feel for others' woes, with a hand guided by benevolence, he always had the respect of the good and the admiration of the bad. The gentleman admired him for his graceful and dignified manner, the rowdy for his inimical jokes and quaint humor.

John Beasley was born on Rocky Comfort Creek in Warren County, Georgia, five miles below Warrenton on October 7, 1787, and is now in the 87th year of his age. His father was Richard Beasley. His mother was Margaret Day. She was a good woman and her life was prolonged to an hundred years. His father died at the age of 63.

The people of Warren County in that early day were a plain people, not much given to wearing fine clothes and not much of any sort. The boys were not permitted to wear britches or hats until their names were placed on the muster roll. The girls wore nothing but loose petticoats until they were of full marriageable age. As soon as a young woman was seen with a frock on, she was considered in the market, making banters and casting "sheeps eyes." They wore only petticoats and in winter stitched down shoes. The boys wore long shirts, tied with a pucker string around the neck which reached half way from the knees to the feet, a bonnet for a hat, which accounts perhaps for that ancient expression: "He has a bee in his bonnet."

The first pants and hat our hero had was a great event in his life. Then sixteen years of age and warned to muster, he must have the necessary outfit. The parents were perplexed as to how it was to be procured. Their ingenuity soon overcame the difficulty. A pair of osnaburg pants, short and small in the legs, and a hat made by drawing on the tan trough for a rawhide, furnished the material, which, while wet, was soft and pliable. The outfit was complete and satisfactory to all concerned.

Bright and soon the next morning, Jack, with pants on and with his rawhide hat on and with his polk stalk for a gun, took up the line of march to the district muster ground with all the "pomp and circumstance of glorious war." Soon the ear-piercing fife and martial drum called to arms and the nation's protectors paraded in martial array.

First the manuel of arms with old guns, polk stalks and walking sticks claimed attention. Then the evolutions of marching, wheeling, etc., followed which, together with the heat of the summer's sun, soon began to tell feelingly on Jack's rawhide hat. It seemed to grow small and tight by degrees with a painful compression on the head and which was becoming intolerable. "What's to become of the thing? It's pinching my head," said Jack. "Take the darn thing off," was the advice of his file leader. An effort to do so was a failure. It was stuck. "Go and stick the darn thing in the branch" was the advice of the sergeant. This was impracticable as it would take a day or two to soften it. His head was being terribly compressed. "In mercy, Peter, take out your knife and cut it loose," said Jake, "and be careful not to cut my head for the hat is buried an inch under the skin." The remedy was applied and with difficulty our hero was relieved, feeling then as now an abhorrence for hats and especially for rawhide hats.

He went to school once to James Gordon, a Scotchman, and studied the old Dillworth spelling book. Having a quick mind, he soon learned to spell in two syllables and his vanity was flattered by his success. Called up by the teacher to say his lesson, he obeyed and with a low bow commenced, "Big A little a r o n ron, Aaron." "Go over that again, Jacob," said the master. It was repeated in the same way as before to the great disgust of the Scotchman, who, imitating his tone, replied: "Big fool, little fool, r o n ron, Foolron. Go back and get it over, Jacob."

Jack, like all the children of that early day, was taught to call his parents by the endearing name of Daddy and Mammy. No pappa and mamma as in these nice and elegant times. Occasionally a family that was getting puffed up a little would teach their children to say Par and Mar, but this was not considered to be a common privilege and was only allowed to those who had come from old Virginia.

A young man who was courting Jack's sister and who was somewhat bashful on the subject, rode up to the cabin one day and not seeing the girl, asked Jake: "Where is your Daddy?" "In the field plowing," was the answer. "And where is your Mar?" says he. "Daddy is plowing her," says Jack, thinking he was referring to the old grey mare. I never knew whether that young man got Jack's sister. I would suppose, if he did, he might have wanted to plow her, too, as her "Mar" was a good plow nag, and she, too, might be.

Captain Beasley is passionately fond of instrumental music. Even now, after he has passed the octogenarian age, the sweet strains of the violin, when touched by the hand of a master, thrill his old heart like the soft strains of a vesper hymn coming over the waters deep and clear at eventide and carry him back to the halcyon days of his young life. He even now in his old age draws the bow as gracefully and scientifically as the ancient and famed Paganini. Yet his first lessons were upon the crude and uncouth gourd fiddle.

> His dim eyes and his hollow cheek
> Show that time had left its trace;
> Hoar with frost his once dark locks
> And wan his once florid face.
> But Uncle Jack keeps young his heart,
> Though his golden age is past
> And the elated spirits keep
> And make his merriment last.

But recently it was the privilege of the writer to be present with his venerable friend at the home of a mutual acquaintance, where we were favored with some beautiful piano music accompanied by a bass violin, and the sparkle of the eagle eye of my old friend and the pat of the foot gave evidence that his inmost soul was stirred. His favorite fiddle, however, was not there.

On the 14th of February, 1810, he was married to Sara Cooper, near Madison, in Morgan County. Squire Garrett performed the ceremony. It was fashionable in that day and was part of the ceremony to require the bridegroom to salute the bride; and it was also the custom for the bride to be kissed by the officiating priest or minister, and it was considered a want of courtesy and respect not to be kissed by all present, especially by the male guests. Women were then not so much in the habit of kissing each other as now, it being considered too great a waste of raw material. This kissing of the bride was annoying to the bridegroom. He did not like that the balm of lips of his beautiful bride should be sipped by any but himself, but it was the custom and he must submit. He had been fascinated by the beauty of Miss Cooper. She was as beautiful as Venus, of queenly grace, soft, melting, blue eyes, rosy lips that might tempt the gods, a form somewhat slight and blithe, a beautiful dancer with grace in every step, heaven in her eyes, and dignity and love in every gesture. Added to these, she gloried in long golden hair, three feet in length and hanging in beautiful ringlets below the waist, and on her feet she wore dainty kid shoes with shining gold buttons. All these stormed the citadel of his heart and he surrendered unconditionally. Sally is still by his side, aged and infirm, having shared his joys and sorrows for sixty-four years. And she and Uncle Jack, like John Anderson my Joe John and his old wife, are tottering down the hill and soon they will sleep together at the foot.

Aunt Sally is a good Christian and has been a church member forty years and it affords the writer great pleasure to bear this testimony to her worth. While her husband was frolicsome and was devoting the prime of his life to revelry and dissipation, greatly to the grief of her heart, her affections nevertheless would cling to him still, like the tendrils of the vine to the oak, riven and blasted though it might be by the raging tempest. And the wayward, too, and this is to his credit, after days and weeks in carousals and dissipations, on his approach to his home, would rejoice to feel

> " 'Tis sweet to hear the watch dog's honest bark
> Bay deep-mouth welcome as we draw near home,
> 'Tis sweet to know there is an eye that will mark
> Our coming and grow brighter when we come."

Several years after the marriage of Captain Beasley and Miss Cooper she informed him that he must go to the mill for the meal was out. He asked that it be postponed and that she could borrow meal from a neighbor. She insisted on his going. He consented and got ready by dressing up in his best clothes. Broadcloth coat, trowsers and vest, ruffled shirt and gaudy breastpin, polished high-top boots and silver knee buckles, arrayed thus he started with his meal sack to Cody's Mill, twelve miles distant on the Augusta road. Arriving at the mill he paid for two and a half bushels of corn with directions that it be ground. He then went to James Collins', three miles away, who was an acquaintance and a boon companion. Soon it was known throughout the settlement of his arrival and a general gathering in of the young men and young women for a frolic followed. For three days and nights they had it with a vim. The theater of their operations was too small and they decided to go to Augusta where he took quarters at the City Hotel, then kept by Phinizy & Byrd. He soon fell in with notorious Phil Thurman, the prince of gambling saloons, and it was hail fellow well met. Many other congenial spirits joined them and they got on a general bender which continued for a month. In calling for his bill when leaving, he was charged with 356 drinks, besides quarts and gallons; and his whole bill was $187.37. This he paid and was satisfied that his expenses were very moderate. He took up the march home by way of Cody's Mill, but the corn was not ground and it was with some difficulty that he could remind the miller that he had paid for it. He had been gone so long it had gone from the miller's mind.

His wife had heard of his coming and dressed up in her best and met him all smiles and goodness and accosted him gladly. "How do you do, Mr. Beasley?" she said. "How do you do, my dear?" he replied. "Well, Mr. Beasley, you are the best mill boy I ever saw." "Why so, my darling?" "Because you never go to mill without bringing the meal." He had been gone to mill forty-three days and spent $187.37.

In politics Uncle Jack was a Troup man in the days of Troup and Clark, and then a Whig up to 1856, when he voted for Buchanan. He has been a democrat ever since.

He was never an aspirant for office—hadn't time for that—

but he held the office of Justice of the Peace in Clark County. He is proud to this day that his commission bears the name of George W. Crawford, Governor, who was a great favorite of his. He was chosen messenger of the state senate in 1843 when Charles Dougherty, another of his special favorites, was its president. It is said that he made a most excellent Justice of the Peace, except that he sometimes leaned a little too far over to mercy under criminal circumstances. Only one of his decisions is reported; and if found at all, it will be found only in Gault's reports, page 502. I give only the substance: Joseph Yancey was arrested under a warrant issued by Squire Beasley, a Justice of the Peace of the 420th District, for stealing one sheep of the value of fifty cents. Upon hearing the case, the defendant entered a plea of guilty. In his exculpatory affidavit, he alleged that at the time thereof he was in a state of intoxication and not responsible for the act. The court asked the prisoner where he got his whiskey, and was informed that he got it at Jack Barnes' still house. The following order was entered on the minutes of the court:

The State vs. Joseph Yancey:

Indictment in Justice Court, 420th District G. M.

Upon the above stated case and the facts connected therewith, it is adjudged by the court that the defendant, Joseph Yancey, be discharged and that the plaintiff pay all the cost accruing on account of this prosecution; and the court gives as a reason for this judgment that the defendant was drunk and got his liquor from Jack Barnes' still house, that he was not responsible for his act to the certain knowledge of the court, for that the said court got drunk on whiskey made at said still house and without malice or evil intent stole all the spoons of his wife, Sally.

At the request of some special friends and with the consent of my old friend, Captain Beasley, I have attempted briefly to give a few incidents in the life of this remarkable man. While the main facts are true as given me by Uncle Jack himself, yet I will say that in some instances I have drawn on my imagination to some extent; but even these are in accordance with the character and peculiarities of the subject. This is but a brief outline, for to write his history would swell into a volume as he expressed it "Larger than Pilgrim's Progress." After all his wanderings and irregularities, his life is still spared beyond the time allotted to human life; and our best prayer is that his effort to be a good man may be crowned with success and though he enters the vineyard at the eleventh hour, we hope that full wages will be his reward.

> And in life's extremity,
> May no fears invade his breast
> And earth's pleasures renouncing
> Inherit eternal rest.

1873

DANIEL LIDDELL

Daniel Liddell was born in Abbeville District, South Carolina, February 19, 1786. He married Isabella Liddell, a distant relative, and a sister of the late Moses Liddell, of whom I wrote in my pen and ink sketches. Their marriage occurred in 1808 and ten years later removed to Franklin County, Georgia. Residing there six years, in 1824 he moved to this county and settled on Beaver Ruin Creek, where he lived until his death, which occurred in November, 1846, in the 61st year of his age.

Mr. Liddell reared eight children, five sons and three daughters. His eldest daughter married Mr. Plaster. His second daughter, Ruth, married Henry Brockman, and his third, Isabella, Dr. Reeder. His oldest son, Moses W., now deceased, married Elizabeth Clower; his second, Thomas Haney, Elizabeth Collier; his third, W. C. P., Evaline Wynn; his fourth, Daniel W., never married; and his fifth, James M., Miss Gober.

His wife, Isabella, survived him until recently and all his children except his first and fourth sons.

I make the following transcript from one of his record books in his own business-like handwriting:

"Lineage or Genealogy of My Kindred of The Liddell Family:"

"I was born in Abbeville District, South Carolina, twelve miles west of the courthouse, February 19, 1786, and was the son of William Liddell, who was born in the city of Annapolis, Md., March 10, 1762. His father was named John and his mother, Rachel. My father was brought from Maryland by an uncle, named Moses, about 1767 to Abbeville. He died in a few years. His aunt died after the commencement of the Revolution. They left no children and was therefore left in the world among strangers. The small estate left by the uncle was taken care of by a Mr. Black, a citizen of Abbeville. My father joined the Whig ranks and served during the war. After the war he married Ruth Keith whose father was a citizen of Pennsylvania."

In regard to his church relations I made an extract from the Old Fairview church book to which I have access. This venerable record of Fairview, running back to the early period of August, 1823, when that church was organized, is to me an interesting relic of the old times of our county, the purusal of which brings up many names in connection with the church, who were the best citizens in this county in those early days.

This old record in itself is a model of neatness as well as of a succinct detail of the admissions, baptisms, deaths, etc., of that church's history from 1823 to 1836 in the handwriting of George

M. Gresham, the first clerk, and Thomas W. Alexander, the second, interspersed occasionally with that of Dr. John S. Wilson. I have seen no church records that equal it as a brief but explicit record of all the church's actions in simplicity and detail.

An extract: "November 8, 1829. The session convened and admitted on profession of faith the following persons: Polly Paden, Rachel Minor, Ruth Liddell, Lucinda Games and Daniel Liddell.
"Thomas W. Alexander, Clerk."

After the death of Mr. Liddell, he was buried at Fairview, and I find on his tombstone the following touching epitaph by his surviving wife:

"Sleep on, my loving husband, sleep!
This marble shall thy memory keep,
But deeper on my heart is graven
The thought that we shall meet in Heaven."

This good wife survived him many years, but recently deceased and is buried by his side in the same old church yard; and ere this, the thought so touchingly expressed by her and engraved on his tablet has been realized and they met in Heaven where death and separation come not.

1873

Levi Loveless

It is with pain that we announce the death of this estimable man who passed on the 24th instant in the 74th year of his age. He had been in feeble health for several years; and although he was able to go about transacting his ordinary business, yet death did not come upon him unexpectedly. It has been but a few months since he was in our office, and though appeared cheerful, he evidently felt that he had about finished his labors. He talked of his approaching death with a calmness that indicated a strong faith in his safety beyond the grave.

Mr. Loveless was born in South Carolina, but had been a citizen of this county for many years. He filled for a long time the office of judge of the Inferior Court and was several times elected to the state legislature. In 1850 he was one of the representatives from this county in the celebrated convention of that year.

For many years, and up to his death, he was a minister in high standing in the Baptist church. Of him it may be truly said that, although Providence had lengthened out his days to a ripe old age, he had not an enemy. With a kind heart and a liberality beyond his means, he went about doing good.

He was quiet and unobtrusive in his manner, gentle and kind in his disposition, but always to be found on the side of morality, whether as a citizen, judge of the Inferior Court, or member of the legislature. He leaves a spotless character and a bright example to those who come after him. Peace to his ashes.

1875

David Winchester Spence

The announcement of the death of Judge Spence fell like a pall on the minds of the readers. A more extended notice is due to his memory.

A history of his remarkable life, his early struggles with adverse fortune, his indomitable energy, his business talents and his wonderful success in life make it proper to be stated.

More than this: For thirty years he was a citizen of our county, active in the discharge of all the various duties as such and contributing largely to her every enterprise of public interest. And more still: Among her present citizens, including those who have moved from her limits during the thirty years of his residence with us, he numbered a host of warm personal friends who will drop a sad tear to his memory.

David W. Spence died at the residence of R. M. Cleveland, near Wartrace, Tennessee, September 13, 1875, after an illness of only five days. The deceased, on his return from New York, stopped at the house of his old friend, Mr. Cleveland, to spend a day or two with him, in good health and exceedingly jovial and full of life. While there he was attacked violently with cholera morbus which failed to yield to medical treatment and from which he died on the fifth day. He was conscious at intervals and recognized his wife and youngest daughter who had been summoned by telegram from their home in Covington and who reached him on Saturday before his death on Monday morning.

He was the youngest son of Nathan and Adaline Spence. The family consisted of three sons and a daughter. A brother, M. H. Spence, now living in Harris County, Georgia, and a sister, Mrs. DeLoach, now living in Mississippi, survive him.

He was born in Jasper County, Georgia, February 21, 1816. His parents were poor, living on rented land, and as a natural consequence the advantages of an early education were denied him. He made use of all the means he had, which consisted of a good mother, who exercised an influence over him for good and which was the foundation of his future greatness. Her marble tablet to be seen in the Lawrenceville cemetery, erected by him, bears on its face evidence of his deep devotion: "A woman of no faults, but many virtues."

With a mother's love his only patrimony, he went forth to

engage in life's battles against poverty and adversity. In 1836 he came to Lawrenceville and engaged to write in the office of the clerk of the Superior Court for Samuel F. Alexander, who at that time was clerk of the court, for seven dollars per month and his board. In the month of June of that year, he joined Captain Garmany's command of Gwinnett Mounted Volunteers and with that gallant company marched to the seat of war near Columbus and participated in the severe battle with the Creek Indians at Shepherd's Plantation. On his return from the war, he resumed his duties in the clerk's office with his accustomed faithfulness. His fidelity to business and his active energy soon attracted the attention of Mr. Cleveland, who procured his services as clerk in his store. With G. W. Wright, he soon bought out Mr. Cleveland and for a short time continued the business as the firm of Spence & Wright.

After a time, Mr. Spence became the sole proprietor and his success in business has no parallel in our section. Commencing business in 1837, a poor young man, without means, scarcely a dollar in his pocket, yet in twenty years he had accumulated a large estate, the result of energy, pluck, good judgment and indefatigable perseverence.

Judge Spence was of peculiar temperament. Strong in his friendships and strong in his dislikes, his temper was brittle and irascible under disappointments or insults. To reflect upon his honor or to attack his interests met with uncompromising resistance at the threshold. In character he was positive in everything, negative in nothing. "Whatever thy hands find to do, do it with thy might." These are the words of inspiration and the command was obeyed fully by Daniel W. Spence, but he hastened to the grave in the prime of his manhood and in the very zenith of his mature life.

Mr. Spence was not well understood by those who only knew him casually. In his rough and tumble life in business he was considered stern, relentless and selfish by many. To have known him well, to have looked at the inner man and the instinct of his better life would have shown that in him was much of the milk of human kindness.

Two years ago it was my privilege to spend a few days with him in his beautiful home in Covington. I had been acquainted with him for more than a quarter of a century and thought I knew him well. I became convinced during that visit that, by seeing him at his hearthstone with his wife and children, his gentle and affectionate deportment to them, especially to his wife and daughters, I had long mistaken the man. I must be permitted to repeat that the whole scene impressed me and the gentleness and affection for his wife and daughters all impressed me and gave me joy and unfolded to me a new chapter in his life. In battling with the world a man may be stern and often irate from the cares of life and its perplexity and may often be misunderstood, but mark him if he is kind and gentle to his wife and you will find a gentleman. Such was David W. Spence.

1875

Robert Steel Brown

It is a sad task to announce the death of an old friend with whom we have associated day after day for years and who has suddenly been cut down in the vigor of manhood and in the midst of a useful life. Within two weeks three of the old citizens of Lawrenceville have passed away. They are D. W. Spence, Thompson Allen and Robert Steel Brown, all of whom are not far from the same age and to all human appearances with many years of usefulness stretching out before them. One after another in quick succession step down from the plain of life into the dark chamber of death.

Mr. Brown was taken sick about two weeks ago. For several days he was able to attend to some business, but the fatal disease had fastened on the fountains of life and he continued to sink. It was soon ascertained that he had a violent attack of typhoid fever which seemed to involve his whole system, mental as well as physical. He appeared to suffer but little, yet the experienced eye could detect a gradual sinking.

He died at 11 o'clock on Sunday, September 26, 1875, and was buried by the Masonic Fraternity on Monday afternoon with the usual ceremonies of that order. A number of members from the Buford lodge was present and assisted in the solemnities.

Perhaps no man ever lived in our community who had more friends and fewer enemies than the subject of this notice. He was remarkable for his evenness of temper and the calm philosophy with which he met the vicissitudes of life.

In every relation of life he was a model man, a good citizen, obliging neighbor, indulgent father, charitable even beyond his own means and a most worthy member of the lodge. The whole community mourn his loss and mingle their grief with his family in the hour of their sad affliction.

1878

David Richardson

The advantages of education in the early settlement of this county were very limited and very imperfect. In the earlier years there were but few school houses in the county. These were scattered far apart and were of rude structure, generally of dirt floors, slab benches, a single door, and no openings but the cracks between the logs and one log cut out to afford light to those learning to write.

These school houses were usually located near a meeting house of the same rude structure, and differed from the school houses by being somewhat larger and ornamented by a high rickety pulpit which was its only distinguishing feature. The seats were of the same material, fixed a little better, with slab floor, and rarely with a plank one, for sawmills were very scarce in those days.

Those who essayed to be school masters in those early times were of very limited education, and what little they knew and taught was imperfectly and generally incorrectly taught, especially in the pronunciation of words.

To be able to read, write and cipher was deemed a sufficient qualification for a school master; and a man thus endowed was considered a paragon of learning and intelligence in the early times of which I write. One possessing these superior gifts was generally deferred to by all the people by general consent. He was the important man in the neighborhood, more so than the justice of the peace, or the preacher, for all agreed that he knew more than both of them.

A few days after the county's organization two academies were established, built by limited endowment by the state, one at Lawrenceville and the other near Gates' ferry in the western part of the county and called Washington Academy. These inaugurated a higher plane of scholastic training—but I am writing about old Davy Richardson, my first schoolmaster. He taught at the old schoolhouse hard by old Mt. Zion meeting house, one mile southeast of Bogan's store, known as the old Hog Mountain house, in 1822 or 1823.

Davy Richardson at that time lived on the Jefferson road leading by Dr. Freeman's, on the hill to the right, east of and but a short distance from the Appalachee River. Not a vestige of the old house now remains and the site is overgrown with old field pines and undergrowth, and there is nothing to indicate that a habitation ever was there. Such is life and the perishing things of this earth.

At the age of six years I was a pupil at Davy Richardson's school at old Mt. Zion, and the first lesson to learn was the alphabet and the most difficult to master of any other in all my subsequent life.

There were many scenes, incidents and circumstances that occurred there that have not nor will ever be blotted from my memory. The unique personal appearance of the man, the childish fears I felt of him, the great dread of his displeasure, the exalted gifts my young mind accorded him because he could spell, write and cipher, impressed me greatly, and I wondered how one small head could carry all he knew.

After this long period of time when I wish to recall the scenes of childhood, it is only necessary to shut my eyes to see him each morning approaching the schoolhouse, coming up the hill with slow and faltering footsteps, with his broad-brimmed old hat tucked up at the right side, with copperas breeches fitting tightly, his slender shanks and his long swallow-tail coat of the same material, and I have again the exact view of my old schoolmaster fifty-five years ago.

This was his picture a hundred yards off. It is only necessary to shut my eyes again and I see him enter the schoolhouse with his long, wrinkled and cadaverous face, his long snaggled teeth highly colored with homemade tobacco juice, his right eye squinted and almond shaped, his left one as round as a bullet and the eyelids immovable. It is a fact that that eye never closed even when asleep. It was said that his sergeant in the War of 1812 complimented him as the best picket in the regiment, for while his right eye slept his left was always on duty. Such are some of the oddities of my first school teacher.

It was the custom in those early days to turn out the master a few days before the expiration of school and make him give a holiday and treat or take a ducking. This school was no exception to the general rule, and I remember well the incidents of that turn out.

There was a large school of Hog Mountain's rustic girls and boys, a number of them grown and hence abundantly able to turn out old Davy Richardson. The plans were laid and tomorrow was the time, and the whole school was notified and the strictest secrecy enjoined. The morning came and all were on hand at an early hour and all were excited. The door was closed and barred with the benches and all things were in readiness. Soon the old master was seen wending his way up the path in slow and measured steps as was his custom and all felt that the supreme hour had come. Upon reaching the house and seeing the situation, he demanded to know in tones of authority what all this meant. Frank Berry, the champion of the occasion, replied: "You must give a holiday, treat to a gallon of rum and three pounds of sugar or take a ducking." This was refused and scouted by the teacher with a threat that he would break the door down. This threat greatly alarmed the little ones and a general cry was the result. An hour or more intervened and no terms could be agreed upon. The ultimatum was again repeated from within and five minutes more were given to decide. The master was unyielding and at the expiration of the time, the barricade was removed, the old man seized and hurried in the direction of the spring, the whole school following. Arriving near the spring, a truce was asked by the master, and finally the terms demanded were agreed upon, and Steve Hill and Anthony Bates were dispatched to Bogan's store for the rum and sugar. They soon returned and the rum and sugar were duly mixed and the whole school, girls and boys, as did the master, partook liberally, all got happy, and the school dismissed for the term and the show was over.

A few years after this, Mr. Richardson left the county and moved to the newer county of DeKalb and settled on the McDonough road, eight miles from Decatur, where he later died. I cherish till yet the memory of my old school master, because he was my first, although he taught me to call the last letter of the alphabet 'izzard,' which took John S. Wilson a whole year afterwards to correct.

His wife, Hannah, was the very opposite of her husband in looks, action and religion. He was lean, sallow and slow, an Universalist in religion, and slept with one eye open. She was fat, florid, quick motivated, a Methodist, and slept with both eyes open, I reckon. She was a good housewife and kept the home neat, was tidy in her dress and wore a hat with a feather in it, but wore no pinbacks and did not hold up her dress to show her underskirt.

1879

THE LAURENCE FAMILY

Old John Laurence was the head-center of the Laurence family that settled here at a very early period of our county's history. They settled on Pugh's Creek, three miles south of town, as early as 1820 or 1821. Where they came from I do not know, but most probably from South Carolina. When I do not know the facts, I always take it for granted that my subject came from South Carolina. Old Billy Brandon used to say, in referring to the large emigration to Georgia fifty or sixty years ago, that "South Carolina had boiled over and the scum had come to Georgia." About this period and after there was evidently a boil-over in that state, but it was not all scum that came here, for a very large part of our early population came from that state and they were our very best citizens.

John Laurence was most probably of the same family as the gallant Captain Laurence of the ship Chesapeake in the War of 1812. The gallantry displayed by him in his engagement with the British ship, Shannon, has rendered the name, Laurence, memorable with Americans for all time to come. His dying words, "Don't give up the ship," have been the battlecry in many a naval engagement since.

John Laurence was old when I first knew him. Though a plain old farmer, he was neat and tidy in his dress when he would visit town, and had some of the bearings of a gentleman, though stern and apparently morose and forbidding in his manners. For this reason he did not take well with our early population. He claimed to be a Revolutionary soldier, but his enemies said he was a Tory. This was not true, however, as he was a Revolutionary pensioner, to obtain which he had to make satisfactory proof to the government.

His family, as I remember, and I write of them only from my personal recollections, consisted of himself, his wife, six sons and one daughter. His sons were George, Thomas, Silas, Martin, Milton and Jackson, and his daughter, Lucy, who married Asa Wade, Jr.

George moved to the wilderness of Paulding County at its first settlement and it was the very place for George Laurence. Its poor lands and broken territory and wild, uncivilized population then, with its abundance of game, was the place for him. I saw him in 1843 with his long, gangling, stooped form, his weather-beaten face, his old slouched hat, his long-tailed blue coat, his buckskin leggins and his stitched-down shoes made at home from leather tanned in his own poplar trough, and if his old blue coat had been substituted for a hunting shirt and his stitched-down shoes by buckskin moccasins, he would have passed currently for a veritable Cherokee. I met one of his sons a few years ago at the convention of the State Agricultural Society, held in Savannah, as a delegate from Paulding County. I found him to be an intelligent, good-looking gentleman, a great improvement on his father.

I don't know what became of Thomas. I remember very little and can say no more about him.

Silas lived here longer than any of them and was better known. In stature he was like George, but was better educated. For a number of years he served as justice of the peace and was a good one and much more efficient than the average 'squire of that day or of this. Added to this, he taught school. He was never out of the state but once. Plucking up courage he went to Charleston on horseback, taking four weeks for the trip. Among his neighbors his trip required an explanation and to their questions about it he said: "I went to see how the big waters sloshed."

Martin and Milton went to Walker County thirty years ago.

Jackson, the youngest, was a Laurence in looks and awkwardness. He had education enough to teach a country school. He got into a scrape, as bachelors and young men sometimes do, and when it culminated, he went to town to consult N. L. Hutchins how to get out of it. The warrant had been issued without his knowledge and was placed in the hands of the sheriff. Getting wind of it and seeing the sheriff approaching him, he ran for his horse to make his escape. He ran so awkwardly that his horse took fright at him, broke loose and the sheriff caught him. He traded that fool horse the first opportunity. He, like Silas, never married, and died soon.

Lucy took after her father in looks and was a Laurence, too. She made an industrious housewife, but quit the world and left no copy.

Mrs. Laurence had a queer name, one hard to understand and pronounce, but when once learned was never forgotten. After the death of her husband it became necessary to show that she was his widow to get his pension, and her affidavit and the certificate of the county court were necessary. I was a sort of chief justice then and it devolved on me to administer the oath. Her name had to be affixed to the affidavit and she could not write. I asked her given name and she mumbled it out, but I could not understand it. I asked my old brother-in-law who had made out the papers and he called it, but it was still all jargon. He said, with his usual Yankee cuteness: "I will spell it," and he commenced, "Me-het-a-bell." Great spoons! Such a name! I never heard such an one before nor since, and I commend it to the parents of these days who dislike the old family names and want new fancy ones. As it must, of course, be abbreviated and have the irrepressible ie to it, they can have it Mehetie, or, if preferable, they can have it Belleie. Either of which I think would be quite as beautiful and appropriate as Mollie, Mamie, Susie, Sallie and all the other innumerable ies now so universal. Though the name to my mind was unique, John Laurence no doubt thought it most beautiful and full of poetry and sweetness in his young days when he wooed and won her, for then she was fresh as the virgin rose, blithe and bonnie, and to his mind lovely to the soul's eye.

Note: In my sketch of the Laurence family I made a mistake as to the name of Mrs. Laurence, as I am reminded by my friend, Judge Byrd. Queer as is the name I gave her, Ba-heth-er-land, her real name, is more so, if possible. I make the correction here for the satisfaction of my friend and one other, they being the only readers of the article who detected it, and, perhaps, the only persons living now who remember her.

1879

ABRAHAM MARTIN

Abraham Martin was born in Spartanburg, S. C., in 1775, and grew up and lived there till 1815 when he moved to Elk River, Tennessee. The lands on Elk River were wonderfully fertile, but there were too many objections to the rich soil in that valley. The Spanish needles and cockleburs grew so rank after the crops were laid by that a heavy brush had to be drug between the rows before the corn could be gathered. This was a serious objection to a South Carolinian. Another objection was that the country was sickly. So he determined to move again. Mr. Martin had heard of the new section of northwest Georgia, of its salubrious climate, and his thoughts turned thither.

In the winter of 1815-16, not being willing to leave his family, he sent his two sons, Sam and Abe, with instructions to go to the Mulberry River in Jackson County and rent a farm and in four weeks or as soon as their mother was able, he would move the family. Sam was eighteen years old and Abe, sixteen, both hardly grown and without experience. They finally reached the designated place and rented a farm. In the meantime they wanted to be at work clearing up the land for a crop, but here was a dilemma. They had no money, no axes, no hoes, no farm implements of any kind to work with, and worse than all, no provisions to live on. But necessity is the mother of invention, and this necessity impelled them to make an effort to obtain these things.

Brandon & Wardlaw had a store nearby, but the boys were strangers just come into the settlement and it was doubtful about getting credit. Sam's motto then, as ever in after life, was there is nothing like trying, and he went to Mr. Brandon and told him that he and his brother had rented a farm for his father, who was then in Tennessee, that they wanted to get to work on it, but had nothing to work with and no provisions to live on; and if they could get these things, their father with the family would be on in four weeks and then settle the account. The story was straightforward and satisfied Mr. Brandon. He sold them the goods. They went to work with a will and worked night and day. In the meantime the four weeks passed and their father had not come. His word to Mr. Brandon had not come true and they were troubled, and his dilemma was worse than at first. All downcast they went back to Mr. Brandon, endeavored to explain their disappointment. They explained to him that in all probability the reason of their father's delay was that their mother was not able to travel as soon as was expected and that he would come soon. Their story was a reasonable one and Mr. Brandon assured them that he was not uneasy and that they could have other supplies. They went back with a great burden lifted from their minds and went to work. Two days later as they were at work, Abe pricked up his ears and said: "Shad, I hear old Brindle's bell." "No you don't. Work on," said Shad. "I'll be durned if I don't," replied Abe, and hurried off to see; and sure enough old Brindle and her bell had come; and the family, too. Sam followed and soon told his tale about Mr. Brandon and the goods; and before unharnessing the team, he was furnished the money and he hurried to the store and paid the bill. I have heard Sam say in his old age that he sought an opportunity during the life time of Mr. Brandon to do him a deed of kindness for the favor he had rendered them, but Mr. Brandon was independent and needed nothing at his hands, and the only thing he could do as a favor was to support with all his might the election of his son, Joe P. Brandon, when he was a candidate for the legislature.

In 1818 the father moved from the Mulberry River to Sweetwater at its junction with Yellow River. Here he lived for many years and here he died in 1832. He was a man of little education, but of strong common sense and good judgment.

He reared a large family, five sons and four daughters. Sam was the oldest and was born in 1795, Abe in 1800, Absolem in 1808, Daniel in 18—, Byrd in 1814.

Sallie, the oldest girl, married Pryor Yates in Tennessee and moved to Texas and for long years has not been heard from. Pollie married David P. Allen and moved to Walker County in its early settlement. Nancy married Miles J. Robinson, son of Tommy Robinson, the wagoner. They went to Harris County and from there to Alabama.

Returning to the sons, Sam was the best informed and to use his own words, was a strong 'polititioner.' He was elected to the legislature in 1844-46. I have written so much of him in the other papers I will not repeat here. He was a fast friend, a Methodist in faith and a Mason in his heart.

I will be indulged here in giving Sam Martin's dream as given me by him in his own peculiar, graphic way. I have met with few men in my life that could tell a story more interestingly than Sam Martin. His blunt and crude expressions and manners of speech made it more so. On my last visit to him, except when on his death bed, he gave me the dream of a few nights before. He had gone back to his old home in Spartanburg which he had not seen in sixty years. There was the old house where he was born as natural as ever, his venerable father sitting in the door mending shoes as was often the case. His mother sat in the other door spinning on a flax wheel as he had often seen her. The old apple tree stood in the yard, redolent with its spring blossoms, and from which he had so often plucked its golden fruit in childhood. The old kitchen in the rear where his mother had so often prepared the family meals, with its creaned chimney of stick and dirt. There was the same old sandy yard, the path to the spring, the old persimmon tree by the side of the path which he had climbed so often for its fruit, the old hollow gum in the spring in which bubbled up the crystal water with which he had slaked his thirst so often in life's young days. All, everything about the old place, was as natural as when he left them sixty years before, and for a while lived over his childhood days again.

No one knows, except the aged, how exquisite is the pleasure of revisiting in long after years the home of childhood and its familiar surroundings even in dreams. It brings back for a time the halcyon days when life was young and sweet. How touchingly and truthfully does Wordsworth sing:

> How dear to my heart are the scenes of my childhood
> When fond recollections present them to view!
> The orchard, the meadow, the deep tangled wildwood
> And every loved spot which my infancy knew;
> The wide spreading pond, and the mill which stood by it,

The bridge and the rock where the cataract fell,
The cot of my father, the dairy house near it,
And e'en the rude bucket that hangs in the well.

Abe, like his brother, Sam, was a strong party man, but never aspired to office. He was a zealous Methodist and Mason. Taking a wild freak in his old age, he moved to Texas. Misfortunes attended after he moved. He was robbed in Atlanta, lost his wife soon after reaching Texas, lost all his children, too, and broken down in health himself he returned to Walker County and soon died.

Absolem was of wonderful manhood, active and strong and of high courage. In many things he was like the others, but with a little of the suave in his manners which was uncommon in the Martins. His politics was the same as the others. I have known three generations of them and in their politics not one of them has degenerated. He held the office of deputy sheriff in this county at one time, the only office he ever held. He died in this county in the prime of life.

Daniel died early in life, not long after becoming of age.

Byrd was of the same type of men as the others of the family. He prospered in business and was hospitable at his home as were all of them. He was a Baptist for several years and a Mason. In his last sickness he adhered to the Old Side Baptists and his Masonry was not questioned. If he had lived, I doubt whether his Masonry would have yielded. He died in 1864.

Old Jack, the negro servant of the old man, gave all the boys nicknames from some peculiar circumstance in each case and these names held on ever after. Samuel was Old Shad, and it is often applied to him still, even since his death. Abraham was Swords, and I have forgotten the others.

The elder Abraham was a Universalist in religion. I have often heard it said that this creed is always renounced on the death bed. In his case at least it was not true. He lived in the faith for fifty years and died in it. I do not defend it, for it is not my faith. It is, however, a liberal view of God's mercy, much more so than that other faith that a large part of the human family was elected to be damned before the world was.

Old Abraham Martin and his wife, Betsy Harris, sleep side by side in old graves at Bethesda. So do Sam and Absolem, and perhaps Daniel and Byrd, and many of the younger members of the family, and probably will many others of them find sepulchers there in this old city of the dead in succeeding years.

1879

THE BERRY FAMILY

During the first decade, or perhaps the early part of the second, of the present century, there came from the backwoods of South Carolina to the poor lands of Hog Mountain and settled near the head spring of the Appalachee a family by the name of Berry, consisting of the old father, then perhaps eighty-five years of age, the aged mother, three sons and three daughters. The father then was very old. Nature with him stood on the very edge of her confines. They were uneducated. None of them could read, write or spell. They were noted for certain traits of character peculiar to them. Of these I propose to speak in this article.

They were among the very first settlers here when all west of the Appalachee was Indian territory, and many of the Cherokees were living within a few miles of the line bordering on that stream. For this reason they are entitled to a place in these sketches.

The father's name was John. Sometimes in his carousals, for old as he was he would drink to excess, he would call himself Old Blue Gray. The first I remember to have seen of him was at the courtground of his district then held at my father's house fifty-five years ago. He was toddling about the grounds, bent almost double with the weight of years, supported by a long staff and drunk as a fiddler. "Hoopee! Old South Carolina forever! The devil and Tom Walker! Here comes Old Blue Gray! Clear the track for Jack Berry." These were some of his utterances that I still remember.

His voice was old and creaky, and his aged and decrepit appearance seemed so unnatural and so unearthly that I was afraid of him and for a time he disturbed my dreams. He died soon after and was buried at the neighboring graveyard. Not a stone or hillock marks his grave and scarcely a man now living remembers him.

John, his oldest son, was not much of the type of his father; not so tall, not so courageous as the father in his young days. He had a family when he came here and was wanting in thrift and industry. By some means he was elected justice of the peace in his district, yet he could not read a summons nor write his name. I never was in his court and do not know how he expounded the law or dispensed justice. From my knowledge of him afterwards, I would think he made a poor squire.

He had but little courage morally or physically, but often prated his manhood and bravery. On one occasion, when he was holding court, he gave offense to one of the Hamiltons, who twitched his nose, but he failed to resent it either personally or officially. In speaking of it afterwards he said in rude rhyme:

If I had not been a 'squire,
I'd have put him behind the fire.

At middle age he became a widower and soon he was gay and dashy. He was attracted by the good looks of the widow of Patrick L. Dunlap, who a few years before killed his wagoner on a trip to Augusta and was executed for it. On his visits to see her, he rode his fine horse, Fly, and always approached her house in a canter to show the movement of his steed and the horsemanship and the gallantry of the rider. These captured her, perhaps, and they were married. She was a nice, clever woman, but as has often been said, there is no accounting for a woman's taste.

Simon, another son, was a different man from John in many particulars. He had more manliness and more courage. He was a man of great physical force and had many encounters at Maltbie's store and at Bogan's and the district courtground with the rough and tumble men of that day. Years afterwards when he became old, he had a terrible affray in Lawrenceville and lost an eye in an encounter with a man who ought to have been his friend. It was a shame.

He, too, became a widower, but was not so gay and gallant as John. I was at his wedding when he married his second wife. He was accompanied on the evening of his wedding by a cavalcade of fifteen or twenty friends on horseback, each one having his lady behind him. On nearing the home of the bride, the speed of the horses was increased to a gallop; and with the same speed, they passed around the house three times, then dismounted and went into the house. The ceremony was said; the bridegroom was required to salute the bride, the 'squire volunteered to do the same, and that part of the show was over.

This was the custom in those days. It was an imposing scene, especially the kissing of the bride, if she was good looking. It had gone out of fashion when I used to marry folks and I did not know whether to be sorry or glad.

The youngest son was James. When he came here he was not married. He was not like Simon, but more like John, both in personal appearance and cast of mind. He delighted in dogs and the chase and always had a pack following his heels. He was as much wedded to his hounds as was Mr. Stephens to his dogs, Rio, Pup and Troup. But his were less behaved about the dinner pots and hens' nests as many of his neighbors' housewives would have testified.

He married the youthful daughter of a respectful gentleman in the neighborhood at the tender age of thirteen. How he succeeded in winning this young girl was only accounted for by an old gentleman who said: "The store coat, green breeches and shoe-boots that he wore captured her, but a school boy with a gingercake could have done the same." This is the best solution of the problem I have ever heard.

An anecdote was attributed to him years ago for the truth of which I cannot vouch. He and his future father-in-law went on a squirrel hunt and were alone for half a day. On their return, just before reaching home, the young man touched him on the shoulder and said: " 'Squire, come this way for I want a word with you." He then asked him for his daughter. To say the least of it the story was well located.

He had a good tract of land and some negroes given him by his wife's father, and by the good management of his wife mainly, he prospered; but his love for the fox chase interested him more than the farm.

At the early settlement of Cobb county he moved there and settled on Big Creek, near the Labon Mills. He was chosen one of the justices of the Inferior Court of that county and was always proud of the title it conferred. It was told of him that in meeting a stranger he would introduce himself as Judge Berry; and as a further introduction would say: "I married the oldest daughter of Squire W., the richest man in Gwinnett County, the granddaughter of Major C., the richest man in Jackson County." This was a weakness he could not help.

After the death of his first wife, he married again and moved to Floyd County. While living there he was accused of robbing the house of William Montgomery. Phil, a negro of Montgomery, made confessions implicating Berry and himself, and Berry was convicted and sent to the penitentiary. Before the expiration of his sentence, the notorious Dr. Roberts was sentenced to the penitentiary from his county, confessed the robbery himself for which Berry was serving. Whereupon Governor H. V. Johnson pardoned Berry. It was a terrible ordeal through which he passed, especially the torture inflicted to force a confession. I never thought him guilty and time proved him innocent. After obtaining his liberty, he moved to Mississippi, and a few years ago, he died at the home of one of his daughters in Cherokee at an advanced age. He reared a large family, and his girls were intelligent, handsome women and all married well.

One more anecdote of him will suffice. Yet many others might be told characteristic of the man. For many years he lived a neighbor to Mathias Bates, near Hog Mountain. He and Mr. Bates were members of the same church and on the best of terms. He would frequently dine with Mr. Bates, who would always ask him to say grace. When Mr. Bates happened to be absent, he would say grace without being asked. Old man Jolly was a shoemaker and a churchman, too. Mr. Bates hired him to come to his house to make his winter shoes. He was as proud to say grace as was Mr. Berry.

During the time he was making these shoes, Mr. Berry happened over one day and remained for dinner, and Mr. Bates was absent. Being seated at the table, both began to say grace at the same time and both continued, one thinking the other would give way. Finally Berry stopped, out of temper, and said: "Jolly, you are a dumed fool. Go on then, dum you." Jolly went on with his grace half as long as a decent prayer, and no doubt felt that he had triumphed.

I had this story from Anthony Bates, a son of old man Bates, who was present and witnessed it. It was a ludicrous scene and excited the risibles of the young man who was afraid to laugh, but couldn't help it. He was afraid of old Jolly and his crutch, was afraid of Berry and afraid of his mother who would tell his father. All these could not restrain him and he laughed.

I cannot refrain at this point from giving a passing tribute to Anthony Bates. He was a clever young fellow of good humor and congenial temperament. He sacrificed his young life in the cause of Texas independence and fell with Fannin and his devoted band near Goliad, Texas, in the fearful massacre ordered by Santa Anna in 1836. Alas! Poor Anthony! I knew him well, a fellow of infinite jest.

Berry never forgave Jolly. He always said afterwards that Jolly was a hypocrite and had no religion.

I turn aside for a moment to moralize. Is it right to give thanks for the blessings of a good Providence who gives us food? This is a duty, but why those long graces? Some seem to think that it is a compliment to their religion to be called on to ask a blessing; and they commence with a grunt and a long breath, a prelude to a long grace. "Be not as the Pharisees who say long prayers to be seen of men." Isaac Adair's grace, "We thank God," was more appropriate than Jolly's or Berry's, usually lasting twenty minutes. In it God was recognized as the Author of the blessings of food and an expression of thanks for the same.

Phil Alston was the first lawyer who came to Lawrenceville when it could boast of a dozen houses, two stores, a blacksmith shop and a jail. Philip was a character. He and others boarded with a widow and she gave them dumplings every day until they had become a sort of nuisance to the boarders. On one occasion the young man who usually asked the blessing was absent and the good hostess called on Colonel Alston. The big dish of dumplings as usual being the prominent dish, the Colonel responded devotedly:

Dumplings are rough, dumplings are tough,
My good Mrs. Simpkins, we've had dumplings enough!

The spirit of the blessing was speedy and dumplings disappeared for a season.

Many other anecdotes peculiar to Mr. Berry could be given, but my space will not allow it. He was for a long time a Methodist, a campmeeting Methodist, and enjoyed the annual recurrences of those occasions. With many natural foibles, imperfect training in his youth and young manhood, at heart I think he was a Christian.

I have narrated with some freedom and at some length the history of the Berry family. They were among the very first settlers in this county and were noted men in the new and crude times of which I write. I have done so with little reserve and perhaps with more liberty than I ought. My main purpose was to delineate character in crude and uncultivated state that was common among our pioneer population fifty or sixty years ago.

I have written freely of my subjects. Some of them were my kin. We may be allowed to talk or write about our kin, if we do not praise them too much. That would be bad taste. I am sure that I will not be thus charged by those who read this article.

A change comes over the spirit of my dream. Fifty years ago the Berrys were a large family. Where are they now? Dead, mostly, and well nigh forgotten. Those of them who survive are scattered to the far southwest and the name here has become extinct. All things are passing away and so we go.

1871

JAMES HAWTHORNE

The subject of this sketch was not among the first settlers of this county, not coming here till 1832, but his uprightness and integrity as a man and citizen deserve a brief biographical sketch in these papers. It must necessarily be brief, for I have but little data to cull from. My personal acquaintance with him was too limited to furnish much from my own recollection of him.

Mr. Hawthorne was born in Abbeville District, South Carolina, on the 15th day of February, 1807, and he came to this county in the fall of 1832. He settled on the poor white lands of Haynes Creek, a section of this county like Hog Mountain, Ben Smith's, and the section from Lawrenceville to Logansville, that our people in the early settlement of the county considered too poor to sprout peas and fit for nothing only to hold the balance of the world together.

Mr. Hawthorne had a number of slaves; and with their labor and his own personal supervision, he soon opened a farm on this poor land and to the astonishment of the old settlers made more cotton and better crops than those living on rich red lands of the county.

Contemporaneous with him was Levi M. Cooper, who settled in the same section upon the same quality of poor land. It was soon found out that James Hawthorne and Levi Cooper were getting rich faster on their poor lands than the farmers on their rich red lands.

I will be indulged to give some of my own personal recollections of the section of Haynes Creek. My father was a stock raiser in the early times. When the range was eaten up on the Appalachee and Yellow Rivers his cattle were moved down on Haynes Creek where the reed was better and the land too poor to even be settled and the range disturbed. This was the idea in those days, but Hawthorne, Cooper and others soon spoiled this calculation and by their demonstration and success dispelled the delusion, and proved that these white lands along Haynes Creek, as well as at Hog Mountain, Ben Smith's, and the section towards Logansville were the best farming lands in the county, and so they are.

An old friend coming from South Carolina many years ago used to say that there was a section of South Carolina in his young days known as the poor lands of Hoo Warry. It was settled by a hardy, industrious people, and when he left there it was called the rich lands of Hoo Warry. So it may be said of these sections of our county referred to; and the fact that much of their value for agricultural purposes was developed by James Hawthorne, Levi M. Cooper and others.

Mr. Hawthorne's wife was Louisa Rutledge, of Anderson, South Carolina, to whom he was married July 30, 1829. She was to my knowledge a most estimable Christian lady. Mr. Hawthorne and his wife were orderly Presbyterians and members at Fairview, but in the absence of the old church book, I can not give the dates of their connection with the church.

They reared a small family. I knew of but three sons. Terrell C. Hawthorne was a man of great energy and enterprise. In 1853 he moved to Mississippi and settled in Tishamingo County, near Corinth, and died there in 1856. My old friend, John Morrow, used to say: "Terrell Hawthorne shortened his days by excessive use of tobacco, and excessive, hard work on his farm.

The other two sons, James O. and David C., are still citizens here and are worthy members of society and honor their father.

Mr. Hawthorne died in May, 1847, in the very prime of life. His wife, after her husband's death, married James W. Plummer.

1871

James Jackson

For plain, unpretending honesty and uprightness in all his aims and purposes in life, not one of our early population surpassed James Jackson. He was one of the old school, now so rare if not entirely extinct, that everybody could trust; one whose word was as good as his bond; one that attended to his own business and meddled with nobody; one that labored diligently with his own hands to provide for his household; one who performed all the duties incumbent upon him as a citizen, a neighbor, a church member and an honest man. Without ambition save to do his duty, to provide for his family, to keep a good repute for honesty and fair dealing, to rear his children to be honest and upright men and women and to serve his Maker faithfully were his chief aims in life.

James Jackson was born in Virginia or North Carolina in 1782. In 1809 he married Nancy Pennall. He came to Gwinnett County in 1821 and settled on Yellow River, five miles west of Lawrenceville, on a tract of land purchased by him and Ely Massey jointly. He lived there 38 years and died there in 1863. He erected a plain, comfortable farm house with outhouses to correspond, cleared a farm and spent more than a third of a century in peace and contentment.

To live in a mansion is desirable with some; to race along the streets and highways in style gratifies the pride of others; to be rich and the possessors of large estates are the aims and aspirations of many; but these bring not happiness. Gilded pleasures are only for the moment and perish in their using. For

> Happy the man whose wish and care
> A few paternal acres bound,
> Content to breathe his native air
> In his own ground.
> Sound sleep by night, study and ease,
> Together mixed sweet recreation,
> And innocence which most doth please
> With meditation.
> Thus let me live unseen, unknown,
> Thus unmolested let me die.
> Steal from the world and not a stone
> Tells where I lie.

Mr. Jackson, in his plain home and in the midst of his few paternal acres, surrounded by wife, children and friends, was contented and happy. Such a life with such surroundings is the sweetest part of earthly enjoyment.

After his death, the old home fell into other hands and soon the old house was torn down and the old patriarchal oaks surrounding it are deadened and the plowshares tear up the old yard and desolation riots around the old place. These old dwelling places of the fathers and their surroundings should be preserved. This is especially true, if they descend to the children. But it is not so here as may be witnessed on every hand. The old homestead of a venerable old man long ago dead and where he resided for half a century is gone. The old house in some cases may be standing, but unoccupied and dilapidated and ready to fall, chimneys down, shade trees dead. Desolation marks the place where life and peace and contentment once reigned supreme. This destruction of the old homes with their wide spreading trees is reprehensible. When thus seen the poet's lines find utterance:

> Woodman, spare that tree,
> Touch not a single bough,
> In youth it sheltered me
> And I'll protect it now.

In his early days Mr. Jackson connected himself with the Redland Baptist Church, a mile and a half west of Lawrenceville. The church stood where the James K. Craig home now is located. Rev. Mitchell Bennett was pastor at that time. When differences arose among the Baptists Mr. Jackson went with neither side, but kept neutral. He, James P. Simmons, B. H. Lamkin, John M. Thompson and others kept the Redland Church alive. Mr. Jackson, however, finally joined Friendship Church. In his religious views he was broad-minded, claiming the right to his own views and conceding the same right to others.

In politics he was rigid and had but little patience with those who were not for General Andrew Jackson. General Jackson was his political polar star. His neighbors were on the other side to his annoyance and disgust. An incident shows his zeal as a Democrat and his fidelity to Old Hickory and his party.

All the neighbors were invited to a corn shucking at Tommy Robinson's. After the corn was shucked and everyone had gathered at the house for supper, Mr. B., who was a Whig and who assumed to know more about politics than any one else, introduced the subject of politics by denouncing General Jackson both in politics and morals. He ridiculed Mr. Jackson for supporting Old Hickory. Mr. Jackson denied the accusations as to morality. Mr. B., to clinch his charge, said: "I will swear to the truth of it." Replying, Mr. Jackson said: "If you will swear to that, you would swear that a crow is a white horse feeding in a meadow." This put Mr. B. on his mettle and the controversy culminated in hot blood that took a long time to cool.

1872

EVAN HOWELL

Evan Howell was born in Cabarrus County, North Carolina, October 23, 1782. In early life he was an invalid and went on crutches. Being poor and disabled to do hard labor, he learned the saddler's trade by which he might earn a livelihood. Recovering in a few years, he married and began farming. He and his wife were the laborers. Soon he borrowed money and purchased a negro girl, and soon after began selling goods on a small scale in his native county.

Fifty years ago, he moved to Georgia and settled on the Chattahoochee River in this county where he died. For half a century he was a citizen of Gwinnett County and one of the best. Here he carried on his farming industry and continued to sell goods, both of which were a success. He did a large credit business for a country store, was indulgent to his customers, yet a close collector.

In those days it was common for people to get in debt and settle by running away. Some at first would attempt to settle with Mr. Howell in this way, but were always unsuccessful. He pursued them, was sure to overtake them and sure always to get his money. The frequent occurrences of this sort and his unvariable success soon established for him such a character that those contemplating settlement in this way would always settle with Mr. Howell before leaving.

I never heard of but one instance in which he was well nigh baffled. James White, who was a shrewd, cunning man, got in everybody's debt, Mr. Howell's as well. He ran away and Mr. Howell pursued him, doubting his ability to collect, for he had a keen insight into White's character and well understood his cunning. White expected it, and afterwards remarked that he feared no one but Howell. He had been gone for several hours and thought by this time Howell must be close after him, and to elude him he took the back track for home, but went in a zigzag way. Howell lost his track which threw him into confusion; but soon recovering from his confusion he concluded that he must have returned home; which was correct, for White had returned, crossed the river, took down its bank and went home. Mr. Howell returned by a different route and getting in the rear of White's house met him starting off again. Of course White had to pay the debt.

Mr. Howell was very unlike old John Phinazy in one particular at least. Phinazy was a merchant and a Dutchman. One of his customers ran away indebted to him and others. Mr. Phinazy was informed of it the next morning by another of the man's creditors. Scratching his head and thinking for a moment he said: "Well, he may go to the debil, I ish got his note."

Mr. Howell was a shrewd business man, with strong sense, keen insight into the character of men, self-reliant and of great perseverance. He amassed a large estate of land, negroes and money, and did it by his energy and good judgment, seldom making a mistake in his business transactions.

He reared four sons, all shrewd, intelligent men, following somewhat in the footsteps of their illustrious father, and three daughters who are all intelligent ladies. The lawsuit growing out of the settlement of his estate may be noted as an unfortunate finale to Mr. Howell. He labored, toiled by day and by night to amass property. He underwent hardships and privations through a long life to heap up the paltry things of this world, not knowing who shall gather them. Bickering, strife and heart burnings result to his offspring therefor and will probably not be healed for generations, for it is easier "to take a city than to reconcile a brother." Such is life. Men toil through summer's heat and winter's cold to make money, and for what? To create enmity and hatred among his children when he is gone. Rather let me die my own executor.

Mr. Howell, for a life long period, was in sentiment a religious man of the Baptist persuasion. He often expressed his great confidence in Christ, His love, His mercy, His justice. He joined the Primitive Baptist Church at Sweetwater in 1867 and was baptized in the blue waters of the Chattahoochee River near his own home at his own request. It was fit and proper. This beautiful stream had rolled onward and onward in its meanderings to the Gulf near by his home for fifty years. No doubt he had many a conflict with the mortal enemy of our race near its limpid waters and it was fit and proper that he should give testimony to his triumph over that enemy in his last days by being buried in baptism beneath its pellucid waters, and it was well.

I always loved the Chattahoochee for the grandeur of its flow, for its gentle waves, its quiet ripples and the poetry of its name. Many years agone its placid waters were ripped by the rude canoe of the Cherokee Indians and its limpid waves washed the tawny limbs of his tribe. Where, now, is that tribe? Where are the agile forms that once sported in its majestic waters? His bones have long since been buried in the far off land of the setting sun and his spirit gone to its happy hunting grounds.

But the noble stream still moves on and on and on in its ceaseless flow.

The writer knew Mr. Howell long. I remember vividly his neat personal appearance, his silvered locks, his peculiar face and gentlemanly deportment. He was always cordial to me and those coming after me. He may have had his foibles, the common inheritance of mortal man, but in this brief passing tribute I will say: For his memory I cherish the kindest regards.

1879

WILLIAM KING

The subject of my present sketch was born in Lancaster District, South Carolina, near the time of the signing of the Declaration of Independence, perhaps a few years before that period. In early life he moved to Georgia and settled on the Mulberry River in Jackson County, where he resided for a number of years. About the date of 1825 he moved to this county and settled on Beaver Ruin Creek where he died in 1852 on his birthday at the age of eighty-three years.

Before coming to Georgia he married Jerusha Harris, of Anderson, South Carolina, in 1808. He reared six sons and four daughters, five of whom are deceased. His son, William, occupies the old homestead of his father, and his youngest daughter, Mrs. F. M. Buchanan, with her husband and children, live nearby the old residence. The others have moved to different parts.

Mr. King was a type of the better class of the population that settled here some sixty years ago. In temperament he was quiet, sedate and circumspect in all his actions and blameless in his life. He had no ambitions to be great in the world's eye, but was ambitious to live in peace with his neighbors, to provide properly for his family and to serve his Maker faithfully in his day and generation. These, and especially the latter, were the acme of his purposes in life and these were fully achieved by him.

Today in company with an old friend who has been here longer than any one living, we passed the old residence of John Boring where he settled sixty years ago. Our conversation turned to the Boring family, who lived there long years ago, of old Johnny, the father, of Isaac and Jesse and other members of the family. He knew them well and so did I. A better family than the Borings never lived here. In speaking of the father my friend said: "When I was a boy living two miles away there were two men in this neighborhood against whom nothing could be said. Their lives and conduct were so orderly and blameless that the tongue of the slanderer did not dare to say one word against them, and these were old Johnny Boring and old Billy King." This was speaking the truth better than I could say it, and a more appropriate eulogy on the lives and memory of these good men than I have the ability to pronounce. Yet, I felt that it was deserved and true in every respect.

Mr. King was a Methodist all his life and a Christian, not in name only but in faith and hope, having the witness of the Spirit through a long life. He lived in a day when there was no incentive to hypocrisy in religion among the pioneer people then living here. His religion was Christianity in earnest. Is it so now? We will not stop to moralize or to criticise.

Recurring to the history of the first Methodist church in the county, erected near the house of Benjamin Watts, not far from the Mulberry River, we find William King, Benjamin Watts, Root Thompson, Joseph Thompson and others among its first members. This was more than 65 years ago. This church soon had a large membership. To make it more convenient to their residences, William King, William Brandon, John Brown, Joseph Comer, Larkin Brown and others branched off and built Sardis Church with William King and William Brandon as first class leaders, and Rev. Wiley Warwick as first pastor.

Sardis Church soon had a large membership. Time in its cycle has carried that devoted band to the grave except William S. Harris, an old friend, who is the last survivor of the first years of Sardis, his membership now being at New Hope.

With the removal of Mr. King to his new home on Beaver Ruin in 1825, he connected himself with Boring's meeting house, now Bethesda. Here he was connected in Christian fellowship with John Boring, Isaac Boring, Sr., Isaac Boring, Jr., Jesse Boring, Daniel Clower and his sons, John and Daniel Pentecost and many others who worshipped in better days of long ago. At a later date and for his own convenience as well as for the convenience of his neighborhood, he and others erected a new church, which from its locality, was called Center. It was southwest from Mt. Carmel, southeast from Flint Hill, due west from Bethesda and about equidistant from each. Center was constituted with Mr. King as its first class leader and was taken into the plan of the circuit. With the other churches in the circuit Center had its regular preaching appointments for a time and had a good membership and fair prosperity. It was finally left out of the preacher's appointments, it was claimed, on account of its proximity to other churches and was thenceforth discontinued. From its organization to its dissolution Mr. King was its class leader as I remember, and its chief supporter; and near the site of this old church lie buried all that is mortal of the venerable William King. A few years before his death it was my privilege to entertain him a day or two at the old Lawrenceville Campground on a campmeeting occasion. He had reached the octogenarian age. I felt it to be a privilege to minister to the temporal comfort of so good a man. His personal appearance then was striking, full six feet in height, of large frame and patriarchal in his bearing, tottering under the weight of years and his head covered with the snows of eighty winters. His garb was in the style of the disciples of Wesley's in the early times of Methodism, straight vested coat with vest to correspond and, taken all in all, he was to my mind an exemplar and type of the old patriarchs in the days of the Savior's sojourn upon the earth.

Briefly and impartially I have attempted to portray the life and Christian character of William King. His life was a living commentary of the truth of the Christian religion and many of his descendants emulate the example of their illustrious predecessor.

1879

John Sammon

Away back in the early times in this county there came to its frontier settlement from the county of Elbert two families, the heads of which were William Richardson and John Sammon. The first named settled on the Maltbie place on the east bank of the Appalachee River, and the other near by at the Isham Williams old place at its head spring. These families were closely related, Mr. Sammon having married the stepdaughter of Mr. Richardson.

Their removal here was at the early period of 1824, two or three years after the county was laid out. Their residences were in the immediate neighborhood of my father's, and although an urchin at the time, I well remember their coming. These families were considered a valuable acquisition to the then rude and rough population that inhabited that new section known as Hog Mountain.

Of Mr. Sammon I come now to speak more directly. I shall probably speak of Mr. Richardson in another chapter.

Mr. Sammon was born in Greenville District, South Carolina, on December 14, 1782. In 1814 he married Elizabeth Harrison who survived but a year or two, leaving one child. After her death he was greatly discomfited and sought relief in travel. Leaving his little girl with her grandmother, he went West, first to Natchez, Miss., and then to New Orleans, but distance and new scenes brought him no relief. The memory of his loved and lost wife preyed upon his working hours as his night's visions were on her sweet babe she had left behind. Soon he returned home and on May 28, 1827, he married Mary B. Harrison, a sister of his former wife. The two wives of Mr. Sammon were the step-daughters of Mr. Richardson, and the daughters of Clem King Harrison, a resident of South Carolina, a gentleman of high spirit and intelligence who, in a difficulty, committed a homicide, and to escape a prosecution fled to Spain, but was afterwards arrested, brought back and suffered the penalty of the law.

Of his children two were the wives of John Sammon, one the wife of James Baskin, another the wife of Mathew Wynn, and his only son, the late Major Mat J. Williams, who is well remembered by many of our people and for a long time a resident of Lawrenceville and a lawyer of great ability. He, like his father, was high spirited and a courtly gentleman. He received his education at the military school at West Point, was an accomplished scholar and every inch a gentleman. I might say much more of him, of his urbanity, his talents, his genial social qualities, but space will not permit.

By his first marriage Mr. Sammon was the father of one child, a little girl, to whom her mother's name was given. Long years ago she and I were pupils of the late Rev. John S. Wilson at the old academy in Lawrenceville. We were near the same age and about fourteen. Mr. Wilson was principal with Miss Emily Cooly, a maiden lady from Massachusetts, as assistant, having charge of the girls. Mr. John Norton, who was prosecuting his studies in the higher branches, would hear the recitations in the advanced classes twice a day.

In referring to Miss Cooly, I desire to say that she was an accomplished lady of perhaps forty-five years, kind and agreeable in the school, a first class instructor, and had the esteem of the whole school, both boys and girls. I had very great respect for her because of her marked kindness to me. Talk about Yankee 'schoolmarms'. They were spoken of with derision sometimes. If a boy had spoken thus of her in my presence, he would have waked up cain in a difficulty at once.

My little friend, Elizabeth, was a beautiful girl just budding into womanhood, with large blue eyes expressive of intelligence and a confiding nature, golden hair in profusion in beautiful ringlets and a young form that was faultless as a fairy. The friendship of our families made us friends; and after these long years when she is dead and I am falling into the sere and yellow leaf, I recall our pleasant times at the old academy in the happy days of life's young dream. When grown to womanhood, she married Cooper Bennett, son of Rev. Mitchell Bennett, for a long time pastor of Redland Baptist Church, and soon moved to Alabama. A few years ago she was left a widow. After the death of her husband, one of her daughters married Nathan Strickland, the youngest son of Oliver P. Strickland, and with them she went to Texas. While engaged in her household duties, she was badly burned which resulted in her death. Alas! A tear glistens in the eye when I think of the horrible death of my early friend.

Mr. Sammon and his second wife reared fourteen children, five sons and eight daughters: John, Menasseh L., William, Edwin D., and Robert; Mrs. O. P. Strickland, Mrs. James C. Dunlap, Mrs. Stiles Liddell, Mrs. G. T. Rakestraw, Mrs. Moncrief, Mrs. John M. Mills, Misses Mary and Laura, both married, but their husbands' names I do not recall. The second wife of Mr. Rakestraw was also one of the daughters. After a year's residence at the old Williams place, Mr. Sammon purchased a place on the Alcova River and settled there the next year where he lived until his death September 12, 1850, being 68 years old.

In his religious faith he was a Baptist, as were his wife and most of her people, but never joined the church for the reason as he said that he could not fellowship many church members whom he knew to be hypocrites and scoundrels. He was a first class citizen for 25 years or more, with good morals and habits, and his life and good example were worthy of emulation by those who come after him.

1879

RICHARD WHITWORTH

The Whitworth family has been an extensive and influential one in this county for over fifty years. The elder members of it were five brothers: Richard, Charles, Hiram, William, and John C.

Richard and Charles were twins. Charles never lived in Georgia, but resided in South Carolina and died there. William lived in Madison County, and represented that county in the legislature, being a Whig in politics. Hiram was also a Whig in his day, but Richard and John were Democrats of the old school.

Richard was born in Pendleton District, now Pickins, South Carolina, on February 3, 1790. From there he moved to Franklin County, now Madison County, Georgia, when he was but a boy. Here he married Mary Barnes December 31, 1811, and lived there ten years. In the land lotteries drawn in Gwinnett, Walton, Hall, and Habersham counties, he drew lot 253 in the fifth land district in Gwinnett County and moved to it in December, 1820. Here he resided from that day till March 24, 1857, the date of his death. The old homestead upon which he lived is now owned and occupied by his son, James O. Whitworth.

Mr. Whitworth reared a large family, eleven in number, five sons and six daughters. The sons are Charles, Hiram, Isaac, Asbury and James. Isaac and Asbury are deceased, but the other three still live here and have a striking resemblance of their father, both in looks and actions. Hiram and James held the office of justice of the peace in their respective districts, and James was deputy sheriff for two terms. The others, like their father, never sought office.

Of the six daughters one married W. A. Nunnally, one Elijah Mathis, one James Morris, one Dozier T. White, one Stephen Etchison, and Miss Sarah, the youngest, is unmarried.

In writing of the father and his sons, I will be pardoned for a seeming digression in referring to Hiram and some incidents in which he and I were the chief actors during the late war. He at the time referred to was nearly exempt by age from the conscript officer, but not quite. His only son was already in the army and he was the only male member left and had entered a branch of the service likely to be nearer home and less arduous than regular service. With this he became dissatisfied and applied to me. I was in position then to relieve him from the heavy duties of a soldier and give him service as carrier of supplies from the railroad, a service as important and valuable to the Confederacy as if in the ranks of the army. This would enable him to visit his home three times a week. With some difficulty this was accomplished and with his wagon and splendid team of mules he transported the supplies from depot No. 12 to Stone Mountain with full satisfaction to the agent.

Another difficulty came up. The impressing officer made his way here after mules and horses and got his eye on Hiram's fine mules and went for them. The owner was indignant, outraged, and the officer was told that he could not get them, that they were already in the service of the government. The officer treated his statement with contempt, said he had heard such tales too often to be cheated by them and should take the mules. Failing to bluff or convince him, he brought him to the Major as a final resort who presided over depot No. 12 to substantiate his statement; and the Major, outranking the Corporal, ordered the mules released. The fact of being taken out of the army when he was getting old and saving his mules will never be forgotten by Hiram Whitworth and he will never be accused of ingratitude so prevalent with many people. And by way of parenthesis I will say that he and one other citizen, G. W. F. C., contributed of their substance for the support of the army more liberally and less reluctantly than any others of our people. Many did well and satisfactory to the agent, many others tried to evade in every way possible. Such is the truth of history.

Richard Whitworth, like all the Whitworths I have known, had a streak of fun and mischief in him. When perpetrated a joke on a friend, as a prelude to it he would take off his hat and put his hand on the top of his head and a joke or some fun was sure to follow at somebody's expense. Anything said at his expense would be followed by an energetic rub on his bald crown.

Many years ago when Madison was the principal market for our people, Mr. Whitworth and his neighbors would carry their cotton there. Early in the season he had sold some bales there and the buyers in sampling would complain of trash in it. This was an excuse for giving less than the top of the market. Upon his return home he decided to pick out one bale with his own hands and have not a bit of trash in it. On his next trip this bale was carried. When sampled not a speck of trash could be seen. "What say you now? I reckon you can give me the top of the market for that." No, it was too white. If it were a little creamy it would bring the top but it was too white. This was too much for Mr. Whitworth. Placing his hand on his head he ejaculated energetically: "Our cotton is never right with you. It is either too trashy or too clean and white. The whole of you cotton buyers ought to be in h---." The experience of Mr. Whitworth is but the experience of farmers generally even till yet.

Long ago before the war and before the enactment of the internal revenue laws, Mr. Whitworth had a distillery. All who wished could still their fruit into brandy and their corn into whiskey without a license from the government for the privilege and without the intervention of the gauger and inspector, and men could sell their liquors by paying a small tax to the state and county for retailing.

Mr. Whitworth had a neighbor who was fond of whiskey and his name was John Harris. I do not mean my old friend, Squire John Cupp Harris, nor Blue John Harris, nor Stiff-leg John, nor either of the forty John Harrises who still live here, but I mean that other John Harris long since gone to Davy Jones or somewhere else and left no kin. One morning especially, and most mornings particularly, John Harris wanted a dram, but had no money or credit, and to obtain it had to resort to strategem. Snow fresh fallen was on the ground. In crossing a stream on his way to the still he came to a large poplar. Taking from his pocket a coon's foot, he made tracks with it in the snow towards the poplar tree as if going up it. Then going on to the still house and knowing Mr. Whitworth's love for a coon fight informed him that he had found a coon's den and the tracks in the snow going to it; and if he would give him a big dram of whiskey, he would show it to him. His terms were complied with. Calling for his boys and others with their axes and dogs, they repaired to the place. There was the big poplar tree and the coon tracks as he had represented. The dogs could not smell it. "Cut it down, boys, for it must be there," said Mr. Whitworth. After some length of time and hard cutting, it fell with a loud crash that could be heard for some distance; but no coon was there nor hadn't been. Rubbing his head nervously he said: "John Harris, you have lied, you made those tracks yourself, you scoundrel." "Now, stop a moment, Mr. Whitworth, you see the big poplar, don't you?" "Yes." "You see the coon tracks, don't you?" "Yes." "But you don't see no coon?" "No." "Well, two truths for one lie does mighty well for John Harris."

Mr. Whitworth was noted in his settlement as a good and generous neighbor. Ready at all times to do good for his friends as many now living can testify. In religion he was a Methodist and was a member at old New Hope Church which was located near the Alcova River a short distance below Harbins bridge, with old Davy Pruett, Joshua Bradford and others of his fellow members.

His remains lie in the graveyard at old Shiloh Church about one hundred yards over the line in Walton County, as do also those of his brothers, Hiram and John C. Whitworth.

1879

Robert S. Adair

Mr. Adair was born in South Carolina in the year 1783, just at the close of the American Revolution. He descended from one of the old families of the Adairs of Scotland where all the Adairs in Europe and America originally sprang from, according to tradition handed down from generation to generation. His great grandfather, Robin Adair, was the boon companion of Robert Burns, the Scottish bard. In one of his lyrics Burns wrote of Adair:

> "There was no fun at the fair
> Because Robin Adair was not there."

It was said of him: "He was a decided character, a good peacemaker, of jovial good humor, witty and wise. At all public places he would have a crowd around him listening to his witticisms and songs." Some of his descendants emigrated to Ireland, some to

England. His son, Robert, went to England, and his son, Robert, married Sir John Sidney's daughter, emigrated to America and settled in the colony of Virginia. Before leaving England he named one of his sons after both grandfathers, Robert Sidney. This son married a widow, Elizabeth Huffman, née Posey, who had two children, Adam and Sally. This marriage took place in 1774, and these were the parents of the subject of this sketch.

At the beginning of the war with the mother country he enlisted in the war for independence and served four years in Virginia, his adopted state. In common with the Whigs of that day, he suffered from the depredations of the Tories. During one of their forays in his absence they captured all his negroes, eighteen in number, his wagons and horses, sacked his house, destroyed his beds and bedding and all the family's subsistence, leaving them destitute of even the necessities of life. On being informed of his family's destitute condition, he obtained a furlough and a transfer to the army of South Carolina. Upon his return home he found that the worst had not been told. All his property was gone and his family penniless. He at once refugeed to South Carolina, where some of his wife's relatives, the Poseys, the Stringers and other old Virginia neighbors, lived. As soon as he could procure a temporary home for his family he reported for duty to General Marion's command. The same troubles awaited them there. The Tories were more numerous and lawless there than in Virginia and to these he gave special attention and many a heartless devil bit the dust.

News of the surrender of Cornwallis reached them and he and others started for their homes. Upon nearing his home, he was fired upon by a squad of Tories and killed. This was three weeks before the birth of our present subject who was well called Robert Sidney in honor of his father.

Mr. Adair's wife, Patsey Lefevre, was related to the distinguished Lefevre family, originally of France, late of South Carolina. Her mother was a widow named Milliner Letcher, whose maiden name was Key. Her father was of the large connection of the Key family, of Virginia, some of whom moved from there to South Carolina and some to Georgia.

In November, 1818, Mr. Adair moved to this county and settled on a farm on Yellow River about four miles north of Lawrenceville. Samuel Maloney, who had married his sister, Nancy, in South Carolina, moved here with him and settled on the other side of the river on what has since been known as the McDill place. They arrived on the first of December and built them a tent as a temporary residence.

This was just before the fifth land district of this county was surveyed. Here he lived four years and then bought a tract of land one and a half miles north of Lawrenceville and moved to it in the fall of 1822. In a few years he had opened a good farm, built a good house and here he lived in peace, quiet and contented, for many years, and here he died.

He was an indulgent parent, but firm in his family government, teaching his children obedience and good morals.

In politics he was an old line Whig, always voting for his political friends. He held the office of justice of the peace in the town district for a term and the position of justice of the Inferior Court four years. When the lands of the Cherokees were to be drawn for, he was appointed to take the names of those in this county entitled to a chance in the lottery.

In 1834 he connected himself with the Baptist Church at New Hope, not far from his residence. His wife was also a member of the same church. He was appointed a delegate from his church to represent it at an association to be held in Walton County. Here he made the acquaintance of the distinguished Jesse Mercer, who was the leading Baptist minister of Georgia in his day. He was much pleased with Mr. Mercer and his preaching. From him Mr. Adair purchased a hymn book, the old Mercer's Cluster, now out of print except an old copy occasionally found in Baptist families and treasured as an heirloom, a relic of a bygone age. At this meeting of the association he subscribed for The Christian Index, then edited by Mr. Mercer, and the organ of the Baptist denomination in Georgia. The Index then, as now, was an exponent of foreign missions, and from time to time published missionary information from Burma, Calcutta and other places, and especially Mr. Judson's letters. Elijah Moore was the pastor at New Hope and would often call on Judge Adair, then the church clerk. On his visits, the preacher would criticise The Index, find fault with its missionary articles, and ridicule Mr. Adair, his friend and brother, for being so weak-minded as to take such a paper, or to indorse its teachings, and for doing so ought to be dealt with by the church. At the next conference, Mr. Adair, the clerk, stated that he had discovered that there was a difference of opinion among the members and that the pastor, Brother Moore, differed radically from them as to the question of missions, as well as on other questions of church polity, and before the storm came, Mr. Adair said: "I move that you authorize your clerk to make out a letter of dismission to each member so that they may be free to connect themselves with any church they please." The motion was put and carried and New Hope from that day ceased to live and has never been reorganized.

The immediate family of Judge Adair consisted of two daughters and four sons. Elizabeth married Moses A. Brandon in 1837 and died of consumption in Cass County in 1847. Patsy married Joseph A. Young in 1843 and died in Cass County in 1846. Madison Lefevre, the oldest son, lives in Lawrenceville, and was for two or more terms the efficient clerk of the superior court of this county, and married the daughter of Berryman Camp of Jackson County. Robert Sidney Adair now lives in Thomasville, Georgia, and married, first, a daughter of James Hood, and then a Miss Price. Terry Jackson Adair died in 1868, and William M. Adair was killed at Gettysburg in the army of Northern Virginia July 4, 1863.

Up to 1853 the health of Judge Adair was remarkably good for one of his age. His health then began to decline and on September 1, 1854, he died of dropsy and was buried at Fairview.

His widow survived until July 23, 1869, and died at the old homestead.

Many other incidents of this family have been furnished me running back to their far off ancestry, which would be interesting to the reader, but for want of space they must be left out of this article. From a long personal acquaintance with Robert S. Adair, I bear testimony of his moral worth, his uprightness as a Christian, his integrity as a citizen, and to his honesty as a man. In all these commendable traits, he had his equals perhaps, but in these he was not excelled.

1879

John Lietch

It would hardly be excusable perhaps if I were to leave out of my sketches the very aged man, lately deceased, whose name heads this article. I have often been requested to write of him since I began my new series, even while he lived, and the request was predicated on the fact that he was so old, the oldest man by far in the county and had been in the county so long. His coming here was so far back in the dim distant past that the memory of the oldest inhabitant now living runneth not to the contrary. And then so little could be said of him, except that he was so old, that I could hardly venture with so scanty material of facts and incidents to attempt even a brief biography of him; but he is dead at last. His sun that brightened his pathway for more than a hundred years has set and after living to see four generations pass away, he at last sleeps in his grave.

What wonderful events have transpired since John Lietch first opened his eyes upon this green earth. Empires have risen, flourished and passed away. Dynasties have come and gone and are forgotten. Britain's idiot king since then ruled this continent; the patriots of his American colonies with Washington at their head wrested them from his control and sent his myrmidons back in defeat to their imbecile master, and American freedom has been established for our beautiful land. All this has occurred since John Lietch lived.

He was a native of Scotland and was born probably between 1770 and 1775. When he first came to the United States no one now living knows. Where he lived before coming to this county is unknown to me. He came to this county at its earliest settlement, as early as 1818 or 1820. The first traces I have of him are that he settled in the western part of the county, near Choice's store, a memorable place in the early annals of the county, with John Choice as its figurehead. He lived in the neighborhood of the place until his death, a period of sixty years.

For many years of his later days he lived in a little old house on the pinnacle of a sharp hill on the Decatur road one mile west of the old store of John Choice on a small, poor farm, upon which he made a scanty subsistence by industry and economy, working with his own hands until he was more than a hundred years old. I never knew him well personally, never talked with him nor was in his company but once.

In the month of December, 1868, eleven years before his death, in passing from Atlanta to my home, I came to his residence near nightfall. He had just driven his little brindle yoke of oxen in front of his house with a load of wood, cut and loaded with his own hands. I was in a hurry, but yielding to the desire to shake hands and have a little talk, I turned my horse and accosted him. "How are you, Mr. Lietch?" He returned my salutation as that of a stranger. "You don't know me, but you know my father," calling his name. "O yes, I knowed your fadder and always voted wid him and Billy Nesbitt." "And you knew my old brother-in-law, William Maltbie." "Yes, yes. He was a good man. I voted for him and Jim Wardlaw for first clerks of this county." "How old are you?" I asked. "Goin' on ninety tree." "That is mighty old, but Uncle Bob Martin of Milton is one hundred and four, they say." "Dat beats me." "How much was your weight when you were in your prime, Mr. Lietch?" "A hundred and terty was my best."

Then grasping his withered hand I bade him goodbye, and never saw him again.

He had been married twice, but I knew nothing of his family except his son, Archibald, who was long a citizen here and was a good, honorable citizen. He went West twenty or more years ago.

In early times, he was a Whig and always voted with Billy Nesbit, his near neighbor. What his religion was I never knew. It is a tradition that he was quite peaceable and industrious, and held the undivided respect of his neighbors. His long life and his death teaches a moral.

God's fiat is: man must die; death comes to all; some in childhood; some in youth's gay morn; some in middle life; some at sexagenarian age; fewer still at seventy; scarce any at eighty; and not one in a million lives to a hundred. Yet John Lietch went beyond this, and yet he, too, died. After his long life, he is now in his grave and sleeps well!

The flight of years long ago with thee begun
Has laid them down in their last sleep.
The dead reign there alone.
So dost thou rest; and thou hast withdrawn
From the living and no friends
Take note of thy departure.
All that breathe will share thy destiny.
The gay will laugh when thou art gone,
The solemn brood of care plod on;
Yet all these shall leave their mirth
And their employment and shall come
And make their bed with thee.

1879

David Pruett

Mr. Pruett was a son of David Pruett of South Carolina. Very little is known of the ancestors of the family. It is believed they came from Virginia to South Carolina, but nothing definite can now be learned of their origin.

The subject of this sketch was born about the year 1772. Of his early life we can gather very little. His education was quite limited, such as was obtained then in what we call the old field or backwoods school. He married Elizabeth Mobley of South Carolina. They were the parents of seven children, four sons and three daughters, all born perhaps before coming to Georgia. Mr. Pruett came to this state in 1822 and settled in what was known as Cut Off district in Walton County, where he remained one year and then moved to Gwinnett County and settled on Shoal Creek, the place where his son, Martin, now lives and remained there until his death, in 1855. He was not very extensively known, seemed never to have a desire to extend his acquaintance beyond the community where he resided.

He was of that class of men who live at home, took very little interest in public affairs, had no great ambition to become rich or great, but pursued the even tenor of his way through a long and pleasant life. He was for many years a member of the Methodist Church.

In those days it was the custom of a great many of our people to have their crop of peaches and apples made into brandy, not at a government still nor under the direction nor by the permit of revenue officials as is now the case, but whoever desired to do so put up his own stills, ground up his fruit, boiled down his singlings and took off his doublings when and where he chose and none dared to molest or make him afraid. It was the custom of Mr. Pruett to have a small amount of brandy made each year. His preacher learned of this and informed him that he must not do this and must cut down his fruit trees and let brandy making alone. Mr. Pruett failed to see it that way and thought he had a right to make a support that way as any other. Hence his connection with the church ceased. He, however, continued to live as he had done for years past, an upright Christian life.

He lived through an eventful period of our country's history. The Revolutionary War began while he was a small boy, but still within his recollection. Then the War of 1812 with Great Britain, the Creek Indian War and the Mexican War were all fought during his life.

Of his sons, Martin, the oldest, lives now on the old homestead, has reared an interesting family, all of whom have reached maturity, is well known to most of our people, and has about lived out the days allotted to man.

William, the second son, lived a long time in the same neighborhood and finally, after the war, moved up on the Chattahoochee in the vicinity of old Sugar Hill, and died a few years ago.

Elisha moved to Alabama many years ago. He was a soldier in the Creek war and then in the Florida war and is supposed to have died there or on his return, as he was never heard from afterwards.

James Marshall, the fourth son, moved to Alabama a number of years ago; died there during the war.

Of his three daughters, only one lived to be grown. She married Mr. Charles Roper. She has been dead several years.

Mr. Pruett's wife died in 1851, and he later married Mrs. Rebecca Bradford. Finally the good old man is gone. He has finished his course, he has run his race; let us forget his faults and emulate his virtues.

Mr. Pruett's custom of converting his fruit into brandy was not singular in his day. With our early population and with the best men who first settled in this county, the first thing to be done after building the cabin was to clear a piece of ground and plant an orchard; and when in bearing a part of the fruit was stilled into brandy, mostly for home use—for the wife's camphor, for medicinal purposes and for the morning dram. If a neighbor paid them a visit, they considered it greatly wanting in hospitality, if a glass of peach brandy sweetened with honey and steeped in spearmint could not be furnished them as part of the entertainment. Yet, there was less drunkenness in those days than now, and much less evil resulting from the use of liquor than in those days when the peach trees must be cut down and the man dealt with by his church, if he makes a little for his own use. This was the habit of our best men, church men, and no evil resulted from it.

Old Sammy Reed, who for many years lived four miles east of Lawrenceville, was a church member, an elder in the Presbyterian Church, and strict in his observance of his church obligations. He was fond of his cups, made his own brandy, drank it at home, and drank until he was exhilarated. He was quiet, orderly, never spoke a loud word, never was unbalanced, and was a model of quietness and good deportment.

My old friend, Samuel Martin, who was related to him, in speaking of his habits years after his death said: "I have no doubt but what he went to Heaven."

Another instance similar to this, but I will not give his name as some of his descendants might object. He lived two miles down the river from me. He was a strict Presbyterian, an orderly, good man, but I have seen him with a brick in his hat.

I do not advocate the custom now. Times have changed and men with them. I refer to these cases to show the degeneracy of these latter times and the necessity of an embargo upon drinking which is now the great evil of the times in which we live.

1879

JOHN STUART AND HIS WIFE

Mr. Stuart moved to this county in 1824 and bought a tract of land on Redland Creek, two and a half miles west of Lawrenceville, where he lived till his death in 1853. He came from South Carolina, his family consisting of his wife, two children, two stepchildren and a few negroes.

His land was fresh and fertile and yielded good crops and he prospered. Having a club foot, he was incapacitated for field work and had learned the trade of a silversmith, which he followed a number of years after he came here.

Mr. Stuart had more than ordinary intelligence and was well read. He was of decided firmness of character, independent and steadfast in his views. A prominent trait in his character was his readiness at all times to accommodate a neighbor. To do this he would often disoblige himself. In acts of good neighborship he always took sincere pleasure.

While he would criticise the conduct of men and censure them, too, often in strong and pointed language, he was never known to speak evil of a woman, no matter what her character might be. I would commend this manly trait of his to the men who read this article, the reverse of which is so common with many. I have known some men in my time whose chief delight seemed to be to slander and calumniate the female sex. I never knew a single one who had a solitary instinct of a gentleman. All such have a deformed and debased existence and when dead will be buried out of sight "unwept, unhonored and unsung."

John Stuart was born in Pendleton District, South Carolina, the date of which is unknown to me. He married in 1817.

I come now to speak more especially of his wife, who was the widow of William Fowler, nee Mary Park, who at the time of their marriage, had three children, Andrew, Nancy who married the late J. P. Hutchins, who still survives, the honored counterpart in looks, kindness, Christian graces and benevolence of her sainted mother, and William, who died in 1837.

Mrs. Stuart was born in Laurens, South Carolina, on April 25, 1785. She married her first husband July 10, 1804. He died in 1815. After two years of widowhood, she married Mr. Stuart on August 21, 1817. They had two children: Mary, the oldest, was the wife of John Montgomery; Elizabeth, the younger, married V. D. Gresham. Mrs. Stuart died April 13, 1872, being then eighty-seven years of age.

She joined the Seceders, a branch of the Presbyterians, and remained a member until she came to Georgia, then joined at Fairview on profession of faith in August, 1827. During her long connection with this church, she was a zealous Presbyterian and a devout Christian.

For fifty years and more it has been the custom of this church to have a yearly meeting beginning on Wednesday before the second Sabbath in August. The first day was devoted to the graveyard, clearing off the rubbish, the briars and weeds that had accumulated during the previous year, and dressing up the graves. At eleven o'clock service was held in the church, a sermon by the pastor, or a prayer meeting, then dinner, and then a resumption of the labor on the graveyard till finished. On Friday after this, a meeting was commenced at the church, which continued for three days, with a large attendance and much interest generally. Mrs. Stuart was always present on the work day, giving directions and encouragement, furnishing help, and subsequently at the meetings as long as she lived.

It was a striking feature to see these annual meetings of the church, the cordial greetings of the old lady members then assembled. I have looked on from my back seat with the highest pleasure at the affectionate shake of the hand, the Christian greetings of these old women as they assembled near the pulpit before the services began and felt that atheism is a lie, infidelity false, skepticism a delusion. Well do I remember at various times these happy occasions, with Mrs. Stuart a prominent figure, and Mrs. Montgomery, and Mrs. Bagby, and Mrs. Moses Liddell, and Mrs. Daniel Liddell, Mrs. Canine, Mrs. Thomas Wright, Mrs. Saye, Mrs. Alexander and others, and Mrs. Morrow, who though a Baptist, seemed to enjoy these occasions as much as any. These mothers in Israel are all dead and most of them sleep in the old churchyard at the old church where they so often met in life. Peace to their ashes and honor to their memory. Better women than they never lived. It was a pleasure to live a near-neighbor to Mrs. Stuart for thirty-five years and for the nineteen years she survived her husband I was her special friend, looking after the business of her farm and advising with her in her business generally. She like her husband was generous and cordial in her hospitalities. None, no matter how poor, or how worthless, was ever turned away from her door empty. To all she was kind and benevolent and to her servants she was good to a fault.

It was my custom to visit her in the late years of her life on Christmas day invariably, because I knew she desired and appreciated it. She invariably saluted by saying: "Well, well! We have lived to see another Christmas and it may be the last." The same was said the last Christmas I ever visited her, and in addition to her usual remarks referred to above, she said: "I can hardly expect to see another. I am eighty-seven years old and can't expect to stay much longer. When I die, I want to be buried at Fairview in the same square with my old man." From this I very cautiously tried to dissuade her, but her mind was fully decided and it was done, and together they sleep in the same grave and her ashes mingle with his who preceded her nineteen years.

She was a dutiful wife to Mr. Stuart and for thirty-five years she was the jewel that hung about his neck and never lost its luster.

1879

ISAAC ADAIR

Isaac Adair was born in Laurens District, South Carolina, in 1808. He came to this county with his father, George R. Adair, about the year 1824. His father had sold his possessions in South Carolina with the view of moving to Georgia, or Alabama. In the fall of 1824, he started on a journey to look for a new home and his route led him through Gwinnett County, his destination being farther west. Passing through Lawrenceville and on three miles west of it, he came to a bold, gushing spring on the roadside and dismounted from his horse to drink of its water. It was a grand spring, gushing out from the hillside in bold currents, pure, limpid and exhilarating to the thirsty traveler. So charmed was he with its cool waters that he at once decided to buy the place, if it could be purchased, for his future home. The land was owned and occupied by Thomas Johnson and Josiah Brown, each owning one-half. Seeking at once an interview with them, the trade was made and his farther journey westward was at an end.

Returning to his home in South Carolina, his preparations for moving were made in due time and his family, including the subject of this sketch, reached here in the year indicated. Isaac Adair, young as he was, had left his heart behind, and soon returned and married Nancy B. Farrow, a daughter of Col. Samuel B. Farrow, of Spartanburg. Sometime after his marriage, he purchased the old Billy Wardlaw place one mile from Lawrenceville, where D. P. Williams now lives and upon which he farmed successfully until 1844, in which year he moved to Russell County, Alabama.

I wish to speak of him from 1836 to 1844, during which time I lived near him and knew him well. He was a driving successful farmer and his great ambition was to get rich, raise better crops than anybody else and have larger mules, and this ambition was not unsuccessful. He was a substantial man, substantial in his person for he was large and stalwart, substantial in the improvements on his farm, and in everything he did. The house that he built was of the best material. The chimneys were of brick made by his own hand on his own farm, and they will last for centuries. The rock fences about the place will stand for generations as a monument to him and his substantial ideas in every improvement he undertook.

My observations are, and I state them as a truism, that a man's home and the fixtures about his premises are a good criterion by which to judge him. If these are substantial, well constructed for service and convenience, it is an infallible index to his character, for attentive and substantial cast of mind is everything. On the contrary, you find a man with his houses dilapidated, some of the roof blown off and not replaced, an old hat stuck in where a pane of glass had been, a hole burned out in the back of the kitchen chimney through which the dinner pot might be thrown, an old gate in front of the house rickety and dragging on the ground, a garden fence with some palings a foot higher than others and others two feet lower than they ought to be, the posts higher than all the palings, then that man may be put down as a shackler in all his notions and ideas. I have known many such in my time and yet they would talk business like a philosopher and act like a fool.

In the fall of 1857, Mr. Adair moved from Alabama to Arkansas and settled in the woods. He at once began to build houses and to open up a farm. By planting time it was said by his neighbors that he had built more houses and cleared more land than had ever been done in that county in so short a time. Here he lived until the war, during which he moved to Texas. The first year there his wife died and his own health failed.

The war swept away well nigh all his property. Broken in health and property gone, his wife and several of his children dead, he eventually decided to return to his sister, Mrs. Nancy Craig, in this county, hoping that he might regain his health in his old home. In the month of April, 1866, accompanied by his faithful colored man, Sandy, he set out in great feebleness for Georgia. After much delay on account of his condition, he finally reached Atlanta, but could go no further, and on April 20, 1866, he died at the home of John J.

Thrasher. His remains were brought here by his relatives and buried in the old graveyard where sleep his mother, a sister, several of his children and other relatives. This is the end of the eventful life of Isaac Adair.

History suggests important lessons in many particulars and in one especially. He had a valuable farm here on which he prospered and enjoyed all the comforts of life. Here he had health and prosperity and the respect and esteem of his neighbors and fellow citizens; but to do better, to get rich faster, to heap up more rapidly the perishing and paltry things of earth, all these allured him to go west still farther and yet again still farther, and his wife and children die from the effects of the climate, and his own robust constitution gives way and he, too, dies before his time.

"Let well enough alone" is a good maxim. Had he remained at his old home in Gwinnett County, with its pure water and health-giving breezes, he most probably would be in this life today.

The faithfulness of Sandy to his old master deserves special notice. He had become a freeman, no longer the slave, and had the right and privilege to go where he pleased, bound to no man, yet he attended and nursed his old master for many months before leaving Texas, accompanied him with all the care and attention of a brother in efforts to get back to Georgia, waited on him at his bedside in his dying hour, followed his remains to their last resting place, assisted in the preparation of the grave, and when the last shovel of dirt was deposited, he, with sorrow in his face and tears in his eyes, said: "I have done all I can for my old master; I nursed him in his sickness, I helped him on his way and tried to get him to the home of his sisters, I stood by him till he died, I followed him to his grave and helped to put him away, and now I must go back to Texas and do what I can for his children for they need me."

For this wonderful devotion on the part of this negro to his old master, Sandy deserves a monument to perpetuate his memory when he, too, is dead. I may be indulged while I moralize briefly on the African and his descendants, of what he was and of what he is. Most of them have many good traits. They are confiding, easily influenced and kind in their impulses. Who does not remember or will ever forget the old black mammy who nourished him in his infancy and watched over him in the absence of his own mother? Our love for her is scarcely less than for our own dear mother, and hers for us scarcely less than for her own offspring. The old 'Uncles,' Jacob, Peter and Gill, and the old 'Aunts,' Rose and Phillis and Suky, who watched over our childhood days with a solicitude almost as sincere as our own parents and told us tales of sights they had seen that greatly excited our credulity and made us superstitious and cowards for life—how can we forget them? Who can forget the anxiety and solicitude of the old servants of the family for their young masters absent in the army during the late terrible conflict, their anxious inquiries from time to time for their safety and welfare and their glad greetings on their return? These make us palliate many of their faults; and the remembrance of Sandy's devotion for Isaac Adair in his last sad days warm up our hearts for this unfortunate race which is destined, in his new sphere, sooner or later, to pass away and his race on this continent to become extinct.

1879

Solomon Hopkins

Few of our people now living remember Solomon Hopkins. He was of quiet turn and mixed but little with the people outside of his own neighborhood. He was in many respects after the type of men who first settled the county. Free and generous in his hospitality, the latch of his door always on the outside to his friends, a stranger or those in want never turned empty away, he knew honesty and truth by instinct and practiced those virtues from principle and instinct.

Some traits in his character would probably be criticised by the straight-laced and fastidious of these days. These may have been his faults; but his faults might have been greater, and if faults at all, they were leaned to the side of virtue. He was old when I first knew him, but I remember him well. His life was spared to a good old age. He died in his 77th year. My personal recollections of him are so meager that I can but give a brief sketch of him. I quote from a memorandum furnished me by his oldest son, George H. Hopkins, now one of our oldest and most worthy citizens and whose integrity and uprightness honor his father.

Solomon Hopkins was born in North Carolina or Greenville, South Carolina, in April, 1781, and was married to his first wife, Elizabeth Terry, an English lady coming to America at eight years of age, soon after he came to his majority. They resided in Greenville until they had born unto them nine children, eight of whom lived to be grown. Mr. Hopkins was one of those men who in his day loved a dram and this love has not abated much with most people of the present day. He sometimes would drink to excess and this was his fault.

He was a fine performer on the violin and fond of the dance, either the round or the square, and would sometimes play the fiddle and at the same time dance a reel with the young people in this section in their innocent amusement. If these pastimes are innocent with church people these days, may they not be with others who are not?

His first wife died in 1822, leaving, besides his other children, an infant, now the wife of George W. Russell of this county. He came to this county in 1822 just after the county was organized and settled on the lot of land now owned by his son, George, on Beaver Ruin Creek. Here he lived one year and then bought a lot on Jackson Creek for $268, and moved to it and lived in a tent till he built a good farm house of hewn logs. With the help of his two sons, George and Thomas, he cleared the acres, the first opened on the place, and by renting some on an adjoining farm he made a support the first year.

In the fall of 1823 he married his second wife, a widow near his age, with whom he lived till his death which occurred November 14, 1858, his wife dying four days later.

Mr. Hopkins was never much a party man, though unwavering in his political principles. Between Troup and Clark in 1825, he was for Clark. In the time of South Carolina nullification he was a Union man and in the days of the Whigs and Democrats, he was a Democrat.

He joined the Baptist Church at Sweetwater in 1831 and was an orderly member for some time, but he loved his cups, drank too much and was excluded from church privileges. Afterwards he abstained and his church desired him to apply for restoration, which he did. In two or three years he was again excluded and was again restored and died in fellowship.

He was remarkable for his horsemanship and had a penchant for cavalry exercises. In South Carolina his cavalry commander was the gallant Dr. Thomas W. Alexander, of whom I wrote my first sketch.

A number of his children yet live, but are now old and passing away. Nancy, the oldest, married John Leitch and moved to Missouri and died soon afterwards. In her day here she was spoken of, I remember, as the most beautiful and sprightly girl in all Beaver Ruin.

Samantha, the second daughter, married James Power, and is still living.

George H., his oldest son, is still here an honored citizen, having filled the office of tax collector of this county years ago and represented this county in the legislature. His first wife was the daughter of Thomas B. Turner. She was a model woman in domestic economy and as a nurse for the sick. In her good management and economy she contributed much to the prosperity of her husband.

Thomas, the second son, was never married. He was in the mercantile business in Chattooga County for a number of years, clerk of the Superior Court of that county, and then held the office of ordinary.

Margaret, the third daughter, married G. B. Turner and died about the close of the war.

John F. married Margaret Baily and now lives in Texas. He is a good Baptist-Methodist, a good Mason and a prosperous farmer.

Eliza is the wife of Willis Jackson and lives in Arkansas.

Elizabeth, the youngest, is the wife of G. W. Russell and as before stated, lives near Norcross in this county.

Old Solomon Hopkins had many good traits of character that were worthy of emulation. Let his faults be written in water, his virtues in brass.

1879

WILLIAM W. DOWNS

My series of biographical sketches have been confined to the dead. The subject of my present article is still in life, though aged and infirm. He has lived to near the Psalmist's limits to human life.

So far as I know he lives in his far distant home in Texas, honored by his friends, loved by his children and grand children, gratified at his eminent success in life and waiting resignedly for his great change now so rapidly approaching.

The success of Mr. Downs is without a parallel among our early population. When we come to consider his early poverty and disadvantages under which he labored in early life and to the time he became the head of a family, it may be said to be marvelous. I knew him as early as 1825. I a mere child, he a young man living on rented land with a wife and one child, and his worldly possessions not worth perhaps more than two hundred dollars. I noticed his progress from then on to 1836 when he left us, his slow but gradual prosperity, his increasing property in proportion to his income. As bailiff of his district he saved his cost and husbanded it. As justice of the peace his profits were increased. As mail contractor on the route from Lawrenceville to Monroe his profits were fair. And from time to time, as his means increased, he engaged in other enterprises successfully until 1836 when he moved, having up to this time increased his estate from nothing to eight thousand dollars.

This was well. How was it afterwards? In 1836 he moved to Decatur, Alabama, and in eleven years his property increased from eight thousand to fifty-five thousand dollars. About this time, with Colonel Abernathy and two others, he purchased the old railroad from Tuscumbia running around Muscle Shoals on the Tennessee River forty miles in length. This old road was sadly out of repair as I well know from personal observation, having traveled over it in 1843. Soon after their purchase, the Memphis and Charleston route was projected and Major Downs and his partners sold to that company for $175,000.

He next invested in cotton, buying 900 bales at 4½ to 5 cents per pound, and sold for 9 to 11½ cents per pound. He then purchased the Leighton property for $12,000 and soon sold it for $32,000. After selling this property he moved to Texas and bought from the late Judge Longstreet, of Georgia, a tract of land for $18,000 and in two years sold it for $36,000. He then invested largely in lands on the Brazos River and in city property in the town of Waco. The farm lands soon doubled in value and the city property increased tenfold. In the meantime he engaged with his sons in the mercantile business and sold largely on a credit. Their business was in successful operation up to the war. Their losses consequent upon the war were $150,000. Major Downs lost individually 97 negroes and there were other losses.

After all these heavy losses he still had left in property and effects $130,000 up to 1873. When I last heard from him he still had a fortune in his old age.

William W. Downs was born in North Carolina, where the town of Weldon now stands, on August 12, 1802. While yet a boy he came to Georgia and was raised to man's estate in Clark County near the little village of Salem. Here he was married to Henrietta Sparks by Rev. Raleigh Green in August, 1823. After his marriage he moved to Morgan County where he resided one year and in the winter of 1824 came to Gwinnett County and rented land on the Hog Mountain road near the Hamilton old place where I first knew him. He remained on this farm one year and then moved to the neighborhood of Lawrenceville and lived one mile south of town on the Monroe road. The place is now owned by P. A. Sterling. Here he remained till he left the county in 1836.

As above stated, he was elected bailiff of the town district and made an active officer. He was then promoted to the office of justice of the peace and then was deputy sheriff for a time, and in all these positions he discharged his duties faithfully and efficiently. During these different periods he encountered many difficulties and much opposition. He gave evidence of a rise in the world. There is a class who cannot stand to see a poor man rise without envy rankling in their bosom. Downs was born poor, reared poor, and the envious class sought to keep him poor and 'On his proper level.' He must not get above his raising! He is not honest. He takes advantages. He deals unfairly. He is an upstart. He has the big-head. All this is mean and low-lived and shows man in his meanest depravity. It is one of the effects of the fall with a class of Adam's race. 'Tis not so with all. It was not so with Stewart Floyd, of Morgan County, who befriended and encouraged him when he lived there. It was not so with William Maltbie and others who befriended him when he came here. It is not so with a class to be found now and then who are ever ready to lend a helping hand to struggling, poverty stricken humanity. This latter class is the noblest work of God. The former the most degenerate sons of Adam's race. Major

Downs treasures the memory of these early friends and their kindness to him in the struggles of his younger days, and will remember them while life lasts.

Major Downs was a kind husband and parent, and I know from personal observation when he lived here, and, as has been fully demonstrated in his case, he educated his children and made large provisions for them since he left. He had born to him eleven children; and at the time when he last communicated with me, three were dead and eight were living. To most of them he gave a classical education, to all a liberal one. Some were educated at Washington College, Virginia, others elsewhere. To them he has given in money and property $45,000.

His son, Major John Wesley Downs, is the able editor and proprietor of the Waco Examiner, the leading paper of Texas, weekly and daily. His other sons are educated farmers in part and others are in the learned professions. His daughters are accomplished ladies, well married and an honor to their sex.

In politics Major Downs in the olden time was a Troup man, then a South Carolina nullifier, then a Henry Clay Whig, and since the war, a southern rights Democrat. In politics, I will say by way of parenthesis, he is always right.

In religion he is a Methodist and was a member of the church in Lawrenceville when it stood down at the old church yard. He left before its removal to its present site. He used to set the tunes for the congregation and sang the old songs well. This was before the modern and French system now in vogue here with its 'queaks and quacks' and ear-splitting discords and incongruities that would put Haydn and Hampden to the blush.

He was appointed class leader of his church in 1833 and after removing held the same position in Alabama. He was licensed to exhort in 1847 and in 1849 licensed to preach. During his long and eventful life, he maintained his religious faith, his church obligations and his hope of Heaven.

While I chronicle briefly some incidents in the eventful life of Major Downs, my memory is fresh with his kind bearing towards me when a boy, his cordiality to me in early manhood, and his kind remembrances of me now when my life has fallen somewhat in the sere and yellow leaf. His letters to me now and then are evidence that he sends a wish and a thought after me and I am happy to know,

"In him I still have a friend
Though a friend I can never see."

To him in his old age and in his far distant home in the soft Southwest, I send greetings, if he is still in life and this should meet his eye. While writing of him this imperfect sketch, many memories come up of 'Auld Lang Syne' and the pleasant days of 'life's young dreams.'

1879

THOMAS MONK AND BURRELL HIGGINS

One incident in the history of these early settlers of our county and which I give hereafter so closely identifies them that I give a chapter of them unitedly.

Old Thomas Monk came to this county when it was still a wilderness, while the Indians still roamed the forests and the wolf and the panther made the night hideous with their howls and yells. The time of his coming the memory of our oldest inhabitants now living runneth not to the contrary.

When first remembered by me, he was domiciled on the Alcova three miles east of where Lawrenceville now stands, for the town was not then laid out, and built a little mill, since known as the Harris mill, but now owned by Dr. Bond. This was in the long ago and those who remember it are now few and far between; and all who were cognizant of the fact have passed to "The undiscovered country," and the grass has long since grown up on their graves.

Mr. Monk was one of the first justices of the Inferior Court of this county, not elected perhaps for his qualifications and fitness for the office, but because suitable material was scarce. The most eventful act in his official life was the marriage ceremony performed by him at the wedding of our former distinguished fellow citizen, now deceased, A. R. Smith. Ministers of the Gospel were scarce in this backwood country; and to get married, our early population was as intent then as now, and with most of them, they were satisfied to be married by a Squire or Judge of the Inferior Court. Most of them would have been satisfied to have "jumped the broomstick."

With Mr. Smith it was "Hobson's choice." He would have preferred a minister, but had to take Judge Monk. I will be pardoned for giving one incident of the marriage as it was given to me by Judge Smith a year before his death.

The young and beautiful bride was an orphan and boarded with Edward Featherstone, who was perhaps her guardian. Mr. Smith and Mr. Featherstone were unfriendly and the marriage took place at the home of a friend in the village. A few friends were present as invited guests, among them being Charles W. Ransom, who came from Massachusetts with Mr. Smith. Judge Monk was on his p's and q's. His best foot was foremost. He had heard something of the Episcopal marriage service and startled the guests by asking in solemn tones: "Who gives the bride away?" For a moment it was painful. No parents, no relatives, no guardian present; but Mr. Ransom, with his Yankee sagacity, came to the relief by saying, "I do." This was satisfactory and the ceremony proceeded. It was said that Judge Monk was always proud that he was honored by marrying Asabel R. Smith and his beautiful bride.

Thomas Monk in his somewhat advanced life joined the church; and as he had been a judge of the Inferior Court, he concluded that he had sufficient gifts to be a preacher. Upon his application being made, his church agreed with him and he was granted a license to preach.

Burrell Higgins lived near him on an adjoining settlement, both on the Alcova River. Mr. Higgins had "hearn" that at Ellison's Mill, down on the Appalachee River, there was a Free Masonic lodge. He wanted to join. Clandestine though it was he knew no better. He thought it "Simon pure." He made application and they took him in. As a part of his initiation they rode him on a rail, stood him on his head and made him drink branch water, applied the hot iron and he was a Mason. The ceremonies were so sad, solemn and painful that they turned his thoughts on the future world and he resolved to be a better man. He made application soon to join the church; and in his experience, which was chiefly his masonic initiation, by which the secret was disclosed, and it being satisfactory, he was received into fellowship. He, too, like his neighbor, Monk, soon felt that it was his duty to "exercise" and licensed to preach. His and Judge Monk's membership was at the same church, old Higginstown, on the Alcova, and was of the Baptist persuasion.

A spirit of rivalry seemed soon to arise between these two brothers, as to which could excel in preaching power. This caused no jar in their personal relations or Christian fellowship. They met on one occasion and the following colloquy ensued:

"How are you getting along preaching, Brother Higgins?"

"Mighty well, Brother Monk. How is it with you?"

"My people say that I preach first rate, Brother Higgins."

"But," said Brother Higgins, "they say I out preach you."

"I don't believe a word of it, Brother Higgins, and I'll bet a bushel of corn against a sifter that I can out preach you."

"Done. I'll take the bet, Brother Monk."

It will be remembered that Brother Monk was a miller and Brother Higgins was a sifter maker.

The time was agreed on for the test and deacons D and R were selected to umpire and settle the contest. The day came, the meeting took place, a great crowd was in attendance. The venerable deacons were on hand.

Brother Monk, as per agreement, took the pulpit first and pronounced as his subject a Scripture to be found somewhere between the lids of the Bible. I can not give the text. After a long period of years it has gone from my memory. It was, however, some passage from Paul's writings that, to his mind, established the doctrine of election and foreordination. He discussed it in that view; and according to the John Calvin hypothesis, that whatever happens was so decided from the beginning. His sermon was able and of the true doctrine and was so considered by the deacons.

Then Mr. Higgins took the pulpit and announced that his subject was from that "Same old book which my hearers may find if they will read their Bibles." In doctrine he agreed with Brother Monk, he was on the same line, of the same faith, of the same creed, and closed with a peroration that greatly edified the deacons and his "lovely congregation."

The deacons then retired to make up their verdict and the contestants and their friends waited in anxious suspense for the award. After a brief conversation it was decided that they could not discriminate between the two sermons. Both were able and of the true doctrine, every sentence and every word were the true gospel, and that they could not distinguish any difference. They returned to the church and Deacon R. delivered the opinion, in accordance with the above statement, and they recommended that they withdraw the wagers, which was done. The preachers shook hands in Christian fellowship, then with the deacons, then with the congregation, and all returned to their respective places of abode well satisfied, especially Brothers Monk and Higgins, though Brother Higgins still contended that he would have out preached Brother Monk if he had stood up straight and not leaned over the "book foard."

This is a story founded on fact. There are a few yet living who can vouch for the correctness of my statements.

I have written this article with no object in view except to delineate in the early times of which I write those happenings peculiar to the period in which those people lived. Both of these men were devout Christians in their day and have long since gone to their reward. Their little wager then in the backwoods country was considered harmless. In these days it would be different and held as sinful and subject the offenders to church discipline.

I remember but little of Judge Monk. I recall him as he would pass up and down the streets of our town fifty years ago in plain garb, bent form and his hands clasped behind him underneath his swallow-tailed coat. He went from here long ago to Sumter County and was drowned in Crooked Creek. That was the end of his earthly career.

I knew Mr. Higgins better for he survived his friend many years and remained a citizen of this county until his death which occurred, I believe, during the war. He was a plain man with but little education. He had the confidence of the people as a man of correct intentions, truthful and honest. I always liked him and my memory now turns towards him, and my occasional intercourse with him with pleasurable emotions.

1879

Samuel Cowser Dunlap

Mr. Dunlap was one of the prominent citizens of this county, coming here soon after its organization, and remaining till his death, a period of thirty-five or forty years. He settled two miles north of Lawrenceville near where the Methodist campground is located. He was a thrifty, energetic farmer. In connection with his farm at home, he owned and cultivated another on Pugh's Creek, adjoining the farm of his brother-in-law, James Hood, working the two together. His hands, negroes and sons, under the management of his faithful black man, Jack, would work over the one at home and move down and work over the other. To his farm he gave much of his personal attention and was successful in raising abundant supplies. He had corn to sell and to keep.

He reared but one daughter, the late Mrs. Dr. Garmany, and six sons, all now living in the state of Arkansas except the oldest son, James C. Dunlap, an intelligent and energetic citizen of Atlanta.

Mr. Dunlap was for a long time tax collector and receiver of this county when those offices were consolidated. The duties of both were discharged with great promptness and correctness, never making mistakes nor subjecting his official conduct to complaints. His tax receipts were always written, for printed ones were then unknown. They were written in his own unique chirography such as no one else could write. He had lost the middle finger of his right hand from the scratch of a briar from which inflammation ensued and it became necessary to have it amputated. The loss of his finger interfered with the use of the pen and made his writing peculiar. It used to be said his receipts looked like bird tracks in the snow. It would have been as difficult to counterfeit his signature as Mr. Springer's, the greenback man of Abe Lincoln's time.

Thirty years ago or more he was elected one of the justices of the Inferior Court of the county and held the office four years. His faithful discharge of the duties of his position is fully verified by me as I was one of his colleagues at the time.

These were the offices he held. His sterling good sense and good judgment qualified him for others, but he never sought them. Judge Dunlap was of kindly nature, remarkably so, and faithful to a friend in distress.

· Many years ago in company with Chas. W. Rawson, one of the early merchants of Lawrenceville, he went west to see the new country of Mississippi with a view of a future location there, if they liked the country. This long journey was to be made on horseback through a new and sparsely settled section, and many portions not settled at all. Far away from home Mr. Rawson was stricken down with a disease and no physician was in reach and no comforts obtainable to be administered. Mr. Dunlap attended him assiduously, day and night, until he died, scarcely closing his eyes for the weeks the sick man lingered. In the solitude of that wild, far-off land, he buried his dead friend, then gathering up his clothes and all that was left of him and packing them on his dead friend's horse, he retraced his steps sad and lonely to his home. I remember to have seen him when he returned, coming up the street leading the horse of his friend and tied upon the saddle his bundle of clothes, and bearing in every lineament of his face the deep desolation of his heart. When interrogated he said: "Rawson is dead," and tears came into his eyes. His looks and all reminded me of one of Shakespeare's female characters who had lost her husband at the hand of an assassin: "But I, an old turtle, will wing me to some withered bough and there lament my fate that's never to be found again."

Mr. Dunlap was not a member of any church, but was a Presbyterian in faith and to which church his wife belonged. While not a churchman, he was exemplary in his deportment and in this was a good model for many who were. His language was always discreet and his habits as circumspect as the conscientious church member. I never heard a profane word from his lips, nor a single expression bordering on it, nor an utterance that might not have been said in the most refined society; and yet I was intimate with him for many years. He was social in his nature but of great modesty and as easy to blush as a girl.

He was prosperous in business and amassed a competency. He used to say he got what he had on two ideas. First, by attending to his own business; and, second, by letting other people's business alone. These were good maxims and by many not practiced. The reverse is true with many people I have known.

It was said of an old citizen who once lived here that he always looked into other people's business more than his own, not for their good but to criticise and find fault. He could tell how much corn his neighbors had to a peck, how much they owed, whether their horses were fat or poor, whether they drank rye coffee or buttermilk, whether they washed in a tin pan or a skillet, all this he knew. This intermeddling in other men's business seems to have been inherited by most of his offspring even to this day. Such a disposition is contemptible.

Judge Dunlap died thirty years ago in Madison, Georgia, on his way to Milledgeville, of strangulated hernia after forty-eight hours of intense suffering, and is buried side by side with his wife, who was Sarah Cowan, at Fairview Church in this county, and here he sleeps in quietness but not in forgetfulness.

"In his grave lurks no treason, no envy swells; here grow no grudges, here are no storms, no noise, but silence and eternal sleep."

www.ingramcontent.com/pod-product-compliance
Lightning Source LLC
Chambersburg PA
CBHW020634300426
44112CB00007B/116